Lawyers and the Rule of Law

Andrew Boon

·HART·
OXFORD · LONDON · NEW YORK · NEW DELHI · SYDNEY

HART PUBLISHING

Bloomsbury Publishing Plc

Kemp House, Chawley Park, Cumnor Hill, Oxford, OX2 9PH, UK

1385 Broadway, New York, NY 10018, USA

29 Earlsfort Terrace, Dublin 2, Ireland

HART PUBLISHING, the Hart/Stag logo, BLOOMSBURY and the Diana logo are trademarks of Bloomsbury Publishing Plc

First published in Great Britain 2022

First published in hardback, 2022

Paperback edition, 2024

Copyright © Andrew Boon, 2022

Andrew Boon has asserted his right under the Copyright, Designs and Patents Act 1988 to be identified as Author of this work.

All rights reserved. No part of this publication may be reproduced or transmitted in any form or by any means, electronic or mechanical, including photocopying, recording, or any information storage or retrieval system, without prior permission in writing from the publishers.

While every care has been taken to ensure the accuracy of this work, no responsibility for loss or damage occasioned to any person acting or refraining from action as a result of any statement in it can be accepted by the authors, editors or publishers.

All UK Government legislation and other public sector information used in the work is Crown Copyright ©. All House of Lords and House of Commons information used in the work is Parliamentary Copyright ©. This information is reused under the terms of the Open Government Licence v3.0 (http://www.nationalarchives.gov.uk/doc/open-government-licence/version/3) except where otherwise stated.

All Eur-lex material used in the work is © European Union, http://eur-lex.europa.eu/, 1998–2024.

A catalogue record for this book is available from the British Library.

A catalogue record for this book is available from the Library of Congress.

Library of Congress Control Number: 2022940553

ISBN:	PB:	978-1-50996-355-3
	ePDF:	978-1-50992-523-0
	ePub:	978-1-50992-522-3

Typeset by Compuscript Ltd, Shannon

To find out more about our authors and books visit www.hartpublishing.co.uk. Here you will find extracts, author information, details of forthcoming events and the option to sign up for our newsletters.

LAWYERS AND THE RULE OF LAW

This book examines lawyers' contributions to creating and maintaining the rule of law, one of the pillars of a liberal democracy. It moves from the European Enlightenment to the modern day, exploring the role of judges, government lawyers, and private practitioners in creating, defining, and being defined by, the demands of modern society.

The book is divided into four parts representing the big themes. The first part considers lawyers' contribution to the growth of constitutionalism; the second, the formulation of roles and identities; and the third the formation of values. The fourth part focuses on the challenges faced by lawyers and the rule of law in the past 50 years – the neoliberal period – and how they challenge both conceptions of lawyers and the rule of law. Each part is illustrated by defining events, from the execution of Charles I, through the Nuremberg Trials, to the insurrection by supporters of Donald Trump in January 2021.

Although the focus is on England and Wales, parallel developments in other jurisdictions (Australia, Canada, New Zealand, and the USA) are considered. This allows analysis of lawyers' historical and contemporary engagement with the rule of law in jurisdictional systems based on the Common Law. Each chapter is thematic, but the passage through the book is broadly chronological.

To (in age order) Mylo, Dottie, Flori, and Romy

Acknowledgements

THIS PROJECT REFLECTS a long-held interest in lawyers, the forces that shape their work and values, and the continuing relevance of collective identity and organisation. I took a broad view of the rule of law as referring to a society depending on consensual observance of law. My intention was to clarify connections between this idea and the role(s) of lawyers in making such a society a reality. Some parts are based on my previous work although, where this is the case, it was substantially re-worked.

I am grateful to colleagues and friends. Professor Richard Abel provided helpful comments on scope. Contributors to the Lawyers and Legal Professions stream at the Socio-Legal Studies Association Annual Conferences provided comments on papers I presented there. I thank Dr Rachel Cahill O'Callaghan, and Professors John Flood and Richard Moorhead in particular. Professors Ian Loveland and Julian Webb read and commented on sections. I was not able to incorporate all the excellent points they made. All errors are obviously mine. Others who have read chapters and provided comments include Natalie Boon, Toni Fazaeli, Helen Taylor and Professor Alan Tuckett. I am grateful to Helen for her understanding and encouragement to focus on this project and for helping me to do so. Thanks go to Tim Boon, John Brownlow, Alma Evans, Ro Gordon, Ruth Miskin, Eleanor Taylor-Scotland, Matt Taylor-Scotland, and Baker Terry for showing interest, having discussions and giving encouragement. I thank Tim for providing several relevant books, Ruth for drawing my attention to Phillipe Sands' *East West Street*, and Baker for highlighting the plight of Steven Donziger.

The Law School at City, University of London, supported two terms of study leave for this project, Catherine Neary at the New Zealand Law Society Library provided materials connected with codes of conduct and Simon Hindley at the Library at Inner Temple (unsuccessfully) searched for some nineteenth century material. Much of the work was carried out from my home office during the COVID-19 pandemic. I am grateful to my daughter Frankie, my 'office buddy' during the final stages of production, for keeping me sane and grounded.

I am thankful for the support and assistance of those at Hart Publishing connected with the project. These include Sinead Moloney, Kate Whetter, Rosie Mearns and Linda Goss. I am particularly thankful to Kate for her encouragement and flexibility over delivery date for the text, extended several times and to Claire Banyard for her careful editing.

There are four Parts, each introduced by a short excerpt. Parts 1 and 4 open with snatches of a poem by Rudyard Kipling *The Old Issue* (1899). Published in several places, including *The Times* and *New York Tribune* before the start of the Boer War,[1]

---

[1] M Hamer, *The Old Issue* (The Kipling Society) www.kiplingsociety.co.uk/readers-guide/rg_oldissue1.htm.

this was a piece of propaganda, particularly the part at the beginning of Part 4. It was directed at President Kruger of the Transvaal, who Kipling cast as a despot. Kipling's verse ignored the fact that liberal opinion worldwide saw Britain as the aggressor in the conflict which followed.[2] These excerpts are nevertheless still relevant to the Parts they open, as demonstrated by the invasion of the Ukraine, which commenced in the week I finally submitted the text.

Andy Boon
London
February 2022

---

[2] ibid.

Contents

Acknowledgements .... *vii*
Table of Cases .... *xvii*
Table of Legislation .... *xxiii*

1. **Lawyers and the Rule of Law** 1
   - I. Introduction 1
   - II. Context 1
   - III. Methodology 6
   - IV. Literature 8
     - A. Part I: Government 8
     - B. Part II: Private Practice 14
     - C. Part III: Professions 17
     - D. Part IV: Futures 21
   - V. Conclusion 25

PART 1
GOVERNMENT

2. **Revolution** 29
   - I. Introduction 29
   - II. Theory 29
   - III. The English Revolutions 31
     - A. Magna Carta 31
     - B. Reformation 32
   - IV. James I and Edward Coke 33
     - A. Divine Right 33
     - B. Institutional Constraints 34
     - C. Sir Edward Coke 35
     - D. Parliament 37
   - V. Charles I and Parliament 38
   - VI. The English Civil Wars 41
   - VII. The Restoration 44
   - VIII. The Glorious Revolution 46
   - IX. The French and American Revolutions 48
   - X. Discussion 48
   - XI. Conclusion 51

x Contents

3. **Constitution** 53
    - I. Introduction 53
    - II. Theory 53
    - III. Forms 55
    - IV. Functions 58
        - A. Diffusing Power 58
        - B. Separating the Three Functions of Law 59
    - V. Judges and the Rule of Law 64
        - A. The Judicial Role 64
        - B. The Interpretative Role 64
        - C. The Control Function 65
    - VI. Other Jurisdictions 72
    - VII. Discussion 75
    - VIII. Conclusion 80

4. **Execution** 81
    - I. Introduction 81
    - II. Theory 81
    - III. Lord Chancellor 82
    - IV. Law Officers of the Crown 84
        - A. History 84
        - B. Responsibilities of the Law Officers 86
    - V. The Constitutional Reform Act 2005 90
        - A. Post-Act Lord Chancellors 90
        - B. Post-Act Law Officers 92
        - C. Senior Government Lawyers and the Rule of Law 94
    - VI. Government Law Officers in Other Common Law Jurisdictions 97
    - VII. Discussion 101
    - VIII. Conclusion 105

5. **Institution** 106
    - I. Introduction 106
    - II. Theory 106
    - III. Open Access Order 108
    - IV. Civil Society 109
    - V. Parliament 113
    - VI. Administration 118
        - A. The Administrative State 118
        - B. The Civil Service 119
        - C. Public Inquiries 122
    - VII. Justice 123
    - VIII. Jurisdictional Differences 128
    - IX. Discussion 129
    - X. Conclusion 131

PART 2
PRACTICE

6. **Identity** 135
    I. Introduction 135
    II. Theory 135
    III. Litigation 136
        A. Groups 136
        B. The Criminal Trial 137
    IV. The Adversary System 138
        A. Transformation 138
        B. Controlling the Courtroom 141
        C. Lawyer and Client Relationship 141
        D. Evidence and Process 142
        E. Cross-examination 143
        F. Trial Strategy 144
    V. Celebrity 145
        A. Reputation 145
        B. The Neutral Partisan 146
        C. Embedding in Culture 150
    VI. Business Lawyers 152
    VII. Discussion 154
    VIII. Conclusion 158

7. **Individuality** 159
    I. Introduction 159
    II. Theory 159
    III. Rights and Liberties 161
        A. Civil Liberties 162
        B. Economic Rights 166
        C. Political Rights 168
        D. Cultural Rights 168
        E. Social Rights 170
    IV. An International Order 171
        A. Citizenship 171
        B. Nuremberg 173
        C. Universalism 177
    V. Discussion 182
    VI. Conclusion 184

8. **Legality** 185
    I. Introduction 185
    II. Theory 185
    III. Legality and Consent 186
    IV. Confidences 189
        A. Integrity 189
        B. Lawyer and Client Relationship 190

		C.	Confidentiality	191
		D.	Legal Professional Privilege (LPP)	193
	V.	Preventing Client Harms to Third Parties		204
		A.	Dangerous Clients	204
		B.	Corporate Clients and Financial Harm	205
	VI.	Discussion		206
		A.	Legal Observance	206
		B.	Client Confidence	207
		C.	Corporate Privilege	210
	VII.	Conclusion		210

9. Morality 212
   I. Introduction 212
   II. Theory 212
   III. Controlling Litigation Lawyers 214
   IV. Hired Stilettoes and Hired Guns 216
       A. The Partisan Prosecutor 216
       B. The Moral Crisis of Adversarialism 218
   V. American Attorneys 223
       A. The Republican Ideal 223
       B. Client Focus 225
       C. Watergate 227
       D. The Standard Conception of the Lawyer's Role 228
       E. The Rule of Law 231
   VI. Other Core Jurisdictions 233
   VII. Discussion 233
   VIII. Conclusion 236

PART 3
PROFESSION

10. Organisation 241
    I. Introduction 241
    II. Theory 241
    III. Prototypes 243
        A. The Bar of England and Wales 243
        B. The Solicitors 245
    IV. Lawyers in the Diaspora 247
        A. The Common Law Tradition 247
        B. The USA 248
        C. Canada 253
        D. Australia 257
        E. New Zealand 258
    V. Discussion 260
        A. Models 260
        B. Roles 261

		C.	Independence 262
		D.	Public Service 264
	VI.	Conclusion 268

11. Regulation 269
    I.   Introduction 269
    II.   Theory 269
    III. From External Regulation to Self-regulation 270
        A. England and Wales 270
        B. The United States 279
        C. New Zealand 281
        D. Canada 283
        E. Australia 284
    IV. Codes of Conduct 284
        A. Supporting the Rule of Law 284
        B. Legalisation 286
        C. Substance: Client and Public Duties 288
        D. Enforcement 290
    V.   Discussion 292
        A. Self-regulation 292
        B. The Role of Rules in Regulation 293
    VI. Conclusion 295

12. Representation 296
    I.   Introduction 296
    II.   Theory 296
    III. Codes of Conduct and the Standard Conception:
        Comparative Analysis 297
        A. Comparing Codes 297
        B. Selecting Markers 298
        C. Assessing Role Differentiation 301
    IV. Neutrality Indicators in Lawyers' Codes of Conduct 301
        A. Neutrality: Accepting Consumers as Clients (N1) 301
        B. Neutrality: Accepting Clients' Lawful Objectives (N2) 304
    V.   Partisanship Indicators in Lawyers' Code of Conduct 308
        A. Partisanship: Duty of Loyalty, Devotion, or Zeal (P1) 308
        B. Partisanship: Using all Lawful Means (P2) 311
    VI. Conformity with Neutral Partisanship in Codes of Conduct 313
    VII. Discussion 314
    VIII. Conclusion 316

13. Incrimination 317
    I.   Introduction 317
    II.   Theory 317
    III. Evaluating Public Duties 318

xiv Contents

    IV. System Duties...320
        A. System Duty: Supporting Legality/Including Reporting
           Requirements (S1) 320
        B. System Duty: The Administration of Justice (S2) 325
    V. Third Party Duties..332
        A. Third Party Duty: Fairness (T1)..332
        B. Third Party Duty: Preventing Harm to Third Parties (T2) 336
    VI. Duties to Legality in the Codes of Conduct....................................339
    VII. Discussion..341
    VIII. Conclusion 344

PART 4
FUTURES

14. Professionalism..347
    I. Introduction 347
    II. Theory..347
    III. Neoliberal Reform of the Legal Services Market............................349
        A. Decline of Professional Society 349
        B. The Politics of Professionalism 350
        C. Professions..353
        D. Judiciary 355
    IV. Independent Regulation...357
        A. Structure...357
        B. Independent Regulators and the Professional Bodies 358
        C. Regulatory Policy 360
        D. Regulatory Practice 361
    V. Discussion..368
    VI. Conclusion 369

15. Corporatocracy 371
    I. Introduction 371
    II. Theory..371
    III. The Rise of Corporate Power..373
        A. The Composition of Government 373
        B. The Corporatised State 375
        C. Legal Services...378
    IV. Lawyers against Corporations..380
    V. Corporate Lawyers 384
        A. Expansion...384
        B. Values 385
        C. Corporate Social Responsibility...387
        D. Pro Bono Legal Services...389
        E. Guantanamo Bay Detention Centre 390
    VI. Discussion..393
    VII. Conclusion 394

16. Globalisation..395
    I. Introduction...395
    II. Theory..395
    III. A Global Order of the Rule of Law? 397
        A. The Washington Consensus..397
        B. Measuring the Rule of Law...399
        C. The Spread of the Rule of Law 401
        D. Alternatives to the Rule of Law..402
    IV. Compromising the Rule of Law 404
        A. Insurgent Cosmopolitanism..404
        B. The Reaction to Terrorist Threats in the UK 406
        C. Lawyers and Special Procedures 409
        D. The Incremental Erosion of Rights..411
        E. Migration 413
    V. The Globalisation of Lawyering...415
        A. Legal Professions..416
        B. Global Law Firms 417
        C. International Lawyer Associations 418
    VI. Discussion..420
    VII. Conclusion 422

17. Democracy 424
    I. Introduction...424
    II. Theory..424
    III. The United Kingdom 426
        A. The 'Brexit' Referendum...426
        B. Notice of Withdrawal..428
        C. Getting Brexit Done 428
        D. Weakening Executive Constraints 431
        E. Legality..434
    IV. The USA 439
        A. The 2016 Election..439
        B. The Russia Investigations 442
        C. Impeachments...443
    V. Discussion..445
    VI. Conclusion 450

18. Epilogue...451
    I. Introduction...451
    II. Lawyers and the Rule of Law 451
        A. Private Practice...452
        B. Government Lawyers...453
        C. Judges...453
    III. Decline of the Rule of Law 453
    IV. Judiciaries 457
    V. Government Lawyers 460

VI.		Private Practice	464
	A.	Roles	464
	B.	The Adversary System	465
	C.	Confidence and Privilege	467
	D.	Legal Professions	468
VII.		Conclusion	474

Appendices *476*
Bibliography *480*
Index *511*

Table of Cases

A and Others v Secretary of State for the Home Department
  [2004] UKHL 56 407
Al Rawi and others (Respondents) v The Security Service and others
  (Appellants) [2011] UKSC 34 ....410, 465
AM&S Europe v Commission (1983) 1QBD 678 (ECJ) cited at 27 210
Anisminic Ltd v Foreign Compensation Commission [1969] 2 AC 147 70
Associated Provincial Picture Houses Ltd v Wednesbury Corp
  [1948] 1 KB 223 71
A and Z and others v Secretary of State for the Home Dept.,
  for example, led to replacement of the Anti-Terrorism,
  Crime and Security 180
B v DPP [2000] 2 WLR 452, 463...67
Baker v Campbell (1983) 153 CLR 52 198
Balabel v Air India [1988] Ch 317 199
Bolton v The Law Society [1994] 1 WLR 512 CA (Civ Div) 512 .....158, 278
Bolkiah v KPMG (a firm) [1999] 2 AC 222 276
Bonham's Case (1610) 8 Co Rep 114a 66
Brett v SRA [2014] EWHC 2974 (Admin).......................................291, 331
Bushell's case (1670) 124 ER 1006 170
Calvin's Case 7 Co. Rep. ia, i3a (1608) 66
Campbell v Mirror Group Newspapers [2004] UKHL 22 192
Carpmael v Powis (1846) 1 Ph 687 198
C v C [2009] EWHC 1491 (Fam)..202
CCSU v Minister for the Civil Service [1985] 1 AC 374........................71–72
Case of Proclamations (1610) 12 Co Rep 74, EWHC KB J22 ....11, 36, 72,
  428–29, 451
The Case of Thomas Skinner, Merchant v The East India Company
  (1666) 6 State Trials 710 (HL)..61
Case of Monopolies 11 Co Rep 84, (1599) 74 ER 1131 70
Cheney v Conn [1968] I All ER 779 66
Cutts v Pickering (1671) 3 Ch. Rep. 66 201
Director of The Serious Fraud Office v Eurasian Natural Resources
  Corporation Limited And The Law Society [2018] EWCA Civ 2006 ...196
Duke of Argyll v Duchess of Argyll 1962 SC (HL) 88..............................201
Entick v Carrington Camden's judgement (1765),
  19 State Trials 1045, 391..62, 69–70,
  78, 111, 429
Five Knights' or Darnell's case (1627) 3 How St Tr 1..................................39

G v Director of Legal Aid Casework (British Red Cross Society intervening)
  [2014] EWCA Civ 1622, [2015] 1 WLR 2247 466
Gartside v Outram [1857] 26 LJ Ch (NS) 113 324
General Mediterranean Holdings SA v Patel [1999] 3 All ER 691 194
Ghaidan v Godin-Mendoza [2004] UKHL 30 [2004] 3 All ER 411 per
  Lord Nicholls at 565, para 9) 184
Gouriet v Union of Post Office Workers [1978] AC 435 104
Greenough v Gaskell 1 M & K 98 .... 197, 203
Jackson and others v Attorney General [2005] UKHL 56 67
Hall v Simons [2000] 3 All ER 673 HL 355
Hirst v UK (No 2) (2005) ECHR 681 181
In re L (A Minor) (Police Investigation: Privilege) [1997] AC 16 .... 186, 195
Liversidge, Appellant v Sir John Anderson and Another Respondents
  [1942] AC 206 163–64
Magor and St. Mellons Rural District Council v Newport Corporation
  [1950] 2 All ER 1226 126
Malone v Metropolitan Police Commissioner [1979] Ch 344 64
McDonald's Corporation v Steel & Morris [1997] EWHC QB 366 380
McE [2009] 1AC 908 411
McKenzie v McKenzie (1970) 3 WLR 472 361
McIlkenny v Chief Constable of the West Midlands [1980] 2 WLR 689 128
Miranda v Secretary of State for the Home Department, the Commissioner
  of Police for the Metropolis and three interveners [2014] EWHC 255
  (Admin) 412
Öcalan v Turkey (2005) 41 EHRR 45 411
O'Connor v Bar Standards Board [2014] EWHC 4324 (QB) 295
Omychund v Barker (1744) 26 Eng Rep 14 66
Padfield v Minister of Agriculture, Fisheries and Food [1968] AC 997 70
Parry-Jones v Law Society [1969] 1 Ch 1 198
Pepper (Inspector of Taxes) v Hart [1993] AC 593 127
Pickin v British Rail Board [1974] AC 765, per Lord Reid 66
Pierson [1998] AC 539 .... 65, 357
Prohibitions del Roy (1608) 12 Co Rep 63 72
Prudential PLC and Prudential (Gibraltar) Ltd v Special Commissioner
  of Income Tax and Pandolfo (HM Inspector of Taxes) [2013] UKSC 1,
  [2013] 2 AC 185 158
R (Anderson) v Home Secretary [2002] UKHL 66
R v Baillie (1778) 145
R (Binyam Mohamed) v Secretary of State for Foreign and Commonwealth
  Affairs [2010] EWCA Civ 65 409
R v Cox and Railton (1884) 14 QBD 153 .... 202–03, 209,
                                                                                            320, 328, 342
R v. Criminal Injuries Compensation Board, Ex parte Lain
  [1967] 2 QB 864 72
R v Derby Magistrates' Court, Ex p B [1996] AC 487 .... 193–94, 201, 208

R v Derbyshire JJ (1759) 2 Keny 299 70
R v Farooqi [2013] EWCA Crim 1649, [2014] 1 Cr App R 8 ....245, 326
R v Home Secretary, ex p Simms [2000] 2 AC 115 67
R v Horseferry Road Magistrates, ex p Bennett 1994] AC 42....................................67
R. (on the application of Jet2.com Ltd) v Civil Aviation Authority
   [2020] EWCA Civ 35..200
R v Derby Magistrates' Court, ex p. B. [1996] 1 AC....................... 193–94, 201, 208
R (On the application of the Good Law Project) v Minister for the
   Cabinet Office and Public First (2021) EWCA 1569 (TTC) 89.......................436
R v Legal Services Board [2015] UKSC 41 357
R (Catherine Lumsdon, Rufus Taylor, David Howker QC, Christopher
   Hewertson) v Legal Services Board v General Council of the Bar
   (acting by the Bar Standards Board), Solicitors Regulation Authority,
   ILEX Professional Standards, Law Society of England and Wales
   [2014] EWCA Civ 1276, [2014] HRLR 29 356
R (on the application of Miller) v Secretary of State for Exiting the
   European Union Divisional Court, Queen's Bench Division
   3 November 2016 [2016] EWHC 2768 (Admin) [2016] HRLR 23 428
R (on the application of Miller and another) (Respondents) v Secretary
   of State for Exiting the European Union (Appellant) REFERENCE
   by the Attorney General for Northern Ireland – In the matter of an
   application by Agnew and others for Judicial Review REFERENCE
   by the Court of Appeal (Northern Ireland) – In the matter
   of an application by Raymond McCord for Judicial Review
   [2017] UKSC 5... 63, 428
R v McIlkenny & others [1992] 2 All ER 417 128
R (Morgan Grenfell & Co Ltd) v Special Commissioner of Income Tax
   [2003] 1 AC 563 ....201, 324
R (on the Application of The Public Law Project) (Appellant) v
   Lord Chancellor (Respondent) [2016] UKSC 39, [2016] AC 1531,
   [2017] 2 All ER 423)..65
R v Secretary of State for Home Affairs. Ex parte Lees [1941] 1 KB 72........... 164–65
R v Secretary of State for the Home Department ex parte Fire
   Brigades Union [1995] 2 AC 513 65
R v Secretary of State for the Home Department, ex p Pierson
   [1998] AC 539... 65, 357
R v Secretary of State for Transport Ex p. Factortame Ltd (No.2)
   [1990] 3 WLR 818...66
R v Shipley 21 St. Tr. 847 (1783–84) 146, 308
R (on the application of Thompson) v Law Society [2004]
   EWCA Civ 167, [2004] 2 All ER 113 466
Rooke's Case (1598) 5 Co Rep 99b 70
Saunders v Punch Ltd [1988] 1WLR 996 209
Shaw v Solicitors Regulation Authority [2017] EWHC 2076 (Admin) 332
Sirros v Moore [1975] QB 118 62

Somerset v Stuart 98 Eng Rep 499 (KB 1772) 172
SRA v Martyn Jeremy Day, Sapna Malik, Anna Jennifer Crowther and Leigh Day (a firm) (2017) SDT case No. 11502–2016 363
Solicitors Regulation Authority v Philip Shiner (2016) SDT Case No.11510/2016 363–64
Stovin v Wise [1996] AC 923 205
Swinfen v Lord Chelmsford (1860) 5 H & N 891 221–22
Three Rivers District Council and others v The Governor and Company of the Bank of England (Three Rivers No 5) [2003] EWCA Civ 474 200
Three Rivers District Council & Others v Governor and Company of the Bank of England (No. 6) [2004] UKHL 48, [2005] 1 AC 610 (House of Lords) 158, 191, 194, 321, 411, 467
United States v Philip Morris Inc (No 1) [2004] EWCA Civ 330, Times, 16 April 2004 343
Waugh v British Railways Board [1980] AC 521 .... 133, 196
Wingate & Anr v Solicitors Regulation Authority and *Solicitors Regulation Authority v Malins* [2018] EWCA Civ 366 278
Williams v Solicitors Regulation Authority [2017] EWHC 1478 (Admin), [2017] 6 WLUK 422 278
X v Morgan-Grampian [1991] 1 AC 1 66
X Ltd and another v Morgan-Grampian (Publishers) Ltd and others [1990] 2 All ER 1 192
Z v Z and others [2016] EWHC 3349 (Fam), [2017] 4 WLR 84 203

EC

Case C-550/07 P *Akzo Nobel Chemicals Ltd and Akcros Chemicals Ltd v Commission of the European Communities* [2011] 2 AC 338 210
Chahal v UK (1996) 23 EHRR 413 406
Lobo Machado v Portugal (1996) 23 EHRR 79 466
Australian Mining & Smelting Europe Ltd v Commission of the European Communities (AM &S) (155/79) [1982] ECR 1575 419

Australia

Daniels Corporation International Pty Ltd v Australian Competition and Consumer Commission (2002) 192 ALR 561 198–99
Dietrich v The Queen (1992) 177 CLR 292 233
George v Rockett (1990) 170 CLR 104 (Supreme Court of Queensland) 166
Parker v R (1963) 111 CLR 610; [1963] ALR 524 258

Canada

Babcock v Canada (Attorney General) [2002] 3 SCR 3 .... 74, 469
*New Brunswick Broadcasting Co v Nova Scotia (Speaker of the House
of Assembly)* [1993] 1 SCR 319 74
British Columbia v Mangat [2001] SCC 67 (CanLII), 3 SCR 113....................469
Canada (Attorney General) v Law Society of B.C., [1982] 2 SCR 307 264
Descoteaux v Mierzwinski (1982) 141 DLR (3d) 590 198
Jones v Smith [1999] 1 SCR 455..196, 198
LaBelle v Law Society of Upper Canada (2001), 56). R [3d] 413 [CA]..................264
Mackin v New Brunswick [2002] 1 SCR 405 469
Reference re: Secession of Québec [1998] 2 SCR 217 .... 73, 458

United States

Bush v Gore 531 U.S. 98 (2000) 447–48
Dandridge v Williams (1974) 397 U.S. 471 ....171, 267
Dred Scott v Sandford 60 U.S. (19 How.) 393 (1857)..........................73, 167–68, 183
Gideon v Wainwright 372 U.S. 335..266
Hamdan v Rumsfeld 548 U.S. 557 (2006)..391–92
Jackson v City of Joliet 715 F.2d 1200, 1203 (7th Cir.), cert. denied,
465 U.S. 1049 (1983) 2 I 170
Legal Services Corporation v Velaquez (531 U.S. 533 (2001) 469
Maranda v Richer [2003] 3 SCR 193 at 215 208
Marbury v Madison (1803) 5 U.S. 137..73
In Re McConnell (370 U.S. 230) 469
Ref re Remuneration of Judges of the Prov. Court of P.E.I.;
Ref re Independence and Impartiality of Judges of the
Prov. Court of P.E.I. [1997] 3 SCR 3 73
United States v Moalin No. 13-50572 (9th Cir. 2020)...412
Upjohn Co v United States (1981) 449 US 383 per Renquist J at 389....................198
Williams v Wallace 240 F. Supp. 100, 106 (M.D. Ala. 1965) 186

New Zealand

IRC v West-Walker [1954] NZLR 191 (CA)...194

Table of Legislation

Administration of Justice Act 1985 349
Courts and Legal Services Act 1990 .... 302, 349, 467
Act of Settlement 1701 .... 62, 76, 110, 148
Act of Union 1706 (England and Wales) 76
Act of Union 1707 (Scotland) 76
Act of Union 1800 (Britain and Ireland) 76
Act Prohibiting Importation of Slaves 1807 2 Stat. 426. (US) 172
Anti-terrorism, Crime and Security Act 2001 .... 180, 406–07
Appellate Jurisdiction Act 1876 62
Banking Act 1987 195
Bill of Rights 1688/9 .... 47, 75–76, 127, 162, 168, 177
British North America Act 1867 73
Claim of Right Act 1689 (Scotland) 76
Commonwealth of Australia Constitution Act 1900 74
Companies Act 1967 384
Constitutional Reform Act 2005 .... 2, 62–63, 68, 76–78, 84, 90–96, 102, 428, 459
Contempt of Court Act 1981 .... 88, 192
Counter-terrorism and Security Act 2015 413
Courts and Legal Services Act 1990 .... 302, 349, 467
Criminal Justice and Courts Act 2015 181
Criminal Justice and Public Order Act 1994 163
District Law Societies Act 1878 (NZ) 259
Equality Act 2010 303
Fixed-term Parliaments Act 2011 .... 77, 430
Freedom of Information Act 2000 .... 89, 118
Human Rights Act 1998 .... 68, 77, 179–81, 194, 407–08, 410, 433, 449
Justice and Security Act 2013 410–11
Law Officers Act 1944 87
Law Officers Act 1997 .... 84, 87
Legal Aid, Sentencing and Punishment of Offenders Act 2012 .... 247, 466
Legal Services Act 2007 .... 2, 276, 287, 295, 349, 352–54, 356–58, 361, 368–69, 380, 471
Police and Criminal Evidence Act 1984 193
Public Disclosure Act 1998 130

Prevention of Terrorism Act 2005 ....180, 408
Prisoners Counsel Act 1836 151–52,
155–56, 218, 221
Proceeds of Crime Act 2002 204
Regulation of Investigatory Powers Act 2000 411
Representation of the People Act 1832..112
Sarbanes-Oxley Act 2002 (US)..205
Solicitors Act 1974 .... 247, 275, 291
Special Immigration Appeals Commission Act 1997.............................406, 409
Terrorism Act 2000 204
Terrorism Prevention and Investigation Measures Act 2011 408

Codes of Conduct and Other Role Guidance

Main Professional Conduct Guides

Australia: Legal Profession Uniform Conduct (Barristers) Rules 2015.
    Law Council of Australia Australian Solicitors' Conduct Rules 2011 298
Canada: Federation of Law Societies of Canada Model Code
    of Professional Conduct 2014.. 285, 298, 314
England and Wales: Bar Standards Board Code of Conduct 2014.
    Solicitor Regulation Authority Code of Conduct 2011 298
New Zealand: Lawyers and Conveyancers Act (Lawyers:
    Conduct and Client Care) Rules 2008 ....260, 283,
298, 326, 330
United States: ABA Model Rules of Professional Conduct 1983....................298, 300,
305, 328, 342

Other Professional Guides

American Bar Association Canons of Ethics 1908 4
American Bar Association Model Code of Professional
    Responsibility 1969.. 280, 284–87, 289,
293, 303, 305,
309–10, 312, 314
Canadian Bar Association, 'Codes of Professional Conduct'
    www.cba.org/Publications-Resources/Practice-Tools/Ethics-
    and-Professional-Responsibility-(1)/Codes-of-Professional-Conduct 284
Council of Bars and Law Societies of Europe, Charter of Core
    Principles of the European Legal Profession Code of Conduct
    for European Lawyers (November 2013) www.ccbe.eu/
    NTCdocument/EN_CCBE_CoCpdf1_1382973057.pdf 419
Federation of Law Societies of Canada, Model Code of Professional
    Conduct (as amended 10 October 2014), first para of preface,
    https://flsc.ca/wp-content/uploads/2014/12/conduct1.pdf 285

General Council of the Bar of England and Wales, Code of Conduct
of the Bar of England and Wales 1981 (London, General Council
of the Bar, 1981) 301
International Bar Association, International Code of Ethics 1988........................418
International Bar Association, International Principles on
Conduct for the Legal Profession (adopted 28 May 2011)
www.ibanet.org/resources 418
Law Society's Code for Advocacy (1993) (UK) 302
Netherland Bar Association, The Rules of Conduct of Advocates 1992,
Introduction 1.2. www.ccbe.eu/fileadmin/speciality_distribution/
public/documents/National_Regulations/DEON_National_
CoC/EN_Netherlands_The_Rules_of_Conduct_of_Advocates.pdf 316
Solicitors Code of Conduct 2007 (UK)... 276, 300, 302, 307,
311, 333, 336, 363, 365–66

Government, Parliamentary and Judicial Guides

*Cabinet Manual: A Guide to laws, conventions and rules on the
operation of government.* https://assets.publishing.service.gov.uk/
government/uploads/system/uploads/attachment_data/file/60641/
cabinet-manual.pdf 77, 87
Code of Conduct for Members of Parliament, https://publications.
parliament.uk/pa/cm201719/cmcode/1882/188202.htm#_
idTextAnchor000 116
Erskine May, https://erskinemay.parliament.uk/ 59, 114
General Council of the Bar of England and Wales, *Code of Conduct
of the Bar of England and Wales* (London, 1981) 251, 273, 286,
301–02, 306, 308, 311,
314, 334, 340, 354
Guide to Judicial Conduct (2019) www.supremecourt.uk/docs/
guide-to-judicial-conduct.pdf 63–64
Ministerial Code (London, Cabinet Office, 2018)
www.gov.uk/government/publications/ministerial-code 61, 104
Ministerial role: Solicitor General. www.gov.uk/government/ministers/
solicitor-general..87
Supreme Court Guide to Judicial Conduct (2009) (UK) 63–64
Securities and Exchange Commission *Implementation of Standards
of Professional Conduct for Attorneys* (US) www.sec.gov/rules/
final/33-8185.htm..206

1
Lawyers and the Rule of Law

> From all outward appearances the ... lawyer is much like everybody else. He is dressed no better than representatives of other occupations or businesses requiring contact with the public ... Certainly he possesses neither the house nor the car which corresponds to the income which others may think he earns based upon his many years of education and the hours he devotes to his profession ... Yet he is surprisingly unpopular. He has been unhappily described as one who gets two other men to strip for a fight and then takes their clothes.[1]

I. INTRODUCTION

THIS BOOK EXAMINES the role of lawyers and argues that it is defined by the rule of law. The relationship was rooted in the European Enlightenment (circa 1600–1800), which led to societies based on the consent of the people, on individuality and on popular observance of law with minimum coercion. The central hypothesis was that this vision of the rule of law and the social role of lawyers were inextricably entwined but needed renewal to survive another 400 years. This chapter briefly contextualises the study. It begins by briefly considering the recent attention to the rule of law and the popular portrayal of lawyers exemplified by the above quotation from Gower and Price. It then explores the approach and structure of the book and outlines the literature underpinning each of four Parts, focusing initially on the literature of the Enlightenment.

II. CONTEXT

In 1885, the British constitutional scholar, AV Dicey identified the rule of law and Parliamentary sovereignty, both concerning the right to make law against the wishes of the monarch or other institutions of government,[2] as twin pillars of

---

[1] LCB Gower and L Price, 'The Profession and Practice of the Law in England and America' (1957) 20(4) *The Modern Law Review* 317, 346 citing AP Blaustein and CO Porter, *The American Lawyer: A Summary of the Survey of the Legal Profession* (Chicago, University of Chicago Press, 1954).
[2] MJC Vile, *Constitutionalism and the Separation of Powers*, 2nd edn (Minneapolis, Liberty Fund, 1998) 252.

the British Constitution.[3] Over 100 years later it made a statutory debut when the Constitutional Reform Act 2005 stated that nothing in it was to affect the 'existing constitutional principle of the rule of law'.[4] In 2007 the Parliamentary Select Committee on the Constitution noted that the section 'begs several questions, the first: what the "rule of law" actually means'.[5] In the Committee's exploration of this question it received evidence from politicians, judges, and academics but no definitive answer.

The Committee received a paper presented by Professor Paul Craig highlighting ambiguities in Dicey's conception of the rule of law.[6] Craig suggested three different ways it could be viewed, starting with the 'core idea' that 'government must have a basis for actions that were regarded as valid by the relevant legal system'[7] or have them struck down by the courts. The second purpose was to guide citizens in organising their lives, which required law to be known, and therefore 'open, clear, stable, general and applied by an impartial judiciary'.[8]

Craig's third purpose of the rule of law was to develop principles of accountable government and justice, mainly through the courts employing mechanisms of judicial review. These were based on and produced principles: 'legality, procedural propriety, participation, fundamental rights, openness, rationality, relevancy, propriety of purpose, reasonableness, equality, legitimate expectations, legal certainty and proportionality'.[9] Craig noted that there was little consensus about whether any such principles were fundamental to the rule of law.

The Select Committee considered these among other possible constructions of the rule of law, from a simple procedural device concerned with the currency and clarity of law to a mechanism for achieving justice. It reached no conclusion on what the 'the existing constitutional principle of the rule of law' meant. The British judge and jurist, Sir John Laws, had reached a similar conclusion: 'a vast academic literature of the rule of law' resulted from 'a remarkable lack of consensus as to what this much-used expression means'.[10] The rule of law made a second statutory appearance two years later, this time in an Act relating to lawyers.

The Legal Services Act 2007 (LSA) reconstructed the legal services market in England and Wales around eight regulatory objectives governing the organisations regulating lawyers. These included 'upholding the constitutional principle of the rule of law'.[11] The Act had an extensive list of defined expressions, but the rule of law was

---

[3] AV Dicey, *Introduction to the Study of the Law of the Constitution* (Boston, Adamant Media Corporation, 2005) (1st edn published 1885).
[4] Constitutional Reform Act 2005, s 1(a).
[5] Select Committee on Constitution Sixth Report, 'Relations between the Executive, The Judiciary and Parliament' Chapter 1: Introduction and Background, para 23, https://publications.parliament.uk/pa/ld200607/ldselect/ldconst/151/15103.htm#a1.
[6] Select Committee on the Constitution Sixth Report, Appendix 5: Paper by Professor Paul Craig: 'The Rule of Law, Section 2: Dicey's conception of the rule of law', https://publications.parliament.uk/pa/ld200607/ldselect/ldconst/151/15115.htm.
[7] ibid.
[8] ibid.
[9] ibid.
[10] J Laws, 'The Rule of Law: The Presumption of Liberty and Justice' (2017) 22(4) *Judicial Review* 365.
[11] Legal Services Act 2007, s 1(1)(b).

not one of them.¹² In 2007, the Law Society, the professional body of the solicitors' profession, sought government approval of a regulatory handbook.¹³ It contained a list of core principles solicitors had to observe and a new code of conduct. The government requested insertion of an additional principle to those proposed, requiring that solicitors support the rule of law. The way in which they did so, beyond performing their occupational legal role, was an opaque consequence of the adversarial justice system.

As the quotation opening this chapter illustrated, lawyers' work role was not widely appreciated. The popular impression was influenced by an early literature Winifred Duke found to be 'unreal and unimpressive', probably because '[f]ictional lawyers are frequently introduced by writers who know little about the law, and who permit their advocates, judges, and attorneys to indulge in grotesque mistakes of procedure and legality'.¹⁴ Duke's conclusion, reached in 1929, may have been challenged by Harper Lee's *To Kill a Mockingbird*, set in a racist community in the American Deep South in the 1930s. Whereas some books on lawyers were relatively unknown outside of their country of origin¹⁵ Lee's tour de force was published in 1960 to instant acclaim. It attracted an international academic literature of its own, much of it concerning the lawyer protagonist, Atticus Finch, well-known enough to be identified simply as Atticus.

In *To Kill a Mockingbird* Atticus was depicted as governed yet torn between loyalty to clients and service to law. He represented Tom Robinson, a black man accused of rape, heroically defending him both in the courtroom and against a lynch mob.¹⁶ Some praised Atticus for the 'warm zeal' he brought to his court appointed and unpaid position, but Freedman suggested he betrayed it when he claimed he had hoped to avoid such a task in his career.¹⁷ Atticus was also criticised for failing the law, concealing the identity of the reclusive Boo Radley, saviour of Finch's daughter and killer of her attacker, to protect his privacy.¹⁸ Here, as elsewhere, legal storylines presented a disjuncture between role and legality, or morality and ethics. A lawyer either acted morally and against their ethics, running the risk of discipline and disbarment, or ethically and against ordinary morals.

The inherent moral ambiguity of the role permeated dramatic legal roles: 'devoted advocate (for good or ill), passionate activist, and reluctant hero'.¹⁹ A US Supreme Court decision in 1915 denied film the free speech protection enjoyed by books.²⁰ The decision resulted in a Production Code governing Hollywood, known as the Hays

---

[12] ibid Schedule 24.
[13] A Boon, 'The legal professions' new handbooks: narratives, standards, and values' (2016) 19(2) *Legal Ethics* 207.
[14] W Duke, 'Lawyers in Literature' (1929) *Juridical Review* 41.
[15] G Morris, 'Devils down under: Perceptions of Lawyer's Ethics in New Zealand Fiction' (2013) *Victoria University Wellington Law Review* 609.
[16] T Dare, 'Lawyers, Ethics and To Kill a Mockingbird' (2001) 25(1) *Philosophy and Literature* 127, S Davies, 'Atticus Finch Alive or dead? A Socio-legal Question' (2019) 36(1) *Law in Context* 36.
[17] MH Freedman, 'Atticus Finch – Right and Wrong' (1994) 45 *Alabama Law Review* 473, 480.
[18] AS Beard, 'From Hero to Villain: The Corresponding Evolutions of Model Ethical Codes and the Portrayal of Lawyers in Film' (2010) 55 *New York Law School Law Review* 961, 967.
[19] ibid 962.
[20] ibid 965.

Code, which from the 1930s dictated what could be shown. This specified that the justice system be shown in a positive light, leading to the film studios portraying lawyers as just, ethical, and moral. This lasted until at least the 1950s. Perhaps coincidentally, this aspirational presentation of lawyers aligned with the moral presentation of lawyers in the American Bar Association *Canons of Ethics* (1908).[21]

When lawyers were introduced to television their silver screen image briefly endured. *Perry Mason*, a series about a criminal defence attorney made between 1957 and 1966, was typical of the genre.[22] Each episode introduced a cast of characters including a murder victim. Mason's client was accused of the murder based on circumstantial evidence, but Mason or his colleagues found the vital evidence to identify the real killer.[23] Mason was upright, ethical, and principled, a position permitted by the innocence of his clientele. This image did not survive beyond the 1970s. Indeed, William Simon, pointing to the preponderance of representations in which lawyers 'broke the rules' to achieve justice, concluded that popular culture found them unattractive when they followed 'narrow' notions of legality.[24]

Simon's suggestion, that a lawyer's inclination to categorical judgement reflected a kind of emotional and intellectual immaturity,[25] was illustrated by the character of French *avocat* Joséphine Karlsson in the French detective series *Spiral*. An ambitious defence lawyer who broke the rules to win cases for despicable clients, Karlsson routinely told criminal clients what lie to tell, concealed evidence and misled the court. By Season 8 she was reformed, a more altruistic and sympathetic character, still breaking the rules but for more deserving causes.

The Australian series *Rake*[26] showed barrister Cleaver Green, a womanising, drug, alcohol and gambling addicted barrister,[27] with clients guilty of something, but not necessarily of the offence they were charged with. Green defended them with evident relish, and legalistically, insisting on the strict meaning of law. In the first episode the client accused of murder had, by arrangement, hosted a suicide and then, at the victim's request, eaten some of the carcass. Green's defence to a murder charge was that his client did not kill anyone: 'cannibalism is not an offence in New South Wales'.[28]

In the episode of *Rake* in which Green defended the cannibal, the popular conception of the legal role was neatly displayed at a dinner party hosted by Joe Sandilands, the State (New South Wales) Attorney General. The conversation turned to the case:

Sal: What would be the point Cleave?

Green: The point of what Sal?

---

[21] ibid.
[22] The series was set in Los Angeles, California and based on books by Erle Stanley Gardner.
[23] A similar structure was found in other examples, eg John Mortimer's *Rumpole of the Bailey*.
[24] WH Simon, 'Should Lawyers Obey the Law' (1996) 38 *William and Mary Law Review* 217, 236–37.
[25] ibid 239.
[26] P Duncan and A Knight, *Rake* (Essential Media and Entertainment, Netflix, 2010).
[27] Historically a rake (short for rakehell) was an immoral character given to these vices who frittered their inheritance.
[28] Duncan (n 26) Season 1 Episode 1: 'R v Murray'.

Sal: You said you were pushing to pursue this to trial. So, what would the point be?

Joe: Yeah. The time and money wasted on an exercise which is gonna make absolutely no difference to your client's future?

Green: Well, to be perfectly Francis [frank] with you, I don't give a shit about my client's future. What I do give a shit about, believe it or not, is the law.

Male guest: Since when?

Green: I don't know about you lot, but I don't want to live in a society where, for purely political reasons, someone can be charged with a crime they didn't commit.

Joe: That's a pretty serious accusation.

Green: Oh please. And it's all kosher because he's got a couple of mental health issues?

[Argument continues good naturedly but with attacks on the client's character]

Male guest: You don't give a rat's arse about the law Cleave. You get low-life crooks off all the time.

Green: 51 per cent of the time. And, once again, you misread me. The very reason I get my low-life crooks off is because I care about the law: It's justice I don't give a toss about.

[All laugh]

Upholding the letter of the law, rather than its spirit, was a common theme of *Rake*. In the second episode the backpack of an Islamic terrorist exploded, killing only him. Green defended his wife, accused of conspiracy in the terrorist plot, but realised during the trial that she had murdered her troublesome and dangerous husband by detonating the bomb where it would hurt no one but him.[29] Green did not reveal this, his behaviour inconsistent with legality but, arguably, consistent with his duty to his client. In another case Green contrived the conviction of his client, partly because he thought that was the right result and for his own reasons. In doing this, he set up his own moral code as superior to law and let self-interest intrude on professional decisions. Since both were acts inimical to the rule of law *Rake* highlighted the risks of replacing compliance with the procedures of law with personal discretion and achieving a popular ideal of justice rather than a legal one.

Another theme of portrayal of the legal role was self-interest, which could, as in *Rake*, be presented as a kind of professional power. This was well-represented in the British television comedy series *Defending the Guilty*. The main character, Will Packham, was one of four pupil barristers serving their apprenticeship while vying for a place in chambers. Discovering that he was trailing in the in-house book on which of them would get the role Will confronted his pupil master, Caroline, a hard-bitten criminal hack, in the court café. Why had no one thought it would be him? Attempting to explain the general perception of his hopelessness, and sensing his total incomprehension:

Caroline: [slow and parental] What are we doing this for?

Will: [tentatively] Just-ice?

Caroline: Shhhh – no, no, no – to win!

---

[29] In 'R v Mohammed' Season 2 Episode 1, Duncan (n 26).

The caricature of lawyers as unprincipled, self-interested proceduralists was part of a larger canon which was not wholly inaccurate. The justification of the role it portrayed was that it was dictated by the needs of a society committed to recognising the dignity of the individual and upholding their rights against the power of the state. This more honourable work role made lawyers champions of their clients but also champions of the rule of law. How this support for the rule of law came about, and whether it could continue under the conditions of the twenty-first century, were issues addressed in this project.

III. METHODOLOGY

The primary focus for investigation was the late medieval period to the present-day. The spread of both the rule of law and the legal role during this period was considered using jurisdictions adopting the British common law: England and Wales, the US, Canada, Australia and New Zealand (the core jurisdictions). This limited range allowed comparison of constitutional systems, law, and lawyers in different locations but with similar starting points. This comparison suggested that the legal role was broadly similar across the core jurisdictions but with some key differences in detail.

Part I (Government) sets out lawyers' role in producing the constitutional order, the institutions characterising that order and the roles of lawyers, judges, and government lawyers. Part II (Private Practice) looks at the ways private practice contributed to the evolution of social order based on the rule of law. Part III (Professions) examines the process of adopting and articulating norms of practice. Part IV (Futures) examines the place of the rule of law and the legal role in modern society.

While the overall structure of the book is broadly chronological, chapters are topical and potentially cover an extended time frame. The analysis drew on legal, historical, philosophical, and sociological sources and existing material comparing the subject jurisdictions.[30] It also looked at some periods and incidents in more depth than others. These provide the heart or core of the academic literature[31] and help to shape perceptions of lawyers and the intellectual environment surrounding the study of them.[32] Some of these stories acquired a mythical quality it was helpful to contextualise.

The analysis of the codes of conduct of core common law jurisdictions set out in the last two chapters of Part III involved a different mode of analysis, comparing the ways certain obligations were presented in lawyers' codes of conduct. The aim was not to use a comparative method to address specific societal or cultural issues, but simply to assess how different legal professions expressed their engagement with the

---

[30] See eg, J Auburn, *Legal Professional Privilege: Law and Theory* (Oxford, Hart Publishing, 2001).

[31] K Economides and M O'Leary, 'The Moral of the Story: Toward and Understanding of Ethics in Organisations and Legal Practice' (2009) 10 *Legal Ethics* 5.

[32] S Scheingold, *The Politics of Rights: Lawyers, Public Policy and Political Change* (Ann Arbor, University of Michigan Press, 2004).

rule of law. The analysis examined rules for approaches to the key rule of law issues related to client autonomy and legality. It used some but not all steps of comparative method.[33] The missing element, how rules operated in practice, was not required for the questions investigated.[34]

While the analysis was restricted to the five core jurisdictions it was arguably of wider relevance. Friedman noted that introduction of Western law to countries often led to the adoption of models of the Western lawyer.[35] Further, institutions like the International Bar Association aimed to spread lawyer organisations worldwide with a view to 'improving the rule of law and defending liberty and justice'.[36] In this task they used a model of lawyers based on those familiar in the core jurisdictions and elsewhere.

It was necessary to identify research questions linking lawyers' engagement with the rule of law to a broad historical context and apparently disparate areas. This involved meeting several objectives:

1. How the roles of judges, government lawyers, and private practice lawyers developed in relation to the rule of law.
2. How these roles supported the rule of law by balancing the demands of individuality and legality.
3. Whether they continued to do so in the changed conditions of modern society and, if not, whether alternative ways of supporting the rule of law were necessary.

My starting point was simply to examine the evolution of lawyers' engagement with the rule of law with a view to illuminating the future. Martin Krygier, an academic who devoted a career to analysing the rule of law, acknowledged difficulties in understanding the motives of social actors in the distant past, arguing that:

> intimations of intellectual dispositions, sensibilities, and traditions of thought and practice that have left significant residues in our culture and seem still able to offer valuable clues about things that matter … So although there is no single understanding of the rule of law that captures it all, there are constellations of themes, preoccupations, and tendencies, some long-lived.[37]

Lawyers often responded to the demands of the rule of law in ways that are just as relevant today.

---

[33] M Van Hoecke, 'Methodology of Comparative Legal Research' (2015) *Law and Method*, www.bjutijdschriften.nl/tijdschrift/lawandmethod/2015/12/RENM-D-14-00001.

[34] The first two steps involve objective and neutral examination of rules and the fourth step is drawing conclusions based on these data. (see further EJ Eberle, 'The Methodology of Comparative Law' (2011) 16(1) *Roger Williams University Law Review* 51).

[35] L Friedman, 'Lawyers in Cross-Cultural Perspective' in RL Abel and PSC Lewis (eds), *Lawyers in Society: Volume 3: Comparative Theories* (Berkeley, University of California Press, 1989).

[36] International Bar Association, 'IBA publishes new code of conduct for the global legal profession' (21 July 2011), www.malaysianbar.org.my/article/news/legal-and-general-news/legal-news/iba-publishes-new-code-of-conduct-for-the-global-legal-profession.

[37] M Krygier, 'The Rule of Law: Pasts, Presents and Two Possible Futures' (2016) 12 *Annual Review of Law and Social Science* 199, 202.

8 *Lawyers and the Rule of Law*

IV. LITERATURE

The early parts of the book link the literature of the Enlightenment to the emergence of constitutional government (Part I) and legal roles (Part II). The purpose of this was to locate lawyers' roles in the society, institutions, and patterns of thought characteristic of the time. The first half of Part III (Professions) is also largely historical, the first two chapters examining engagement with the rule of law through professionalisation and codes of conduct. The second half of Part III is empirical, relating current codes of conduct to the rule of law. Part IV explores recent and contemporary engagements of lawyers with the rule of law focusing on professions, corporations, globalisation, and democracy. There was a potentially large literature overall. Professor Craig's evidence to the Parliamentary Select Committee on the Constitution suggested he had found 16,810 citations to books and articles on the rule of law alone.[38] Not all of this was considered here.

A. Part I: Government

i. *The Enlightenment and the Social Contract*

Aspects of the modern rule of law, for example, that the law should be general and applied by judges to individuals using discretion, were present in Greek or Roman constitutional provisions.[39] The European Enlightenment (roughly 1600–1800) resulted from the earlier exposure of Western religious scholars, such as Thomas Aquinas (1225–74) to the works of Greek philosophy, but also involved applying the method of reason to understanding the universe and the human condition. This revolution in scientific inquiry produced the ideas underpinning the liberal order. Central individuals, identified by Stephen Holmes, included: Milton, Spinoza, Locke, Montesquieu, Hume, Voltaire, Beccaria, Blackstone, Smith, Kant, Bentham, Madison, Hamilton, Constant, De Tocqeville, and Mill.[40]

In political philosophy John Locke, Jean-Jacques Rousseau and Immanuel Kant developed a view of the world which gained wide influence. It built on a theory proposed by Thomas Hobbes (1588–1679) that humans were motivated by basic impulses of survival. In *Leviathan*, Hobbes imagined humans in a 'State of Nature' living by the 'Law of Nature' composed of nine universal rules creating trustworthy and stable social relations. Other philosophers reconceived and embroidered Hobbes' idyl.

John Locke (1632–1704) thought that people were born without an innate condition, therefore 'being all equal and independent, no one ought to harm another in his life, liberty, or possessions'.[41] Charles-Louis Montesquieu (1689–1755) saw humans

---

[38] Craig (n 6).
[39] Vile (n 2) 48–49.
[40] S Holmes, *Passions and Constraint: On the Theory of Liberal Democracy* (Chicago, University of Chicago Press, 1995).
[41] J Locke, *Second Treatise of Government* 1689 (New York, MacMillan, 1952) para 6.

as naturally avoiding violence. Jean-Jacque Rousseau (1712–88) saw the state of nature as one of harmony ended by the division of labour, and the need to protect wealth and property.[42] Another influential device used by Hobbes was the idea of a 'social contract' between ruler and ruled. Under this the natural freedoms of the state of nature were subjugated, traded for protection by a strong state. Later scholars exploited the concept's radical potential.

Hobbes' successors thought that the social contract should produce a society in which people were not governed by coercive force. Rousseau predicted that a 'naturalized social contract', protecting the 'haves' from the 'have nots' would be superseded by a normative social contract based on agreement,[43] leading to a free and equal society.[44] Locke proposed a state respecting individual autonomy in return for the citizen's observance of positive law.[45] In *The Spirit of the Laws*, Montesquieu conceived of liberty as the 'tranquility of mind' provided by protection from harm by law, arguing that people should be allowed the freedom to engage in the widest possible range of activity in confidence that, if they obeyed laws, the power of the state would not be directed against them.[46]

ii. Liberty and the Individual

The individual's right to liberty was at the centre of Enlightenment scholarship. One of Hobbes' laws of nature, respecting others' liberty, required 'that every man acknowledge another for his equal by nature; no man require to reserve to himself any right, which he is not content should be reserved to every one of the rest; if a man be trusted to judge between man and man, that he deal equally between them'.[47] Others tended to agree with this idea of individuality, only Rousseau urging subordination of the individual to society, arguing that rights should be controlled by the community: equality was the prime value of social organisation, subordinating the individual.[48] One of Rousseau's more influential ideas was that government be distinguished from the sovereign power of the People. If government was committed to the good of the People, it obeyed the law. If it exceeded the boundaries set by the People, they could remove it and constitute another government.

Society based on law was a powerful and revolutionary idea during the late medieval period. Tom Paine's advocacy of violent rebellion against oppressive rule influenced the course of events in Britain's North American colonies. A signal contribution by Montesquieu to the political philosophy of the Enlightenment was a model

---

[42] JJ Rousseau, 'On the Social Contract, or, Principles of Political Rights' (1762) and 'The Discourse on the Origin and Foundations of Inequality Among Men' in *Jean-Jacques Rousseau: The Basic Political Writings* (trans DA Cress) (Cambridge, MA, Hackett Publishing Company, 1987).
[43] ibid.
[44] ibid 'On the Social Contract'.
[45] J Locke *Second Treatise of Government* (Indianapolis, Hackett, 1980).
[46] C de Montesquieu, *The Spirit of the Laws* 11.4. cited in H Bok, 'Baron de Montesquieu, Charles-Louis de Secondat' in EN Zalta (ed), *The Stanford Encyclopedia of Philosophy* (Summer 2014 Edition), https://plato.stanford.edu/archives/sum2014/entries/montesquieu/.
[47] These are the 9th, 10th and 11th laws (ibid).
[48] Rousseau (n 42).

for constitutional government. This aimed to embody the supremacy of law and preserve the liberty of the subject. His constitutional arrangement distributed the functions of law's creation, formulation, execution, and interpretation, to different parts of the state. This distribution, known as the separation of powers, facilitated liberty by minimising the risk of abuse of power by any one of the bodies discharging the functions.[49]

iii. Legality and Order

The separation of state and society following the Enlightenment, Saunders suggested, 'de-theologised' government and 'de-politicised religion'[50] leading to conscience becoming a private rather than a public or political concern and positive law an instrument of pacification. Separating religion from politics minimised conflict between factions and created 'a sphere of civil life independent of the empire of religion'.[51] The growth of civil society was a vital factor in providing avenues for contestation and continuing debates about morality. The market exchanges, coffee houses and academies constituted a new civil society populated by privileged but politically powerless aristocrats, nouveau riche tradesmen, merchants and financiers and intellectuals.[52] From the eighteenth century, intellectuals became centres of moral authority, able to criticise political authority.[53] This caused political tensions first manifest in the French Revolution.

The new civil sphere provided a secure social platform to project a vision of moral society based on inalienable rights and fundamental freedoms to which the state posed a threat.[54] The source of these rights, the common law, was promoted by William Blackstone (1723–80), a former barrister and University administrator. His early legal treatise, written while an Oxford University librarian, led to him becoming the first Vinerian Professor of Law at Oxford in 1758. His *Commentaries on the Laws of England*, published between 1765 and 1770,[55] helped to establish the common law in other core jurisdictions.[56] The idea of inalienable rights embodied in a common law was at odds with the separation of law and morality in the political philosophy of the Enlightenment, beginning with Hobbes' observation that law was that which the sovereign commanded.

The noted utilitarian philosopher, John Austin (1790–1859) took issue with Blackstone's assertion that the source of all law was God's law and that which

---

[49] Vile (n 2) 260.
[50] D Saunders, *Anti-Lawyers: Religion and the Critics of Law and State* (Abingdon, Routledge, 1997) citing, at 4–7, R Koselleck, *Critique and Crisis: Enlightenment and the Pathogenesis of Modern Society* (Oxford, Berg, 1988) 39.
[51] Saunders (n 50) 3.
[52] ibid 7–9 citing Koselleck (n 50) 65–66.
[53] Koselleck (n 50).
[54] Saunders (n 50) 9.
[55] W Blackstone, *Blackstone's Commentaries on the Laws of England* (1765–1770). See The Online Library of Liberty, http://files.libertyfund.org/files/2140/Blackstone_1387-01_EBk_v6.0.pdf.
[56] AS Miles, 'Blackstone and his American Legacy' (2000) 5(2) *Australia & New Zealand Journal of Law and Education* 1327.

contradicted it was not law.[57] Based on Hobbes, Austin argued that all law was human creation and that there was no necessary connection between law and morality. This insight was often attributed to the more lauded Jeremy Bentham (1747–1832) and was championed, with some modifications, during the second half of the twentieth century by HLA Hart.

Hart's work exposed schisms in legal philosophy scholarship between those who saw the rule of law as a set of procedural principles and those who argued that it had substantive and/or moral dimensions. Lon Fuller, a Professor of Jurisprudence at Harvard, accepted the procedural dimensions of the rule of law but argued that the 'inner morality of law' was a condition of legality.[58] Later philosophers followed and developed one or other of these positions. Some accepted Aristotle's line that the rule of law depended on both good constitutional arrangements and an overall aim (telos) or sought authority for such additions in the social contract or in values such as individual liberty and the freedom of the subject.

iv. The Rule of Law

Aristotle had argued that the rule of law was preferable to the (arbitrary) rule of man,[59] but the modern significance attached to the phrase originated with Dicey. He identified three requirements of the rule of law, the first that personal liberty should not be interfered with or punished except for breaches of existing law determined by ordinary courts. This asserted '… the absolute supremacy or predominance of regular law as opposed to the influence of arbitrary power … [excluding] the existence of arbitrariness, of prerogative, or even of wide discretionary authority on the part of the government …'.[60] The second of Dicey's requirements of the rule of law was that everyone, whatever their position in society, was subject to ordinary law.

The third element of Dicey's rule of law was that it included constitutional rights established by the common law courts in deciding the cases of citizens. This echoed Blackstone's idea that sovereign power was constrained by the common law, judge made law, rooted in antiquity. The ambiguity in the idea of the rule of law, between a set of essentially procedural mechanisms constraining central power and a set of more substantive rights was unresolved by Dicey[61] and received relatively little academic attention until the 1960s, when Selznick proposed that it should be a central focus of legal sociology.[62] Krygier noted that interest accelerated dramatically from the 1980s and from several viewpoints.[63]

---

[57] SE Stumpf, 'Austin's Theory of the Separation of Law and Morals' (1960–1961) 14 *Vanderbilt Law Review* 117.
[58] L Fuller, *The Morality of Law* (New Haven, Yale University Press 1969).
[59] Vile (n 2) 25.
[60] ML Principe, 'Albert Venn Dicey and the Principles of the Rule of Law: Is Justice Blind? A Comparative Analysis of the United States and Great Britain' (2000) 22 *Loyola of Los Angeles International & Comparative Law Review* 357, 359 citing AV Dicey, *Introduction to the Study of the Law of the Constitution*, 10th edn (London, Macmillan, 1961) 42.
[61] See *Case of Proclamations* (1610) 12 Co Rep 74, EWHC KB J22.
[62] P Selznick, 'The sociology of law' in DL Sillis and RK Merton (eds), *The International Encyclopedia of the Social Sciences, Vol. 9* (New York, Macmillan 1968) 52.
[63] Krygier (n 37) 199, 200.

Marxist jurisprudence, seeking to expose the structure of law and domination in capitalist society, located the rule of law as 'the centrepiece of liberal political philosophy'.[64] The conservative political economist Francis Fukuyama, meanwhile, identified it as an essential component of effective modern states along with state institutions and accountable government.[65] Other works located the rule of law among a broader range of factors necessary for successful states[66] or considered what conditions may be prerequisite in establishing it.[67]

Despite general acceptance of the importance of the rule of law, the lack of clarity and scope in its formulation led Krygier to despair of finding a 'correct' definition or agreement on the values served by the rule of law:

> the term has become too protean, the purposes for which it is invoked too many and varied, the freight carried by this short phrase too distant from anything that could be derived from dictionary definitions of its component words. Not enough, because the phrase is part of old and ongoing moral and political arguments about fundamental matters of political organization, concerns, and ideals, much affirmed and much contested.[68]

Despite these doubts, Krygier suggested, the central concern the rule of law addressed was controlling the 'perversions and pathologies of power', particularly its arbitrary exercise.[69]

Krygier identified three kinds of arbitrary power. One was where power was exercised at the whim of a body under no routine or regular control.[70] A second was where those affected could not anticipate or understand what was required, so could not comply, and a third was where there was no opportunity to respond. The first kind was synonymous with a sovereign or sovereign body with limitless discretion. The second concerned prescriptions for the clarity and transparency of law and requirements that it be prospective rather than retrospective. The third suggested a need for procedural constraints on agents of the state so that those affected by law were afforded dignity.[71] While the state was a principal source of the first threat, it had to be strong enough to control non-state actors[72] and to have discretion to avoid them perpetrating the second and third kinds of arbitrariness.[73] This need for flexibility meant that the rule of law could not depend purely on constitutional arrangements.

Although the control of arbitrariness was central to the rule of law, there were arguments that it necessarily involved more. This was implicit in the third limb of

---

[64] H Collins, *Marxism and Law* (Oxford, Clarendon, 1982) cited in G Baars, *The Corporation, Law and Capitalism* (Leiden, Boston, Brill Nijhoff, 2019) 9.
[65] F Fukuyama, *Origins of Political Order: From Prehuman Times to The French Revolution* (New York, Farrar, Straus, and Giroux, 2011).
[66] D Acemoglu and JA Robinson, *Why Nations Fail: The Origins of Power, Prosperity, and Poverty* (UK, Crown Business, 2013).
[67] JJ Heckman, RL Nelson and L Cabatingan (eds), *Global Perspectives on the Rule of Law* (London and New York, Routledge, 2010).
[68] Krygier (n 37) 202.
[69] ibid 203.
[70] ibid.
[71] J Waldron, 'The rule of law and the importance of procedure' (2011) 50 *Nomos* 3.
[72] Krygier (n 37) 221–22.
[73] ibid 204–5.

Dicey's formula, defining the rule of law with reference to fundamental rights established by British courts. At a minimum these might be summarised as a right to human dignity, the position adopted by British Law Lord and jurist, Tom Bingham.[74] The necessities for ensuring human dignity were debatable, covering a spectrum of basic political rights to philosophical arguments for egalitarian social arrangements. A key thinker was Immanuel Kant, who proposed that the social contract should be based on political arrangements producing autonomous persons, treated as 'ends in themselves'.[75] Kant regarded politics as subordinate to what was right, a standard against which rulers could be judged.

A recent exponent of the Kantian tradition, John Rawls, considered the constitution of a just society in *A Theory of Justice*.[76] Rawls proposed that the fundamental conditions in which law could be imposed on a pluralistic society were legitimacy and stability, which encouraged people to follow rules against their own interests when they were fair. By the device of a hypothetical 'Original Position', Rawls conceived rational people determining fair social arrangements[77] behind a 'veil of ignorance' concealing what one's situation in society might be.[78] They would assume the value of certain primary goods, wealth, rights, and the opportunity to allocate them based on two Principles of Justice.

Rawls' first principle of justice was that all citizens had as much freedom as possible consistent with the equal freedom of others. The second principle was that social and economic advantages were equally available, but not necessarily evenly distributed. Nevertheless, arrangements would benefit the least advantaged. These principles would inform the 'basic structure of society; the political constitution, forms of property, family structure and economy'.[79] Rawls concluded that civil liberties would be widely distributed and that the least well off would be better off than they would have been under any alternative system.

The protean tendencies of the rule of law called for the kind of synopsis provided by Brian Tamanaha, reproduced in Table 1.[80] The multiple versions of the rule of law were simplified by juxtaposing two levels, formal and substantive, each with three positions. The beginning of each row (boxes 1 and 4) represented bare, or 'thin', conceptions of the rule of law and the end (boxes 3 and 6) more developed, 'thick', versions. So, the beginning of the formal scale, 'rule *by* law', envisaged that government followed its own laws. Formal legality embodied Dicey's requirements that law was general, prospective, and clear and all were equal before the law. The final step required the consent of the governed through active democracy.

---

[74] T Bingham, *The Rule of Law* (London, Penguin, 2011).

[75] D Boucher and P Kelly, 'The Social Contract and Its Critics' in D Boucher and P Kelly (eds), *The Social Contract from Hobbes to Rawls* (London and New York, Routledge, 1994) 7–9.

[76] J Rawls, *A Theory of Justice* (Cambridge, MA, Harvard University Press, 1971).

[77] There are differences in how the original position might be perceived; from the viewpoint of one representative, rational person (eg Rawls) or more than one person with potentially divergent views eg F D'Agostino, *Incommensurability and Commensuration: The Common Denominator* (Burlington, VT, Ashgate, 2003).

[78] Rawls (n 76).

[79] J Rawls *Political Liberalism* (New York, Columbia University Press, 1996).

[80] BZ Tamanaha, *On the Rule of Law: History, Politics, Theory* (Cambridge, Cambridge University Press, 2004).

Table 1 Tamanaha's model of formal and substantive versions of the rule of law

Formal Versions	1. Rule by law law as an instrument of government action	2. Formal legality general, prospective, clear, certain	3. Democracy + legality consent determines content of law
Substantive Versions	4. Individual rights property, contract, privacy, autonomy	5. Right of dignity and/or justice	6. Social welfare substantive equality, welfare, preservation of community

Source: B Tamanaha, *One the Rule of Law: History, Politics, Theory* (Cambridge, Cambridge University Press, 2004) 91.

Along a 'substantive' row, the content of law, the first box contained protection of individual rights to property, contract, privacy, and autonomy. The mid-range position asserted the individual's right to dignity and justice. The final step on the substantive row promised equality, welfare, and preservation of community. Tamanaha saw no necessary relationship between the formal and substantive positions but thought they could align in practice. A totalitarian state might meet the requirements of the first box on each line, combining rule by law with basic rights to property, while Western democracies were most clearly situated in the middle box on each line (2 and 5) because of failures in fully achieving boxes 3 and 6.

B. Part II: Private Practice

Although lawyers were well-established in Europe and elsewhere during the Enlightenment, they were not the subject of the new craze for scientific analysis. This changed in 1831 when the French government funded a study of the prison system in the US. The work was carried out by Alexis de Tocqueville (1805–59) and Gustave de Beaumont[81] who both wrote books. De Tocqueville's *Democracy in America* (1835) expressed the difficulty of finding a suitable political form, for '[w]hen the rich alone govern, the interest of the poor is always endangered; and when the poor make the laws, that of the rich incurs very serious risks'.[82]

De Tocqueville considered aristocratic government superior to democracy when '… the representatives of the people do not always know how to write correctly'[83] but, since government based on aristocracy was in terminal decline, a 'new political science' was needed to 'instruct democracy'. Mediating institutions could prevent a 'tyranny of the majority' and the loss of individual rights. In America, lawyers were

---

[81] See further JT Schleifer, *The Making of Tocqueville's Democracy In America*, 2nd edn (Indianapolis, Liberty Fund, 1980), https://oll.libertyfund.org/titles/schleifer-the-making-of-tocquevilles-democracy-in-america.
[82] A de Tocqueville *Democracy in America* (trans H Reeve) (Penn State Electronic Classics Series, 1831) 266, http://seas3.elte.hu/coursematerial/LojkoMiklos/Alexis-de-Tocqueville-Democracy-in-America.pdf.
[83] ibid 227.

the obvious choice to perform that role, belonging 'to the people by birth and interest, to the aristocracy by habit and by taste, and they may be looked upon as the natural bond and connecting link of the two great classes of society'.[84] For these reasons, and despite recognising their inherent faults, De Tocqueville considered it necessary for the health of the American republic that lawyers' influence in public business increased proportionately to the broadening of the franchise.

De Tocqueville thought that lawyers displayed the tastes and habits of the aristocracy and entertained 'the same secret contempt of the government of the people'.[85] They were able to 'mingle the taste and the ideas of the aristocratic circles in which they move with the aristocratic interests of their profession'.[86] Other factors made them ideal arbiters between democracy and power:

> The special information which lawyers derive from their studies ensures them a separate station in society, and they constitute a sort of privileged body in the scale of intelligence. This notion of their superiority perpetually recurs to them in the practice of their profession: they are the masters of a science which is necessary, but which is not very generally known; they serve as arbiters between the citizens; and the habit of directing the blind passions of parties in litigation to their purpose inspires them with a certain contempt for the judgment of the multitude. To this it may be added that they naturally constitute a body, not by any previous understanding, or by an agreement which directs them to a common end; but the analogy of their studies and the uniformity of their proceedings connect their minds together, as much as a common interest could combine their endeavors.[87]

The situation in America reinforced de Tocqueville's point about controlling democracy. America had 'no nobles or men of letters, and the people is apt to mistrust the wealthy',[88] therefore lawyers, the bench and the Bar, were 'the highest political class, and the most cultivated circle of society'.[89]

Lawyers benefitted from democracy, because 'when the wealthy, the noble, and the prince are excluded from the government, they are sure to occupy the highest stations, in their own right, as it were, since they are the only men of information and sagacity, beyond the sphere of the people, who can be the object of the popular choice'.[90] Even the English aristocracy conferred 'a high degree of importance and of authority upon the members of the legal profession' and co-opted them.[91] English lawyers did not occupy the first rank but were content with their station as a 'younger branch of the English aristocracy'.[92]

De Tocqueville was intrigued by the fact that lawyers did not always appear to pursue the same collective strategies or seek the same political outcomes. Their influence in European political life had been volatile, working with the aristocracy in

---

[84] ibid 305.
[85] ibid 302.
[86] ibid.
[87] ibid.
[88] ibid 307.
[89] ibid.
[90] ibid.
[91] ibid 306.
[92] ibid.

England and against it in France, or first supporting the Crown and then opposing it.[93] Lawyers were not always 'friends of order and the opponents of innovation' but were usually so. Having nothing to gain by innovation made them more conservative and fostered their natural taste for public order.[94] They could be co-opted by the monarchy or aristocracy by high station and would then be conservative and anti-democratic[95] but they used institutions such as the jury system to promote counter-majoritarian values with the public. Their influence in government was a phenomenon that de Tocqueville thought it useful to investigate, 'since it may produce analogous consequences elsewhere'.

De Tocqueville asked whether lawyers were 'swayed by sudden and momentary impulses' or were 'impelled by principles which are inherent in their pursuits, and which will always recur in history'. He continued:

> I am incited to this investigation by reflecting that this particular class of men will most likely play a prominent part in that order of things to which the events of our time are giving birth. Men who have more especially devoted themselves to legal pursuits derive from those occupations certain habits of order, a taste for formalities, and a kind of instinctive regard for the regular connection of ideas, which naturally render them very hostile to the revolutionary spirit and the unreflecting passions of the multitude.[96]

Despite his description of lawyers as formalistic individuals, de Tocqueville thought English and American lawyer resembled 'the hierophants of Egypt, for, like them, he is the sole interpreter of an occult science'.[97]

De Tocqueville was not unusual in detecting lawyers' mystique. In the same period, the early nineteenth century, Jeremy Bentham referred to legal practice as 'lawyer craft', comparing it to religion and priest craft, but not as benign.[98] He criticised English lawyers for accepting injustice as natural and using legal jargon as an instrument of mystification. He thought this served to create a bond between lawyers, setting them apart, reinforcing their complacency, generating business, and keeping critics at arm's length.[99] The reality was more dynamic, according to the accounts of developments of the legal system in the eighteenth and nineteenth centuries by John Langbein and others.[100] Early comparison of lawyers to sorcerers, tribal shamans or priests continued in discussion of their role in modern business contexts, where legal form assumed a quasi-religious quality sanctioned by trust in the mystery of law.[101]

---

[93] ibid 301.
[94] ibid 307.
[95] ibid 303.
[96] ibid 302.
[97] In this, he was comparing the impenetrability of common law, compared to the French Civil Code (de Tocqueville, ibid 306).
[98] HLA Hart, 'Bentham and the Demystification of the Law' (1973) 36(1) *The Modern Law Review* 2, 9.
[99] ibid.
[100] JH Langbein, *The Origins of Adversary Criminal Trial* (Oxford, Oxford University Press, 2003); S Landsman, 'The Rise of the Contentious Spirit: Adversary Procedure in Eighteenth-Century England' (1990) 75(3) *Cornell Law Review* 498.
[101] J Flood, 'Lawyers as Sanctifiers: The Role of Elite Law Firms in International Business Transactions' (2007) 14(1) *Indiana Journal of Global Legal Studies* 35, Harari suggested that the uniquely human capacity to accept 'fiction' was exemplified by 'belief' in business corporations, but see CR Hallpike, 'A Response to Yuval Harari's *Sapiens: A Brief History of Humankind*' New English Review, https://aipavilion.github.io/docs/hallpike-review.pdf, citing Harari at 31.

C. Part III: Professions

i. Professional Rationality

In the twentieth century one of the founders of the emerging discipline of sociology, Max Weber (1864–1920) had a muted influence on the sociology of the professions because his work was not translated until 1968.[102] In *Economy and Society*, first published in Germany in the 1920s, Weber had suggested that the structures of market, bureaucracy and professions explained the emergence of Western rationality.[103] He argued that the nature of society determined the role of lawyers, while the work of lawyers shaped society. Legal systems were determined both by political and cultural factors operating on them and by the needs and preferences of stakeholders. Together, these institutions created the conditions for the advent of industrial capitalism.[104] Weber also explored the link in Western society between religion, capitalism and the kind of professional calling typified by lawyers.

In *The Protestant Ethic and the Spirit of Capitalism* (1905) Weber claimed that Protestantism created the physiological conditions for the development of constitutional government and capitalism.[105] The processes through which this occurred emanated in the Puritan theology of Jean Calvin. Weber saw economic rationalism as a system based not on custom 'but on the deliberate and systematic adjustment of economic means to the attainment of the objective of pecuniary profit'.[106] Based largely on the writings of English Puritans at the end of the seventeenth century, Weber detected a change in attitude legitimising pursuit of wealth. No longer anti-social or immoral, it became a religious duty. Weber proposed that Calvinism was linked to the development of the professions, capitalism, and bureaucracy because it focused on impersonal, rational goals.[107]

In *The Protestant Ethic and the Spirit of Capitalism* Weber noted that Catholicism demanded asceticism of the priest or monk: self-discipline, self-denial, abstinence, and avoidance of indulgence. Calvin demanded it of all believers. There was no hope that denial would bring redemption,[108] because a small number had already been chosen by God, or 'elected'. Their identity, or why they were chosen, was unknowable.[109] The 'extreme inhumanity' of God's decrees, fixed for eternity, gave Protestants 'a feeling of

---

[102] G Ritzer, 'Professionalization, Bureaucratization and Rationalization: The Views of Max Weber' (1975) 53(4) *Social Forces*.

[103] M Weber, *Economy and Society: An Outline of Interpretative Sociology* (G Roth and W Wittich, eds) (Totowa, New Jersey, Bedminster, 1968) and 2nd edn (Berkeley, University of California Press, 1978) https://archive.org/details/MaxWeberEconomyAndSociety/mode/2up.

[104] For critical summaries see DM Trubek, 'Max Weber on Law and the Rise of Capitalism' (1972) 3 *Wisconsin Law Review* 720 and M Albrow, 'Legal Positivism and Bourgeois Materialism: Max Weber's View of the Sociology of Law' (1975) 2 *British Journal of Law and Society* 14.

[105] M Weber, *The Protestant Ethic and the Spirit of Capitalism* (trans T Parsons) (London, George Allen and Unwin Ltd, 1930) 16.

[106] ibid Foreword 1.

[107] Ritzer (n 102) 627, 628, citing Weber (n 103) 1200.

[108] Weber (n 105) 117. Catholics believed that the priest was a magician who could offer atonement for sins, and who held the key to eternal life.

[109] Weber (n 105) 103.

unprecedented inner loneliness'.[110] God's plan meant spiritual isolation for the Puritan,[111] where all sociability, luxury, or inactive contemplation was time lost and valueless.[112]

Calvin urged his followers to believe themselves saved and apply themselves to intense worldly activity.[113] The elected Christian could serve the glorification of God only by fulfilling his commandments and serving the mundane requirements of the community through 'a calling',[114] in a task set by God. The calling was a novel idea in Christian thought derived from Luther's reading of the Bible, but not, as it had been for Luther, a station in God's schema to which one was born, but an enterprise chosen by the individual.[115] It made 'labour in the service of impersonal social usefulness appear to promote the glory of God and hence to be willed by Him'.[116] Labour in a calling was the ideal ascetic activity, God's approval was shown by the success of His chosen ones.[117] Good works, although useless in gaining salvation, demonstrated the believer's conviction of it.[118]

Weber thought that man's nature was 'simply to live as he is accustomed to live and to earn as much as is necessary for that purpose'.[119] Later Puritans rejected possession of goods as indicating people succumbing to idleness and pleasure.[120] Yet the combination of intense acquisitive activity and limited consumption produced the accumulation of capital.[121] While ascetic Puritanism rejected lust for worldly goods or luxury, the use of wealth for the good of the community was approved as rational. In the eighteenth century John Wesley's Methodism surrendered predestination but continued to advocate good works as a sign of belief:[122] 'we must exhort all Christians … to grow rich', but also to give all they can.[123] These beliefs laid a foundation for both occupational organisation and for capitalism.

Weber noted that religion tended to break down under the secularising influence of wealth,[124] 'giving way to utilitarian worldliness'.[125] What remained was what Weber perceived to be the English national character 'unspoiled naïve joy of life … a strictly regulated, reserved self-control, and conventional ethical conduct'.[126] Thus, he concluded, of Protestant doctrine, Calvinism 'appeared to be more closely related to the hard legalism and active enterprise of the bourgeoise-capitalistic entrepreneurs'.[127] Weber's notion of a calling fitted neatly with John Stuart Mills'

---

[110] ibid 104.
[111] ibid 107.
[112] ibid 157–58.
[113] ibid 111–12.
[114] ibid 108.
[115] ibid 160.
[116] ibid 109.
[117] ibid 133.
[118] ibid 115.
[119] ibid 60.
[120] ibid 157.
[121] ibid 172.
[122] ibid 141
[123] ibid 175–76.
[124] ibid 174.
[125] ibid 176.
[126] ibid 173.
[127] ibid 139.

advocacy of the division of labour, allowing the acquisition of skill and social contribution through methodical work.[128] This interpreted the activity of both the factory hand and the factory owner as 'a calling'.[129]

Weber suggested a trajectory of rationality whereby the non-rational role of shaman or sorcerer gave way to that of the rational priest.[130] The priest was distinguished from the sorcerer by possession of professional knowledge, fixed doctrine, and theoretical vocational qualifications, which allowed acceptance by rational society.[131] The professionalisation of lawyers resulted from the need for specialised legal knowledge generated by increased commerce.[132] Priesthood shared characteristics with other 'professions', specifically their rational and theoretical training.[133] A logical end point of Weber's projection of the rationalisation of society could have been that faith in law would replace religion as a common belief system, however he did not go that far.

ii. Professional Roles

The effect of roles on expectations, identity, and behaviour patterns occupied several disciplines, notably anthropology, psychology, and sociology, in the 1920s and 1930s.[134]

Roles were defined as 'patterns of behaviour that are characteristic of persons and contexts'.[135] The disciplines often disagreed about the differential impact of roles and other factors on behaviour[136] but minimal generalisations could be made: behaviour was sometimes patterned and characteristic of people in a particular context; similar behaviour could be observed among people sharing an identity or social position; behaviour could be affected by awareness of role; roles persisted because they were embedded in wider social systems; and people could be taught roles but were sometimes not happy in them.[137]

Some difficulties concerning occupational role theory were less pronounced in relation to professions. Once it was accepted that human behaviour could be affected by collaborative activity it was easier to accept it as a feature of institutions governed by hierarchies, rules, and norms. During the emergence of legal roles, professional associations were key groups in civil society with distinctive processes of socialisation instilling internal cultures and norms,[138] including in codes of conduct. Rules were

---

[128] ibid 161.
[129] ibid 178.
[130] Ritzer (n 102) 631.
[131] Ritzer (n 102) 631 citing Weber (n 103) 425.
[132] ibid 629.
[133] ibid 630–31.
[134] BJ Biddle, *Role Theory: Expectations, Identities and Behaviors* (New York and London, Academic Press, 1979).
[135] ibid 20.
[136] For example, regarding the difference between norms and expectations and the extent to which there must be agreement regarding behaviour for it to be part of a role (Biddle (n 134) 13–16).
[137] Based on Biddle (n 134) 8.
[138] D Sciulli, *Professions in Civil Society and the State: Invariant Foundations and Consequences* (Leiden and Boston, Brill Publishing, 2009).

enforced as a matter of professional discipline, potentially leading to exclusion from professional legal work.

In the legal field it was proposed that normative cultures differed across fields of practice within the same professions.[139] It therefore seemed quite likely that lawyers in different jurisdictions would develop in different ways. There was, indeed, some evidence that norms developed from pre-liberal roots[140] and developed along quite distinct paths.[141] From the 1980s, however, material on the social role of lawyers was dominated by American literature, and by a model identified primarily from the rules of its influential professional body, the American Bar Association. The standard conception of the lawyer's role (hereafter 'standard conception') cast lawyers as morally neutral in choosing clients and pursuing their purposes, partisan in pursuit of their goals and non-accountable for the outcomes of representation.

Although it was an American construction based on American rules, the founding scholarship often cited English antecedents and values as a common 'basic narrative':[142] loyalty to clients, confidentiality and candour to the court.[143] The literature on lawyers and legal professions contained notable historical analyses[144] including the role lawyers played in developing political liberalism in England, France and America.[145] It proposed a legal role consistent with constitutionalism: acceptance of individual perceptions of the good provided they were lawful, the liberty of the individual from interference by the state, and the need for all to understand the law, enabling compliance. The standard conception, therefore, reflected a jurisprudence of modernity. Some of the literature on the legal role, notably contributions by David Luban and William Simon, criticised the implicit severance of law and morality and the distinctive 'role morality' it produced.[146] Recent contributions returned to the underlying justifications of the lawyers' role in political philosophy, Bradley Wendel, for example, arguing that the pursuit of clients' *lawful* objectives was balanced by the deference to legality implicit in the rule of law.[147]

---

[139] P Bourdieu, *Outline of a Theory of Practice* (Cambridge, Cambridge University Press, 1977).

[140] CR Andrews, *Standards of Conduct for Lawyers: An 800-Year Evolution* (2004) 57 *SMU Law Review* 1385.

[141] RG Pearce, 'Rediscovering the Republican Origins of the Legal Ethics Codes' (1992) 6(24) *Georgetown Journal of Legal Ethics* 241.

[142] GC Hazard, Jr, 'The Future of Legal Ethics' (1991)100 *YALE L.J.* 1239, 1249.

[143] ibid.

[144] See eg JH Baker, *The Legal Profession and the Common Law: Historical Essays* (London and Ronceverte, The Hambledon Press, 1986); MS Larson, *The Rise of Professionalism: A Sociological Analysis* (Berkeley CA, University of California Press, 1977); RL Abel, *The Legal Profession in England and Wales* (Oxford, Basil Blackwell, 1988).

[145] See eg TC Halliday and L Karpik (eds), *Lawyers and the Rise of Western Political Liberalism* (Oxford, Clarendon Press, 1997); RW Gordon, 'The Role of Lawyers in Producing the Rule of Law: Some Theoretical Reflections' (2010) 11 *Theoretical Inquiries in Law* 441.

[146] D Luban, *Lawyers and Justice: An Ethical Study* (New Jersey, Princeton University Press, 1988); W Simon, 'The Ideology of Advocacy: Procedural Justice and Professional Ethics' (1978) *Wisconsin Law Review* 29.

[147] WB Wendel, *Lawyers and Fidelity to Law* (Princeton University Press, 2010).

D. Part IV: Futures

Part IV concerns the future of lawyers' role in relation to the rule of law. Efforts to install the rule of law in countries around the world had stalled, and core jurisdictions experienced a growth in populism threatening the rule of law. These developments raised larger questions about the rule of law and human history. Relevant literature included 'big histories' such as Yuval Noah Harari's *Sapiens*, depicting the development of complex human society as a story of the growth of co-operation,[148] Francis Fukuyama's *The End of History and the Last Man*, suggesting liberal democracy was the end point of human experimentation with forms of government,[149] and Mark W Moffett, a biologist studying insects,[150] reflecting on the mechanics of social organisation.

i. The Sweep of History

Complex human societies began to appear only around 12,000 years ago, when agriculture led to settled communities. Moffett observed that the transition from tribal organisation to the formation of states[151] led to political authority being based on descent, religion, and monopoly of force.[152] This led to development of infrastructure and organisation capable of dominating and controlling large populations. Moffett observed that some propensities of these large human societies were present in ant colonies and other animal society, and possibly served evolutionary functions.

Moffett suggested that Hobbes was probably right to suggest that in pre-agrarian human existence, groups had no leaders, or even hierarchies. Archaeological finds and studies of surviving hunter-gatherer bands suggested that they operated as fission-fusion societies,[153] dispersed in small 'factory efficient' bands not exceeding 150 people[154] and only occasionally coming together as a larger group not exceeding 500.[155] Surviving hunter-gatherer societies manifested strong egalitarian tendencies. Groups becoming too large to accommodate participative decision-making tended to divide. To the extent that tribal societies had leaders they were exemplary group members characterised by 'humility, integrity, and steadfastness' using mechanisms of inclusion such as informal councils.[156]

Fukuyama suggested that Hobbes' and Rousseau's vision of humans in a state of innocence was contradicted by evidence of chimpanzee hunting groups, generally male and based on kin connections.[157] It was no small leap, he said, to imagine such

---

[148] YN Harari, *Sapiens: A Brief History of Humankind* (Israel, Dvir Publishing House Ltd, 2011).
[149] F Fukuyama, *The End of History and the Last Man* (New York, Free Press, 1992).
[150] MW Moffett, *The Human Swarm: How Our Societies Arise, Thrive and Fall* (London, Head of Zeus Ltd, 2019).
[151] ibid ch 10.
[152] CR Hallpike, *The Principles of Social Evolution* (Oxford, Clarendon Press, 1986).
[153] Moffett (n 150).
[154] ibid 121.
[155] ibid 266.
[156] ibid 130.
[157] F Fukuyama, 'Women and the Evolution of World Politics' (1998) 77(5) *Foreign Affairs* 24.

groups being the basis of cooperation and of tribes and armies. There was certainly archaeological evidence that intra-community violence, including massacres of whole communities, was a feature of life in post-agrarian, prehistoric Europe.[158] Linguist and psychologist Stephen Pinker suggested that declining social violence was due to trends rooted in the culture of reason.[159]

Pinker suggested more peaceful societies arose because of increased literacy, state bureaucracy and commerce. Contributing trends since the European Enlightenment included a Humanitarian revolution, solidifying respect for the rights of women, and antipathy to slavery and cruel punishments. According to Pinker, liberal democracy provided a system capable of regulating propensities derived from an evolutionary past based on competition for resources. Rights were functional in capitalist systems geared to harnessing the potential of available populations, including creative and entrepreneurial capacities.

A common theme of the big histories was the inexorable movement towards Fukuyama's predicted triumph of liberal democracy. He argued that an obvious rationale for liberal social and political systems was that they mitigated human potential to cause harm by the constraints of institutions, laws, and norms: 'It does not always work, but it is better than living like animals.'[160] Harari reached a similar conclusion, presenting human development as a series of leaps of imagination, religion, first polytheisms and then monotheisms, the development of money, and then credit, of trade and then capitalism. The unique ability to believe in these 'fictions', intangible things, whether gods, money or human rights made complex society possible, maintaining order without coercion. The end point was a process of 'unification' currently taking place through capitalist globalisation.

ii. The Political Divide

Barriers to inexorable realisation of the liberal vision materialised in the twenty-first century, when established democracies developed internal tensions exacerbated by migration and globalisation. Big history contributed to the understanding of this phenomenon, Moffett suggesting that 'every society is a community that has to be socially constructed in the imaginations of its people', including the details of how the society operates.[161] This national narrative of 'shared imaginings' defined the framework within which people operated, and what was important to them.[162] It was the psychology underlying the narrative rather than the specifics that were important. Difference was tolerated in bushman society provided it was not dysfunctional, but scale complicated matters. Psychologists suggested that individuality was not prized

---

[158] A Roberts, *Ancestors: The Pre-history of Britain in Seven Burials* (London and New York, Simon and Schuster, 2021) 174–77.
[159] S Pinker, *The Better Angels of Our Nature: The Decline of Violence in History and Its Causes* (London, Viking Books, 2011).
[160] Fukuyama (n 157) 39–40.
[161] Moffett (n 150) 162.
[162] ibid 18, 162.

until the Middle Ages[163] and most societies had trouble accommodating outsiders. Moffett attributed this to the fact that existing large groups could be regulated by shared beliefs, referred to as 'social markers' passed from generation to generation as values and moral codes: when to be generous or helpful and what was 'fair and proper'.[164] Markers were central to citizenship and to rights, reflecting reciprocal obligations: 'the duty to behave properly and participate in matters important to the group'.[165]

Historical problems in accommodating 'outsiders', which Wade attributed to deep evolutionary patterns,[166] Moffett argued, could be managed when there was institutional support for diversity. Groups defined by their ethnicity tended to see themselves in that way when in a minority. Prejudice between groups declined when there were positive interactions, but minorities often felt as if they had to fit in. Only members of the majority were free to consider their positions as individual 'idiosyncratic' persons'.[167] The accommodation of difference in large societies was a matter of states managing relationships between groups,[168] but they were not necessarily disposed to. In fact, some modern societies chose to redirect discontent to 'outsiders' including ethnic groups within the society.[169]

Moffett suggested that existing large groups were comprised of two main factions roughly corresponding in size, patriots, and nationalists,[170] both strongly committed to their society, but with different perceptions and orientations. Nationalists admired national identity distinctively associated with their own ethnic group, were less open to change, more committed to the status quo and likely to exclude outsiders. Patriots were more open to diversity and cooperation outside their own immediate group, their prejudices were less overt, and they were more inclined to be critical of their own society. These features mapped onto political divides, and parties, becoming more exposed in times of tension, whether social, political, or economic.

iii. Global Spread of the Rule of Law

The global spread of the rule of law was a goal of individual countries and international institutions, perhaps because, as Fukuyama noted, liberal democracies tended not to fight one another.[171] The reasons for this were not established, but probably

---

[163] Moffett (n 150) 115, citing RF Baumeister, *Identity: Cultural Change and the Struggle for Self* (New York, Oxford University Press, 1986).
[164] ibid 82.
[165] ibid 119.
[166] N Wade, *A Troublesome Inheritance* (New York, Penguin Books, 2014). Generalised conclusions based on evolutionary theories were often criticised on the ground that data or science is misinterpreted, as with Wade's interpretation of genetic science, criticised by J Yoder, 'The Molecular Ecologist' (*Portside*, 4 July 2014) https://portside.org/2014-07-04/how-troublesome-inheritance-gets-human-genetics-wrong#:~: text=In%20his%20new%20book%20A%20Troublesome%20Inheritance%2C%20Nicholas,or%20 autocratic%2C%20warlike%20or%20peaceable%2C%20prosperous%20or%20poor.
[167] Moffett (n 150) 360.
[168] ibid chs 23 and 24.
[169] ibid 362.
[170] ibid 340.
[171] Fukuyama (n 157).

included factors such as the rule of law, respect for individual rights, and the priority of commerce. Fukuyama observed that liberal societies also involved women in the franchise and political decision-making more than authoritarian states.[172] This made the stalled spread of the rule of law across the global community a question of interest.

Weingast suggested that societies wishing to observe the rule of law needed to meet three 'doorstep conditions': effective control of military force, the establishment of a rule of law for elites and, finally, arrangements, including institutions, that survived changed leadership, a condition of *perpetuity*.[173] Empirically, there were two social orders for controlling violence. The first, a limited access order, gave powerful individuals and groups rights and privileges incentivising cooperation with each other and the state. This would include bribes or the right to control of assets, rent creation. The second, an open access order, based on 'impersonal relations and impersonal exchange'[174] controlled violence through open institutions and economic competition.

Limited access orders, based on personal relations and personal exchange, became open access orders by creating the conditions for entrepreneurship. A basic form of government, the natural state, had to progress through stages, fragile, basic, or mature but, in whatever form it took, it had a 'limited access order'. To satisfy the doorstep conditions for an open access order a mature natural state achieved political control over sources of violence, including the police and military, provided mechanisms for change of leadership, preserved institutions, and impersonalised the relations between elites to regularise privileges.[175] Open access orders provided the conditions to support a rule of law culture.

In states with an open access order, it did not matter who was presently in charge; the character and institutions of the state would be the same in the future. This built trust reinforced by: (1) institutions to provide law, and (2) credible commitments to the preservation of systems based on equality and incorporation.[176] Being based on impersonal treatment of citizens, open access orders were characterised by equality before the law: accountability through open reporting, effective opposition in a democratic order, and competitive markets.

States with an open access order often had large governments providing benefits to citizens on an impersonal basis,[177] controlled bureaucracy to avoid corruption, and ensured the honesty of local officials by paying them direct from central funds. These features encouraged citizen participation in a rule of law regime based on confidence in equality.

---

[172] ibid 35–36.
[173] This theory is described in BR Weingast, 'Why Developing Countries Prove So Resistant to the Rule of Law' in Heckman, Nelson and Cabatingan (n 67) 28 drawing on earlier work; DC North, JJ Wallis and BR Weingast, *Violence and Social Orders: A Conceptual Framework for Understanding Recorded Human History* (Cambridge, Cambridge University Press, 1989).
[174] Weingast (n 173) 29.
[175] ibid 37.
[176] ibid 33.
[177] ibid 33–35.

iv. Lawyers

While some of the literature on lawyers made connections between them and the rule of law, the big histories accorded them little significance. Exceptionally, Harari, as an example of the continuing relevance of fictions, suggested that businesspeople and lawyers were modern versions of a sorcerer or tribal shaman. As noted previously, the comparison invited the suggestion that law replaced religion as part of the process of Western rationalisation but as indicated, law and morality were still in a kind of conflict manifested in conceptions of the rule of law.[178] While lawyers remained key advocates of the rule of law, their authority, like that of priests, declined in the consumer society and was under constant threat from authoritarianism.

V. CONCLUSION

The rule of law emerged from the European Enlightenment as a set of procedures for the administration of a state, primarily, as a check on the abuse of power by government. It was manifest in control of government by distributing the functions of law between arms of government, by vesting rights against government in citizens, and creating a society governed by a condition of legality. The system was based on the idea of support for and observance of rule of law principles, by politicians, judges, and the people. Lawyers played various roles in this system, as judges, as legal officers in government or as practitioners in private practice. While they had different roles and responsibilities for the rule of law, all were bound by common membership of legal organisations rooted in civil society.

It was tempting to see the rise of the rule of law as a kind of secular successor to religion, a powerful belief in legality that had the capacity to bind society. The connection of lawyers and this idea was often regarded with cynicism. In his Reith Lectures in 2019, the former Supreme Court judge Jonathan Sumption asked 'what do we mean by the rule of law, the phrase that so readily trips of the tongues of lawyers? Is it, as cynics have sometimes suggested, really no more than a euphemism for the rule of lawyers?'.[179] Any consideration of the future of lawyers and the rule of law must address this among a range of relevant questions.

---

[178] D Saunders, *Anti-Lawyers: Religion and the Critics of Law and State* (Abingdon, Oxfordshire, Routledge, 1997).

[179] J Sumption, 'Lecture 1'Law's expanding empire' (The Reith Lectures, BBC broadcast Wednesday 22 May 2019).

Part 1

Government

All we have of freedom, all we use or know –
This our fathers bought for us long and long ago.
Ancient Right unnoticed as the breath we draw –
Leave to live by no man's leave, underneath the Law.
Lance and torch and tumult, steel and grey-goose wing
Wrenched it, inch and ell and all, slowly from the King.
Rudyard Kipling *The Old Issue* (1899)

2
Revolution

I. INTRODUCTION

THE REVOLUTIONS CONVULSING the Western world in the seventeenth and eighteenth centuries established constitutional orders in place of monarchy. In England, the Glorious Revolution of 1688 marked the beginning of the rule of law. The independence of the US and French Revolutions followed similar patterns more than a century later. The question addressed in this chapter concerns the part played by lawyers, focusing on the English revolutions of the 1600s. It examines the part played by a government law officer, senior judge and politician, Sir Edward Coke (1552–1634), by John Cook, solicitor general, and by a Parliament including many barristers. These lawyers helped to formulate, articulate, and defend the rule of law as an alternative to autocracy.

II. THEORY

Philosophers of the classical era were ambivalent about tyrannical power. They thought it could be used for good or ill, distinguishing between tyrants who ruled by consent and those that did not. Aristotle argued, however, that tyranny could not achieve human well-being because it curtailed individual decision making and the equality of citizens, both necessary to living a good life.[1] He claimed that those who gave power over the law to any individual, 'gives it to a wild beast, for such his appetites sometimes make him',[2] but thought preferred individuals should be guardians or ministers of law.[3] Plato argued that the obligation of obedience to law occurred only when it was '(i) freely and honestly made, and (ii) made with good reason'.[4] In classical societies assassination for the public good, such as that of Julius Caesar, was a duty of elites.

---

[1] *Aristotle's Politics: A Treatise On Government* (trans W Ellis) (London, George Routledge and Sons, 1895).
[2] ibid 117–18.
[3] M Krygier, 'The Rule of Law: Pasts, Presents and Two Possible Futures' (2016) 12 *Annual Review of Law and Social Science* 199, 205 citing Aristotle, *The Politics* (Cambridge, Cambridge University Press 1988) 1279a, 19–22.
[4] SK Brincat, '"Death to Tyrants": The Political Philosophy of Tyrannicide – Part I' (2008) 4(2) *Journal of International Political Theory* 212, 217.

In about 48 BC, fire destroyed the library at Alexandria holding surviving copies of works by Aristotle. The North African theologian, Augustine (354–430), drew on Plato in developing Christian doctrine, creating a tradition of resignation to tyranny.[5] In the 1100s, Anna Komnene, a Byzantine princess, commissioned translations of student notes on Aristotle's *Nicomachaean Ethics*, held at the library at Constantinople.[6] These found their way, through the visits of monks to the Middle East to Thomas Aquinas (1224/6–74) and into mainstream Christianity.

In the late medieval period, political theorists adopted an empirical approach to politics. Machiavelli (1469–1527) depicted the abuse of power as a means of maintaining tyrannical rule. Other thinkers of the European Enlightenment developed political theory influenced by the moral perspective of natural law. This began with publication of Thomas Hobbes' *Leviathan*,[7] two years after the execution of King Charles I in 1649, towards the end of the English Civil War (1642–51). Hobbes' intention was to justify absolutism or the 'Divine Right' of a monarch to rule. This reflected a mood throughout Europe that the killing of Charles I was 'morally reprehensible'.[8]

Hobbes' analysis imagined a 'State of Nature' governed by the 'Law of Nature' based on reason: 'For whatsoever men are to take knowledge of for Law, not upon other mens' words, but every one from his own reason, must be such as is agreeable to the reason of all men; which no Law can be, but the Law of Nature'.[9] The Law of Nature nurtured individual freedom: a man should 'be contented with so much liberty against other men, as he would allow other men against himself; that men perform their covenants made; that no man by deed, word, countenance, or gesture, declare hatred or contempt of another'.[10]

Hobbes argued that people enjoyed liberty in the State of Nature, but that it was likely to be conflictual; a permanent war of all against all, with little commerce, knowledge, or security. He reasoned that since most people feared violent death they should surrender their liberty, renounce their rights against each other in the state of nature and accept a sovereign, an entity with supreme and ultimate power to hold them to this bargain. The idea of a social contract being the basis of political legitimacy, although not new,[11] dominated political theory. In the early medieval period, the claim that rights were endowed on humans by God, justified resistance to tyranny.

---

[5] ibid.

[6] P Frankopan, *The Silk Roads: A New History of the World* (London, Bloomsbury, 2015) 147.

[7] T Hobbes, *Leviathan or the Matter, Forme and Power of a Common-wealth Ecclesiastical and Civill*, www.gutenberg.org/files/3207/3207-h/3207-h.htm#link2H_4_0306.

[8] Brincat (n 4), and see DK Van Kley, *The Religious Origins of the French Revolution: From Calvin to the Civil Constitution: 1560–1791* (New Haven and London, Yale University Press, 1996) ch 1; CE Olmstead, *History of Religion in the United States* (Englewood Cliffs, NJ, Prentice-Hall, 1960) 9–10.

[9] Hobbes (n 7) ch XXVI: Of Civill Lawes. These ideas were also expressed as early as 1625 by Hugo Grotius (1583–1645).

[10] These are the 2nd, 3rd and 8th laws (*Leviathan*, ch 15).

[11] The notion of a social contract (neither to harm or be harmed) was also proposed by Epicurus (c341–270 BC) as essential to a well ordered society (JJ Thrasher, 'Reconciling Justice and Pleasure in Epicurean Contractarianism' (2013) 16(2) *Ethical Theory and Moral Practice* 423).

In *Two Treatises of Government*,[12] John Locke (1632–1704) proposed alternative interpretations of the Law of Nature. Written in 1679–70, probably against the Restoration of Charles II,[13] Locke argued that the social contract conferred the right to live as one chose, free from interference and in an ideal state of liberty, with shared and equal rights to life and property. In his first treatise, Locke rebutted the proposition that a Divine Right of Kings could be derived from religious authority. In the second he turned Hobbes' theory and conclusion regarding the State of Nature on its head. The need for sovereign authority arose with a need to protect property. Such a regime would perpetuate social inequality and could only be justified by the greater well-being of the people.

III. THE ENGLISH REVOLUTIONS

A. Magna Carta

Some research suggested that some Dark Age cultures of Northern Europe were less autocratic than others. The population of the British Isles, including in England in the modern day, was predominantly Celtic. At the Synod of Whitby in 664AD the King of the dominant Anglo-Saxon kingdom, Northumbria, Oswys, opted to follow Rome, a move that was said to have 'anathemised the Celtic population and legitimised English lordship over them'.[14] Noting several examples of Celtic insurrection well into the medieval period, Wall observed that 'Rebelliousness against tyranny was not a peculiarly Irish or Welsh trait, but seems to be characteristic of the Celts'.[15] The Celts did not operate the principle of primogeniture, leading to diffusion of power compared to later arrivals in the British Isles.

While the Anglo-Saxons had a more centralising culture, their monarchs ruled with advice from counsellors. The Danish King, Canute, briefly the Lord of a Scandinavian and British empire, aspired to protect the people.[16] The Normans retained much Anglo-Saxon law following their conquest of England in 1066, but maintained order by brute force. In the medieval period, law was seen as the custom of the community embodying the law of God. Monarchs were judges interpreting this law, legislative acts mere clarification. This was the basis of the theory of sovereignty, a power to command: order or prohibit.[17] So, when William the Conqueror established a Great Council comprising heads of the church and nobility, its role was purely consultative.

---

[12] J Locke, *Two Treatises of Government In the Former, The False Principles, and Foundation of Sir Robert Filmer, and His Followers, Are Detected and Overthrown. The Latter Is an Essay Concerning The True Original, Extent, and End of Civil Government* (London, Awnsham Churchill, 1690).

[13] P Laslett (ed), 'Introduction' in *Locke: Two Treatises of Government* (Cambridge, Cambridge University Press, 1960) 34, 59–61.

[14] M Wall, *Warriors and Kings: The 1500-year Battle for Celtic England* (Glocs, Amberely, 2017) 144.

[15] ibid 227.

[16] Sir Stephen Sedley, *Lions Under the Throne: Essays on the History of English Public Law* (Cambridge, Cambridge University Press, 2015) 3.

[17] MJC Vile, *Constitutionalism and the Separation of Powers*, 2nd edn (Minneapolis, Liberty Fund, 1998) 28.

The Norman feudal system was based on unique personal relationships between monarch and barons. Their potential for violence was controlled by allocating land in return for military service and favours according to power, military prowess, and loyalty. In 1215 the barons imposed Magna Carta,[18] a peace treaty constraining King John (1166–1216),[19] re-establishing their customary rights, and interpreting them in the interests of their heirs.[20] It began with several provisions controlling the King's discretion to deal with estates after death. Under the feudal system baronial lands reverted to the monarch on the death of the Lord and could then be granted to a favourite or, sometimes, a potentially more useful magnate.

The Barons' wanted their heirs to inherit their estates on payment of a fee, Magna Carta providing that:

> (2) If any earl, baron, or other person that holds lands directly of the Crown, for military service, shall die, and at his death his heir shall be of full age and owe a 'relief', the heir shall have his inheritance on payment of the ancient scale of 'relief'. That is to say, the heir or heirs of an earl shall pay £100 for the entire earl's barony, the heir or heirs of a knight 100s. at most for the entire knight's 'fee', and any man that owes less shall pay less, in accordance with the ancient usage of 'fees'.[21]

Magna Carta was significant because it formalised control over royal power, removed arbitrariness from the process of allocating land, and introduced the idea of perpetuity to land ownership. These were elite privileges, and it took many centuries to establish a general principle of *primogeniture*, the right of a firstborn child to inherit real property, and then the right to divide land between beneficiaries.[22]

Magna Carta did not establish any lasting institutions. John excised from reissues of the treaty a clause establishing a committee of 25 barons to keep him to its terms. Nor did it establish common rights as opposed to elite privileges. Even the promises to the barons were broken by John and by subsequent monarchs. During the minority of John's young son, Henry III, the royal finances were supervised by members of the King's Council. This led to a convention later attributed to Magna Carta that the monarch did not raise non-feudal taxes without the consent of the Council.

B. Reformation

In 1521 at the Diet of Worms, Martin Luther challenged the claim of the church to intermediation with God and its right to sell indulgencies for the remission of sins. He asserted the Bible was the only source of divine knowledge and the scriptures the support for individual conscience. The Protestant movement taking hold across

---

[18] A Arlidge and I Judge, *Magna Carta Uncovered* (Oxford, Hart Publishing, 2014) particularly ch 3.
[19] RV Turner, *King John: England's Evil King?* (Stroud, History Press, 2009).
[20] Arlidge and Judge (n 18) 23.
[21] The National Archives, *Magna Carta, 1215*, www.nationalarchives.gov.uk/education/resources/magna-carta/british-library-magna-carta-1215-runnymede/.
[22] BR Weingast, 'Why Developing Countries Prove So Resistant to the Rule of Law' in J Heckman, R Nelson and L Cabatingan (eds), *Global Perspectives on the Rule of Law* (London and New York, Routledge, 2010) 28, 41.

much of Northern Europe resulted in Henry VIII breaking with the Catholic Church and, by the Act of Supremacy 1534, becoming the 'Supreme Head on earth of the Church of England'. In the reign of his Protestant daughter, Elizabeth I, a compromise between Catholic and Lutheran theology through the liturgy of the Church was attempted in the Elizabethan Settlement of 1559.[23]

In Tudor times, large parts of the populations of the British Isles, particularly in England, belonged to Puritan sects, the largest including Congregationalists, and Presbyterians. During Elizabeth's reign, and that of her successor, James I, Protestantism was heavily influenced by the central tenets of the teachings of Jean Calvin (1509–64), a French theologian and a leading light of the Reformation. Calvin preached predestination and the absolute sovereignty of God.[24] During the reign of Charles I Puritan forces in the Church of England lost the fight on several issues, notably the removal of bishops, to a high church faction. Their sensibilities were offended when James I and then Charles I promoted a *Book of Sports*, encouraging Sunday games, contrary to the Puritan ascetic doctrine which only allowed physical activity necessary for health.[25] Unfortunately for the Stuarts, Calvin's religious philosophy crossed into the political sphere. He advocated that a ruler who challenged God lost their divine right to rule and could be deposed. Thus, many opponents of absolutist monarchy believed that they were 'weapons in the hand of God, and executors of His providential will'.[26]

IV. JAMES I AND EDWARD COKE

A. Divine Right

James VI of Scotland acceded to the English throne on the death of Elizabeth I in 1603 becoming James I of England. He was an autocrat with no respect for law. Journeying to London for his coronation he had a cutpurse plaguing the royal retinue summarily hanged.[27] He interfered in the conduct of courts in his own causes and those of his favourites.[28] He saw no fault in this: he was from a tradition in which monarchs ruled by divine right, wielding power that was absolute.

In *The Trew Law of Free Monarchies*, James outlined his argument for the supremacy of monarchy, by which he claimed a free hand in governance:

> The king towards his people is rightly compared to a father of children, and to a head of a body composed of divers members. For as fathers the good princes and magistrates of

---

[23] MAR Graves, *Elizabethan Parliaments 1559–1661*, 2nd edn (London, NY, Routledge, 1996) 24.
[24] These ideas were taken back to England by Protestant exiles who had fled to the continent during the reign of Mary Tudor.
[25] M Weber, *The Protestant Ethic and the Spirit of Capitalism* (trans T Parsons) (London, Butler and Tanner, 1930) 166–67.
[26] ibid 125.
[27] P Ackroyd, *The History of England Volume III: Civil War* (London, Pan Books, 2015) 2.
[28] G Robertson, *The Tyrannicide Brief: The story of the man who sent Charles I to the scaffold* (London, Chatto & Windus, 2005) 23.

the people of God acknowledged themselves to their subjects. And for all other well-ruled commonwealths, the style of *Pater patriae* (father of his country) was ever and is commonly used to kings. And the proper office of a king towards his subjects agrees very well with the office of the head towards the body and all members thereof. For from the head, being the seat of judgment, proceedeth the care and foresight of guiding and preventing all evil that may come to the body or any part thereof. The head cares for the body, so doth the king for his people.[29]

Since 1066 institutions with a degree of independence such as Parliament and the common law had emerged and in 1600 stood as opponents to James' autocracy.

B. Institutional Constraints

The common law originated in efforts by Henry II (1133–89) to establish a unified court system 'common' across the country. It integrated systems of local custom into principles and precedents established in previous cases. Decisions began to be published and applied by judges travelling on different circuits around the country. By the fifteenth and sixteenth Centuries three Common Law Courts, King's Bench, Common Pleas and Exchequer,[30] were in competition with a court of equity, the Court of Chancery.[31]

Differences between the common law and other courts were substantive and procedural. The Common Law Courts required claims to fit within narrow forms of action, were slow, procedurally complex and bound by precedent. Chancery had a wide jurisdiction, was less procedurally hidebound and offered novel remedies. The resentment of the common law judges for the arbitrariness of Chancery was nothing compared with their antipathy of the prerogative courts.

In the early medieval period courts were established out of the King's Council, their authority deriving from his prerogative powers, such as deploying armed forces, making international treaties, and granting honours. The Court of Star Chamber was established to hear cases against powerful individuals who were intimidating to ordinary judges.[32] It comprised a mix of Privy Councillors and common law judges without a jury, with more effective interrogation procedures than the Common Law Courts. It used the 'cruel trilemma', placing a party under oath and demanding answers to questions leading to either self-incrimination, perjury or contempt of court. Under Henry VIII, the Star Chamber gained an infamous reputation for political trials and arbitrary judgments.

---

[29] *The Trew Law of Free Monarchies* (Edinburgh, Robert Waldegrave, 1598). For the rest of this excerpt see the text at www.wwnorton.com/college/english/nael/noa/pdf/27636_17th_U42_James-1-2.pdf.
[30] Common Pleas dealt with disputes between subjects, and King's Bench those affecting the Crown.
[31] This jurisdiction emerged from the role of Chancery as the place where writs for the Common Law Courts were purchased (see further ch 5).
[32] A good example was Parliamentary candidates, the selection of which often led to bitter local conflict (MA Lishlansky, *Parliamentary Selection: Social and Political Choice in Early Modern England* (Cambridge, Cambridge University Press, 1986) 18.

Magna Carta was part of the tradition invoked to legitimise resistance to royal prerogative by common law judges. Although it addressed elite concerns, many of its terms were expressed broadly. Several provisions characterised what we now know as the rule of law:

> (38) In future no official shall place a man on trial upon his own unsupported statement, without producing credible witnesses to the truth of it.
>
> (39) No free man shall be seized or imprisoned, or stripped of his rights or possessions, or outlawed or exiled, or deprived of his standing in any way, nor will we proceed with force against him, or send others to do so, except by the lawful judgment of his equals or by the law of the land.
>
> (40) To no one will we sell, to no one deny or delay right or justice.[33]

Another centre of power in struggles between the King and the courts was Parliament. Throughout the Tudor period both Henry, and then Elizabeth I, maintained an uneasy and untested relationship with Parliament. It had acquired privileges such as the right of free speech in the chamber, and James I was therefore forced to work with institutions with established claims to independence.

C. Sir Edward Coke

In the reign of Elizabeth I, Coke was an MP and Speaker of the House. She made him Solicitor General in 1592 and Attorney General in 1594.[34] He was knighted within two months of the arrival of James I in London in 1603 and shortly after conducted the prosecution of Sir Walter Raleigh, a great hero and favourite of the Elizabethan age, on charges of treason. Raleigh was accused of conspiring to place an alternative to James, 'a pretender', on the English throne and accepting a Spanish bribe to do so. The King asked Coke to secure the conviction of Raleigh.

The prosecution was noted for the viciousness of Coke's cross-examination, which began:

> Thou art a scurvy fellow; thy name is hateful to all the realm of England for thy pride. I will now make it appear to the world that there never existed on the face of the earth a viler viper than thou art.[35]

Required by the court to curb his invective and allow Raleigh to respond, Coke sat down, so piqued he had to be cajoled to continue. The conviction was achieved using the tainted evidence of one very unreliable witness.[36] In June 1606 Coke became the

---

[33] National Archive (n 21).
[34] AD Boyer, *Sir Edward Coke and the Elizabethan Age* (Stanford, Stanford University Press, 2003).
[35] *A complete collection of state-trials and proceedings for high-treason, and other crimes and misdemeanours; from the reign of King Richard II to the end of the reign of King George I* (London, J Walthoe etc, 1730) 205.
[36] A signed confession of his friend and alleged co-conspirator, Henry Brooke, who was not produced to give evidence in person. Raleigh was sent to the Tower of London for 10 years, then pardoned on condition he did not engage in any action against the Spanish, but against his orders, a party from an expedition he led to Guyana attacked a Spanish settlement. On his return the death sentence was reinstated.

Chief Justice of the Common Pleas, a post usually filled by the Attorney General on the departure of the previous incumbent.

The move from Attorney General to Chief Justice changed Coke's disposition. An apparently loyal Crown servant became an independent and troublesome judge, a thorn in the King's side, and a saboteur of his claim to absolute authority. In 1608 James wished to adjudicate a jurisdictional dispute between the Court of Common Pleas and the Court of High Commission, a prerogative court which ruled on ecclesiastical matters. At a meeting on the case Coke disputed James' right to rule on questions of law above the jurisdiction of the Common Law Courts.

On hearing Coke's views, the King exploded, 'Then I am under the law, which is treason to affirm'.[37] Despite the express threat Coke continued, arguing that although the King was not subject to man he was 'subject to God and Law'.[38] James protested that he protected the Law, not the other way round, but Coke said the King had no knowledge of the 'artificial reason' of the Law, which required long study. Sensing the need for an act of self-preservation, Coke fell to his knees, saved only by the intercession of a ministerial favourite.[39] Even so, the next day, he sealed a prohibition and sent it to the Court of High Commission.

Coke also resisted James' claims in cases he heard, particularly *The Case of Proclamations*[40] in which he declared that law binding the sovereign power was given by Common Law Courts exercising prerogative powers derived from the Crown. This acknowledged the King as the source of legitimate power but subjected him to process; he could appoint and dismiss judges but was bound by whatever law they declared. This argument probably derived from Bracton, who in the thirteenth century had argued that the King was subject to the law because the law makes him King.[41] In 1613 the King transferred Coke from the Court of Common Pleas to the King's Bench, a forum that traditionally favoured the King.

Coke's relocation did not quell his rebelliousness. In *Peacham's Case* (1616) he refused to convict a Puritan preacher accused of preparing an undelivered sermon contemplating the death of the King. James had the case retried by other judges. Within two years Coke was on a bench which refused to recognise a writ in which James gave the benefits of a bishopric to a favourite. Coke instigated a letter advising James that the proposed action was illegal. The King summoned the bench before him and ripped the letter up. The other judges prostrated themselves begging pardon, but Coke declared that 'I shall do that which shall be fit for a judge to do'.[42] Shortly after, James removed him from office.

Following Coke's dismissal from the King's Bench he returned to Parliament in 1621. Although this was at the King's instigation Coke joined a group opposing the King's interests. It particularly opposed granting royal awards of monopolies,

---

[37] Arlidge and Judge (n 18).
[38] ibid 122.
[39] ibid 122.
[40] *The Case of Proclamations* (1611) 12 Co Rep 74, [1610] 77 ER 1352, [1610] EWHC KB J2277.
[41] L Mosesson, 'Dr Bonham in Woolf's Clothing: Sovereignty and the Rule of Law Today' (2007) *Mountbatten Yearbook of Legal Studies* 5, 7.
[42] J Hostettler, *Sir Edward Coke: A Force for Freedom* (Chichester, Barry Rose Law Publishers, 1997) 91.

which were often detrimental to consumers but provided revenue to the Crown. James tried to compromise but Parliament persisted. He warned it not to meddle in matters of state. Parliament responded with a Remonstrance to the King, which James rejected, attending Parliament to rip it from the Journal of the Commons. He dissolved Parliament and committed Coke to the Tower for nine months. A Statute of Monopolies was passed in 1624.

D. Parliament

A significant step toward an independent constraint on royal power occurred in 1265 when the rebel baron, Simon De Montfort, sought to muster support by summoning commoners, knights, and local representatives to a Parliament.[43] Henry III's son, Edward I, continued this practice when he established a model Parliament in 1295 and in 1307 agreed not to raise tax without Parliamentary consent. Controlling taxation was important in establishing Parliament's legitimacy but did not make it essential to government. Monarchs raised money by seeking loans or requiring subjects to make them. Struggles over finance were part of the conflict between the Stuart Kings and Parliament, but another significant factor was religion.

On the accession of James I, large parts of the population of the British Isles, particularly in England, belonged to Puritan sects like the Congregationalists and the Presbyterians, sharing central tenets of the teachings of Jean Calvin. They stood apart from the Church of England and were justified in fearing persecution and a return of a Roman Catholic monarch. James was particularly hostile to Presbyterians, some of whom had challenged his authority in Scotland.[44] There were also concerns over James' favouritism towards Catholics and Spanish influence at court and abroad.[45]

Parliament was anxious to protect Puritans while James was absorbed with dynastic and other considerations. His disdain for Parliament was reflected in the scant use he made of it. By the early seventeenth century, the government legislative programme was small.[46] In 1604 bills were proposed to recognise title to the throne and to confirm Magna Carta. In 1614, James put forward 11 grace bills; concessionary measures to get Common's approval for taxation. Between 1604 and 1629 Parliament was nearly redundant. The gap left by the lack of government legislation was filled by bills proposed by members or outside organisations in their personal or corporate interests.[47]

In March 1610 James addressed Parliament claiming the right of Kings 'to make and unmake their subjects' and to '… have the power of raising and casting down,

---

[43] P Ackroyd, *A History of England Volume I: Foundation* (London, Macmillan, 2011) 199.
[44] P Ackroyd, *A History of England Volume III: Civil War* (London, Pan, 2015) 8.
[45] C Hill, *The Century of Revolution, 1603–1714* (London and NY, Routledge, 1961) 58–59.
[46] A Thrush and JP Ferris, *The History of Parliament: The House of Commons 1604–1629* (Cambridge University Press, 2010) ch XI: History. and John P. Ferris, 2010 he and John P. Ferris, 2010
[47] Crown legislation proposed in this period concerned the Union, the Great Contract and Tunnage and Poundage.

of life and of death ... and make of their subjects like men at the chess'.[48] Parliament responded by delivering a Petition of Grievances, referring to the 'dear and precious' freedom 'to be guided and governed by the certain rule of law which giveth both to the head and members that which of right belongeth to them and not by any uncertain or arbitrary form of government'.[49]

The contestations continued through James' reign, with Parliamentarians arguing that Magna Carta restrained the monarch and supported their privileges, including free speech in the House.[50] Monarchists asserted the superiority of the King to law, claiming Magna Carta was a bogus document extracted by force.[51] Common law judges and Parliament argued that there were fundamental laws of the kingdom that countered claims of Divine Right. The beauty of this fundamental law was that it was impossibly vague.[52]

V. CHARLES I AND PARLIAMENT

When James I died in 1625, his son Charles I brought stronger abhorrence of Parliamentary authority to the throne. He conducted show trials of members of Parliament who displeased him and insisted that his judges impose punishments and detention at his pleasure.[53] The bitter differences included resentment of Charles' favourite, the Duke of Buckingham and his inept conduct of foreign wars, his attempts to convert Charles to Catholicism, and his secret sympathies with Spain.[54] In 1626 the King dismissed Parliament, arresting Dudley Digges and Sir John Eliot for leading attempted impeachment of Buckingham by both Houses of Parliament. Charles needed Parliament's financial support for an expensive war with Spain but instead he resurrected defunct levies,[55] exploited his royal prerogatives, and demanded loans from rich subjects.

In 1625 Charles sought approval of Parliament to raise the taxes of tonnage and poundage[56] but Parliament delayed voting until its grievances were aired. It was prorogued early because of plague in London, but tonnage and poundage was collected without parliamentary consent. In 1627 Charles imprisoned five knights for failing to make loans. Writs of *habeus corpus* were countermanded by order of the

---

[48] Arlidge and Judge (n 18) 123 citing James I, *The Works of the Most High and Mighty Prince* (London, 1616) 528–31.

[49] Arlidge and Judge (n 18) 123 citing H Hallam, *The Constitutional History of England* (Vol.1) (London, 1973) 441.

[50] Arlidge and Judge (n 18) 124–5.

[51] Of these the most famous was probably Robert Filmer's *Patriarcha*, probably written in 1620 but only published in in 1680 (Arlidge and Judge (n 18) 124).

[52] Hill (n 45) 65.

[53] Robertson (n 28) 36.

[54] P Ackroyd, *The History of England Volume III: Civil War* (London, Pan Macmillan, 2015) 118–21.

[55] Distraint of knighthood had not been levied for nearly 100 years. One of Charles' ruses was to confer knighthoods on subjects with good annual earnings.

[56] Tonnage was a customs duty levied on each tun (cask) and poundage a proportional tax on imported and exported goods, www.britannica.com/topic/tonnage-and-poundage.

King. The King's Bench agreed this was justified by state necessity[57] but the same year the courts declared it illegal to imprison those refusing loans to the Crown, forcing Charles to call a Parliament.[58]

At its first session in 1628, Coke presented Parliament with a Petition of Right asserting popular liberties and criticising abuses of royal authority. It demanded Parliamentary approval of taxation, respect for *habeus corpus*, and prohibitions on the imposition of Martial Law, particularly the billeting of troops in people's houses. Hearing that the Petition had been accepted by the Lords, Charles forbade Parliament from considering it further. Coke nevertheless spoke in favour of the Petition, citing Magna Carta, and the Lords approved it.

Charles tried, but failed, to have a clause inserted into the Petition acknowledging the sovereign power or royal prerogative.[59] After the Lords assented the King was forced, very reluctantly, to give the traditional royal assent. The publication of the Petition of Right was acclaimed throughout England and celebrated with bonfires and church bells.[60] It was then discovered that it had been printed with Charles' words of equivocation and without the words of royal assent.

When the second session of the 1628 Parliament opened early in 1629, Charles gave a speech justifying tonnage and poundage. The response was hostile, and Charles called for an adjournment. The Speaker, Sir John Finch rose to leave, signalling the end of the session, but several Parliamentarians rose and Denzel Holles and Benjamin Valentine held him in his chair. Sir John Eliot's resolutions on tonnage and poundage were read and carried. Although the Speaker was seen as the King's official, Sir William Heyman suggested a new Speaker be chosen, telling Finch he was sorry that he was a Kentish-man, 'and that you are of that name which hath borne some good reputation in our own county'.[61]

Another Parliament was not called for 11 years, Charles preferring to make peace with France and Spain. Forced to use royal prerogative powers to raise finance, in 1634 he tried to broaden the tradition that royal ports provide a ship for the navy by requiring the general population to contribute. A leading Parliamentarian, John Hampden, was prosecuted for failing to pay. In 1637, a bench under intense pressure from the Crown held against him by 7 to 5. Even a royalist, the future Lord Clarendon, said that the case was decided 'upon such grounds and reasons that every stander-by was able to swear was not law by a logic that left no man anything which he might call his own'.[62] Consequently, 'people ... no more looked upon it as the case of one man, but the case of the kingdom'.[63] Hampden's case united the propertied classes and only a fraction of the ship money was collected.

Forced to the brink of bankruptcy, in 1640 Charles summoned Parliament and then dissolved it when it refused funding to intervene in the bishops' war in Scotland. He sent an army, nonetheless. The Scots defeated it and occupied much of the north of England.

---

[57] Arlidge and Judge (n 18) 130.
[58] *Five Knights*' or *Darnell's case* (1627) 3 How St Tr 1.
[59] Hill (n 45) 53.
[60] See Arlidge and Judge (n 18) 134–36.
[61] https://en.wikisource.org/wiki/Heyman,_Peter_(DNB00).
[62] *Westminster Review* Vol. XIX July-October (London, Robert Heward, 1833) 365.
[63] Hill (n 45) 55.

In November 1640 Charles was forced to summon the so-called Long Parliament. It promptly sought to impeach Lord Strafford, principal adviser to the King, on his record as Lord Deputy of Ireland and John Finch, the former Speaker and latterly a judge.[64]

Strafford advised the King to accuse leading Parliamentarians of treason to pre-empt the impeachment. The plan was discovered, making any defence of Strafford within the Commons almost impossible. Finch, meanwhile, fled to Holland. The evidence of misconduct by Strafford was thin until a note of a discussion in Privy Council came to light. Threatened with invasion by a Scottish army the previous year, Strafford had advised Charles he was absolved from rules of government. He would be justified, Strafford advised, to use his army in Ireland to 'reduce the kingdom'.[65] Although in the circumstances it was ambiguous whether 'the kingdom' referred to Scotland or England, it was seen as damning.

Attempts to impeach Strafford in the House of Lords having failed the Commons issued a bill of attainder, accusing Strafford of treason and demanding his execution. Some advocated sparing him, but a failed plot to release him by force poisoned the mood. The bill was passed but required Charles' signature. Despite his assurances to Strafford that his person and property would be safe, in May 1641 Charles signed a document assenting to Strafford's death and forfeiture of his estates.

Strafford's execution was an act of provocation by Parliament. The previous December it had delivered an incendiary document, the Grand Remonstrance, comprising a detailed list of objections to domestic and foreign policy. It was precipitated by an Irish rebellion but listed grievances such as the intimidation of judges and sale of offices.[66] Late in December the King delivered a rebuttal of many of the points but adopted a reconciliatory tone. During 1641 an emboldened Parliament went on to abolish the Courts of Star Chamber and High Commission and pass an Act requiring that it be summoned every three years, without the King's consent if necessary.

Burrage suggested that the course to war was determined in March 1642, when Parliament demanded the removal of judges who had supported the King's right to ship money.[67] It was signalled in May 1641, when a Protestation, effectively an oath of allegiance, promising to defend the Protestant religion, the liberties and rights of subjects, and the privilege of Parliament was sworn by members of the House of Commons and circulated to all parishes of the realm.[68] This reflected growing Protestant fears and doubts about the King's religious allegiances.

---

[64] Finch became Chief Justice of Common Pleas in 1634 and played a key role in the ship money case against John Hampden. Impeachment proceedings against him alleged that he tried to bend other judges to the King's desired outcome, see *State Trials* Volume IV (Cobbett's Complete Collection) 151 'Proceedings in Parliament Against John Lord Finch, Baron of Fordwich, Lord Keeper, for High Treason: 16 Charles I. AD 1640' (4 Rushworth, 124. 2 Cobb. Parl. Hist. 685, 12–14).

[65] PC Yorke, 'Thomas Wentworth, Earl of Strafford' *Encyclopaedia Britannica*, https://en.wikisource.org/wiki/1911_Encyclop%C3%A6dia_Britannica/Strafford,_Thomas_Wentworth,_Earl_of.

[66] Robertson (n 28) 60.

[67] M Burrage, *Revolution and the Making of the Contemporary Legal Profession: England France and the United States* (Oxford, Oxford University Press, 2006) 410.

[68] Rushworth and John, 'Historical Collections: May 1641' in *Historical Collections of Private Passages of State: Volume 4, 1640–42* (London, 1721) 239–79. British History Online, www.british-history.ac.uk/rushworth-papers/vol4/pp239-279; MJ Braddick, *God's Fury, England's Fire: A New History of the English Civil Wars* (London, Penguin, 2009) 137.

In January 1642 Charles came to Parliament with 400 troops, accused five members of treason, and demanded to know their whereabouts.[69] On this occasion the Speaker answered with 'May it please your Majesty, I have neither eyes to see nor tongue to speak in this place but as the House is pleased to direct me, whose servant I am here and humbly beg your majesty's pardon that I cannot give any other answer than this is to what your majesty is pleased to demand of me'.[70] The English Civil War was a misnomer; it had three phases and involved fighting in both Scotland and Ireland. The first phase began after Charles failed to arrest the five members.

VI. THE ENGLISH CIVIL WARS

On leaving Parliament, Charles fled north and raised an army. It met Parliamentary forces at Edgehill in September 1642, but after early successes it was destroyed following engagements at Naseby and then Langport in 1645. Charles threw himself on the mercy of a Presbyterian Scottish army who handed him over to Parliamentary forces. From prison he encouraged his supporters to continue the fight and between 1648 and 1649 royalist plots and insurgencies were foiled or defeated. Royalists taken prisoner had promised not to take up arms against Parliament and their breach of parole led to the execution of many aristocrats.

The problem of dealing with a captured King faced the English Parliament in 1649. Oliver Cromwell, the leader of the Parliament and its New Model Army sought an agreement that would establish Charles as a constitutional monarch. Despite failure of this initiative, and the King's role in fermenting continuing strife, some Parliamentarians favoured either a continuing role for him or abdication. He negotiated possible futures while writing to his wife that he would only be bound by any agreement until he had regained sufficient power.[71] Amid rumours of an imminent invasion by an Irish and Dutch force, the Parliamentary Army ended negotiations and expelled potential royal collaborators from Parliament. The remaining 75 members, the so-called Rump Parliament, were instructed by the Army commanders to try Charles I for treason in the name of the people.

Two leading Parliamentary lawyers advised Cromwell that the legality of prosecution was doubtful:[72] the King was the Law and therefore above it. The House of Lords rejected the Bill and adjourned to avoid its re-presentation. The House of Commons turned to biblical interpretation portraying the authority of kingship as emanating from the people rather than from God.[73] On 4 January 1649 the House of Commons declared:

> That the People are, under God, the Original of all just Power: And do also *Declare*, that the Commons of *England*, in Parliament assembled, being chosen by, and representing the People, have the Supreme Power in this Nation: And do also *Declare*, That whatsoever is

---

[69] The attempt to arrest five Members of Parliament for treason, was based either on their suspected involvement in supporting a Scottish rebellion or to pre-empt a plot to impeach the Queen.
[70] *House of Commons Manuscript Journal*, 4 January 1642. Parliamentary Archives, HC/CL/JO/1/22, https://archives.blog.parliament.uk/2019/01/04/i-see-the-birds-have-flown/.
[71] Robertson (n 28) 101–9.
[72] ibid 129.
[73] ibid 127.

enacted, or declared for Law, by the Commons, in Parliament assembled, hath the Force of Law; and all the People of this Nation are concluded thereby, although the Consent and Concurrence of King, or House of Peers, be not had thereunto.[74]

By this seismic declaration Parliament purported to dispense with the idea that the state depended on royal authority.

A High Court was established 'to the end that no chief officer or magistrate may hereafter presume traitorously or maliciously to imagine or contrive the enslaving or destroying of the English nation and expect impunity for doing so'.[75] In January 1649, 135 commissioners were summoned to participate in the trial. Many refused. None of the leading lawyers wanted what Geoffrey Robertson QC dubbed *The Tyrannicide Brief*.[76] Cromwell's Lord Chancellor and his Chief Justice fled to the country to avoid it.[77]

The court met on 8 January, but it was 10 January before John Cook, the son of a Leicestershire farmer and a practising barrister,[78] accepted the brief to prosecute Charles and became Solicitor General to the Commonwealth.[79] His task was to prepare the case for presentation by the Attorney General, William Steele. A few days later Steele sent a note to Parliament pleading illness. Cook and two others had two days to draw up charges against the King. Cook was said to have taken the lead and following several edits by Cromwell and others the long list was made into a manageable indictment: *A Charge of High Treason, and Other High Crimes*.[80]

The indictment accused Charles of being a 'tyrant, traitor, murderer, public and implacable enemy of the Commonwealth of England' and, calling for justice, averred 'that the blood that had been spilt cried out for it'.[81] Robertson suggested that much of this was legally dubious, but that, in identifying tyranny as the King's crime Cook found a credible legal basis of responsibility for two wars, the first prosecution for war crimes.[82] Charles' personal correspondence with foreign powers, captured towards the end of the war, made the charges difficult to refute.

The trial began on 20 January 1649 with Charles refusing to enter a plea. Advised by a bevy of high-profile lawyers, he claimed no court had jurisdiction over a monarch. In Robertson's account, Cook played his role well. As he read the

---

[74] *House of Commons Journal Volume 6: 4 January 1649*, 110, www.british-history.ac.uk/commons-jrnl/vol6/pp110-111.
[75] Robertson (n 28) 12.
[76] ibid.
[77] ibid 9.
[78] ibid and see RS Kirby in *The Biographical History of England from Egbert the Great to the Revolution* (London, William Baynes and Son, 1824) 127.
[79] Robertson (n 28) 11–12.
[80] ibid 147.
[81] ibid 149, citing The Hon Justice Michael Kirby 'The Trial of King Charles I – Defining Moment for our Constitutional Liberties' An address to the Anglo-Australasian Lawyers' Association at Gray's Inn, London, January 1999. www.hcourt.gov.au/assets/publications/speeches/former-justices/kirbyj/kirbyj_charle88.htm#.
[82] Robertson (n 28) 150.

indictment.[83] Charles twice tried to stop him by crying 'Hold' and tapping him with his cane.[84] On both occasions Cook continued. The third time Cook ignored Charles. The King stood up and struck Cook so hard across his shoulder that the silver tip flew off his cane. Charles signalled to Cook to pick it up. After a brief stand-off Charles was forced to retrieve it himself.[85] This incident was symbolic; the divine monarch bowing to human law.[86]

In four days of trial the King was continuously asked to plead to the charges. He denied the court's authority, the following exchange typical:

> King: I have a trust committed to me by God, by old and lawful descent; I will not betray it, to answer to a new unlawful authority: therefore resolve me that, and you shall hear more of me ...
>
> Lord President: If you acknowledge not the authority of the court, they must proceed.
>
> King: I do tell them so; England was never an elective kingdom, but an hereditary kingdom for near these thousand years; therefore let me know by what authority I am called hither ... [and] I will answer it; otherwise I will not answer it.
>
> Lord President: Sir, how really you have managed your trust, is known: your way of answer is to interrogate the Court, which beseems not you in this condition. You have been told of it twice or thrice.[87]

The King was brought back and forth but on 22 January the court ruled he could not challenge its legitimacy.[88] Cook argued that the lack of cooperation with the court should be read as a confession and demanded judgment. The King was not finished and continued to demand to know the source of the court's authority. As he was ordered to be taken down, he appeared to be moving towards a plea, his final utterance of the second session: 'I never took up arms against the people, but for the laws.'[89]

Cook's closing speech was not required since refusal to participate was taken as confession. His request for judgment in default of plea was more anodyne than the closing he had prepared for a contested hearing.[90] This would have suggested that the King's bad faith was manifest from the very beginning of his reign. He had required the archbishop administering his coronation oath to leave out the words 'which the people shall chuse [choose]' from the description of laws he would uphold. Cook

---

[83] Others claimed that the charge was read by the chief judge, John Bradshaw, see CN Trueman, 'The Trial And Execution Of Charles I' (*The History Learning Site*, 17 March 2015) www.historylearningsite.co.uk/stuart-england/the-trial-and-execution-of-charles-i/.
[84] 'Killing the King: The Trial and Execution of Charles I', www.historyinanhour.com/2012/12/11/trial-and-execution-of-charles-i-summary/.
[85] Robertson (n 28) 154–55, see TB Howell (compiler), *A Complete Collection of State Trials and Proceedings for High treason and Other Crimes and Misdemeanours from the Earliest Period to the Year 1783*, Volume IV (24: Charles I, 1649: Trial of Charles the First) (London) 995, https://babel.hathitrust.org/cgi/pt?id=hvd.hxj2f4;view=1up;seq=512.
[86] G Robertson, *Crimes Against Humanity: The Struggle for Global Justice*, 2nd edn (London, Penguin Books, 2002) 5.
[87] Howell (n 85) 996.
[88] Robertson (n 28) 164.
[89] ibid 167.
[90] ibid 169–70.

stated that there was 'no light presumption, that from that very day he had a design to alter the fundamental laws, and to introduce an arbitrary and tyrannical government',[91] that:

> the Kings of England are trusted with a limited Power to govern by law, the whole stream and current of legal Authorities run so limped [limpid] and clear, that I should but weary those that know it already ... for it is one of the fundamentals of law, That the king is not above the law, but the law is above the king.[92]

An evidentiary hearing took evidence from 33 witnesses. They swore that Charles had personally commanded his armies, overseeing the torture of prisoners and the abuse of civilians.[93] The Commissioners were invited to sign his death warrant and 57 did so at the time with two adding their names later. On 30 January 1649 Charles I was beheaded and his son, also Charles, went into exile. Parliament rewarded Cook with a judicial appointment and land in Ireland.

By May 1649 the House of Commons, under pressure from factions in the army, had enacted legislation creating a Commonwealth, declaring itself sovereign and abolishing the monarchy and the House of Lords. By 1653 Oliver Cromwell dismissed the Rump Parliament, for tardiness in producing constitutional proposals, and placed himself in charge of a 'Protectorate'. An Instrument of Government ended military rule and established a written Constitution with a distinct legislature and executive and measures to prevent the domination of government by each.[94] Executive power was exercised by a Council of State established under the direction of Cromwell.

VII. THE RESTORATION

On Cromwell's death in 1659 conflict between factions within Parliament and the army made government impossible. The attempt to establish a stable and durable republic had failed and the life squeezed from an emergent civil society,[95] but many ideas and principles survived the restoration of the Stuarts.[96] The role of kingmaker fell to General George Monck, commander of the Parliamentary army in Scotland. Fearing descent into chaos, Monck responded to overtures by the exiled Charles Stuart. The Long Parliament finally dissolved itself in 1660 having agreed to his return. Charles made the Declaration of Breda, which offered reconciliation and promised moderation in religious and political matters on his return.

Charles II reached London on 29 May 1660. An Indemnity and Oblivion Act 1660 granted amnesty to Parliamentary supporters in general, except those most directly

---

[91] Howell (n 85) 1020.
[92] ibid 1019.
[93] Robertson (n 28) 173–75.
[94] RC Brown, 'The Law Of England During The Period Of The Commonwealth' (1931) 6(6) *Indiana Law Journal* 359, 370–72. The pamphlet defending the Instrument, *A True State of the Case of the Commonwealth*, was at the time attributed to Marchamont Nedham (see further Vile (n 17) 53).
[95] The Levellers' influence waned with the formation of the Rump Parliament and the increased political reach of the Army.
[96] Brown (n 94) 382.

implicated in the execution of his father. Under pressure from the royalist faction this number grew until, eventually, 104 persons were excluded from amnesty.[97] Many were publicly executed, others tracked and murdered abroad. One of the 104 was John Cook, Chief Justice of Ireland, who was seized and sent to England.

Edmund Ludlow, one of the few regicide Parliamentarians to escape the wrath of Charles II,[98] said of Cook:

> Being brought to his trial, he was accused of preferring, in the name of all the good people of England, an Impeachment of High Treason to the High Court of Justice against the late King; that he had signed the said impeachment with his own hand; that upon the King's demurrer to the jurisdiction of the Court, he had pressed that the charge might be taken for confessed; and therefore had demanded judgment from the Court against the King: but this indictment being more particularly charged upon him in the three following articles: First, that he, with others, had propounded, counselled, contrived, and imagined the death of the late King. Secondly, that to bring about this conspiracy, he, with others, had assumed authority and power to accuse, kill and murder the King. Thirdly, that a person unknown did cut off the King's head; and that the prisoner was abetting, aiding, assisting, countenancing and procuring the said person so to do.[99]

Cook's defence was classically legalistic; he could not have contrived or counselled the death of the King, because the proclamation for the trial was published on the day before he was appointed solicitor to the High Court of Justice. He had not 'assumed authority' being authorised by Parliament, a lawful authority, to do what he did. Finally, not having been 'accuser, witness, jury, judge, or executioner' he could not have abetted or procured the death of the King.

Cook urged that 'the High Court of Justice, though now called tyrannical and unlawful, was yet a court, had officers attending them, and many thing had authority, there being then no other in this nation than that which gave them their power; and if this will not justify a man for acting within his own sphere, it will not be lawful for anyone to exercise his profession unless he may be sure of the legality of the establishment under which he acts'.[100]

Commissioners appointed to decide Cook's fate included those expelled from the long Parliament and other royalist sympathisers such as John Finch, the former Speaker, lately returned from Holland. As one of many regicides prosecuted, Cook received scant attention.[101] He was hung, drawn and quartered at Charing Cross.[102] In a letter to his wife from the Tower shortly before his execution he wrote: 'We fought for the public good and would have enfranchised the people and secured the

---

[97] It was originally planned to exclude seven regicides from the amnesty, but, encouraged by a largely Anglican Parliament, the list grew (CH Firth (ed), *Memoirs of Edmond Ludlow Lieutenant-General of the Horse in the Army of the Commonwealth of England, 1625–1672* (Oxford, Clarendon Press, 1894) 275, 285).

[98] Despite several attempts (ibid 359–76).

[99] Firth ibid 309–10.

[100] ibid 311.

[101] Robertson was motivated to write his book on Cook as a response to Kirby J, the trial of Cook being more marked by abuse than that of Charles I.

[102] D Jordan and M Walsh, *The King's Revenge: Charles II and the Greatest Manhunt in British History* (London: Little, Brown Book Group, 2013) 174–75.

welfare of the whole groaning creation, if the nation had not delighted more in servitude than freedom.'[103]

Charles II was a popular despot but during his reign, from 1660–85, there were tensions, even with a sympathetic Parliament, over the funding of military ventures. The period was marked by the emergence of prototype political parties; Whigs and Tories, terms of abuse used by the other side. They were largely defined by support or opposition to the prospect of Charles' unpopular younger brother, James, succeeding him. Tories supported James' right of accession, while the ultra-protestant Whigs advocated his exclusion from the throne as a suspected Roman Catholic. To reassure the nation, Charles encouraged the marriage of James' daughter, Mary, to the Protestant William of Orange, but he also frustrated Parliamentary attempts to block the succession by packing it with his supporters.[104] He had the Whig leader, Lord Shaftesbury, committed to the Tower where, from 1666, he was advised by John Locke.[105]

VIII. THE GLORIOUS REVOLUTION

James II came to the throne in 1685, initially supported by the High Church, Anglican Tories of The Loyal Parliament. Early in his reign he dissolved Parliament when it protested about the enlargement of the standing army and allocation of military commands to Catholics. He did not recall it during the remaining three years of his reign. He racked up tension by trying to establish a King's Party and issued a Declaration of Indulgence in favour of religious tolerance.[106] He created a Catholic led standing army and purged Protestants in the English army based in Ireland.

In 1687 James prepared to pack Parliament with supporters in readiness for Catholic emancipation. He tried to control government offices and corporations to give himself a permanent electoral advantage. Seven bishops who petitioned the Crown against the legislative plans were prosecuted for seditious libel. The final straw was the announcement of the Queen's pregnancy, which dashed hopes that James' Protestant daughter, Mary, would succeed him. The Whig's were provoked to act, inviting William of Orange to accept the throne.

William landed at Brixham on 5 November 1688, by which time James had fled to France, deemed by Parliament to have abdicated. William's wife, Mary, James II's daughter, arrived three months later, accompanied by John Locke. On December 26,

---

[103] G Robertson, 'My Hero: John Cook', *The Guardian* (23 April 2011), www.theguardian.com/books/2011/apr/23/john-cooke-my-hero-geoffrey-robertson.

[104] M Burrage, 'Mrs Thatcher Against the "Little Republics": Ideology, Precedents and Reactions' in TC Halliday and L Karpik (eds), *Lawyers and the Rise of Western Political Liberalism* (Oxford, Clarendon Press, 1997) 137, 149–50.

[105] PA Schouls, 'John Locke And William III: A Dutchman's Rule In England Curtailed By An Englishman To Whom The Dutch Had Extended Political Asylum' (1985) 6:2 *Canadian Journal Of Netherlandic Studies* 60, 61.

[106] For example, Henry Compton, the anti-Catholic Bishop of London and Protestant fellows of Magdalen College, Oxford (*New World Encyclopaedia*, 'Glorious Revolution'), www.newworldencyclopedia.org/entry/Glorious_Revolution.

William accepted government duties and called a Parliament excluding the Tories of the Loyal Parliament of 1685. William refused to accept a regentship, so he and Mary became joint rulers. On 13 February 1689, Mary II and William III jointly acceded to the throne of England in a coup known by the victors as the Glorious Revolution.[107] At their coronation a Declaration of Rights proclaimed the 13 ways in which James had sought to subvert the Protestant religion and the People's rights and liberties. A Bill of Rights set out in similar form was enacted in 1688.

John Locke, the architect of the settlement following the Glorious Revolution, expressed his manifesto in the Bill of Rights: 'to establish the throne of our great restorer, our present King William; to make good his title in the consent of the people; which being the only one of all lawful governments'.[108] This, the defining document of the new constitutional order, declared:

> That the pretended Power of Suspending of Laws or the Execution of Laws by Regall Authority without Consent of Parlyament is illegall.
>
> That the pretended Power of Dispensing with Laws or the Execution of Laws by Regall Authoritie as it hath beene assumed and exercised of late is illegall.
>
> That the Commission for erecting the late Court of Commissioners for Ecclesiasticall Causes and all other Commissions and Courts of like nature are Illegall and Pernicious.
>
> That levying Money for or to the Use of the Crowne by pretence of Prerogative without Grant of Parlyament for longer time or in other manner then the same is or shall be granted is Illegall.
>
> That it is the Right of the Subjects to petition the King and all Commitments and Prosecutions for such Petitioning are Illegall.
>
> That the raising or keeping a standing Army within the Kingdome in time of Peace unlesse it be with Consent of Parlyament is against Law.
>
> That the Subjects which are Protestants may have Arms for their Defence suitable to their Conditions and as allowed by Law.
>
> That Election of Members of Parlyament ought to be free.
>
> That the Freedome of Speech and Debates or Proceedings in Parlyament ought not to be impeached or questioned in any Court or Place out of Parlyament.
>
> That excessive Baile ought not to be required nor excessive Fines imposed nor cruell and unusuall Punishments inflicted.
>
> That Jurors ought to be duely impannelled and returned ...
>
> That all Grants and Promises of Fines and Forfeitures of particular persons before Conviction are illegall and void.
>
> And that for Redresse of all Grievances and for the amending strengthening and preserveing of the Lawes Parlyaments ought to be held frequently.

This ended absolute monarchy and the possibility of a Catholic head of state. It made all significant state activity, suspending laws, levying taxes, maintaining a standing

---

[107] Although their succession to the English throne was peaceful, force was required to establish the new regime's authority in Ireland and Scotland.

[108] Schouls (n 105).

army during peacetime, subject to Parliamentary approval. William was said to have experienced the Crown on his head as a 'confining band'.[109] He complained he 'had more power as Stadtholder in Holland then as King in England'.[110]

IX. THE FRENCH AND AMERICAN REVOLUTIONS

In 1774 representatives of 12 of 13 States of the American colonies met to discuss a response to the British blockade of Boston harbour since December the previous year. The First Continental Congress met from 5 September to 26 October 1774. Its unsuccessful attempts to agree new terms for governance of the colonies led to the American Revolutionary War (1775–83). In 1776 the outcome of the conflict was in doubt, with many Americans in favour of remaining under the Crown and eschewing the help of the French against British forces. A factor in turning the tide in favour of independence was the arguments of a British immigrant, Thomas Paine (1737–1809).

In 1776 Paine published a pamphlet, *Common Sense*, in America. It attacked the English mode of government, claiming that it was ineffective in curbing the King's power. *Common Sense* was published in time to influence the Declaration of Independence by the Second Continental Congress on 4 July 1776. The American War of Independence provided both cause and inspiration for the French Revolution of 1789. The cause was French military and material support for the Americans, which drained French national resources and forced government to impose unpopular taxes. The inspiration was the liberal, radical, and republican ideals articulated in the American struggle.

X. DISCUSSION

The judicial excesses of the civil war underlined the importance of principles of legality in the imagination of lawyers. Accused parties received little protection in the legal process. The bill of attainder by which Parliament impeached the Earl of Strafford nullified his rights. The contemporary Australian judge, Kirby J described the trial of Charles I as a 'travesty' dressed up in formal procedure but unconcerned with substance.[111] Robertson felt that John Cook was similarly maligned and mistreated. He was not an anti-monarchist, having spoken in support of his former patron, the Earl of Strafford, providing legal arguments for his defence to impeachment and even offering to testify.[112] Robertson attributed the origin of the right of defendants to keep silent under questioning, and the principle that lawyers should not be accountable for who they represent, to Cook.

Lawyers such as Coke, Cook and Hampden were leading protagonists in the English revolution, but they were not isolated. An Inn of Court had existed as a centre

---

[109] ibid.
[110] ibid.
[111] Robertson (n 28).
[112] Robertson (28) 55.

for legal advocacy at the Temple, since at least 1340. During the seventeenth century court advocates and barristers, belonged to one of four Inns of Court covering a square mile of London at Holborn on the edge of the City of London. The Inns provided lawyers with residence, workspace, and social functions, including communal dining.[113] In the 1500s the Inns began admitting and training around 250 students a year,[114] acting as legal universities based on the collegiate model of Oxford and Cambridge.

In the early 1600s about 40 per cent of the Inns' residents were from the nobility, 40 per cent from the gentry and 12 per cent the sons of clergy, doctors, merchants, and lawyers.[115] They were often finishing schools for nobility,[116] and training schools for the others. Training increased hierarchy in what were collegial organisations, resulting in physical confrontations between benchers and students, which the King was forced to call the judges to resolve. They were also a hotbed of ideas, including ideas about the pre-eminence of law.

James I, Parliament, and the judges all tried to control or co-opt the Inns of Court. They were, however, independent, unpredictable, and potentially violent institutions. In 1608 James had granted the land occupied by the societies of the Inner Temple and Middle Temple jointly in perpetuity for the accommodation, entertainment and education of students and practitioners of the law.[117] No doubt hoping to draw on the goodwill generated, James wrote shortly after to suggest that the Inns formed a militia, a suggestion they declined to follow.[118] In 1613 the Inns again risked the King's displeasure by rejecting his nomination of a lecturer.[119]

Charles I 'deluged' the Inns with missives on disturbances, military training, loans and contributing to the rebuilding of St Pauls.[120] These were also largely ignored. Charles's lack of traction with the Inns may have been because of anti-absolutist thinking affecting students, the serjeants, drawn from the ranks of utter barristers, and the judges of the Common Pleas and King's Bench, drawn from the serjeants. Those most influential on the contestations between King and Parliament often had close connections with the Inns. This may have been the basis of De Tocqueville's speculation that, where lawyers were denied a political role, they would 'be the foremost agents of revolution'.[121] Pue suggested that all the English, American and French revolutions may have resulted from too many lawyers having insufficient work.[122]

---

[113] Burrage (n 67) 394.
[114] ibid 392–94.
[115] ibid 394.
[116] ibid 400.
[117] www.barcouncil.org.uk/about-the-bar/what-is-the-bar/inns-of-court/.
[118] Burrage (n 67) 402.
[119] ibid 401.
[120] ibid 403.
[121] A de Tocqueville *Democracy in America* (trans H Reeve) (Penn State Electronic Classics Series, 1831) 266, 303, http://seas3.elte.hu/coursematerial/LojkoMiklos/Alexis-de-Tocqueville-Democracy-in-America.pdf.
[122] WW Pue, 'Lawyers and Political Liberalism in Eighteenth and Nineteenth Century England' in Halliday and Karpik (n 104) 167, 168, citing D Duman, *The English and Colonial Bars in the Nineteenth Century* (London, Croom Helm, 1983) 206–9.

Sedley observed that the resistance to royal power offered by Coke and others was based on an assumed culture of the common law rather than precedent.[123] The basis in local custom legitimised resistance of autocracy. Judges of the Common Pleas were convinced that prerogative courts like the Court of High Commission, an ecclesiastical court with powers of arrest and detention, exercised powers contrary to Magna Carta. They resisted issuing orders of prohibition and countermanded arrests. This led to the jurisdictional dispute between the courts and King in which Coke was the most noted judicial participant. Coke was not the only judge to be sacked for ruling against Stuart Kings.[124] In seventeenth century England decisions of the King's courts still largely operationalised the King's policies.

While Coke was not the only notable judge of the period his law reports afforded him a prime position.[125] They were prepared between 1572, when he attended courts as a student to watch cases being argued, and 1615, when his judicial career ended. Baker referred to them as some of the most influential named reports[126] and they were seen to have affected many areas of the US Constitution. When James I sacked Coke, he recommended he spend his time correcting such 'novelties and errors and offensive conceits as are dispersed in his Reports'.[127] In 1634, Coke's papers, including the materials used to prepare his later reports, were seized by the Crown, only to be returned in 1641 after Coke's death, to his son.

The outbreak of judicial resistance in the seventeenth century did not represent an attempt to return to a golden age of judicial discretion under the Tudors. Rather, it reflected the emergence of Parliament as a competitor sovereign. The re-alignment of judicial loyalty with Parliament gradually followed.[128] Parliament and some of the common law judges were engaged in a joint operation to constrain and contain the Royal prerogative and the ecclesiastical courts deriving their authority from the Crown.[129]

Many of the Parliamentarians challenging the right of the King to dictate to Parliament were lawyer members of the Inns. John Hampden, admitted as a student of Inner Temple in 1613 and as an MP in 1621, was identified by Macaulay as the central figure of the Civil War, his statue at the entrance to the House of Commons. Other notable figures were members of Inns or had close connections with them: Sandy, Pym and Phelips (Middle Temple) and Digges (Gray's Inn).[130] These lawyers and others, like Coke, were incensed that Charles' ruses to raise finance without consent offended the ancient laws declared in Magna Carta. In 1628, when Charles I

---

[123] Sedley (n 16) 2.
[124] In 1627 Justice Crew was dismissed for declaring that Charles I's imprisonment of those who refused to make him loans was illegal. In 1634 Justice Heath were sacked (SC Stimpson, *The American Revolution In the Law: Anglo-American Jurisprudence before John Marshall* (Princeton, Princeton University Press, 1990) 24).
[125] ibid 6.
[126] J Baker, *An Introduction to English Legal History* (London, Butterworths, 2002) 183.
[127] J Baker, 'Law Reporting in England 1550–1650' (2017) 45(3) *International Journal of Legal Information* 209, 216 citing J Spedding (ed), *The Letters and the Life of Francis Bacon* (1872) vi, 76–7.
[128] ibid.
[129] Hill (n 45) 66.
[130] Arlidge and Judge (n 18) 126–27.

contemplated summoning Parliament to raise funding for disastrous foreign wars, he considered banning lawyers from membership.[131] In the event he often made his leading Parliamentary opponents, such as Coke, High Sheriffs, confining them to their counties.

For their role in preventing the dissolution of the 1628 Parliament, Charles had nine members committed to prison: Sir John Eliot, John Selden, William Coryton, Denzil Holles, Benjamin Valentine, Sir Miles Hobart, Sir William Heyman (or Haymon), Walter Long and William Strode. Most of these also had connections with the Inns. Eliot, Selden, Hobart, Holles and Strode were educated there, while Valentine's father was probably a member of Inner Temple. Walter Long's parents had died while he was young and 'his welfare was commended to the family's "special friend", a serjeant, Speaker of the House and master of the Rolls Sir Edward Phelips'.[132] Although Phelips was ostensibly a royalist, his son, Sir Robert, was an implacable opponent of tax levied without Parliamentary consent. Seven of the nine prisoners therefore had strong connections with the Inns or with lawyers in the Inns.

The five members of Parliament Charles I failed to arrest immediately before the outbreak of the Civil War in 1642 were Denzil Holles, John Pym, Sir Arthur Haslerig, John Hampden and William Strode. Most were lawyers previously imprisoned, Pym in 1602, Hampden in 1610 and Holles and Strode for preventing dissolution of the 1629 Parliament. Sir Arthur Haslerig, according to Clarendon, was an acolyte of Pym. Lawyers from the Inns of Court were therefore the formulators and carriers of grievance in the English revolutions. The same could be said of the American revolution. The Continental Congress which led to the War had 55 members of which 35 were lawyers.[133] Of the 56 signatories of the American Declaration of Independence, 26, including its author Thomas Jefferson, were lawyers.[134]

Locke's idea of replacing despotic rulers was not new, but justification differed in the classical, medieval, and liberal periods. In the classical period it was rooted in the functional role of leadership in public life, in the medieval period it was natural law doctrine and then social contract theory.[135] While these theories can be united by some notion of the people's right of self-defence they can also be seen as a rejection of arbitrary government, the first stage in establishing the rule of law.

XI. CONCLUSION

In the seventeenth century lawyers were at the forefront of efforts to subject monarchical power to formal legal constraint. The Stuart period consolidated opposition

---

[131] ibid 131.
[132] www.historyofparliamentonline.org/volume/1604-1629/member/long-walter-ii-1592-1672.
[133] MC Miller, *The High Priests of American Politics: The Role of Lawyers in American Political institutions* (Knoxville, University of Tennessee Press, 1995) 31.
[134] RR Lounsbury, 'Lawyers in the Constitutional Convention' (1927) 13 *ABA Journal* 720.
[135] Brincat (n 4); DK Van Kley, *The Religious Origins of the French Revolution: From Calvin to the Civil Constitution: 1560–1791* (New Haven and London, Yale University Press, 1996) ch 1; CE Olmstead, *History of Religion in the United States*, (Englewood Cliffs, New Jersey, Prentice-Hall, 1960) 9–10.

to arbitrariness focusing on the legacy of Magna Carta. William and Mary were the 'principled principals' Levi and Epperley identified as necessary to establish the rule of law.[136] They accepted constraints on power in a constitutional order, particularly Parliamentary control of finance. Establishing that a monarch could not be the sole repository of power was only the beginning of the process of establishing the rule of law. The next stage was to find arrangements to constrain power.

---

[136] M Levi and B Epperly, 'Principled Principals in the Founding Moments of the Rule of Law' in Heckman, Nelson and Cabatingan (n 22) 192, 208.

3

Constitution

I. INTRODUCTION

THE ENLIGHTENMENT IDEA of diffusing the power of Law produced options like mixed government, a separation of powers and a balanced constitution.[1] Mixed government distributed institutions between classes or interests, people, monarchy, and aristocracy. In a balanced Constitution the power of each individual or institution of government was checked by another. This ensured the power of government over law could only operate as a coercive force when acting in concert. Lawyers with a central role in this system were members of the judiciary. This chapter examines the role that they played with other lawyers in designing constitutional arrangements to promote and protect the rule of law.

II. THEORY

Hobbes recognised that, for power to be effective, the person or body that made the law had to be free to change the law; to be sovereign:

> The Soveraign of a Common-wealth, be it an Assembly, or one Man, is not subject to the Civill Lawes. For having power to make, and repeale Lawes, he may when he pleaseth, free himselfe from that subjection, by repealing those Lawes that trouble him, and making of new; and consequently he was free before. For he is free, that can be free when he will: Nor is it possible for any person to be bound to himselfe; because he that can bind, can release; and therefore he that is bound to himselfe onely, is not bound.[2]

Hobbes proposed three possible forms of sovereign power, a Monarchy, an Assembly of men, or an Aristocracy.[3] Concentrated power ensured an effective state but posed a threat to freedom. A central problem was defining a 'set of rules which effectively restrains the exercise of government power'.[4] The ideal arrangement should not

---

[1] J Morrow, *History of Political Thought* (Palgrave, London, 1998) ch 9: 'Mixed Government, Balanced Constitutions and the Separation of Powers'.
[2] T Hobbes, *Leviathan or the Matter, Forme and Power of a Common-wealth Ecclesiastical and Civill*, www.gutenberg.org/files/3207/3207-h/3207-h.htm#link2H_4_0306. Chapter XXVI: 'Of Civill Lawes – The Soveraign is Legislator – And Not Subject to Civill Law'.
[3] ibid.
[4] MJC Vile, *Constitutionalism and the Separation of Powers*, 2nd edn (Minneapolis, Liberty Fund, 1998) 252) 8.

impose constraints on government action which would unduly restrict necessary change, prevent accumulation of private power, and allow it to stop oppression of minorities. The beneficiaries included the minority whose economic freedom led to great wealth. The quest for a form of government that could control society but was itself under control led to experimentation with the doctrine of the separation of powers.

Three key centres, the US, the UK, and France, developed systems depending on variables such as prevailing circumstances, the theories of government propounded by intellectuals and politicians and pragmatic decisions. Locke had envisaged a separation of powers based on the Law of Nature: the legislative power derived from man's power of preservation within the state of nature and executive power from the power to punish crimes against the Law of Nature.[5] Locke's system envisaged executive power being vested in one person (a monarch or Protector)[6] and did not allow for an autonomous judicial function. He thought that political elites should be checked by other elites.[7]

In *The Spirit of Laws* (1748) Montesquieu identified three possible forms of government, Despotic, Monarchical and Republican.[8] He observed that Despotic and Monarchical forms of government placed executive and legislative powers in the same hands and that such concentrated power was likely to be abused.[9] He proposed that different people or bodies should exercise the main functions of government, the first of the Enlightenment scholars to clearly articulate[10] a tripartite separation of powers: a legislature making law, a body applying law and an executive enforcing law:[11]

> By virtue of the first, the prince or magistrate enacts temporary or perpetual laws, and amends or abrogates those that have been already enacted. By the second, he makes peace or war, sends or receives embassies, establishes the public security, and provides against invasions. By the third, he punishes criminals, or determines the disputes that arise between individuals. The latter we shall call the judiciary power, and the other, simply, the executive power of the state.[12]

Montesquieu thought that republican government could take an aristocratic or democratic form.

Montesquieu was an exception among Enlightenment scholars in paying attention to the judicial function. He thought the type of constitutional system would determine the judicial role. The judicial function in a monarchy was to reconcile conflicting

---

[5] ibid 63–74.

[6] ibid 73.

[7] M Qvortrup, *The Political Philosophy of Jean-Jacques Rousseau: The Impossibility of Reason* (Manchester, Manchester University Press, 2003) ch 3.

[8] CL Montesquieu, *The Spirit of the Laws* (trans/ed AM Cohler, BC Miller, and HS Stone) (Cambridge, Cambridge University Press, 1992) 63.

[9] ibid.

[10] Vile (n 4) suggested (at 60) that these institutions were proposed by George Lawson in 1657 and 1660 but with the executive having different functions (G Lawson, *An Examination of the Political Part of Mr Hobbs in his Leviathan* (London, 1657).

[11] Vile (n 4) 105.

[12] Montesquieu (n 8) Book XI: Of the Laws which establish Political Liberty, with Regard to the Constitution, Chapter VI: Of the Constitution of England.

rules, whereas the law of a republic was more predictable, so judges merely had to follow law. Montesquieu also emphasised the role of judicial procedures in protecting individual rights. Despotic governments ensured speedier proceedings, but formality was the price of freedom.[13]

Montesquieu's ideal arrangement was for the judicial function to be performed by an occasional ad hoc body comprising ordinary people and a revolving membership:

> By this method, the judicial power, so terrible to mankind, not being annexed to any particular state or profession, becomes, as it were, invisible. People have not then the judges continually present to their view; they fear the office, but not the magistrate. In accusations of a deep and criminal nature, it is proper the person accused should have the privilege of choosing, in some measure, his judges, in concurrence with the law … The judges ought likewise to be of the same rank as the accused, or, in other words, his peers; to the end, that he may not imagine he is fallen into the hands of persons inclined to treat him with rigour.[14]

In England, Montesquieu argued, the verdict was the work of a jury, following which the sentence determined by the judge was dictated by law.[15] This account of the justice system focused on these two dimensions: the institutions, specifically the jury, and attitudes to the judicial role, reflected in the liberal jurisprudence of legal positivism.

III. FORMS

When the civil war broke out in 1643 the main bone of contention was the location of sovereign legal authority.[16] The idea that it resided wholly in Parliament was not fully realised in practice. The failure to establish credible institutions after the civil war led to the Restoration and the return to mixed government, with monarch, Commons and Lords sharing power. Charles II promised to heed the legislature, albeit subject to his veto, while William and Mary agreed to work with it. Montesquieu saw these arrangements as enlightened constitutional monarchy although, in modern terms, they remained despotic; total power was exercised but not in an arbitrary way.[17]

The British system of government remained mixed until well into the nineteenth century. Monarchs consulted trusted advisers, but the first recorded usage of the term 'Cabinet' was in Francis Bacon's *Essays* in 1605.[18] Procedures were formalised during the reign of Charles I until, gradually, Cabinet comprised the heads of various ministries. Both George I and II made increased use of the arrangement because of their poor command of English. The executive power of Cabinet increased during the period of Robert Walpole between 1721 and 1742, a Whig regarded as the first

---

[13] Vile (n 4) 98.
[14] Montesquieu (n 8) Book XI: Of the Laws which establish Political Liberty, with Regard to the Constitution, Chapter VI: Of the Constitution of England.
[15] Vile (n 4) 97.
[16] ibid 47.
[17] A republic disguised as a monarchy (Vile (n 4) 92).
[18] As a remedy for poor advice 'the doctrine of Italy, and practice of France, in some kings' times, hath introduced cabinet counsels; a remedy worse than the disease'. F Bacon, *Essays, Civil and Moral* (XX Of Counsel, The Harvard Classics, 1909–14), www.bartleby.com/3/1/20.html.

Prime Minister, but the monarch remained the head of government in practical and legal terms.

Agitation against government increased in the eighteenth century, a main criticism being the failure of the House of Commons as a check on government. Tom Paine's *Rights of Man* (1791) claimed that the British system was corrupt, the Cabinet being comprised of men who were both members of parliament and servants of the Crown, advising on policy and carrying it out.[19] In 1807 Cobbett and others demanded the exclusion of Cabinet members from the Commons.[20] Vile argued that the American Revolution of 1789 and the French Revolution of 1848 reflected similar patterns of unrest to those in the UK in the period between 1770 and 1832.

Sir William Blackstone (1723–80) endorsed Sir Edward Coke's observations about the antiquity of English rights. In the *Commentaries on the Laws of England* (1765–69) he declared Magna Carta had been 'for the most part declaratory of the principal grounds of the fundamental laws of England', but, he said, Coke had identified 32 'corroborating statutes' up until the Petition of Right accepted by Charles I at the beginning of his reign, and the 'more ample concessions' made after.[21] To these were now added the *habeas corpus* act of Charles II and the recognition by William and Mary of the 'undoubted rights and liberties' and 'indubitable rights of the people of this kingdom'.[22]

Bailyn suggested that the ideological foundation of the American rebellion was provided by a mixture of the republican ideas of Enlightenment thinkers and Protestant theology.[23] He suggested that their motivation was as much fear that the English government would corrupt liberty as concerns about taxation or other economic anxiety. The so-called the Federalist Papers contained 85 essays written by Alexander Hamilton, John Jay, and James Madison under the name 'Publius' in six months from late 1787.[24] Published in newspapers they were written to persuade New Yorkers to ratify the Constitution over existing Articles of Confederation, but were then used in courts to understand the intention of the drafters.

Principal drafters of the second American Constitution, such as Madison and Hamilton, aimed to give each part of an unevenly populated country a stake, while avoiding fluctuating and inconsistent government. They each envisaged different forms and members of government.[25] Madison desired a deliberative spirit in government, with large electoral districts and solid landowners. Hamilton sought stability, with the dynamism of the commercial and professional classes harnessed in autonomous administrative institutions.

---

[19] Vile (n 4) 122.

[20] ibid 122.

[21] W Blackstone, *Blackstone's Commentaries on the Laws of England* (1765–70) Book the First, Chapter The First: Of the Absolute Rights of Individuals, Chapter 1, https://avalon.law.yale.edu/subject_menus/blackstone.asp.

[22] ibid.

[23] B Bailyn, *The Ideological Origins of the American Revolution* (Cambridge, The Belknap Press of Harvard University Press, 1967).

[24] 'Federalist Papers: Primary Documents in American History' *Library of Congress*, https://guides.loc.gov/federalist-papers/full-text#:~:text=The%20Federalist%20Papers%20were%20written%20and%20published%20to,explain%20particular%20provisions%20of%20the%20Constitution%20in%20detail.

[25] BJ Cook, *The Fourth Branch: Reconstructing the Administrative State for the Commercial Republic* (Kansas, University Press of Kansas, 2021).

Blackstone influenced the American Constitution, adapting Montesquieu and proposing that the executive should be a branch of the legislature, but not the whole of it, and that the executive, not the monarch, should be the repository of prerogative power.[26] The second Constitution, proposed in 1787 and coming into force in 1789, vested legislative powers in a Congress consisting of a Senate and House of Representatives.[27] A President elected by representatives of constituent States for four years[28] was part of the legislature, his veto only overcome by a special majority. Executive power was also vested in the President. A reconciliation of the separation of powers and popular sovereignty was implemented in most of the new State constitutions.[29]

The opening of the ratified Constitution 'We the People' appeared to create popular sovereignty, although the system was representative and militated against it.[30] The alternative was that the Constitution itself was sovereign. The solution to controlling power adopted in the US Constitution reflected local political preoccupations as well as political theory. The first 10 articles, known as the Bill of Rights, embodied constraints on government and guarantees of rights, the first three being concerned with a formal separation of the powers of government.

The unwritten British Constitution failed to achieve the conceptual clarity of its US equivalent, with its formal separation of powers. With progress towards a broader democracy during the 1800s, the British Cabinet began to assume more executive control[31] but Queen Victoria quietly influenced legislation and policy.[32] William Ewart Gladstone, Liberal politician and British Prime Minister for four terms between 1868 and 1894, claimed that while the British Constitution was 'the most subtle organism which has proceeded from progressive history, so the American Constitution was the most wonderful work ever struck off at a given time by the brain and purpose of man'.[33] Gladstone opined that, although the American Constitution was new, its principles were drawn from the English common law, given 'certain original conceptions and novel adaptations'.[34]

In his 1867 book *The English Constitution* Walter Bagehot minimised theories about balanced constitutions or separated powers.[35] He claimed that government could only be understood by looking at power. The government of Britain was divided between elements that were 'dignified': the monarch and House of Lords, and those that were efficient: Cabinet government and the legislature. The monarch,

---

[26] Vile (n 4) 112.
[27] The Constitution of the United States, Article 1, section 1, www.archives.gov/founding-docs/constitution-transcript.
[28] ibid Article 2, section 1.
[29] G Casper, 'An Essay in Separation of Powers: Some Early Versions and Practices' (1989) *William and Mary Law Review* 211.
[30] S Levinson, 'Popular Sovereignty and the United States Constitution: Tensions in the Ackermanian Program' (2014) 123 *Yale Law Journal* 2644.
[31] Vile (n 4) 244.
[32] P Ackroyd, *The History of England Volume V: Dominion* (London, Macmillan, 2018).
[33] RR Lounsbury, 'Lawyers in the Constitutional Convention' (1927) 13 *ABA Journal* 720, 724–25.
[34] ibid 725.
[35] W Bagehot, *The English Constitution* (London, Chapman and Hall, 1867).

as the main dignified element, commanded the loyalty and obedience of the uneducated and politically unsophisticated, but had limited rights: to be consulted, to encourage and to warn. The efficient elements of the Constitution, the government, were the centre of power; they ran the country. This arrangement worked, barely, Bagehot conceded, because a competent middle class elected competent representatives. Within 20 years of Bagehot, Albert Venn Dicey, Vinerian Professor of English Law at Oxford, provided a more theoretical and less critical analysis in *Introduction to the Study of the Law of the Constitution* (1885).[36] Gladstone read Dicey aloud, in Parliament, as 'an authority on the Constitution'.[37] Until that point, the British arrangements had little theoretical underpinning. Dicey identified two constitutional pillars: the rule of law and Parliamentary sovereignty.

IV. FUNCTIONS

A. Diffusing Power

Concentrations of government power could be diffused vertically and horizontally. Vertically, both central and local government had distinct spheres of political influence, whether federal or simply pluralistic. Horizontally, there could be a constitutional separation of powers between executive, legislative and judicial functions. Montesquieu provided no clear model for a Constitution based on a separation of powers because he preferred a mixed Constitution. In a stricter separation the three powers he proposed may have been able to inhibit abuse by the other functions. A legislature comprising two houses could impede each other, the legislature could deny funding to the executive and the executive could veto proposals of the legislature and the judicial function declare acts of the legislature and the executive to illegal.[38]

Montesquieu proposed the most advanced constitutional theory, but it left much to authors of constitutional arrangements to decide. A formal separation of the powers of government allocated the functions of government, making law, applying law, enforcing law, to different constitutional bodies. Therefore, in Vile's conventional formulation of the separation of powers:

> Each branch of the government must be confined to the exercise of its own function and not allowed to encroach upon the functions of the other branches. Furthermore, the persons who compose these three agencies of government must be kept separate and distinct, no individual being allowed to be at the same time a member of more than one branch. In this way each of the branches will be a check to the others and no single group of people will be able to control the machinery of the State.[39]

---

[36] AV Dicey, *Introduction to the Study of Law of the Constitution* (Boston, Adamant Media Corporation, 2005) (1st edn published 1885)).
[37] Vile (n 4) xi.
[38] Montesquieu (n 8) Book XI: Of the Laws which establish Political Liberty, with Regard to the Constitution, Chapter VI: Of the Constitution of England.
[39] Vile (n 4) 14.

Before considering the operation of the judicial function elsewhere, this chapter looks at its operation in the separation of powers in the UK.

B. Separating the Three Functions of Law

i. Creating Law: The Legislative Function

In Dicey's conception, the constitutionally sovereign body was the Queen in Parliament. Provided the legislature observed correct formality, including the monarch's assent, the power to legislate was subject to no legal limitations, and the courts had no power to review the validity of Acts of Parliament. The monarch's role was purely 'dignified', as Bagehot said, a vestige of the balanced constitution.[40] Legislation still passed between both Houses of Parliament and received the royal assent, so the monarch could theoretically refuse consent.[41] This power was untested and constitutionally uncertain. It might be refused if proposed laws did not serve the interest of the people or were contrary to established principles of international law protecting the rights of individuals or groups (see chapter seven).

Lord Bingham claimed that the rule of law and Parliamentary democracy were uniquely linked in the UK.[42] Unlike most similar countries, Parliament, not the Constitution was the ultimate authority. Sir John Laws argued that the power of a democratically elected Parliament was a function of the autonomy of citizens.[43] The proposition that Parliament held power in trust for the people was, Laws suggested, not just a moral proposition but a legal fact. The current edition of the bible of Parliamentary procedure, Erskine May, unambiguously asserted that democracy conferred legitimacy on Parliament and specifically the House of Common:

> The dominant influence enjoyed by the House of Commons within Parliament may be ascribed principally to its status as an elected assembly, the Members of which serve as the chosen representatives of the people. As such, the House of Commons possesses the most important power vested in any branch of the legislature, the right of imposing taxes upon the people and of voting money for the public service. The exercise of this right ensures the annual meeting of Parliament for redress of grievances, and it may also be said to give to the Commons the chief authority in the State.[44]

Like Hobbes' sovereign, Parliament controlled the creation or repealing of law, but despite the theoretical ascendancy of Parliament, there were weaknesses in the theory that it controlled the executive.

---

[40] Vile (n 4) 230
[41] V Bogdanor, *The New British Constitution* (Oxford, Hart Publishing, 2009) 16.
[42] Lord Bingham (Cornhill), 'The Rule of Law and the Sovereignty of Parliament?' (2008) 19(2) *King's Law Journal* 223.
[43] J Laws, 'The Rule of Law Today' in J Jowell and D Oliver (eds), *The Changing Constitution*, 5th edn (Oxford, Oxford University Press, 2000) ch 1.
[44] UK Parliament 'Erskine May', https://erskinemay.parliament.uk/, Part II, Chapter 11, para 11.3: Principal Power of the Commons.

Dicey had noted the risk of government administration placing executive activity beyond the scope of Parliament. In the 1920s Lord Hewart, the Lord Chief Justice, caused controversy, noting it was 'steadily increasing the range and the power of departmental authority and withdrawing its operations more and more from the jurisdiction of the Courts'.[45] Other criticisms were added in the late twentieth century by Vile. He noted, first, that governments needed time between elections to deliver their legislative agenda, during which there was little pressure to consider the electorate. Secondly, effective control of government by the House of Commons was hampered by the partisan party system. Governments with large majorities controlled Parliament rather than the other way round.

ii. Carrying Out Law: The Executive Function

In the UK the executive function was supervised by the Cabinet, mainly comprising politicians responsible for one of the Ministries of State. The modern system was initiated by David Lloyd George during World War I as a response to need of greater efficiency. Innovations included creation of a Cabinet Office and Secretariat and lines of responsibility for departmental Cabinet ministers. Cabinet's range of responsibilities cut across other possible functions: preparing legislation (legislative function), carrying out law and policy (executive function) and maintenance of law and order (administrative function). After World War II tasks of government were increasingly performed by a large army of neutral administrators, civil servants, and a range of bodies, prosecution services, police forces, prisons, and local authorities.

Centralisation of power in Cabinet increased the power of the Prime Minister. Bagehot had conceived of the role as *primus-inter-pares*, but Prime Ministers gained increasing power. From 1873 only they were able to summon Cabinet and from 1903 dismiss ministers,[46] increasingly as a matter of political calculation.[47] As party leadership became a significant factor in elections the post became more significant and, in some analyses, almost Presidential.[48] In fact, a Prime Minister's power, in Cabinet and Parliament, depended on a number of electoral factors: the majority they commanded, their popularity in their party and their perceived strength as an electoral asset.

The great power given to government ministers was counterbalanced by a framework of conventions covering ministers' collective and individual responsibilities. Collective responsibility involved all ministers backing a Cabinet decision collectively and resigning if the government was defeated. A minister unable to live with a Cabinet decision also had to resign. Individual responsibility meant that ministers

---

[45] G Hewart, *The New Despotism* (London, Ernest Benn Limited, 1929) 12.

[46] A Blick and G Jones, 'The Institution of Prime Minister' (UK Government), https://history.blog.gov.uk/2012/01/01/the-institution-of-prime-minister/.

[47] A King and N Allen, '"Off With Their Heads": British Prime Ministers and the Power to Dismiss' (2010) 40(2) *British Journal of Political Science* 249.

[48] G Allen, *The Last Prime Minister: Being Honest About the UK Presidency* (London, House of Commons, 2003); (2002) 56(2) *Parliamentary Affairs* 359.

took responsibility for personal failings or political failures by resigning their post. These conventions could be uncertain in scope and operation.[49]

Questions of Procedure for Ministers was a guidance document issued from at least the 1980s, but it became known as the Ministerial Code during the 1990s (see chapter four). It was issued by the Prime Minister at the beginning of a period of government following the same format, if not the letter, of previous codes. A well-known extract related to an aspect of individual responsibility, the truthfulness of ministers in dealing with Parliament:

> It is of paramount importance that Ministers give accurate and truthful information to Parliament, correcting any inadvertent error at the earliest opportunity. Ministers who knowingly mislead Parliament will be expected to offer their resignation to the Prime Minister.[50]

The Prime Minister, the notional author of the code, judged whether the code was breached and what consequences should follow.

iii. Interpretating the Law: Judicial Function

The separation of executive and judicial functions was established in the seventeenth century,[51] but recognition of the judicial function as the third limb of the separation of powers was slow. Historically, justice and the courts were expressly political. Interpreting legislation was seen as a legislative function, whether the legislator was monarch or Parliament. In the early Middle Ages both Houses of Parliament heard petitions for the judgments of lower courts to be reversed.[52] In 1399 the House of Commons stopped considering petitions[53] and the numbers presented to the House of Lords declined. The jurisdiction was revived in 1621 when James I asked the Lords to consider the case of a particularly persistent petitioner. In 1670 a jurisdictional dispute between the Lords and the Commons, over a case involving the East India Company, led Charles II to intervene.[54] Following this, the Lords resolved to only receive petitions the lower courts had failed to resolve.

One of Parliament's key demands before the civil war was judicial independence.[55] In 1642, Charles I agreed to the appointment of judges 'during good behaviour'. On the restoration of the monarchy in 1660 four judges in each of the Common Law

---

[49] Bogdanor (n 41) 15–19.
[50] *Ministerial Code* (London, Cabinet Office, 2018) 1.3.c., www.gov.uk/government/publications/ministerial-code.
[51] Vile (n 4) 32.
[52] This process was not an appeal in the modern sense: that it was based on what had happened in the inferior court.
[53] The Supreme Court: Appellate Committee of the House of Lords, www.supremecourt.uk/about/appellate-committee.html.
[54] *The Case of Thomas Skinner, Merchant v The East India Company* (1666) 6 State Trials 710 (HL) cited in BP Sahni, 'A Legal Analysis of the British East India Company' (2013) 54(4) *Acta Juridica Hungarica* 317, fn 16.
[55] G Robertson, *The Tyrannicide Brief: The Story of the Man who sent Charles I to the Scaffold* (London, Chatto & Windus, 2005) 60.

Courts, 12 in all, remained in office. This was recognition that judicial appointments should not be political. In 1668, however, appointment 'during pleasure' was reintroduced. The increased tension caused by alleged plots in the 10 years prior to 1688, created a volatile political atmosphere.[56] Charles II sacked 11 judges in 11 years and his brother, James II, sacked 12 in just three years.[57] Since their tenure was so insecure, judges were only independent in a narrow sense, when ruling on private disputes.[58]

The Heads of Grievances presented to William III in 1688 included demands that judges only be removed 'by due cause of law' and that they be paid salaries from public funds. Judicial independence from the executive was formally adopted in the Act of Settlement 1701. The arrangements involved secure tenure and immunity from action.[59] The path to recognising the full constitutional significance of the judiciary arguably began around the 1770s. This was the time the celebrated *Entick v Carrington*[60] case was heard (see below) and Blackstone converted Montesquieu's proposal for democratic and ad hoc juries into a blueprint for an independent judiciary with responsibility for the common law.[61]

Blackstone's proposals became concrete 100 years later when the Appellate Jurisdiction Act (1876) made the House of Lords a final court of appeal and regulated is hearings.[62] Lords of Appeal in Ordinary were to be appointed as professional judges, working full time on the judicial business of the House,[63] but also as life peers, with positions protected by statute.[64] This elevated the status of the judicial function but, contrary to the theory of the separation of powers, located it within Parliament. Law Lords heard appeals in the chamber of the House of Lords until World War II, when they moved to a nearby committee room.[65] They could vote on legislation in the House of Lords, but rarely did so.

The Constitutional Reform Act 2005 reconstituted the Appellate Committee of the House of Lords as the Supreme Court,[66] locating it outside Parliament physically

---

[56] The Popish Plot, Meal Tub Plot, Rye House Plot, Duke of Monmouth's Rebellion (SC Stimpson, *The American Revolution In the Law: Anglo-American Jurisprudence before John Marshall* (Princeton, Princeton University Press, 1990) 23–24).

[57] H Brooke, 'The History of Judicial Independence in England and Wales' (2015) *European Human Rights Law Review* 446.

[58] Stimpson (n 56).

[59] Current arrangements provided for retirement at the age of 75, or 70 if first appointed to a judicial office after 31 March 1995 (Constitutional Reform Act 2005, s 33). They had immunity from actions in tort or other civil proceeding arising from acts in their judicial role (*Sirros v Moore* [1975] QB 118, per Lord Denning at 134).

[60] *Entick v Carrington* Camden's judgment (1765), 19 State Trials 1045, 391–97.

[61] Vile (n 4) 114.

[62] Appellate Jurisdiction Act 1876.

[63] Under the Act, Lords of Appeal in Ordinary were required to be holders of high judicial offices for at least two years or practising barristers for not less than 15 years (Appellate Jurisdiction Act 1876, s 6).

[64] They would hold office during good behaviour and could not be removed except on address of both Houses of Parliament (Appellate Jurisdiction Act 1876, s 6).

[65] The House of Commons was bombed, and the Lords' chamber moved to escape the noise of the building repairs.

[66] Constitutional Reform Act 2005, s 40 and Sch 9 (The Supreme Court was actually established in 2009). See also Constitutional Reform: A Supreme Court for the United Kingdom (Department of Constitutional Affairs, July 2003). For background, see https://publications.parliament.uk/pa/cm200405/cmselect/cmconst/275/27504.htm.

and constitutionally by removing the right of senior judges to attend or vote.[67] The Act also re-allocated the judicial responsibilities of the Lord Chancellor, a member of government, to a judge, the president of the Supreme Court[68] with statutory power to create Supreme Court rules.[69] The Lord Chief Justice, the new President of the Courts of England and Wales, except the Supreme Court,[70] became responsible for the training, guidance and deployment of judges[71] and was given statutory authority to lay before Parliament any representations about the judiciary or administration of justice.[72]

There were signs that the Constitutional Reform Act 2005 had reinforced the independence of the senior judiciary. In 2012, the Supreme Court resisted draft legislation allowing the chief executive of the court to be appointed by a government minister.[73] In *Miller (No 1)* it asserted the fundamental importance of the independence of the judiciary and its recognition in the founding constitutional statutes, stating that 'in the broadest sense, the role of the judiciary is to uphold and further the rule of law; more particularly, judges impartially identify and apply the law in every case brought before the courts'.[74] The decision itself manifested determination not to bow to considerable political pressure (See further chapter seventeen).

A judicial code of ethics for the Supreme Court[75] and a similar document for other courts and the tribunal service[76] claimed the institutional independence of the judiciary since the early eighteenth century.[77] They alluded to six 'values' underpinning the judicial function including independence, as 'a prerequisite to the rule of law and a fundamental guarantee of a fair trial'.[78] Maintaining public trust in the system of justice depended on judges demonstrating both institutional and personal independence.[79] Institutional independence, involved determination to apply the law irrespective of adverse consequences for government. Personal independence,

---

[67] Constitutional Reform Act 2005, s 137.
[68] ibid s 23(5).
[69] ibid s 45.
[70] ibid ss 7 and 7(4).
[71] ibid s 7(2)(b).
[72] Constitutional Reform Act 2005, s 3(1), s 5(1) and s 5(5)(a).
[73] O Bowcott and R Syal, 'Judges take on ministers over supreme court' *The Guardian* (17 December 2012). The Constitutional Reform Act 2005, s 48(2) gave the power of appointment to the Lord Chancellor.
[74] *R (on the application of Miller and another) (Respondents) v Secretary of State for Exiting the European Union (Appellant) REFERENCE by the Attorney General for Northern Ireland – In the matter of an application by Agnew and others for Judicial Review REFERENCE by the Court of Appeal (Northern Ireland) – In the matter of an application by Raymond McCord for Judicial Review* [2017] UKSC 5, para 41.
[75] The *United Kingdom Supreme Court Guide to Judicial Conduct* (2009) was based on the Bangalore Principles of Judicial Conduct, a model code endorsed by the United Nations Human Rights Commission in 2003 and published with a commentary in 2007. It was revised and republished in 2019 (www.supreme-court.uk/docs/guide-to-judicial-conduct.pdf).
[76] First published in 2003 the current version is the *Guide to Judicial Conduct* (2019) (www.judiciary.uk/wp-content/uploads/2018/03/Guide-to-Judicial-Conduct-March-2019.pdf).
[77] *United Kingdom Supreme Court Guide to Judicial Conduct* (2019) (n 75), para 2(1), www.supreme-court.uk/docs/guide-to-judicial-conduct.pdf.
[78] ibid para 1(2)i.
[79] ibid, the subsection continues 'A judge shall therefore uphold and exemplify judicial independence in both its individual and institutional aspects'.

involved doing so irrespective of popular opinion or consequences for the rich and powerful.[80] The other values were impartiality, integrity, propriety, competence, and diligence.[81]

V. JUDGES AND THE RULE OF LAW

A. The Judicial Role

The first two of Dicey's three principles of the rule of law made ordinary judges arbiters of constitutional rights.[82] The first asserted the predominance of regular law excluding arbitrariness, prerogative, or even wide discretionary power in government: 'A man can be punished for breach of law, but he can be punished for nothing else'.[83] Secondly, equality before the law meant all classes were subject to the ordinary courts.[84] These two principles controlled arbitrary and discretionary power. The third principle gave judges a role setting constitutional rules, which were 'the consequence of the rights of individuals, as defined and enforced by the courts'. Therefore, 'the principles of private law were extended to determine the position of the Crown and its servants; thus, the Constitution is the result of the ordinary law of the land'.[85]

B. The Interpretative Role

The judges' interpretative role was central to constitutionalism.[86] Systems of formal legality demanded that judges were rational, neutral and dispassionate, but mainly predictable. In the English system the two sources, common law and statute, allowed scope to 'develop' the common law, largely a judicial creation in the first place. The convention was, however, to proceed incrementally, for example extending rights to privacy,[87] not simply inventing 'new' causes of action in Tort.[88] Creativity in making law was the preserve of Parliament.[89] Subjection of the judicial role to Parliamentary sovereignty meant that judges' role in interpreting legislation was also restricted by self-imposed procedures and rules.[90]

---

[80] This distinction is made in the Canadian case *Valente* (1983), cited by K. Malleson, *The New Judiciary: The Effects of Expansion and Activism* (Aldershot, Ashgate, 1999) 44.
[81] *United Kingdom Supreme Court Guide to Judicial Conduct* (2019) (n 75) para 1(2)i-vi.
[82] AV Dicey, *Introduction To The Study Of The Law Of The Constitution*, 3rd edn (London, Macmillan, 1889) ch 4. For the summary of principles below see Vile (n 4) 120–21.
[83] Dicey (n 82) 175.
[84] ibid 180–81.
[85] ibid 182–83.
[86] Vile (n 4) 360.
[87] L Dolding and R Mullender, 'Tort Law, Incrementalism, and the House of Lords' (1996) 47(1) *Northern Ireland Legal Quarterly* 12.
[88] T Bennet, 'Privacy and Incrementalism' in A Koltay and P Wragg (eds), *Comparative Privacy and Defamation* (Cheltenham, Edward Elgar, 2020) 24.
[89] Bennet (ibid) citing *Malone v Metropolitan Police Commissioner* [1979] Ch 344, per Megarry VC, 372: 'it is no function of the courts to legislate in a new field. The extension of the existing laws and principles is one thing, the creation of an altogether new right is another'.
[90] J Raz, *The Authority of Law: Essays on Law and Morality* (Oxford, Clarendon Press, 1979).

New law students learned that the starting point in interpreting statutes, the 'literal rule', gave effect to the presumed intention of the lawmaker, divined from the ordinary meaning of the words of the statute. The 'golden rule' allowed a deviation from the literal rule if the interpretation would be absurd. The 'mischief rule', derived from Coke's decision in *Heydon's Case*,[91] permitted consideration of whatever failing in the law the statute addressed. These methods envisaged only limited exploration beyond the actual words of the statute to interpret meaning. Anything else was to usurp the legislative function.

Decisions of senior courts bound all the courts below them. The government's judiciary website claimed that, although annual civil appeals represented a minute proportion of the number of annual cases, they were crucial to the rule of law.[92] There were two overlapping reasons, identified by the Roman legal scholar Justinian. The private function of appeals was to satisfy individual litigants' need for accountability. The public functions, eliminating errors in decision-making and providing guidance to lower courts, reduced the risk of future errors and encouraged certainty. Legal outcomes that were predictable, based on clear and extant laws, encouraged confidence in law and obedience to law.[93] Latterly, the courts indicated that legislation would be interpreted consistently with the rule of law principles of substantive and procedural fairness, 'unless there is the clearest provision to the contrary'.[94]

C. The Control Function

i. Control of the Legislature

British judges had no power to review or declare invalid, primary legislation.[95] This was attributable to the late recognition of the significance of the judiciary and because there was no authoritative reference point, such as a written Constitution, against which to assess the validity of legislation.[96] The third principle in Dicey's formulation of the rule of law, enthusiastically embraced at the time by Gladstone, set up that possibility. It created a potential conflict between: (a) the common law as the source of the rights of the people and basic constitutional norms, and (b) the doctrine of Parliamentary sovereignty and the interpretative function of the judiciary. The interpretative role therefore constrained the judiciary in controlling the legislature.

---

[91] (1584) 76 ER 637.

[92] For example, in 2011 there were 1,553,983 civil (non-family) cases started, but only 1,269 appeals filed in the Court of Appeal Civil Division, www.judiciary.uk/about-the-judiciary/the-judiciary-the-government-and-the-constitution/jud-acc-ind/right-2-appeal/.

[93] Per Lord Mustill in *R v Secretary of State for the Home Department ex parte Fire Brigades Union* [1995] 2 AC 513 at 567.

[94] *R v Secretary of State for the Home Department*, ex p Pierson [1998] AC 539 at 581.

[95] Secondary legislation, made under an authorising statute, found to be *ultra vires* could be declared invalid (see eg *R (on the Application of The Public Law Project) (Appellant) v Lord Chancellor* (Respondent) [2016] UKSC 39, [2016] AC 1531, [2017] 2 All ER 423).

[96] States with a written Constitution may not have legislative review on the grounds that one branch of government should not meddle in the activities of another.

In cases pre-dating the Glorious Revolution, Coke CJ asserted the supremacy of the common law to Parliament. In his report of *Calvin's Case*,[97] he said that the judges had agreed that Parliament could not change the protection conferred by 'a law eternal, the Moral law, called also the Law of Nature', recognised by common law as common right and reason.[98] Similarly, in *Bonham's Case* 1610, Coke stated that 'When an Act of Parliament is against Common Right and Reason, or repugnant, or impossible to be performed, the Common Law will controll it, and adjudge such Act to be void'.[99] When the Glorious Revolution established the supremacy of Parliament, Coke's position was said to be 'obsolete'.[100] Parliamentary supremacy became 'the paramount principle of our constitution'.[101] Judges accepted they could not declare statutes invalid but only divine Parliament's assumed intention.[102]

While British judges had little formal role in policing legislation, they used the rule of law as a yardstick in legislative interpretation. Sir John Laws suggested that although they were ostensibly seeking the ordinary meaning of the text of a statute, the exercise was often 'normative rather than descriptive'.[103] He illustrated this with the example of a case, heard before commissioners in India, in which a Hindu witness refused to swear a Christian oath.[104] The future Lord Mansfield, William Murray, appearing for a party in the proceedings, observed that those passing a statute requiring this could not have considered the prevailing circumstances. The common law, he said, was superior to an Act of Parliament because its rules were drawn from the fountain of justice.[105]

The doctrine that the UK Supreme Court had no role regarding the legality of primary legislation was tested when the UK joined the European Union (EU) in 1973. From that point, British domestic law became subject to EU law in specified areas.[106] Acting within the European constitutional framework compromised the theory of Parliamentary sovereignty.[107] This point was brought home by the decision in *R v Secretary of State for Transport ex p Factortame Ltd (No 2)*[108] where UK legislation affecting part-time employees was 'dis-applied' because it violated an EU directive. It was followed shortly by cases where judges asserted a residual constitutional role for the rule of law.

In *X v Morgan-Grampian* Lord Bridge stated that 'The maintenance of the rule of law is in every way as important in a free society as the democratic function'.[109]

---

[97] *Calvin's Case* 7 Co. Rep. ia, i3a (1608).
[98] DO McGovney, 'The British Origin of Judicial Review of Legislation' (1944) 93(1) *University of Pennsylvania Law Review* 1, 2.
[99] *Bonham's Case* (1610) 8 Co. Rep. 114a, 118a at 2.
[100] *Pickin v British Rail Board* [1974] AC 765, per Lord Reid.
[101] *R (Anderson) v Home Secretary* [2002] UKHL 46 per Lord Steyn at 39.
[102] Ungoed-Thomas J in *Cheney v Conn* [1968] I All ER 779.
[103] J Laws, 'The Rule of Law: The Presumption of Liberty and Justice' (2017) 22(4) *Judicial Review* 365.
[104] *Omychund v Barker* (1744) 26 Eng Rep 14.
[105] Laws (n 103) para 12.
[106] M Elliott, 'United Kingdom: Parliamentary sovereignty under pressure' (2004) 2(1) *International Journal of Constitutional Law* 545.
[107] ibid 553.
[108] *R v Secretary of State for Transport ex p Factortame Ltd (No 2)* [1990] 3 WLR 818.
[109] *X v Morgan-Grampian* [1991] 1 AC 1, 48.

In *R v Horseferry Road Magistrates, ex p Bennett* Lord Bridge said: 'There is, I think, no principle more basic to any proper system of law than the maintenance of the rule of law itself'.[110] Around the time of these cases, in 1995, an article in a leading public law journal by the recently retired Lord Chief Justice, Lord Woolf, stated that:

> if Parliament did the unthinkable, then I would say that the courts would also be required to act in a manner which would be without precedent ... Ultimately there are even limits on the supremacy of Parliament, which it is the courts' inalienable responsibility to identify and uphold. They are limits of the most modest dimensions, which I believe any democrat would accept. They are no more than are necessary to enable the rule of law to be preserved.[111]

Lord Woolf gave no example of what legislative breach of the rule of law would justify judicial intervention. In 2000 Lord Hoffmann proposed that the courts could query primary legislation when its 'constitutionality' could be questioned using principles 'little different from those which exist in countries where the power of the legislature is expressly limited by a constitutional document'.[112] In the same year, in *B v DPP*, Lord Steyn observed that 'the sovereignty of Parliament is the paramount principle of our constitution; but Parliament legislates against the background of the principle of legality'.[113]

The high point in judicial indications that Parliamentary sovereignty was subject to the rule of law was probably reached in *Jackson and others v Attorney General*.[114] Lord Hope made several pertinent points, noting: 'The rule of law enforced by the courts is the ultimate controlling factor on which our constitution is based. The fact that your Lordships have been willing to hear this appeal and to give judgment upon it is another indication that the courts have a part to play in defining the limits of Parliament's legislative sovereignty'.[115] He also said that 'Parliamentary sovereignty is an empty principle if legislation is passed which is so absurd or so unacceptable that the populace at large refuses to recognise it as law'[116] and finally: 'The principle of parliamentary sovereignty which in the absence of higher authority, has been created by the common law is built upon the assumption that Parliament represents the people whom it exists to serve'.[117]

In 2004 Lord Woolf gave a speech in which he claimed that: 'Ultimately, it is the rule of law [upheld by the independent judges] which stops a democracy descending into an elected dictatorship.'[118] Again he gave no examples but, earlier, in a Centenary lecture at Cambridge University, he proposed that the rule of law required access to

---

[110] *R v Horseferry Road Magistrates, ex p Bennett* [1994] AC 42, 67.
[111] Lord Woolf, 'Droit Public – English Style' (1995) *Public Law* 57, 68–69.
[112] *R v Home Secretary, ex p Simms* [2000] 2 AC 115, 131.
[113] *B v DPP* [2000] 2 WLR 452, 463.
[114] *Jackson and others v Attorney General* [2005] UKHL 56.
[115] ibid Lord Hope at para 107.
[116] ibid para 120.
[117] ibid para 126.
[118] L Mosesson, 'Dr Bonham in Woolf's Clothing: Sovereignty and the Rule of Law Today' (2007) *Mountbatten Yearbook of Legal Studies* 5, 14, citing Lord Woolf's Squire Centenary Lecture at Cambridge on 3 April 2004.

independent courts, a fair trial, a reasoned judgment within a reasonable time, effective enforcement powers, fair and reasonable court procedures, and a system of law that is 'reasonably certain, readily ascertainable, proportionate and fair'.[119] These essentially procedural requirements echoed the aims of new Civil Procedure Rules he had introduced, so the prospect of courts challenging parliamentary sovereignty seemed to have receded.

A fresh potential constraint on the executive was the introduction of the Human Rights Act 1998. Its aim was to bring UK law into line with the European Convention on Human Rights, obliging Parliament to consider the rights represented in creating all future legislation. Further, if a senior court found that primary legislation contradicted a Convention right it could make a declaration of incompatibility, allowing, but not requiring, Parliament to review the identified incompatibility and decide whether to change the incompatible statute.[120] Lord Bingham, a judge particularly identified with the rule of law through authorship and the University Centre dedicated to him, said the inability to declare incompatible legislation invalid was evidence of the constitutional supremacy of Parliament.[121] He rejected the suggestion that the House of Lords had ever, or would ever, act as a constitutional court.[122]

When the House of Lords Select Committee on the Constitution asked the Lord Chief Justice, Lord Phillips, whether the Supreme Court could strike down action that conflicted with the rule of law, such as legislation that removed a sphere of executive action from judicial review, he referred to the Act.[123] Noting the duty to consider compatibility[124] he thought that, if Parliament refused to legislate accordingly that would be contrary to 'what I would call rule of law', but it would be the end of the argument because Parliament 'is in that field supreme'.[125]

The Constitutional Reform Act 2005 was an opportunity to revise the relationship between judges and Parliament. There were however no provisions suggesting that courts act as a kind of constitutional backstop. This appeared to end the matter. Since the Act declared that it was subject to the 'existing principle of the rule of law' there remains a remote possibility that a future court might ground such a challenge in common law, 'constitutionality', the 'principle of legality' or 'rule of law'.[126] This would provoke a constitutional crisis.[127]

---

[119] ibid 14 citing Speech to the Commonwealth Law Conference in September 2005, reported by Joshua Rozenberg in *The Telegraph* on 22 September 2005.
[120] Human Rights Act 1998, s 4(2).
[121] Lord Bingham (Cornhill), 'The Rule of Law and the Sovereignty of Parliament?' (2008) 19(2) *King's Law Journal* 223.
[122] Bogdanor (n 41) 57.
[123] House of Lords, Select Committee on the Constitution *5th Report of Session 2005–06: Constitutional Reform Act 2005* (London, The Stationery Office, 2005) para 43.
[124] Human Rights Act 1998, s 4.
[125] House of Lords, Select Committee on the Constitution, *6th Report 2007*, 'Relations between the Executive, the Judiciary and Parliament' para 26, https://publications.parliament.uk/pa/ld200607/ldselect/ldconst/151/15103.htm#a8.
[126] Mosesson (n 118) 13.
[127] Bogdanor (n 41) 83.

ii. Control of the Executive

While Parliamentary sovereignty precluded judicial review of primary legislation, courts could review secondary legislation; statutory instruments created by ministers or regulations created by other bodies using enabling provisions in an Act of Parliament. This was an essential part of the courts' more expansive role in controlling unlawful actions by the executive. It included reviewing executive action taken under primary legislation by subordinate bodies, including any public body established by statute or given statutory authority, including utilities, local authorities, and government ministers. The acts of all such bodies affecting individuals were subject to judicial review.

Sir John Laws noted that judicial review was the invention of the judiciary.[128] He claimed that the underlying basis was a presumption of liberty that was 'the touchstone of a free, but organised, community': 'For the individual citizen, everything which is not forbidden is allowed; but for public bodies, and notably government, everything which is not allowed is forbidden.'[129] The presumption of liberty implicit in the first position is 'critically dependent on the efficacy of the second.'[130] The reverse of both propositions, and denial of the rule of law, was true in totalitarian states where, for the individual citizen, everything which was not allowed was forbidden, but for the state, everything which was not forbidden was allowed.

For Laws, the notion of justice was Kantian in nature, focused on rights and duties, rather than consequentialist, based on utilitarian principles. A judge should not deny a judicial review remedy because to do so would cause political damage any more than she should convict an innocent person to please or reassure the public. Rather, the presumption of liberty demanded careful examination of the power a statute gave to an executive agency, without bias in favour of the sovereign, through a four-stage process established by the common law: precedent, experiment, history, and distillation. Since every intrusion on individual freedom by the state 'needed objective justification'[131] Parliament should never curtail judicial review. The clarity of statute law depended on it.[132]

The consequences, and benchmarks, of the presumption of liberty were basic human rights and the rule of law. This was illustrated in the celebrated case of *Entick v Carrington* heard in 1765.[133] The defendant, an agent of the secretary of state, had been instructed to search the plaintiff's property for evidence of seditious libel. In defence to an action for trespass, the agent claimed that he interpreted his instruction from a minister to be authority to 'sweep all'. Lord Camden CJ found that state agents had no authority based on an executive instruction without clear statement in law: 'The king himself has no power to declare when the law ought to be violated for reason of state.'[134]

---

[128] Laws (n 103) and see *ex p Bennett* [1994] 1 AC 42, p 62 cited by Malleson (n 80) 11.
[129] Laws (n 103) 16–17.
[130] ibid 18.
[131] ibid 21.
[132] ibid 38.
[133] *Entick v Carrington* Camden's judgment (1765), 19 State Trials 1045, 391–97.
[134] ibid.

Entick v Carrington was not seriously challenged for two centuries, but Sir Stephen Sedley suggested that modern public law developed from the 1960s, largely through large numbers of cases made possible by legal aid.[135] Yet he also showed how modern case law followed principles from older cases.[136] Based on Sedley's collection of essays Sir John Laws drew on three examples 'honed over generations' to illustrate his proposition that judicial review was based on a presumption of liberty: illegality, procedural propriety and rationality.[137] He used two cases to illustrate each requirement, one from a case going back to at least the 1700s and one more recent.

The principle of illegality required misapplication of statutes to be rectified even if the consequences were beneficial. In the *Case of Monopolies*[138] a man sought to enforce a monopoly granted, according to a preamble, to advance the public good. Popham CJ held that the Queen had been deceived in making the grant because the monopoly had not served that purpose. Laws suggested that the same principle applied in the modern case, *Padfield v Minister of Agriculture, Fisheries and Food*.[139] Milk producers challenged a minister's refusal to hold an inquiry into the cost of distributing milk under a national scheme. The House of Lords decided that the refusal could be reviewed to see whether it frustrated the policy and objects of the enabling Act. Lord Upjohn reasoned that, if the minister gave no good reason for refusal, the court could conclude that he had no good reason.

Procedural propriety meant following fair procedure even if this produced undesirable consequences. In the eighteenth century case *R v Derbyshire JJ*[140] the court had disregarded an Act of Parliament preventing senior courts from granting *certiorari*, a writ inviting them to quash decisions of inferior courts exceeding their jurisdictional powers.[141] This was the principle applied in the case of *Anisminic Ltd v Foreign Compensation Commission*[142] where an Egyptian government agency purchased mining properties from a British company following the Suez crisis, then claimed a share of compensation the Egyptian government paid to the British government. The governing Act had stated that the decision of the commission distributing the funds could not be reviewed in a court of law. The House of Lords held that a court could examine the validity of the refusal. It decided that the commission had misconstrued the Act and its decision was null.

Rationality referred to the application of statute to the individual case, ignoring beneficent policy outcomes the statute did not justify. In *Rooke's Case*[143] the commissioners of sewers sought recovery of riverbank repair costs from the owner of the property adjoining the section of river rather than all those benefitting from access

---

[135] S Sedley, *Lions under the Throne* (Cambridge, Cambridge University Press, 2015).
[136] ibid 28.
[137] Laws (n 103) para 34.
[138] *Case of Monopolies* 11 Co Rep 84, (1599) 74 ER 1131, cited by Laws at para 31.
[139] *Padfield v Minister of Agriculture, Fisheries and Food* [1968] AC 997.
[140] *R v Derbyshire JJ* (1759) 2 Keny 299.
[141] Since the Senior Courts Act 1981, s 29(1) orders of *certiorari* have been known as quashing orders.
[142] *Anisminic Ltd v Foreign Compensation Commission* [1969] 2 AC 147, discussed by Sedley (n 135) (p 61, fn 36) and cited by Laws (para 32).
[143] *Rooke's Case* (1598) 5 Co Rep 99b.

to it. Sir Edward Coke held that the statutory discretion given to the commissioners was 'bound with the rule of reason and law' and not theirs to exercise 'according to their wills and private affections'.[144] In *Associated Provincial Picture Houses Ltd v Wednesbury Corp*[145] the Court of Appeal set out the grounds of a power to ensure that a public body could not act unreasonably in the performance of its public functions. This principle was evident in the earlier case amidst the medieval language, not least in the reference to 'the rule of reason'.[146]

Wednesbury was a mundane but important case heard only a few years after the end of World War II. A cinema operator had been licensed to show films on Sunday, but the local licensing authority, which had wide discretion to impose conductions under the Sunday Entertainments Act 1932, had specified that no child under 15 could be admitted. This was because the council, controlled by Sabbatarians, was restricting access by children to keep parents at home on Sundays. Sedley suggested that the decision was eminently reviewable, but the courts followed a long tradition of describing wide powers of review while declining to use them.[147]

While not assisting local cinema enthusiasts, the *Wednesbury* decision confirmed that judicial power could be used to constrain executive power not simply as an appellate function of senior courts. The authority to adjudicate on the reasonableness of executive action included consideration of both the process of reaching a decision and the quality of the decision itself. Courts could ask whether the authority had considered matters it should not or failed to consider matters it should. Importantly, even if the process was faultless, the decision itself was still reviewable if it was a decision no reasonable local authority could ever have come to. The test of executive excess was therefore unreasonableness, also known as irrationality.[148]

The modern basis of judicial review was laid out by the House of Lords in *CCSU v Minister for the Civil Service*[149] in 1985. The Government Communications Headquarters (GCHQ) was the centre of a national security network charged with securing military and official communications and providing government with signals intelligence. In 1947, GCHQ employees were allowed for the first time to belong to trade unions. In December 1983, Margaret Thatcher, the Prime Minister, suddenly and unilaterally required that terms of service of GCHQ staff be amended to exclude membership of trade unions. The justification for this was not obvious. Between 1979–81 there had been seven industrial disputes at GCHQ, most minor. The most serious had been in 1981, a protest about abolition of pay research machinery. The motive for the action probably lay in government irritation that the trade union was resisting use of polygraphs in the recruitment process, but this did not feature in the case.

A civil service trade union and six individuals challenged the ban in the High Court. Glidewell J held that the Unions had a reasonable expectation of consultation

---

[144] Cited by paras 28–29.
[145] *Associated Provincial Picture Houses Ltd v Wednesbury Corp* [1948] 1 KB 223.
[146] Laws (n 103) para 30.
[147] Sedley (n 135) 24–25.
[148] Which, as Professor Loveland observed in his comments, indulged a wide degree of political autonomy.
[149] *CCSU v Minister for the Civil Service* [1985] 1 AC 374 at 410.

and that Mrs Thatcher's instruction had no effect. The government appealed and argued, for the first time, that its failure to consult the trade union arose from national security concerns. The evidence, an affidavit by the Cabinet Secretary, Sir Robert Armstrong, claimed that: 'To have entered such consultations would have served to bring out the vulnerability of areas of operations to those who have shown themselves ready to organise disruption.' This proved to be the decisive point in both the Court of Appeal and then the House of Lords. Both accepted that courts were not competent to consider matters of national security. The Lords found that national security considerations affected the mind of the minister and the decision she reached was justified.[150]

The government had won the day, but the House of Lords made important points on the scope of judicial review. The majority rejected the idea that executive action was immune from judicial review because it was an exercise of prerogative power. Depending on its subject matter, ministers exercising such powers were under the same duty to act fairly as those acting under statutory powers. Lord Scarman found cases where prerogative powers were subject to the jurisdiction of the courts[151] referring to Sir Edward Coke's argument in *The Case of Proclamations* that royal prerogative was part of and subject to the common law:[152] 'Today, therefore, the controlling factor in determining whether the exercise of prerogative power is subject to judicial review is not its source but its subject matter'.[153] The GCHQ case was significant in basing the decision of a 'duty to act fairly' rather than 'natural justice', the test adopted in earlier cases.[154]

Sir John Laws argued that apparent confusion about the standards applied by judges in judicial review reflected the norms necessary for independent and impartial adjudication to take place and for the operation of the rule of law. He suggested three, reason, fairness, and the presumption of liberty, based on existing principles. Reason, he suggested, had morphed from *Wednesbury* reasonableness to proportionality and fairness from natural justice to legitimate expectations.[155] These standards he suggested were not culturally specific but were appropriate for the regulation of any people or bodies subject to regulation by law.

VI. OTHER JURISDICTIONS

All of the core jurisdictions incorporated a version of the separation of powers into constitutional arrangements and, in some cases, reinforced it later. In the US for example, this happened with the court system. The Constitution vested judicial power in a

---

[150] *CCSU* ibid 393.
[151] For example, *Reg v Criminal Injuries Compensation Board, ex parte Lain* [1967] 2 QB 864, where a decision of a body established under prerogative power was reviewed.
[152] Citing *Prohibitions del Roy* (1608) 12 Co Rep 63.
[153] *CCSU* (n 149) per Lord Scarman 407.
[154] See *CCSU* per Lord Roskill
[155] Laws (n 103) paras 13–15.

Supreme Court, with inferior courts to be established by Congress.[156] Until the early 1800s senior judges were political appointments and openly partisan. This changed with the appointment of the fourth Supreme Court Chief Justice, John Marshall, in 1801 by John Adams. After the election of Thomas Jefferson as President in the same year, and Senate proceedings against some senior judges, Marshall's neutral posture became the benchmark of behaviour.[157]

The Constitution gave the Supreme Court wide jurisdiction but did not enable it to review legislation. An important development was the court's claim to powers of legislative review based on common law.[158] This 'clarification' occurred during a period of aggressive assertion of the Supreme Court led by Marshall. The decisive case was *Marbury v Maddison* (1803) in which the Supreme Court established the principle that legislation contradicting a State Constitution, or the Constitution of the US, could be declared invalid.[159] It did not happen until *Dred Scott* in 1856 (see chapter six) but there were small numbers of annual cases thereafter.[160] This reinforced the separation of powers.

Canada's Constitution was set out in a British Act of Parliament, the British North America Act 1867, adopted with minor amendements as the Constitution Act in 1982, when full sovereignty was ceded. The Constitution reflected the federal pattern dictated by geographical provinces, but the preamble to the Act described the Constitution as 'similar in principle to that of the United Kingdom'.[161] In 1997 the Supreme Court of Canada described it as 'an actual order of positive laws' consistent with the rule of law.[162]

In the *Secession Reference* case the Supreme Court of Canada declared that the Constitution Act 1982 did not exhaustively define the Constitution.[163] It was said to include unwritten foundational principles: federalism, democracy, constitutionalism and the rule of law, and respect for minorities. In another Canadian case, it was said that the provisions of the Act were only specific expressions of these underlying principles[164] which were also said to have the 'full force of law'.[165] The rule of law was a foundational principle because it protected everyone's interests: without it, there would be 'anarchy, warfare and constant strife'.[166] The Canadian Supreme Court

---

[156] US Constitution Article 3, section 1.
[157] S Landsman, 'A brief survey on the development of the adversary system' (1983) 44(3) *Ohio State Law Journal* 713, 732.
[158] LC Keith, 'The United States Supreme Court and Judicial Review of Congress, 1803–2001' (2007) 90(4) *Judicature* 166.
[159] *Marbury v Madison* (1803) 5 US 137 decided that the claimant had good grounds but ruled against him on the grounds that the Act allowing him to bring his claim to the Supreme Court was unconstitutional.
[160] Keith (n 158).
[161] British North America Act 1867, C3 Preamble, www.legislation.gov.uk/ukpga/Vict/30-31/3/contents.
[162] *Ref re Remuneration of Judges of the Prov. Court of P.E.I.; Ref re Independence and Impartiality of Judges of the Prov. Court of P.E.I.* [1997] 3 SCR 3, https://scc-csc.lexum.com/scc-csc/scc-csc/en/item/1541/index.do.
[163] R Millen, 'The Independence of the Bar: An Unwritten Constitutional Principle' (2005) *Canadian Bar Review* 84.
[164] *Reference re: Remuneration of Judges* (n 162) at 64 cited by Millen at fn 11.
[165] *Reference re: Secession of Québec*, [1998] 2 SCR 217 at 249 cited by Millen (n 163).
[166] Millen citing in Reference re: Manitoba Language Rights.

further declared that Canadian courts could strike down legislation inconsistent with these constitutional principles.[167]

Various theories were offered for recognition of the unwritten principles of the Constitution by the Supreme Court of Canada. In the *Secession Reference* case, these were the vital, unstated assumptions upon which the text of the Act was based. In another case, an additional reason was offered: that the preamble to the Act stated the Canadian Constitution was 'similar in principle to that of the UK'.[168] Each of these approaches gave scope to courts to extend sections in the Act.

The Australian Constituion of 1900 was based on meetings, so-called Constitutional Conventions, conducted throughout Australia in the 1890s. These approved a draft by Sir Samuel Griffith, a barrister and later a judge[169] which was enacted by the British Parliament with modest amendments. The Australian Parliament comprised two Houses, a lower house with representatives selected on a nationwide vote and an upper house with representatives of the States.[170] An authoritative overview of the Act noted that it followed a conventional but incomplete separation of powers, with executive government composed of members of Parliament on the British model.[171] The original Constitution, with minor amendments, continued following independence. This was mainly because the mechanisms for amendment were onerous. The legitimacy of the Constituion was, however, then seen to rest on consent of the people rather than the Act.[172]

Britain established a first permanent settlement at Wellington, New Zealand in 1840 as part of the Australian colony of New South Wales. In 1841 it became a separate colony and was made self-governing in 1852. A Constitution Act was passed by the British Parliament in the same year, declaring New Zealand a federalised state and a constitutional monarchy with the Queen as head of state.[173] The Act was drafted by Governor-in-Chief, Sir George Grey, a former soldier and explorer. It was a very practical document rather than a statement of high principle. New Zealand attained Dominion status in 1907 and full independence in 1931, although this was not ratified until 1947.

The New Zealand Parliament passed the Constitution Act 1986 setting out a conventional separation of powers. The contemporary New Zealand government maintained that the 1986 Act formed only part of the Constitution, which also comprised other New Zealand legislation, such as the New Zealand Bill of Rights

---

[167] *Babcock v Canada (Attorney General)* [2002] 3 SCR 3 at 29 (Millen at fn 24).

[168] McLachlin J in *New Brunswick Broadcasting Co v Nova Scotia (Speaker of the House of Assembly)* [1993] 1 SCR 319. Cited by Millen at fn 5.

[169] See generally J Macrossan, K Saunders, S Berns, C Sheehan and K McConnel, *Griffith, the Law, and the Australian Constitution* (Brisbane, Royal Historical Society of Queensland, 1998).

[170] Commonwealth of Australia Constitution Act 1900, Chapter 1: The Parliament.

[171] Australian Government Solicitor, *Australia's Constitution* (Canberra, Parliamentary Education office, 2010).

[172] GJ Lindell, 'Why is Australia's Constitution Binding? – The Reasons in 1900 and Now, and the Effect of Independence' (1986) 16(1) *Federal Law Review* 29.

[173] The New Zealand Constitution Act 1852, HTTP://NZETC.VICTORIA.AC.NZ/TM/SCHOLARLY/TEI-GOVCONS-T1-BODY-D1-D1.HTML.

1990 and regulation such as the *Cabinet Manual*.[174] 'Ancient British law', Magna Carta and the Bill of Rights 1689, were also said to form part of it.

VII. DISCUSSION

The role of lawyers in formulating constitutional arrangements embedding the rule of law were sometimes clear. In the US, lawyers dominated the constitutional conventions following the Declaration of Independence. An American Constitutional Convention took place in Pennsylvania between 25 May and 17 September 1787, leading eventually to the publication of the US Constitution in 1789. Lawyers made up more than half this Convention. Of its 55 members, 39 had been members of the first or second Continental Congress.[175] The Constitutional Convention included among its 55 sitting members, soldiers, farmers, physicians, educators, financiers, and merchants; but 32 or 33 were lawyers and some of these were judges of State Courts.

Of the 55 Constitutional Convention members, 29 were college and university educated and some had studied or qualified in England. Five were at Middle Temple, four the Inner Temple, one at Oxford and two at Scottish institutions. Others were graduates of American colleges: Yale, Harvard, Princeton, Columbia, the College of Philadelphia and William and Mary. The Second Continental Congress ratified Articles of Confederation, the first national Constitution. Under the influence of lawyers James Madison and Alexander Hamilton, a new Constitution and government emerged under George Washington.

Draft proposals were debated before the Constitution of the United States was agreed. They were prepared by a Committee of Detail comprising Rutledge, Randolph, Gorham, Ellsworth and Wilson, and all except Gorham were lawyers. The Committee of Style, appointed to phrase and arrange the Constitution, consisted of Johnson, Hamilton, Gouverneur Morris, Madison and King, all of whom were lawyers. Morris was said to be responsible for the distinctive literary style. The so-called 'Virginia Plan', which formed the nucleus of the Constitution, was probably largely drafted by Madison.

Many of the lawyers serving in the American Constitutional Convention went on to senior positions of state. Madison became President of the United States while Hamilton was Secretary of the Treasury. Wilson, Rutledge, Ellsworth, Blair, and Paterson became Supreme Court judges. Rutledge and Ellsworth were, respectively the second and third Chief Justices of the United States.[176] The heavy involvement of lawyers in the creation of the US Constitution did not make it immune from criticism, particularly regarding its flawed separation of powers.

---

[174] Legislation Design and Advisory Committee, *Fundamental constitutional principles and values of New Zealand law* 'Chapter 4: Fundamental Constitutional Principles and the Rule of Law', http://ldac.org.nz/guidelines/legislation-guidelines-2021-edition/constitutional-issues-and-recognising-rights-2/chapter-4/part-1/.
[175] Lounsbury (n 33).
[176] ibid.

Critics suggested that the US separation of powers was compromised by formal powers given to one function to countermand the other. The President could veto legislation and the Senate approve appointments of judges. Madison claimed that Montesquieu had insisted that power not be concentrated, not that the functions should not interact.[177] He contended that no structural design could prevent the accumulation of power. Rather, it depended on those with administrative control of the different parts having 'constitutional means and personal motives to resist encroachments of the others'.[178]

In the UK, a government paper recently described Magna Carta as 'the bedrock and the Glorious Revolution as the beginning of the "modern British Constitution"'.[179] There was little written detail of that Constitution. The Bill of Rights of 1689 had purported to protect 'ancient rights and liberties' but most of the rights asserted reflected the failings of Stuart monarchs, and particularly those of James II. It touched on Parliamentary authority as a control of royal and arbitrary power, declaring illegal 'pretended power of suspending the laws and dispensing with laws by regal authority without consent of Parliament', forbidding the keeping of a standing army without Parliament's consent and raising taxes using prerogative powers.

The Select Committee on the Constitution, established by the House of Commons to 'examine the constitutional implications of all public bills coming before the House; and to keep under review the operation of 'the constitution', defined the Constitution as:

> the set of laws, rules and practices that create the basic institutions of the state, and its component and related parts, and stipulate the powers of those institutions and the relationship between the different institutions and between those institutions and the individual.[180]

The Committee recognised there was no single constitutional statement, but identified Magna Carta and legislation, the Bill of Rights 1689, the Parliament Acts of 1911 and 1949 and the Constitutional Reform Act 2005, as key documents. The majority in the key constitutional law case of *Miller (No 1)* identified a similar list of statutes enacted in the 20 years between 1688 and 1707 as of 'particular legal importance'.[181] This legacy was also seen as important in other former British colonies.

While the British system sought a separation of the power over law, Vile identified confusion about how to achieve it. Three aspects were critical: function. structure, and process.[182] The British Constitution was based on a partial separation of the

---

[177] 'Separation Of Powers And Checks And Balances' Legal Information Institute, Cornell Law School (undated) citing *The Federalist* Nos. 47–51 (J Cooke Ed, 1961) 323–53 (Madison), www.law.cornell.edu/constitution-conan/article-1/section-1/separation-of-powers-and-checks-and-balances.
[178] ibid 349.
[179] Ministry of Justice, *The Governance of Britain* (CM 7170, 2007) 12–14, https://assets.publishing.service.gov.uk/government/uploads/system/uploads/attachment_data/file/228834/7170.pdf.
[180] Constitution Committee, *First Report of Session 2001–02*, Reviewing the Constitution: Terms of Reference and Method of Working (HL Paper 11), Chapter 2.
[181] Those statutes were the Bill of Rights 1688/9 and the Act of Settlement 1701 in England and Wales, the Claim of Right Act 1689 in Scotland, and the Acts of Union 1706 and 1707 in England and Wales and in Scotland respectively. (Northern Ireland joined the UK pursuant to the Acts of Union 1800 in Britain and Ireland). *R (on the application of Miller and another)* (n 74).
[182] Vile (n 4) 347.

personnel of government, and of the functions of government, but had never implemented a strict, formal separation of powers. Indeed, the British system confused functions, institutions, and personnel.[183] Vile noted that France and Britain had attempted, unsuccessfully, to adapt parliamentary government to the rule of law and the separation of powers[184] creating different problems to those in the US.

Writing in 2009 Bogdanor suggested that, although Dicey remained authoritative on many constitutional matters, there had been such critical changes in the UK's constitutional arrangements that a new Constitution was in the process of being created.[185] The changes included membership of the EU, devolution of government powers to Wales, Scotland, and Northern Ireland and to mayors in London and Manchester. Bogdanor proposed that the cornerstone of any new Constitution was the Human Rights Act 1998, because it provided a means of breaching the wall of the unwritten Constitution, Parliamentary sovereignty, through intervention by the courts.

Many of the changes Bogdanor referred to resulted from initiatives of the Labour governments of Tony Blair (1997–2007) and Gordon Brown (2007–10), who had ambitions to clarify constitutional arrangements. Blair's government introduced the Constitutional Reform Act 2005, apparently to reinforce the separation of powers, but without a clear end view. In 2007 Gordon Brown's government put forward proposals to remove or limit executive powers to:

> deploy troops abroad; request the dissolution of Parliament; request the recall of Parliament; ratify international treaties without decision by Parliament; determine the rules governing entitlement to passports and for the granting of pardons; restrict parliamentary oversight of the intelligence services; choose bishops; have a say in the appointment of judges; direct prosecutors in individual criminal cases; and establish the rules governing the Civil Service.[186]

Brown's government also promised to increase parliamentary scrutiny of public appointments.[187] Some of these proposals were enacted in part. For example, the Fixed-term Parliaments Act 2011, setting a Parliamentary timescale for General Elections, was enacted by the Tory government of David Cameron. It removed the power of the Prime Minister to call an early election when conditions were favourable.[188]

In 2009 Gordon Brown raised the idea of a written Constitution[189] and a *Cabinet Manual*, setting out the operation and procedures and rules and practices of government, was produced as a possible basis. The idea stalled, but the *Cabinet Manual* became a guide for those working in government.[190] While the foreword[191] modestly

---

[183] ibid 3, 13.
[184] ibid 263–64.
[185] Bogdanor (n 41).
[186] Ministry of Justice (n 179).
[187] ibid.
[188] Fixed-term Parliaments Act 2011.
[189] 'Gordon Brown on constitutional reform – prime minister's statement in full' *The Guardian* (10 June 2009) www.theguardian.com/politics/2009/jun/10/gordon-brown-constitutional-reform.
[190] *The Cabinet Manual: A Guide to laws, conventions and rules on the operation of government*, https://assets.publishing.service.gov.uk/government/uploads/system/uploads/attachment_data/file/60641/cabinet-manual.pdf.
[191] By Gus O'Donnell, the Cabinet Secretary.

claimed it was not intended to be authoritative, it was probably the most neutral and respected statement of current constitutional understandings and conventions. It also suggested that the conventions of the Constitution were evolving.

The Constitutional Reform Act 2005 had appeared to sharpen the position of the judiciary as custodians of the separation of powers and rule of law by establishing a separate and independent Supreme Court. The House of Lords Select Committee on the Constitution suggested that the Act had weakened the judges' informal influence by disqualifying senior judges from the House of Lords and removing the direct channel to government provided by the Lord Chancellor as head of the judiciary.[192] The Lord Chief Justice could make written representations to Parliament, but Lord Judge referred to this as a 'nuclear option'.[193] Lord Woolf thought that a need for judicial representation in Parliament, presumably via the House of Lords, would increase with time.[194]

The Committee on the Constitution suggested that Parliament had a role in upholding the rule of law through legislative scrutiny and oversight of government action, particularly through the work of parliamentary select committees, informed by the views of the senior judiciary.[195] The then Lord Chancellor, Mr Grayling, told the select committee in evidence:

> I would not be hostile to a route of last resort … [for senior judges] if something is going badly wrong – the Government of the day are misbehaving, the Lord Chancellor is paying no attention – to have the ability to say to Parliament, 'Help'.[196]

This proposition was supported by former Lord Chancellors Lord Falconer and Mr Clarke, provided it was used sparingly. The ability to enlist Parliament to defend the rule of law depended on Parliamentary representatives following their conscience. Large numbers of politicians, however, often up to one third of the ruling party, were on the government payroll or hoped to be, and the rest were subject to party discipline.

Even before the Glorious Revolution, judges made significant contributions to the British Constitution, defining the rights Dicey identified as bedrock. Bagehot and Dicey were both trained as lawyers, although only Dicey practised.[197] Lawyers played important roles in designing constitutional arrangements, although in Britain these contributions were often hidden. They were also active in bringing cases to court and making the arguments on which constitutional principles were founded. Cases like *Entick v Carrington* underpinned Dicey's concept of the rule of law.[198] His second principle assumed that equality before the law was better protected by ordinary courts than specialist administrative courts.

---

[192] House of Lords Constitution Committee, *The Office of Lord Chancellor* Chapter 2: The Rule Of Law And Judicial Independence (2014–15), https://publications.parliament.uk/pa/ld201415/ldselect/ldconst/75/7505.htm, paras 82–87.
[193] ibid para 85.
[194] ibid para 84.
[195] ibid para 83.
[196] ibid para 86.
[197] Bagehot was called to the Bar in Lincoln's Inn in 1852, but never practised. Dicey was called in Inner Temple in 1863 and practised between 1872 and 1883, serving as junior counsel to the Commissioners of the Inland Revenue for a few years from 1876 (n 36) 'Introduction' xiv.
[198] AW Bradley and KD Ewing, *Constitutional and Administrative Law: Volume 1* (London, Longman, 2002) 96.

The constitutional role of the Common Law Courts was not just to establish rights but to hold the other functions of government to account. The test of the judiciary lay not just in asserting power to resist executive excess but in doing so. This seemed assured after the late 1970s, when Gavin Drewry suggested that the approach of the court in the GCHQ case marked a step in 'a steady resurgence of judicial activism'.[199] He argued, however, that the GCHQ case could not be understood except in the context of the Thatcher government's policies on trade unions, which built up to a decisive confrontation with trade union power in the Miners' Strike of 1984.

The GCHQ litigation brought together two political streams that became more pronounced during the first Thatcher government: '... determination to face down the trade unions in general and the public sector unions in particular, and a wish to "de-privilege" the civil service'.[200] A third stream, heightened sensitivity to issues of national security, reflected tensions between government and sections of the population. Fears that matters might end in court were generally exaggerated.

While the trade unions were organisations whose social role was increasingly questioned by government, they did not to see the courts as 'either sympathetic or natural avenues for redress'.[201] This suspicion, Drewry suggested, was justified in the GCHQ case, where the House of Lords was too easily assuaged by weak evidence on the national security point, particularly when Scarman had emphasised its late emergence. He had indicated however, that a future court might push open the door left ajar. Although the case was undoubtedly significant constitutionally, especially on the justiciability of ministerial decisions based on royal prerogative, Drewery declared the case was 'hardly an example of stirring judicial heroism'.[202]

Asked to review potential restrictions on judicial review, the barrister Amy Street suggested that judicial review was remarkable because:

> not only do individuals have the power to subject government decisions to an independent review of lawfulness, but such power is exercised on the premise that the government abides by the outcome in its exercise of executive power. Judicial review thus defines our constitutional climate. It plays a key role in ensuring that the executive acts only according to law. Without it, we are closer to an authoritarian or even totalitarian state. With it, we live under the rule of law.[203]

Members of the executive often appeared resentful about judicial review of their actions, but it was for the benefit of the state, a fact underlined by the Crown taking over successful applications for judicial review as claimant.

---

[199] See also Malleson (n 80) 44–47.
[200] G Drewry, 'The GCHQ Case – A Failure of Government Communications' (1985) 38(4) *Parliamentary Affairs* 371, 374.
[201] ibid 374.
[202] ibid 380.
[203] A Street, *Judicial Review and the Rule of Law: Who's in Control?* (London, Constitution Society, 2013) 12.

VIII. CONCLUSION

In Western constitutionalism, there was belief in limited government but uncertainty about how to achieve it. The separation of powers, 'the grand secret of liberty and good government',[204] tackled the problem identified by Hobbes; controlling government while still allowing the executive power to be effective.[205] In Britain in the eighteenth century a theory of balanced Constitution evolved,[206] with checks and balances operating between government functions which gave way to a system where fused legislative and executive powers were subject to the control of parliament and the courts.[207] This system depended on a judiciary holding government to account without exploiting the inherent *indeterminacy* of law to pursue personal or political agendas.[208] In order to control other agents of the state, judges had to be shielded from state institutions, and protected from purges, manipulation of selection procedures, abuse of pay or career incentives, creation of special courts, legislative reversals of decisions and intimidation.[209] Ideally, they were selected through independent procedures, guaranteed security, and had remuneration set by independent bodies.[210] As Locke noted, declarations of rights were flimsy protections against state power:[211] judges had to limit the state.

---

[204] Vile (n 4) at 3 (citing Nedham?) *A True State of the Case of the Commonwealth* (London, 1654) 10.
[205] Vile (n 4) 417.
[206] This envisaged, for example, that the legislature might be captured by popular parties and that another part of the legislature might be required to block or slow down change (Vile (n 4) 37).
[207] ibid 254.
[208] BZ Tamanaha, *On the Rule of Law: History, Politics, Theory* (Cambridge, Cambridge University Press, 2004) 90.
[209] T Ginsburg, 'The Politics of Courts in Democratisation' in in J Heckman, R Nelson and L Cabatingan (eds), *Global Perspectives on the Rule of Law* (London and New York, Routledge, 2010) 175.
[210] See eg US Constitution, Article 3, section 1.
[211] J Locke, *Second Treatise of Government* (Indianapolis, Hackett, 1980).

4

Execution

I. INTRODUCTION

Societies based on the rule of law depended on government lawyers to ensure that executive action was legal. In Britain these lawyers were the Lord Chancellor and two Law Officers of the Crown, the Attorney General and Solicitor General. Other jurisdictions had no Lord Chancellor, and either or both the other two often at both national and local level. Among different and varied responsibilities, a primary duty was upholding the legality of government. This obligation was often complicated by vagueness in defining it and the political nature of appointment. This chapter explores the effectiveness of government lawyers in monitoring and protecting the rule of law in the British system and variations in other jurisdictions.

II. THEORY

According to De Tocqueville the Anglo-American lawyer valued legality above any other public virtue. If a legislature deprived people of liberty, lawyers would not complain, they were 'less afraid of tyranny than of arbitrary power'.[1] Dictators, he said, would do well to introduce lawyers to their government; despotic power would 'assume the external features of justice and of legality in their hands'.[2] Lawyers close to power became part of state bureaucracy,[3] an effective way of ensuring the regularity and predictability on which the rule of law depended. A continuing debate concerned the continuing value of the role of Lord Chancellor or whether it had outlived its historic purpose.[4]

Since medieval times the Lord Chancellor was a lawyer, an executive role with judicial dimensions and formal parliamentary duties. The Law Officer roles originated in court work for the Crown and became a step towards Lord Chancellor.[5]

---

[1] *A de Tocqueville Democracy in America* (trans H Reeve) (Penn State Electronic Classics Series, 1831) 266, http://seas3.elte.hu/coursematerial/LojkoMiklos/Alexis-de-Tocqueville-Democracy-in-America.pdf.
[2] ibid.
[3] M Krygier, 'The Rule of Law: Pasts, Presents and Two Possible Futures' (2016) 12 *Annual Review of Law and Social Science* 199, 210.
[4] D Woodhouse, *The Office of Lord Chancellor* (London, Bloomsbury, 2001).
[5] Examples included Francis Bacon, Attorney General for England and Wales between 1613 and 1617 and Lord Chancellor from 1617 to 1621.

Other possibilities included senior judicial roles such as Lord Chief Justice. The modern roles of senior government lawyers adapted considerably in the twentieth century, with more explicit and positive obligations to the rule of law. A substantial literature covered the role of Lord Chancellor,[6] and the individuals who filled it, the British law officers,[7] and the law officer role in general.[8] Other relevant material included speeches by appointees including Frederick Elwyn-Jones, a barrister and Labour politician who was Attorney General for England and Wales (1964–70) and Lord Chancellor (1974–79) and Oliver Heald, a barrister MP who was Solicitor General to the government of David Cameron (2012–14).

III. LORD CHANCELLOR

An office like Lord Chancellor existed in Ancient Rome, where bishops had administrators for secretarial tasks.[9] In England, the office evolved in the late Saxon period, notably in the reign of Ethelbert, and was continuously occupied after the Norman Conquest.[10] The post holder was a Privy Councillor, a member of the inner group expected to advise the monarch, and custodian of the Royal Seal[11] which had symbolic significance as the expression of royal will in an age of limited literacy.[12] The Lord Chancellor, often a senior representative churchman on a path to bishopric was literate and therefore able to fulfil administrative tasks.

In the reign of Henry III (1216–72) the office was separated from the King's household and established as an office of writing, or Chancery, in Chancery Lane in Holborn. The role acquired a legal dimension in the reign of Edward 111 (1327–77), when the Chancellor attended the *Aula Regia*, a court which advised the King. Matters relating to the King's grants were delegated to the office.[13] Campbell suggested this legal role became functionally divided between cases needing a writ in other courts ('the hamper') and those reserved for the Lord Chancellor's special attention (the 'petty bag'). As he had no power to determine issues of fact, cases requiring a jury were passed to the King's Bench.

By the reign of Richard II (1377–99) the Lord Chancellors had a jurisdiction concerning appeals to the King for legal remedies not offered by the common law.[14] The Common Law Courts only recognised legal title in land for example whereas equity invented the idea of trusts of land. As the volume of cases grew, they were

---

[6] J Campbell, *The Lives of the Lord Chancellors and Keepers of the Great Seal of England: From the Earliest Times Till the Reign of George IV*, Volume I (Philadelphia, Lea and Blanchard, 1847).

[7] JLJ Edwards, *The Attorney General, Politics and the Public Interest* (London, Sweet and Maxwell, 1984).

[8] G Appleby, *The Role of the Solicitor-General: Negotiating Law Politics and the Interest* (Oxford, Hart Publishing, 2018).

[9] Campbell (n 6).

[10] There are references to such a position as early as 605AD (ibid 47–52).

[11] ibid 26–27.

[12] In 1442 ambassadors refused to carry out the King's supplementary instructions in relation to candidates for royal marriage until they were confirmed by a document issued under the seal (ibid 42–43).

[13] ibid 29.

[14] ibid 30–31.

delegated to the Lord Chancellor as 'keeper of the King's conscience' in legal matters, a so-called equitable jurisdiction. Campbell suggested that the implication that Lord Chancellors acted capriciously was unfair since Equity observed its own jurisprudential conventions.[15]

Lord Chancellors risked being dangerous to the monarch as alternative sources of power and authority.[16] In the reign of Henry VIII, Lord Audley managed to hold onto the role for 11 years by executing the royal will and avoiding the limelight. Thomas Cromwell, whose many titles included Lord Privy Seal, but not Lord Chancellor, dissolved the monasteries with Audley's enthusiastic assistance, but he plotted Cromwell's fall.[17] His power was illustrated by policy on religious matters, described by a foreign observer: 'subjects who were against the Pope were burned while those who were for him were hanged'.[18]

In the late medieval period, the Lord Chancellor was often Prime Minister, but the Earl of Clarendon in the reign of Charles II was the last to formally have that role.[19] Lord Chancellors then became important members of Cabinet, regarded as superior in status to Prime Minister. A Lord Keeper was appointed if there was no suitable candidate for Lord Chancellor and in 1591, and during the Commonwealth, Commissioners of the Seal were appointed.[20]

After 1707, and the union with Scotland, Queen Anne appointed William Cowper, the Keeper at the time, to the re-designated post of Lord High Chancellor of Great Britain. During the eighteenth century the Lord Chancellor was torn between loyalty to the monarch and party politics. When Pitt the Younger died and the government dissolved, the Lord Chancellor, Lord Eldon surrendered the seals to George III, who said: 'Lay them down on the sofa for I cannot and will not take them from you. Yet I admit you cannot stay when all the rest have run away.'[21]

In the eighteenth century the political eminence of the Lord Chancellor declined as monarchs withdrew from politics. By the mid-nineteenth century, Campbell suggested Lord Chancellors were no longer a 'casuist for the sovereign' but the giver of 'honest advice for which he is responsible in Parliament'.[22] With the rise of the Prime Minister, the Lord Chancellor was powerful but without purpose, becoming a kind of constitutional and legal figurehead. Writing in 1847, Campbell described the role as 'the guardian of personal liberty': 'anyone unlawfully imprisoned could apply to him for a writ of *habeus corpus* in term or in vacation'.[23] A degree of detachment

---

[15] ibid 34.
[16] Thomas Moore (1529–32), and Thomas Becket who, having served as Lord Chancellor (1155–62), was murdered for attempting to extend the rights of the Church.
[17] Campbell (n 6) 467–68.
[18] Audley did not object to the execution of protestants who denied transubstantiation but insisted on the execution of Catholics who refused to swear under the Act of Supremacy (ibid 470).
[19] ibid 39.
[20] Commissioners were declared to have the same power as a Lord Chancellor in the Great Seal Act 1688, one of the first statutes of William III and Mary.
[21] JM Rigg, 'Scott, John (1751–1838)' in *Dictionary of National Biography, 1885–1900* Vol 51; L Stephen and S Lee (eds), *Dictionary of National Biography*: from the earliest times to 1900 (London, Oxford University Press, 1949).
[22] Campbell (n 6) 40.
[23] ibid 34.

from politics became evident because, although Speaker of the House of Lords, the Lord Chancellor did not sit in treason trials of peers.[24]

In the twentieth century the Lord Chancellor's responsibilities spanned the functions of the legislature, executive and judiciary. By virtue of office, postholders were members of Cabinet, Speakers of the House of Lords[25] and played a central role in selecting senior judges. As a judge, the Lord Chancellor could hear challenges to executive action but, by convention, was the defender of the rule of law in government. This contradiction was addressed by the Constitutional Reform Act 2005, considered below.[26]

IV. LAW OFFICERS OF THE CROWN

A. History

In England and Wales and Northern Ireland the Law Officers of the Crown were the Attorney General and Solicitor General.[27] The origin of the role of Attorney General began with appearances in court on behalf of the sovereign, who could not plead cases in his own courts.[28] Records from 1243 showed a King's attorney receiving a regular fee for defending the interests and prerogatives of royalty, but there were probably a few such appointees. The need for regular advice on litigation, and growing complexity in state administration, led to a more formal arrangement.

The first record of the use of the title Attorney General was in 1461 when John Herbert was called on by the House of Lords,[29] with the King's Serjeants, to advise on the claim of the Duke of York to the throne.[30] This was also the time when the first record of a King's solicitor appears. It is unclear whether this choice of title reflected the postholder's expertise in Chancery, solicitors' principal function at the time, or the fact that, like solicitors, he assisted the attorney.[31] The title Solicitor General first appeared in 1515, from when there was one appointment to each law officer post, with both having power to appoint deputies.[32]

In the medieval period law officers pursued the monarch's purpose with scant regard for legal propriety. One of the early collators of the records of State Trials condemned the many Attorneys General 'who with rude and boisterous language abuse and revile the unfortunate prisoner; who stick not to take all advantages of

---

[24] Although he could preside over the impeachment of commoners for 'high crimes and misdemeanours' (ibid 38).
[25] ibid 36.
[26] Constitutional Reform Act 2005.
[27] Historically, Attorney General was the senior role, but the Law Officers Act 1997 provided that any function of the Attorney General was exercisable by the Solicitor General.
[28] E Jones, 'The Office of Attorney-General' (1969) 27 *Cambridge Law Journal* 43.
[29] The first law officer to bear the title of Attorney General was in 1461.
[30] Jones (n 28), Appleby (n 8) 25–26. The practice of advising the upper House ended in 1742, although the law officers still attended as counsel.
[31] Appleby (n 8) 21.
[32] ibid 21.

him, however hard and unjust ... and who browbeat his witnesses as soon as they appear'.[33] The trial of Thomas Moore for treason in the reign of Henry VIII was a case in point. Moore was key to breaking popular resistance to the King as head of the church so, when it seemed the jury would acquit Moore of denying the King his dignity and title, Solicitor General Richard Rich falsely accused Moore of telling him in conversation that Parliament could not make the King supreme head of the church.[34] Moore suggested the inherent unlikelihood of such carelessness, saying: 'In good faith Rich I am more sorry for your perjury than for mine own peril.'[35]

In the late medieval period, the Attorney General operated as a link between the Houses of Parliament. The Commons suspected he was an agent of the Crown and the Lords and, when Francis Bacon performed the role in 1614, the lower house resolved that he 'remain in the House for this Parliament but never any Attorney-General to serve in the Lower House in future'.[36] Despite this, law officers continued to be drawn from the lower house and, if there was no suitable candidate, a safe Parliamentary seat was found for the appointee. By the seventeenth century the law officers were responsible for prosecution in notable cases, but it was not clear whether both had authority.

The relative positions of the Law Officers were clarified in 1768 when there was no appointed Attorney General and Jon Wilkes challenged charges brought against him by the Solicitor General. The chief justice of the Common Pleas held that the Attorney General had no right inherent in his office, but merely exercised powers entrusted by the Constitution to the monarch.[37] Therefore, it did not matter who brought charges in the King's name. The implication of this decision was that neither law officer had any responsibility other than to the King. As Attorney General, Sir John Scott, the future Earl of Eldon, led the imposition of repressive legislation: the Traitorous Correspondence Act 1793, Habeas Corpus Suspension Act 1794, the Treasonable Practices and Seditious Meetings Acts 1795 and the Newspaper Proprietors' Registration Act 1798.[38]

By the nineteenth century the law officers' advocacy role declined and they played a more significant role in Parliament.[39] By this point they were the King's chief legal advisers and George III directed that the law officers be recognised as heads of the Bar in 1814.[40] This may have been partly because they were generalist lawyers but also because their loyalty was more assured than that of the Sergeants who, being common lawyers, generally supported the supremacy of law and Parliament over the Crown. This displaced the sergeants at the Bar and their role sharply declined.

---

[33] S Emlyn, *A complete collection of state-trials and proceedings for high-treason: and other crimes and misdemeanors; from the reign of King Richard II. to the reign of King George II* (London, John Walthoe, 1730) cited by Jones (n 28) 45.
[34] Campbell (n 6) 436–37.
[35] ibid 437.
[36] Jones (n 28) 44.
[37] Appleby (n 8) 22–23.
[38] In his second spell as Lord Chancellor (1807–27) Eldon opposed the abolition of slavery and Catholic emancipation (Rigg (n 22)).
[39] WS Holdsworth, *A History of English Law*, Vol VI (Methuen, 1924) (1937 reprint) 457; Appleby (n 8) 22.
[40] Appleby (n 8) 22.

As with the Lord Chancellor, expectations of the law officers began to change in the nineteenth century. They were no longer seen as simply 'bloodhounds of the Crown'.[41] Thomas Denman, a noted Whig and briefly Attorney General (1830–31), was praised for conducting prosecutions in a way that was 'temperate' and 'humane'.[42] The King wrote to him expressing appreciation that this had an 'important effect upon the public mind'.[43]

By 1911, the Attorney General defended his role as being the assertion of the Crown's prerogative powers rather than the defence of executive power. It was only recently that the Attorney General was cast as 'the guardian of the rule of law and the public interest'.[44] Edwards dated the idea that the Attorney General's powers should be exercised independently to the nineteenth century,[45] but Barendt felt that it could only have clearly taken hold after 1924. In that year, Ramsay MacDonald's Labour government instructed Sir Patrick Hastings to drop the prosecution of the editor of a Communist paper for an article construed as incitement to mutiny, and he did so.[46]

Growing expectations of independence and accountability in the Attorney General's prosecutorial role were exemplified in 1951. The Attorney General, Sir Hartley Shawcross, had to explain to the House of Commons his decision to prosecute gas workers for taking prohibited industrial action.[47] In what became a 'classic' statement of decisions in the public interest,[48] Shawcross pointed to constitutional convention that the Attorney General could consult Cabinet colleagues about whether to prosecute in a specific case, but must exercise their own judgement, in the light of relevant public policy when it came to a deciding whether to prosecute.

B. Responsibilities of the Law Officers

The responsibilities of the Law Officers reflected historical origins and in some way conflict with increased responsibility for the rule of law. They included management, investigation, prosecution decisions, advocacy for, and advice to, government. In Scotland the Advocate General performed these functions for the Scottish government.

---

[41] ibid 24, citing H Shawcross, *The Office of the Attorney General* (Law Society, 1953) 3.
[42] ibid 24, citing JW Norton-Kyshe, *The law and privileges relating to the Attorney-General and Solicitor-General of England: with a history from the earliest periods, and a series of King's Attorneys and Attorneys and Solicitors-General from the reign of Henry III. to the 60th of Queen Victoria* (London, Stevens and Haynes, 1897) 18–19.
[43] Appleby (n 8) 24, citing Norton-Kyshe ibid 61.
[44] See eg O Heald, 'The role of the Law Officers' Speech by Solicitor General Oliver Heald QC MP to Kent Law School 18 October 2012, www.gov.uk/government/speeches/the-role-of-the-law-officers.
[45] Edwards (n 7).
[46] Book review by E Barendt (1985) 34 *International and Comparative Law Quarterly* 413.
[47] Appleby (n 8) 38–39.
[48] House of Commons Constitutional Affairs Committee, *Constitutional Role of the Attorney General: Fifth Report of the Session 2006–7* (London, HC306, 2007) para 16.

i. Managerial

The Attorney General had management responsibility for government legal institutions: the Government Legal Department, the Crown Prosecution Service, the Service Prosecuting Authority, HM Crown Prosecution Service Inspectorate, and the Serious Fraud Office. Each had a hierarchy of officers so, for example, the Director of Public Prosecutions acted under the Attorney General's superintendence and direction. The Attorney General also had specific responsibilities within each area. In relation to criminal proceedings, for example, specific tasks included: (a) giving consent to prosecute certain categories of criminal offence, relating to Official Secrets, corruption, explosives, incitement to racial hatred, and terrorism offences with overseas connections, (b) referring unduly lenient sentences to the Court of Appeal, (c) terminating criminal proceedings on indictment by issuing a *nolle prosequi*, and (d) referring points of law in criminal cases to the Court of Appeal.[49]

As noted, during the twentieth century the right of the Solicitor General to perform any function of the Attorney General was confirmed by statute.[50] The Solicitor General was therefore a deputy or agent of the Attorney General in managing legal government bodies, advising on civil litigation, civil law matters and on the public interest function of government.[51] An Attorney General's Office helped the Law Officers perform their duties.[52] This, as with many other areas of their work had clear rule of law implications; imposing correct sentences contributed to the predictability and proportionality of law.

Another example of the Attorney General's contribution to legality was reviewing sentences which may be too lenient. According to Heald, there were a small but significant number of cases every year where the Court of Appeal was asked to intervene in sentencing. In 2011, for example, 263 sentences were drawn to the attention of the Attorney General, of which 112 were referred to the Court of Appeal. The sentence was increased in 95 cases.[53] The detailed analysis of suitable cases was the kind of work conducted by the Attorney General's Office.

ii. Parliamentary

The Law Officers were responsible to Parliament for their agencies. They were often full-time members of parliamentary committees dealing with Bills with mainly legal content and were expected to help steer some legislation through the House.[54] As members of any Cabinet Committee considering government Bills, the Attorney General advised government on 'lawful and proper' ways to achieve its

---

[49] ibid para 12.
[50] Law Officers Act 1944, Law Officers Act 1997 (Appleby (n 8) 23).
[51] UK Government 'Ministerial role: Solicitor General', www.gov.uk/government/ministers/solicitor-general.
[52] *The Cabinet Manual: A Guide to laws, conventions and rules on the operation of government*, Chapter 6, https://assets.publishing.service.gov.uk/government/uploads/system/uploads/attachment_data/file/60641/cabinet-manual.pdf.
[53] Heald (n 44).
[54] Jones (n 28) 51.

legislative objectives. They had responsibility for blocking bills not meeting criteria of legality or propriety, for example retrospective legislation,[55] and then working with Parliamentary Counsel and government lawyers to rectify problems.

iii. Investigation, Prosecution and Advocacy

In 1893 an office was created to support the Law Officers but it only assumed a legal character in the twentieth century.[56] The generalist nature of the operation reflected the fact that, until the end of the nineteenth century, law officers combined the role with private practice at the Bar.[57] In 1892 the law officers' fees from private practice were banned, only to be reintroduced three years later for contentious work, together with criteria for cases in which they should be instructed.[58] In 1946 it was decided that any fees the law officers earned should be set off against salary.

Attorney-Generals remained responsible for Crown litigation. Since, by convention, they were senior barristers they could appear in court on behalf of the Crown and 'lead' the prosecution team. The cases where this might happen involved important constitutional issues, cases before the International Court of Justice and occasionally, important murder trials. When appearing for the Crown in important matters of state, Attorneys General were supported by the Government Legal Department.

The Law Officers' responsibility for litigation in the public interest was expressed in decisions on whether to prosecute for contempt of court or refer unduly lenient sentences to the Court of Appeal.[59] Prosecutions of the media for the reporting of trials offending the Contempt of Court Act 1981 and requirements of fair trial were not uncommon. In a notable case, following a murder in 2017, a neighbour of the victim who appeared in television interviews was subject to a campaign in *The Sun* and *Daily Mail* newspapers.[60] Proceedings against the newspapers alleged a risk of serious prejudice in any trial. The Attorney General at the time claimed that the successful prosecution of the papers served as 'a reminder to the press that the Contempt of Court Act applies from the time of arrest'.[61] Other examples of the public interest dimension of the Law Officers' role were protection of the public interest by initiating legal proceedings or investigating serious accidents and preventing recurrence.[62]

iv. Advice to Government

A core area of the Law Officers' responsibility for the rule of law lay in the Attorney-General's role as legal adviser to government. Since this was a responsibility of

---

[55] Heald (n 44).
[56] Appleby (n 8) 30.
[57] Jones (n 28) 46.
[58] Appleby (n 8) 28–29.
[59] Heald (n 44).
[60] The witness, Mr Jefferies, was a neighbour of the victim, a young woman called Joanna Yates. He was arrested on suspicion of murder but was later found to be wholly innocent. (Heald (n 44)).
[61] ibid.
[62] Jones (n 28) 52.

potentially vast scope,[63] much of the advice was prepared by civil servants expert in a particular field, for example EU law.[64] The principal area in which the Attorney General was personally involved was advice to Cabinet and government departments.[65] General guidance was given in 1953, when Lord Shawcross suggested the law officers should be consulted when there were legal problems of special importance, including the high value of a matter, or special difficulty.[66] He added, almost as an afterthought, that these might involve constitutional matters or international tribunals.

The rule of law dimension of the Law Officer role was protected by a relatively weak kind of structural independence. In the twentieth century it was decided that the Law Officers should not be members of Cabinet but attend as required. Jones observed of the Attorney General that 'it has been considered more appropriate, in recent times at any rate, that the independence and detachment of his office should not be blurred by his inclusion in a political body – that is to say the Cabinet – which may have to make policy decisions upon the basis of the legal advice the law officers have given'.[67] When the Attorney-General was not at a Cabinet meeting, the Lord Chancellor drew matters requiring advice to their attention.[68]

The current *Cabinet Manual* stated that the core function of the Law Officers was 'to advise on legal matters, helping ministers to act lawfully and in accordance with the rule of law'.[69] The Attorney General's advice was often communicated orally at meetings of the Cabinet and Cabinet Committees but could be a written answer to a set question. An early chance to comment on legislation was afforded by requiring circulation of bills before consideration by Cabinet. Attorney-General opinions were confidential but could be published with the permission of the law officers of the day if they were of historical interest.[70] The opinions were, however, exempted from the Freedom of Information Act 2000.[71]

The issue of the independence of the Attorney General's advice arose at the time of the Iraq war in 2003. Participation in the war was approved by a comfortable Parliamentary vote. This was achieved by the Prime Minister's assurance that the war was legal, and that the Iraqi regime posed a threat to British security. The Attorney General, Lord Goldsmith, gave advice which was equivocal. Focusing on whether Iraq was in breach of an UN ceasefire resolution made following the first Gulf war in 1991, it suggested the government should probably obtain a further UN Security Council resolution.[72] Three days before the conflict began, Goldsmith presented a

---

[63] Following devolution of legislative responsibility to a Scottish Assembly, an Advocate General for Scotland advised the UK Parliament on Scottish law.
[64] House of Commons Constitutional Affairs Committee (n 48).
[65] While the Lord Chancellor could contribute an opinion in Cabinet it was not his role to do so and was inconsistent with his office as head of the judiciary (Jones (n 28) 46).
[66] Appleby (n 8) 33 citing Shawcross (n 41) 6.
[67] Jones (n 28) 47.
[68] Evidence of Lord Mackay of Clashfern, a former Lord Chancellor, to the Select Committee, para 70.
[69] *Cabinet Manual* (n 52) para 6.4.
[70] Jones (n 28) 47.
[71] Freedom of Information Act 2000, s 35(1).
[72] S Jeffrey, 'Lord Goldsmith's legal advice and the Iraq war' *The Guardian* (27 April 2005), www.theguardian.com/world/2005/apr/27/iraq.iraq2.

nine-paragraph statement to the House of Lords which did not reflect earlier doubts. The government exercised the convention against disclosure to prevent publication of the full advice[73] but, after pressure, published it in 2005.[74]

In evidence to public inquiry under Sir John Chilcott in 2009, given in 2011, Goldsmith denied having responded to pressure to change his advice. Rather, he claimed, he had changed his mind on the legality of war before making the statement to the Lords.[75] Even so, there were concerns that the advice to the Prime Minister was kept from other ministers who had jointly commissioned it, and that the Prime Minister made statements about legality which Goldsmith said did not accord with the advice.[76] These alleged misstatements were not publicly corrected at the time.[77] Despite the currency of concerns about the Attorney General's role, no clarification was provided by time the Constitutional Reform Act 2005 was enacted.

V. THE CONSTITUTIONAL REFORM ACT 2005

A. Post-Act Lord Chancellors

In the twentieth century the Lord Chancellor's role, spread across the functions of government, negated the separation of powers. The Labour government of Tony Blair considered abolishing the post, but the Constitutional Reform Act 2005 merely addressed accumulated anomalies. It replaced the Lord Chancellor as presiding Officer in the House of Lords, removed judicial functions,[78] and by establishing a Judicial Appointments Commission, ended selection of judicial candidates.[79] The Lord Chancellor became a member of the House of Commons rather than of the House of Lords, holding a ministerial portfolio in a new Ministry of Justice (MoJ). The department was responsible for the courts and tribunal service, prisons and probation, legal aid, and criminal injuries compensation.[80]

The ministerial role retained the Lord Chancellor's responsibility for the pay and conditions for judges, implementing recommendations for judicial appointments, including a right to veto senior appointments, and overseeing disciplinary proceedings against judges. Specific responsibilities included: administration of the courts and tribunal service; ensuring an efficient and effective courts system;[81]

---

[73] Appleby (n 8) 42–43.

[74] House of Commons Constitutional Affairs Committee (n 48) para 47.

[75] BBC News, 'Iran Inquiry: Blair to deal with Goldsmith Claims' (*bbc.co.uk*, 18 January 2011), www.bbc.co.uk/news/uk-politics-12209604.

[76] A McSmith, 'Tony Blair showed "little appetite" to ensure Iraq War was legal, Chilcot report says' *The Independent* (6 July 2016) www.independent.co.uk/news/uk/politics/chilcot-report-lord-goldsmith-legal-advice-iraq-war-tony-blair-verdict-latest-news-a7122756.html.

[77] BBC News, 'Iran Inquiry' (n 75).

[78] Judges in the Appellate Committee of the House of Lords and Judicial Committee of the Privy Council and President of the Supreme Court of England and Wales.

[79] A Judicial Appointments Commissions now sits for each of the three jurisdictions in the United Kingdom (see Constitutional Reform Act 2005, s 61). Formally, the appointment is made by the monarch, see Constitutional Reform Act 2005, s 14(a).

[80] House of Commons Constitutional Affairs Committee (n 48) para 30.

[81] Courts Act 2003.

providing legal aid; and making appointments to maintaining a new Legal Services Board, which was to oversee the regulation of the legal services market. The result of these changes was a stricter separation of the judicial function from the other two functions of state.

Since 1672 every Lord Chancellor had been a lawyer.[82] Removal of the Lord Chancellor's judicial functions was said to negate this requirement. The Constitutional Reform Act 2005 provided Lord Chancellors need only appear to the Prime Minister to be qualified by experience[83] as Minister of the Crown, membership of either House of Parliament, of qualifying practice, teaching law in a university or anything equivalent.[84] In 2012 Chris Grayling MP became the first non-lawyer to be appointed Lord Chancellor for 350 years.

The Constitutional Reform Act stated that it did not adversely affect '(a) the existing constitutional principle of the rule of law or (b) the Lord Chancellor's existing constitutional role in relation to that principle'.[85] It also provided Lord Chancellors swear an oath promising to 'respect the rule of law, defend the independence of the judiciary and discharge my duty to ensure the provision of resources for the efficient and effective support of the courts for which I am responsible'.[86] This oath was to replace two sworn under the Promissory Oaths Act 1868,[87] a generic oath of allegiance and a judicial oath undertaking to 'do right to all manner of people after the laws and usages of this realm, without fear or favour, affection or ill will'.[88] Neither of the two oaths previously sworn mentioned the rule of law.

The Constitutional Reform Act 2005 contained no definition of the rule of law but provided specific detail of the Lord Chancellor's responsibility for the judiciary. The tenor was set by section 3(6) which stated that:

the Lord Chancellor must have regard to—

(a) the need to defend that independence;
(b) the need for the judiciary to have the support necessary to enable them to exercise their functions;
(c) the need for the public interest in regard to matters relating to the judiciary or otherwise to the administration of justice to be properly represented in decisions affecting those matters.

The Act also imposed an obligation on the Lord Chancellor to support the effectiveness of the court system,[89] to uphold the independence of the judiciary[90] and not,

---

[82] After Henry VIII sacked Thomas Wolsey in 1529 the post of Lord Chancellor was filled by non-lawyers but lawyers were always appointed from 1672.
[83] Constitutional Reform Act 2005, s 2.
[84] ibid s 2(2).
[85] ibid s 1.
[86] Constitutional Reform Act 2005, s 17.
[87] House of Common Library 'Lord Chancellor's Oath and the Rule of Law' (13 October 2020) https://commonslibrary.parliament.uk/research-briefings/cdp-2020-0107/.
[88] ibid.
[89] Constitutional Reform Act 2005, s 10.
[90] Constitutional Reform Act 2005, s 3(1).

whether alone or with other Ministers of the Crown, seek to influence particular judicial decisions through any special access to the judiciary.'[91]

Apart from the generality of section 1 of the Act, and the oath, the provisions might have been interpreted to limit the post-holder's responsibility for the rule of law to judicial matters. When the House of Lords Select Committee on the Constitution considered this issue it expressed concern at this but reported that, apart from the Lord Chancellor, guardians of the rule of law included the government law officers, the Attorney-General and Solicitor-General, and that their roles might expand to fill any void.[92]

B. Post-Act Law Officers

The Constitutional Reform Act 2005 focused on the Lord Chancellor and the judiciary, but not the Law Officers. It was, however, just the beginning of the Labour government's programme of constitutional reform. Shortly after the Act was passed a green paper, *The Governance of Britain*, was presented.[93] The foreword to the report, written by Prime Minister Gordon Brown and Lord Chancellor Jack Straw envisaged forging a new relationship between government and citizen, and a new constitutional settlement addressing two fundamental questions: how should we hold power accountable, and how should we uphold and enhance the rights and responsibilities of the citizen?'[94]

A section of the green paper concerning the Attorney General hinted at concern about the 'complexity' of the role as chief legal adviser and guardian of the public interest.[95] It went on to express commitment 'to enhancing public confidence and trust in the office of Attorney General' and to ensuring 'that the office retains the public's confidence'.[96] The government would consult on alleviating the conflicts (or the appearance of them) and promised to have regard to a report of the House of Commons Constitutional Affairs Committee, published in 2007.

The Committee report on the role of the Attorney General (2007) noted the complexity of the constitutional role as it had developed and the fact that the Constitutional Reform Act 2005 had left the Attorney General as the only member of government required to be legally qualified.[97] It also noted 'three particular controversial matters that had highlighted further concerns'; potential prosecutions regarding 'cash for honours'; Goldsmith's advice regarding the Iraq War, and the decision of the Serious Fraud Office to discontinue investigation into BAE systems.[98]

---

[91] Constitutional Reform Act 2005, s 3(5).
[92] The office of Lord Chancellor – Report of the House of Lords Select Committee on the Constitution (Debated in Chamber on 7/7/2015) Summary, p 4, https://publications.parliament.uk/pa/ld201415/ldselect/ldconst/75/7505.htm.
[93] Ministry of Justice *The Governance of Britain* (CM 7170, 2007), https://assets.publishing.service.gov.uk/government/uploads/system/uploads/attachment_data/file/228834/7170.pdf.
[94] ibid.
[95] ibid para 53.
[96] ibid para 54.
[97] House of Commons Constitutional Affairs Committee (n 48).
[98] ibid Summary, 3.

The last two of these raised questions about the independence of advice provided by Attorneys General.[99]

Much of the evidence referred to by the Committee was supplied by Attorney General Lord Peter Goldsmith, who was in post when the matters referred to in the report had occurred. The other two instances cited by the Committee were prosecution decisions with political implications. The 'cash for honours' case involved allegations that donors to the Labour Party election campaign had received promises of future honours.[100] The Attorney General had a conflict of interest if senior colleagues were implicated. In an earlier inquiry into the case the Committee had been told by the Lord Chancellor that the Attorney General would not be involved in a decision to prosecute, but Goldsmith refuted this in his evidence. The Committee accepted his assurances that the matter would be handled transparently. The Crown Prosecution Service subsequently announced there would be no prosecutions because, although donors had made loans to Labour there was no evidence of promises of honours.

The last case considered was an investigation of the arms firm BAE. The company was alleged to have bribed Saudi Arabian officials to win an order. A decision by the Serious Fraud Office (SFO) to drop charges had attracted controversy and raised questions about whether the Attorney General had affected the Head of the SFOs decision not to prosecute.[101] The Committee noted the view of several distinguished commentators that that the BAE case thew up questions about how the public interest was identified, calling into question the inadequate protection provided to the rule of law by the Attorney General's divided loyalty.[102]

Lord Goldsmith gave written evidence reminding the Committee of previous controversies in which Attorneys General had been accused of allowing political considerations to affect their judgement on prosecution. The list included Sir Peter Rawlinson not prosecuting a Palestinian activist, Leila Khalid, for attempted hijack of an Israeli airliner in 1970 and Labour Attorney General Sam Silkin not prosecuting the Clay Cross parish councillors for not implementing legislation raising rents.[103] It featured Sir Michael Havers' prosecution of a civil servant, Clive Ponting, under the Official Secrets Act for leaking information about the sinking of the Argentinian battleship Belgrano in the Falklands War, contradicting the account Margaret Thatcher gave to the House of Commons. It also mentioned Sir Nicholas Lyell's handling of the failed prosecution of the machine tool firm Matrix Churchill for supplying material to Iraq on advice of government.[104]

Despite these controversies, Lord Goldsmith denied that the Attorney general's political involvement was problematic in the exercise of the role. He described it as to give 'legal advice and take decisions based on a scrupulous approach to the law and to evidence; where I am exercising my public interest functions, to act on the basis of an objective, dispassionate assessment of the public interest, without regard to party

---

[99] ibid para 5.
[100] ibid paras 38–42.
[101] ibid paras 43–46.
[102] ibid paras 46–47.
[103] ibid para 37.
[104] ibid para 52.

political considerations; and to act independently, fairly and with accountability'.[105] Goldsmith considered it anomalous that the Act had given the Lord Chancellor specific responsibility for the rule of law but not the Law Officers.[106] The Committee agreed, observing that such responsibility should pervade the general responsibilities of Law Officer posts and not just the advisory role.[107]

In a section of the report entitled 'A "Guardian of the Rule of Law"?' the Committee noted that Lord Goldsmith had claimed 'upholding the Rule of Law' as a key function.[108] This was ensuring 'compliance with the law', meaning both 'domestic and international obligations'; subjecting Government 'to the scrutiny of the independent courts' and respecting their judgments; 'basic values which it is important to stand up for', for example, those in the European Convention'.[109] Goldsmith told the Committee that 'for better or worse Government operates in a world where the law, and the need for the Rule of Law, plays an increasingly important role' and that 'it is right that there should be a lawyer at the heart of Government ... to ensure that the law is properly respected'.[110]

The Committee concluded that perceived lack of independence and political bias inherent in the role, exacerbated by recent examples, risked a loss of public confidence in the decision making of the Attorney General that 'was not sustainable'.[111] It suggested that 'the purely legal functions should be carried out by an official outside party political life while the ministerial duties should be carried out by a minister in the MoJ'.[112] This would involve the separation of the functions of the Attorney General into the legal (prosecution and legal advice to government) and political (ministerial).

The government followed up the Committee report with a consultation on the main issues raised by the Committee but claimed this revealed little support for changing the Attorney General's role. Despite the Committee's report, and a further report by the equivalent House of Lords Committee, nothing substantial resulted. A reference to the rule of law was added to the Attorneys General' oath, provision for an annual report to Parliament made and a protocol introduced to govern prosecutions.[113]

C. Senior Government Lawyers and the Rule of Law

In 2006, the House of Lords Select Committee on the Constitution focused attention on the Constitutional Reform Act provision combining the office of Lord

---

[105] ibid fn 11 citing Ev 58.
[106] ibid paras 26–27.
[107] ibid para 28.
[108] ibid para 58.
[109] ibid para 21, response to question 6.
[110] ibid para 31.
[111] ibid para 56.
[112] ibid.
[113] Appleby (n 8) 46.

Chancellor with that of the Secretary of State for Justice.[114] It expressed concern that responsibility for the rule of law was inconsistent with a ministerial role with 'added responsibilities for politically contentious areas of public policy'.[115] It returned to the issue in 2015 in a review of the changes.[116] Its report began with reductions in the scope of judicial review and drastic cuts to legal aid,[117] measures that apparently weakened the rule of law and called into question the Lord Chancellor's effectiveness in upholding it.

Andrew Le Sueur, a Professor of Constitutional Justice, gave evidence that before the 2005 Act Lord Chancellors' advice to government had been 'at very best … sporadic and peripheral'.[118] The Committee examined the nature of the Lord Chancellor's 'continuing' obligation under the Act, noting it said nothing about scope. The Committee decided that the Lord Chancellor's duty to defend the rule of law was key to its inquiry.[119] The Committee's curiosity about whether the Lord Chancellor's duty went beyond defending judicial independence and, if so, how was vindicated by the diverse views expressed by witnesses.[120]

The non-lawyer Lord Chancellor, Mr Grayling, said the duty related to 'an independent justice system, free from interference from outside, free from corruption, free from influence, that is respected and treated as independent by those in government and those in Parliament, and that ultimately … we respect the ability of the courts and the responsibility of the courts to take decisions according to their best judgement about what the law of the land requires'.[121] Grayling's interpretation of his duties was supported by the former Attorney-General, Dominic Grieve, who said that, before the 2005 Act, the Lord Chancellor had a wider guardianship role in government,[122] but that afterwards, it was restricted to upholding the independence of the judiciary and the integrity of the justice system. The extent to which future incumbents took an interest in the rule of law beyond their departments would, he said, depend on their interests 'and their legal qualifications'.[123] Others found this unduly narrow.

Lord Falconer of Thoroton, Lord Chancellor when the Act was passed, told the Select Committee that it aimed 'to retain and entrench his or her role as being a defender of the rule of law and the justice system'[124] as the 'constitutional conscience

---

[114] House of Lords, Select Committee on the Constitution *5th Report of Session 2005–06: Constitutional Reform Act 2005* (London, The Stationery Office, 2005) Chapter 1, para 1, https://publications.parliament.uk/pa/ld200506/ldselect/ldconst/83/83.pdf.
[115] ibid.
[116] *The Office of Lord Chancellor – Report of the House of Lords Select Committee on the Constitution 2014–15* (HL Paper 75, 2014), https://publications.parliament.uk/pa/ld201415/ldselect/ldconst/75/75.pdf.
[117] ibid para 1. See also O Bowcott, 'Downing Street under pressure on plans to restrict judicial review access' *The Guardian* (26 November 2014), www.theguardian.com/politics/2014/nov/26/downing-street-under-pressure-plans-restrict-judicial-review-access.
[118] *The Office of Lord Chancellor* (n 116) para 57.
[119] ibid para 14.
[120] ibid para 43.
[121] ibid para 18.
[122] This view was supported by Dr Patrick O'Brien, Research Associate at University College London, called a 'special constitutional guardian of the principles of judicial independence and the rule of law within cabinet' (ibid para 35).
[123] ibid para 44
[124] ibid para 14.

of Government'.[125] This was a 'special role' to protect the rule of law, and that to think otherwise would 'undermine what the Constitutional Reform Act had sought to do'.[126] The balance of evidence the Committee received favoured Lord Falconer's wider interpretation of the role.

Sir Hayden Phillips, a former senior civil servant, said that the Lord Chancellor should provide singular leadership in relation to the rule of law 'taking responsibility for constitutional issues in the broadest sense'.[127] Dr Gabrielle Appleby, Deputy Director of the Public Law and Policy Research Unit at the University of Adelaide, referred to 'responsibilities to warn and advise on how proposed policies and actions may impact on the different aspects of the rule of law'.[128] Sir Alex Allan, former Permanent Secretary of the Department for Constitutional Affairs, argued that all ministers must 'uphold the law and not to do things that are illegal ...' but that the Lord Chancellor had 'a general fallback, oversight role'.[129]

The Committee explored whether the functions of Lord Chancellor could be performed by someone else. Lord Phillips of Worth Matravers argued that the title was unimportant but the oath taken by Lord Chancellors was.[130] A Judicial Appointments Commission witness thought both the oath and ministerial functions of the Lord Chancellor in judicial appointments were reasons for retaining the role.[131] A former Lord Chancellor and Secretary of State for Justice, Jack Straw, argued that the post was 'a bulwark within the Executive against interference in the judiciary' a feature which might be lost if the role were subsumed into that of Secretary of State for Justice.[132]

The Select Committee considered that someone in government must have responsibility for monitoring compliance with the rule of law. It considered that Lord Chancellors now had advantages and disadvantages in that respect. By becoming more explicitly political appointees they were positioned to 'observe and intervene in the development of wider policy decisions that could affect the rule of law'.[133] The disadvantage, wider political responsibilities, interfered with monitoring rule of law issues in Cabinet Committees.[134] Nor, after 2005, were Lord Chancellors members of the Parliamentary Business and Legislation Committee, which kept them abreast of the legislative and policy agenda.[135] The political dilemmas and risks, including loss of office, complicated risk monitoring and compliance roles.

The Committee found that the evidence it received suggested pre-reform Lord Chancellors had not been 'scrutinising policy proposals for threats to the rule of law' but that the new, political versions were less likely to be independent and stand up to colleagues.[136] It concluded that Lord Chancellors had responsibility 'to ensure that

[125] ibid.
[126] ibid para 35.
[127] ibid para 46.
[128] ibid para 47.
[129] ibid.
[130] ibid para 136.
[131] ibid para 137.
[132] ibid para 138.
[133] ibid para 76.
[134] ibid para 53.
[135] ibid para 55.
[136] ibid para 62.

the rule of law is upheld within Cabinet and across Government'.[137] It did not accept that individual post-holders could determine their own responsibility for the rule of law. It regretted the fact that the Ministerial Code and *Cabinet Manual* only defined the Lord Chancellor's responsibility in terms of upholding judicial independence.[138] It recommended that the Ministerial Code and the *Cabinet Manual* be revised and that the Lord Chancellor's oath be amended so that incumbents promised to 'respect and uphold the rule of law' rather than just respect it.[139]

Although the Select Committee accepted that the Lord Chancellor's responsibility for the rule of law was a more limited and 'reactive' role,[140] it concluded that the responsibility was shared. The Lord Chancellor had never been the sole guardian of the rule of law, either within government or more broadly, and the others had become more significant. Grayling stressed the obligation on all ministers, not just the Lord Chancellor, to uphold the rule of law. The Committee thought that Parliament had a crucial role in securing government compliance with the rule of law[141] and the significance of the Law Officers had also increased.

The Select Committee proposed that, after the 2005 Act, the Lord Chancellor and Attorney General had complementary roles. The Lord Chancellor attended Cabinet as of right, the Attorney General by invitation.[142] The Attorney General scrutinised government bills and, unlike the Lord Chancellor, sat on the Cabinet Committees most likely to throw up rule of law issues at an early stage.[143] The Law Officers monitored and alerted the Lord Chancellor to potential breaches. Lord Falconer considered that 'the Attorney and the Lord Chancellor acting together are quite a powerful force in government'.[144]

VI. GOVERNMENT LAW OFFICERS IN OTHER COMMON LAW JURISDICTIONS

No British colonies or former colonies had a Lord Chancellor but Attorney General or Solicitor General were common posts at national level and in States or provinces.[145] The role and duties associated with it took different forms. Appleby suggested that where there was an Attorney general and a Solicitor-General, the latter was usually a government courtroom advocate. Where there was only a Solicitor General, they tended to also be government advisers.[146] The roles sometimes did not carry the conventional titles. In Canada, for example, the Attorney General title was held by the Minister of Justice, while the Solicitor General role was part of the Minister of Public Safety portfolio. Executive responsibilities and responsibilities for the rule of

---

[137] ibid para 50.
[138] ibid para 49.
[139] ibid para 51.
[140] ibid para 77.
[141] ibid paras 87–88.
[142] ibid para 75.
[143] ibid para 73.
[144] ibid para 77.
[145] In Australian provinces a Solicitor General advised state executives on constitutional and public law issues providing a conduit to the judiciary.
[146] Thus, a Solicitor General was the main legal adviser to Australian State governments (Appleby (n 8)).

law varied. The national model least like the Westminster model was the US, where Attorney General was a significant appointee leading the Department of Justice and a member of Cabinet[147] and a Solicitor General represented government in the Supreme Court.

As an appointee of the US President the Attorney General was a political post but it was unpredictable whether they would be politically partisan or defenders of the rule of law. Shugerman's study of the post-revolutionary period suggested that the backgrounds of appointees could be classified in three ways: a politico with an established electoral base, a professional established in private practice government service or the judiciary, or an insider connected to the president.[148] He found professional appointees to be the most independent and principled but that insiders could be independent once in office.

There were often periods where one of the three types of appointment predominated. In the nineteenth century, an age of patronage, Attorneys General were surprisingly professional in background. In the twentieth century it became common for appointees to be 'partisan insiders, hacks, and fixers'[149] to the point that some Presidents saw the postholder as their 'personal lawyer and fixer'.[150] John F Kennedy fulfilled a long-term desire of his father Joe by appointing his brother Bobby, 35 years old and never tried a case. Despite clampdowns on the mafia during the Kennedy presidency, there was no investigation of the patriarch's mafia connections.[151]

Richard Nixon appointed a former colleague, John Mitchell, whom he had befriended in private practice and who ran his 1968 presidential campaign, as Attorney General, and persuaded the FBI director not to do a background check on him. Mitchell resigned as Attorney General to direct Nixon's 1972 election campaign and was replaced by Deputy Attorney General, Richard Kleindienst. In his first Presidential term Nixon had instructed Kleindienst to drop an antitrust suit against International Telephone & Telegraph Corp (ITT) a former, and possibly future, campaign donor, about which Kleindienst lied to Congress.

In 1972, men arrested at a break-in at the Democratic Party Convention Headquarters at the Watergate Office Building in Washington DC were linked to Nixon's re-election committee. Mitchell involved Kleindienst in trying to limit the investigation. The cover-up involved various illegal acts and was partly successful.[152] Nixon was re-elected in November 1972 as reporters at *The Washington Post* began to uncover the Watergate conspiracy. The body responsible for the administration of justice, the House of Representatives Judiciary Committee, required an investigation. Kleindienst resigned as Attorney General as the scandal escalated and was replaced by Elliot Richardson. Shugerman classified Richardson as a politico with

---

[147] Attorneys General at state level were elected posts with responsibilities in law enforcement.
[148] JH Shugerman, 'Professionals, Politicos, and Crony Attorneys General: A Historical Sketch of the U.S. Attorney General as a Case for Structural Independence' (2019) 87 *Fordham L Rev* 1965.
[149] ibid 1966.
[150] ibid.
[151] ibid 219–20.
[152] At one point, Mitchell had his wife held by secret service agents to prevent her talking to the press.

strong secondary professional characteristics, unlike Mitchell and Kleindienst, who were both insiders.

In May 1973 Richardson appointed Archibald Cox as special investigator. The Judiciary Committee insisted, and Richardson promised, that Cox would only be removed 'for cause', on grounds of misuse of office. In October, Cox served a *subpoena* for surrender of tape recordings of conversations in the President's Oval Office. Some negotiation followed over what might be disclosed. Nixon then instructed Richardson to sack Cox, but he refused and resigned. The Deputy Attorney General William Ruckelshaus was then given the same instruction, refused to follow it, and resigned.

After the resignation of the two senior law officers, Nixon swore in the Solicitor General, Robert Bork, as Attorney General and instructed him to sack Cox. Bork claimed at the time that the departing law officers had requested that he comply, but his posthumous memoir claimed that Nixon had promised to nominate him to the Supreme Court. What became known as the Saturday Night Massacre was announced by NBC anchor John Chancellor as possibly 'the most serious constitutional crisis in its history'.[153] An editorial in the *New York Times* opined that 'The nation is in the hands of a president overcome with dictatorial misconceptions of his constitutional authority'.[154] There was an unprecedented postbag from the public calling for action against Nixon, including impeachment.

In February 1974 the House Judiciary Committee conducted a formal impeachment inquiry, a constitutionally prescribed process used when an official was guilty of 'treason, bribery, and other high Crimes and Misdemeanors'.[155] In May, the Committee began receiving evidence on three charges against Nixon, including obstructing justice and abusing power. Belief that Nixon's guilt would be proved by the Oval Office tapes was now strong. Cox's replacement, appointed by Bork, continued to press for release of the tapes and some were eventually handed over with heavy redactions.

Limited publication of the Watergate tapes led to Nixon's resignation. Some recordings were said to have been accidentally erased by Nixon's long-serving secretary. A tape released in August 1974 showed Nixon's complicity in a cover up. In light of the inevitable impeachment and almost certain conviction, Nixon resigned on 4 August 1974. A month later he was pardoned by his successor, former Vice President Gerald R Ford. Sixty-nine government officials were indicted and 48 convicted, including Mitchell for perjury and Kleindienst, who refused to answer questions and pleaded guilty to contempt of court.

Richardson emerged from the Watergate scandal with credit. He was accused by Nixon's vice president, Spiro Agnew, of being motivated by political ambition, but was generally seen to have taken a principled stand, dictated by his agreement with Congress that Cox could only be fired for 'extraordinary impropriety'. Richardson concluded that Cox's position in demanding the Oval Office tapes was 'not only

---

[153] W Shapiro, 'Lessons from Saturday Night Massacre for Trump and Democrats' Roll Call' (*Roll Call*, 29 December 2017), https://rollcall.com/2017/12/29/lessons-from-saturday-night-massacre-for-trump-and-democrats/.
[154] ibid.
[155] US Constitution Article II, Section 4.

defensible but right'.[156] His obituary in the New York Times called it 'a special moment of integrity and rectitude'.[157]

In an article in *The Atlantic* magazine in 1976, Richardson attributed Watergate to 'an amoral alacrity to do the president's bidding … traceable less to flaws in his own political character (although it was reinforced by them) than to the political and cultural evolution of 20th century America'.[158] He blamed the predominance of 'get-ahead, go-along organization men' adopting prevalent organisational values. Richardson's prediction, that Watergate would lead to 'reassertion of old ideals and the renewal of government processes',[159] proved true in the short term. In Shugerman's analysis, the next three Attorneys General fitted the 'professional profile', but when Ronald Reagan appointed his close friend, William French Smith in 1981, the previous pattern was restored.[160]

Appleby compared the Australian Constitution to the Westminster model; both being defined by shifting conventions. In the Australian national government, the Solicitor General had a ministerial portfolio but no separate title. During the 1990s the role of Attorney General to the Australian Government became increasingly political. A shadow Attorney General queried the postholder's constitutional duty to act independently of the Executive or to defend the courts from political attacks.[161] In the ensuing debate, Appleby suggested, it was noted that the role was vaguely defined. It was accepted that Australian Attorney Generals engaged with the executive more than the English tradition allowed. This was because the role of government advisor had increasingly devolved to the Solicitor General, a state employee rather than a politician in Australia.

Despite the overtly political nature of the Australian Attorney General's role, appointees still had responsibilities for the rule of law. They were responsible for judicial appointments and prosecution. Prominent on the government website, the Attorney General's page devoted a section to supporting the rule of law 'through our daily work', by ensuring that:

- laws are clear, predictable and accessible;
- laws are publicly made and the community is able to participate in the law-making process;
- laws are publicly adjudicated in courts that are independent from the executive arm of government; and
- dispute settlement is fair and efficient where parties cannot resolve disputes themselves.

---

[156] NA Lewis, 'Elliot Richardson Dies at 79; Stood Up to Nixon and Resigned' *New York Times* (1 January 2000) https://archive.nytimes.com/www.nytimes.com/library/magazine/home/obit-e-richardson.html.
[157] ibid.
[158] E Richardson, *The Atlantic Monthly* (March 1976) (this article is not archived and the quotations below are taken from the obituary and a short review, J Goldberg, 'Impeachment: An Argument' (*The Atlantic*, March 2019) www.theatlantic.com/magazine/archive/2019/03/impeachment-an-argument/580420/.
[159] ibid.
[160] Shugerman (n 148) 1971.
[161] Appleby (n 8) 11.

Separate from, but immediately below, this list a statement suggested that the Attorney General supported the Australian Government 'in being accountable for actions, making rational decisions and protecting human rights'.[162] The office claimed to 'advance the rule of law internationally by actively promoting adherence to the global rules-based system and helping to build effective governance and stability in our region'.

New Zealand had an Attorney General from 1841 and a Solicitor General from 1867. The roles and their duties developed in a unique way. The Attorney General's Act was amended in 1876 so that the post could be a political appointment.[163] The Solicitor General became a non-political, permanent appointment and head of the Crown office in 1875 and remained so for most of the time thereafter. It operated most of the 'apolitical' law officer functions, including advice to government, acting as prosecutorial and constitutional officer in matters including the appointments of judges and QCs.[164] After the Public Sector Act 1988, which created some largely autonomous agencies, legal advice on constitutional questions and the exercise of executive power had to be referred by the Crown Office to a lawyer free of any conflict of interest.[165]

VII. DISCUSSION

Effective constitutional government required lawyers working with the executive, identifying relevant issues, monitoring performance and, occasionally, insisting on compliance with the rule of law despite executive pressure. The core conundrum was balancing sufficient proximity to the executive to enable observation with the independence of those entrusted to reinforce the rule of law. The US experience showed that lawyers embedded in government placed political loyalty above public interest and were complicit in illegality and its concealment. Since the prevention of corruption was a central goal of legality, the question was 'how could government lawyers be encouraged to resist and reveal threats to the rule of law?'.

Shugerman showed that norms of independence eroded when presidents made campaign managers or national party chairmen Attorney General. Almost every president from Roosevelt to Reagan had appointed a partisan Attorney General, apparently inconsistently with the constitutional oath appointees they took to 'faithfully execute' their offices.[166] Shugerman argued that Congress should constitute them in an independent agency 'to restore professionalism, structural independence, and the impartial rule of law'.[167] He speculated, however, that structural change could run up against a constitutional problem.

---

[162] Australian Government Attorney General's Department, *The Rule of Law*, www.ag.gov.au/about-us/what-we-do/rule-law.
[163] D Collins, 'The Role of Solicitor General in Contemporary New Zealand' in P Keyser and G Appleby (eds), *Public Sentinels: A Comparative Study of Australian Solicitors-General* (London, Taylor and Francis, 2016) 171.
[164] ibid 173.
[165] ibid 175–76.
[166] Shugerman (n 148) 1994.
[167] ibid.

Separating the Attorney General and perhaps the Department of Justice from the executive may have contravened Article II of the US Constitution. This laid out the separation of powers, vested executive power in the President and designated the role of the principal officers of government departments as tendering advice. It was unclear from the text whether the Attorney General fell within this executive sphere, and could be appointed, directed and removed by the President at will, or whether it is a 'quasi-judicial' role which could be more easily moved outside the sphere of direct Presidential influence. This ambiguity could obscure making rule of law obligations more explicit.

The lack of clarity surrounding the Westminster system was exposed by the Constitutional Reform Act 2005 and the Parliamentary inquiries into the Lord Chancellor and Law Officer roles in 2005 and 2015. While evidence suggested that the Lord Chancellor's responsibility went beyond dealing with the justice system, how far beyond was unclear. The 'existing constitutional role' referred to in the Act could have been a ragbag of tasks, such as receiving petitions for judicial review of detention without charge,[168] or it could be the broader conception favoured by Lord Falconer, guardian of the rule of law across government. In its 2014 review, the House of Lords Select Committee did not clarify what ensuring governance 'in accordance with constitutional principles' or 'respect for the rule of law within Government'[169] would require of the Lord Chancellor.

While Lord Falconer claimed that the Constitutional Reform Act 2005 aspired to strengthen constitutionality, it was not necessarily motivated by principle and potentially had unintended consequences. Helena Kennedy QC criticised Falconer for abandoning the legal requirement 'on the back of an envelope' because 'his old friends Tony Blair and David Blunkett had got tired of hearing the judiciary being defended by [Lord Chancellor] Lord Derry Irvine'.[170] She argued that, while the role needed reforming, it had the advantage of being filled by experienced but unambitious lawyers who 'would therefore fearlessly defend the rule of law and the independence of lawyers and judges against bullying authoritarian cabinet colleagues … Someone with weight who would counter the voice of the home secretary'.[171]

Kennedy's point related to the appointment of another non-lawyer, Liz Truss, as Lord Chancellor in 2016. She was widely criticised for failing to speak out when the *Daily Mail* branded judges 'enemies of the people' for a judgment finding that government needed to consent of Parliament to give notice of leaving the European Union.[172] This assumed, of course, that a lawyer would have known better. Nevertheless, diminishing the role of Lord Chancellor potentially weakened support for the rule of law by hobbling the person with the clearest advocacy role. The Select Committee placed reliance on the Law Officers' enhanced role after the Constitutional Reform Act 2005, but divided responsibility risked rule of law issues not being picked up or pursued.

---

[168] Under the *Habeus Corpus* Act 1679 the Lord Chancellor remains one of the persons who can be petitioned.
[169] *The Office of Lord Chancellor* (n 116) Summary, pp 4, 8.
[170] H Kennedy, 'Charlie Falconer to blame for Lord Chancellor folly' *The Guardian* (27 July 2016) www.theguardian.com/law/2016/jul/27/charlie-falconer-to-blame-for-lord-chancellor-folly.
[171] ibid.
[172] J Slack, 'Enemies of the People' *Daily Mail* (4 November 2016).

The Select Committee's 6th Report of 2014/15 perceived that Mr Grayling's narrow view of the Lord Chancellor's duty was at odds with that of many other witnesses and, indeed, that his opponents alleged that his policies were a breach of the rule of law.[173] The Committee accepted that Lord Chancellors could differ in perceiving what constituted rule of law issues or threats to it.[174] It also accepted that their effectiveness in protecting the rule of law depended on personal authority and that significant ministerial or other experience enabled them to hold their own in Cabinet. It also accepted inherent flaws in the system. Even if Lord Chancellors fulfilled a more general monitoring responsibility, committee agendas could be incomplete or unclear or ministerial actions not reviewed by Cabinet.[175] These weaknesses in the Lord Chancellor's oversight role, both in detecting issues and taking effective action, were likely to increase after the Act.

The Law Officers' role had potentially evolved to provide more direct support to the rule of law. Oliver Heald's article described an 'order of loyalties' he had resolved to honour. These were influenced by the autobiography of a former Solicitor and Attorney General, Peter Rawlinson,[176] who recounted how, on becoming Solicitor General in 1962, the Prime Minister, Harold Macmillan:

> honoured him with a 'scholarly review of mediaeval office holders', a review which flowed into the 16th and 17th centuries, embraced approvingly the career of Samuel Pepys, and concluded with the admonition that the loyalties of a Law Officer must be first to the Crown, second to Parliament, and only thirdly, almost incidentally, to the administration.[177]

It was noticeable that Heald's order of loyalties did not include expressly the rule of law, although it may be implied by relegation of loyalty to the administration. Heald suggested that the advisory role was essential in ensuring the predictability, stability, and reliability needed to make decisions. Law Officers were, however, less likely than the Lord Chancellor to have oversight of the range of government actions.

Problems attended the Attorney General's task of excluding political considerations from prosecution decisions. In cases where a decision not to prosecute *appeared* to reflect a political interest, confidence in law, and hence the rule of law, would be undermined.[178] The Attorney General's role, while politically detached was inevitably political. That is why Shawcross favoured an unelected, apolitical public service role which could more effectively support the rule of law.[179] The contrary argument, accepted by the Committee and articulated by Heald was that:

> ... the core function of the Attorney General was and is to make sure that government, that ministers, act lawfully, in accordance with the rule of law. The current arrangement, as awkward as it may look on paper, like so many of the eccentricities in our constitution,

---

[173] Select Committee on the Constitution 6th Report: 2014/15 (n 116) para 56.
[174] ibid para 56.
[175] ibid para 54.
[176] P Rawlinson, *A Price Too High* (London, Orion Publishing Co, 1989).
[177] Heald (n 44).
[178] For example, whether there had been bribery of officials of foreign governments and whether political donors had been promised honours in return (Appleby (n 8) 41–42).
[179] ibid 40–41.

works because it puts at the heart of government an independent lawyer who is trusted by those he advises because he is one of them.[180]

This assumed that issues were detected, referred for advice, the advice was followed, and if not that remedial or other action was taken.

When government did not heed legal advice, or used it as cover for a dubious action, there was no clear duty to whistle-blow. Although Attorneys General were not covered by Cabinet collective responsibility, the secrecy accorded advice achieved a similar affect. The conventions set out in the Ministerial Code were that:

> 2.10 The Law Officers must be consulted in good time before the Government is committed to critical decisions involving legal considerations.
>
> 2.11 By convention, written opinions of the Law Officers, unlike other ministerial papers, are generally made available to succeeding Administrations.
>
> 2.12 When advice from the Law Officers is included in correspondence between Ministers, or in papers for the Cabinet or Ministerial Committees, the conclusions may if necessary be summarised but, if this is done, the complete text of the advice should be attached.
>
> 2.13 The fact that the Law Officers have advised or have not advised and the content of their advice must not be disclosed outside Government without their authority.[181]

The House of Commons 2007 Committee report on the Attorney General heard voices raised for and against publication of advice in the Committee.[182] The argument for secrecy apparently succeeded, probably because it encouraged the Law Officers to give Cabinet frank advice. Although it was not decisively determined whether the Attorney General's decision was reviewable by the courts,[183] publication of advice at the time a decision was made would be necessary for effective judicial review.

The 2015 Select Committee report on the future of the Lord Chancellor supported the notion of complementary roles but argued that diffused responsibility should be clear and widely understood.[184] Attorneys General should attend Cabinet meetings, ministers should consult the Law Officers as necessary,[185] and, as described in the *Cabinet Manual*, the Law Officers should help ministers to act in accordance with the rule of law.[186] The effectiveness of senior lawyers' roles depended on politicians following their advice on the rule of law. There were no clear mechanisms to enforce compliance, apart from public opinion. The Committee urged Parliament to be vigilant, to 'scrutinise the actions and policies of Government to ensure it governs in accordance with the rule of law'.[187] These conclusions seemed complacent given the importance attached to the rule of law by the 2005 Act, the acknowledged weaknesses in structural support for the rule of law at that time, and the weakening of that support by the politicising of the Lord Chancellor's role under the Act.

---

[180] Heald (n 44).
[181] *Ministerial Code* (London, Cabinet Office, 2018) (www.gov.uk/government/publications/ministerial-code).
[182] The Attorney General 2007 paras 48–50.
[183] *Gouriet v Union of Post Office Workers* [1978] AC 435.
[184] Select Committee on the Future of the Lord Chancellor 2014/15 (n 116) para 81.
[185] ibid para 65.
[186] ibid para 71.
[187] ibid para 140.

VIII. CONCLUSION

Lawyers occupied a wide range of government positions, in government offices, as state prosecutors and as law officers. They often had responsibility for maintaining the rule of law and in many systems, government law officers' opinions carried authority. There were, however, suspected conflicts of interest with political loyalties. The notion of diffused responsibility did not necessarily help. Paradoxically, increasing the numbers of people with *some* responsibility often magnified the risk of issues being missed or ignored. There seemed to be two obvious solutions. The first was to increase the robustness, transparency, and accountability of processes by providing more support for both the existing monitoring and advice roles, publishing advice and providing publicly accessible performance data. A second was to establish an independent office to advise government and monitor its performance in observing the rule of law.

5
Institution

I. INTRODUCTION

ON SOME ANALYSES a society governed by the rule of law must be an open society, supported by institutions like the financial and market system, Parliament, and a civil society including authoritative non-government organisations and a free press. The contribution of such institutions lay in demonstrating accessibility to levers of power, equality before the law and freedom from corruption. These features of an open society encouraged voluntary compliance with law by most of the population most of the time, encouraged by consensus in the appropriateness of laws, widespread compliance, and the real risk of punishment for non-compliance. This chapter concerns the role of lawyers in creating and maintaining social and political institutions protecting the rule of law, including Parliament, civil society, and the justice system.

II. THEORY

The institutions of Western society were produced by specific circumstances. Tawney agreed with the jurist and ground-breaking sociologist Max Weber (1864–1920) about the impact of Calvinism, noting it promised a balance between 'prosperity and salvation, retaining the theology of the master but repudiating his scheme of social ethics'.[1] He wondered however whether the bourgeois revolution in Holland and England was because religious attitudes affected the economic base or vice versa. A driving force was arguably the 'dynamic individualism' inspired by John Locke which contended for the prime social role of the individual, the right to hold property, and the state as neutral facilitator of individual enterprise.

Another pioneering sociologist, Émile Durkheim (1858–1917), saw the state as an ultimate moral force, but it was too remote from the individual to understand personal needs or so close that it risked suffocating them. It needed to support secondary groups to promote 'moral individualism' in community identity.[2] Churches,

---

[1] M Weber, *The Protestant Ethic and the Spirit of Capitalism* (trans T Parsons) (London, Butler and Tanner, 1930) Foreword 10.
[2] MS Cladis, *A Communitarian Defence of Liberalism: Emile Durkheim and Contemporary Social Theory* (Stanford, Stanford University Press, 1992).

corporations, and professions counterbalanced each other and the state. Weber similarly saw a role for mediating institutions. The nineteenth century Utilitarian theorists advocated Liberal themes[3] concerned with the purpose of law. John Austin argued that law should promote the happiness of the society and Bentham argued for 'demystification' of legal institutions[4] and accessibility by ordinary people.[5]

Vile recognised a problem of modern government was 'the arbitrariness of a great machine staffed by well-intentioned men, possessing, of necessity, a limited range of vision, and a limited ability to judge where a succession of expedient decisions will lead'.[6] He noted that groups established outside conventional frameworks developed their own understanding of their work or cause. Internal mechanisms of such groups distinguished them and supported desired behaviour.[7] They were able to increase the accountability of those holding power by voicing authoritative criticism. The effectiveness of this network of controls depended on the standing and discipline of the groups, their perception of their roles, and on the integrity of their members.

North and Weingast argued that institutions were essential in creating and perpetuating the rule of law.[8] Feudal England was a fragile natural state based on a limited access order, doorstep conditions for the rule of law being met only when the Glorious Revolution established constitutional government.[9] There was then effective control of military force, but social mechanisms for perpetuity, continuation of institutions, had to be developed. The key was the Enlightenment idea that quiet pursuit of rational self-interest, primarily through commercial opportunities, was a way of taming humans' wilder impulses.

The term 'civil society' was known to classical civilisations[10] but had distinctive connotations in the Enlightenment. Christenson suggested two possible origins.[11] The first, drawing on Hobbes and Pufendorf, cast civil society as areas enabled by a strong state: free association, commerce, free expression and religious tolerance. The second, drawing on Locke and Scottish Enlightenment thinkers such as Hutcheson, saw equal citizenship as a prerequisite of a society capable of ensuring that government avoided corruption and served the common good. Both conceptions were

---

[3] Control of power, even in the hands of benign reformers; freedom of speech; a free press; the right of association; the need to publish and disseminate law; control administrative agencies; no criminal liability without fault and no punishment except for extant crimes (*nulla poena sine lege*) (HLA Hart, 'Positivism and the Separation of Law and Morals' (1958) 71(4) *Harvard Law Review* 593, 595–96).

[4] Hart noted that Bentham shared with Karl Marx a belief in the necessity for demystification of social convention, he described Bentham as a 'sober reformer' seeking to remodel society along bourgeois, Utilitarian lines (HLA Hart, 'Bentham and the Demystification of the Law' (1973) 36(1) *The Modern Law Review* 2, 5).

[5] ibid 9.

[6] MJC Vile, *Constitutionalism and the Separation of Powers*, 2nd edn (Minneapolis, Liberty Fund, 1998) 261–62.

[7] ibid 356.

[8] DC North and BR Weingast, 'Constitutions and Commitment: The Evolution of Institutions Governing Public Choice in Seventeenth-Century England' (1989) 49(4) *Journal of Economic History* 803.

[9] BR Weingast, 'Why Developing Countries Prove So Resistant to the Rule of Law' in JJ Heckman, RL Nelson and L Cabatingan (eds), *Global Perspectives on the Rule of Law* (London and New York, Routledge, 2010) 28.

[10] Initially in ancient Greece, although Cicero used the term *societas civilis*.

[11] GA Christenson, 'World Civil Society and the International Rule of Law' (1997) 19 *Human Rights Quarterly* 724.

consistent with the goal of producing a population able to share liberty. The common link lay in the need for institutions to develop citizen's awareness and promote their interests, but Locke's version envisaged citizens actively sustaining the rule of law.

III. OPEN ACCESS ORDER

In Liberal theory free markets were essential to open society, expressing belief that economic freedom must include the right to accumulate wealth. Changes to the legal framework covered areas from the enforcement of contracts to reform of real property law, allowing it to be used as collateral and saleable debt. An open access order developed slowly with the establishment of a financial system and administrative state.[12] The need for a centralised financial system was highlighted when the French Navy defeated the English in 1690 at the Battle of Beachy Head. Re-building funds were raised by establishing a long-mooted Bank of England in 1694.[13]

The idea of the Bank of England split political opinion. The Tories opposed the bank as a republican institution, favouring a Land Bank, launched in 1696, which failed within a year. The Bank of England was private but actively supported by William III who contributed to it. Whigs came to support it when they realised that credit could finance both war and manufacture.[14] The Bank offered generous interest on loans and was quickly oversubscribed, probably because investors were reassured that the state would not abandon financial commitments.[15]

The return of the Stuarts would have ruined the Bank of England and for several generations it was 'emphatically a Whig body'.[16] Macaulay wrote that it 'constantly in the scale of the Whigs, almost counterbalanced the weight of the Church, which was as constantly in the scale of the Tories'.[17] The impact of the Bank effectively supported manufacturing rather than landed interests by assisting the growth of the financial system,[18] but the economic infrastructure was determined by invention of the corporation.

In his commentaries, Blackstone wrote that the corporation was a Roman invention designed to mitigate conflict between factions by establishing 'separate societies of every manual trade and profession'.[19] They were adopted by the canon law for the maintenance of ecclesiastical discipline before being refined and improved 'according to the usual genius of the English nation'. Blackstone defined corporations as 'one person in law' with one will 'collected from the sense of the majority of the

---

[12] GM Hodgson, '1688 and all that: property rights the glorious revolution and the rise of British capitalism' (2017) 13(1) *Journal of Institutional Economics* 79.

[13] W Thornbury, 'The Bank of England' in *Old and New London: Volume 1* (London, 1878) 453, 455, www.british-history.ac.uk/old-new-london/vol1/pp453-473.

[14] S Pincus and A Wolfram, 'A Proactive State? The Land Bank, Investment and Party Politics in the 1690s' in P Gauci (ed), *Regulating the British Economy, 1660–1850* (Abingdon, Routledge, 2016).

[15] R Harris, 'Law, finance and the first corporations' in Nelson et al (n 9) 145, 149.

[16] Thornbury (n 13) 455.

[17] ibid.

[18] Pincus and Wolfram (n 14).

[19] W Blackstone, *Blackstone's Commentaries on the Laws of England* (1765–1770) Book the First – Chapter: The Eighteenth: Of Corporations.

individuals', the rules established for 'this little republic' forever vesting 'the privileges and immunities, the estates and possessions' as 'a person that never dies: in like manner as the river Thames is still the same river, though the parts which compose it are changing every instant'.[20]

Parliament responded to the corporation slowly. Almost 100 years after Blackstone, the Joint Stock Companies Act 1844 created a right to incorporation other than by royal or statutory grant. The Limited Liability Act 1855, which meant investors only risked the capital put into a company, aimed to stop companies incorporating under competing regimes in the US or France.[21] The corporation, which government used to exploit overseas territories, became a vehicle to incorporate or invest, in theory at least, available to all. The Industrial Revolution, beginning in the 1820s[22] was arguably the final step in opening the economic and political systems to civil society.[23]

IV. CIVIL SOCIETY

A population able to sustain the rule of law had to be informed and educated and the impact of the printing press, economically, socially, and politically, was considerable. Between 1500 and 1600, cities with printing presses grew 60 per cent faster than similar cities without and between 1500 and 1800 they grew at least 25 per cent faster.[24] As the 1600s progressed, printed materials expanded. More pamphlets were published in England between 1628 and 1660 than in the American and French Revolutions put together. By the seventeenth century the printed word affected public mood. The cavalier establishment blamed the execution of Charles I on the pulpit and press, but Rahe suggests that the press was probably the main influence.[25] Charles II was advised to curb the press to avoid the conflict of his father's reign.[26]

Print was an urban technology and Parliamentary support was strongest in major cities and ports. At the outbreak of the civil war Charles had the support of about half of Parliament, the Nobles and gentry, Catholics and the poorer areas of the North and West. It drained away partly because of the publication of the first newsbook, the forerunner of newspapers, in 1641 by John Thomas. The topic was the Grand Remonstrance. The pamphlet invited the public to consider the cause of the complaint, putting forward the view of Parliament, and probably that of Thomas' political ally, John Pym.

The news book was a broad platform for political journalism. The Levellers, a political movement with a strong power base in London and in the Parliamentary

---

[20] ibid.
[21] G Baars, *Law, Capitalism and the Corporation: A Radical Perspective on the Role of Law in the Global Political Economy* (Leiden, Boston, Brill, 2019) 65.
[22] Weingast (n 9) 29.
[23] Other cultures used elements of the rule of law without integrating them in a single or sustained system (see A Sen, 'Global Justice' and T Kuran, 'The rule of law in Islamic thought and practice: a historical perspective' both in Nelson et al (n 9) at 55 and 71).
[24] JE Dittmar, 'Information technology and economic change: the impact of the printing press' (2011) 126(3) *The Quarterly Journal of Economics*.
[25] ibid 57.
[26] R Cust, 'News and Politics in Early Seventeenth-Century England' (1986) 112(1) *Past & Present* 60.

army, used *The Moderate*, to advocate sovereignty of the people based on wide suffrage, annual elections, religious tolerance, equality before the law and an end to arbitrary detention.[27] They laid the foundation for the separation of church and state in Britain,[28] continental Europe and the US.[29] Whether or not it promoted cultural enlightenment or reinforced existing prejudices,[30] the printed word helped carve out a space for what we now recognise as the public sphere, providing a platform for the 'public intellectual', and making 'censors and judges of ordinary readers'.[31] Journalism ensured that at the time of the English Civil War, the English people 'had become what it had never been before: a *public* – a wakeful community able to judge'.[32] There were new expectations of individuality and liberty.

Following the Glorious Revolution an anonymous pamphlet appeared: *Political Aphorisms*, based on the writings of John Locke and others. This tract and those such as *Voxpopuli, vox dei* and *The Judgment of Whole Kingdoms and Nations*, published later, contained 'true maxims of government', decrying the despotism of the later Stuarts and justifying the Glorious Revolution. These tracts were influential in establishing the Whig view of the world during the 1700s. The first edition of *The Judgment* included a recommendation that it was 'proper to be kept in all families, that their children's children may know the birth right, liberty, and property belonging to an Englishman'.[33]

Three editions of *The Judgment* quickly sold 8,000 copies, and, in four years, 11 editions appeared. Potential patrons were offered the opportunity to buy and return it in two days for a full refund. It was republished in 1747 and in 1771, a few years before the classic liberal economic text, Adam Smith's *Wealth of Nations*. In *The Commentaries* Blackstone wrote that a free press was essential to a free state, but that such a press must be responsible for anything 'improper, mischievous, or illegal'.[34]

The availability and distribution of rationally grounded opinion created an environment in which civil society flourished and in the eighteenth and nineteenth centuries independent 'publics', clubs, organisations, and professions proliferated.[35] After the Act of Settlement 1701, judges began to act in a more fair-minded way and litigants began to assert political rights, such as resisting enclosures of common land in the period between 1710–20.[36] By the 1760s, it was possible for determined individuals to claim civil and political rights against reluctant government.

---

[27] R Foxley, *The Levellers: Radical Political Thought in the English Revolution* (Manchester, Manchester University Press, 2013).

[28] PA Rahe, 'An Inky Wretch: The Outrageous Genius of Marchamont Nedham' (2002–2003) 70 *The National Interest* 55.

[29] *The Excellence of Free State* was excerpted in John Adams' *Defense of the Constitutions of the United States of America* in the 1780s (see https://founders.archives.gov/documents/Adams/06-18-02-0290).

[30] Rahe (n 28).

[31] Rahe (n 28) 57.

[32] ibid 56.

[33] R Ashcraft and MM Goldsmith, 'Locke, Revolution Principles, and the Formation of Whig Ideology' (1983) 26(4) *The Historical Journal* 773, 793 citing the preface to *The Judgment*.

[34] *Blackstone's Commentaries* (n 19) Volume 4.

[35] TC Halliday and L Karpik, 'Politics Matter: A Comparative Theory of Lawyers in the Making of Political Liberalism' in TC Halliday and L Karpik (eds), *Lawyers and the Rise of Western Political Liberalism* (Oxford, Clarendon Press, 1997) 15, 19.

[36] S Landsman, 'The Rise of the Contentious Spirit: Adversary Procedure in Eighteenth-Century England' (1990) 75(3) *Cornell Law Review* 498, 582–83.

A leading proponent of political reform, and an astute user of law to achieve it, was John Wilkes, a member of the Literary Club with Samuel Johnson and David Garrick, the famous actor.[37] Wilkes was self-styled champion of 'the middling sort'[38] who, at the start of the 1760s, produced *The North Briton*, a weekly publication appearing between 1762–63. In 1763, issue number 45 criticised a speech by George III and accused him of lying about the war with France. Imprisoned on a charge of seditious libel, Wilkes issued a writ of *habeus corpus*, addressed the court on freedom of speech, and won on a technicality.[39] Following his acquittal Wilkes won an award of £1,000 against the government for false arrest, trespass, and theft of personal papers. Wilkes fled abroad in 1764 when a more solid case of seditious libel charge was laid against him.[40] A year later *Entick v Carrington*[41] established, in a case of seditious libel against the *Monitor*, that such acts were illegal.[42] The English rights trumpeted by Blackstone were achieved by this campaign of court challenges.[43]

Wilkes returned in 1767 and won a seat in Parliament before surrendering. Lord Mansfield sentenced him to 22 months in prison. Before the new Parliament met, an unruly crowd formed outside his jail. A magistrate named Gillam authorised troops to use arms and at least one innocent bystander was killed. The victim's wife was persuaded to bring a prosecution and Gillam and a soldier stood trial for murder. Although they were acquitted the authorities exercised restraint at later demonstrations.[44] When Wilkes' seat was given to his electoral rival, 60,000 people from all over the country signed a petition citing this example of 'governmental tyranny'.[45] It had little obvious impact on its actions, but 'generated immense pressure on the government to conform its conduct to established legal principles'.[46]

In 1769 the Society of the Supporters of the Bill of Rights (SoBR) was established to support Wilkes financially. Chairman John Glynn and about 10 per cent of the members were lawyers[47] the remainder printers and less prosperous businessmen.[48] In 1770 Parliament granted a print monopoly for publishing its proceedings, resolving to arrest printers producing unlicensed reports. To counter Parliament, a printer called Wheble was arrested by his own servant and brought before Wilkes, now a magistrate, who released him on a technicality. Parliamentary messengers trying to arrest other printers were charged with assault and false imprisonment.[49]

---

[37] AH Huguenard, 'Dr. Johnson on the Law and Lawyers' (1933) 8 *Notre Dame Law Review* 195.
[38] Landsman (n 36) 583.
[39] ibid 585.
[40] ibid 586.
[41] *Entick v Carrington* (1765) 2 Wils KB 275.
[42] Landsman (n 36) 585.
[43] A Tomkins and P Scott (eds), *Entick v Carrington: 250 Years of the Rule of Law* (Oxford, Hart Publishing, 2015).
[44] Landsman (n 36) 586.
[45] ibid 587.
[46] ibid 587.
[47] WW Pue, 'Lawyers and Political Liberalism in Eighteenth and Nineteenth Century England' in TC Halliday and L Karpik (eds), *Lawyers and the Rise of Western Political Liberalism* (Oxford, Clarendon Press, 1997) 167, 178.
[48] Landsman (n 36) 583.
[49] ibid 588.

Despite internal disagreements[50] Wilkes' supporters published numerous pamphlets in support of liberty and the rule of law. In 1771 one demanded the end of corrupt political practices, support for wider democracy and no taxation without consent in the Americas. In 1814 *The Times* was produced by steam power.[51] Cheaper newspapers allowed a radical press, like William Cobbett's *Political Register*, which campaigned against political corruption and first called for a reformed Parliament in 1816.[52] These campaigns bore fruit when the Representation of the People Act 1832 widened the franchise, abolishing 'rotten boroughs', and extending voting qualification to property owners and leaseholders paying more than £10 a year.[53]

Modern definitions of civil society were contentious. Requirements that civil society organisations had a political focus, like political parties, protest movements or Trade Unions, or simply brought people together, charities, churches and clubs, seemed too narrow.[54] Broader definitions of the 'civil society ecosystem'[55] included NGOs (non-government organisations) 'that have an organized structure or activity'.[56] Non-political organisations supporting democracy or the rule of law arguably deserved inclusion for their role in representing the interests of citizens.[57]

Civil society contributed to the rule of law by counterbalancing the monopoly of expertise by the state and providing the capability, the platforms, organisation, and social capital, to hold institutions of the state to account. Non-governmental organisations on the left and right invoked the rule of law from different perspectives. The sum of such groups in civil society arguably produced an equilibrium in which all views and all interests were considered,[58] reducing the chance that government agencies and ideologies monopolised the social framework.[59]

The Freedom Association described itself as 'a non-partisan, centre-right, classically liberal campaign group',[60] with 'Eight Principles of a Free Society': Individual Freedom, Personal and Family Responsibility, The Rule of Law, Limited Government, Free Market Economy, National Parliamentary Democracy, Strong National Defences, and A free press and other media. Leading lights of the Freedom Association were Conservative politicians on the right-wing of the Party. The causes they espoused, from South African apartheid, anti-trade unionism, and anti-British Broadcasting Corporation, which it saw as too left wing, were often illiberal and inconsistent with balanced, rights-based notions of the rule of law.

---

[50] They disagreed over diverting the society's funds to help the printers and Glynn and other left to form the Constitutional Society in 1771.
[51] P Ackroyd, *A History of England, Volume V: Dominion* (London, MacMillan, 2018) 14.
[52] Cobbett was not a lawyer but was briefly a clerk in Gray's Inn. See GDH Cole, *The Life of William Cobbett* (London, Routledge, 1924) 22).
[53] Representation of the People Act 1832.
[54] E Gellner, *Conditions of Liberty: Civil Society and Its Rivals* (Toronto, Hamish Hamilton/Penguin, 1994).
[55] World Economic Forum, *The Future Role of Civil Society* (Geneva, Switzerland, 2013).
[56] ibid.
[57] RD Putnam, R Leonardi and RY Nanetti, *Making Democracy Work: Civic Traditions in Modern Italy* (Princeton, Princeton University Press, 1994).
[58] Vile (n 6) 364.
[59] ibid 365.
[60] Freedom Association, www.tfa.net/about.

At the libertarian end of the spectrum of non-governmental civil society organisations, the campaigning organisation Justice claimed to 'scrutinise and challenge developments in the justice system that threatened adherence to human rights and the rule of law'.[61] Its wide membership was 'drawn primarily from the legal profession … using their networks and influence to change the justice system for the better'.[62] Other campaigning groups dominated by lawyers included the Public Law Project and Good Law Project. Both used legal actions strategically to reinforce the legality of government decision making.[63] The Good Law Project had a more explicit focus on litigation and was active in exposing corruption in the award of government procurement contracts during the COVID-19 pandemic.[64]

V. PARLIAMENT

On their accession in 1688, William and Mary tried to balance the interests of the Whig and Tory parties in government. Mary's sister, Anne, who succeeded on William's death in 1702, favoured the Tories. On Anne's death in 1714, Tories attempted to return her half-brother, the son of James II, also James, to the throne. Whig support for Protestant Hanoverian, George I, led to Whig domination of government offices which lasted until 1850.[65] By the 1800s the 'Whig supremacy' had embedded liberal thought in public discourse. It embraced constitutional monarchy, the supremacy of Parliament and wider suffrage, free trade, the abolition of slavery and, in distinct contradiction of Whig origins, Catholic emancipation.

Whigs opposed the Church of England for fostering the habit of passive obedience to royal authority. Government power was limited to three key groups, ministers, civil servants, and the House of Commons,[66] who shared the rule-making power and limited party power. In the nineteenth century Parliament became more open and, while elder sons of upper-class families inherited and cared for the land, younger sons aspired to careers at the Bar, in the Army and Navy, the established clergy, and the civil and diplomatic services. Many leading eighteenth and nineteenth century Members of Parliament (MPs) were barristers and a few were solicitors. In the twentieth century around a fifth of MPs were lawyers.[67]

An argument for lawyer MPs was that they reinforced the culture of legality and reduced the two types of corruption that plagued the executive function. This distinction was described in the literature as 'grand corruption' involving large sums or upper levels of government, and 'petty corruption' concerning small sums or officials

---

[61] Justice, 'About Us', https://justice.org.uk/about-us/.
[62] ibid.
[63] Public Law Project, https://publiclawproject.org.uk/what-we-do/, Good Law project, https://goodlawproject.org/about/.
[64] D Conn, '"Apparent bias": Gove acted unlawfully, judge rules' *The Guardian* (19 June 2021) https://goodlawproject.org/case/procurement-case/.
[65] R Ashcraft and MM Goldsmith, 'Locke, Revolution Principles, and the Formation of Whig Ideology' (1983) 26(4) *The Historical Journal* 773, 789.
[66] Vile (n 6) 355.
[67] J Hyde, 'Legal background is ticket to seat in new parliament' (*Law Society Gazette*, 21 May 2015) www.lawgazette.co.uk/news/legal-background-is-ticket-to-seat-in-new-parliament/5048967.article.

lower down the political ladder.[68] Grand corruption was likely to be 'political' and the norms infringed, such as 'fairness', second order and vague. Lower-level administrative or bureaucratic corruption violated first order norms such as legal rules. The risk of corruption was exacerbated when standards were vague, behaviour unmonitored, and accountability weak.

The melange of customs, conventions, and assumptions operating as constraints on government were set out in a book originally published in 1844 by Thomas Erskine May. The book, *A treatise on the law, privileges, proceedings and usage of Parliament*, commonly referred to as '*May*', was the authoritative guide to parliamentary practice and procedure.[69] May was arguably an exemplar of lawyer influence on parliament. He began work as a Parliamentary Assistant Librarian in 1831, at the age of 16, but entered Middle Temple in 1834 and was called to the Bar in 1838. His book became so important in rulings by the Speaker of the House of Commons Parliamentary procedures that the 25th edition was published online in 2020.[70]

The need for *May* underlined the point, made by Vile and others, that infrequent elections were a poor way to discipline government.[71] This was brought home in 1994, when allegations of the purchase of privilege led to a major review of public standards. The owner of the elite department store Harrods, Mohamed Al-Fayed, claimed he had paid ministers to ask questions in the House.[72] In the wake of the so-called 'cash for questions' scandal the Prime Minister, John Major, asked Lord Nolan to chair a new Parliamentary committee examining standards in public life. Nolan had a relatively unprofitable career at the Bar, spending years in lower judicial positions before appointment to the Court of Appeal in 1991. In 1994, on being appointed to the standards brief, he had just been appointed to the Judicial Committee of the House of Lords.

Having decided that a senior lawyer should lead the inquiry Major had asked his Lord Chancellor, Lord Mackay of Clashfern, for advice. Mackay, a strict Presbyterian, thought Nolan, a devout Catholic, would bring a suitably moral approach to the role.[73] Nolan's record as a judge, in which he delivered principled judgments in diverse cases, not failing to criticise the establishment, may also have been a factor. Nolan promptly demonstrated being 'independently minded', by ignoring Major's suggestion that the Committee 'probably sit in private' and announcing public sittings.[74]

The first report of Nolan's Committee in 1995 reviewed a long history of Parliamentary scandals. In 1695 the Speaker was expelled for receiving money to assist the passage of Bill, a high crime and misdemeanour found to be 'to the subversion of the Constitution'.[75] In 1858, in a move directed at barristers, members were

---

[68] SD Morris, *Forms of Corruption* (2011) 9(2) *CESifo DICE Report* 10.
[69] UK Parliament, 'Erskine May', https://erskinemay.parliament.uk/.
[70] ibid.
[71] Vile (n 6) 363.
[72] *Britannica*, 'Cash-for-questions scandal', www.britannica.com/topic/cash-for-questions-scandal.
[73] A Roth, 'Obituary: Lord Nolan' *The Guardian* (26 January 2007) www.theguardian.com/news/2007/jan/26/guardianobituaries.obituaries.
[74] ibid.
[75] Lord Nolan (Chair), *Standards in Public Life: First Report of the Committee for Standards in Public Life* (London, HMSO, 1995) (cm 2850-1) para 24.

forbidden from bringing forward or advocating any measure for which they had received payment.[76] In 1947 a wordy statement banned any contractual constraint on members' 'independence and freedom of action in Parliament'.[77]

Nolan's review of the modern history of scandals adopted Lord Blake's observation that financial impropriety went in cycles.[78] There had been little of note from 1865 to 1895 but then a lot until the 1930s. A notable episode occurred in 1911, when David Lloyd George profited handsomely from buying shares in the American Company, Marconi, before announcing that the British government had awarded it a lucrative contract. Lloyd George tried to conceal the fact, then denied wrongdoing, but Parliament divided on Party lines and declined to condemn him. The press, and consequently the public, showed little interest in the matter.[79]

In the relatively stricter period after World War II, a minister called John Belcher resigned his ministerial position and his seat having been found to have improperly issued licences to businessmen friends in return for gifts.[80] Nolan noted that the 1950 and 1960s were marked by sexual scandals and the 1970s by a large financial scandal around the award of contracts to the architect, John Poulson, leading to the imprisonment of local government officials and criticism of the Home Secretary and two MPs.[81] Lord Blake attributed increased petty corruption in the previous 20 years to a 'get rich quick mentality' among MPs.[82]

Nolan's brief, to examine 'current concerns' about activities of office holders, including their financial and commercial activities,[83] was intended to ensure 'the highest standards of propriety' for ministers, civil servants, advisers, and other public office holders in bodies such as government quangos (executive non-departmental public bodies and the National Health Service). Nolan found no major scandals since the 1990s but, rather, numerous resignations for sexual impropriety, payments to MPs to ask questions in the house, political appointments to public bodies, corruption in local councils and reluctance of ministers to resign over mistakes.[84] He called this a 'pervasive atmosphere of "sleaze"', where examples of governmental misconduct were 'indifferently linked'.[85]

Nolan found that 30 per cent of MPs held paid consultancies related to their Parliamentary role. He thought work for lobbying companies should be banned but other outside employment could be allowed. He recommended that arrangements, including trade union sponsorship of MPs, should be declared and that a review should decide whether they were allowed at all. He resisted calls that MPs' discipline be enforced by the courts, arguing that the House of Commons should be responsible for enforcing its own rules.

---

[76] ibid para 25.
[77] ibid para 26.
[78] ibid Appendix 1: Lord Blake, 'Standards in Public Life: Twentieth Century cases of misconduct and current public opinion' (p 104).
[79] ibid.
[80] ibid p 105.
[81] ibid pp 105–6.
[82] ibid extract from letter quoted at p 104.
[83] Hansard 25 October 1994, col 758, cited in Nolan (n 75).
[84] Nolan (n 75) p 106.
[85] ibid p 106.

Nolan informed John Major that the public had expressed great interest in his task and considerable concern over failures to observe standards.[86] He warned the Prime Minister of a risk that, without corrective measures, public 'anxiety and suspicion' over the situation would give way to 'disillusion and growing cynicism'.[87] Nolan's 'restatement' of general principles underpinning public life was, summarised, as follows:

1. Selflessness: acting solely in terms of the public interest.
2. Integrity: avoiding placing themselves under any obligation to people or organisations that might try inappropriately to influence them in their work; not acting or taking decisions to gain financial or other material benefits for themselves, their family, or their friends; declaring interests and relationships.
3. Objectivity: acting and taking decisions impartially, fairly and on merit, using the best evidence and without discrimination or bias.
4. Accountability: being accountable to the public for their decisions and actions and submitting themselves to the scrutiny necessary to ensure this.
5. Openness: acting and taking decisions in an open and transparent manner; not withholding from the public unless there are clear and lawful reasons for so doing.
6. Honesty: being truthful.
7. Leadership: exhibiting these principles in their own behaviour; actively promoting and robustly supporting the principles and being willing to challenge poor behaviour wherever it occurs.[88]

Nolan recommended that these principles be incorporated into binding codes of conduct in all public bodies[89] with clear disciplinary procedures and penalties.[90] A code was created for Members of Parliament comprising 21 rules including the Nolan principles.[91]

Nolan recommended that a register of MPs' financial interests, which had existed since 1974, should be more detailed, focused on conflicts of interest, and maintained by a new Parliamentary Commissioner for Standards. The Commissioner would investigate allegations against members and publish the results. Where further action was recommended a sub-committee of the Committee of Privileges would conduct a public hearing and recommend a penalty. Since then, a handful of cases were investigated annually. A notable case, involving former MP Charlie Elphicke, was relevant to the rule of law because it illustrated expectations of MPs regarding observance of the separated functions of government.[92]

---

[86] He also referred to surveys showing declining trust in politicians including ministers (Letter from Lord Nolan to Prime Minister (n 75) pp 106–8).
[87] ibid.
[88] Nolan Report (n 75) p 14.
[89] ibid Recommendations, p 3.
[90] ibid paras 95–96.
[91] The Code of Conduct for Members of Parliament, https://publications.parliament.uk/pa/cm201719/cmcode/1882/188202.htm#_idTextAnchor000.
[92] UK Parliament Committees, 'Committee on Standards publishes report on the conduct of Mrs Natalie Elphicke, Sir Roger Gale, Adam Holloway, Bob Stewart, Theresa Villiers' (21 July 2021) https://committees.parliament.uk/committee/290/committee-on-standards/news/156736/committee-on-standards-publishes-report-on-the-conduct-of-mrs-natalie-elphicke-sir-roger-gale-adam-holloway-bob-stewart-theresa-villiers/.

Elphicke was charged with sexual assault and awaited sentencing. The Parliamentary Commissioner for Standards investigated letters written by five MPs to the Senior Presiding Judge for England and Wales and the President of the Queen's Bench Division in connection with the case.[93] They expressed concern that character references provided for Elphicke should be made public, arguing that this would be a 'radical change to judicial practice'. The presiding judge in the case, Mrs Justice Whipple, was sent a copy, shortly before considering the issue. The Lord Chief Justice's private secretary rebuked the MPs for trying to influence the judge, breaching the separation of powers and independence of the judiciary. The MPs then wrote again, this time directly to Mrs Justice Whipple, acknowledging that it was her decision to make.

The commissioner concluded that the letters sought to interfere in the judicial process and were a breach of paragraph 17 of the MPs' Code of Conduct, 'an action likely to cause significant damage to the reputation and integrity of the House'. Since this could not be part of the Members' Parliamentary duties, their use of House of Commons stationery for the letter also breached paragraph 16 of the Code: 'Members shall ensure that their use of public resources is always in support of their parliamentary duties'.

The standards committee noted that MPs had routes to raise judicial issues, including though the Lord Chancellor. It agreed with the Commissioner for Standards that the MPs had breached the code of conduct, stating: 'Such egregious behaviour is corrosive to the rule of law and, if allowed to continue unchecked, could undermine public trust in the independence of judges.' It took account of aggravating and mitigating factors in deciding appropriate sanctions. It regarded the fact that two of the MPs had 'substantial legal experience' and the third, the 'longest standing ... still does not accept his mistake' as aggravating factors. All five were required to apologise, but these three were suspended because they 'should have known better'.[94]

In his review of standards of public life Lord Nolan was circumspect about procedures for dealing with allegations against ministers.[95] He recommended a revision of existing guidance in *Questions of Procedure for Ministers*, focusing on what he identified as fundamental issues. These formed the core principles of ministerial conduct set out in the Ministerial Code in 1967. The current code stated:

a. The principle of collective responsibility applies to all Government Ministers;
b. Ministers have a duty to Parliament to account, and be held to account, for the policies, decisions and actions of their departments and agencies;
c. It is of paramount importance that Ministers give accurate and truthful information to Parliament, correcting any inadvertent error at the earliest opportunity. Ministers who knowingly mislead Parliament will be expected to offer their resignation to the Prime Minister;

---

[93] A member of the House of Lords had also written, but that case was not part of this review.
[94] G Davies, 'Tory MPs set to be suspended for trying to influence trial of ex-MP Charlie Elphicke' *The Telegraph* (21 July 2021) www.telegraph.co.uk/news/2021/07/21/tory-mps-set-suspended-trying-influence-trial-ex-mp-charlie/.
[95] Nolan (n 75) Recommendation 21.

d. Ministers should be as open as possible with Parliament and the public, refusing to provide information only when disclosure would not be in the public interest, which should be decided in accordance with the relevant statutes and the Freedom of Information Act 2000;
e. Ministers should similarly require civil servants who give evidence before Parliamentary Committees on their behalf and under their direction to be as helpful as possible in providing accurate, truthful and full information in accordance with the duties and responsibilities of civil servants as set out in the Civil Service Code;
f. Ministers must ensure that no conflict arises, or appears to arise, between their public duties and their private interests;
g. Ministers should not accept any gift or hospitality which might, or might reasonably appear to, compromise their judgement or place them under an improper obligation;
h. Ministers in the House of Commons must keep separate their roles as Minister and constituency Member;
i. Ministers must not use government resources for Party political purposes; and
j. Ministers must uphold the political impartiality of the Civil Service and not ask civil servants to act in any way which would conflict with the Civil Service Code as set out in the Constitutional Reform and Governance Act 2010.[96]

Nolan thought that the Prime Minister should take advice from the Cabinet Secretary on ministerial misconduct, which should remain private.[97] The current version of *May* emphasised the importance of ministers being open with Parliament.[98]

VI. ADMINISTRATION

A. The Administrative State

Enlightenment thinkers considering diffusion of state power did not anticipate the growth or impact of the administrative state. As it became more complex, interpretation and execution of law was performed by police, prosecutors, and civil servants. This raised the question of why the judge was distinguished from these others. Vile argued that it was because of the authoritative quality of judicial interpretation.[99] It was also because of the unique detachment and independence of the judge from other affiliations and concerns.

Dicey had already warned that the growth of the British administrative state posed a threat to the rule of law. By the end of the nineteenth century, it was clear that remote parts of the ever more complex state machinery were not subject to

---

[96] Ministerial code (Cabinet Office, 2019) 1(3), https://assets.publishing.service.gov.uk/government/uploads/system/uploads/attachment_data/file/826920/August-2019-MINISTERIAL-CODE-FINAL-FORMATTED-2.pdf.
[97] Nolan (n 75) paras 18–22.
[98] Erskine May (n 69) Chapter 11.40.
[99] Vile (n 6) 360.

effective Parliamentary control.[100] Judicial review, while essential, could not be the only control of the administrative machine.[101] Vile concluded: 'the aspiration towards a government of laws and not of men is inherently incapable of being realized, but a government of men subject to the restraints of certain rules is not'.[102] The best way of countering threats to the rule of law not redressed in courts depended on circumstances.

In 1929 the Committee on Ministers' Powers considered powers exercised by ministers by delegated legislation and quasi-judicial decision making by executive bodies. The Committee's brief was to identify safeguards for securing the sovereignty of Parliament and the rule of the law. The Committee did not however, see much of a problem. Broadly, it rejected the suggestion that the relevant actions of ministers and civil servants threatened the separation of powers. The justifications for this position seemed controversial: administrative decisions were not judicial decisions but simply applied policy;[103] delegating legislative and judicial power to the executive was essential to modern government and could be subject to adequate safeguards;[104] the separation of powers was a rule of political wisdom rather than a principle of the English Constitution. The Committee failed to take seriously risks of corruption, the abuse of public power for personal gain.[105]

B. The Civil Service

The shortcomings of the mid-nineteenth century civil service, small and based on patronage, were exposed by the Crimea War (1852–56). The Northcote and Trevelyan Report (1853) which claimed the civil service attracted those 'whose abilities do not warrant an expectation that they will succeed in the open professions, where they must encounter the competition of their contemporaries' led to a Civil Service Commission recruiting by open competition.[106] After the electoral reform of 1867, entry by examination became the norm for higher and lower entry echelons, but a Treasury-based elite ensured that exam content favoured Oxbridge candidates.[107] The British civil service was distinctive for a notion of service inspired in the public schools by the study of Plato and Aristotle and by aristocratic disdain for financial reward.[108]

---

[100] ibid 255 and 399.
[101] ibid 401.
[102] ibid 328.
[103] ibid 258.
[104] ibid 256.
[105] Morris (n 68) citing JS Nye, 'Corruption and Political Development: A Cost-Benefit Analysis' (1967) 61(2) *American Political Science Review* 417.
[106] SH Northcote and CE Trevelyan, *Investigation and report into The Organisation of the Permanent Civil Service* (1853), www.politicsweb.co.za/news-and-analysis/the-northcotetrevelyan-report.
[107] S Horton, 'The Public Service Ethos in the British Civil Service: An Historical Institutional Analysis' (2006) 21(1) *Public Policy and Administration* 32, 35.
[108] ibid citing M Weiner, *Culture and the Decline of the Industrial Spirit 1850–1980* (Cambridge, Cambridge University Press, 1981).

The commitment to a public service ethos was attributed to Sir Warren Fisher, Head of the Civil Service between 1919–39. He referred to an 'unwritten code of ethics' with the sanction being 'public opinion of the Service itself [demanding] a standard of integrity and conduct not only inflexible but fastidious'.[109] The public service ethos was manifested in 'behavioural traits such as honesty, integrity, impartiality, and objectivity; loyalty to the organisation and its goals; a commitment to public service; and accountability through and to political authorities'.[110] Expansion of the state after 1900 afforded the civil service a greater role, which solidified into an ethos of loyalty to the government of the day during World War I.

Despite the success of 'irregular' recruitment during World War II the civil service reverted to Oxbridge to control the experts managing the welfare state. The Fulton report in 1968 criticised the amateurism, exclusiveness, and lack of managerial skills of this senior elite. The Tory government of Margaret Thatcher elected in 1979 confronted civil service tradition, relying on special advisers and think tanks for policy advice and reviewing Permanent Secretary appointments to ensure they were 'one of us'.[111] Traditional civil service work was hived off, leaving the civil service and ministers to manage agencies. With internal changes, the mindset of civil servants became more attuned to private sector values.[112]

In 1984 the future of the public service ideal was called into question when the civil servant, Clive Ponting, revealed to Parliamentarians that government was misleading the public and Parliament about the sinking of the Argentine battleship Belgrano during the Falklands war. He was prosecuted under the Official Secrets Act. A jury acquitted Ponting, whose defence was a provision in the Act allowing disclosure 'in the interests of the state'.[113] The civil service demanded a code of ethics clarifying the relationship between loyalty to government and the service ethos.

In the 1980s and 1990s the involvement of civil servants in government scandals involving the sale of military equipment called their integrity into question.[114] Reports and a white paper affirmed the importance of civil service traditions of integrity and probity.[115] In 1997, at the end of the Tory period beginning with Thatcher, the civil service was seen to be more overtly political, partisan and identifiable. The Blair government of 1997 continued the practice of having special advisers and keeping senior civil servants out of policy. Parliamentary Committees advocated returning to the public service ethos[116] but promised legislation was not enacted.

---

[109] ibid 36, citing E Gladden, *Civil Services in the United Kingdom 1855–1970* (London, Frank Cass, 1967) 167–69.
[110] ibid 33.
[111] ibid 38.
[112] ibid 39.
[113] D Leigh, 'Obituary: Clive Ponting' *The Guardian* (6 August 2020) www.theguardian.com/politics/2020/aug/06/clive-ponting-obituary.
[114] See the Westland Helicopter and 'Arms to Iraq' affairs.
[115] See Horton (n 107) 41, citing Public Accounts Committee, *The Proper Conduct of Public Business* (PAC, 1994), The Treasury and Civil Service Committee, *The Role of the Civil Service* (1994) and the Cabinet Office, *Continuity and Change* (1994).
[116] Horton (n 107) 42, citing the House of Commons Public Administration Select Committee's *Public Service Ethos* (2002)

During its 160 years the civil service went through changes which undermined its original regulatory ethos. It transformed into a public or social service role in the late nineteenth century and then a welfare state role after World War II, and an enabling state role in the late twentieth century. The increase in managerial and administrative duties, at the expense of a policy role, transformed ideal civil servants into different kinds of official: 'business-like, concerned with efficiency and effectiveness and achieving results, displays leadership qualities, is able to defend policies and wants to succeed'.[117] As a result, civil servants' autonomy was reduced, and accountability increased, and their potential to support good government decreased. This was perhaps less true of government lawyers, whose work roles explicitly supported the rule of law.

The civil service contained large numbers of lawyers in legal roles. The Treasury Solicitor's Department has existed since 1876, when it was invested with legal powers as a corporation sole. It became the Government Legal Department in 2015, supporting Ministerial Departments in legal matters and employing most of approximately 2,000 lawyers engaged full-time in government work. When it examined the role of the Lord Chancellor in 2015, the Select Committee on the Constitution was told that departmentally-based lawyers were expected to refer rule of law issues to the Law Officers.[118] The Permanent Secretary of the Ministry of Justice and the Treasury Solicitor or First Parliamentary Counsel had specific obligations to speak on issues touching on the rule of law.[119]

Treasury counsel or government department standing counsel usually appeared in cases involving the Crown. James Eadie QC, a barrister in Middle Temple was appointed First Treasury Counsel in 2009 and appeared in controversial litigation about Britain leaving the EU. The government also employed independent counsel, usually barristers in private practice, to represent it in legal matters. The 'Treasury Devil' was the common term for the First Junior Treasury Counsel, a private practitioner barrister who represented government in Common Law Courts.

The Law Officers, through the Government Legal Department, were responsible for maintaining large panels of junior counsel in private practice. An Attorney General's panel of over 400 juniors undertook civil and EU work for government departments. They could also 'work outside the panel' for the government.[120] Although appointment to a panel provided minimum work, members were encouraged to also maintain public and private practice. It was considered beneficial for counsel to have experience of acting against government. All government counsel had responsibility for upholding the rule of law.

---

[117] Horton ibid 44.
[118] Evidence given to the Select Committee on the Constitution by Sir Alex Allen, a senior civil servant, para 67, https://publications.parliament.uk/pa/ld201415/ldselect/ldconst/75/7505.htm#note89.
[119] ibid para 66.
[120] There are London Panels, Regional Panels and Public International Law Panels, comprising tiers of counsel according to experience. Those in the top, A panel, have over 10 years' advocacy experience. The Attorney General also administers three panels of junior counsel undertaking public international law for government departments. See UK Government 'Attorney General's civil panel counsel: appointments, membership lists and off panel counsel', www.gov.uk/guidance/attorney-generals-panel-counsel-appointments-membership-lists-and-off-panel-counsel.

Sir Stephen Sedley recalled a case in 1988, in his early career as a barrister, representing a prisoner found guilty of a breach of discipline by the prison governor. Sedley sought judicial review because the governor had not heard the prisoner's defence. John Laws, the Treasury devil, declined to take an obvious defence, non-justiciability, because if upheld it would have affected the duty of boards of prison visitors hearing disciplinary charges.[121] This was a clear example of a government lawyer prioritising rule of law principles.

C. Public Inquiries

Public inquiries were a means of exploring failings in the operation of the state which were matters of public concern by addressing three questions: what happened and why, who was to blame, and what could prevent reoccurrence?[122] Since 1997, there was never fewer than three at one time and at the end of 2017 nine were open.[123] An insight into when inquiries were held was outlined in a revealing restricted memorandum prepared by the Cabinet Secretary in 2010.[124] The immediate issue was whether there should be an investigation of revelations that journalists at a national newspaper were hacking the phones of people in the news for stories. The note observed that statutory inquiries were called to investigate, inter alia, instances of failed regulation, corruption, and breaches of the rule of law raising issues of public concern. From 2005 the procedure was governed by Inquiries Act 2005 which, the memo noted, merely *allowed* a minister to hold a statutory inquiry.[125]

Lawyers, and particularly judges, were often appointed chairs of public inquiries.[126] The working and failures of the system were illustrated in 1989, when a Public Inquiry under Taylor LJ followed the death of 96 football fans at a football match at the Hillsborough Stadium in Sheffield. The corruption concerned efforts of the police authority to blame members of the crowd[127] involving critical changes to the evidence and testimony of 68 police officers. Nevertheless, the report, published in 1990, concluded safety failings at the ground and mismanagement by South Yorkshire police caused the disaster. There was no correction of the corrupted evidence before an inquest in 1991 brought in findings of accidental death.

The 1991 coroner's verdict was overturned in 2012 and a verdict of gross negligence by the officer in charge was substituted. No criminal charges were brought

---

[121] S Sedley, *Lions under the Throne* (Cambridge, Cambridge University Press, 2015) 16–17.
[122] Institute for Government, 'Public inquiries' (21 May 2018 www.instituteforgovernment.org.uk/explainers/public-inquiries.
[123] ibid.
[124] G O'Donnell, 'Public Inquiries' (19 March 2010) https://assets.publishing.service.gov.uk/government/uploads/system/uploads/attachment_data/file/60808/cabinet-secretary-advice-judicial.pdf.
[125] These had the advantage of being able to compel evidence. Other means of investigation included non-statutory inquiries, which could safely be used for investigation of government because compellability was not an issue.
[126] If judges were used in a statutory inquiry, a specified senior member of the judiciary had to be consulted (Inquiries Act 2005, s 10).
[127] D Conn, 'Hillsborough: why has the trial collapsed and what happens next?' *The Guardian* (26 May 2021) www.theguardian.com/football/2021/may/26/hillsborough-why-has-the-trial-collapsed-and-what-happens-next.

until 2021 when the police authority solicitor and two officers from the Inquiry team were charged with perverting the course of justice. All three were acquitted because, the judge ruled, Taylor had conducted a non-statutory inquiry, which was 'an administrative exercise' rather than a 'course of public justice'. This raised the question of whether the obligations of public employees, such as the police, were sufficiently robust or whether a statutory 'duty of candour' might improve transparency and promote public trust.[128]

VII. JUSTICE

Barbara Shapiro identified two convulsions in the court system reflecting changes in ways of thinking.[129] The first, and deepest, occurred in in the eleventh century when irrational trial methods, such as ordeal, were replaced by trial based on evidence. Verdicts produced by 'findings of fact guided by common sense and common knowledge' marked the beginning of a change from superstition to reason.[130] By the thirteenth century distinctions between law and fact were made in decisions and case procedures. The emergence of trial based on evidence and cross-examination of witnesses were introduced around 1400 but attendance of witnesses only became compulsory, and perjury a crime, in 1563.[131]

Before the civil war courts were tools of the monarch.[132] Following the civil war, Parliament struggled to justify the execution of Charles I and half of the 12 common law judges refused to continue.[133] Parliament was guilty of similar abuses to those of the Stuart kings[134] and during the Protectorate, when the purged Parliament shared authority with the Army,[135] pamphlets reflected a common feeling deeply hostile to law and to courts.[136] Cromwell failed to implement several proposals to make courts more accessible.[137] Foreign wars, a new government order and problems in raising finance meant 'it would be difficult to pick a period in English history … when the prospect of legal progress would seem less inviting'.[138]

The administration worked hard to assuage the scruples of the six remaining common law judges.[139] From 1640 significant procedural changes in criminal cases

---

[128] S Gardiner, D Morrison and S Robinson, 'Integrity in Public Life: Reflections on a Duty of Candour' (2021) *Public Integrity*, www.tandfonline.com/doi/full/10.1080/10999922.2021.1903165.

[129] B Shapiro, '"To a Moral Certainty": Theories of Knowledge and Anglo-American Juries 1600–1850' (1986) 38(1) *Hastings Law Journal* 153.

[130] ibid 155.

[131] ibid 156.

[132] In 1346, judges swore that 'they would in no way … give advice to any man, great or small, in any action to which the King was a party himself', www.judiciary.uk/about-the-judiciary/history-of-the-judiciary/.

[133] M Burrage, *Revolution and the Making of the Contemporary Legal Profession: England France and the United States* (Oxford, Oxford University Press, 2006) 411.

[134] For example, it refused to agree not to interfere in private law suits (RC Brown, 'The Law Of England During The Period Of The Commonwealth' (1931) 6(6) *Indiana Law Journal* 359).

[135] ibid 363.

[136] Burrage (n 133) 412.

[137] ibid 420–21.

[138] Brown (n 134) 361.

[139] ibid 364.

reflected Parliament's desire to reassert 'legality' after the excesses of revolution.[140] The Rump Parliament fixed salaries for judges, removed the practice of paying them from fees and reduced competition between courts and, with it, the risk of corruption. It also required that law books and records be in English. The 'Barebones Parliament' following it proposed an unimplemented right to legal counsel.[141] Stability was achieved in the court system.

From the seventeenth century, the second great transition in the court system saw new ideas about evidence and rational deduction. Shapiro attributed this second convulsive change to an intellectual climate produced by overlapping groups; Protestant theologians, questioning religious dogma, and naturalists, basing truths on observable phenomena.[142] Subjection of religious truths to sceptical attack contributed to sophisticated theories of knowledge. Three kinds were identified: the physical, which was proven by sense data, the mathematical, which was provable by logical demonstration, and the moral, which depended on witness and second-hand reports of sense data. Sceptics argued that facts must be distinguished from probability.

Moral knowledge was, according to John Locke, a kind of probability depending on evidence that could rise to almost certain knowledge.[143] Locke's Essay *Concerning Human Understanding* (1690) set an intellectual climate in law and history by highlighting factors affecting the reliability of human evidence in a forum like a court of law: 'the number of witnesses, their integrity, their skill at presenting evidence, and its agreement with the circumstances, and lastly, the presence or absence of contrary testimony'.[144] Enlightened attitudes, ending cruel punishment and providing jury trial, were supported by lawyers. In 1616 John Selden, barrister of Inner Temple and MP, published an edition of *Fortesque* advocating the 'right' of trial by jury.[145]

When Blackstone published his *Commentaries*, he defined trial as 'the examination of the matter of fact in issue' but which 'varied it's examination of facts according to the nature of the facts themselves' to achieve the 'best method of trial, as the best evidence upon that trial, which the nature of the case affords'.[146] The characteristics were that 'all witnesses, that have the use of their reason, are to be received and examined, except such as are infamous, or such as are interested in the event of the cause. All others are competent witnesses; though the jury from other circumstances will judge of their credibility'.[147] Blackstone claimed ancient roots to jury trial, lauding it as part of the impartial administration of justice and 'the great end of civil society'.[148]

---

[140] Vile (n 6).
[141] Brown (n 134) 369.
[142] Shapiro (n 129) 157.
[143] ibid 158.
[144] ibid at 161 citing J Locke, *An Essay Concerning Human Understanding* (London, 1690) b10, bk. IV, ch. XV, § 5
[145] A Arlidge and I Judge, *Magna Carta Uncovered* (Oxford, Hart Publishing, 2014) 125.
[146] W Blackstone, *Blackstone's Commentaries on the Laws of England* (1765–1770). Book the Fourth – Chapter: The Twenty Second: of the several Species of Trial.
[147] ibid Book the Fourth – Chapter: The Twenty Third: Trial by Jury.
[148] He asserted that 'the nature and method of the trial by jury' might be traced to 'the Britons themselves', but that they were certainly used by the earliest Saxon colonies, their origins 'being ascribed by Bishop Nicolson to Woden himfelf, their great legislator and captain'. See Blackstone (n 146) Book the Fourth – Chapter: The Twenty Third: Trial by Jury).

Blackstone claimed the advantage of juries was heightened in criminal cases.[149] When a magistracy was 'selected by the prince' it was not human nature for those few to 'be always attentive to the interests and good of the many'.[150] In France or Turkey he said, the authorities might 'imprison, dispatch, or exile any man that was obnoxious to the government, by an instant declaration, that such is their will and pleasure'.[151] However, the English laws demanded that 'the truth of every accusation, whether preferred in the shape of indictment, information, or appeal, should afterwards be confirmed by the unanimous suffrage of twelve of his equals and neighbours, indifferently chosen, and superior to all suspicion'.[152]

The right to trial by jury became an essential feature of criminal justice because, according to Stephens:

> The very essence of trial by jury is its principle of fairness. The right of being tried by his equals, that is, his fellow citizens, taken indiscriminately from the mass, who feel neither malice nor favor, but simply decide according to what in their conscience they believe to be the truth, gives every man a conviction that he will be dealt with impartially, and inspires him with the wish to mete out to others the same measure of equity that is dealt to himself.[153]

More recently, Lord Devlin claimed trial by jury was 'more than an instrument of justice and more than one wheel of the constitution: it is the lamp that shows that freedom lives'.[154]

The system of justice was not based on the Utilitarian view that the good of the greatest number was inevitably a decisive consideration, nor of teleologists, like Aristotle, that ends were significant. Rather, it followed Kant's view that what was right took priority over what was good. A legacy of Utilitarianism was Jeremy Bentham's conviction that law was human creation, not something natural or 'discovered' by judges. This was a precursor to the rise of formalism in late nineteenth century, a project undertaken between practitioners and judges in Germany, England, and the US creating a common 'frame of mind' in traditions of legal thought.[155]

In the 1970s, the British legal philosopher HLA Hart, paid tribute to Bentham's legacy in a lecture at Harvard on legal positivism and the interpretative function. He argued that natural, procedural justice demanded objectivity and impartiality so that rules were applied only to genuine cases of the relevant rule.[156] This involved distinguishing 'core cases' covered by the rule and 'penumbra cases', not considered by the creators of the law, where judges needed to 'interpret' the provision.

Hart's hypothetical 'penumbra case' involved a law banning vehicles from a park. This clearly covered the core case, motor vehicles, but not necessarily bicycles, roller

---

[149] Blackstone (n 146) Book the Third – Chapter: The Twenty Third.
[150] ibid Book the Fourth – Chapter: The Twenty Third: Trial by Jury.
[151] ibid Book the Fourth – Chapter: The Twenty Seventh: Of Trial and Conviction.
[152] ibid Book the Fourth – Chapter: The Twenty Seventh: Of Trial and Conviction.
[153] JER Stephens, 'The Growth of Jury Trial in England' 10(3) (1896) *Harvard Law Review* 150, 160.
[154] P Devlin, *Trial By Jury* (Stevens, London, 1956) 164.
[155] EM Wise, 'The Transplant of Legal Patterns' (1990) 38 *American Journal of Comparative Law Supplement* 1, 15.
[156] Hart (n 3) 624.

skates, toy automobiles or airplanes.[157] Hart argued that deciding penumbra cases involved some notion of what law ought to be, but this was not 'ought' in the sense of moral judgement. Hart acknowledged that 'the intelligent decision of penumbral questions was one made not mechanically, and with a view to aims, purposes, and policies, but not in the light of anything we would call moral principles'.[158]

Hart's lecture provoked a response by the American legal philosopher, Lon Fuller.[159] Fuller took issue with Hart's idea that law had a core not open to interpretation. The example of the prohibited vehicles in the park, for instance, needed to be viewed in context. The rule was only easily applied because the aim of the rule seemed obvious, but the mischief (noise or safety) was not, so the clear core was insecure. If, Fuller said, some locals wanted to display a fully functioning World War II truck in the park, would opponents be able to rely on the 'no vehicle rule' to frustrate the plan?

Fuller argued that applying rules was a purposive exercise. Judicial interpretation recognised law had a structural integrity, sometimes called 'the intention of the statute'. Fidelity to law allowed a judge a creative role in the framework, but not beyond. Judges bound by superior courts or making judgments antithetical to their views had to embrace responsibility for making law what it ought to be.[160] Fuller's perspective drew on a history of 'interpretative scepticism' associated with the legal realist movement.

Fuller drew support from the German legal philosopher, Radbruch, who argued that the legal positivism advocated by Hart smoothed the path to dictatorship in pre-Nazi Germany.[161] Ignoring the moral ends and inner morality of law primed German lawyers to accept anything appearing to be law. Corruption of the legal system was effected because: '[t]he first attacks on the established order were on ramparts which, if they were manned by anyone, were manned by lawyers and judges. These ramparts fell almost without a struggle'.[162]

English courts first experimented with a 'purposive approach' to statutory interpretation in the Court of Appeal in the 1950s.[163] Lord Denning, a controversial judge, suggested resolving difficult cases by considering Parliament's intention in making law, 'filling in the gaps and making sense of the enactment'. On appeal Lord Simmons said this was 'a naked usurpation of the legislative function under the thin disguise of interpretation ... if a gap is disclosed, the remedy lies in an amending Act'. By the 1970s English judges, possibly influenced by civil law jurisdictions in Europe and the European Court of Justice, accepted more purposive interpretative techniques.[164]

---

[157] ibid 607.
[158] ibid 614.
[159] LL Fuller, 'Positivism and Fidelity to Law – A Reply to Professor Hart' (1958) 71(4) *Harvard Law Review* 630.
[160] ibid 647.
[161] ibid.
[162] ibid 659.
[163] *Magor and St. Mellons Rural District Council v Newport Corporation* [1950] 2 All ER 1226, per Lord Denning.
[164] Lord Reid, 'The Judge as Lawmaker' (1972–73) *Journal of the Society of the Public Teachers of Law* 22 and K Malleson, *The New Judiciary: The Effects of Expansion and Activism* (Aldershot, Ashgate, 1999).

The convention that courts could not refer to proceedings in Parliament in construing statutory provisions, because this would involve looking beyond the ordinary meaning of words, was relaxed by the House of Lords in *Pepper v Hart* (1993). A taxpayer challenged taxation of a benefit, the difference between a standard school fee and the reduced fee paid by a teacher for his child's place in a school where he taught.[165] It was not clear what the statute meant by the 'cash equivalent' of the benefit. It was argued on the taxpayer's behalf that, when the measure was debated in Parliament, a Treasury spokesman claimed tax would be calculated on the *extra* cost to the employer of providing a benefit. In this case, that was negligible because the school had empty places. The House of Lords held that this information was relevant in interpreting the statute and reduced the estimated benefit value. This established that courts could take account of Parliamentary statements by ministers or other promoters of primary legislation in construing ambiguity or obscurity in statutory drafting.

Pepper v Hart was referred to the Joint Committee on Parliamentary Privilege as a potential breach of the Bill of Rights (1689), Article 9[166] which provided that 'the freedom of speech and debates or proceedings in Parliament ought not to be impeached or questioned in any court or place out of Parliament'. Guaranteeing members freedom of speech and freedom of debate was seen as a 'cornerstone of parliamentary democracy'[167] but the Committee agreed with the court that *Pepper v Hart* did not infringe Article 9 because it did not 'question' the proceedings of Parliament. *May* was duly amended to reflect this.[168]

In the US, the known ideological orientations of judges, as revealed by political party affiliations, were the most significant factor in predicting their decisions, especially at Supreme Court level.[169] Recent work by Cahill O'Callaghan looking at Supreme Court judgments in the UK, found that in 'hard cases', where there was no clear outcome dictated by precedent, the exercise of discretion was significant.[170] One of the relevant factors, the personal values of justices, revealed stark differences in the value profiles of individuals which were important subconscious influences on outcomes. Two examples from a file of cases illustrated that aspirations for a perfectly rational and fair justice system were as flawed as those that worked in it.

Judicial subversion of the rule of law was often shocking, as in the Profumo scandal in 1963. John Profumo resigned as a Conservative minister over lies he told to the House of Commons about a brief affair with Christine Keeler, an alleged call girl. A recent book by Geoffrey Robertson QC suggested that the prosecution of a friend of Keeler, Stephen Ward, for living off earnings of prostitution was a politically

---

[165] *Pepper (Inspector of Taxes) v Hart* [1993] AC 593.
[166] C Littleboy and R Kelly, 'Pepper v Hart' Parliament and Constitution Centre, Standard Note: SN/PC/392 (House of Commons Library, 2005) https://researchbriefings.files.parliament.uk/documents/SN00392/SN00392.pdf.
[167] ibid.
[168] Erskine May (n 69) '"Impeached" and "Questioned"' Part II, Chapter 13, 11.
[169] DP Currie, 'Positive and Negative Constitutional Rights' (1986) 53 *U Chi L Rev* 864, 906–7.
[170] R Cahill O'Callaghan, *Values in the Supreme court: Decisions, Division and Diversity* (Oxford, Hart Publishing, 2020).

motivated witch hunt[171] driven by the Home Secretary, with the active support of senior judges in a spirit of 'Christian solidarity'. Ward killed himself on the last day of the trial while the prosecution knew, but did not reveal, that Keeler, the critical witness, was a liar.

Another judicial weakness was credulousness concerning executive assurances of propriety. In *McIlkenny v Chief Constable of the West Midlands*,[172] men convicted of a terrorist bombing had claimed that confessions were extracted by torture. While they served prison terms, the Court of Appeal halted their civil action for assault against the police because, Lord Denning said, the allegations were too serious to be believable. In 1992, the scientific evidence was thrown into doubt as, 'in the absence of any explanation, police witnesses were at least guilty of deceiving the court'.[173] The accused men were therefore exonerated.

VIII. JURISDICTIONAL DIFFERENCES

De Tocqueville's study of American lawyers convinced him that they brought respect for legality to society, formal procedure to government and tempered popular government.[174] These indicators of responsibility were evidenced by Rogers in his brief account of the American Bar Association, where he claimed colonial lawyers were historically attuned to participate in politics and other community activities 'to become known, deservedly known'.[175] Miller suggested that lawyer politicians in the US tended to be younger when elected, longer in office, often in positions of leadership in the legislature and more likely to run for high office.[176]

Historically, the majority of the US Senate and House of Representatives were lawyers. After 1850, State governors were usually lawyers, with a high of 66 per cent in 1983.[177] By the 1990s, 25 of 41 Presidents had been lawyers with four in the twentieth century: Roosevelt, Ford, Nixon and Clinton.[178] Rogers claimed that legal representation in Congress promoted constitutional stability because lawyers 'preached the value and sacredness of our Constitution' and 'are much the most responsible single element in our population'.[179] Early studies did not bear this out, detecting little difference in the voting patterns of lawyers and non-lawyers.[180]

---

[171] G Roberston, *Stephen Ward was Innocent OK?: The Case for Overturning his Conviction*. (London, Biteback Publishing, 2013).
[172] *McIlkenny v Chief Constable of the West Midlands* [1980] 2 WLR 689.
[173] *R v McIlkenny & others* [1992] 2 All ER 417, 431j to 432a.
[174] A de Tocqueville, *Democracy in America* (trans H Reeve) (Penn State Electronic Classics Series, 1831) http://seas3.elte.hu/coursematerial/LojkoMiklos/Alexis-de-Tocqueville-Democracy-in-America.pdf.
[175] JG Rogers, 'History of the American Bar Association' (1953) 39(8) *American Bar Association Journal* 659, 662.
[176] MC Miller, *The High Priests of American Politics: The Role of Lawyers in American Political institutions* (Knoxville, University of Tennessee Press, 1995).
[177] ibid 31.
[178] ibid 31 (and Truman attended night classes in law).
[179] Rogers (n 175) 662.
[180] Miller (n 176) citing H Eulau and JD Sprague, *Lawyers in Politics: A Study in Professional Convergence* (Indianapolis, Bobbs-Merrill, 1964) found that lawyer and non-lawyer legislators displayed little difference in roll-call voting

Miller argued that looking at lawyer voting patterns gave a misleading idea of their influence. Advocating a neo-institutional approach, he analysed internal political environment and organisational context to understand the US legislature. Examining members' professional training and backgrounds[181] he argued Congressional procedures clearly reflected lawyers' 'pre-occupation' with process,[182] their preference for incremental rather than radical change and their way of thinking.[183] Lawyers were more likely to conceive of themselves as 'trustees' than as 'delegates', to view courts in positive terms and to pay attention to court decisions. They were less likely to see judicial decisions as politically biased. The incremental, rights-based, lawyerly approach was probably at the expense of vision, but it supported the rule of law.

IX. DISCUSSION

Successful embedding of the rule of law was not simply a matter of institutional organisation but depended also on cultures of legality, in government, administration and civil society, which were mutually reinforcing. There were no simple solutions. Hamilton's constitutional legacy was administrative institutions intended to perform some of the functions of the other powers, particularly the executive, constituted in a spirit of public service and staffed with professionals. They arguably constituted a fourth power of state.[184] Eleven such institutions existed before the Civil War and a further six were created before 1900. In the 1930s, Roosevelt's New deal necessitated creation of agencies to administer increased levels of state activity.

The proliferation of administrative agencies led to concerns about the growing significance of the administrative function. They often had limited legislative and judicial powers for which there was no constitutional authority. In 1941 a committee established by the Attorney general identified 51 federal agencies including executive departments and independent agencies.[185] The Administrative Procedure Act 1946 aimed to 'improve the administration of justice by prescribing fair administrative procedures'.[186] It established a regulatory framework for state administrative agencies with a view to promoting public information about them, public involvement in their processes, the promotion of common standards across agencies and judicial review of the exercise of any formal adjudicatory function.[187]

Reconfiguring the role of administrative agencies was not a panacea and was sometimes problematic, either creating legislative spaces or too much regulation. Administrative encroachment resulted from neglect by executive and legislative

---

[181] Miller ibid 4.
[182] ibid 12.
[183] ibid 18.
[184] BJ Cook, *The Fourth Branch: Reconstructing the Administrative State for the Commercial Republic* (Kansas, University Press of Kansas, 2021).
[185] *Final Report of Attorney General's Committee on Administrative Procedure* (Senate Document No. 8, 77th Congress, First Session, 1941) Library of Congress Web Archives.
[186] Administrative Procedure Act 1946, PUBLIC LAW 404–79TH CONGRESS] [CHAPTER 324–2D SESSION].
[187] ibid ss 3–5, and the *Attorney General's Manual on the Administrative Procedure Act* (US Department of Justice, 1947).

functions. Congressional failure to enact clean air legislation, for example, encouraged the Environmental Protection Agency to fill the gaps[188] whereas comprehensive regulatory schemes often led to agencies abusing powers 'to defer, exempt, and dispense'.[189]

Administration in the British system had sought, through the civil service, to internalise an ethic of public good as an operational rationale. As a result of Nolan's concerns about loss of the public service ethos the *Civil Service Code of Ethics* (1996) acknowledged a right to appeal conflicts of interest and like other employees, civil servant whistleblowers were protected by legislation.[190] These responsibilities informed different aspects of the work of government lawyers. Public prosecutors, for example, had specific obligations in criminal cases[191] and rules of fairness applied to the conduct of civil litigation on behalf of government.[192]

The culture of the rule of law was manifest in positivist jurisprudential theory. Critics suggested it was undermined by social welfare legislation, which often used open-ended concepts, such as fairness or reasonableness, requiring use of judicial discretion.[193] The rapid pace of social change also meant that courts were left to develop law in controversial areas, such as genetic experimentation, without legislative guidance. Finally, there was increasing awareness that judicial decision making was not value free,[194] but subject to bias. Controlling the indeterminacy of law while serving constitutionality is a continuing problem for the rule of law.

Theories of constitutionalism made much of separating the power of the legislature, executive and judiciary to maintain the rule of law but little of the role of institutions, administration, and culture. Vile observed that the literature was silent about procedural checks, but that 'due process' was an essential part of constitutional government in antiquity. In modern times it ran parallel with ideas of good government and the separation of powers but was rarely an integral part of those theories.'[195] Jürgen Habermas noted that civil society was important in controlling state institutions[196] and Krygier suggested that civil society networks, even those coordinated by the state, were an effective counter to abuse of power.[197]

---

[188] MS Greve and AC Parrish, 'Administrative Law without Congress' (2015) 22 *George Mason Law Review* 501.
[189] ibid 546.
[190] Public Disclosure Act 1998.
[191] For a critique see A Wooley, 'Reconceiving the Standard Conception of the Prosecutor's Role' (2017) 95(3) *Canadian Bar Review* 795.
[192] JW Diehm, 'The Government Duty to Seek Justice in Civil Cases' (2000) 9 *Widener Journal of Public Law* 289; BA Green, 'Must Government Lawyers "Seek Justice" in Civil Litigation?' (2000) 9 *Widener Journal of Public Law* 235, but there is an argument that similar duties of fairness apply (see RE Rodes Jr, 'Government Lawyers' (2000) 9 *Widener Journal of Public Law* 281).
[193] FA Hayek, *The Political Ideal of the Rule of Law* (Cairo, National Bank of Egypt, 1955); R Unger, *Law in Modern Society* (New York, Free Press, 1976).
[194] Since the 1930s 'legal realists' suggested judges' values inevitably affect their decisions.
[195] Vile (n 6) 21.
[196] J Habermas, *Between Facts And Norms* (trans W Rehg) (Oxford, Polity Press/Blackwell, 1996) 367, cited by Christenson (n 11) fn 23.
[197] M Krygier, 'The Rule of Law: Pasts, Presents and Two Possible Futures' (2016) 12 *Annual Review of Law and Social Science* 199, 224.

Holmes contended that the state committed to an open society needed to 'institutionalise, at a bare minimum, religious toleration, freedom of discussion, personal security, free elections, constitutional government and the freedom to buy and sell in a market for goods and services'.[198] Institutions were important in establishing a framework for the rule of law and a normative consensus in which to operate. They ranged from financial institutions existing in perpetuity, like corporations, to a free press, which supported legality by educating the population and exposing corruption.[199] Institutions encouraged participation, debate, and campaigning. The value of these contributions was recognised by public consultation on important proposed legislation. This had arguably hardened into a new constitutional convention.[200]

Institutions played an important role in controlling corruption. Civil society was informed by an active press reporting on organisations campaigning against executive failings. These mechanisms for dealing with breaches of the rule of law traditionally relied on a culture of shame to deter executive or judicial overreach. This mechanism arguably had reduced effectiveness in societies with increasingly diverse values. This made civil society organisations that were willing to challenge government malpractice in court increasingly important.

X. CONCLUSION

Lawyers played diverse roles in creating institutions supporting the rule of law. Individual contributions to creating the market economy, civil society, and scientific method, were lost.[201] They contributed to the intellectual climate of the seventeenth and early eighteenth centuries, when the growth of 'possessive individualism', made the person the owner of their own capacities, owing nothing to society.[202] This placed emphasis on specific aspects of legality: 'impartial hearings, uniform procedures and an independent judiciary, as well as laws that were clearly framed, publicly proclaimed and fairly enforced'.[203] These were principles of the rule of law fundamental to a society based on Libertarian principles. They also contributed to a condition of legality in which law was seen to be less arbitrary, more predictable, and more directed to control power.

---

[198] S Holmes, *Passions and Constraint: On the Theory of Liberal Democracy* (Chicago, University of Chicago Press, 1995) 13–14.
[199] J Raz, *The Authority of Law: Essays on Law and Morality* (Oxford, Clarendon Press, 1979) 218–19.
[200] Vile (n 6) 375.
[201] Landsman (n 36) 602–3.
[202] CB Macpherson, *The Political Theory Of Possessive Individualism: Hobbes To Locke* (Oxford, Oxford University Press, 1962).
[203] Holmes (n 198) 15.

Part 2

Practice

Dr Johnson (1709–84), who at the age of 30 was refused admission to the Bar for want of a degree,[1] explained the function of lawyers to James Boswell, who was a lawyer:

> As it rarely happens that a man is fit to plead his own cause, lawyers are a class of the community who, by study and experience, have acquired the art and power of arranging evidence, and of applying to the points at issue what the law has settled. A lawyer is to do for his client all that his client might fairly do for himself, if he could.[2]

---

[1] AH Huguenard, 'Dr. Johnson on the Law and Lawyers' (1933) 8 *Notre Dame Law Review* 195, 200.
[2] *Boswell's Life of Johnson* vol 5, p 26 (Birkbeck Hill, 1950) cited by Lord Simon of Glaisdale in *Waugh v British Railways Board* [1980] AC 521, 535 and Lord Carswell in *Three Rivers District Council and Others v Governor and Company of the Bank of England (No 6)* [2004] UKHL 48, para 114.

6
Identity

I. INTRODUCTION

THIS CHAPTER CONSIDERS how the collective identity of lawyers – history, name, work performed, clientele served, and values – affected the nature of lawyers' engagement with the rule of law. In England, historical groupings of lawyers had specific identities from soon after the Norman Conquest. Early legal occupations tended to form around two main kinds of work, litigation, the bringing of cases to court, and business activity, particularly dealings in land. Although this was not inevitable it was broadly true across pre-capitalist Europe and in the jurisdictions examined. Identities changed radically after the English civil wars, leaving legacies which had a powerful influence on the legal imagination and conceptions of the rule of law.

II. THEORY

In *Economy and Society*, Weber claimed that lawyers played a reciprocal role in developing a rational system of formally elaborated law.[1] First, they formulated rules which institutionalised values as part of an intellectual system. Then they maintained the unique skills and modes of thought of that system to engage with commerce. In this way, lawyers contributed to the rational development of the state and the rationalisation of institutions. Weber suggested that this pattern of cause and effect was not limited to lawyers. The rise of professional priesthood, exemplified by salaried, hierarchical positions and prescribed and distinctive duties, reflected the rationalisation of the church just as the modern church led to a professional priesthood.[2]

Theorists noted that fundamental changes in society inevitably brought about changes in justice systems. Foucault identified changes in criminal punishments[3] while Habermas suggested that courts were subject to the influence of civil society.[4]

---

[1] M Weber, *Economy and Society* (Totowa, NJ, Bedminster, 1968) 775, cited by G Ritzer, 'Professionalization, Bureaucratization and Rationalization: The Views of Max Weber' (1975) 53(4) *Social Forces* 627, 628.
[2] Ritzer ibid 628 citing Weber ibid 1164.
[3] M Foucault, *Discipline and Punish: The Birth of the Prison*, 2nd edn (trans A Sheridan) (New York, Random House, 1995).
[4] J Habermas, *Between Facts And Norms* (trans W Rehg) (Oxford, Polity Press/Blackwell, 1996) 367, cited by Christenson fn 23.

Sward said that justice systems reflected two influences; a desire for fair dispute resolution and shared social values.[5] The range of objectives achieved involved conflict resolution, rulemaking, and behaviour modification as primary goals. The function of rulemaking was particularly pronounced in common law systems, where judges were invested with discretion to change law through a process of interpretation. Their decisions had a function of behaviour modification. Therefore, for example, allowing class actions was a procedural quirk emphasising this function.

The American legal philosopher John Rawls proposed a notion of justice suggesting equality was a logical basis of society. He adopted Kant's view of justice as a prior value in political systems:[6] 'the priority of right over good means that principles of right invariably outweigh considerations of welfare or satisfaction of desire, however intense, and constrain in advance the range of desires and values properly entitled to satisfaction'.[7] Justice could not be based on outcomes, which were inevitably subjective, but on impartial and regular administration of public rules. In later work Rawls limited his theory to liberal conceptions of justice, where government was neutral regarding competing notions of the good.

III. LITIGATION

A. Groups

By the thirteenth century there were different representative roles in the litigation process. Among the groups were elite pleaders, the serjeants, who were educated in Roman Civil and Canon law at universities and often represented the Crown.[8] Attorneys were also well established,[9] their role being to stand alongside the countor, a kind of legal representative or advocate in court, in place of litigants. This assisted clients with many cases or cases in remote courts.[10] The First Statute of Westminster (1275) and a London ordinance (1280) both applied to serjeants, but cases of deceit often involved attorneys.[11]

From the fourteenth century apprentices to the serjeants, *utter barristers*,[12] established distinct forms of practice in the middle of London and regional Assize courts.[13] A small and elite band of serjeants had exclusive rights of audience in Common

---

[5] EE Sward, 'Values, Ideology, and the Evolution of the Adversary System' (1989) 64(2) *Indiana Law Journal* 301, 306.
[6] J Rawls, *Political Liberalism* (New York, Columbia University Press, 1993).
[7] J Sandell, *Liberalism and the limitations of justice* (Cambridge, Cambridge University Press) 17–18.
[8] JH Baker, 'Solicitors and the Law of Maintenance 1590–1640' (1973) 32 *Cambridge Law Journal* 56.
[9] Attorneys probably had other roles (Baker ibid), CR Andrews, *Standards of Conduct for Lawyers: An 800-Year Evolution* (2004) 57 *SMU Law Review* 1385, 1391, https://scholar.smu.edu/smulr/vol57/iss4/3/.
[10] Andrews ibid 1385.
[11] ibid 1403, citing J Rose, 'The Ambidextrous Lawyer: Conflict of Interest and the Medieval and Early Modern Legal Profession' (2000) 7 *University of Chicago School of Law Roundtable* 137.
[12] Entrants to an Inn made speeches as part of the process of call to the Bar. Becoming an utter barrister was only the beginning of 10 years' apprenticeship to a serjeant (M Burrage, *Revolution and the Making of the Contemporary Legal Profession: England, France and the United States* (Oxford, OUP, 2006) 388).
[13] Until replaced by permanent Crown Courts in 1972.

Pleas,[14] and their apprentices appeared in King's Bench and Exchequer.[15] By the sixteenth century barristers had monopoly rights of audience in the main Common Law Courts.[16] Identities began to take a modern form in the seventeenth century, when the barristers' role as technical pleaders of civil cases was transformed into that of courtroom advocate.

B. The Criminal Trial

In Tudor society judges were the main means of enforcing criminal law,[17] there being no police force or other civil authority for maintaining order. Charges were brought by victims of crime and trials were cursory affairs with procedures designed to secure convictions. In the 1560s a Justice of the Peace read an account of their interviews with defendant and witnesses.[18] Witnesses then gave accounts of events, frequently interrupted by the judge or jurors, and followed by more detailed judicial questioning. Defendants interceded if they could.[19]

At the beginning of the 1700s the procedural protection offered to defendants in serious cases was scant. They could be committed to trial at an assize not knowing the charges they faced. The weight of evidence was measured by the number of sworn witnesses. Only prosecution witnesses swore an oath, enhancing the credibility of their evidence. Witnesses might include details they had been told by parties not in court. Jurors could ask questions of witnesses and might make evidential statements without being sworn.[20] Lawyers were rarely present, the rationale being that the truth was more likely to be had from the accused's own mouth than from an intermediary.

At the beginning of the eighteenth century victims of serious offences prosecuted their own cases and seldom hired lawyers. Only defendants charged with minor offences (misdemeanours) were allowed representation by counsel as of right.[21] When charged with the most serious offences (felonies), they could receive advice from lawyers but were not allowed to be defended by them in court.[22] The requirement that defendants spoke for themselves was a vital requirement in decisions about which defendants should be hung 'as examples'.[23]

---

[14] By the 16th century, those who became serjeants occupied their own Inn (Burrage (n 12)).
[15] A small number of the third group, doctors, obtained a doctorate of civil law and worked in Ecclesiastical and Admiralty Courts.
[16] Burrage (n 12) 387–89.
[17] S Landsman, 'The Rise of the Contentious Spirit: Adversary Procedure in Eighteenth-Century England' (1990) 75(3) *Cornell Law Review* 498, 507.
[18] This process was based on a single first-hand account of such a trial so may not be representative (ibid 504–5).
[19] JM Beattie, 'Scales of Justice: Defense Counsel and the English Criminal Trial in the Eighteenth and Nineteenth Centuries' (1991) 9(2) *Law and History Review* 221, 323.
[20] JH Langbein, 'The Criminal Trial Before the Lawyers' (1978) 45 *Chicago Law Review* 263, 288.
[21] This was to do with the fact that misdemeanours covered many matters that were more civil in nature, like failure in the upkeep of roads (Langbein (n 20) 308).
[22] And in some cases prevented the accused using notes prepared by lawyers. Langbein (n 20) 309.
[23] Beattie (n 19) 231.

The only professional lawyer in the room was usually the judge, who was to protect the interests of defendants; to act as their counsel. The judge supposedly provided elementary procedural protections, but did not assist the defence and indeed, often introduced their own political views.[24] In 1689, Hawles dismissed the idea that judges were well placed to help defendants in cases involving the state: '[betraying] their poor Client, to please, as they apprehended, their better Client, the King'.[25]

In 1696 the legal counsel and representation of defendants was allowed in treason cases.[26] This was a Whig response to experience under the Stuarts,[27] the prosecutions in the Popish Plot (1678–70), the Rye House Plot (1683) and Bloody Assizes (1685), and the biased trials, false convictions and executions that followed.[28] The right to counsel in other serious cases did not follow at this time, presumably because the state was not so directly involved in other cases, but also because treason was seen as 'uniquely problematic'.[29]

IV. THE ADVERSARY SYSTEM

A. Transformation

Important changes, protecting the rights of the accused, occurred in the eighteenth century. Determining exactly how this happened was made difficult by the relative absence of reliable reports.[30] The record of State Trials, recorded from the Normans onward[31] mostly involved political defendants, although some notorious cases were included. These cases were not representative of what happened in ordinary criminal courts. An insight into more serious criminal matters was gained by John Langbein and others using the Old Bailey Session Papers (OBSP), a record of trials of the most serious crimes committed in England from around 1670.

In the early days, the OBSP were 'sensation-mongering pamphlets written by non-lawyers' providing little information about process, evidence, or advocates.[32] More detail was provided as time progressed. Comparing later OBSP with other reliable reports, Langbein concluded that they were generally accurate, but not necessarily complete.[33] What the OBSP showed was that during the 1700s the criminal trial was transformed by allowing defendants to be represented by lawyers. The methods they

---

[24] Landsman (n 17).
[25] Langbein (n 20) 309, citing J Hawles, *Remarks Upon The Tryals Of Edwin Fitzharris, Stephen Colledge, Count Coninosmark, The Lord Russel, Colonel Sidney, Henry Cornish And Charles Bateman* 22 (London, 1689).
[26] Beattie (n 19).
[27] ibid 224.
[28] J Langbein, *The Origins of the Adversary Criminal Trial* (Oxford, Oxford University Press, 2003) 3.
[29] ibid.
[30] Accurate law reporting typically followed the involvement of lawyers.
[31] Langbein (n 20) 246–66.
[32] ibid 268.
[33] JH Langbein, 'Shaping the Eighteenth-Century Criminal Trial: A View from the Ryder Sources' (1983) 50 *University of Chicago Law Review* 1 at 25.

brought to the court were not necessarily new. Langbein suggested that they had probably already been developed before the eighteenth century in civil litigation and minor criminal cases, where lawyers had freedom of access. Nor were they confined to representation but formed part of a wider social transformation.

An important innovation from 1700 was in the role of juries. Based on records from Sussex, Langbein noted that in 1595 juries were often composed of those who had performed the role many times before.[34] Records from the Old Bailey in London suggested that jury panels continued into the 1730s.[35] The switch from juries acting as witnesses to hearing the evidence occurred in the reigns of Queen Anne and George I.[36] Juries began to be composed more randomly, determined the facts of the case, and applied the law, as directed by the judge, to reach a verdict. This move to a fairer jury system reflected wider social changes which also led to the introduction of lawyers to the criminal process.

In 1692 a statute offered a reward of £40 for the capture of highway robbers.[37] This encouraged a class of men who made careers from 'thief taking' and bringing cases based on 'confessions, admissions, and hearsay'.[38] Doubts about the process surfaced when one of the most famous thief takers, Jonathon Wild, faced trial. In 1722, Wild was at the top of his profession, heavily involved in proofing witnesses,[39] appearing as advocate, sometimes for the defence, or making decisive interventions in trials.[40] In 1725 he was exposed as the leader of a criminal gang and hung. The similarity of the evidence in the cases he presented, his conversations with apprehended prisoners, often the decisive evidence, should have raised suspicions. His victims were often former accomplices or rivals. The introduction of counsel for the defence reflected anxiety about unsafe convictions based on tainted evidence.[41]

The second major factor that brought defence lawyers into serious criminal cases was the involvement of lawyers in prosecution. Under Queen Anne the state took new interest in ordinary crimes and financed some prosecutions.[42] In the reign of George I (1714–27) the Prime Minister, Robert Walpole, extended this support to a wider range of offences. Independent barristers were briefed to appear as prosecutors in the most notorious cases and several government departments appointed officers responsible for investigation and prosecution. Prosecuting counsel handled nearly all questioning of defendants, while questioning of the prosecution depended on defendants' abilities or help from the judge.[43]

The OBSP suggested that in the early 1700s even serious criminal trials proceeded with 'extraordinary rapidity', probably because accused persons representing

---

[34] Langbein (n 20) 276.
[35] Landsman (n 17) 505.
[36] JER Stephens, 'The Growth of Jury Trial in England' (1896) 10(3) *Harvard Law Review* 150.
[37] The classes of crimes covered was extended over the next century to 'burglars, horsethieves, coiners' and others (Landsman (n 17) 573).
[38] ibid 575.
[39] ibid 502.
[40] ibid 572–77.
[41] Langbein (n 20) 311.
[42] D Lemmings 'Criminal trial procedure in eighteenth-century England: The impact of lawyers' (2005) 26(1) *Journal of Legal History* 73.
[43] Landsman (n 17) 520.

themselves misguidedly threw themselves on the mercy of the court.[44] Judges exercised 'arrogant and caustic' humour, usually at the expense of prisoners,[45] and demanded deference from all involved. The OBSP indicated that representation of defendants began in earnest in the 1730s.[46] By the mid-1730s there were enough cases, nine in 1736, to suggest the practice was becoming established.[47] Numbers gradually increased thereafter, achieving a high of 37 per cent of the 546 cases heard at the Old Bailey in 1795.[48] In every year of comparison after 1730, the defence engaged counsel more often than the prosecution.

At the beginning of the 1730s counsel did not appear as of right, but with permission of the judge,[49] but regular, almost routine, appearance of counsel suggested the active cooperation of the bench. By 1800, though they appeared in a small number of cases, the practice of the defendant managing their own case was largely replaced, with advocacy conducted by barristers. This changed criminal trials so that lawyers gained control of process and of the relationship with clients in ways recognisable in modern courtrooms. The transformation was so marked the new system became known as the adversary trial.

The rationalisation of the trial process began to transform the nature of advocacy. At the beginning of the 1700s it 'was often loud, long and declamatory, frequently diffuse and meandering, full of pathetic description, florid, extravagant in words and gestures to the point of theatricality'.[50] The adversary system made it detailed, focused, and strategic. The criminal trial turned advocacy into a form of public entertainment, with proponents as heroes.[51] This was aided by the techniques of cross-examination as a tool to expose unreliable and perjured evidence. This turned the Old Bailey into what Landsman dubbed 'a slaughterhouse of reputations'.[52]

Individuals contributed to the identity and mythology of the Bar during the development of the adversary system. Before 1780 the OBSP did not record the names of barristers appearing, but two stand out as celebrities after then, Thomas Erskine (1750–1823) and William Garrow (1760–1840). Being a little more senior, Erskine's appearances were not always recorded in the OBSP while Garrow, who only practised for 10 years, recorded at least 1,000 appearances in OBSP cases.[53]

Garrow was a clergyman's son who trained with an attorney before joining Lincoln's Inn as a student in 1778. His first case was a prosecution at the Old Bailey in 1784, but he was more associated with criminal defence and ordinary crimes such as highway robbery. He was celebrated for the assertion of clients' rights and

---

[44] Langbein (n 20) 277–82.
[45] Landsman (n 17) 515–16.
[46] Langbein (n 20) 311–13.
[47] Beattie (n 19) 225.
[48] Because of the inaccuracy of records, the number of cases at the main criminal court in London involving defence counsel may be underrepresented (ibid 227).
[49] Lemmings (n 42).
[50] A Watson, *Speaking in Court: Developments in Court Advocacy from the Seventeenth to the Twenty First Centuries* (Gewerbestrasse, Palgrave MacMillan, 2019) 327.
[51] Beattie (n 19) 247–48.
[52] Landsman (n 17) 553.
[53] ibid 567.

willingness to argue with judges.[54] Few demonstrated Garrow's innovation and flair. He was particularly celebrated as an exponent of the forensic and aggressive cross-examination style, which Landsman described as 'slashing'.[55]

B. Controlling the Courtroom

By the end of the eighteenth century, lawyers usually had de facto control of the courtroom, while judges were habituated to the role of neutral umpire. In *Smith*, a judge declined a party's request for guidance from the court with the declaration that 'this is not a court of inquisition'.[56] In 1777, a judge appeared almost deferential to counsel's argument about the admissibility of evidence, suggesting reliance on counsel was well established.[57] Contrary to this was an incident in 1786, when Garrow was reminded that he still appeared with the permission of the judge. Garrow was arguing against a deaf mute being allowed to give evidence against his client through an interpreter when Mr Justice Heath told him he could not speak until he had been formally 'assigned' to the case and that this would not happen until he behaved with 'decency'.[58] This suggested that judges did not always allow counsel, but Garrow's response, 'I have not been used to be interrupted. I am here to argue points of Law for the prisoner', suggested it was routine.[59]

C. Lawyer and Client Relationship

The adversarial criminal process changed the relationship between lawyers and their clients. Over the period of the 1700s counsel became increasingly responsible for making strategic decisions about the conduct of the case on behalf of their client. This was a significant change. When lawyers first became involved, they acted as counsel, advisers, to the victim or accused, who were the main protagonists. By the end of the period, counsel ran proceedings, at least in the courtroom. In 1782 a defendant who interjected while a prosecution witness was giving evidence was rebuked by his own counsel: 'Mr. Graham do you chuse to leave your defence to me or not?'.[60]

Another consequence of the adversary trial for the lawyer and client relationship was to introduce a higher degree of loyalty. In 1717, in a rare appearance, defence counsel took a technical point on his client's behalf and made a point of saying that he did not seek to justify his client's behaviour.[61] From 1730 there was evidence of more loyalty to clients and, in many cases, a more partisan approach by lawyers.[62]

---

[54] Beattie (n 19) 239.
[55] Landsman (n 17) 563.
[56] *Smith* (OBSP 1782) ibid 524.
[57] ibid 523 (*Dodd* OBSP 1777).
[58] Beattie (n 19) 246.
[59] ibid 246.
[60] *Graham* OBSP 1782 (Landsman (n 17) 558).
[61] *Howell* OBSP 1717 (Landsman (n 17) 538)
[62] Landsman (n 17).

An obligation to accept the client's factual account and their instructions appeared to be quite well established by a 1747 case in which counsel for the defendant was upbraided by the judge for alleging that senior church officials may have sanctioned damage to their own church property. In response he stated, 'I must follow my Instructions, and will not go from them.'[63]

As the eighteenth century progressed, loyalty may explain why counsel used increasingly hostile methods to undermine prosecutions. This was evident in a practice of threatening victim prosecutors with perjury charges if their allegations were not backed by witnesses.[64] Although they were still constrained in what they could do for the accused, advocates pushed harder against constraints on acting in client interests and the rules under which they worked. This might explain why more criminal defendants engaged lawyers.[65] It may also explain an increase in ill-tempered exchanges between counsel.[66]

D. Evidence and Process

From the 1730s defence counsel at the Old Bailey were inclined to seek proof of the constituent elements of the offence charged. In a bigamy case, for example, it insisted the prosecution produce evidence of a first marriage.[67] Yet the obligation on the prosecution to prove all the elements of offences was still not clear by the 1750s. In *R v Fuller*, a case of alleged smuggling heard in 1747, the prosecution produced several witnesses prepared to swear that the defendant had contraband in his saddle bags, but none who provided direct evidence.[68] Defence counsel asked a witness in cross-examination whether he could tell what was under his hat. When he could not, counsel told him: 'Thou canst just as well tell, what was in those Casks, as what is in my Hat. There might be Tobacco in the Bags. Or thou canst not tell, but there might be Vinegar or Verjuice [a non-alcoholic juice made from unripe grapes used in cooking] in the Casks.' At this point, the prosecutor, the Solicitor-General, intervened:

> *Solicitor-General.* You must show it was Verjuice.
>
> *Counsel for the Defendant.* I think otherwise.
>
> *Solicitor-General.* That you don't.

Over the following decades doubts about the burden of proof were gradually resolved in favour of the defendant.

Langbein noted that, around 1762, there was sharper insistence on proof beyond suspicious circumstances. In a case that year, the victim of a burglary accused the defendant of stealing items from his house because he had been 'lurking' in the vicinity.[69] The defendant was arrested and searched but nothing was found except for some tools

---

[63] ibid 520.
[64] ibid 529 (*Kite* 1762) Miss Kite had accused a customs officer of taking liberties while searching her.
[65] Beattie (n 19) 229.
[66] Landsman (n 17) 543.
[67] *Sommers* (OBSP, 1736) (Landsman (n 17) 537)
[68] *Fuller* (OBSP 1747) (Landsman (n 17) 527).
[69] (*Delaney* 1762) (Landsman (n 17) 528).

that might have been used in a burglary. In court the judge asked the victim 'Then you charge him upon suspicion only?'. The victim agreed and the defendant was acquitted.

By 1780 suspicion of circumstances had hardened into a standard of proof 'beyond reasonable doubt'.[70] At the same time, clarification of the burden of proof, whether the defence had to prove innocence, or the prosecution prove guilt, was also established. This could result in the defence submitting that, on evidence presented, there was no case to answer.[71] Later in the century, Garrow coined the phrase 'innocent until proven guilty',[72] thereby focusing on the prosecution burden. In a 1790 case he was so confident in the principle that he told the court he would present no evidence and advise his client to remain silent on the charge.[73]

Developments in evidence and what constituted fair proof occurred quite rapidly after 1730.[74] The defendant's previous convictions, which were allowed as part of the evidence against them in the early 1700s, were gradually excluded.[75] Langbein suggested that by the early 1700s judges could exclude hearsay evidence, that given by a party of what another party had said, or allow juries to assess what credit it was given.[76] By 1730 hearsay appeared to have become inadmissible, the judge in one case declaring: 'What was said by the Man or the Woman at the Cow's Face is no Evidence on either side, except they were here to swear it themselves.'[77]

More leeway may have initially been given for the admission of hearsay in murder cases, especially where it was evidence that the accused had threatened the victim.[78] By the 1780s, the rules against hearsay covered even murder, but clever advocates found forms of questioning to avoid exclusion. In *Carter* Garrow successfully defended an abusive husband accused of drowning his wife by showing that she was suicidal.[79] The court blocked Garrow's questions, which were leading a witness to say that the deceased had said she intended to 'make away with herself'[80] but he recovered by seeking the witness' opinion that the dead woman was in low spirits after conversations with the accused.

E. Cross-examination

Restrictions on hearsay compelled the production of more live testimony.[81] If parties alleged that a witness had said something relevant to the cause, the court would

---

[70] Langbein (n 28) 33.
[71] Landsman (n 17) 537.
[72] Garrow may not have been first to make the claim, but he did so in a case in 1791 (OBSP 1791 case 312) (Beattie (n 19) 249).
[73] *Hayward* (OBSP 1790) The defendant, a coachman, was accused of keeping a harness in lieu of wages when sacked. The judge directed the jury to return a verdict of not guilty. (Lemmings (n 42) 75).
[74] Langbein (n 20) 307.
[75] ibid 303.
[76] ibid 301–2.
[77] *Mason* (OBSP 1731) (Landsman (n 17) 567–68).
[78] Landsman (n 17) 567.
[79] *Carter* (OBSP 1787) (Landsman (n 17) 571–72).
[80] Landsman (n 17) 572.
[81] ibid 565.

provide an opportunity for the defendant to call the witness.[82] The production of more witnesses increased the scope for examination of oral evidence, drawing out inconsistencies and addressing juries on cogency. The right of lawyers to ask prosecution witnesses questions was established slowly. The OBSP showed that the right of defence counsel to cross-examine as they chose took time to establish.

Initially, cross-examination occurred only with the consent of the court. This was a constraint on how counsel approached the task. In 1731 a jury objected to a vigorous cross-examination of a victim, telling the judge that 'We desire his Lordship would please to ask the Questions that are proper, and that the Man may not be interrupted.'[83] In a 1741 murder trial in Bristol the prosecution objected to counsel for the defendant cross-examining on grounds that the right to do so was still variable.[84] As the right to cross-examine became established, it was used creatively to present the defendant's case.

Defendants could address juries but concerns that oratory might persuade jurors to acquit meant that lawyers could not address juries on their behalf. Lawyers used various pretexts to nibble away at the convention. They might claim the defendant was too ill to speak or ask to set out the defence without commenting on the prosecution evidence.[85] Garrow was adept at exploiting the uncertainty of courtroom regulation. A ploy to overcome the handicap of not being able to address the jury was to outline his case under the guise of explaining it to the judge: 'I wish I could also address that Jury on this trial. I should be glad to ask them whether they should chuse to convict a man of felony upon the testimony of a man with whom they could not hold a conversation'.[86]

The inability to comment on evidence in closing speeches forced lawyers to use cross-examination to comment on evidence. Highlighting inconsistencies and other weaknesses in the prosecution case produced a highly stylised form of witness interrogation. It was often conducted with such brutal sarcasm that witnesses refused to answer questions. Landsman notes that, during the eighteenth century, cross-examination developed to allow defence counsel to develop a case strategy: present a 'theory of the case, refute an opponent's claims, develop favorable proof, discredit opposing witnesses, and generally advance his client's position before the jury'.[87]

F. Trial Strategy

Control of the presentation of the case allowed defence counsel to play to juries' sensitivities and prejudices. The last thief catcher scandal occurred in the 1750s, but advocates continued to suggest that rewards encouraged victims and their witnesses

---

[82] ibid 521–22, referring to *R v Perry* (OBSP 1762).
[83] ibid 512.
[84] Langbein (n 20) 313.
[85] Landsman (n 17) 546.
[86] Beattie (n 19) 246.
[87] Landsman (n 17) 535.

to lie. Garrow's handling of thief takers invariably played on the jury's suspicions, questioning witnesses' character, their motive and emphasising the reward they would take on conviction:

> Garrow: Perhaps you do not know that there is a reward for these men if they are convicted?
> A: How should I know?
> Garrow: What is the price of the blood of these men, if they are convicted?
> A: I shall not tell you.[88]

Garrow was also said to have introduced the tactic of eliciting perverse verdicts from juries for capital crimes that were relatively minor offences. In theft cases attracting the death sentence for goods over a certain value, he invited juries to find that the goods were less valuable than the threshold for execution.

V. CELEBRITY

A. Reputation

The careers of Erskine and Garrow were examples of how lawyering offered fortune and status to impecunious aristocrats and minor gentry. Erskine was the younger son of an aristocratic Scottish family fallen on hard times. He joined the Royal Navy in his teens and then the Army. On the advice of Lord Mansfield, a family friend, he joined Lincoln's Inn in 1775. To shorten the period of study until qualification he enrolled at Cambridge University and, as an Earl's son, received a degree without examination. Erskine had a gift for oratory before joining the Bar, having preached sermons in the Army and won a prize at Cambridge for a presentation on the Glorious Revolution. James Boswell's *Life of Johnson* noted Erskine's fluency and vivacity.

After his call to the Bar in 1778 Erskine's rise was meteoric.[89] He quickly gained his first case acting for the governor of the Seaman's Hospital in Greenwich. Thomas Baillie had published a pamphlet criticising the Admiralty's running of the hospital, and a case of criminal libel was laid against him.[90] Erskine thought he had been appointed as Baillie's barrister and was disappointed to find he was one of five, the others more senior. Despite his lowly status, Erskine unexpectedly delivered a coruscating final speech threatening to expose the corruption of the First Lord of the Admiralty. He was widely credited with Baillie's acquittal, a stunning success which meant that, unusually for a barrister, he was busy from early in his career.

Erskine's speeches were particularly feared. In a case in 1787, in which Garrow was a prosecution junior, the jury was warned of Erskine's eloquence:

> You will admire his talents; you will say, pity so much ingenuity should be exerted in behalf of men so undeserving; pity it is that his great abilities are not employed on the other side, to bring these men to justice; if they had, he would have made us all shudder at their iniquity; and we should have sat down, lamenting, that such men ever existed, and that the

---

[88] *Levy* (OBSP 1784) (Beattie (n 19) 243).
[89] J Hostettler, *Thomas Erskine and Trial by Jury* (Hook, Hants, Waterside Press Ltd, 2010).
[90] *R v Baillie* (1778) also known as the *Greenwich Hospital* case.

Court had it not in their power to inflict a more exemplary punishment on such atrocious offenders .... Gentlemen, if the evidence comes up to but half of what I have opened, you will not let the able harangue of my learned and eloquent friend, Mr. Erskine, outweigh the testimony of so many witnesses.[91]

Ten years later, when Garrow was at the height of his career at the Bar, more often appearing for the prosecution than defence, such a speech was used against him.[92]

B. The Neutral Partisan

Trials allowed barristers like Erskine and Garrow to present the Bar as a defender of citizens' rights. The anti-establishment bent established in the Seaman's Hospital case followed Erskine through his early career. In 1781 he defended Lord George Gordon, accused of constructive treason for his role in instigating an anti-Catholic riot.[93] In 1783 he entered Parliament as a Whig but lost his seat in 1786. Returning to the Bar he defended William Davis Shipley (1784) and John Stockdale (1789) against charges of seditious libel.

R v Shipley concerned a vicar re-publishing a pamphlet written by his brother-in-law[94] supporting electoral reforms already proposed in a Bill brought to the House of Commons by Pitt the Younger. A Society for Constitutional Information was formed to raise funds for legal representation. Erskine was briefed to appear before Buller J, who declared the publication libellous, as the law then entitled him to do, leaving the jury to decide only whether it had been published. Erskine convinced the jury to return a verdict of 'guilty of publication only', but the judge then sentenced the defendant for the full offence.

During the case Erskine argued with Buller over the way in which the jury's verdict would be recorded. Finally, the following exchanged occurred:

Buller, J.: Sir, I will not be interrupted.

Erskine: I stand here as an advocate for a brother citizen, and I desire that the [record be complete].

Buller, J.: Sit down, Sir; remember your duty or I shall be obliged to proceed in another manner [by this he probably meant with imprisonment for contempt of court].

Erskine: Your Lordship may proceed in what manner you think fit; I know my duty as well as your Lordship knows yours. I shall not alter my conduct.[95]

---

[91] *Priddle* OBSP 1787 (Landsman (n 17) 561).

[92] Knowles OBSP 1797 (Landsman (n 17) 563–64).

[93] These began as protests against legislation ending discrimination against Catholics (Catholic Relief Act 1778). Gordon, the leader of the Protestant Association, was concerned that allowing Catholics into the Army risked creating a dangerous 'fifth column'. He attended the House of Commons accompanied by a large mob, which quickly became violent and assaulted members. Army units were mobilised resulting in hundreds of deaths (Hostettler (n 89) 34–42).

[94] *R v Shipley* 21 St. Tr. 847 (1783–84). (Landsman (n 17) 589, based his discussion on P Devlin, *The Judge* (Oxford, Oxford University Press, 1979) 118–25.

[95] *Campbell's Lives of the Lord Chancellors of England* (1857) VIII, 277, cited by A Periman in 'A 150 Year Old Example of Zealous Advocacy' (relating research undertaken by Monroe Freedman) April 2007, www.legalethicsforum.com/blog/2007/04/index.html.

Campbell opined: 'This noble stand for the independence of the Bar would of itself have entitled Erskine to the statue which the profession affectionately erected to his memory in Lincoln's Inn Hall .... The example had a salutary effect in illustrating and establishing the relative duties of Judge and Advocate in England.'[96]

Erskine appealed from the local court to the King's Bench, arguing that the judge had negated the jury's right to nullify an unjust law. The appeal court upheld the principle that juries could not decide whether material was technically libellous, but released Shipley on a technicality, to popular rejoicing. Erskine pursued the principle with leading Whig politicians, resulting in the reversal of the law by the Libel Act 1792.[97] He later wrote that he had originally pressed the point with the jury 'from no hope of success' but to expose the iniquity of the law.[98]

In 1791 Thomas Paine's *Rights of Man* was published. It found a large and sympathetic audience but was incendiary to the political establishment.[99] One part was a response to the Whig politician Edmund Burke, who had been critical of the French Revolution.[100] The other was an account of the Revolution written from Paine's perspective as an active participant and member of the French National Assembly. Sections were also critical of the English aristocracy and monarchy. It intensified the paranoia of the English ruling class, already at fever pitch following the French Revolution in 1789.[101]

In 1792 Paine was prosecuted *in absentia* for seditious libel. Erskine was put under considerable pressure by a hostile press to reject the brief. He was warned off by the Lord Chancellor, Lord Loughborough, while walking on Hampstead Heath. Erskine was attorney-general to the Prince of Wales, who also asked him to reject the case. His friends advised him that he was putting at risk prospective elevation to Lord Chancellor by continuing with it.

Records of the trial did not make it clear what prompted Erskine's most often quoted words.[102] It was said to have been in response to a jibe by the prosecutor, the Attorney-General, Sir Archibald Macdonald, who opined that, in the light of Paine's obvious guilt, it was 'disgraceful for Erskine to represent a cause he did not believe in'.[103] Erskine stated:

> I will for ever, at all hazards, assert the dignity, independence, and integrity of the English Bar, without which impartial justice, the most valuable part of the English constitution,

---

[96] ibid.
[97] Landsman (n 17) 590.
[98] ibid.
[99] It quickly sold a million copies to skilled workers, reformers and Protestant dissenters (G Rudé, *Revolutionary Europe: 1783–1815* (Oxford, Blackwell, 1964) 183)
[100] E Burke, *Reflections on the Revolution in France* (1790) www.bl.uk/collection-items/reflections-on-the-revolution-in-france-by-edmund-burke.
[101] MH Freedman, 'Henry Lord Brougham – Advocating At The Edge for Human Rights' (2007) 36 *Hofstra Law Review* 311, 313.
[102] The most complete record of the case does not contain the paragraph. See *The trial of Thomas Paine: for a libel, contained in The second part of rights of man, before Lord Kenyon, and a special jury, at Guildhall, December 18. With the speeches of the Attorney General and Mr. Erskine, at large* (Eighteenth Century Collections Online) https://quod.lib.umich.edu/e/ecco/004809446.0001.000/1:2?rgn=div1;view=fulltext.
[103] W Wesley Pue, 'Lawyers and Political Liberalism in Eighteenth and Nineteenth Century England' in TC Halliday and L Karpik (eds), *Lawyers and the Rise of Western Political Liberalism* (Oxford, Clarendon Press, 1997) 167.

can have no existence. From the moment that any advocate can be permitted to say that he *will* or will *not* stand between the Crown and the subject arraigned in the court where he daily sits to practise, from that moment the liberties of England are at an end. If the advocate refuses to defend, from what he may think of the charge or of the defence, he assumes the character of the judge; nay, he assumes it before the hour of judgment; and in proportion to his rank and reputation, puts the heavy influence of, perhaps, a mistaken opinion into the scale against the accused, in whose favour the benevolent principle of English law makes all presumptions ...[104]

Despite Erskine's nine-hour speech, Paine was convicted by a carefully selected jury.[105]

Outside the court a confused and chanting crowd damned Paine but exalted the king, freedom of the press and Erskine. They unhitched the horses from his carriage and carried it to his rooms in Serjeants Inn. In 1794 Erskine had more success representing other anti-establishment figures. He was briefed to represent seven members of a group of 12 leading radicals charged with treason.[106] Success in the first case also caused popular celebration. Two further successes led to the abandonment of the remaining cases and other prospective prosecutions. Hostettler suggested that this may have pre-empted a government 'reign of terror'.[107]

Watson dated the principle that barristers accepted clients, irrespective of considerations such as their reputation, to the Paine case, although he acknowledged that it was built on 'pre-existing rules of professional etiquette'.[108] This was consistent with earlier allusions to it, including John Cooke's defence to charges of regicide (see chapter two). If it was a strongly established feature of the barrister's role it was surprising that Erskine felt the need to defend the principle so vigorously. Nevertheless, his description of the obligation to represent was one of two principles which came to define the Bar. The other was strong and exclusive devotion to client interests, evoked by the term 'fearless advocacy' exemplified by Erskine in the *Shipley*. This was associated with Erskine's younger contemporary, Henry Brougham (1778–1868).

Brougham joined Lincoln's Inn in 1803 and was called to the Bar in 1808. He won his first Parliamentary seat in 1810 only two years after qualifying as a barrister. The case he was identified with was the so-called Trial of Queen Caroline. In 1785, at the age of 21, George, the Prince of Wales and heir apparent, secretly married Maria Fitzherbert, a Roman Catholic. This breached the Act of Settlement 1701, preventing a Catholic succeeding to the throne, and the Royal Marriages Act 1772, which required the heir to have the monarch's consent to marry. In 1795 George was persuaded to a dynastic marriage, to Caroline of Brunswick, without having obtained a divorce from Maria. George and Caroline hated each other at first sight and separated in 1796.

---

[104] Hostettler (n 89) 93, LP Stryker, *For the Defense: Thomas Erskine, the most enlightened liberal of his times, 1750–1823* (New York, Doubleday, 1949).

[105] He did not return to England but was elected to the French National Convention. In 1793 he was imprisoned following factional infighting but released after intervention by James Monroe, future President of the US.

[106] As was the custom in treason trials the seven were represented pro bono.

[107] Hostettler (n 89) xvii.

[108] Watson (n 50) ch 2.

In 1814 Caroline went to live in Italy and George explored the possibility of divorce. His agents found no definitive evidence of a rumoured affair with her Italian servant. When George came to the throne in 1820, Caroline returned to England, intending to be Queen. London was 'in a frenzy of delirious excitement' with crowds shouting 'The Queen! The Queen'.[109] Lord Eldon, the Lord Chancellor, wrote that 'the lower orders here are all the Queen's folk'.[110] George IV began divorce proceedings but, to avoid Caroline raising the matter of Fitzherbert, a Pain and Penalties Bill aimed for divorce by decree, removing Caroline's title. Caroline was represented by a legal team including Brougham.

Legal process required the Bill be presented in the House of Lords and then to the Commons. Following presentation of Caroline's petition:

> Mr. Brougham and Mr. Denman, her Majesty's Attorney and Solicitor-General, were then called in to support the petition, which prayed that their Lordships would not prosecute a secret inquiry against her, – and they began that series of orations in her defence, which raised the reputation of British forensic eloquence.[111]

Brougham's opening described loyalty to clients:

> An advocate, by the sacred duty which he owes his client, knows, in the discharge of that office, but one person in the world, that client and none other. To save that client at all expedient means – to protect that client at all hazards and costs to all others, and among others to himself – is the highest and most unquestioned of his duties; and he must not regard the alarm, the suffering, the torment, the destruction, which he may bring upon any other.[112]

Freedman related how Lord Erskine, now a member of the House of Lords, left the chamber in tears on the opening statements. It was, he explained, 'one of the most powerful orations that ever proceeded from human lips'.[113] Recovered, he spoke against the proceedings, noting their exceptional nature, the power arrayed against the Queen, including the King, and the 'unparalleled generality of accusation'.[114]

Erskine's proposal that the Queen be afforded the same rights as any subject in a criminal or treason case was defeated on a division. Having failed to secure details of the charges, Erskine examined witnesses against her, highlighting their 'fraud and perjury'.[115] The proceedings lasted 11 weeks and Caroline was cheered by crowds as she went to the House of Lords each day. Monroe Freedman suggested that Caroline was widely perceived to be guilty of the charges and was in fact so.[116] The Pain and Penalties Bill narrowly passed in the House of Lords but was withdrawn before being put before the House of Commons.

---

[109] Hostettler (n 89) 218.

[110] J Campbell, *The Lives of the Lord Chancellors and Keepers of the Great Seal of England: From the Earliest Times Till the Reign of George IV* Volume 10, 5th edn (London, John Murray, 1868) 6.

[111] ibid 10.

[112] This version is quoted in L Ray Patterson, 'Legal Ethics and the Lawyer's Duty of Loyalty' (1980) 29 *Emory Law Journal* 909, citing S Rogers, 'The Ethics of Advocacy' (1899) 15 *Law Quarterly Review* 259, 269.

[113] M Freedman, 'Henry Lord Brougham & Resolute Lawyering' (2010–2011) 37 *The Advocates' Quarterly* 403, 407.

[114] Hostettler (n 89) 220.

[115] ibid.

[116] Freedman (n 113) 407.

After withdrawal of the bill, addressing the Lords, Erskine rejoiced that his life whether 'for good or evil, has been passed under the sacred rule of law. In this moment I feel my strength renovated by that rule being restored ... There is an end to that horrid and portentous excrescence of a new law ... retrospective, oppressive and iniquitous. Our Constitution is once more safe'.[117] Weeks after the end of the Bill, George's coronation took place. Caroline was denied entry by armed sentries and was tended by George's retainer. Suspiciously, she fell ill that night and died soon after.

Although Brougham actively courted establishment displeasure and animosity by representing Caroline, his reference to the 'alarm, the suffering, the torment, the destruction' of the other was ambiguous.[118] Patterson interpreted the speech as meaning that a lawyer must 'tell the truth' notwithstanding the social or political cost.[119] Brougham suggested in his autobiography, that his statement was a 'menace'; a threat to expose the secret marriage, proving that George had forfeited the crown.[120] Monroe Freedman suggested that there was also an implicit threat of insurrection,[121] possible because of George's unpopularity and Caroline's popularity which carried into factions of the Army.[122] Whatever Brougham's precise intent, Freedman suggested that this was possibly the earliest case of 'graymail'; a threat to embarrass government if prosecution continued.[123]

C. Embedding in Culture

i. High Office

Pue suggested that the 'Whiggish' character of the Bar, exemplified by the principles of neutrality and partisan loyalty, was attributable to the likes of Erskine and Brougham occupying high offices of state.[124] Erskine entered Parliament twice as a Whig MP (1783 and 1790) becoming Lord Chancellor and a life peer in 1806, choosing as his motto 'trial by jury'. He lost the role in 1807 when the government fell, an event he may have unintentionally caused.[125] For 25 years either side of this brief tenure, the Tory Lord Eldon was Lord Chancellor. He shared the unpopularity of the administrations of George IV but was said to have impartially summed up the case

---

[117] Hostettler (n 89) 222 citing Hansard iii. 1747, 1820.
[118] Patterson (n 112) 909.
[119] ibid 910.
[120] MH Freedman, 'Henry Lord Brougham And Zeal' (2006) 34(4) *Hofstra Law Review* 1319 citing (at 1320 fn 8) H Brougham, *The Life And Times Of Henry Lord Brougham, Written By Himself* (1871) at 309 (see also Cambridge, Cambridge University Press, 2015).
[121] Freedman, ibid 1321, citing Brougham at 380–81.
[122] There were attacks on the residencies of the King and his allies, mutinies and, according to Brougham, a cavalry regiment prepared to 'fight up to their knees in blood for their queen' (Freedman, ibid 1320).
[123] ibid 1321.
[124] Pue (n 103).
[125] He had spoken to George III to dissuade him from resisting a bill allowing Catholics to hold rank in the Army, which apparently convinced the King a change of government was necessary (Hostettler (n 89) 188–91).

against Queen Caroline on the second reading of the Bill of Pains and Penalties.[126] Holding office prevented Erskine returning to practice at the Bar.

After serving several constituencies Brougham was Lord Chancellor between 1830 and 1833 when the Reform Act 1832 and Abolition of Slavery Act 1833 were passed. He was identified with campaigns to promote free trade and the equal rights of women. Freedman claimed his liberal credentials outshone those of Abraham Lincoln who, in 1858, made a 'white-supremacist' speech on slavery.[127] Brougham had demanded the total equality of slaves in the House of Lords 20 years before.[128] He also had many enemies, including in his own party, and his flawed character was partly to blame for the fall of the government in which he served. He became an active member of the House of Lords for 30 years from 1834, helping to create University College London and establishing Nice, in France as a resort.[129]

Beattie suggested that Garrow was encouraged to enter Parliament because the government was, in the wake of the French Revolution, gearing up to prosecuting political trials by the 1790s. He was both Solicitor General (1812–13) and Attorney General (1813–17) before becoming Baron of the Exchequer until 1832. Although he entered Parliament as a Whig, Garrow became an ally of Gladstone's Tory government in the 1790s, yet in 1811 Erskine praised him for knowing 'more of the real justice and policy of everything connected with the criminal law than any man I am acquainted with'.[130] It is undeniable that aspects of Whig philosophy, independence, individual rights, and anti-authoritarianism, were a current of Bar ideology. This built on aspects of group identity present before the advent of the adversarial system but which apparently grew because of it.

Appreciation of the achievements of the popular face of advocacy presented by Erskine and Brougham was widespread. According to Freedman, 'Erskine and independence' was a common toast at Inns of Court dinners during Brougham's time at the Bar. Despite political differences Erskine, Garrow and Brougham shared mutual admiration and a common view of proper practice at the Bar.[131] Twenty years after Garrow had appeared in his last case as defence advocate,[132] a House of Lords committee hearing evidence on the Prisoners Counsel Act 1836, was told that 'it is not every man who has the firmness to stand a speech with the power that Mr Garrow could exert, and which he always did exert in defence of his client'.[133] The Act arguably represented the triumph of a Bar reinventing itself as servant of the people.

---

[126] In anticipation of his coronation and by patent dated 7 July 1821 George IV made Scott Viscount Encombe.

[127] 'I am not nor ever have been in favor of making voters or jurors of negroes, nor of qualifying them to hold office ... I as much as any other man am in favor of having the superior position assigned to the white race' (Freedman (n 113)).

[128] 'The slave ... is as fit for his freedom as any English peasant, ay, or any Lord whom I now address. I demand his rights; I demand his liberty without stint ... I demand that your brother be no longer trampled upon as your slave!' (ibid).

[129] Freedman (n 113) 312.

[130] Beattie (n 19) 238–39 citing A Aspinall (ed), *The Correspondence of George, Prince of Wales* (London, Cassell, 1963).

[131] As illustrated by the Queen Caroline case, see JA Lovat-Fraser, *Erskine* (Cambridge, Cambridge University Press, 1932) 93.

[132] He became Kings Counsel in 1793 and took up civil practice.

[133] Beattie (n 19) 239 citing House of Lords Sessional Papers (130) 1835, xlvi, 317 (App IV): 52.

ii. The Prisoners Counsel Act 1836

By the 1830s lawyers could cross-examine witnesses but could not organise a defence or address juries on behalf of defendants. Between 1821 and 1828, and then between 1833 and 1836, a total of 10 bills were introduced, initially to allow representation by counsel in capital cases. These were sponsored by John Martin, a civil and religious freedom campaigner and independent member of Parliament, supported by several Whigs members, but rejected by a Tory dominated Commons.[134] Later in the first period, a bill allowing defence by counsel in all cases failed.

The campaign for representation was renewed with a more receptive government in 1833. Successive Bills were introduced by William Ewart, a Liverpudlian lawyer and MP. The campaigns involved arguments over principles and practicalities. Proponents of changing the law focused on the unfairness in distinguishing between capital felonies and misdemeanours which could both end in execution.[135] Opponents argued that prosecutors could be relied on to be fair to defendants and that judges acted as their counsel.[136] Despite warnings that lawyers made proceedings lengthy, the Prisoners Counsel Act 1836 finally provided a right to legal representation in all criminal cases.[137] Clauses enabling lawyers to be assigned by the court to impecunious defendants and allowing defence counsel to make a final submission to the jury did not survive the Parliamentary process.

VI. BUSINESS LAWYERS

By the seventeenth century various occupations could claim to be business lawyers. Solicitors were established by the sixteenth century as legal adviser and in the seventeenth century as specialists in chancery. Attorneys focused on common law[138] but were more numerous and their core work unsettled. From the sixteenth century successful barristers required clients to go through intermediaries. The OBSP showed that in the later 1700s, attorneys assumed a primary role in organising litigation[139] including the new tasks of collection, verification, and analysis of evidence and preparing witnesses. The appearance of lawyers spread to the country, but with attorneys often instructed to undertake both preparatory work and advocacy.[140]

As the 1700s progressed, increasing prosperity and the growth of business created demand for new kinds of legal services: transferring property, drafting wills, creating trusts and family settlements and moneylending.[141] From the 1750s attorneys became

---

[134] ibid 250–51.
[135] ibid 252.
[136] ibid 253.
[137] Prisoners Counsel Act 1836.
[138] CR Andrews, *Standards of Conduct for Lawyers: An 800-Year Evolution* (2004) 57 SMU Law Review 1385, 1392.
[139] In *Annesley* (OBSP 1742) an attorney had attended the coroner and interviewed witnesses for the defendant (Landsman (n 17) 545).
[140] Lemmings (n 42).
[141] AJ Schmidt, 'The Country Attorney in Late Eighteenth-Century England: Benjamin Smith of Horbling' (1990) 8(2) *Law and History Review* 237, 238.

generally more significant in rural settings.[142] This was probably due to the increase from the early 1600s in enclosure, where manorial land held by multiple tenants in common was taken into single ownership by the lord. The Glorious Revolution accelerated applications as Parliament became more amenable to the interests of landed gentry.[143]

Attorneys assisted landlords with applications,[144] coordinated consultation in parish meetings, prepared petitions to Parliament for an Enclosure Act, provided supporting documents, and made representations to local commissioners about the implementation of the scheme.[145] This experience advertised attorneys' utility to rural landowners as representatives, dependable figures to administer other local matters: clerking for Justices of the Peace at Quarter Sessions or appearing on turnpike or drainage commissions. This often led attorneys to become commissioners. This general elevation in status and trust made the attorney a suitable occupation for younger sons of noble families and for the gentry.[146] In 1804 a Stamp Act gave attorneys a legal monopoly of land transfers: conveyancing. With the massive growth in house building from the Victorian era, this would become bedrock of work for the next 200 years.[147]

By the early 1800s the enclosure process forced dispossessed peasants to industries providing work in the cities. In Karl Marx's critique, *Capital*, this was the proletariat[148] struggling under a legal structure forming the ideological superstructure of capitalism. Lawyers helped to turn the demands of the material world into abstract legal ideas, concepts, and institutions with the appearance of being natural, logical, and automatic. Attorneys advised and conducted transactions for the new corporations, constantly generating legal work.[149] They adapted the corporate form from its use by monasteries, gilds and boroughs, inspired by the religious corporation initially employed by Medieval Popes.[150] They gained a de facto monopoly of business transactions for the industrialist, financial, and merchant classes.

The modern English solicitors' profession was dominated by elite global firms originating in the pre-capitalist period. An example was Freshfields Bruckhaus Deringer, one of five City of London firms designated the 'magic circle', which claimed links with an attorney instructed by the Bank of England in 1743.[151] In 1788 an antecedent firm advised the entrepreneur Richard Arkwright, whose inventions ushered in the Industrial Revolution. In the early nineteenth century, as Freshfields, it acted for Lloyds of London. In 1974, it switched focus to corporate law in time for the 1980s 'Big Bang' de-regulation of financial services in the City of London. In 2000 it

---

[142] ibid.
[143] G Baars, *The Corporation, Law and Capitalism: A Radical Perspective on the Role of Law in the Global Political Economy* (Chicago, Haymarket Books, 2020) 53.
[144] Schmidt (n 141) 246.
[145] ibid 247.
[146] ibid 239.
[147] This was also the basis for an arrangement with the Bar that solicitors would not seek to be advocates in higher courts.
[148] K Marx, *Capital* (Hamburg, Verlag von Otto Meisner, 1867).
[149] Baars (n 143) 26.
[150] Baars suggests that in the 12th century Pope Innocent IV used the idea of the artificial corporate body for ecclesiastical chapters which were immune from religious punishment such as excommunication (ibid 46).
[151] Freshfields Bruckhaus Deringer, www.freshfields.com/en-gb/about-us/our-history/.

merged with two European firms to consolidate its global presence. It still acted for the Bank of England.

VII. DISCUSSION

An open society needed a system of justice perceived to be fair.[152] The advent of the adversary system from the 1720s was part of a shift in intellectual climate. Among a host of changes, considering defendants innocent until proven guilty[153] was an advance on its predecessor, but opinion was divided on whether decisions were based on accurate representations of facts. The changes did satisfy one of the central principles of the rule of law identified by Stephen Holmes; irrespective of the content of law procedural rules were applied impartially.[154] This alone could be said to have enhanced the freedom of subjects, while increased confidence, dignity and moral equality enhanced possibilities for social cooperation.[155] The adversary system was a central reason why, according to Pue, English barristers and a handful of attorneys played, between 1700 and 1800, 'a central – perhaps even indispensable – role in relation to three components of political liberalism: (1) Judicial constraint on executive power, (2) the creation of "publics", an essential feature of civil society, and (3) the enhancement of individual rights'.[156]

Krygier noted that from the medieval period to the eighteenth century, the rule of law was concerned with binding arbitrary monarchical power.[157] From the 1700s onwards, both in England and Europe, it focused on a second manifestation of arbitrariness, the clarity and transparency of law. Concern with the third manifestation, the execution of law, was present through the whole period, with lawyers advocating the necessity of jury trials, the presumption of innocence and the promotion of other defendants' rights. The adaptation of lawyers to participating in these systemic changes was illustrated by developments in the court work of barristers, in the rationalisation of the various groupings of business lawyers, and the settlement between these occupations leading to the split profession.[158]

Landsman speculated that the reason that the adversary system evolved was the advent of industrial production and the rise of the capitalist classes.[159] Features such as party control and neutral adjudication were particularly attractive at a time of profound social change. Pue suggested that procedural changes were a response to the

---

[152] Sward (n 5) 303.
[153] Beattie (n 19) 248.
[154] S Holmes, *Passions and Constraint: On the Theory of Liberal Democracy* (Chicago, University of Chicago Press, 1995)
[155] M Krygier, 'The Rule of Law: Pasts, Presents and Two Possible Futures' (2016) 12 *Annual Review of Law and Social Science* 199; P Gowder, *The Rule of Law in the Real World* (Cambridge, Cambridge University Press, 2016).
[156] Pue (n 103) 169–70.
[157] Krygier (n 155).
[158] Andrews 1402, citing D Duman, 'The English Bar in the Georgian Era' in WR Prest (ed), *Lawyers in Early Modern Europe and America* (London, Croom Helm, 1981) 86.
[159] S Landsman, 'A brief survey on the development of the adversary system' (1983) 44(3) *Ohio State Law Journal* 713.

exercise of state power and were liberal or proto-liberal in character.[160] Notable trials in the period reflected liberal hostility to state power and to class prerogative, manifesting 'faith in rationality (especially in this period as regards the process of "proof") and an overall inflation of the value attached to the individual'.[161]

In the second half of the 1700s the catastrophic loss of the American colonies shocked the British state and caused a period of severe government repression. Fear of revolution meant that questioning social conditions was treason. The homes of assumed revolutionary sympathisers were ransacked by mobs.[162] The treatment of the American colonies, and their eventual loss, caused distrust of the establishment in the intellectual classes. From the 1770s, tensions were reflected in a battle over reform of Parliament, the electoral system and institutional corruption. The result was a crisis from 1776 to 1783 in which many Whigs were in secret sympathy with radicals like Tom Paine. Later, the unpopularity of George IV made republicanism more attractive. Pue suggested that English lawyers of the late eighteenth and early nineteenth centuries were less radical than their French counterparts, but the ease with which barristers moved between the courtroom and politics helped to turn 'private grievance into *cause celebre*'[163] and refine the 'languages of liberty'.[164]

In the later 1700s, criminal trials became spectacles.[165] Lawyer control of the criminal courtroom provided opportunities to channel liberal hostility to class privilege as challenges to state power.[166] There was a dramatic increase in trials with a political dimension from 1787[167] and an increase in anti-government rhetoric in the Old Bailey Session Papers.[168] Garrow told a jury 'The King cannot break down, or infringe, or invade any one of the rules of evidence; he has no prerogative to say that innocence shall not be protected.'[169] Whig lawyers believed that constitutional objectives could be achieved as effectively through the courts as through Parliament.[170] This was the period in which the identity of the Bar was formed.

It is likely that the reputations of Erskine and Brougham helped to establish Bar identity, but the values represented were held widely. The failed Jacobite plot supported by Tory magnates, in 1715, led to Tories being mistrusted in public life, including at the Inns of Court for over 100 years[171] but, Pue suggested, the Benchers of the Inns were conservative and hostile to radicals.[172] The eventual triumph of the adversary system, represented by the Prisoners Counsel Act, may have been due to the support of a few individuals for the radical strand of Bar thinking. Although it was

---

[160] Pue (n 103) 181.
[161] ibid.
[162] Hostettler (n 89) 89.
[163] Pue (n 103) 178–79.
[164] ibid 180.
[165] ibid 175–76.
[166] ibid 180–81 citing Landsman (n 17) 503.
[167] Landsman (n 17) 530.
[168] ibid 513.
[169] *Reilly* OBSP 1787 (Landsman (n 17) 560).
[170] Pue (n 103) 184–85 citing Beattie (n 19) 238.
[171] R Ashcraft and MM Goldsmith, 'Locke, Revolution Principles, and the Formation of Whig Ideology' (1983) 26(4) *The Historical Journal* 773, 789.
[172] ibid.

promoted by Brougham, and seen as a triumph of Whig individualism, the Act split political and professional thought.[173]

Only two barristers gave evidence to a Royal Commission on prisoners' counsel, both against the changes, but the Bar was silent on the issue.[174] This was attributed to its fragmentation and public unpopularity. Crime victims were said to be reluctant to bring cases for fear that they or their witnesses would become confused by counsel's questions.[175] A Tory peer, Lord Wharncliff reflected a common view that 'permitting counsel to address juries on behalf of the party accused, would have the effect of increasing that uncertainty upon which professed rogues were accustomed to calculate'.[176] William Garrow, who had twice been Attorney-General and was now a senior judge, noted that judges could help defendants but not advise on their best defence.[177] This was influential and may have been decisive.

Systemic adaptation, reflecting greater attention to the rule of law, would not have occurred in an intellectual vacuum. Allowing accused parties to have lawyers reflected changes in patterns of thought. Dramatic changes in laws of evidence occurred in the eighteenth century, but whether this was due to the influence of lawyers or attempts by courts to control either them or juries was unclear. No doubt, the increasing rationality of evidential requirements reflected a more scientific intellectual climate, social opinion and, possibly, the desire of juries for a sound basis to execute others or deprive them of liberty. Thus, the adversary system was one of many ways to mitigate revulsion at the 'bloody code' of criminal law.[178]

Procedural change was a continuation of trends in relation to credibility issues.[179] After the Act of Settlement 1702 guaranteed their independence, judges precipitated moves towards procedural protections for clients. The OBSP showed higher expectations of party responsibility, participation, and initiative,[180] but the pace of change was slow. Blackstone noted that the fact that capital offenders had no counsel 'unless some point of law shall arise proper to be debated' was 'not at all of a piece with the rest of the humane treatment of prisoners by the English law' nor 'part of our ancient law'. He added that 'to say the truth, the judges themselves are so sensible of this defect in our modern practice, that they seldom scruple to allow a prisoner counsel to stand by'.[181] Judges strived to ensure trials happened, persuading those admitting guilt of capital offences to change their plea.[182]

The development of the adversarial trial demonstrated the capacity of the common law to develop systems and doctrine incrementally. Even so, it was unlikely

---

[173] CC Griffiths, 'The Prisoners' Counsel Act 1836: Doctrine, Advocacy and the Criminal Trial' (2014) 4(2) *Law, Crime and History* 28, 40.
[174] ibid.
[175] Beattie (n 19) 236.
[176] HL Deb 14 July 1836 vol 35, 171.
[177] Beattie (n 19) 254.
[178] See eg Griffiths (n 173) 39.
[179] For example, by the later 17th century there was recognition of the flaw in the medieval practice of treating all evidence given on oath equally.
[180] Landsman (n 17) 519.
[181] W Blackstone, *Commentaries on the Laws of England* (1765–1770). Book the Fourth – Chapter: The Twenty Seventh: Of Trial and Conviction.
[182] Langbein (n 20) 279.

that change would have occurred without some wider intellectual consensus. Shapiro's research, which examined the influence of values external to the justice system,[183] showed that shifts in attitude to the standard of proof resulted from intellectual developments outside of the courts, and therefore beyond the internal logic of the common law.

Shapiro's focus was the phrase 'moral certainty' which, with reasonable doubt, was part of the instruction to juries in most states of the US in 1986.[184] In 1680, Whig lawyers referred to the notion of a 'satisfied conscience', linked to rational persuasion by credible testimony, when considering issues of guilt.[185] This refined Locke's observation, discussed in Part I, that it was possible to be 'morally certain' of a proposition based on compelling witness evidence. In eighteenth century England Christian jurors were afraid of eternal damnation should they give incorrect verdicts, particularly for cases that could end in the execution of the accused, so called 'blood crimes'.[186]

Authors found different origins of the reasonable doubt formula, most religious.[187] Shapiro suggested that it assuaged religious uncertainty, making it easier for those of conscience to convict. It was, Whitman said, not a proof procedure but a 'moral comfort procedure' aimed at relieving 'the moral anxieties of persons who feared engaging in acts of judgment', sixteenth century judges or early modern criminal jurors.[188] Jurors 'could convict without risk to the safety of their salvation, as long as their "doubts" were not "reasonable"'.[189] Therefore, Whitman suggested:

> In its original form, it had nothing to do with maintaining the rule of law in the sense that we use the phrase, and nothing like the relationship we imagine to the values of liberty. It was the product of a world troubled by moral anxieties that no longer trouble us much at all.[190]

This evidence suggested to Shapiro that law did not develop autonomously but borrowed key ideas from other areas of thought.

The creation of a new professional identity of solicitors in the 1830s reflected their growing significance as servants of the new economic order. The industrial revolution fuelled the rapid acceleration of capitalism and the demand for new kinds of legal services. With the rapid growth and dominance of the capitalist system, solicitors

---

[183] B Shapiro, '"To a Moral Certainty": Theories of Knowledge and Anglo-American Juries 1600–1850' (1986) 38(1) *Hastings Law Journal* 153, 154.

[184] In 1986, California had recently proposed removing moral certainty from the jury instruction because it was not understood (ibid).

[185] ibid 165.

[186] JQ Whitman, 'What Are the Origins of Reasonable Doubt?' (History News Network, George Mason University, 25 February 2008) https://digitalcommons.law.yale.edu/cgi/viewcontent.cgi?referer=https://www.google.com/&httpsredir=1&article=1000&context=fss_papers.

[187] ibid (at 10–11 cites Franklin as a proponent of a 16th century root (J Franklin, *The Science of Conjecture: Evidence and Probability before Pascal* (Baltimore, Johns Hopkins Press, 2001) 63) and B Shapiro, *Probability and Certainty in Seventeenth-Century England: A Study of the Relationships between Natural Science, Religion, History, Law and Literature* (Princeton, NJ, Cambridge University Press, 1983) 167–93 for evidence of a 17th century origin.

[188] Whitman (n 186) 9.

[189] ibid 7.

[190] ibid 8.

were indispensable. But for Marx, lawyers served a bourgeoise expansion obtaining, as he observed, with the other 'unproductive classes [civil servants, physicians, scholars] ... a share of the surplus product, of the capitalist's *revenue*'.[191]

VIII. CONCLUSION

From the seventeenth century, both English legal professions changed identifying characteristics in response to social change. First in time were the barristers, whose role in creating the adversary system reflected the growing individualistic and entrepreneurial nature of society.[192] The flexibility of the common law allowed a critical transformation, taking a medieval criminal trial procedure and, through the involvement of prosecution and defence counsel,[193] achieving a clearer focus on evidence, greater awareness of issues of cogency, witness credibility and probability.[194]

By the early 1830s, right to counsel for criminal trials had been established, control of process had largely passed from judges to the litigants' lawyers and evidential and procedural rules had been developed.[195] A party was encouraged to argue selfishly and entitled to a statement of the reasons confirming that 'the decision was based on the relevant substantive and procedural rules, and that his arguments were considered'.[196] This expanded a culture of rights, considered in the next chapter.

As agents of business for the merchant classes and bourgeoisie, solicitors came closer to Halliday and Karpik's characterisation of nineteenth century lawyers' work: accommodating capitalism to the framework of the rule of law.[197] They depended heavily on 'integrity', the assurance, as Lord Bingham said in the 1990s, that every member of the profession, 'of whatever standing, may be trusted to the ends of the earth'.[198] This emphasised legality as much as rights, a dual focus reflected in solicitors' obligation to preserve the secrecy of their communications with clients from courts.[199] Legal Professional Privilege was a legacy of the Elizabethan period, but became a cornerstone of the rule of law.[200] Both barristers and solicitors were bound by it, but solicitors were more likely repositories of intimate private and business secrets, the subject of chapter eight of this book.

---

[191] K Marx, *The Grundrisse* Notebook 4, 1857–22 January 1858 (1857).
[192] Sward (n 5).
[193] Langbein (n 20).
[194] Beattie (n 19), citing Shapiro (n 183).
[195] Pue (n 103) 180–81 citing Landsman (n 17).
[196] Sward (n 5) 310.
[197] TC Halliday and L Karpik, 'Postscript: Lawyers, Political Liberalism, and Globalisation' in Halliday and Karpik (n 103) 349; D Nicol, *The Constitutional Protection of Capitalism* (Oxford, Hart Publishing, 2010) 38.
[198] *Bolton v The Law Society* [1994] 1 WLR 512 CA (Civ Div) 512, 518.
[199] Solicitors' competitor professions, such as accountants, could not claim LPP when providing legal advice (see *Prudential PLC and Prudential (Gibraltar) Ltd v Special Commissioner of Income Tax and Philip Pandolfo (HM Inspector of Taxes)* [2013] UKSC 1, [2013] 2 AC 185) advantaging elite London firms in competition for international clients.
[200] *Three Rivers District Council & Others v Governor and Company of the Bank of England (No. 6)* [2004] UKHL 48, [2005] 1 AC 610 (House of Lords) per Lord Scott para 34.

7
Individuality

I. INTRODUCTION

DICEY ASSERTED THAT constitutional rules were 'the consequence of the rights of individuals, as defined and enforced by the courts', suggesting a core of recognised constitutional rights. Bingham also thought the rule of law must incorporate citizens' fundamental rights.[1] What was the scope of these fundamental rights? Enlightenment scholars urged that liberty required that 'every man may enjoy the same rights as are granted to others'.[2] The logic of this was that society should allow individuals to live a preferred life, but since different people valued different things, those who had rights and which rights were recognised was a political issue depending, as Kant argued, on social circumstances or as 'reason' revealed new rights.

II. THEORY

The concept of individuality referred to characteristics sufficiently marked to distinguish one member of a group from others. Human societies prioritised individuality to different degrees. Classical societies of the Eastern Mediterranean diminished human agency, attributing events to fate. They recognised a public sphere and a domestic sphere related to the institutions of the family or the city. Both were hierarchical and institutionalised inequality. Siedentop argued Christianity brought about a focus on the individual, Saint Paul claiming that God created humans equally, with free will.[3] Ideas of agency and moral equality appealed to those marginalised in classical society, such as women and slaves.[4] Martyrdom emphasised the power of the individual, democratising heroism.[5]

---

[1] T Bingham, *The Rule of Law* (London, Penguin, 2011) 68.
[2] J Locke, *Letter Concerning Toleration* (1689) 101 cited by R Faulkner, 'Faith of Our Modern Fathers: Bacon's Progressive Hope and Locke's Liberal Christianity' in DA Gish and DP Klinghard (eds), *Resistance to Tyrants, Obedience to God: Reason, Religion and Republicanism, at America's Founding* (Lanham US, Lexington Books, 2013) 38.
[3] L Siedentop, *Inventing the Individual: The Origins of Western Liberalism* (London, Allen Lane, 2014).
[4] ibid 66.
[5] In classical thinking the hero was an aristocratic warrior, an ideal characterised by Achilles. Christian martyrdom was available to anybody.

Individualism became entrenched in the Roman social structure and institutionalised in the church. In the early medieval period, the four Catholic mendicant orders were influenced by newly rediscovered Aristotelian philosophy. Thomas Aquinas (1225–74), a Dominican friar, formulated principles of Natural Law emanating from God but interpreted by human rationality. The basic principle was to do good and to avoid evil. Aquinas held that people intuitively knew good actions; life, procreation, knowledge, society, and reasonable conduct.[6] The Franciscan order of monks promoted a notion of justice built on individual conscience.[7] During the seventeenth century, Enlightenment thinkers questioned religious conformity from the perspective of reason.

In *Tractatus Theologico-Politicus* (*TTP*) Baruch Spinoza (1632–77) criticised established religion for confusing theology, conformity to established teaching, and philosophy, based on rationality.[8] Jonathan Israel identified two ways in which this influenced radical attitudes to religion.[9] First, it contradicted philosophers, such as Descartes, who tried to reconcile reason with traditional religious teaching.[10] Secondly, God was an abstract entity, properly understood as Nature, which was impersonal, immune to appeal by prayer, and incapable of intervening in everyday events. There was no divine plan and no meaning in the events of nature, which were projections of human fears and desires. This justified rejection of religious authority and practice.

Israel contended that Spinoza encouraged religious scepticism leading to separation of the state and religion. His work contributed to that of John Locke[11] who argued that people could not be brought to belief by force.[12] Religious choice was supported by European Protestant scholars such as Hugo Grotius (1583–1645) and Samuel Pufendorf (1632–94), whose natural law was distinct from divine law, civil law, and national law. This laid the foundation for the theory of rights of Immanuel Kant (1697–1737), a secular variant of Christian natural law theory. Kant's conception of rights derived from his notion of a moral law, a version of Aristotle's good life, in which autonomous individuals chose to do good.

Kant argued that rights supported autonomy and enlightenment.[13] They prevailed over sociocultural and political arrangements[14] including the claims of

---

[6] DJ O'Connor, *Aquinas and Natural Law* (London, Macmillan International Higher Education, 1967).
[7] Siedentop (n 3) 77.
[8] B Spinoza, *Tractatus Theologico-Politicus* (Hamburg, Henricus Künraht, 1670).
[9] JI Israel, *Radical Enlightenment: Philosophy and the Making of Modernity, 1650–1750* (Oxford, Oxford University Press, 2001).
[10] Spinoza thought that Descartes' contention that the mind and body were distinct (and that humans could therefore possess a soul) would lead to a failure of coordination. He thought humans had no free will but did have freedom of action. They misunderstood their appetites or motivations but became more virtuous by their efforts to actively gain knowledge.
[11] J Locke, *Letter Concerning Toleration 1689 American History*, www.let.rug.nl/usa/documents/1651-1700/john-locke-letter-concerning-toleration-1689.php.
[12] The second proposition was doubted contemporaneously, and more recently (see Locke's Political Philosophy *Stanford Encyclopaedia of Philosophy*, https://plato.stanford.edu/entries/locke-political/, citing J Proast (1690), 'The Argument of the Letter concerning Toleration Briefly Consider'd and Answered' in M Goldie (ed), *The Reception of Locke's Politics*, Volume 5 (London, Pickering & Chatto, 1999 and 1993) and J Waldron, 'Locke, Toleration, and the Rationality of Persecution' in *Liberal Rights: Collected Papers 1981–1991* (Cambridge, Cambridge University Press, 1993) 88.
[13] G Beck, 'Immanuel Kant's Theory of Rights' (2006) 19(4) *Ratio Juris* 371, 374.
[14] ibid 371.

the majority.[15] Kant acknowledged that societies needed order, and reasoned that a liberal, republican society would emerge 'as the result of spontaneous social, economic and political development'.[16] The legitimacy of the state and law was guaranteed by negative liberty, the right to be left alone by government, and a fair system of justice.[17] The pursuit of economic self-interest was subject to the overriding norm of fairness[18] so that welfare and education would help individuals achieve their potential. In *Esprit de Lois*, Montesquieu argued that the state owed citizens 'nourishment, suitable clothing, and the opportunity for a healthy life'.[19]

Montesquieu saw unnecessary law as consistent with tyranny: it should be as easy as possible to live without committing crime. Therefore, law should not establish offences that were difficult to prove or where it was difficult to establish innocence.[20] Montesquieu advocated focusing state power on threats to public order and security. In theory, the low volume of law may lead to people living freer lives with less likelihood that criticising the state or its agents would be a crime. Law should not be vague, inhibit public debate, require positive acts, or penalise thoughts or religious beliefs.

From the 1760s, the liberal view was projected to the colonies in Blackstone's *Commentaries*. Building on foundations laid by Hobbes, Grotius and Putendorf, Blackstone claimed that rights were inherent in the state of nature. He stated the principal aim of society was to 'protect individuals in the enjoyment of those absolute rights, which were vested in them by the immutable laws of nature'.[21] The 'absolute rights of man, considered as a free agent ... consisted 'in a power of acting as one thinks fit, without any restraint or control, ...' consistent with his 'faculty of freewill'.[22] These rights were, Blackstone claimed, confirmed in the Act of Settlement 1702, protecting 'the birth-right of the people of England according to the ancient doctrine of the common law'.[23]

III. RIGHTS AND LIBERTIES

Isaiah Berlin suggested that the difference between negative and positive liberty was that the first required government to leave you alone and the second to do something

---

[15] ibid 371.
[16] ibid 373.
[17] ibid 376 citing C Taylor, 'Kant's Theory of Freedom' in Z Pelczynski and J Gray (eds), *Conceptions of Liberty in Political Philosophy* (London, Athlone, 1984) 118.
[18] S Holmes, *Passions and Constraint: On the Theory of Liberal Democracy* (Chicago, University of Chicago Press, 1995) 27.
[19] DP Currie, 'Positive and Negative Constitutional Rights' (1986) 53 *U Chi L Rev* 864, 867 citing Baron De Montesquieu *Esprit Des Lois* (V Pritchard ed, 1898).
[20] For example, Law should not criminalise witchcraft, which was difficult to prove, or sodomy, which might encourage 'witnesses' to lie (*Spirit of the Laws* 12.6).
[21] W Blackstone, *Blackstone's Commentaries on the Laws of England* (1765–1770) Book the First – Chapter: The First. Of the Absolute Rights of Individuals Chapter 1, https://avalon.law.yale.edu/subject_menus/blackstone.asp.
[22] ibid.
[23] ibid.

to help you.[24] Civil liberties and other 'basic' rights tend to be negative, while other categories, particularly social rights tend to be positive. The Universal Declaration of Human Rights 1948 set out a schema covering civil, economic, political, cultural and social rights. Civil rights and property rights, which fell in the economic classification, tended to be first chronologically, followed by political, cultural and social rights. Most of these areas developed in interconnected fits and starts, so claims to religious freedom, a cultural right, necessarily involved assertion of civil rights.

A. Civil Liberties

The Bill of Rights 1688 entrenched negative liberty, providing that 'the pretended power of suspending the laws and dispensing with laws by regal authority without consent of Parliament is illegal'. By the mid-eighteenth century, Blackstone confidently asserted in his *Commentaries* that liberties, the 'absolute rights of every Englishman', were 'coeval with our form of government' and that, if suppressed by tyranny, when 'the struggle have been over, the balance of our rights and liberties has settled to its proper level … and asserted in parliament, as often as they were thought to be in danger'.[25]

Blackstone advocated only such human laws as were 'necessary and expedient for the general advantage of the public', so that every 'wanton and causeless restraint of the will of the subject, whether practiced by a monarch, a nobility, or a popular assembly, is a degree of tyranny'.[26] There was only a need for 'legal obedience and conformity' necessary to secure 'political or civil liberty'.[27] Blackstone gave two examples of legal restrictions consistent with tyranny or liberty. Edward IV's ban on anyone below aristocratic station wearing 'pikes upon their shoes or boots of more than two inches in length' was oppressive, but Charles II's decree that the dead only be buried in woollens was 'consistent with public liberty' because it encouraged a trade essential to the good of the nation.[28]

As negative rights, basic liberties were difficult to remove, but could be interpreted differently. Blackstone argued for the accused's right to silence, arguing that 'his fault was not be wrung out of himself, but rather to be discovered by other means, and other men'.[29] Blackstone said that in finding its verdict the jury ought to be cautious in its acceptance of 'presumptive evidence of felony … for the law holds, that it is better that ten guilty persons escape, than that one innocent suffer'.[30]

---

[24] I Berlin, 'Two Concepts of Liberty' in *Four Essays on Liberty* (London, Oxford University Press, 1969) 118.
[25] Blackstone (n 21).
[26] ibid.
[27] ibid.
[28] ibid.
[29] W Blackstone, *Commentaries on the Laws of England: A Facsimile of the First Edition of 1765–1769* (Chicago, University of Chicago Press, 1979) Volume 5, Amendment VIII, Document 4, http://press-pubs.uchicago.edu/founders/documents/amendVIIIs4.html.
[30] Blackstone (n 21) Book IV, Ch 27, 352 (and see JM Beattie, 'Scales of Justice: Defense Counsel and the English Criminal Trial in the Eighteenth and Nineteenth Centuries' (1991) 9(2) *Law and History Review* 221, fn 74).

Jeremy Bentham criticised this as an incorrect framing of the issue.[31] Rather, the balance was between freedom of the innocent versus the specific harm and general alarm caused by acquitted criminals.

Bentham reluctantly accepted that the presumption of innocence provided a fixed starting point,[32] but saw the right to silence as residual distrust of courts like Star Chamber rather than rational policy. 'Sentimental' reasons for retaining such a rule included guilty persons not being the cause of their own conviction and providing a fair chance of escape (the foxhunter's reason). He considered both plainly wrong, arguing that silence should at least count against a defendant.

Recent legal philosophers, such as HLA Hart, disagreed with Bentham on the right to silence, conceding that if he 'fails to persuade he still forces us to think'.[33] The Law Commission was at the time proposing amendments, but Hart argued: 'that there is something profoundly wrong with a legal system which imposes on citizens, guilty of no crime, duties sanctioned by the risk of conviction to give an account of themselves to the police; and that a society where this was accepted with docility, even if it meant that the guilty never escaped conviction, would be a worse society than one where there was a right to silence even though some criminals escape'.[34] In the 1990s the right to silence was amended by statute in the UK in line with Bentham's argument that inferences should be drawn from silence,[35] but it remained a fundamental constitutional right in the US.

There was recurring tension between rights and executive power in time of emergency. In the US, Abraham Lincoln suspended *habeus corpus*, regarded as *the* guarantee of liberty, during the Civil War, so that Southern sympathisers could be detained.[36] Lincoln reasoned: 'Must I shoot a simple-minded soldier boy who deserts, while I must not touch a hair of a wiley agitator who induces him to desert? ... I think that in such a case, to silence the agitator, and save the boy, is not only constitutional, but, withal, a great mercy'.[37] In Britain the outbreak of World War II in 1939 led to restrictions on civil liberties widely considered necessary. Against a background of anxiety that 'liberties shall not be unnecessarily sacrificed'[38] Parliament passed the Emergency Powers (Defence) Act 1939.

Draft subordinate regulations proposed under the emergency legislation allowed the Secretary of State wide powers of detention when satisfied it was 'necessary ... for public safety or the defence of the Realm'[39] but this was amended so that he needed

---

[31] HLA Hart, 'Bentham and the Demystification of the Law' (1973) 36(1) *The Modern Law Review* 2, 14.
[32] Beattie (n 30) 249–50.
[33] Hart (n 31) 17.
[34] ibid.
[35] Criminal Justice and Public Order Act 1994, ss 34–39.
[36] M DeLong, 'To Save a House Divided: Lincoln's Suspension of Habeas Corpus' (1996) *Senior Research Projects* 118, https://knowledge.e.southern.edu/senior_research/118.
[37] ibid citing F.J Jacob, *President Lincoln's Views* (Peoria, Illinois, Jacob's own press, 1929) 1–2.
[38] Frank Kingsley Griffith, MP, House of Commons Debate, 31 October 1939, 7.14pm. (cited in *Liversidge v Anderson*, Sir Harry Gibbs Legal Heritage Centre, Supreme Court Library, Queensland, Australia, https://legalheritage.sclqld.org.au/liversidge-v-anderson-1942-ac-206).
[39] Defence (General) Regulations 1939.

'reasonable cause to believe any person to be of hostile origin or associations'.[40] Jack Perlzweig, known as Robert Liversidge, was arrested without formal charge or stated reason and held for over a year.[41] He brought an action for false imprisonment. In a previous case[42] the Home Secretary had produced an affidavit claiming he had 'considered reports and information from persons in responsible positions'[43] but no grounds were offered for holding Liversidge. Even so, the Court of Appeal refused to inquire further.

In November 1941, the House of Lords considered whether the Home Secretary had 'reasonable cause to believe' Liversidge had hostile associations. It was argued that, in *habeas corpus* cases, any interference with liberty must be justified. The decision followed the line taken by the Court of Appeal, Viscount Maugham stating that 'if there is a reasonable doubt as to the meaning of the words used, we should prefer a construction which will carry into effect the plain intention of those responsible for the Order in Council rather than one which will defeat that intention'.[44] The Home Secretary must have acted on confidential information which should not leak out[45] and if, acting in good faith, and he thought he had reasonable cause to believe it, the onus was on the appellant to show otherwise.

Lord Macmillan thought that '[t]he liberty which we so justly extol is itself the gift of the law and as Magna Carta recognizes may by the law be forfeited or abridged'.[46] Detention was a relatively mild deprivation when citizens could be conscripted, or their goods requisitioned. Lord Atkin's dissent in Liversidge was controversial. The minister's claim to an absolute power of detention had 'so far as I know, never been given before to the executive, and I shall not apologize for taking some time to demonstrate that no such power is in fact given to the minister by the words in question'.[47] Atkin argued that 'the words in question' had only one plain and natural meaning so that there was a clear justiciable issue.

Atkin asked whether a person might be accused of having a 'hostile origin' when they '… had been a loyal subject for thirty or forty years, was a supporter of this country's war effort, and had never taken any part in any hostile activity'.[48] He protested 'against a strained construction … giving an uncontrolled power of imprisonment to the minister'.[49] The appellant's right to the particulars justifying his detention was based on '… a principle which again is one of the pillars of liberty in that in English law every imprisonment is prima facie unlawful and that it is for a person directing imprisonment to justify his act'.[50]

---

[40] ibid reg 18B
[41] *Liversidge, Appellant v Sir John Anderson and Another Respondents* [1942] AC 206.
[42] *Rex v Secretary of State for Home Affairs. Ex parte Lees* [1941] 1 KB 72.
[43] ibid 216.
[44] ibid 219.
[45] ibid 221.
[46] ibid 257.
[47] ibid 226.
[48] ibid 243.
[49] ibid 244.
[50] ibid 245.

Lord Atkin criticised both the prosecution and his fellow judges:

> I view with apprehension the attitude of judges who on a mere question of construction when face to face with claims involving the liberty of the subject show themselves more executive minded than the executive. Their function is to give words their natural meaning, not, perhaps, in war time leaning towards liberty, but ... [i]n a case in which the liberty of the subject is concerned, [constrained by] ... the natural construction of the statute. In this country, amid the clash of arms, the laws are not silent. They may be changed, but they speak the same language in war as in peace. It has always been one of the pillars of freedom, one of the principles of liberty for which on recent authority we are now fighting, that the judges are no respecters of persons and stand between the subject and any attempted encroachments on his liberty by the executive, alert to see that any coercive action is justified in law. In this case I have listened to arguments which might have been addressed acceptably to the Court of King's Bench in the time of Charles I.[51]

The Lord Chancellor, Viscount Simon, tried to persuade Atkin to delete a passage from Lewis Carol's *Through the Looking Glass* in which Humpty Dumpty told Alice that a word meant 'just what I choose it to mean'.[52] The Lord Chief Justice censured him for his reference to executive minded judges. Many of Atkin's judicial peers ostracised him. The press was divided as were junior judges, lawyers, and academics. Among the letters of support Atkin received one, from Stable J, stated: 'Bacon, I think, said the judges were the lions under the Throne, but the House of Lords has reduced us to mice squeaking under a chair in the Home Office.'[53]

The Times published a letter from Viscount Maugham which he claimed was necessary because prosecution counsel could not respond, even to 'so grave an animadversion' as the allusion to Charles I's courts. He had, he said, 'listened to every word of their arguments, and I did not hear from them, or anyone else, anything which could justify such a remark'.[54] Maugham was himself criticised in Parliament for the letter.[55] In his review of a book by AWB Simpson, Sir Stephen Sedley suggested that the case was a rare aberration in the 'long sleep' of judicial review for 70 years after World War I.[56]

Sedley attributed judicial alignment with the executive, a 'process of judicial abdication', to the confidence and trust judges reposed in 'an Oxbridge-led professional civil service'.[57] He thought Atkin was probably not opposed to the outcome but rather the process. Therefore, while Atkin's language 'still cheers lawyers and judges up when the system comes under criticism', he would have been quite content had the executive invoked the public interest, and more specifically national security,

---

[51] ibid 244.
[52] Lord Bingham of Cornhill, 'The Case of Liversidge v. Anderson: The Rule of Law Amid the Clash of Arms' (2009) 43(1) *The International Lawyer* 33, citing RFV Heuston and A Goodhart, *The Lives of the Lord Chancellors: 1940–1970* (Oxford, Clarendon Press, 1987) 59.
[53] Bingham ibid 37.
[54] Cited in *Liversidge v Anderson*, Sir Harry Gibbs Legal Heritage Centre (n 38).
[55] ibid.
[56] S Sedley, 'When Judges Sleep' (1993) 15(11) *London Review of Books*, reviewing AWB Simpson, *In the Highest Degree Odious: Detention without Trial in Wartime Britain* (New York, Clarendon Press of Oxford University Press, 1992).
[57] ibid 28.

to justify non-disclosure. Lord Atkin's judgment was, however, significant in the common law diaspora, notably in India, Australia, New Zealand, Canada and the US.[58] Considering objectively whether there were reasonable grounds for executive decisions became orthodox.[59]

Later events vindicated Atkin's insistence that the executive decisions should be justified whatever the circumstances. The file of evidence against Liversidge was later found to be insubstantial; eight short paragraphs contained one with vague allegations of association with Germans connected to the Nazi security services. The remainder was 'a combination of antisemitism and character assassination'.[60] This may have reflected a casual wartime attitude to grounds for internment, even among notable judges,[61] but there were also reasons to doubt the motives of Anderson, the Home Secretary and the named defendant.

Anderson had expressed support for Nazi domestic policy[62] and, at a Bengal conference in 1937, advocated suppressing political parties and trade unions and arresting their leaderships, as in Germany.[63] The Emergency Powers regulations were aimed at organisations like Oswald Moseley's British Union of Fascists (BUF), but he had argued in Cabinet against r18(B) on the ground that there was no evidence that the BUF was engaged in disloyal activity. When, in June 1940, Anderson acquired new powers to ban organisations he delayed banning the BUF.

B. Economic Rights

Economic rights, including rights to private property and the use of assets, were, according to Blackstone, among the oldest and most basic of rights. He thought that property would be held in common in the state of nature, but citing Grotius and Puffendorf, explained the vesting of property on a 'right of occupancy'.[64] The need for 'constant subsistence' would lead to a concept of title to the land, for who would endure the 'pains of tilling it, if another might watch an opportunity to seize upon and enjoy the product of his industry, art, and labour?'.[65] Without the notion of property 'the world must have continued a forest, and men have been mere animals of prey'.[66]

---

[58] ibid 44.
[59] eg *George v Rockett* (1990) 170 CLR 104 (Supreme Court of Queensland).
[60] Sedley (n 56).
[61] Sedley pointed to evidence in Lord Denning's account of his wartime work, legal adviser to the North East region, where he ordered detention of a parson under r18(b) because he holidayed in Germany.
[62] A member of Hugh Gaitskell's Cabinet he was initially kept on by Churchill (Sedley (n 56)).
[63] Sedley (n 56), citing M Carritt, *A Mole in the Crown: Memoires of a British official in India who worked with the communist underground in the 1930s* (East Sussex, London, Rupa 1986).
[64] Sir William Blackstone, *Commentaries on the Laws of England in Four Books. Notes selected from the editions of Archibold, Christian, Coleridge, Chitty, Stewart, Kerr, and others, Barron Field's Analysis, and Additional Notes, and a Life of the Author by George Sharswood. In Two Volumes* (Philadelphia, JB Lippincott Co, 1893). Vol. 1 – Books I & II. Chapter I: Of Property, In General. https://oll.libertyfund.org/page/blackstone-on-property-1753.
[65] ibid 8.
[66] ibid.

Blackstone argued that natural justice led to temporary possession of other property creating rights superior to those of anyone else.[67] The notion of ownership led to the possibility of and transfer of and hence, 'commercial traffic, and the reciprocal transfer of property by sale, grant, or conveyance', for 'it was found, that what became inconvenient or useless to one man, was highly convenient and useful to another, who was ready to give in exchange for it some equivalent that was equally desirable to the former proprietor'.[68]

Blackstone applied his view that all private property in land was derived directly or remotely from the sovereign power of a country to colonised land. This led to several blind spots. He noted that Native Americans recognised no private property in land; 'but the territory or hunting-grounds belonged to the tribe, who alone had the power to dispose of them. In the confederacy of the Six Nations, this power was vested in the general council-fire, so that the separate tribes had no right to sell or transfer'.[69] He held that discovery of foreign lands did not give title to the explorer but 'to the nation to which he belongs or under whose flag he sails'.[70] A more contentious property issue for liberals of the period was posed by slavery. Britain was active in transporting hundreds of thousands of slaves from Africa to America and the West Indies until the trade ended in 1807.[71]

Slaves were property and denied basic rights but might become legally emancipated. The US Supreme Court considered an emancipation claim in 1857 in which one of the applicants, Dred Scott, was born in Virginia around 1799 as the property of Peter Blow.[72] Scott was sold to military surgeon Dr John Emerson in 1830 because of the Blow family's financial problems. Emerson was posted in Illinois and Wisconsin, a Northern part of the vast territory covered by the Louisiana purchase of 1803. Slavery was prohibited there by the Missouri Compromise of 1820.[73] While there, Emerson married Irene Sandford and Scott married Harriet Robinson, another slave, before returning to St Louis in 1842. Emerson died and Scott, his wife Harriet and their two children were hired out to other families by Irene Emerson.

In 1846, the Scotts launched actions claiming that their time in free territories brought them within a principle applied by some courts at the time 'once free, always free'.[74] John Anderson, Scott's abolitionist minister, collaborated with Peter Blow's children to finance the action. After contradictory decisions in lower courts the Missouri Supreme Court denied relief. The US Supreme Court upheld that decision on the ground that people of African descent, free or enslaved, could not sue in federal courts because they were not citizens. The Fifth Amendment, it was said,

---

[67] ibid.
[68] ibid 9.
[69] Blackstone (n 64) fn 1.
[70] ibid.
[71] D Eltis, *Economic Growth and the Ending of the Transatlantic Slave Trade* (New York, Oxford University Press, 1987).
[72] *Dred Scott v Sandford* 60 U.S. (19 How.) 393 (1857).
[73] This legislation provided that all the territory gained in the Louisiana purchase from France, apart from Missouri, would be slave free.
[74] Missouri Supreme Court decisions including *Winny v Whitesides* (1824) were precedents (Missouri State Archives, 'Missouri's Dred Scott Case, 1846–1857') www.sos.mo.gov/archives/resources/africanamerican/scott/scott.asp.

protected slave owner rights not to have their property taken without due process. When the decision in *Dred Scott* was handed down in 1857, Irene had married her second husband, congressman and abolitionist Calvin Chaffee. The Scott family were sold to Taylor Blow, the son of Peter Blow, Scott's original owner, who freed them. Dred Scott died from tuberculosis the following year.

C. Political Rights

Slavery, as a legally recognised condition, ended with the passing of the Thirteenth Amendment in 1865, but its impacts, for example on political rights, continued. In the US, black men were given the vote in 1870 under the fifteenth amendment, but the adherence of individual states was patchy until the Voting Rights Act 1965. White women had the vote from 1920, but people of other ethnicities acquired rights of citizenship or voting spasmodically. Asian Americans were only enfranchised in 1952.

In England during the early nineteenth century, electoral reform was blocked by Tory governments but Earl Grey, a new Whig Prime Minister, forced through legislation at the third attempt by threatening to create extra peers in the House of Lords.[75] The Reform Act 1832 extended suffrage to all men who were householders or paid rent of more than £10 a year. Disraeli's Second Reform Act 1867 extended the franchise to only 16 per cent of the population. Adult male suffrage (over 21) was only achieved in 1918. Women over the age of 30 meeting property qualifications could vote from 1918 but women were fully enfranchised from 1928.

In liberal society the rule of law was assumed to embrace democracy, formal legality, and individual rights.[76] Ideas of equality, justice and fairness demanded equal access to participation in the legislature and voting in elections. Recognition of rights did not, however, follow reason but reflected stages of economic, social, and political development.

D. Cultural Rights

While the Bill of Rights of 1689 addressed Protestant concerns about persecution, discrimination on religious grounds persisted until the Catholic Emancipation Act 1829 allowed participation in the military. Even then the prohibition on a Catholic monarch remained in force. This was a blot on what Hobbes, and other Enlightenment thinkers, considered the most significant area for the expression of liberty. Freedom of religion was the right to believe what one wished, to practice a religion publicly or to belong to any religious group without discrimination or persecution.[77]

---

[75] The Reform Act 1832, www.parliament.uk/about/living-heritage/evolutionofparliament/houseofcommons/reformacts/overview/reformact1832/.

[76] BZ Tamanaha, *On the Rule of Law: History, Politics, Theory* (Cambridge, Cambridge University Press, 2004) 110–11 citing TRS Allan, *Law Liberty and Justice: The Legal Foundations of British Constitutionalism* (Oxford, Oxford University Press, 1993) 21–22.

[77] Despite Hobbes' Christianity, he did not prescribe laws on belief.

Religious freedoms were contested throughout the reigns of Henry VIII and James I, both zealous supporters of the official state religion, Anglicanism, and suppressors of other beliefs and congregations. This was a source of conflict between ordinary people and the state. Juries selected or bribed to return a guilty verdict often refused to convict in religious cases. So-called 'jury nullification' occurred in 1554 when Throckmorton was acquitted of complicity in the attempted overthrow of Mary I.

In the seventeenth century Puritan agitator John Lilburne, a serial martyr, was put on trial for his life three times, deliberately exposing procedural unfairness in the legal system.[78] 'Freeborn John' and a co-defendant were first brought before Archbishop Laud and the Star Chamber in the 1630s. He was charged with publishing pamphlets without licence, infringing a monopoly of the stationers' company, but was probably targeted as a member of the Puritan underground.[79]

Before the Star Chamber, as in later trials, Lilburne refused to take the oath, asserting the rights of all 'freeborn Englishmen' to know the charge against him, to face his accusers and not to make self-incriminating statements.[80] He suffered whipping through the streets, the pillory and further torture in prison, writing that execution would have been preferable.[81] He continued to agitate from prison, stirring up the London apprentices to attack Laud's palace, the kind of 'Puritan populism'[82] which led to the Civil War. In 1640 the House of Lords was inundated with petitions complaining about abuses of executive power[83] leading to abolition of Star Chamber.

Lilburne was charged with treason when, during the trial of Charles I's adviser, Strafford, he claimed that an armed crowd of up to 50,000 would attend the next day 'to have either the deputy or the King'.[84] The House of Lords dismissed the case for want of evidence and a Star Chamber order for Lilburne's imprisonment was also quashed.[85] Despite distinguishing himself in the Civil War on the side of Parliament, Lilburne was twice called before the House of Commons Committee for Examinations in 1645 for asserting rights to freedom of conscience and free speech. After a period of self-imposed exile, he was put on trial in 1649 for plotting to restore the monarchy. The jury refused to convict him, leading to half an hour of cheering in court.

Perverse verdicts by juries[86] increased from the 1640s and included a famous case against William Penn.[87] Penn became a Quaker in his teens and spent two periods as a law student without practicing.[88] He used the courts to confront religious persecution

---

[78] M Braddick, *The Common Freedom of the People: John Lilburne and the English Revolution* (Oxford, Oxford University Press, 2018).
[79] ibid 21.
[80] Lilburne was said to be the inspiration and authority for the Fifth Amendment of the American Constitution, against self-incrimination.
[81] Braddick (n 78) 27–29.
[82] ibid 48.
[83] ibid 42.
[84] ibid 49.
[85] ibid 46.
[86] Also known as jury equity, (UK) and Jury nullification (US).
[87] AR Murphy, *Liberty Conscience and Toleration: The Political Thought of William Penn* (Oxford, Oxford University Press, 2016).
[88] ibid 10.

when an Act first passed in 1644 to prevent large religious assemblies other than those of the Church of England was renewed in 1670. Penn and William Mead were arrested while preaching outside the Quaker meeting house in Gracechurch Street and charged with riot. They were held for several weeks before facing a hostile bench at the Old Bailey. A heroic account of the trial, *The people's ancient and just liberties asserted* (*The people's*), was used as propaganda for a decade.[89]

The people's was significant because it captured 'the exercise of legal, social and political power in the early modern world … a politics of dissent against arbitrary authority, of clear written law against prosecutions built on vague appeals to common law, and of juries as defenders of popular liberties against power-hungry judges'.[90] The account had Mead challenging the legality of the charges and the judge. Sir Samuel Starling, Lord Mayor of London, told Mead that he 'deserved to have his tongue cut out'. Contemporary practice required juries to give reasons and allowed judges to disagree and demand deliberation until the 'right' verdict was reached.[91]

The stand-off led to one of the most celebrated rule of law decisions, *Bushell's case*.[92] Starling directed the jury to convict and threatened to hold them until they did. The jury returned a 'not guilty' verdict, but Penn and Mead were returned to jail for contempt of court. The jury was fined and the Chairman, Bushell, appealed. The chief justice, Sir John Vaughan 'clarified' that judges had no right to fine disobedient jurors. Although the right of juries to follow their consciences was established it made little practical difference to jury trials for about a century.[93]

E. Social Rights

Social rights were often positive rights, including entitlements to welfare, work, reside and health provision. The documents framing the British Constitution, from Magna Carta to the Bill of Rights, promised no positive rights. In nineteenth century Britain, serious failure of staple crops led to famine, but Corn Laws kept the price of bread artificially high to protect farming landowners. A coordinated programme of social rights only followed World War II. Large parts of this programme, including legal aid, declined mainly because of lack of electoral support for these kinds of rights.

Analysis of the US Constitution detected concern that government may do too much for people rather than too little.[94] Despite this backdrop, the US States of Alabama, Alaska, Kansas, Montana, and Wyoming enacted constitutional rights to welfare. The Alabama Constitution stated that it 'shall be the duty of the legislature to require the several counties of this state to make adequate provision for

---

[89] ibid ch 3.
[90] ibid 57.
[91] JH Langbein, 'The Criminal Trial Before the Lawyers' (1978) 45 *Chicago Law Review* 263, 288, 291–96.
[92] *Bushell's case* (1670) 124 ER 1006.
[93] Langbein (n 91) 298.
[94] Currie (n 19), citing Judge Posner in *Jackson v City of Joliet* 715 F.2d 1200, 1203 (7th Cir.), cert. denied, 465 U.S. 1049 (1983) 2 I.

the maintenance of the poor'.[95] Data from the States in the US mandating welfare suggested that the poor did not necessarily fare better than they did in non-welfare States.[96]

Uncertainty regarding the best way to address poverty was reflected in the Supreme Court decision in *Dandridge v Williams*, which decisively rejected a constitutional basis for relief of poverty and the notion that courts should police poor law.[97] Judicial decisions characterised rights as being 'a constitutionally recognized, judicially enforceable restraint on popular government'.[98] The practical impact was illustrated by abortion law, where courts could support a woman's right to choose while denying any state obligation to support the procedure.[99]

IV. AN INTERNATIONAL ORDER

A. Citizenship

Historically, rights accrued as an adjunct of citizenship. Blackstone displayed awareness of the inherent problem posed to natural law by colonisation and empire. He deemed discovery of new and unoccupied lands, as practised 'by the Phœnicians and Greeks, and the Germans, Scythians, and other northern people' consistent with the 'laws of nature'[100] but queried whether 'seizing on countries already peopled, and driving out or massacring the innocent and defenceless natives … was consonant to nature, to reason, or to Christianity' proposing that this 'deserved well to be considered by those who have rendered their names immortal by thus civilizing mankind'.[101] Consideration did not necessarily mean regarding all people, beyond citizens, as equal. This notion, although not the reality, was being expressed by the end of the century.

In 1776 the US Declaration of Independence maintained that 'all men are created equal' and the 1788 Constitution conferred 'the blessings of liberty' on the population. This was, however, a concept of citizenship for white property-owning men, the Naturalization Act 1790 having only specified that 'free white persons' were eligible for citizenship. In 1789 the French Constituent Assembly adopted the Declaration of the Rights of Man and the Citizen,[102] based on Enlightenment thinking, notably Rousseau. The first Article declared: 'Human Beings are born and remain free and equal in rights.' These expressions of universal rights took much longer for groups such as women or non-white ethnicities to achieve. In the US, this distinction became clear during the period of territorial expansion in the nineteenth century.

In 1845 journalist and editor John L O'Sullivan wrote that it was 'the right of our manifest destiny to overspread and to possess the whole of the continent which

---

[95] ibid 894.
[96] ibid.
[97] *Dandridge v Williams* (1974) 397 U.S. 471.
[98] Currie (n 19) 860.
[99] ibid 866.
[100] Blackstone (n 64) p 7.
[101] ibid.
[102] Drafted by the Marquis de Lafayette with Thomas Jefferson.

Providence has given us for the development of the great experiment of liberty and federated self-government entrusted to us'.[103] European settlement led to conflict with Native American tribes, accelerating from the 1830s and, after the American Civil War, with mass migration west.[104] Manifest destiny was deplored by leading Whigs as 'belligerent' and 'pompous', but the idea was popular and promoted by the Democratic Party.[105] Whig campaigns against the transatlantic slave trade gained momentum in the late 1700s led by abolitionists such as Granville Sharp. In 1772 a writ of *habeus corpus* was issued when a slave called James Somerset claimed freedom on arrival in England with his American master.[106] After a long delay Lord Mansfield declared Somerset's emancipation.

The 1770s also marked the start of campaigns in the US to end the slave trade. By 1808 President Thomas Jefferson legislated to make bringing slaves from abroad a federal crime.[107] In 1841 the Supreme court heard a case concerning a cargo of intended slaves seized by Spanish slavers on the West African coast. They had been sold in Cuba and taken aboard the ship *Amistad* destined for a Caribbean plantation. The intended slaves seized the ship, but the plantation owners misdirected them and they were detained by the US Navy while moored off Long Island, New York.

Charges of murder of the captain and cook and piracy were dropped, but actions were launched for ownership of the men. The plantation owners claimed property rights and the naval officers claimed the ship and contents as salvage. A group of abolitionists paid for a team of lawyers from New Haven and New York. The district court denied claims to ownership because the Africans were illegally held as slaves. The case came to the Supreme Court and abolitionists again paid for representation; John Quincy Adams, former President and member of the House of Representatives.[108] He was 74, had not argued a case for 30 years and was at odds with some of the abolitionists.[109]

Adams had campaigned against slavery in Congress and criticised the US President, Martin Van Bueren, for overreaching his executive powers in trying to return the ship to Cuba under pressure from the Spanish government. Having reluctantly agree to take the case, Adams spoke for almost nine hours arguing against Hobbes that war was the natural state of man and asserting the men's right to freedom on moral, legal and constitutional grounds, claiming: 'The moment you come to the Declaration of Independence, that every man has a right to life and liberty, an inalienable right, this case is decided.'[110] Senior Chief Justice Joseph Story related that the men had been 'kidnapped and transported illegally, they had never been slaves', and upheld their right to use force to resist. Abolitionists paid for a ship to return the men,

---

[103] DS Heidler, 'Manifest Destiny' *Encyclopedia Britannica*, www.britannica.com/event/Manifest-Destiny.
[104] D Brown, *Bury My Heart at Wounded Knee: An Indian History of the American West* (London, Vintage Books, 1991).
[105] ibid.
[106] *Somerset v Stuart* 98 Eng. Rep. 499 (K.B. 1772) (S Landsman, 'The Rise of the Contentious Spirit: Adversary Procedure in Eighteenth-Century England' (1990) 75(3) *Cornell Law Review* 590).
[107] The Act Prohibiting Importation of Slaves 1807 2 Stat. 426.
[108] GV Wood and JQ Adams, *Heir to the Fathers: John Quincy Adams and the Spirit of Constitutional Government* (Lanham Maryland, Lexington Books, 2004).
[109] ibid 173.
[110] ibid 188.

accompanied by Christian missionaries, to Africa.[111] The *Amistad*, by recognising the rights of non-citizens, was a step towards practical implementation of a universalistic notion of human rights law.

B. Nuremberg

After World War I the German state had promised to prosecute those accused of crimes against other states' nationals in the German Supreme Court in Leipzig. In the event a few military personnel were charged with attacking hospital ships or executing or mistreating prisoners of war. Cases against other defendants were abandoned.[112] During World War II the Allies published the Joint Declaration for the Punishment of War Criminals 1942, promising to punish Nazi persecution of civilians.[113] Demands for accountability remained strong until the end of World War II in May 1945, when the Allies held several high-profile Nazis. Rumours of atrocities were confirmed by the ghastly evidence of Concentration Camps. The British Prime Minister, Winston Churchill, favoured summary execution, but US President Harry S Truman was persuaded by the Head of the US War Department, a lawyer named Stimson, to conduct a judicial process.[114] The plan was pushed by elite US lawyers who 'as part of their class and profession had a keen sense of the ideological and material role and purpose of law'.[115]

No legal framework existed for criminal proceedings against foreign state officials, so one was set out in the London Charter for the International Military Tribunal. Truman appointed Robert Jackson, former solicitor-general and attorney-general and acting US Supreme Court justice, as lead counsel. As a practitioner Jackson was known as a trenchant defender of individual rights against abuses of power by executive agencies.[116] When the trials began at the end of 1945 there were 22 defendants. They included Hermann Goring, the most senior captured member of the Nazi government and creator of the Gestapo, Rudolf Hess, Hitler's former deputy, and Alfred Rosenberg, author of the Nazi racial theories.

Jackson was given a wide brief to devise a strategy for the Nuremberg trials[117] but there was a team of Nuremberg prosecutors comprised of lawyers nominated by each of the allied countries. The defendants were represented by German lawyers. There were disagreements between the allies on the charges and their scope.[118]

---

[111] ibid.
[112] G Hankel, 'Leipzig War Crimes Trials' *International Encyclopaedia of the First World War*, https://encyclopedia.1914-1918-online.net/article/leipzig_war_crimes_trials.
[113] P Sands, *East West Street* (London, Wiedenfeld and Nicolson, 2016) 99; G Baars, *The Corporation, Law and Capitalism: A Radical Perspective on the Role of Law in the Global Political Economy* (Chicago, Haymarket Books, 2020) 141.
[114] Baars (n 113) 141.
[115] ibid 141–42 citing T Taylor, *The Anatomy of the Nuremberg Trials* (New York, Bloomsbury, 1992).
[116] He was notable for not having a law degree, having qualified by a practice route.
[117] Baars (n 113) 142.
[118] A sensitive area was whether charges should cover the period of the Third Reich, or Third German Empire, from 1933–45, or only those committed during World War II. The Americans wanted to avoid the wider period because of sensitivity about their treatment of Native Americans.

Other lawyers played important roles in resolving these issues and providing the legal framework for Nuremberg. This was demonstrated in a recent book by Philippe Sands, *East West Street*, in which he described the roles of Hersch Lauterpacht (1897–1960) and Rafael Lemkin (1900–59), Eastern European Jews who escaped Nazi invasion.[119] Both left relatives behind, but their intellectual interest lay in the charges brought at Nuremberg.

Lemkin enrolled to study Law at Lwów, now known as Lviv in Ukraine, in 1926 and, after working as a public prosecutor in Warsaw, barely escaped the Nazi invasion of Poland in 1939. His interest in oppressed peoples led to an argument with a professor at Lwów over the case of an Armenian, Tehlirian. charged with the murder of a Turkish official who had overseen the extermination of a million Armenians.[120] Lemkin had argued that the conviction was unjust, given that the official was unaccountable because of state sovereignty. Lauterpacht studied Law at Lemburg University in Ukraine and went to Vienna and then London, becoming a barrister in 1933.[121] In 1937 he was elected to the Whewell Chair of International Law at Cambridge University.[122] Lauterpacht studied the relationship between state law and international law.[123] His PhD, from the London School of Economics in 1925, examined Private Law Sources and Analogies of International Law. A theme of his work was the potential for 'state customary laws' to act as a source of international law that could 'rein in the power of the state'.[124]

Lauterpacht delivered a lecture in the US asserting the fundamental rights of man and those oppressed under Nazi regimes and he was contacted by Robert Jackson. Lauhterpacht argued for a focus on crimes against the individual, an extension of the criminal law of the state. Rafael Lemkin argued that the Nazis' crimes against groups should also be recognised. During the War, he worked on German legal documents, including those from occupied territories, detecting a systematic plan and pattern of behaviour by the German authorities.

German occupation was typically followed by removal of a country's intelligentsia and enslavement of the remaining population. In relation to the Jews and other minorities a two-step process was undertaken, to: (1) de-nationalise targeted groups by withdrawing legal documentation, and (2) de-humanise the group by the removal of rights and property, the introduction of rationing and gradual starvation. Lemkin conceived of the crime of Genocide, (from *genos*, Greek for tribe or group and *cide*, Latin for killing) to describe the systematic extermination of ethnic groups. In *Axis Rule in Europe* (1944) he detailed the process from definition of the group to its liquidation.[125]

A lawyer was also one of the Nuremberg defendants. Hans Frank defended Adolf Hitler in numerous court cases during the rise of the Nazi party and was a prominent

---

[119] Sands (n 113).
[120] ibid 148.
[121] ibid 87.
[122] 'Hersch Lauterpacht' Lauterpacht Centre for International Law, University of Cambridge, www.lcil.cam.ac.uk/about-centrehistory/sir-hersch-lauterpacht.
[123] This was spurred by the opening of the Permanent Court of the International Court of Justice in 1922.
[124] Sands (n 113) 82.
[125] ibid 181.

jurist of National Socialism with a central role in exterminating Polish jews. Frank was aware of debates concerning individual rights and the rule of law. In 1935 he made a speech opposing the 'individualistic, liberalistic, atomizing tendencies of the egoism of the individual'.[126] Lemkin noted papers he had given in which he stated that law 'was that which is useful and necessary to the German nation' and justified the right of 'the nation' to persecute minorities.[127]

Lauterpacht influenced the draft charges against the Nuremberg defendants, suggesting titles for sections of the text laying out the charges. These included the name for atrocities in the field ('war crimes') and against civilians ('crimes against humanity'). Article 6 of the Charter of the International Military Tribunal (1945) gave the tribunal power to punish individuals guilty of crimes against humanity, murder, extermination, enslavement, deportation, whether or not these were in in violation of the domestic laws of the country where they were perpetrated.

Jackson borrowed Lemkin's book for a year, returning it in October 1946,[128] but Lemkin tried in vain to interest the prosecutors in charging the defendants with Genocide. Lemkin was added to Jackson's War Crimes office but was sent back to the US from London because of his emotional approach and failings as 'a team player'.[129] Sands suggested, however, that Lemkin's ideas gained no traction with the Americans because Jackson was under pressure not to open up the US to claims by Native Americans.[130] Jackson may also have been influenced against Lemkin's ideas because of Lauterpacht's concern that focusing on crimes against the group cut across the focus on the individual and had no precedent in state law.[131] His persistence paid off when the word Genocide was mentioned in the charges.[132]

The Allies agreed that the defendants should appear as individuals and the tribunal decided that defendants could not claim that they were merely following the policies of the German state. This confronted the main problem at Nuremberg: '… the notion that an individual had rights against the state was inconceivable … in short, the state could do whatever it wanted to its nationals. It could discriminate, torture or kill'.[133] Lauterpacht wrote to his wife that the Nuremberg trials placed a state in the dock for the first time.[134] It fell to Jackson to justify this position.

Jackson's qualities included writing legal speeches. His opening defended the Nuremberg process, invoking Enlightenment reason:

> The wrongs which we seek to condemn and punish have been so calculated, so malignant, and so devastating, that civilization cannot tolerate their being ignored, because it cannot survive their being repeated. That four great nations, flushed with victory, and stung with injury, stay the hand of vengeance and voluntarily submit their captive enemies to the

---

[126] ibid 135.
[127] ibid 174.
[128] ibid 184.
[129] ibid 187.
[130] ibid 298.
[131] ibid 106–7.
[132] Lemkin was disappointed that Genocide was included in charges under Count 3 (War Crimes) of the 4 counts, but not under Count 4, crimes against humanity, as he had hoped (Sands (n 113) 188).
[133] Sands (n 113) 76.
[134] ibid 281.

judgement of the law is one of the most significant tributes that power has ever paid to reason ...[135]

He also argued for procedural fairness, noting the 'dramatic disparity between the circumstances of the accusers and of the accused that might discredit our work if we should falter, in even minor matters, in being fair and temperate'.

Over several hours, Jackson urged the need for fair process:

> We must never forget that the record on which we judge these defendants today is the record on which history will judge us tomorrow. To pass these defendants a poisoned chalice is to put it to our own lips as well. We must summon such detachment and intellectual integrity to our task that this Trial will commend itself to posterity as fulfilling humanity's aspirations to do justice.[136]

The speech was widely admired and the only defendant to admit guilt, Albert Speer, a close ally of Hitler and the Minister of Armaments and War Production, declared it 'devastating'. In closing, Jackson echoed John Cook's proposed closing against Charles I, invoking the inalienable rights of the individual. He asked the judges to create a world where people of goodwill would, henceforth, wherever they were, in Kipling's words, have 'leave to live by no man's leave, underneath the Law'.[137]

Sir Hartley Shawcross, barrister, Labour politician, and serving Attorney General, led for the British with Tory MP David Maxwell-Fyfe as his deputy.[138] Maxwell-Fyfe employed the concept of Genocide several times in trying to show that Konstantin Von Neurath, Reichsprotektor of Bohemia and Moravia, had planned to eliminate the Czech intelligentsia.[139] Shawcross' speeches used a draft written by Luaterpacht in opening. In closing, addressing the legitimacy of the proceedings, he urged that, if war was justified to protect populations, how could judicial proceedings not be?[140]

The court found that the obligations of individuals transcended their obligations to the state. It condemned 12 of the 22 defendants, including Frank, to death by hanging.[141] Resolution 95(1) of the UN General Assembly, passed late in 1946, affirmed the principles of international law recognised by the Charter of the Nuremberg Tribunal and the judgment of the Tribunal. This 'set in motion the process for turning the principles at issue into general principles of customary law binding on member States of the whole international community'.[142] Genocide was recognised as an international crime distinct from crimes against humanity in 1946.[143] A Convention on Genocide was adopted in 1948 with states being obliged to prevent it from 1951.

---

[135] Robert H. Jackson: Opening Statement Nuremberg Trials, 1945 (The Supreme Court), www.thirteen.org/wnet/supremecourt/personality/print/sources_document12.html.

[136] ibid.

[137] Sands (n 113) 289.

[138] Maxwell-Fyfe, a member of Gray's Inn, was called to the Bar in 1922 and Parliament in 1929.

[139] He had been in post when 1,200 protesting students were sent to concentration camps and nine shot (Sands (n 113) 337).

[140] Sands (n 113) 349.

[141] ibid 366–72.

[142] A Cassese, *Affirmation of the Principles of International Law recognized by the Charter of the Nürnberg Tribunal General Assembly resolution 95 (I)*, https://legal.un.org/avl/ha/ga_95-I/ga_95-I.html.

[143] UN General Assembly (1946) Resolution 96.

C. Universalism

While there was no treaty on Crimes Against Humanity, Lauterpacht was influential in the creation of the Universal Declaration of Human Rights 1948. In 1945 he published a book supporting his plan for an international bill of the rights of man.[144] It received some acclaim in the US but was criticised for 'harking back to a long-disappeared constellation of 19th century ideas'.[145] Henri Laugier, Assistant Secretary-General at the newly formed United Nations (UN), invited the Canadian John Peters Humphrey, a former practitioner and legal academic, to accept directorship of the UN Human Rights Division.[146] Eleanor Roosevelt, a member of the US delegation to the UN was elected chair of a subcommittee drafting a declaration on rights.

The multi-national committee drafted a declaration based on Magna Carta (1215), the English Bill of Rights (1689), the American Declaration of Independence (1776), the American Bill of Rights (1791), and the French Declaration of the Rights of Man and of the Citizen (1789). The final version reflected the diverse perspectives of members of the drafting committee and consultees. At the suggestion of the Chinese vice-chair, Peng-Chung Chan, religious references were removed to promote universalism while the Chilean judge Hernán Santa Cruz argued, against the North Atlantic nations, that socio-economic rights should be included.[147]

The Universal Declaration of Human Rights (1948) elaborated four freedoms identified by the US president Franklin D Roosevelt as war aims in 1941: freedom of speech, of religion, freedom from fear, and from want. A drafter, Rene Cassin, envisaged the 30 articles comprising four groups: the rights of the individual, the individual in political society, spiritual and political freedoms and economic and social freedoms.[148] It reflected first generation rights, to life, liberty, dignity, asylum, personal security and specified procedural protections such as freedom from torture, arbitrary detention or arrest and the presumption of innocence. The last three Articles were general, with Article 28(1) stating that 'everyone has duties to the community in which alone the free and full development of his personality is possible'.

Presenting it to the UN General Assembly 1948 the chair of the commission, Eleanor Roosevelt, expressed hope that the Universal Declaration of Human Rights 'might become one of the cornerstones on which peace could eventually be based'.[149] In 1966 the UN adopted a resolution establishing an International Bill of Rights, comprising the Universal declaration and two multi-lateral treaties, the International

---

[144] H Lauterpacht, *An International Bill of the Rights of Man* (New York, Columbia University Press, 1945).
[145] Sands (n 113) 109.
[146] Biography: John Peters Humphrey: Father of the modern human rights system, www.humphreyhampton.org/john-peters-humphrey.
[147] United Nations, 'Drafting of the Universal Declaration of Human Rights', https://research.un.org/en/undhr/draftingcommittee.
[148] UN Universal Declaration of Human Rights, www.ohchr.org/en/press-releases/2021/01/saotome-and-principes-human-rights-record-be-examined-universal-periodic?LangID=E&NewsID=26680.
[149] A Black, 'Eleanor Roosevelt and the Universal Declaration of Human Rights' (25 June 2020) www.nps.gov/elro/learn/historyculture/udhr.htm.

178 *Individuality*

Covenant on Civil and Political Rights (1966)[150] and the UN International Covenant on Economic, Social and Cultural Rights 1966.[151] Despite receiving enough signatories to come into force in 1976, there were continuing concerns about breaches. Offenders included the US, which ratified in 1992, but failed to enact legislation enabling enforcement of rights.

Lauterpacht's hope that Nuremberg would lead to an international criminal court[152] was frustrated by the Cold War. It progressed when the UN established ad hoc tribunals to hear cases arising out of conflict in the former Yugoslavia (1993) and Rwanda (1994). A permanent International Criminal Court (ICC) was finally established in 1998.[153] The Nuremberg concepts of war crimes and genocide were recognised in the statutes of court investigations of Yugoslavia, Rwanda and the ICC, but their definitions had evolved.[154] The new jurisprudence had difficulties,[155] but the offences, developed in the courts' statutes and in the international and national courts, now represented customary international law.[156] They were represented in a *Code of Crimes against the Peace and Security of Mankind*, adopted in 1996.[157]

In 1949, the Council of Europe was formed with the broad political purpose of preventing wars, protecting human rights and the rule of law, and promoting democracy across Europe.[158] Britain played a central role, with David Maxwell Fyfe one of the key authors of the European Convention on Human Rights and Fundamental Freedoms 1950 (ECHR)[159] comprising 14 Articles.[160] The European Court of Human Rights (ECtHR) was established as an independent and representative tribunal to enforce the Articles in 1959[161] and the UK accepted the right of individuals to petition it in 1966. By 2011 the ECHR covered 820 million people in 47 countries. Of all ECtHR judgments finding at least one violation in 2011, 36 per cent involved a

---

[150] Adopted by United Nations General Assembly Resolution 2200A (XXI) on 16 December 1966, and in force from 23 March 1976

[151] Adopted and opened for signature, ratification, and accession by General Assembly resolution 2200A (XXI) of 16 December 1966, entry into force 3 January 1976.

[152] Sands (n 113) 339.

[153] Rome Statute of the International Criminal Court 1998.

[154] Crimes against humanity now included 'widespread or systematic attack against a civilian population' (Article 7 ICC Statute). The ICC Statute also contains four new categories of punishable acts as crimes against humanity: torture (Article 7(1) (f)), sexual crimes (Article 7(1) (g), enforced disappearance of persons (Article 7(1) (i)) and the crime of apartheid (Article 7(1) (j)) (see Cassese (n 142)).

[155] Genocide was seen as more serious, encouraging claims and exacerbating conflict.

[156] Cassese (n 142).

[157] *Yearbook of the International Law Commission* (1996) Vol. II (Part Two).

[158] Treaty of London (1949) (UN treaty number I:1168, Vol 87, p 103).

[159] The British Institute of Human Rights, 'The European Convention on Human Rights', www.bihr.org.uk/theconvention#:~:text=The%20UK%20played%20a%20significant%20role%20in%20 creating,to%20sign%20the%20ECHR%20on%204%20November%201950.

[160] 1 – obligation to respect rights; 2 – right to life; 3 – prohibition of torture and inhuman or degrading treatment or punishment; 4 – prohibition of slavery and forced labour; 5 – right to liberty and security; 6 – right to a fair hearing; 7 – no punishment without law; 8 – right to respect for private and family life, home and correspondence; 9 – freedom of thought, conscience and religion; 10 – freedom of expression; 11 – freedom of assembly and association; 12 – right to marry; 13 – right to an effective remedy; 14 – prohibition of discrimination.

[161] The Parliamentary Assembly of the Council of Europe elected judges to the Court from a list of three candidates nominated by each member state.

violation of the right to life, the prohibition against torture or inhuman or degrading treatment.[162]

Principe noted that, between 1965 and 1990, twice as many human rights petitions were lodged with the ECHR against the UK than any other nation.[163] Since 1966, ECtHR judgments against the UK often involved breaches of basic civil liberties, such as the right to a fair trial (30 per cent of adverse judgments) or the right to life (four per cent) and the prohibition of torture and inhuman or degrading treatment (four per cent).[164] The UK also lost more significant cases than any other nation.

The Human Rights Act 1998 was partly a bid to stem the embarrassing tide of successful claims by providing a domestic mechanism for dealing with abuses[165] and by introducing a 'human rights culture' in public services.[166] It may have also anticipated the Charter of the Fundamental Rights of the European Union, which aimed to introduce rights as a background for EU law. The first, foundational Article declared 'Human dignity is inviolable. It must be respected and protected' the text declaring it: 'not only a fundamental right in itself but [that it] constitutes the real basis of fundamental rights'.[167]

Human rights observance benefited from statutory protection.[168] Following the Human Rights Act, the UK reduced its 'rate of defeat' in Strasbourg cases. Of 12,000 applications brought against the UK between 1999 and 2010 only three per cent (390 applications) passed the 'substantial merit' threshold for admissibility.[169] Successful cases also declined from one in 50 before the Act to one in 200 by 2011. New rights were established[170] relating to retention of innocent people's DNA profiles, unnecessary secret surveillance, indiscriminate stop and search, forced labour and servitude, rights for lesbian, gay, bisexual or transgender people, banning of corporal punishment in schools, restricting the physical punishment of children in the family, protecting journalists' sources and investigative journalism.[171]

Despite the international regime of rights, there remained difficulties in applying the rule of law to host states' relations with non-nationals.[172] In Britain this reflected some historical antagonism in the Tory party to the ECtHR, although both Margaret Thatcher in 1989 and John Major in 1993 declared support for the system.[173] Ostensibly, opponents objected to the subjection of national sovereignty to

---

[162] A Donald, J Gordon and P Leach, *The UK and the European Court of Human Rights* Equality and Human Rights Commission Research report 83, www.equalityhumanrights.com/sites/default/files/83._european_court_of_human_rights.pdf.
[163] ML Principe, 'Albert Venn Dicey and the Principles of the Rule of Law: Is Justice Blind? A Comparative Analysis of the United States and Great Britain' (2000) 22 *Loyola of Los Angeles International & Comparative Law Review* 357, 363.
[164] Donald et al (n 162) viii.
[165] Principe (n 163) 365.
[166] Donald et al (n 162).
[167] https://fra.europa.eu/en/eu-charter/article/1-human-dignity.
[168] Principe (n 163) 366.
[169] Donald et al (n 162) vii.
[170] ibid viii.
[171] ibid.
[172] M Kanetake, 'The Interfaces Between the National and International Rule of Law: A Framework Paper' in M Kanetake and N Nollkaemper (eds), *The Rule of Law at the National and International Levels* (Oxford, Hart Publishing, 2016) 11.
[173] Donald et al (n 162) 10.

an overseas court, but the irritant concerned the rights of suspected terrorists against executive action and legislative provisions.[174] Bogdanor speculated that the judiciary may have regarded it as their duty to defy legislation on the issue.[175]

In 2003 the Labour government and the Home Secretary, David Blunkett proposed legislation excluding asylum claims from judicial review and holding foreign terrorist suspects without trial.[176] Lord Woolf told the House of Lords that criticisms of judicial review were 'inconsistent with the rule of law' and that unfair criticism of judges was damaging and 'undermines the confidence of the public in the justice system'.[177] This was part of a wider disagreement in which Blunkett was said to have referred to Woolf, as a 'muddled and confused old codger'.[178] In the event the Asylum and Immigration (Treatment of Claimants Act 2004) made a harsher environment for asylum seekers.

In the three years to 2011, the ECtHR adopted conclusions reached by UK courts[179] and the UK generally implemented judgments of the ECtHR.[180] Nevertheless, UK politicians on both the left and right criticised the 'activism' of the ECtHR.[181] What was perceived to be the UK's negative attitude caused fear of a 'contagion' which would undermine the authority of the ECtHR across Europe leading to 'weakening of the rule of law'.[182] The Attorney General, Dominic Grieve, reasserted commitment as 'fundamental to our national interest'.[183] In 2009, a backbench Tory MP called Dominic Raab published a book claiming 'The spread of rights has become contagious and, since the Human Rights Act, opened the door to vast new categories of claims, which can be judicially enforced against the government through the courts'.[184] In 2011 Donald et al concluded that the Human Rights Act had not inculcated the intended culture of human rights.[185]

In 2011 a report noted hostility from senior British politicians, including David Cameron the Prime Minister, to the ECtHR particularly regarding adverse decisions

---

[174] *A and Z and others v Secretary of State for the Home Dept*, for example, led to replacement of the Anti-Terrorism, Crime and Security Act 2001 with the Prevention of Terrorism Act 2005.

[175] V Bogdanor, *The New British Constitution* (Oxford, Hart Publishing, 2009) 72–74.

[176] D Taylor, 'Top judge attacks Blunkett' *Evening Standard* (17 May 2002); C Dyer and P Wintour, 'Woolf leads judges' attack on Ministers' *The Guardian* (4 March 2004).

[177] F Gibb, 'Woolf rejects Blunkett criticism' *The Times* (22 May 2003).

[178] F Elliott, 'Britain's top judge forced out by bullying Blunkett' *The Independent* (31 October 2004).

[179] Donald et al (n 162) reporting a survey by Sir Nicolas Bratza, President of the ECtHR.

[180] The exception, prisoner suffrage, was an issue from 2005.

[181] See eg David Davis MP, 'Today's vote on prisoners' rights is an historic opportunity to draw a line in the sand on European power' (*Conservative Home*, 10 February 2011) and Jack Straw MP, Hansard, HC Vol. 523, Col. 502, 10 February 2011 (both cited by Donald et al (n 162) p 1, fns 1 and 2).

[182] Donald et al (n 162) x.

[183] ibid 186, citing D Grieve, 'European Convention on Human Rights – Current Challenges' (Speech at Lincoln's Inn, London, 24 October 2011), www.gov.uk/government/speeches/european-convention-on-human-rights-current-challenges.

[184] D Raab, *The Assault on Liberty: What Went Wrong With Rights?* (see R Syal and H Siddique, 'Dominic Raab's paper seen as fulfilment of quest to destroy Human Rights Act' *The Guardian* (14 December 2021) www.theguardian.com/politics/2021/dec/14/dominic-raabs-paper-seen-as-fulfilment-of-quest-to-destroy-human-rights-act?s=08.

[185] Donald et al (n 162) viii.

on the rights of suspected terrorists[186] and prisoners' suffrage.[187] The authors of the report suggested that calls from MPs and commentators to withdraw from the ECHR, or the jurisdiction of the ECtHR, appeared likely to undermine the reputation of the UK and the European system of human rights.[188] Lord Neuberger, president of the Supreme Court, attacked the Home Secretary for criticising judges in human rights cases.[189] A conference to mark the UK's Chairmanship of the Council of Europe in November 2011 concluded that politicians and other public figures should 'tread with conscience' when discussing human rights.[190]

In 2013 Cameron proposed excluding categories of judicial review[191] and making all cases more difficult to bring.[192] A Ministry of Justice review claimed that it was being used 'inappropriately' as a campaigning or delaying tactic.[193] It consulted on further restrictions. The Constitution Society commissioned an administrative law barrister, Amy Street, to consider whether the proposals threatened the rule of law. Her report observed that the doctrine of Parliamentary sovereignty was a judicial invention[194] therefore: 'if Parliament were to legislate in a way which the courts considered to be contrary to the rule of law, the courts would need to confront whether they consider their primary obligation to be to the will of Parliament, or to the constitutional principle of the rule of law'.[195]

The Criminal Justice and Courts Act 2015 contained provisions requiring courts to refuse judicial review if the outcome for the applicant would not have been substantially different if the conduct complained of had not occurred.[196] Other provisions made those providing third party funding and intervening in judicial review more prone to risk.[197] The measures were resisted in the Lords, where Tory peers voted against them. The shadow justice secretary promised to overturn the Act on a return to government.[198] In 2021 government consulted on replacing the Human Rights Act with a Bill of Rights.[199] Presented by Dominic Raab, now Deputy leader of the Tory Party, as an attempt to restrict criminal deportees claiming a right to family life, it was seen as an attempt to dilute rights generally[200] and subject ECtHR decisions to British courts.

---

[186] Donald et al (n 162) fn 530 citing '"Human rights laws put lives at risk": Cameron tells Euro court it harms fight against terror' *Mail Online* (26 January 2012); 'The Prime Minister must defy the European Court' *Daily Express* (11 February 2011).
[187] *Hirst v UK* (No 2) (2005) ECHR 681.
[188] Donald et al (n 162) 174.
[189] O Bowcott 'Judge defends court role over terror suspects' *The Guardian* (5 March 2013).
[190] Donald et al (n 162) 187.
[191] P Wintour and O Boycott, 'David Cameron plans broad clampdown on judicial review rights' *The Guardian* (19 November 2012).
[192] T Dyke, 'Why Cameron has got it wrong on judicial review reform' (*The Lawyer*, 29 January 2013).
[193] Ministry of Justice, *Judicial Review: Proposals for further reform* (2013), https://consult.justice.gov.uk/digital-communications/judicial-review/.
[194] A Street, *Judicial Review and the Rule of Law: Who's in Control?* (London, Constitution Society, 2013).
[195] ibid 8.
[196] Criminal Justice and Courts Act 2015, s 84.
[197] ibid ss 85–86.
[198] O Bowcott, 'Khan will reverse curbs on judicial review' *The Guardian* (2 March 2015).
[199] Ministry of Justice, *Human Rights Act Reform: A Modern Bill Of Rights* CP 588 (London, HMSO, 2021).
[200] H Siddique and R Syal, 'Raab to claim overhaul of human rights law will counter "political correctness"' *The Guardian* (14 December 2021) www.theguardian.com/law/2021/dec/14/raab-to-claim-overhaul-human-rights-law-counter-political-correctness.

V. DISCUSSION

A tradition of rights was not created by lawyers, but often reflected social movements using the logic of rights to air causes in court. In seventeenth century England, it was religious agitators such as Lilburne and Penn who presented rational arguments hoping for sympathetic decisions from juries. Lawyers were not involved, although Penn had legal training and Lilburne probably had activist training. Later, common law rights were established as a joint venture of litigants, courts, juries, and lawyers, often recognising a community view of morality.[201] The same process arguably continued into modern times, with judges expected to do what legislators should have done had they confronted hot political issues with no moral consensus; abortion, animal rights or the environment.[202]

The role of lawyers in establishing rights became less obscure in the eighteenth and nineteenth centuries. Lawyers enlisted by notable abolitionists or sympathisers, provided representation to Dredd Scott.[203] Samuel Mansfield Bay, a New Yorker by birth and former Missouri legislator and attorney general, became the attorney of record in June 1847. For the federal cases, Charles Edmund LaBeaume who began hiring the Scotts from Mrs Emerson in 1851, consulted Roswell M Field who worked on the case without a fee. Rights cases reflected the continuation of politics through the courts.

David and Daniel Barnhizer argued it was politics rather than rights that decided *Amistad* and *Dredd Scott*.[204] Allowing the *Amistad* salvage claim would have created a loophole for importation of slaves, antagonising Northern opinion. Allowing Dredd Scott his freedom would have threatened established property rights in the South, antagonising opinion there. The line of least resistance was to free the slaves in *Amistad*, while the opposite was true in *Dredd Scott*. A political dimension was undeniable in *Dredd Scott*; five of the nine justices were from slave holding families. Chief justice Roger B Taney, who represented Southern 'planter aristocracy', declared that the words 'all men were created equal' in the Declaration of Independence, were not intended to apply to black people.[205] The Barnhizers argued that these were political outcomes 'dressed up' with legal reasoning, requiring belief in the rule of law to have 'a degree of hypocrisy and suspension of disbelief'.[206] Scheingold also referred to the mythic quality of rights in general.[207] claiming they were either seldom enforceable through courts or failed to change political reality.

---

[201] R Dworkin, 'Political judges and the rule of law' (1978) 64 *Proceedings of the British Academy* 259 (cited by Tamanaha (n 76) 102).

[202] Tamanaha (n 76) 103 citing A MacIntyre, 'Theories of Natural law in the Culture of Advanced Modernity' in EB McLean (ed), *Common Truths: New Perspectives on Natural Law* (Wilmington, Del, ISI books, 2000).

[203] For fuller information on this and the various judges see Missouri State Archives (n 74).

[204] D Barnhizer and D Barnhizer, *Hypocrisy and Myth: The Hidden Order of the Rule of Law* (Florida, Vanderplas Publishing, 2009).

[205] He had released his own slaves and given the longest serving pensions, but represented a constituency view (M DeLong, 'To Save a House Divided: Lincoln's Suspension of Habeas Corpus' (1996) *Senior Research Projects* 118) https://knowledge.e.southern.edu/senior_research/118.

[206] Barnhizer and Barnhizer (n 204) 10.

[207] S Scheingold, *The Politics of Rights: Lawyers, Public Policy and Political Change* (Ann Arbor, University of Michigan Press, 2004).

Scheingold's criticism that rights were mythic were largely true in relation to welfare rights. He qualified his second charge, that courts did not change political realities, by accepting that the mythology of rights encouraged acceptance of the political order and motivated people to tackle social ills. Lovell reviewed later scholarship and qualified Scheingold's conclusions further.[208] He found that people did not have an idealised view of rights, saw judicial decision-making and politics as related, yet subscribed to the legitimacy of law, accepted legal authority, and were not motivated to mobilise politically.[209] He argued litigation strategies were somewhat effective in establishing rights, but that judicial conservatism dampened enthusiasm for them.[210]

Currie identified two problems with relying on courts to enforce such positive rights. The first was the financial and economic barriers, which disadvantaged the impoverished groups welfare rights would protect. The second was overt political bias in court composition, a view which echoed the Barnhizers' argument that *Dred Scott* and *Amistad* undermined the legitimacy of the rule of law.[211] Both of these views depended on simplistic notions of how rights were established. The failure to establish welfare rights did not indicate a failure of courts or the rule of law unless progressive versions of the social contract, such as that envisaged by Rawls, were adopted. The failure of courts to uphold rights ignored the fact that they were often a stepping-stone, not always the end point in rights claims.

Dred Scott led to a political change that better realised the rule of law. It created a public mood in the North that made civil war inevitable,[212] 'propelling' Abraham Lincoln to the Presidency in 1861 and leading to the abolition of slavery.[213] In other situations rights were slowly established by an infrastructure comprising financial support, advocacy organisations and appropriate legal resources, whether in-house or external and sometimes pro bono.[214] A concept of rights based on equality was generally the background to rights being established. Thus, the poor lacked welfare rights when electorates did not prioritise social justice.

Prosecutors in the Nuremberg trials drew on the political theory of the Enlightenment thinkers, Hobbes, Kant and Blackstone, to establish human rights as inherent 'natural rights'. These were essential to life as a human being, for the development of the distinctive human qualities of reason and conscience, for enjoying autonomy and being accorded dignity. The Nuremberg judges recognised rights

---

[208] GI Lovell, 'The Myth of the Myth of Rights' (2012) 59 *Studies in Law, Politics and Society* 1, citing JF Handler, EJ Hollingsworth and HS Erlanger, *Lawyers and the Pursuit of Legal Rights* (New York, Academic Press, 1978).

[209] Lovell ibid citing JL Gibson and GA Caldeira, 'Has legal realism damaged the legitimacy of the U.S. Supreme Court?' 45 *Law & Society Review* 195.

[210] Lovel ibid, citing eg MW McCann, 'Law and social movements: Contemporary perspectives' (2006) 2 *Annual Review of Law and Social Science* 17.

[211] Barnhizer and Barnhizer (n 204) 4.

[212] Questioning the constitutional validity of the Missouri Compromise undermined restrictions on slavery in the northern area of the Louisiana purchase, causing consternation in the Northern states. Smithsonian, 'The Human Factor of History: Dred Scott and Roger B. Taney', https://nmaahc.si.edu/explore/stories/human-factor-history-dred-scott-and-roger-b-taney.

[213] Ironically, Taney swore in Abraham Lincoln as president of the United States in 1861.

[214] Currie (n 19) 880.

inherent in any person against a state occupying a jurisdictional space, no matter what a person's relationship to that state.[215]

The international rhetoric of rights was not realised in all countries, and they differed in the degree to which they recognised different freedoms.[216] This was often because, as Kant anticipated, a right depended on social acceptance of a reciprocal freedom. Rights to creations began to be recognised following the industrial revolution. Sexual rights were relatively recently recognised on grounds of fairness,[217] as were modern conceptions of cultural rights, use of the mother tongue and rights to study.

VI. CONCLUSION

Spinoza argued that religious and philosophical toleration was compatible with sovereign power and beneficial to it.[218] Power, manifest as obedience, was more easily achieved when policy was popular. Law which forbade expression of views or beliefs created a sullen and hostile population.[219] Therefore, it was rational to allow the expression of opinion not disturbing the peace or threatening the state as a condition of spontaneous order. Rights were integral to Western democratic states governed by the rule of law.[220] Limiting the power of the state gave rise to different kinds of liberty. Through elections, all citizens played a role in determining the laws that govern them (political liberty), government officials were bound to act in accordance with law declared in advance (legal liberty), and a core of individual rights, for example, civil liberties, was treated as inviolable and protected by law (personal liberty). Recognition of these rights was more likely to advance the rule of law.

---

[215] A-M Berghian, 'Fundamental Human Rights and Liberties: Concept and Classification' (2007) 10 *Annales Universitatis Apulensis Series Jurisprudentia* 38.

[216] DW Carbado, 'Black Rights, Gay Rights, Civil Rights'(2000) 47 *UCLA L Rev* 1467.

[217] The House of Lords held that to interpret the Rent Act 1977 to deprive a homosexual couple of protection would be discriminatory (*Ghaidan v Godin-Mendoza* [2004] UKHL 30 [2004] 3 All ER 411 per Lord Nicholls at 565, para 9).

[218] This suggested that Spinoza read Hobbes (N Malcom, 'Hobbs and Spinoza' in JH Burn (ed), *Cambridge Histories Online* (Cambridge University Press, 2008) 530, www.johnjthrasher.com/wp-content/uploads/2014/01/Hobbes-and-Spinoza-Noel-Malcolm.pdf

[219] Spinoza (n 8) ch 20.

[220] See further, Tamanaha (n 76) ch 3.

8
Legality

I. INTRODUCTION

THIS CHAPTER LOOKS at the corollary of rights, legality, and the way the legal role served this aspect of the rule of law. It examines how lawyers balanced the task of representing individual interests with public responsibilities to legality. The baseline obligations were not participating in client wrongdoing, or providing facilitative advice, or undermining the integrity of public processes such as litigation. These requirements potentially limited the principle of client loyalty by constraining what lawyers did for clients. A contentious area concerned whether lawyers had a specific obligation to prevent clients harming others by illegal actions. This potentially placed different kinds of obligations, duties of loyalty to clients and public responsibility, in conflict. The two areas were held in balance by a duty of confidentiality covering client communication and lawyers' legal obligation to respect clients' Legal Professional Privilege.

II. THEORY

Hobbes asserted that law was what the sovereign decreed, apparently severing the link between law and justice, or morality, as represented by the medieval tradition of natural law. The social contract bound people to comply with law in return for security. Dicey's insistence on legal rules that were certain, ascertainable, and not retrospective suggested a culture of legality in which people were encouraged to understand and observe law. These notions of the rule of law influenced the law and lawyers by making legality rather than personal morality the organising principle of society.

Two legal traditions, positivism and adversarialism, may have influenced the legal mindset. Positivism was the focus of the analytical jurisprudence of HLA Hart, who suggested that legal systems reached decisions by following facts (previous legal rules). Morality, in contrast, was not fact and could not be subject to the same methods of proof. The tradition of Legal Positivism had negative connotations, a 'positivist' mindset suggesting willingness to apply law whether 'pointless or wrong',[1] but it underpinned the requirements of the adversarial system, which insisted on strict protocols of proof.

The legalistic view of the lawyer's role was exemplified by the doctrine of Legal Professional Privilege, which made the confidentiality of client information a higher value than truth. In such cases, Lord Nicholls of Birkenhead suggested: 'The public interest in a party being able to obtain informed legal advice in confidence prevails over the public interest in all relevant material being available to courts when deciding cases.'[2] Lawyers were obliged to work with this principle, ignoring the fact that, in many cases, the truth of a situation was sacrificed to a procedural device or a rule of evidence. The justification of this was that society gained greater benefit from the trust implicit in lawyer and client relations than decision-making based on truth.

III. LEGALITY AND CONSENT

The legality dimension of the rule of law contributed to law-abiding communities by enabling citizens to live as they wished, asserting their own morality, within the bounds of law. The context of their consent was the constitutional arrangement, although this might be compromised in crises, such as the American civil war or the Troubles in Northern Ireland.[3] These events arguably reflected the failed promise of the rule of law to protect minority interests, justifying rebellion. This raised the issue of when violence was justified in a society governed by the rule of law.

Hart proposed that the rule of law was maintained by citizens' habits of obedience. These could be internal – acceptance of law as right, or external – fear of sanction.[4] Mechanisms for stimulating debate, rights such as free speech and protest, gave society an opportunity to respond to dissent and therefore strengthened the rule of law. There was significant debate about whether disruptive civil disobedience and violent protest could be placed on the same spectrum as these rights since, on the face of it, they denied the rule of law.

In 1965, the federal court in Montgomery, Alabama in the US sanctioned a civil rights march from Selma to Montgomery to protest about discrimination, including suppression of black voter registration.[5] The march, which would take a week, would cause considerable traffic disruption and divert resources. In deciding whether the march should take place the judge, Frank Johnson, stated that the 'extent of the right to assemble, demonstrate and march peaceably along the highways and streets in an orderly manner should be commensurate with the enormity of the wrongs that are being protested and petitioned against'.[6] This test might also

---

[1] See further 'Legal Positivism' in Stanford Encyclopedia of Philosophy, https://plato.stanford.edu/entries/legal-positivism/.
[2] *In re L (A Minor) (Police Investigation: Privilege)* [1997] AC 16, 32.
[3] JE Finn and JD Finn, *Constitutions in Crisis: Political Violence and the Rule of Law* (Oxford, Oxford University Press on Demand, 1991).
[4] HLA Hart *The Concept Of Law* (Oxford, Clarendon Press, 1994) 51–61.
[5] *Williams v Wallace* 240 F. Supp. 100, 106 (M.D. Ala. 1965).
[6] B Marshall, 'The Protest Movement and the Law' (1965) 51(5) *Virginia Law Review* 785, 789.

apply to disruptive protest not sanctioned by courts, which nevertheless promotes the rule of law.

Hall referred to a literature arguing that civil disobedience manifesting compulsion to break law could serve 'as a firebreak between legal protest and rebellion ... providing a safety valve through which the profoundly disaffected can vent dissent without resorting to more extreme means'.[7] This, he argued, might promote the rule of law when consistent with a belief in the validity of the law. This kind of civil disobedience commanded society's respect as morally justified. Hall suggested a definition that met these conditions: 'a political protest over an unjust law or policy committed by violating law conscientiously, openly, and non-violently, with respect for the interests of others and with acceptance of punishment'.[8] This test can be applied to recent controversies over public statues.

In the US, statues of Confederate soldiers were erected in Southern States from the late nineteenth century until the mid-1960s, a period of segregation in many States. Recently, many were removed, mainly because of associations with slavery.[9] In 2017 it was suggested that the statue of Admiral Horatio Nelson, on the column in Trafalgar Square in London, should be removed because he had opposed the abolition of slavery in the House of Lords.[10] The argument was contested, partly because the evidence that Nelson supported slavery was ambiguous[11] and because Nelson only spoke in the House of Lords six times, always on naval matters.[12]

In the summer of 2020, demonstrations over the killing of a black man, George Floyd, by a policeman in the US spread to Britain. Participants in a Black Lives Matter demonstration in Bristol pulled down a statue of Edward Colston, applied graffiti and threw it in the harbour. Colston was commemorated in 1895 as a local philanthropist, but since the 1920s his links to the Atlantic slave trade had made him controversial. The largest local concert venue was renamed in 2017 and a petition with 11,000 signatures had called for removal of the statue. A local council committee had been locked in disagreements over wording of a plaque to place on the plinth acknowledging Colston's role in slavery. This delay was offered as justification for the crowd's action.

The organiser of the demonstration said, 'People have been trying to get it taken down "the right way" for decades, but they have been completely disregarded'.[13]

---

[7] MR Hall, 'Guilty but Civilly Disobedient: Reconciling Civil Disobedience and the Rule of Law' (2007) 28(5) *Cardozo Law Review* 2083.

[8] ibid 2085–86.

[9] J Ruck, 'Confederate statures removed across Southern US States' *The Guardian* (15 August 2017) www.theguardian.com/us-news/gallery/2017/aug/15/confederate-statues-removed-across-southern-us-states-in-pictures.

[10] A Hirsch, 'Toppling statues? Here's why Nelson's column should be next' *The Guardian* (22 August 2017) www.theguardian.com/commentisfree/2017/aug/22/toppling-statues-nelsons-column-should-be-next-slavery.

[11] The claims mainly derived from the content of one letter, which was ambiguous and may have been forged in parts by anti-abolitionists. See further, 'Lord Nelson and Slavery: Nelson's dark side' (*History Extra*, 8 June 2020) www.historyextra.com/period/georgian/lord-nelson-slavery-abolition-william-wilberforce-dark-side/; C Brett, 'Deceit and Defamation: The Nelson-Taylor Letter' (*The Nelson Society*) https://nelson-society.com/nelson-letter-a-forgery/.

[12] S Anderson, 'Did Nelson really back the slave trade?' *Eastern Daily Press* (21 October 2020) www.edp24.co.uk/lifestyle/heritage/lord-nelson-slave-trade-simon-taylor-letter-doctored-6408146.

[13] T Wall, 'How Bristol dumped its hated slaver in the docks, and a nation searched its soul' *The Guardian* (14 June 2020).

What followed apparently vindicated this claim to a higher purpose. The statue was recovered from the harbour, but there were no plans to reinstall it. It was displayed in a museum, complete with graffiti applied during the incident, and with placards recovered in the aftermath of the demonstration. The museum surveyed opinion on whether it should be a permanent exhibit in that condition. It was argued that removal of the statue was justified by the strength of feeling against Colston commemorations in Bristol and the length of the campaign to remove them.

Some journalists argued that violent public protest brought the issue to attention, stimulated debate and quickened desirable change. It drew attention to historical inequality, confronting British people's complacency on colonialism and the legacy of empire.[14] This might, in turn, have shifted public opinion on contemporary inequality and forced the establishment to consider changes to address them. It stimulated a continuing national debate about other statues, like one of Cecil Rhodes at Oriel College Oxford and those of Nelson and Winston Churchill, who was accused of holding imperialist and racist views. Oriel College resolved to remove the statue of Rhodes, but eventually resorted to a plaque acknowledging his exploitation of Southern Africans.[15]

A columnist defended the Colston action arguing that 'processes' were used by conservatives to 'stymie change'.[16] She argued: 'process by its very nature is conservative. ... the rights we now take for granted were won by people who knew when the time had come to give up on the establishment. Civil disobedience, strikes, riots and boycotts are not the hijacking of process: they are its continuation by other means'. This conflated legitimate protest, boycotts, with illegitimate, riots, and ends with means. The removal of statues in the US was the result of local political decisions, or legal cases[17] while removing the Colston statue was violent.

Five people accepted police cautions and four were charged with criminal damage and elected for jury trial at Bristol Crown Court. At the end of 2021, a historian gave evidence that Colston was 'heavily involved' in the Royal Africa Company, which shipped 84,000 slaves.[18] One of the four defendants stated 'this was not a violent act. This was an act of love for the people of Bristol'.[19] Her barrister submitted that the statue was 'forcibly and, we submit, lawfully removed from its plinth', because veneration of Colston was an act of abuse in a multicultural city. He urged the jury to be 'on the right side of history'.[20]

---

[14] D Olusoga, 'The toppling of Edward Colston's statue is not an attack on history. It is history' *The Guardian* (8 June 2020) www.theguardian.com/commentisfree/2020/jun/08/edward-colston-statue-history-slave-trader-bristol-protest; D Olusoga, 'A year on, the battered and graffitied Colston is finally a potent memorial to our past' *The Guardian* (6 June 2021) https://amp.theguardian.com/commentisfree/2021/jun/06/year-on-battered-graffitied-colston-finally-potent-memorial-to-our-past.

[15] Wall (n 13).

[16] N Malik, 'When petitions and pleas are ignored, protest is essential' *The Guardian* (15 June 2020).

[17] 'Confederate statue removed from city hall in Louisiana after 99 years' *The Guardian* (18 July 2021) www.theguardian.com/us-news/2021/jul/18/confederate-statue-removed-city-hall-louisiana.

[18] D Gayle, 'Colston's firm enslaved more Africans than any other, Olusoga tells court' *The Guardian* (17 December 2021).

[19] ibid.

[20] D Gayle, '"Be on the right side of history", jury in Colston statue trial is urged' *The Guardian* (5 January 2022).

Prosecuting counsel argued that the case was 'fundamentally about the rule of law ... If we can simply pull down what offends us regardless of the views of others then what statues, institutions or buildings are next, you might ask'.[21] The jury disagreed, acquitting the defendants in 2022, in a clear case of jury nullification. Defence barristers were at pains to emphasise that the decision was justified, the case turning on the particular facts and not justifying any other violent acts, but government threatened more draconian punishment as part of a proposed raft of legislation designed to deter protest.[22] Both protesters and government diminished the rule of law according to test of legitimate civil protest proposed by Hall J at Selma.

IV. CONFIDENCES

A. Integrity

Lawyers' contribution to legality was the flip side of their role in vindicating client rights. By acting as intermediaries between individuals and the state they explained the law, assisting clients against more powerful opponents and ensuring equality of arms. Their advice to clients was intended to enable them to obey the law.[23] The fact that they might contribute to illegality, allowing guilty clients to walk free on technicalities, was an acceptable cost for the condition of freedom. Other risks to legality included enabling clients contemplating illegal actions or undertaking work for clients not in itself illegal, but which facilitated illegal or immoral actions.[24] Where these actions fell in the range of lawyers' ethical responsibilities depended on one's philosophical position.

The secrecy of the counselling role created a risk that lawyers might become involved in clients' illegal activity, facilitate it by providing advice, minimise their risk of being caught or even anticipate the investigation process. This would be antithetical to the idea behind a system built of the rule of law. Because of the importance of lawyers in maintaining legality a high premium was placed on integrity. This was one of many words with a broad range of meaning, suggesting a state of wholeness embracing straightforwardness, honesty, principled behaviour, consistency, and an absence of corruption.

The Canadian McRuer Report referred to professionals as the broad class of technical expert society depended on. The designation commanded the personal confidence individuals could place in the technical competence and integrity of practitioners to provide a service. A key part of this relationship of trust was that

---

[21] ibid.
[22] A Allegretti and D Gayle, 'Shapps vows "loophole" will be closed as Tories rage at Colston acquittal' *The Guardian* (7 January 2022).
[23] An example of the 'traditional republican ideal' in action was using authority with clients to promote respect for Law (RG Pearce, 'Rediscovering the Republican Origins of the Legal Ethics Codes' (1992) 6(24) *Georgetown Journal of Legal Ethics* 241) citing RW Gordon, 'The Independence of Lawyers' (1988) 68 *Boston University Law Review* 1, 14).
[24] A Boon, *Lawyers' Ethics and Professional Responsibility* (Oxford, Hart Publishing, 2015) 127–33.

professionals would not exploit intimate details disclosed to them.[25] They were also independent, not controlled by their clientele and there were extreme circumstances where they owed a higher duty to a public value or interest than to the individual client. Recognising those circumstances and acting accordingly was a defining aspect of professional practice.

B. Lawyer and Client Relationship

The rule of law typically protected client secrets told to lawyers in two ways, by a duty of confidentiality and a professional privilege of more limited application. Although the circumstances where they arose were similar, they were not related branches of a single doctrine.[26] Confidentiality derived from equitable principles based on a public interest, so could be ousted by countervailing public interest concerns.[27] The privilege accorded lawyer and client communication was a common law doctrine to which public interest arguments were irrelevant. It was recognised by the state as the client's right, which lawyers had no discretion to ignore. Recognition of the privileged nature of communication prevented any court investigation.

An extended academic analysis by Jonathan Auburn in 2000 found privilege for lawyer and client communication was ubiquitous in leading common law jurisdictions, though called Legal Professional Privilege (UK), attorney client privilege (US) and both Legal Professional Privilege and client-legal privilege (Australia).[28] Auburn suggested that, by the first half of the twentieth century such privilege generally had an instrumental or utilitarian basis.[29] It was justified by reference to the complexity of legal matters, the need for lawyers, competent advice depending on full factual knowledge, and protected communication encouraging client disclosure. This brought about social benefits, including confidence in lawyers and, through their advice, the encouragement of lawful behaviour.

In English law, the confidential nature of a communication or document was a pre-requisite of Legal Professional Privilege (LPP). The privilege was lost if information became public, even without a positive intention to surrender it, because the quality of confidence was lost.[30] Litigants could be ordered to give full disclosure of privileged information if part was given, and it would be unfair to conceal the remainder.[31] Other jurisdictions recognised the privilege of lawyer and client

---

[25] F Schindeler, 'Hon. J. C. McRuer, Royal Commission Inquiry into Civil Rights: Report No. 1. Toronto: Queen's Printer, 1968, Pp. Lix, 1331' (1969) 2 *Canadian Journal of Political Science* 131. Royal Commission, *Inquiry Into Civil Rights*. Ontario Report No 1, Volume 3, at p 1161, cited by WR Flaus 'Discipline within the New Zealand Legal Profession' (1971) 6 *Victoria University of Wellington Law Review* 337, fn 2.

[26] For a summary see J Auburn, *Legal Professional Privilege: Law and Theory* (Oxford, Hart Publishing Ltd, 2000) 18.

[27] *Robb v Green* [1895] 2 QB 315, suggested that the obligation was an implied contract or equitable principle but *Seager v Copydex Ltd No 1* [1967] 1 WLR 973 confirmed the basic principle as equitable (and see Auburn (n 26) 59).

[28] Auburn, (n 26) 1 and my thanks to Julian Webb for explaining the Australian position.

[29] Auburn (n 26).

[30] ibid 196–97.

[31] ibid ch 11.

communications in similar ways. In the US the duty was absolute and permanent once it applied, enabling lawyers 'successfully to perform the duties of his office'.[32] Most common law jurisdictions required disclosure of non-privileged material in litigation through a formal disclosure process.[33]

Privilege from production in court could be claimed for communications between lawyer and client, and between both and third parties, such as witnesses. All were admissible as evidence but not compellable. The rationale was that the legal process was a contest between the evidence assembled by the parties. As the American judge, Justice Jackson observed: 'Discovery was hardly intended to enable a learned profession to perform its functions either without wits or on wits borrowed from the adversary'.[34] Rules could provide privilege was lost if a party no longer had an interest in the confidentiality of a communication (for example, where he was dead or otherwise beyond prosecution). In one US case, however, the permanency of LPP prevented two lawyers from providing exculpatory evidence of a confession by a deceased client which could have exonerated a defendant in a capital murder case.[35]

C. Confidentiality

A distinct lawyer's duty of confidence to clients was established by the eighteenth century as an obligation owed by a 'gentleman of character' both as a matter of honour and to facilitate the conduct of business.[36] From the mid-nineteenth century, the English common law recognised a general protection from disclosure where information attracted an obligation of confidence,[37] the provider had a reasonable expectation of confidence,[38] and unauthorised use was detrimental to the communicator.[39] Any duty was subject to a public interest in disclosing information in breach of confidence.[40]

Unlike lawyers, journalists were unable to claim that communications with sources were privileged. They therefore relied on confidentiality laws to protect them. The consequences were illustrated in the case of a journalist who refused

---

[32] *Hatton v Robinson* 31 Mass (12 Pick.) 416 (1834) per Chief Justice Lemuel Shaw, Supreme Judicial Court of Massachusetts at 422.
[33] Auburn (n 26) 175.
[34] *Hickman v Taylor* (1947) 329 US 495, 516 (cited by Lord Roger in *Three Rivers District Council & Others v Governor and Company of the Bank of England (No 6)* [2004] UKHL 48, [2005] 1 AC 610 (House of Lords) hereafter *Three Rivers*).
[35] *State v Macumber* 112 Arizona 569,544 PZd 1084 (1976).
[36] *Annesley v Anglesey* 17 How. St. Tr. 1140, 1223-226, 1241 (Ex., 1743); JT Noonan, 'The Purposes of Advocacy and the Limits of Confidentiality' (1966) 64 *Michigan Law Review* 1485.
[37] Hence, there is no duty in relation to information that is public knowledge.
[38] *Duke of Queensberry v Shebbeare* (1758) 2 Eden 329.
[39] *Prince Albert v Strange* (1849) 2 De G & Sm 652, on Appeal 1 Mac & G 25; *Coco v AN Clark (Engineers) Ltd* [1968] FSR 415, [1969] RPC 41, per Megarry J at 47; *Attorney-General v Guardian Newspapers Ltd (No 2)* [1990] 1 AC 109, per Lord Goff at 281 (and see further *Halsbury's Laws* Vol 8(1) paras 401–6).
[40] *Attorney General v Observer Ltd and other respondents* [1990] 1 AC 109.

to reveal the source of stolen confidential corporate information.[41] Lord Bridge asserted that:

> In our society the rule of law rests on twin foundations: the sovereignty of the Queen in Parliament in making the law and the sovereignty of the Queen's courts in interpreting and applying the law. While no one doubts the importance of protecting journalists' sources, no one, I think, seriously advocates an absolute privilege against disclosure admitting of no exceptions.[42]

The journalist had sworn an affidavit stating, 'I cannot therefore see a moral justification for breaking my undertaking [of confidentiality]'. Lord Bridge of Harwich suggested that this assertion of the right of the journalist to determine justification, rather than the court, 'wholly undermines the protestations of a high-minded determination to seek a martyr's crown in conscientious defence of an indissoluble obligation'.[43]

Under the Contempt of Court Act 1981, s 10, the House of Lords had to decide whether the journalist was in contempt of court or could be exempted because disclosure was not in the interests of justice, state security or crime prevention.[44] Since the last two circumstances did not apply, the court had to decide if it was in the interests of justice to order the journalist to disclose the source. Protecting the source was more important if illegally obtained information exposed iniquity. Lord Bridge observed that he had not noticed any campaign claiming the law was unjust or the exceptions too broad:

> But if there were such a campaign, it should be fought in a democratic society by persuasion, not by disobedience to the law ... The journalist cannot be left to be judge in his own cause and decide whether or not to make disclosure. This would be an abdication of the role of Parliament and the courts in the matter ... [T]o contend that the individual litigant, be he a journalist or anyone else, has a right of 'conscientious objection' which entitles him to set himself above the law if he does not agree with the court's decision, is a doctrine which directly undermines the rule of law and is wholly unacceptable in a democratic society ... Freedom of speech is itself a right which is dependent on the rule of law for its protection and it is paradoxical that a serious challenge to the rule of law should be mounted by responsible journalists.[45]

Recent cases in which courts developed the tort of breach of confidence to incorporate a right to privacy[46] did not generally affect the nature of the obligation of lawyers to clients. The lawyer's legally binding promise of confidentiality was already broad. It potentially included the fact that they were acting for that client at all if that was material to the client.[47] It was also less relevant where the client communication was also privileged.

---

[41] *X Ltd and another v Morgan-Grampian (Publishers) Ltd and others* [1990] 2 All ER 1.
[42] ibid, see extracts at *Loveland: Constitutional Law, Administrative Law and Human Rights 8e: Online casebook*, https://learninglink.oup.com/static/5c0e79ef50eddf00160f35ad/casebook_199.htm.
[43] ibid.
[44] Contempt of Court Act 1981, s 10.
[45] ibid.
[46] *Campbell v Mirror Group Newspapers* [2004] UKHL 22.
[47] 'JK Rowling wins breach of confidence damages' (*Solicitors Journal*, 31 July 2013).

D. Legal Professional Privilege (LPP)

In the UK LPP originated in common law but was defined in a statute governing police criminal investigation.[48] This identified two categories, the first covering communication to obtain legal advice and the second applying only to litigation. Litigation privilege was broader than advice privilege in that it covered communications with witnesses and experts and the products of such investigations, the material gathered. This distinction could be important since one privilege might be allowed without the other. This also made the antecedents of the privileges relevant.

The origin of LPP in litigation was suggested by Sir George Mackenzie's allusion to it in 1755 to the context of advocacy:

> An Advocate is by the Nature of his Imployment tied to the same Faithfulness that any Depositor is: For his Client has depositate in his Breast his greatest Secrets; and it is the Interest of the Common-wealth, to have that Freedom allowed and secured without which Men cannot manage their Affairs and private Business: And who would use that Freedom if they might be ensnared by it? This were to beget a Diffidence betwixt such who should, of all others, have the greatest mutual Confidence with one another; and this will make Men so jealous of their Advocates that they will lose their private Business, or succumb in their just Defence, rather than Hazard the opening of their Secrets to those who can give them no Advice when the case is Half concealed, or may be forced to discover them when revealed.[49]

Blackstone's *Commentaries*, which referred to 'a cause' also suggested privilege was limited to litigation:

> no counsel, attorney, or other person, entrusted with the secrets of the cause by the party himself, shall be compelled, or perhaps allowed, to give evidence of such conversation or matters of privacy, as came to his knowledge by virtue of such trust and confidence: but he may be examined as to mere matters of fact, as the execution of a deed or the like, which might have come to his knowledge without being entrusted in the cause.[50]

Blackstone may also be taken to suggest a possible exception for matters divulged without 'being entrusted in the cause'.

Despite suggestions that privilege originated in litigation, Auburn found evidence of a distinct advice privilege in the Elizabethan period.[51] It was, despite competing rationales, a logical reaction to testimonial compulsion at the time.[52] In this, Auburn contradicted the evidence scholar, John Henry Wigmore, who suggested the rule was based on respect for the honour of the lawyer. The potential of origin to affect rationale and scope became relevant around the 1980s, when state agencies sought

---

[48] In England and Wales they are set out in the Police and Criminal Evidence Act 1984, s 10(1) and 10(2).
[49] *Sir George Mackenzie's Works*, Vol 2 (1755) at p 44, cited by Lord Rodger of Foscote in *Three Rivers* (n 34) para 54.
[50] W Blackstone, *Commentaries on the Laws of England in Four Books*. Book the Fourth – Chapter: The Twenty Third: Trial by Jury.
[51] Lord Taylor of Gosforth CJ traced antecedents in the 16th century reports in *R v Derby Magistrates' Court, Ex p B* [1996] AC 487, 507 et seq and see JH Wigmore and JT Mcnaughton, *Evidence in Trials at Common Law* (Boston, Little, Brown & Co, 1961) cited by Auburn (n 26) 16–17.
[52] Auburn (n 26) 61–62.

documents or testimony in regulatory investigations or created for administrative tribunals.[53] This raised the issue of whether privilege could be claimed by both individuals and corporations and whether the protection was different.

The first issue was whether privilege applied in the same way to litigation and advice. Auburn suggested two routes were possible. One was to confine the privilege to a 'rule of evidence' in litigation, and the other to conceive of it as a broader and more substantive right. In the initial phase, the more restrictive view prevailed. The validity of search warrants in Canada, Australia and South Africa were upheld on the ground that privilege did not apply on the particular facts of the cases presented. The New Zealand Court of Appeal was exceptional in deciding that privilege prevented disclosure of information to the Commissioner for Inland Revenue.[54]

Auburn argued that the instrumental rationale for privilege gradually declined across jurisdictions as it was augmented or supplanted by rights-based arguments.[55] By this point, many countries had legislation superimposing a framework of rights on the common law. There was little point in providing accused parties with rights to consult lawyers if whatever they said was not confidential. Of the common law jurisdictions considering the issue in the 1980s, only South Africa failed to recognise privilege as a substantive legal right. Auburn expected the binding framework of rights introduced by the Human Rights Act 1998 in the UK,[56] with incorporation of Articles 6 (right to a fair trial) and 8 (right to respect for private and family life) to English law,[57] would lead to a substantive common law right of LPP.[58]

A move towards recognition of LPP as a right was the House of Lords' decision in *R v Derby Magistrates' Court, ex p B*[59] where Lord Taylor referred to the privilege as 'more than an ordinary rule of evidence ... [and] a fundamental condition on which the administration of justice as a whole rests'.[60] This appeared to elevate LPP beyond a legal right to a constitutional principle, but it was not clear whether it covered corporations. The argument was that it should not because 'human' rights were not at stake and because of corporate capacity to cause harm on a massive scale.

An opportunity to test the limits of LPP was provided very soon after Auburn's book was published. *Three Rivers District Council and Others v Governor and Company of the Bank of England (No 6)*[61] (*Three Rivers*), decided four years later, had narrow facts, but provided considerable illumination of corporate claims to privilege. The principles that emerged, particularly regarding the scope of advice privilege, were significant and potentially enduring. In the House of Lords, Lord Scott of Foscote set out the facts in the leading judgment.[62]

---

[53] ibid 17.
[54] *IRC v West-Walker* [1954] NZLR 191 (CA).
[55] Auburn (n 26) ch 2.
[56] ibid 17.
[57] Human Rights Act 1998, Sch 1, Part 1.
[58] *General Mediterranean Holdings SA v Patel* [1999] 3 All ER 691 per Toulson J, cited at 25.
[59] *R v Derby Magistrates' Court, ex p B* [1996] 1 AC.
[60] ibid 507.
[61] *Three Rivers* (n 34).
[62] ibid 1275.

The case arose out of the collapsed Bank of Credit and Commerce International SA (BCCI) in July 1991 with a huge excess of liabilities over assets. The Chancellor of the Exchequer announced in Parliament that there would be an independent inquiry chaired by Bingham LJ, whose terms of reference included consideration of whether action taken by all the UK authorities was 'appropriate and timely'.[63] Under the Banking Acts of 1979 and 1987 the Bank of England (the Bank) had a supervisory role over the UK banking sector and so was the principal subject of investigation.

In preparation for the Inquiry the Governor of the Bank appointed three officials to deal with all communications with the inquiry. They became known as the Bingham Inquiry Unit (BIU). The City of London solicitors' firm Freshfields were retained to advise the Bank in relation to the inquiry. The BIU prepared information and instructions to Freshfields and received advice on the preparation and presentation of evidence to the inquiry. Paperwork comprised a substantial volume of communications including witness statements and a 258-page overarching statement setting out the Bank's case and material evidence. The Bingham Inquiry Report was published on 22 October 1992.

In 1993 the claimants, over 6,000 people with interests at stake, depositors, shareholders, liquidators, and creditors, sued the Bank of England. Under the relevant legislation the Bank was not liable for negligence, but only for discharging its functions in regulating BCCI in bad faith.[64] The claimants therefore had to show a failure of regulatory supervision amounting to misfeasance in public office. Lord Scott observed that:

> This requirement plainly placed before the claimants in the action (the respondents before your Lordships) a very high hurdle and it is not in the least surprising that they have been, and still are, seeking the widest possible discovery from the Bank in order to assist their efforts to jump it.[65]

Numerous applications sought discovery of documents held by the Bank. It could not claim litigation privilege because the Bingham Inquiry was an inquisitorial proceeding, not an adversarial proceeding[66] and a previous House of Lord's decision, *In re L* blocked litigation privilege for material produced in inquisitorial matters.[67] The Bank's claim, that advice privilege covered all documents prepared for the dominant purpose of obtaining or recording legal advice from Freshfields or counsel, was accepted by the first instance judge, Tomlinson J. He held that internal confidential documents were privileged from production, as were documents prepared by third parties for the same purpose.

The Court of Appeal upheld the first part of this decision. Privilege covered communications between the BIU and Freshfields seeking or giving legal advice

---

[63] ibid.
[64] Banking Act 1987, s 1(4).
[65] Lord Scott para 7.
[66] ibid para 10.
[67] In *re L (A Minor) (Police Investigation: Privilege)* [1997] AC 16 per Lord Jauncey of Tullichettle, Lord Lloyd of Berwick and Lord Steyn at 26, 30 and 37 (Lord Mustill and Lord Nicholls of Birkenhead dissenting).

and no one else was to be treated as the client for privilege purposes. The Bank was refused leave to appeal and so began disclosing documents provided by non-members of the BIU, including the Governor of the Bank who, not being a member of the BIU, was but a 'single officer however eminent'.[68] A dispute arose over whether advice from Freshfields covering presentational advice was covered. Tomlinson J, following the Court of Appeal, held privilege only covered advice concerning the Bank's rights and obligations. The Bank again appealed, and the Court of Appeal confirmed that advice to BIU on how to present its submission to the Bingham Inquiry did not qualify for privilege.

Having outlined these material facts in the House of Lord appeal, Lord Scott suggested they raised three questions; what sort of communications were covered by LPP, what constituted legal advice or assistance, and were all communications between lawyers and employees of corporate clients covered? He added however, that a coherent view of the issues could not be expressed without considering first the policy reasons for establishing advice privilege and then for retaining it. The scope of the privilege should reflect the outcome. In the US, New Zealand and Australia, Scott said, the privilege, once found, was absolute.[69] Only Canada qualified secrecy on the grounds of compelling and higher public interest, such as public safety.[70]

i. Litigation Privilege

Lord Carswell indicated that the modern case-law, supported by key nineteenth century cases, limited it to cases where: (a) litigation was in progress or contemplated; (b) communications were made for the sole or dominant purpose of conducting that litigation; and (c) the litigation was adversarial, not investigative, or inquisitorial.[71] The last of these had been recently confirmed. Thus, a report of a railway accident prepared to review safety issues and to seek legal advice was not covered and a report prepared for a dual purpose must anticipate litigation as the main or dominant purpose.[72] These restrictions made litigation privilege narrow and the scope of advice privilege crucial.

The potential narrowness of litigation privilege was illustrated in a recent case involving a Serious Fraud Office investigation of allegations of fraud at subsidiaries of a mining corporation operating in Eastern Europe and Africa.[73] The High Court upheld a claim for advice privilege in respect of only some documents held by the corporation, so protection of the remainder depended on litigation privilege. The High Court rejected the claim because the documents had not been created when criminal legal proceedings were in reasonable contemplation. The judge decided that the point of 'reasonable contemplation' began when a prosecuting authority

---

[68] *Three Rivers* (n 34) per Scott para 14.
[69] ibid para 24.
[70] *Jones v Smith* [1999] 1 SCR 455.
[71] *Three Rivers* (n 34) per Carswell at para 102.
[72] *Waugh v British Railways Board* [1980] AC 521 per Lord Edmund-Davies at 542.
[73] *The Director of The Serious Fraud Office v Eurasian Natural Resources Corporation Limited And The Law Society* [2018] EWCA Civ 2006.

had sufficient evidential basis for prosecution. Possible future charges would be too remote to satisfy the test.

On appeal the Court of Appeal found that most of the documents were covered by litigation privilege and the High Court had incorrectly aligned reasonable contemplation of litigation with a decision to prosecute. The dominant purpose test was satisfied when a prosecuting authority indicated a prospect of a criminal prosecution and a company instructed lawyers in response. The court said that advice with the dominant purpose of avoiding legal proceedings, or given with a view to settlement, was as much protected by litigation privilege as advice given for the purpose of defending proceedings.

The Law Society intervened in the action arguing that, allowing litigation privilege to arise at a late stage in criminal proceedings would deter corporations from consulting lawyers during investigations or engaging in self-reporting. This would undermine lawyers' ability to advise them, the corporations' right not to self-incriminate, and the rule of law. This highlighted the significance of a central issue in *Three Rivers*, the class of persons in a corporation entitled to receive privileged communication. The Law Society argued that the House of Lords had defined this too narrowly.

ii. Advice Privilege

In *Three Rivers* Lord Carswell traced the origin of the modern law on advice privilege to a case decided by Lord Brougham LC in 1833.[74] The defendant solicitor objected to producing materials relating to professional legal advice to his client, and Brougham said:

> To force from the party himself the production of communications made by him to professional men seems inconsistent with the possibility of an ignorant man safely resorting to professional advice and can only be justified if the authority of decided cases warrants it. But no authority sanctions the much wider violation of professional confidence, and in circumstances wholly different, which would be involved in compelling counsel or attorneys or solicitors to disclose matters committed to them in their professional capacity, and which, but for their employment as professional men, they would not have become possessed of.[75]

Brougham scotched any limitation of the privilege to proceedings pending or in contemplation: 'for a person oftentimes requires the aid of professional advice upon the subject of his rights and his liabilities, with no references to any particular litigation, and without any other reference to litigation generally than all human affairs have, in so far as every transaction may, by possibility, become the subject of judicial inquiry'.[76]

---

[74] *Greenough v Gaskell* 1 M & K 98, (per Lord Carswell at para 90).
[75] Cited by Lord Carswell in *Three Rivers* (n 34) para 90.
[76] ibid.

Other cases of the period followed a similar line. In *Carpmael v Powis* Lord Lyndhurst LC upheld privilege for communications concerning bids on a sale of land, holding, 'the privilege extends to all communications between a solicitor, as such, and his client, relating to matters within the ordinary scope of a solicitor's duty'.[77]

The outcome of *Three Rivers* was unpredictable in terms of whether the House of Lords would allow a wide or narrow scope. The Law Reform Committee had reported in 1967 that 'its true rationale is as a privilege in aid of litigation'[78] suggesting that advice privilege be confined to counselling on 'rights and liabilities enforceable in law by litigation'.[79] This would have given rise to argument about the prospect, however vague, of future litigation. Lord Carswell thought that this conclusion may have been partly due to the presence of Lord Denning MR and Diplock LJ on the Committee, both having expressed similar views in a later case.[80]

When *Three Rivers* reached the House of Lords Lord Rodger noted that the lower courts had been 'less than enthusiastic about the very notion of legal advice privilege' with Lord Phillips wondering or 'why it should attach to matters such as the conveyance of real property or the drawing up of a will'.[81] The restricted scope of advice privilege favoured by the Law Reform Committee and the Court of Appeal had run counter to the recent cases and, as Lord Scott and Lord Carswell observed, the trend in other major common law jurisdictions.

In the US, the Supreme Court had argued advice privilege promoted 'broader public interests in the observance of law and administration of justice ...'.[82] Australia and Canada had developed it with no limitation as a rule of evidence.[83] The High Court of Australia had argued that privilege was 'serving the ends of justice because it is facilitating the orderly arrangement of the client's affairs as a member of the community'.[84] The Supreme Court of Canada had noted that 'family secrets, company secrets, personal foibles and indiscretions all must on occasion be revealed to the lawyer by the client'.[85] In Canada the privilege covered any circumstances in which a client consulted a solicitor, whether or not litigation was anticipated.[86]

Beyond the common law jurisdictions, continental jurisprudence recognised a fundamental interest in a broad-based privilege. Lord Scott quoted Advocate General Slynn who said:

[The privilege] springs essentially from the basic need of a man in a civilised society to be able to turn to his lawyer for advice and help, and if proceedings begin, for representation;

---

[77] *Carpmael v Powis* (1846) 1 Ph 687 at 692.
[78] 16th Report of the Law Reform Committee, *Privilege in Civil Proceedings* (Cmnd 3472) 1967 page 9, para 18.
[79] ibid para 19.
[80] *Parry-Jones v Law Society* [1969] 1 Ch 1 (see Lord Carswell at para 104).
[81] Lord Rodger 55 citing [2004] QB 916, 935, para 39, per Lord Phillips of Worth Matravers MR.
[82] *Upjohn Co v United States* (1981) 449 US 383 per Renquist J at 389.
[83] *Baker v Campbell* (1983) 153 CLR 52, citing Wilson J in the High Court of Australia at p 94, followed in *Daniels Corporation International Pty Ltd v Australian Competition and Consumer Commission* (2002) 192 ALR 561, 573, para 44, per McHugh J.
[84] *Baker v Campbell* (1983) 153 CLR, Wilson J, 95.
[85] *Jones v Smith* [1999] 1 SCR 455, pp 474–75, para 46.
[86] *Descoteaux v Mierzwinski* (1982) 141 DLR (3d) 590 per Lamer J in the Supreme Court of Canada 604–5.

it springs no less from the advantages to a society which evolves complex law reaching into all the business affairs of persons, real and legal, that they should be able to know what they can do under the law, what is forbidden, where they must tread circumspectly, where they run risks.[87]

In line with the general trend in support of advice privilege, the House regarded limitations on advice privilege canvassed in the Court of Appeal, whether the client had legal liabilities and obligations, whether they arose in private law or public law, or whether litigation was in prospect, as diversions.

Their Lordships considered that the only required limitation was identified by Taylor J in *Balabel v Air India*: a 'relevant legal context'.[88] Lord Rodger had no doubts that a testator's private worries about his son's ability to fend for himself were worthy of protection when communicated to his solicitor in a legal context. Unless privilege applied, people having legitimate interests in keeping such matters private would be inhibited in seeking informed legal advice. Only if, Scott suggested, a solicitor was simply a client's 'man of business', might communications not be covered.[89]

Examples of contexts in which advice might not be legal were canvassed in argument. Counsel for the claimants had proposed that a developer seeking planning permission at a planning inquiry could claim LPP, whereas an objector would not because, following the Law Reform Committees' proposed test, the developer's rights, liabilities, and obligations were in issue, whereas the objector had no rights under planning law. This, Scott concluded, could not be right. It reflected irrelevant concerns about litigation privilege covering non-adversarial proceedings, but it was not relevant to advice privilege. Upholding privilege in the objector's communication would not 'extend litigation privilege to inquiries, but give legal advice privilege its due scope'.[90]

Counsel for the claimants had also argued that legal advice privilege would obviously not cover communication about joining a private club. Lord Scott agreed, not because legal rights or obligations were not involved but because the example 'had no legal context whatever'.[91] Were it given one, he said, a right to advice privilege might emerge. If a previous application to join the club had been rejected in breach of the club rules, for example, advice on a new application to test the rules would clearly be protected by legal advice privilege.[92]

Applying these considerations to the present facts led Lord Scott to the conclusion that communications between the BIU and Freshfields were covered by advice privilege. There would always be marginal cases, he said, but this was not one. The 'relevant legal context' was the Bingham Inquiry, Freshfields would use their legal

---

[87] *Three Rivers* (n 34) per Scott at 33 citing Case 155/79 *AM & S Europe Ltd v Commission of the European Communities* [1983] QB 878, 913, a passage cited by Kirby J in *Daniels Corporation International Pty Ltd v Australian Competition and Consumer Commission* (2002) 192 ALR 561, 584, para 87.
[88] *Balabel v Air India* [1988] Ch 317 Taylor LJ, 330.
[89] *Three Rivers* (n 34) per Scott para 34.
[90] ibid para 39.
[91] ibid para 42.
[92] ibid para 44.

skills to advise properly,[93] and evidence submitted to the Bingham Inquiry for the Bank aimed to persuade that it had blamelessly discharged its public law obligations under the Banking Acts: 'The defence of personal reputation and integrity was at least as important to many individuals and companies as the pursuit or defence of legal rights whether under private law or public law.'[94] Lord Brown was confident that such assistance had the character of legal business.[95]

In summary, advice privilege attached to legal advice given by a lawyer to his or her client where the communication or document was made confidentially for the purpose of obtaining or giving legal advice, including what should be done in a relevant legal context, on an occasion on which it was objectively reasonable to expect the privilege to apply.[96] The Bank was entitled to claim advice privilege for discussions about presentation, as would promoters of private Bills or parliamentary counsel preparing public Bills.[97]

The position taken by the Court of Appeal in *Three Rivers no 5*, that only discussion between the BIU and Freshfields were covered,[98] had caused concern in the legal community regarding the reduced scope of advice privilege. The Attorney General, the Law Society and the Bar Council were given leave to intervene in the litigation by making written submissions. The interveners argued that the Court of Appeal had gone too far in declining advice privilege to communications between Freshfields and Bank employees outside the BIU. In the House of Lords, Lord Scott noted the importance of this for corporate clients but decided that the appeal could be decided without resolving that issue.[99]

The Court of Appeal had indicated that it would have departed from a narrow definition of 'client' but for precedent. The Court of Appeal normally being bound by its own decisions, it was a situation only the House of Lords, or later the Supreme Court could change. The House of Lords may have anticipated that a suitable case would allow proper consideration of the issue, but the expected flood of cases did not materialise, and it may not have anticipated so many years passing before a chance arose.[100] It therefore remained uncertain which individuals within a company could have conversations with a lawyer and be covered by privilege.

iii. Privilege and the Rule of Law

Three Rivers confirmed that advice privilege had acquired a wide public interest rationale. This was outlined by Lady Hale:

> It is in the interests of the whole community that lawyers give their clients sound advice, accurate as to the law and sensible as to their conduct. The client may not always act

---

[93] ibid per Lord Rodger para 60.
[94] ibid per Lord Scott para 44.
[95] ibid per Lord Brown of Eaton-Under-Heywood, para 120.
[96] ibid per Lord Scott para 38.
[97] ibid para 40.
[98] *Three Rivers District Council and others v The Governor and Company of the Bank of England (Three Rivers No 5)* [2003] EWCA Civ 474.
[99] *Three Rivers* (n 34) 21.
[100] In a recent case (*R (on the application of Jet2.com Ltd) v Civil Aviation Authority* [2020] EWCA Civ 35) the Court of Appeal expressed doubt about *Three Rivers No 5* but was obliged to follow it on this point.

upon that advice (which will sometimes place the lawyer in professional difficulty, but that is a separate matter) but there is always a chance that he will. And there is little or no chance of the client taking the right or sensible course if the lawyer's advice is inaccurate or unsound because the lawyer has been given an incomplete or inaccurate picture of the client's position.[101]

It was essential she said that lawyers have full information if they are to 'be able to give the client sound advice as to what he should do, and just as importantly what he should not do, and how to do it'.[102]

Lord Rodger observed that 'the public interest justification for the privilege is the same today as it was 350 years ago: it does not change, or need to change, because it is rooted in an aspect of human nature which does not change either'.[103] The justification was to guarantee confidence in full disclosure to enable the best advice to be given: 'the effect, and indeed the purpose, of the law of confidentiality is to prevent the court from ascertaining the truth so far as regards those matters which the law holds to be confidential'.[104] Lord Scott confirmed that orderly arrangement of clients' affairs was strongly in the public interest because it encouraged clients to be candid.

In *Three Rivers* the House of Lords explicitly linked LPP with the rule of law. Lord Scott suggested that:

> in a society in which the restraining and controlling framework is built upon a belief in the rule of law, that communications between clients and lawyers ... should be secure against the possibility of any scrutiny from others, whether the police, the executive, business competitors, inquisitive busybodies or anyone else ... This, ['the rule of law rationale'] ... justifies, in my opinion, the retention of legal advice privilege in our law, notwithstanding that as a result cases may sometimes have to be decided in ignorance of relevant probative material.[105]

Lord Carswell noted other Commonwealth jurisdictions had elevated advice privilege into 'something more nearly resembling a basic constitutional principle, expressed in the rhetoric of rights'[106] and that a similar transition had occurred in the UK. Lord Taylor's opinion that privilege was a 'fundamental condition for the administration of justice'[107] and Lord Hoffmann's that it was a 'fundamental human right long established in the common law',[108] was evidence of this.

iv. The Crime, Fraud, or Iniquity 'Exception'

The principle that 'no secrecy [was] due to the client in crimes',[109] the so-called iniquity exception to LPP, meant that a client's criminal or fraudulent intent took a

---

[101] *Three Rivers* (n 34) per Baroness Hale of Richmond para 61.
[102] ibid para 62.
[103] ibid per Lord Carswell para 54.
[104] Citing Lord Reid in *Duke of Argyll v Duchess of Argyll* 1962 SC (HL) 88, 93.
[105] *Three Rivers* (n 34) per Scott at para 34.
[106] ibid per Carswell at para 87.
[107] *R v Derby Magistrates' Court, Ex p B* [1996] AC 487 Lord Taylor of Gosforth CJ, with whose reasons the other members of the House agreed, stated, at p 507.
[108] Lord Hoffmann in *R (Morgan Grenfell & Co Ltd) v Special Commissioner of Income Tax* [2003] 1 AC 563, 606, para 7.
[109] *Cutts v Pickering* (1671) 3 Ch Rep 66.

lawyer's advice outside the scope of the lawyer and client relationship.[110] Late cases clarified that the fraud or 'iniquity' exception was not limited to criminal or civil fraud but applied to dishonest conduct in general. This presented problems to conscientious practitioners in deciding what to do about the confidentiality of renegade clients whose right to confidentiality or LPP *may* have been abrogated by such conduct.

In considering whether to negate LPP the court balanced the gravity of the charge against the public policy grounds for protection.[111] The main case, *R v Cox and Railton*, illustrated the practical difficulty.[112] In 1882 Lord Munster brought an action for libel against RJ Railton & Co., the publishers of the *Brightonian* newspaper. Lord Munster obtained damages for libel, but a bailiff sent to seize goods faced a Bill of Sale in favour of Mr Cox, Railton's former partner. The deed of partnership between Cox and Railton concerning *The Brightonian* was produced. It bore a note dissolving the partnership dated before Lord Munster's action. At the defendants' trial for conspiracy to defraud, a solicitor, Mr Goodman, was called by the prosecution.

Goodman gave evidence that he had been consulted by Cox and Railton after judgment in Lord Munster's libel case. He had advised there was no point in transferring the company assets from Railton to Cox because they had been partners at the time the time of the judgment. Assured that this was the only problem, and that Goodman and his clerks were the only ones who knew the details of the partnership,[113] Cox and Railton paid, and he heard no more from them. The defendants were convicted on the conspiracy charge and appealed. One ground was that Goodman's evidence concerned privileged legal advice and should not have been received.

The Court for Crown Cases Reserved[114] considered whether Goodman's evidence was properly received when there was no other evidence that Cox and Railton had committed fraud. It was submitted for the appellants that their communication with Goodman, 'if not absolutely privileged from disclosure, must at least be *primâ facie* privileged, so that the evidence should not have been admitted without some reasonable foundation having first been laid by evidence to destroy the presumption of privilege'.[115] Coleridge CJ, feeling 'the necessity of protecting all legitimate communications between clients and their legal advisers',[116] announced that the five judges then present would be expanded to 10 judges.

When the full court assembled, Lopes J expressed concern at the absence of facts destroying Cox and Railton's privilege. It could not be justified by Goodman's evidence: 'It is impossible to say you are to have the secret of the client disclosed in public, so as to see if it ought to be disclosed.'[117] The conviction was upheld, the reasons delivered later by Stephen J confirmed that the intent of committing a crime

---

[110] Auburn (n 26) ch 8.
[111] See eg Munby J in *C v C* [2009] EWHC 1491 Fam, at para 35.
[112] *R v Cox and Railton* (1884) 14 QBD 153 (and see Auburn (n 26) 151).
[113] *Cox and Railton* ibid 156.
[114] This was a review court later superseded by the Court of Criminal Appeal.
[115] E Clarke QC in *Cox and Railton* (n 112) 157.
[116] ibid 158.
[117] ibid per Lopes J, 161–62.

or fraud negated any professional relationship and privilege.[118] It would he said, 'work most grievous hardship on an attorney, who, after he had been consulted upon what subsequently appeared to be a manifest crime and fraud, would have his lips closed, and might place him in a very serious position of being suspected to be a party to the fraud, and without his having an opportunity of exculpating himself'.[119]

The judgment of the Court for Crown Cases Reserved lamented that the privilege of Cox and Railton had been 'violated in order to ascertain whether it exists'.[120] Had the appeal been about whether to receive Goodman's evidence, the outcome may have been different. In future, courts would need to consider on the facts of the case 'whether it seems probable that the accused person may have consulted his legal adviser … before the commission of the crime for the purpose of being guided or helped in committing it'.[121] Stephen J noted that the power to admit potentially privileged evidence must be used with 'the greatest care … and every precaution should be taken against compelling unnecessary disclosures'.[122]

The 'iniquity' exception to LPP was applied by courts in routine cases. A wife claiming financial provision sought disclosure of insurance arrangements for a valuable art collection her husband moved out of the jurisdiction.[123] The husband's solicitors came off the court record two weeks before trial but gave evidence he was retained 'in general terms' by the husband and two other respondents, P Ltd and C Ltd. He refused to answer further questions on the ground that advice privilege applied. The court refused advice privilege, first, because the solicitor had simply acted as the husband's man of business and any advice lacked a relevant legal context. Its second reason invoked the iniquity exception. Suspicion that property was fraudulently put beyond the jurisdiction was 'determinative' in justifying examination of LPP, irrespective of the decision on legal advice.[124]

The approach in *R v Cox and Railton* was adopted in Canada, Australia, New Zealand, South Africa and the US.[125] Subin noted of the US, clients had no 'right' to use attorneys for achieving unlawful goals.[126] If they conspired with lawyers, the relationship was not professional and if he did not reveal the purpose he did not place confidence in the lawyer.[127] Auburn suggested that this rationale was unsatisfactory. If, for example, at the time of imparting information, Cox and Railton had not formed a clear, dishonest purpose, a lawyer and client relationship existed. If they subsequently formed a criminal plan based on the advice, this could not change that relationship retrospectively.[128] There was no other plausible interpretation than that

---

[118] This was contrary to a strict reading of *Greenough v Gaskell* (n 74) where Lord Brougham suggested the privilege was absolute.
[119] Stephen J (at 175) quoting Bovill CJ in *Tichborne v Lushington*
[120] *Cox and Railton* (n 112) 175.
[121] ibid 175.
[122] ibid 176.
[123] *Z v Z and others* [2016] EWHC 3349 (Fam), [2017] 4 WLR 84, per Haddon-Cave J.
[124] ibid paras 13–18, 27.
[125] Auburn (n 26) 152, *Cox and Railton* (n 112) 168. This rationale was adopted in the US case of *Clark* (1933) 289 U.S. at 15.
[126] HI Subin, 'The Lawyer as Superego: Disclosure of Client Confidences to Prevent Harm' (1985) 70 *Iowa Law Review* 1091, 1162.
[127] Auburn (n 26) 153.
[128] ibid 172.

the privilege had been overridden.[129] This undermined the rationale for advice privilege, that clients were encouraged to be candid and, to echo Lord Scott on another issue, this could not be right.

Over the last 30 years, most jurisdictions imposed statutory duties to report some kinds of client wrongdoing, such as dangerous or high-risk criminal activities. In the UK statutory offences of failing to report suspected terrorism[130] and money laundering[131] or 'tipping off' clients that reports had been made, applied to workers in legal and financial sectors. While exceptions were made where the lawyer came across information in privileged circumstances,[132] the obligations were significant incursions into lawyers' duties of loyalty, candour, and confidentiality.

When Canada imposed money-laundering provisions on lawyers they were challenged by two local Law Societies; the Federation of Law Societies of Canada and the Law Society of British Columbia.[133] These bodies sought declarations that legislative reporting requirements were unconstitutional because they violated the independence of the bar. On an interlocutory application, Justice Allan ordered suspension of such lawyer related provisions pending a full hearing. She concluded that irreparable harm would otherwise result from 'unprecedented intrusion into the traditional solicitor-client relationship'.[134] Similar decisions followed in Alberta, Saskatchewan, Ontario and Nova Scotia. The government repealed the regulations relating to lawyers. Subsequent decisions said that lawyers should not be forced to be sources of information against their clients. Parties seeking information from lawyers would have to show it could not be obtained in other ways, otherwise the principle of lawyer-client confidentiality would not be impaired by a disclosure order.

V. PREVENTING CLIENT HARMS TO THIRD PARTIES

A. Dangerous Clients

Because of their counselling role, lawyers were sometimes positioned to prevent crimes. Examples included client threats to cause physical harm or substantial financial losses to third parties. While common law judges left open the possibility of liability, depending on circumstances, imposing broad legal obligations to prevent harms to others went to the heart of the freedom of the individual. As a Law Lord explained: 'it is less an invasion of the individual's freedom for the law to require him to consider the safety of others in his actions than to impose on him a duty to

---

[129] ibid 127.
[130] Terrorism Act 2000 (as amended), s 38B.
[131] Proceeds of Crime Act 2002 (as amended).
[132] ibid ss 19(5)(a) and 21A(5)(b) and see 'Anti-Terrorism Practice Note' issued by the Law Society, July 2007.
[133] See R Millen, 'The Independence of the Bar: An Unwritten Constitutional Principle' (2005) *Canadian Bar Review* 84.
[134] ibid.

rescue or protect'.[135] The existence of privilege covering communication between lawyer and client was another complication. If a client left a lawyer threatening to immediately visit serious physical harm on a third party, the lawyer might invoke the iniquity principle to justify warning the third party. The risk was that if the client was letting off steam but with no intention of hurting anyone, the lawyer would have broken privilege and besmirched the client's reputation for nothing.

B. Corporate Clients and Financial Harm

The sheer scale of large corporations, and the need to control the risk they posed was highlighted by financial damage to investors, shareholders, and even the world economy by notable cases of corporate collapse. Accountants were more obvious participants in these cases but lawyers, sometimes 'in-house' at the corporation or external law firms, knew of financial malpractice, participated in, or facilitated it or helped to cover it up after the event, sometimes allowing further harm to third-party interests. These scandals included Lincoln Savings and Loan, Enron, WorldCom, Allied Irish Bank, Stanford Financial Group and Tyco International. A substantial American literature bemoaned lawyer's roles in corporate collapse and debated imposing whistleblowing responsibilities or liability.[136]

Its role in the Enron scandal led one of the five leading accountancy firms in the world, Arthur Anderson, to be dissolved but there were relatively few consequences for numerous lawyers involved.[137] The US regulatory response, the Sarbanes Oxley Act 2002, tightened up regulatory infrastructure, emphasising the duty owed by company auditors to corporate stakeholders, like shareholders, rather than directors or company officers. The Act said information filed with the US Securities Exchange Commission must represent a full and reliable account of a company's position and required much more openness, particularly by directors.

During the legislative process, proposals for imposing a duty on attorneys to disclose corporate client wrongdoing to regulatory authorities were canvassed and dismissed. The main problem was reconciling such a duty with confidentiality and attorney-client privilege. Instead, the Act provided that the financial sector regulator, the Securities Exchange Commission (SEC), prescribe minimum standards of professional conduct for attorneys representing issuers.[138] The Act delegated the task of drafting subordinate rules to the SEC.

---

[135] *Stovin v Wise* [1996] AC 923 (per Lord Hoffmann).
[136] See eg WH Simon, 'The Kaye Scholer Affair: The Lawyer's Duty of Candor and the Bar's Temptations of Evasion and Apology' (1998) 23 *Law and Social Inquiry* 243; DC Langevoort, 'What Was Kaye Scholer Thinking?' (1998) 23 *Law and Social Inquiry* 297; RW Gordon, 'A Collective Failure of Nerve: The Bar's Response to Kay Scholer' (1998) 23 *Law and Social Inquiry* 315; E Wald, 'Lawyers and Corporate Scandals' (2004) 7 *Legal Ethics* 54.
[137] D Rhode and P Paton, 'Lawyers, Ethics and Enron' (2002–3) 8 *Stanford Journal of Law Business and Finance* 9; SM Solaiman, 'The Enron collapse and criminal liabilities of auditors and lawyers for defective prospectuses in the United States, Australia and Canada: A Review' (2006–7) 26(8) *Journal of Law and Commerce* 81.
[138] The Sarbanes-Oxley Act 2002, s 307.

In November 2002, the SEC adopted new standards of professional conduct, requiring attorneys to report 'evidence of a material violation'.[139] The obligation was triggered by 'credible evidence, based upon which it would be unreasonable, under the circumstances, for a prudent and competent attorney not to conclude that it is reasonably likely that a material violation has occurred, is ongoing or is about to occur'.[140] The report was, however, to be reported 'up-the-ladder' of the issuer company, to the chief legal counsel or the chief executive officer or a committee established for the purpose.[141] If there was still no remedial response the lawyer was to withdraw from the representation and notify the SEC, not of the suspected violation, but of the suspicion. This process, 'noisy withdrawal', warned the regulator of problems.

The SEC also 'allowed' an attorney, without the consent of an issuer client, 'to reveal confidential information related to his or her representation to the extent the attorney reasonably believes necessary': (1) to prevent the issuer from committing a material violation likely to cause substantial financial injury to the financial interests or property of the issuer or investors; (2) to prevent the issuer from committing an illegal act; or (3) to rectify the consequences of a material violation or illegal act in which the attorney's services have been used.[142]

The weakness in Sarbanes-Oxley was revealed by the collapse of the American merchant Bank, Lehman Brothers, in 2008. This was generally recognised as a factor in a devastating world financial crisis.[143] Illustrating the global reach of corporate finance and corporate law, Lehman Brothers had instructed the City of London 'magic circle' solicitors, Linklaters, to provide a letter which allowed it to conceal over exposure in sub-prime mortgages. American law firms could not supply such a letter for regulatory reasons. Although Sarbanes-Oxley, and the SEC regulations, impacted positively on lawyer conduct[144] it was ineffective in matters outside the regulatory scope of the SEC.

VI. DISCUSSION

A. Legal Observance

William Simon criticised Positivism because citizens often ignored law (speed limits) or were 'entitled' to act contrary to law to achieve substantively fair results (civil rights protests). Thus, he argued, 'Substantivism', citizens' violation of legal norms to vindicate more basic ones, fulfils a basic obligation to 'law'. In fact, Simon argued,

---

[139] Securities and Exchange Commission, *Implementation of Standards of Professional Conduct for Attorneys*, www.sec.gov/rules/final/33-8185.htm.
[140] ibid.
[141] ibid.
[142] ibid.
[143] L Elliott and J Treanor, 'Five years on from Lehman: "We had almost no control"' *The Guardian* (13 September 2013).
[144] A Afrati, 'The Stanford Affair: Another Bad Day for Proskauer's Tom Sjoblom' (*Wall Street Journal Law Blog*, 27 August 2009) www.wsj.com/articles/BL-LB-18063.

reasons for obeying law did not apply if they led to 'compliance with jurisdictionally adequate but morally evil laws like the Nazi enactments requiring reporting Jews and dissidents or the antebellum Fugitive Slave Laws'.[145] Nor did he think that there was a categorical reason to obey law unless failing to do so precipitated a threat to a legitimate legal order.[146]

Simon's argument raised issues about the balance between rights such as protest, legality, and the legitimacy of a cause. Hall noted that some critics of disruptive civil disobedience argued that it always damaged the rule of law, impinging on the rights of others as a coercive means to an end.[147] Violent demonstration risked provoking opposition and a cycle of escalation. Escalating disorder did not improve discourse and inevitably ruptured the consensus for obedience to law. Legitimising violent protest encouraged protesters to think of themselves as 'mere subjects aggrieved by the sovereign rather than as citizens with responsibility and opportunity for participation'.[148]

The only avenue for those charged with violent civil disobedience was jury nullification, which conveyed disregard for the rule of law. Hall argued that bringing civil disobedience into the legal structure would diminish conflict by allowing pleas of 'guilty but civilly disobedient' to defendants who acted conscientiously, openly, and respectfully in breaking the law.[149] This did not involve pleading guilty, but willing acceptance of punishment upheld respect for law.[150] Since retribution usually reflected the gravity of the offence, a guilty but civilly disobedient verdict could attract lesser punishment on conviction.[151] It did, however, maintain the idea of respect for law.

B. Client Confidence

De Tocqueville observed that lawyers in the US and in England were legalistic.[152] The English seemed 'indifferent to the real meaning of what they treat, and they direct all their attention to the letter, seeming inclined to infringe the rules of common sense and of humanity rather than to swerve one tittle from the law'.[153] He attributed this to the nature of the common law. Adherence to precedent reflected respect for 'the opinions and the decisions of their forefathers' and encouraged 'a love of regular and

---

[145] WH Simon, 'Should Lawyers Obey the Law' (1996) 38 *William and Mary Law Review* 217, 224.
[146] ibid, Simon suggested that his alternative, Substantivism (see next chapter) might lead to a decentralised legal system, albeit one considered by a Positivist as a form of anarchy.
[147] Hall (n 7).
[148] ibid 2100.
[149] ibid 2114.
[150] ibid 2105.
[151] MC Loesch, 'Motive Testimony and a Civil Disobedience Justification' (1991) 5 *Notre Dame Journal of Law, Ethics & Public Policy* 1069.
[152] A de Tocqueville, *Democracy in America* (trans H Reeve) (Penn State Electronic Classics Series, 1831) 305–7, http://seas3.elte.hu/coursematerial/LojkoMiklos/Alexis-de-Tocqueville-Democracy-in-America.pdf.
[153] ibid 307.

lawful proceedings'.[154] This reverence for custom was not found in a French advocate, who was more concerned with 'what should have been done, and hence his own opinion'. This created different dispositions towards cases; the former, De Tocqueville said, produced precedents, the latter reasons.[155]

In the core countries the legal role reflected a legalistic mindset. Common lawyers only recognised responsibilities legally imposed, not consideration of causal questions (why or in who's interest?), simply how to achieve their client's goals.[156] Their obligation to legality was not to counsel or further client illegality. The client's right to confidential counsel was in line with the nature of adversarial advocacy, but explicitly applied to advice since Lord Brougham's intervention in the mid-1800s. The modern British law was asserted by the House of Lords in the *R v Derby Magistrates* declaration that 'if a balancing exercise was ever required ... it was performed once and for all in the 16th century, and since then was applied across the board in every case, irrespective of the client's individual merits'.[157] *Three Rivers* confirmed that the counselling dimension of the lawyer's role was a decisive policy consideration. The law gave lawyers an opportunity to dissuade clients from wrongful actions, maximising liberty.

Auburn noted a tendency in Commonwealth jurisdictions to regard privilege as absolute. Treating privilege as sacrosanct could, Auburn predicted, be problematic, since there were circumstances in which privilege either assisted or impeded a fair trial. A question of whose rights were enforced therefore arose. Auburn argued that Commonwealth courts paid insufficient regard to arguments for the disclosure of evidence,[158] even when privilege produced unjust results.[159] Canada appeared most sympathetic to privilege, Millen suggesting that a rebuttable presumption operated in favour of privileged client and lawyer communication, to prevent the lawyer's office becoming 'archives for the use of the prosecution'.[160]

Auburn noted that American rules on privilege were more relaxed, with each case depending on its merits. This position seemed counterintuitive given constitutional rights to counsel and against self-incrimination and a view, identified by Subin, that confidentiality was the pre-requisite of individual autonomy and the primary objective of the legal system.[161] The justification of privilege, that clients would not otherwise reveal the unvarnished truth, was often doubted.

Academics suggested clients did not understand the differences between privilege and confidentiality[162] or were unaware that disclosures to lawyers were protected at all.[163] A bare majority of people expected their behaviour would be affected if there were no

---

[154] ibid 305.
[155] ibid 305.
[156] G Baars, *The Corporation, Law and Capitalism: A Radical Perspective on the Role of Law in the Global Political Economy* (Chicago, Haymarket Books, 2020) 266.
[157] *R v Derby Magistrates Court Ex p. B* [1996] AC 487 Lord Taylor, para 65.
[158] Auburn (n 26) 8,101.
[159] ibid ch 13.
[160] *Maranda v Richer* [2003] 3 SCR 193 at 215, cited by Millen (n 133) fns 48 and 56.
[161] Subin (n 126) 1160.
[162] Auburn (n 26) ch 4.
[163] FC Zacharias, 'Rethinking Confidentiality' (1989) 74 *Iowa LR* 351; R Cranston (ed), *Legal Ethics and Professional Responsibility* (Oxford, Clarendon Press, 1995) 9.

protection.[164] This, Auburn argued, meant that privilege rules could be more restrictive[165] but he did not favour exceptions once privilege was found to apply.[166] This would make it easier, he reasoned, to forewarn clients when conversations were not privileged.[167] It would also give scope to specify circumstances when privilege would not survive a client's death.[168]

Whatever changes might be made to LPP, arguments based on client awareness seemed unconvincing. People may have been unaware of the details of their right to secrecy, but they were surely aware that disclosures to their lawyers were not the same as disclosures to police officers. Changes to English law weakening privilege did not seem likely following *Three Rivers*. The judges there seemed united behind the argument that privilege promoted frank disclosure. An exception was Lindsay J who, before *Three Rivers*, had argued that this argument was exaggerated.[169] He observed that *R v Cox and Railton* had not obviously inhibited clients in what they told their legal advisers.

R v Cox and Railton did not provide a sound basis for lawyers warning third parties of impending harm by their clients. The lawyer in that case, Goodman, should not have breached his client's privilege without a court ruling, and the delay would surely inhibit lawyers aware of clients' malign illegal intentions towards third parties in an emergency. Allowing any action was inconsistent with a client's presumed privilege, creating a conflict between legality and rights.[170] Subin advocated a legal duty on lawyers in relation to prospective acts where some third-party harm was avoidable,[171] and serious.[172] He argued that neither constitutional rights nor privilege presented insuperable barriers to disclosure for purposes clearly in the public interest. On the constitutional issue, he argued that a stipulation that information leading to a kidnap victim could not be used against the accused, who might then go free. Ultimately, whether the public interest was best served by candid disclosure or a duty to report was a matter to be decided in each case.[173]

Practical problems arose when contemplating obligations to report dangerous clients. A chance remark in a discussion of criminal charges did not undermine the purpose for which the client was consulting a lawyer. Therefore, the normal reasons for vitiating confidence or privilege, abuse of the fundamental relationship of trust between lawyer and client, did not apply. It would also be difficult to prescribe the point when a risk should be taken seriously. Absent the decision of a court, the risk would have to be so clear and present that it overwhelmed the need for an order negating client privilege.

---

[164] See Auburn (n 26) 72–75.
[165] ibid 77.
[166] ibid 508.
[167] ibid 123.
[168] ibid 66–67.
[169] *Saunders v Punch Ltd* [1988] 1 WLR 996.
[170] Subin (n 126).
[171] ibid 1176.
[172] ibid 1172–73.
[173] ibid 1152–53.

C. Corporate Privilege

Corporations enjoyed the benefit of privilege in the UK to the extent allowed by *Three Rivers*. The logic of equating personal and corporate rights to privilege was not followed on the European continent, where advice privilege was important but usually not extensive. Auburn noted that judges in the key case in the European Court of Justice were supportive of a rights-based approach,[174] describing the European approach to privilege as at a formative stage. However, while common law jurisdictions extended the privilege to in-house lawyers in competition investigations, EU jurisprudence argued they lacked the necessary independence.[175] The EU also tended to exempt company regulatory investigations from privilege protections.[176]

Differences in treatment were irrelevant when considering lawyers' reporting obligations regarding corporate misconduct. As the Lehman Brother example showed, the scale of risk could exceed those posed by money laundering or terrorism. It was arguable that any responsibility on lawyers for breaching corporate clients' privilege should be equally formal and unambiguous, that is statutory and specific. This presented the problem of identifying prescribed conduct in statutory or regulatory terms without undermining the trust between lawyers and clients. Such duties could be attached to process such as corporate disclosure, preparing, verifying, and assessing documentation for financial sector regulation purposes.[177]

Corporate enjoyment of privilege was not wholly secure. In 2016, the Law Society called a meeting to discuss the application of LPP.[178] The context was reports by corporate law firms that regulators and law enforcement agencies were increasingly pressuring lawyers to advise clients to waive claims to LPP. As a result, the Law Society issued advice reassuring solicitors that no action could be taken against lawyers for asserting it or against clients for refusing waivers sought by regulators. It warned, however, that claims 'advanced in bad faith' could expose lawyers 'to liability for conspiracy to pervert the course of justice'.

VII. CONCLUSION

Observing requirements of legality was the citizen's obligation to a society governed by liberty. Lawyers contributed to legality both by articulating rights, but also by minimising the possibility of client wrongdoing. Communications with clients

---

[174] *AM&S Europe v Commission* (1983) 1 QBD 678 (ECJ) cited at 27.
[175] Auburn (n 26) 28, Case C-550/07 P *Akzo Nobel Chemicals Ltd and Akcros Chemicals Ltd v Commission of the European Communities* [2011] 2 AC 338.
[176] For background and context see E Gippini-Fournier, 'Legal Professional Privilege in Competition Proceedings before the European Commission: Beyond the Cursory Glance' (2005) 28 *Fordham International Law Journal* 967.
[177] Solaiman (n 137).
[178] 'Is legal professional privilege under threat? A roundtable discussion at the Law Society' (*Law Society*, 28 October 2016) www.lawsociety.org.uk/topics/the-city/.

were protected on the basis that lawyers would dissuade clients from illegal actions, not participate in illicit schemes, and, in a narrow range of cases, report client wrongs. The nature of the counselling role could bring lawyers close to involvement in illegal plans. In these cases, they generally could not continue to act but nor could they inform on clients. This caused difficulty in preventing harms to third parties. The rationale for not imposing duties on lawyers to prevent harm was the state's commitment to both protect and promote the individual and to respect the rule of law.

9

Morality

I. INTRODUCTION

FROM THE 1970S, academic lawyers and moral philosophers in the US criticised the morality of the lawyer's role. These criticisms coalesced around a dominant theory called the standard conception of the lawyer's role (the standard conception), based on a reading of the American Bar Association Model Rules of Conduct, case-law and other materials.[1] It comprised three principles: neutrality, partisanship and non-accountability. Neutrality described the basic orientation of the lawyer. The main feature was that lawyers should not refuse clients on the grounds of unpopularity or causes they disagreed with morally. This suggested a kind of emotional detachment enabling dispassionate advice regarding client goals.[2]

The principle of partisanship demanded that lawyers do what they could within the law to achieve client objectives and protect their best interests. The risk that the two main principles would bring public opprobrium necessitated invoking a third principle, non-accountability, meaning that lawyers were not morally responsible for the consequences of representation. A leading critic of the standard conception, William Simon, suggested that it represented the ideology of advocacy.[3] Producing unjust outcomes, such as the guilty going free, resulted from the procedural requirements demanded by the rule of law, but could neutral partisanship be justified, in the courtroom or otherwise? What account should lawyers take of morality in representing clients?

II. THEORY

Kronman lamented the loss of the lawyer statesman ideal, invoking a golden age in which lawyers were characterised by wisdom and public spiritedness. He evoked

---

[1] See eg ML Schwartz, 'The Professionalism and Accountability of Lawyers' (1978) 66(4) *California Law Review* 669; D Luban, *Lawyers and Justice: An Ethical Study* (Princeton, Princeton University Press, 1988).
[2] TJ Johnson, *Professions & Power*, (London, MacMillan, 1972) 36; V Denti, 'Public Lawyers, Political Trials and the Neutrality of the Legal Profession' (1981) 1 *Israel Law Review* 20.
[3] WH Simon, 'The Ideology of Advocacy: Procedural Justice and Professional Ethics' (1978) *Wisconsin Law Review* 29.

a tradition of civic republicanism, an Enlightenment ideal associated with mixed government and the rule of law.[4] This proposed that laws, institutions, and norms should be configured to promote the connection between freedom through active citizenship and civic virtue. In public life procedures would screen candidates for public office and configure rules and norms to minimise corruption. High levels of public accountability would render the function of lawyers in the criminal process to be producing wise and informed decisions based on truth.[5]

Kronman's resentments were for the bureaucracy of the legal system, large law firms, and the technocratic nature of legal practice and legal education. His was a critique of what he perceived to be the legal role these forces had produced. A long list of US critics of the standard conception argued it produced an image of American lawyers as hired guns.[6] Lawyers' complicity in actual illegal behaviour was blamed on this client centred 'mind-set'.[7] It ignored third-party harms, damaged the public interest, and was psychologically harmful to lawyers. The standard conception was also criticised in other jurisdictions where it was assumed to apply. This included England[8] where criticism aligned with accusations that lawyers were excessively self-interested.[9]

The implicit function of the standard conception was to provide a baseline measure for criticism of the social role of lawyers. Its philosophical justifications invoked rule of law principles and legality requirements rooted in Enlightenment thinking. One was that traditional legal roles helped citizens resist the state,[10] the other that they were dictated by the rule of law.[11] An alternative view of the legal role, contrary to the standard conception, was that it was essentially paternalistic, with lawyers defining client needs and how to meet them.[12] This perspective was consistent with the high levels of responsibility for clients imposed on lawyers, equivalent to fiduciary relationships such as trusteeship. On this reading, the moral problem with the legal role was that it failed to recognise clients as individuals.

---

[4] For an introduction see 'Republicanism' *Stanford Encyclopedia of Philosophy*, https://plato.stanford.edu/entries/republicanism/#CriJusRulLaw.
[5] JT Noonan, 'The Purposes of Advocacy and the Limits of Confidentiality' (1966) 64 *Michigan Law Review* 1485.
[6] See eg Schwartz (n 1); D Nicolson and J Webb, *Professional Legal Ethics: Critical Interrogations* (Oxford, Oxford University Press, 1999); D Rhode, *In the Interests of Justice* (New York, Oxford University Press, 2000); Luban (n 1); Simon (n 3).
[7] RG Pearce, 'Rediscovering the Republican Origins of the Legal Ethics Codes' (1992) 6(24) *Georgetown Journal of Legal Ethics* 241, 277.
[8] Nicolson and Webb (n 6).
[9] R Moorhead and R Cahil-O'Callaghan, 'False Friends? Testing commercial lawyers on the claim that zealous advocacy is founded in benevolence towards clients rather than lawyers' personal interest' (2016) 19(1) *Legal Ethics* 30.
[10] See particularly Schwartz and Luban (n 1).
[11] T Dare, *The Counsel of Rogues? A Defence of the Standard Conception of the Lawyer's Role* (Farnham, Ashgate Publishing Ltd, 2009) (New Zealand); WB Wendel, *Lawyers and Fidelity to Law* (NJ, Princeton University Press, 2010).
[12] Johnson (n 2).

III. CONTROLLING LITIGATION LAWYERS

Historic concerns about lawyers encouraging litigation were reflected in actions prohibiting maintenance, champerty, and barratry, crimes and torts. Maintenance prevented anyone encouraging or 'maintaining', financing, a legal action. Champerty prevented uninterested parties from taking a share of the award. Barratry proscribed bringing vexatious litigation. In England, but not the US, these prevented lawyers taking contingency fees, payment depending on the outcome of litigation. Strict confinement to performance of their legal role reflected concerns about lawyers fermenting litigation dating from the medieval period, expressed in statutes of the period and the oaths sworn as a requirement of appearance in courts.

Andrews' study of medieval legal systems suggested that oaths were effective because of fear of divine punishment.[13] They indicated predominant contemporary concerns. An oath imposed by Frederick II of Germany in 1221 prescribed removal from office and a fine for advocates who 'allege anything against their sound conscience', who undertake 'desperate causes' or who, having undertaken a case find it is unjust, do not abandon it.[14] English ecclesiastical courts required practitioners to swear oaths in 1237.[15] One administered to advocates in the ecclesiastical Court of Arches in London in 1273 required that they reject unjust causes, not seek unjust delays and not knowingly infringe on ecclesiastical liberties, diligently and faithfully serve their clients, not charge excessive fees and not take a stake in the litigation.[16]

Lawyers were treated as officers of the courts in classical society and Medieval Europe.[17] The Statute of Westminster 1275, the first general statute applying to English lawyers, threatened imprisonment to those guilty of deceit or collusion in the courts.[18] In a speech to new serjeants in 1648 Lord Commissioner Whitlocke laid out duties of secrecy, diligence and fidelity, including respect for client confidentiality, and duties to respect and be truthful with the courts.[19] Obligations to courts trumped duties to clients. One of the four provisions of The *Mirror Des Justice* (circa 1285) was that a pleader or serjeant 'will not knowingly maintain or defend wrong or falsehood but will abandon his client immediately that he perceives his wrongdoing'.[20]

In 1274 a royal ordinance required French lawyers to swear an oath which included the core duties imposed on English lawyers at that time.[21] This was periodically updated, and a duty of secrecy added in 1816.[22] In the same year the Canton

---

[13] CR Andrews, *Standards of Conduct for Lawyers: An 800-Year Evolution* (2004) 57 SMU Law Review 1385, 1392–93.
[14] ibid.
[15] ibid 1393.
[16] The oath is attributed to Archbishop Kilwardy (ibid 1393).
[17] EW Timberlake, 'The Lawyer as an Officer of the Court' (1925) 11(4) *Virginia Law Review* 263.
[18] Andrews (n 13) 1392–93, 1395.
[19] ibid 1400.
[20] ibid 1388–89.
[21] ibid 1409.
[22] ibid 1411–12.

of Geneva, Switzerland, instituted a new oath incorporating the medieval French oaths, as follows:[23]

> I swear before God-
>
> To be faithful to the republic and the canton of Geneva;
>
> Never to depart from the respect due to the tribunals and authorities;
>
> Never to counsel or maintain a cause which does not appear to be just or equitable, unless it be the defense of an accused person;
>
> Never to employ knowingly, for the purpose of maintaining the causes confided to me, any means contrary to truth, and never to seek to mislead the Judges by any artifice of false statement of fact or law;
>
> To abstain from all offensive personality, and to advance no fact contrary to the honour or reputation of the parties, if it be not indispensable to the cause with which I *may* be charged;
>
> Not to encourage either the commencement or the continuance of a suit from any motive of passion or interest;
>
> Not to reject, for any considerations personal to myself, the cause of the weak, the stranger, or the oppressed.[24]

The last of these, the lawyer's obligation of representation, was also found in England, from at least 1425, when serjeants took an oath to serve the King's people and accept any instructions for a fee, payable in advance.[25] This suggests deep roots of the neutral and partisan role.

Burrage suggested that before the Civil War accessibility was one of the English Bar's three rudimentary values: 'to act in the public interest, to represent all comers, not to tout or to enter into improper contracts with particular solicitors for the supply of business'.[26] John Cooke's defence of his part in the execution of Charles I was that, 'having acted only as counsel, he was not answerable for the justice or injustice of the cause he had managed; that being placed in that station by a public command, it could not be said he acted maliciously or with a wicked intention'.[27] The fact that the defence did not succeed was not decisive, since he faced other allegations.[28] Geoffrey Robertson suggested that this was a first assertion of 'the cab rank principle',[29] but Cooke's language suggested the idea of non-accountability was current.

---

[23] ibid 1412.

[24] Oath for advocates of the Canton of Geneva (cited by L Ray Patterson, 'Legal Ethics and the Lawyer's Duty of Loyalty' (1980) 29 *Emory Law Journal* 909, 942, fn 129).

[25] JH Baker, *The Legal Profession and the Common Law: Historical essays* (London, The Hambledon Press, 1986) 104–5.

[26] M Burrage, *Revolution and the Making of the Contemporary Legal Profession: England, France and the United States* (Oxford, Oxford University Press, 2006) 398, citing JH Baker, *The Common Law tradition: Lawyers, Books and the Law* (London, Hambledon Press, 2000) 81–82.

[27] G Robertson, *The Tyrannicide Brief: The story of the man who sent Charles I to the scaffold* (London, Chatto & Windus, 2005) 311.

[28] Cooke's prosecutors alleged that he colluded with Puritans in Massachusetts, who sent agents to London to assist in the trial. The brief was endorsed with an instruction to use criminal law to end the impunity of tyrants (Robertson ibid 7).

[29] ibid 8.

IV. HIRED STILETTOES AND HIRED GUNS

A. The Partisan Prosecutor

In mid-seventeenth century England, prosecution was not a neutral exercise and later critics sometimes confused it with the legal role in general. In the 1830s Thomas Babbington, Lord Macaulay, a Cabinet member in nineteenth century Whig governments wrote a review of a new edition of a book on the Elizabethan courtier Francis Bacon.[30] In it he was critical of lawyers' morality. Bacon, from a wealthy and influential family left poor by the father's death, worked as a lawyer in Gray's Inn in the 1570s. He was befriended by the Earl of Essex who, despite Bacon's youth, tried to have him installed as Attorney General in 1594. When Edward Coke was appointed instead Essex gave Bacon a small estate. In 1597, Queen Elizabeth made Bacon her legal adviser, the first Queen's Counsel. Bacon went on to be Attorney General and Lord Chancellor to James I.

Around 1601 Elizabeth fell out with Essex and charges of treason were laid against him for plotting a rebellion. Bacon served in the prosecution team led by Coke. Macaulay condemned Bacon's willingness to betray his benefactor and exceed his professional duty:

> ... [F}rom the nature of the circumstances there could not be the smallest doubt that the Earl would be found guilty. The character of the crime was unequivocal. It had been committed recently, in broad daylight, in the streets of the capital, in the presence of thousands. If ever there was an occasion on which an advocate had no temptation to resort to extraneous topics, for the purpose of blinding the judgment and inflaming the passions of a tribunal, this was that occasion.[31]

Macaulay said that 'many wise and virtuous men' followed the professional rules and that if Bacon had, he would be 'blameless, or, at least, excusable'[32] but, Macaulay said, he did not.

Bacon compared Essex to Pisistratus, a tyrant of Athens in the classical period who had sought to fool the populace into supporting rebellion. Of this Bacon spoke at the trial:

> ... And this I must needs say; It is evident that you, my Lord of *Essex*, had planted a Pretence in your heart against the Government; and now, under colour of Excuse, you must lay the Cause upon particular Enemies. You put me in remembrance of one *Pisistratus*, that was come into a City, and doting upon the Affections of the Citizens unto him (he having a Purpose to procure the Subversion of a Kingdom, and wanting Aid for the accomplishing Humour) thought it the surest means for the winning of the hearts of the Citizens unto him, and so in that Hope entred the City, and cut his Body over-thwart, to the end they might conjecture he had been in danger: and so by this Means held the same Conceit as you

---

[30] B Montagu, *A review of The Works of Francis Bacon, Lord Chancellor of England: A new Edition* (London, 1825–34).

[31] Thomas Babington, Lord Macaulay, *Critical and Historical Essays, Vol. 2* [1832], Lord Bacon July 1837, 280 at 320, https://oll.libertyfund.org/titles/macaulay-critical-and-historical-essays-vol-2.

[32] ibid 318.

and your Complices did, entring the City of *London*, perswading your selves, if they had undertaken your Cause, all would have gone well on your side.[33]

Seen in the context of contemporary advocacy, which encouraged fierce and extreme posturing, Bacon's performance was restrained.[34] His moderate tone compared favourably with Coke's treatment of Sir Walter Raleigh and his intemperate cross-examination of Essex.

Macaulay claimed that Bacon exceeded the requirements of the prosecutor role. He cited Parliamentary debate in the period following the Glorious Revolution, on whether the judges and prosecutors who prosecuted Parliamentarians should be held accountable. A case in question was raised by the family of Sir Thomas Armstrong, tried and executed after the Rye House plot, a scheme to assassinate Charles II and James in 1683.[35] The trial judges were led by the notorious Jeffreys, and the three prosecutors were Sawyer, the Attorney-General, Graham and Burton. There was no evidence against Armstrong, apart from the fact that he fled abroad, and he was condemned without being heard.

The dead man's daughter said that she had attended Sawyer to plead her father's case only to be told he must die[36] and he called for Armstrong's execution in court. Some Parliamentarians were sympathetic to Sawyer's defence that he had done no more than his duty as prosecutor demanded. Mr Hawles said 'he is bound to pursue the interests of his client, and it was for the interest of the King to preserve his subjects',[37] but others argued that Sawyer went too far. Hampden senior stated that 'If the profession of the law gives a man authority to murder at this rate, it is the interest of all men to rise and exterminate that profession'.[38]

The balance of opinion was that Sawyer should compensate the Armstrong family by paying £5,000. Some thought him lucky.[39] Sir William Williams, a lawyer who had acted as Counsel for the Crown, argued that lawyers prosecuting prisoners who had no counsel must 'exercise a discretion' in how to conduct the case.[40] The House of Commons agreed that every lawyer who neglected this obligation was a 'betrayer of the law'.[41] It may have been a natural impulse for Parliament to seek revenge against members of the former regime, but it took a more ameliorative approach, drawing a line under prosecutorial abuse. The Treason Act 1695 then provided that the accused could have a copy of the indictment, no evidence

---

[33] The Arraignment And Tryall Of Robert Earl Of Essex And Henry Earl Of Southampton At Westminster The 19th Of February, 1600. And In The 43 Year Of The Reign Of Queen Elizabeth, 20, https://quod.lib.umich.edu/e/eebo/A25875.0001.001/1:2?rgn=div1;view=fulltext.

[34] A Watson, *Speaking in Court: Developments in Court Advocacy from the Seventeenth to the Twenty First Centuries* (Gewerbestrasse, Palgrave MacMillan, 2019) ch 2.

[35] *Debates in the House of Common from the year 1667 to the year 1694: Volume 9* (Monday 20 January) 529.

[36] Macaulay (n 31).

[37] ibid 535.

[38] ibid 528.

[39] ibid 551.

[40] ibid 319.

[41] ibid 320, Macaulay is here quoting Sir William Williams in the HC debates at 527.

could be brought not referred to there, there must be two witnesses against accused persons and that they could be represented by two counsel.[42]

By the early 1800s, litigation was adversarial in the way anticipated in the Treason Act. Jeremy Bentham, a critic of many aspects of legal process, approved of innovations such as oral testimony, interrogation, and zealous advocacy.[43] There were also concerns. Erskine's view of the professional obligation of barristers to represent had prevailed, but there were fears that counsel would adopt the 'passions and prejudices of clients'[44] or bamboozle juries. In Lord MacAulay's article on Bacon, he asked:

> whether it be right that a man should, with a wig on his head, and a band round his neck, do for a guinea what, without those appendages, he would think it wicked and infamous to do for an empire; whether it be right that, not merely believing but knowing a statement to be true, he should do all that can be done by sophistry, by rhetoric, by solemn asseveration, by indignant exclamation, by gesture, by play of features, by terrifying one honest witness, by perplexing another, to cause a jury to think that statement false.[45]

Macaulay's much quoted criticism of the practice of advocacy, common in the 1830s, was inappropriately applied to the case of Bacon and Essex. Parliament had decided that lawyers had a duty to prosecute if instructed and were to be held to account only if they exceeded their role. If they did exceed their role they may justify Macaulay's claim: 'they would be a more hateful body of men than those bravoes who used to hire out their stilettoes in Italy'.[46] This somehow conflated the injustice of the Stewart treason trials and adversary trial in general. In fact, the seventeenth century treason cases cried out for the adversarial defence required by the Treason Act 1695.

B. The Moral Crisis of Adversarialism

In the eighteenth century, Samuel Johnson expressed what may have been a lawyer's view of the ethics of representation:

> Boswell asked the Doctor whether the practice of the law in some degree hurt the nice feeling of honesty. The Doctor had fixed ideas on the subject and began: 'Why no, Sir, if you act properly. You are not to deceive your clients with false representations of your opinion; you are not to tell lies to a judge.' Boswell led him on: 'But what do you think of supporting a cause which you know to be bad?'
>
> Johnson: 'Sir, you do not know it to be good or bad till the Judge determines it.'[47]

It may be significant that Macaulay's intervention came later, during the 15-year period it took to pass the Prisoners' Counsel Act 1836. Often seen as a period of progress beyond superstition, acceptance of the principle of representation was not

---

[42] See ch 6 'Identity'.
[43] S Landsman, 'The Rise of the Contentious Spirit: Adversary Process in Eighteenth Century England' (1992) 75 *Cornell Law Review* 479, 602 citing *Jeremy Bentham, Rationale Of Judicial Evidence* (1827) 228, 274–75 and 406–7.
[44] Landsman ibid 602.
[45] Macaulay (n 13) 318.
[46] ibid 321.
[47] AH Huguenard, 'Dr. Johnson on the Law and Lawyers' (1933) 8 *Notre Dame Law Review* 195, 200, 203.

universally accepted by Whigs, Bar and Bench. Indeed, adversarial advocacy was a focus of moral struggle as Victorian politicians, authors, the press, lawyers, and the newly engaged middle classes, sought a new approach to criminality. This process turned society's attention 'from the scaffold towards the forensic process itself'.[48]

In 1840, six years after the Act, Brougham responded to a petition presented by the Bishop of London on behalf of Londoners complaining that 'prisoners charged with felony were allowed to employ counsel for their defence'.[49] The bishop sought only to have the matter referred to Commissioners of Criminal Law Inquiry, adding that 'there were passages of God's word which he could not reconcile with the propriety of any man taking a reward to prove that to be otherwise which the accused himself had distinctly confessed'.[50]

Brougham's response to the petition resuscitated elements of Erskine's speech in the Paine case:

> The privilege of the exercise of which they complained was not that of the counsel, but of the prisoner; it was a privilege upon which the elucidation of truth, the prevention of injustice depended, and the life, liberties, and property of the subject were not worth an hour's purchase if the freest scope, he would say more, the most unrestrained license was not given to the bar. Whether in a case which was right or wrong this was the rule, the sacred rule of the profession, and it was one upon which the safety of the administration of justice depended ... If once a barrister were to be allowed to refuse a brief, and to say he would not defend a man because he was in the wrong, many would be found who would refuse to defend men, not on account of the case, but because they were weak men, under the pressure of unpopularity, against whom power had set its mark, because they were the victims of oppression, or were about to be made so, or because it would not be convenient for parties at all times to beard power on behalf of individuals, in the situation of prisoners.[51]

The bishop responded that 'the noble and learned Lord had admirably demolished the phantom of his own creation'.

The Bishop accepted it 'was not competent for a counsel to refuse a brief' but 'lamented the hardship of the law, which ... might compel a man to do that which was against his own conscience, namely, defend by a speech a man whom he knew to be guilty'.[52] Despite the bishop's protest, his objection was partly to the obligation on barristers to accept a brief, the cab rank principle[53] although he did not name it, and Brougham did address this as a warning against pre-judgement. The Bar addressed the core objection by requiring that barristers receiving a confession could not present a case or positive evidence inconsistent with that confession.

---

[48] J-M Schramm, '"The Anatomy Of A Barrister's Tongue": Rhetoric, Satire, And The Victorian Bar In England' (2004) 32 *Victorian Literature and Culture* 285, 300.
[49] House of Lords (1840) 55 *Parliamentary Debates*, House of Lords (5th Series) 10 August 1840, cols 1401-2.
[50] ibid.
[51] ibid 1401.
[52] ibid 1402.
[53] See eg D Pannick, *Advocates* (Oxford, Oxford University Press, 1992) 141 and Watson (n 34) ch 2.

Allowing lawyer speeches to the jury was particularly controversial. The power of legal rhetoric was exemplified by Charles Phillips, a member of Middle Temple and the Irish Bar since 1812. Phillips, a poet and barrister, did not strive to separate his callings, and his speeches were widely published. Early in his career he orated for the wife in a matrimonial cause casting doubt on the motive of the husband:

> But here is an ambition – base, and barbarous, and illegitimate; with all the grossness of the vice, with none of the grandeur of the virtue; a mean, muffled, dastard incendiary, who, in the silence of sleep, and in the shades of midnight, steals his Ephesian torch into the fane, which it was virtue to adore, and worse than sacrilege to have violated![54]

He continued in similar vein. When he had finished, the jury was in tears and the court room applauding.

Following publication of Phillips' rhetoric an anonymous article appeared in the Edinburgh Review in 1816 criticising the advocacy:

> Its characteristics are, great force of imagination, without any regularity or restraint; great copiousness of language, with little selection or propriety; vehemence of sentiment, often out of place; warmth of feeling, generally overdone; a frequent substitution of jingling words for ideas; and such a defect in skill (with reference to the subject in view), as may be supposed to result from the intemperate love of luxuriant declamation, to which all higher considerations are sacrificed.[55]

Schramm speculated that the author was Brougham, writer of articles in the Edinburgh Review praising examples of Erskine's eloquence. The criticism of Phillips' rhetoric, she said, reflected 'an expression of that English insistence on the language of plain fact which appeared with puritanism and the work of the Royal Society in the seventeenth century'.[56] It was also a warning of cultural limits on the partisan lawyer.

Phillips appeared in a notable case in 1840 which crystalised misgivings about the Bar's ascendancy. The accused, Courvoisier, a Swiss valet to Lord William Russell, was charged with murdering his master and stealing several items. After some prosecution evidence, Philips received a confession but continued to present the case as if his client was innocent, implicating others in the crime, accusing the police of planting evidence, and attacking the credibility of a witness.[57] The accused admitted everything on conviction, making Phillips' defence indefensible.

One review criticised Phillips' tactics, and his florid closing speech, as 'adversarial excess', damning lawyers acting in this way as accessories after the fact.[58] This was not the last such excess. In a trial of the murderer Tarwell in 1845, Sir Fitzroy Kelly was accused of encouraging the 'impunity of crime'. He shed tears while reading an affectionate letter to the accused from his wife, then argued that a guilty verdict

---

[54] Schramm (n 48).
[55] 'Irish Eloquence' *Edinburgh Review* (1816) cited by Schramm (n 48) 291.
[56] Schramm (n 48) 291.
[57] ibid 292.
[58] ibid 292–93.

would deprive her and the children of a father.[59] This attracted extreme criticism in the Press and merciless parody in *Punch*.[60]

In the period after the Prisoners' Counsel Act the image of the barrister as fearless partisan vied with the accusation of guilt by association. The right to representation was according to Pue 'raised to high constitutional principle where "political" issues were involved'.[61] The Bar's pride in members as 'champions of liberty' was reflected back in the media:

> When Lord Erskine withstood Mr. Justice Buller, with propriety and taste equal to his courage, and began the exposure of the monstrous doctrine that, in prosecutions for libel, the fact of publishing was all the jury could investigate, to which the Press is indebted for that statute which deserves to be considered as the charter of its freedom he set an example of independence of mind, not of class, of which any profession might be proud. Still nobler was the sacrifice which he made to the claim of professional duty, and that a duty he would gladly have avoided for its own hardships, when he resigned his office of attorney-general to the Prince of Wales, rather than abandon the defence of the prosecution instituted against Paine's Rights of Man.[62]

Memory of the Bar's contribution to liberty and the Constitution, albeit 50 years old, informed a debate encompassing public hostility to lawyers.

Controversy surrounding the role of barristers in the adversarial system came to a head in a five-year period beginning in 1860. A central controversy surrounded the will of Samuel Swinfen leaving a substantial part of his estate, worth £60,000, to Patience, the wife of his deceased son.[63] The will was challenged by Samuel's nephew Frederick. Patience instructed a legal team headed by Frederick Thesiger QC, an MP and former solicitor general. At the end of the first day of the trial, Thesiger consulted his team of three other barristers who agreed the case had gone badly.

Against Patience Swinfen's express instructions, Thesiger entered a compromise with Frederick's lawyers. The case was reopened, and won, by another barrister, Charles Rann Kennedy, who then acted in a malpractice action against Thesiger. This suit alleged that Sir Creswell Creswell, the judge in the case and one of the most noted of the period, had secretly and improperly communicated with Thesiger at the end of the first day expressing the thought that the cause had little chance of success. The case came to trial before a jury in 1859,[64] an event Pue described as 'a scalper's dream'.[65]

Thesiger and Creswell were noted Conservative politicians. Thesiger became Lord Chancellor in 1859 and was sued in his new title, Lord Chelmsford. Rann had

---

[59] ibid 293.
[60] ibid 294–95.
[61] W Pue, 'Moral Panic at the English Bar: Paternal vs. Commercial Ideologies of Legal Practice in the 1860s' (1990) 15(1) *Law & Social Inquiry* 49, 55.
[62] Pue (n 61) fns 11 and 18 citing 'On the Principle of Advocacy as Developed in the Practice of the Bar' 20 (ns) *Law Magazine & Review: Quarterly Review Jurisprudence* 265, 266 (Feb-May 1854) (vol 51 of Old Series, No 103) (reprinted from No 84 of *Law Magazine*).
[63] Pue (n 61) 60–75.
[64] *Swinfen v Lord Chelmsford* (1860) 5 H & N 891.
[65] Pue (n 61) 63.

recently run for Parliament as a Liberal and was assisted by George Denman, son of the noted Whig reformer. The court was packed with spectators, mainly barristers. Guest judges observed from the bench and Chelmsford and Cresswell gave evidence alongside them dressed in full judicial regalia. Chelmsford agreed he had greeted Creswell at the end of the day and had 'formed the impression' that it had not gone well. Thesiger denied that he wished to settle because he had been booked to appear in another case in another town.

The established facts favoured Kennedy's case. Chelmsford admitted he had received an intimation from Creswell and settled the case without the client's agreement. In his defence he invoked a tradition that distinguished barristers of the utmost integrity arranged their client's matters for the best, as a kind of public duty. He saw himself 'serving lay clients who presumptively might not sufficiently "understand" their own best interests'.[66] This paternalistic view of the legal role was in sharp contradiction to the idea of the client's right of self-determination, promoted by Kennedy, where what was 'best' for the client was a matter for the client.[67] This was a commercial and contractual view of the lawyer and client relationship. What had happened was also contrary to the new spirit of the adversarial court, where judges kept their opinions private.

The outcome of *Swinfen v Lord Chelmsford* swung on divergent notions of the lawyer's role in litigation. In his summing up, Chelmsford's barrister, Sir Fitzroy Kelly, placed great reliance on the standing and status of his client and the three other noted barristers who had agreed to the compromise.[68] Having failed to persuade the claimants to withdraw the charges, or at least the allegation of conspiracy, the judge invoked the independence of the Bar, directing the jury that a barrister need only 'discharge his duty towards his client as best he could'.[69] He suggested that putting the charges on the record outraged 'public decorum and decency.'[70]

While the middle-class press was critical of Kennedy's 'vindictiveness', it was sceptical of the view of lawyer responsibility the outcome conveyed. Generally, it extolled the virtues of open justice represented in the adversarial process. It was critical of secret justice and the complacency of senior members of the Bar, which the case was seen to exemplify.[71] Their attitudes were seen as inconsistent with the principles of a '"free-trade" political economy'.[72] While Chelmsford survived an appeal, the Inns of Court announced an inquiry into improper conduct.[73] This led to constraints which led to the norms surrounding the practice of advocacy taking something like a modern form. This curbed controversy in England but it took a different path in America.

---

[66] ibid 68.
[67] ibid 64.
[68] ibid 68.
[69] ibid 71.
[70] ibid 70.
[71] ibid 72.
[72] ibid 72.
[73] ibid 76.

V. AMERICAN ATTORNEYS

A. The Republican Ideal

Russell Pearce argued that analyses of American legal ethics misread the evidence of a republican ethical ideal.[74] Michael Hoeflich identified a tradition prioritising public interest concerns which remained prominent well into the 1800s[75] but declined after the 1840s.[76] Winsberg described an early nineteenth century legal world 'obsessed with the dangers of excessive zeal'.[77] This was exemplified in Joseph Story's eulogy for John Marshall in 1835, noting his sense of deep responsibility 'not to his client alone, but to the court, and to the cause of public justice ... of being a minister at [the law's] altars'.[78] Story castigated lawyers who perverted such principle 'to swell the trophies of cunning, or avarice, or profligacy'.[79]

Winsberg's description of early nineteenth century ideal incarnations of American attorneys as 'anti-adversarial, morally weighted, and even pious',[80] was at odds with the ethic of the Bar in England at the time. The juxtaposition of the republican ideal and Brougham's justification of the defence at the trial of Queen Caroline, well-known at the time, was the context for early work on lawyers' ethics by two American scholars, David Hoffman published in 1836[81] and George Sharswood in 1854.[82] They were probably aware of Brougham, but neither entirely embraced his client-centric approach.

Hoffman reflected a moralistic, Christian tone. His professed objective in publishing 'Resolutions In Regard to Professional Deportment'[83] as part of his book *Course of Legal Study* was to guide 'a young man of the soundest morals, and of the most urbane, and honorable deportment'.[84] His 'resolutions' placed moral considerations over lawyers' actions on behalf of clients and were explicit in dismissal of the partisan lawyer. His first resolution pledged that 'I will never permit professional zeal to carry me beyond the limits of sobriety and decorum, but bear in mind, with Sir Edward Coke, that "if a river swell beyond its banks, it loseth its own channel"'.[85]

---

[74] Pearce (n 7) 241.
[75] M Hoeflich, 'Legal Ethics in the Nineteenth Century: The "Other Tradition"' (1998) 47 *University of Kansas Law Review* 793.
[76] Some doubt a republican legal ethic existed (NW Spaulding, 'The Myth of Civic Republicanism: Interrogating the Ideology of Antebellum Legal Ethics' (2003) 71 *Fordham Law Review* 1397).
[77] S Winsberg, 'Attorney "mal-practices": an invisible ethical problem in the early American republic' (2016) 19(2) *Legal Ethics* 187.
[78] Winsberg (n 77) 190 citing J Story, *A Discourse Upon the Life, Character, and Services of the Honorable John Marshall, L.L.D., Chief Justice of the United States of America* (Boston, James Munro and Company, 1835) 63.
[79] Winsberg (n 77).
[80] ibid 188.
[81] D Hoffman, *Course of Legal Study: Addressed To Students And The Profession Generally*, 2nd edn (Baltimore, Joseph Neal, 1836).
[82] G Sharswood, An *Essay on Professional Ethics*, 5th edn (Philadelphia, T and JW Johnson, 1907).
[83] DC Hoffman, *Fifty Resolutions in Regard to Professional Deportment* (1836) HTTPS://LONANG.COM/COMMENTARIES/CURRICULUM/PROFESSIONAL-DEPORTMENT/.
[84] Andrews (n 13) 1427 citing Hoffman (n 83) 751.
[85] Hoffman (n 83).

Hoffman was also dismissive of neutrality, arguing that attorneys should not bring bad claims. Which claims were bad was conflated with the identity of the person whose claim it was: 'Persons of atrocious character' were merely entitled to have their case investigated, not 'special resorts to ingenuity'.[86] Anything more, Hoffman deemed unprofessional and described his process accordingly:

> [i]f, after duly examining a case, I am persuaded that my client's claim or defense (as the case may be), cannot, or rather ought not to, be sustained, I will promptly advise him to abandon it. To press it further in such a case, with the hope of gleaning some advantage by an extorted compromise would be lending myself to a dishonorable use of legal means in order to gain a portion of that, the whole of which I have reason to believe would be denied to him both by law and justice.[87]

Hoffman concluded that lawyers should not put forward technical defences to debt claims such as limitation or infancy, 'for if my client is conscious he owes the debt, and has no other defense than the legal bar, he shall never make me a partner in his knavery'.[88] Hoffman described the worst kind of lawyer: 'Smart, unprincipled, reckless, persevering, bold, cunning, worthy, and grinding'.[89] His work was a lament for a tradition that never was and a professional exclusivity fast disappearing.[90]

Sharswood, the more obviously influential of the two struck a more obvious balance between clients and the legal system. He thought it impractical to have lawyers only representing just causes, describing the 'prevailing tone of professional ethics' accordingly: 'all causes are to be taken by [a lawyer] indiscriminately, and conducted with a view to one single end, success'.[91] He cited approvingly Sir Matthew Hale, who claimed to have investigated cases rejected by other attorneys, often finding them 'very good and just'.[92] Sharswood believed that lawyers should defend accused parties with zeal even if convinced of their guilt.[93] He also proposed, after the adversarial fashion, that clients should have cases decided on the law and the evidence. Lawyers, he argued, were not morally responsible for the unjust causes of clients, nor for the decisions of courts in their favour. He still, however, advocated declining a case offending the lawyer's 'sense of what is just and right'.[94]

Sharswood came close to the spirit of Brougham in describing what was required in defending client rights.[95] An attorney, he said:

> owes entire devotion to the interest of his client, warm zeal in the maintenance and defense of his cause, and the exertion of the utmost skill and ability to the end, that nothing may be taken or withheld from him, save by the rules of law, legally applied. No sacrifice or peril,

---

[86] ibid.
[87] ibid 11.
[88] ibid Resolution 12.
[89] Winsburg citing David Hoffman (pseud. Anthony Grumbler), 'Miscellaneous Thoughts on Men, Manners, and Things' 326 (1837) see also Kessinger Reprints, 2010.
[90] MS Ariens, 'Lost and Found: David Hoffman and the History of American Legal Ethics' (2014) 67 *Arkansas Law Review* 571, 625.
[91] Pearce (n 7) citing Sharswood (n 82) 257.
[92] ibid 258.
[93] A Marston, 'Guiding The Profession: The 1887 Code Of Ethics Of The Alabama State Bar Association' (1998) 49(2) *Alabama Law Review* 471, 495.
[94] Andrews (n 13) 1430.
[95] Patterson (n 24) at 930–31.

even to loss of life itself, can absolve from fearless discharge of this duty. Nevertheless, it is steadfastly to be borne in mind that the great trust is to be performed within and not without the bounds of the law which creates it. The attorney's office does not destroy the man's accountability to the Creator, or loosen the duty of obedience to law, and the obligation to his neighbor; and it does not permit, much less demand, violation of law, or any manner of fraud or chicanery, for the client's sake.[96]

Sharswood's was a modern compromise, echoing the view of Pennsylvania Chief Justice Gibson, that lawyers held duties to the public and the court as well as to the client.[97] Sharswood did not shirk from providing examples of the balance between client and public duties. Lawyers should not act as private prosecutors of the innocent[98] or use opponents' mistakes to defeat just claims.[99] They should observe etiquette and conduct fair dealings with other lawyers.[100] They should make statements to the court that were accurate and carefully distinguish what was in their knowledge and what was in their instructions.

Andrews suggested that the work of Hoffman and Sharswood was a linear development of lawyer morality from the medieval period. Hoffman's resolutions addressed five of the six core duties of lawyers from medieval oaths: litigation fairness, competence, loyalty, reasonable fees, and service of the poor.[101] In addition to providing 'another level of detail'[102] these works were more than merely developmental because they began to translate the oath 'do no falsehood' to modern conditions. There was broad agreement among US writers that some adjustment of this narrative was needed to reflect a new focus on clients.

B. Client Focus

There were three possible reasons for the adoption of a more client-centric approach, the failure of the republican ideal, the self-interest of lawyers, or the adoption of the adversarial process. All were probably relevant. The Republican legal ethic created a risk that lawyers would fail their clients and systemic failings would be inadequately addressed.[103] Winsberg suggested that in the early 1800s, the court's inherent jurisdiction was misused to suspend lawyers who displeased judges, or for political reasons.[104]

In the 1820s and 1830s actions for malpractice and attorney fraud injuring clients increased but failed to make an impression on judicial scepticism and media indifference. Winsberg focused on New York attorney George Niven, who successfully defended numerous cases of obvious misconduct. He apparently avoided

---

[96] ibid 938 citing *Alabama Code Of Ethics*, Rule 10.
[97] Patterson (n 24).
[98] Marston (n 93) 495.
[99] Andrews (n 13) 1430.
[100] ibid 1428.
[101] ibid 1431.
[102] ibid.
[103] Winsburg (n 89) 188.
[104] ibid 204.

accountability because courts were reluctant to confront the reality of abuse. Nor did lawyers committing malpractice suffer reputational damage, many rising to judicial office despite malpractice claims. The republican ideal blinded the legal profession and judiciary to the fact that lawyers often failed clients badly.

Self-interested lawyers led to the compromise of the republican ideal, but there was also pressure to allow more active forms of business generation and loosen constraints on what lawyers could do for clients. Patterson suggested that Brougham provided a justification for client-centredness.[105] US treatises on ethics in the second half of the nineteenth century provided attorneys with convenient rationalisations for morally dubious conduct for clients.[106] This may well be attributable to the influence of the adversarial trial. In the mid-1700s, well before American Independence, its virtues were extolled in Blackstone's *Commentaries*. This may have been evident in stiffening of requirements on confidentiality, which tended not to be mentioned in medieval codes. A dozen of Hoffman's resolutions concerned litigation, but not confidentiality.[107] Sharswood focused on aspects of litigation, including respect for the courts, but only briefly addressed confidentiality.[108]

Patterson noted that, until the advent of the emphasis on confidentiality, the allocation of authority between lawyer and client depended on the presenting issue. Context determined who was principal or agent in the relationship. The notion of the lawyer-client relationship could 'best be characterized as one of reciprocal agency rather than one of simple agency'.[109] Reciprocal agency ended with the rise of confidentiality, which shifted authority in the relationship to the client. This hypothesis synthesised the three explanations of the decline of a republican legal ethic. The adversarial ethic may have been favoured by lawyers, but it also addressed fundamental deficits in the treatment of clients.

The balanced ethic, tilted towards clients but with a strong tinge of public responsibility, was a staple and relatively unexamined ethos of US lawyers until the 1960s. It became controversial when Monroe H Freedman, an academic who chaired the American Civil Liberties Union, published an aggressive interpretation of its obligations.[110] He argued that advocates acting for criminal defendants should treat trials as 'battles' in which they *should* discredit witnesses known to be telling the truth, allow their witnesses to give perjured testimony and advise clients in a such a way that enabled them to give perjured evidence. Freedman's argument was based on a variation of the constitutional argument that underpinned the adversary system in England: defendants must have a champion when facing the awesome power and resources of the state.

A response to Freedman by John Noonan, a noted federal judge, argued that 'the advocate plays his role well when zeal for his client's cause promotes a wise and

---

[105] Patterson (n 24) 912.

[106] ibid at 913 citing M Schudson, 'Public, Private, and Professional Lives: The Correspondence of David Dudley Field and Samuel Bowles' (1977) 21 *American Journal of Legal History* 191, 193.

[107] Andrews (n 13) 1427.

[108] ibid 1429.

[109] Patterson (n 24).

[110] MH Freedman, 'Professional Responsibility of the Criminal Defense Lawyer: The Three Hardest Questions' (1966) 64 *Michigan Law Review* 1469.

informed decision of the case'.[111] Freedman poured scorn on Noonan, asserting the impracticality of his guiding principle: 'It is hard to believe that Professor Noonan either wants or expects members of the bar to act on this advice'.[112] Future chief justice of the US, Warren E Burger, called for Freedman's disbarment[113] and although this failed, he was said to be instrumental in excluding him from an ethics panel at George Washington University.

In 1998, Freedman received an award from the American Bar Association for his 'original and influential scholarship' in the field.[114] One of his University employers claimed him as a founder of the discipline of lawyers' ethics, acknowledging he was also a 'disruptor [who] helped us to question the status quo and made us think deeply about the complexity of legal representation, particularly for those marginalized by society'.[115] While this was fair, Freedman's assertion that lawyers' duty required that they ignore and subvert legal process was uncomfortable for the profession. The implications of that debate were revived by Watergate.

C. Watergate

Concerns about the morality of the lawyer's role reignited with the Watergate scandal (see chapter four 'Execution'). It began in June 1972 and ended with the resignation of President Richard Nixon in 1974. Post-Watergate Congressional hearings into the bugging of Democratic headquarters implicated 13 lawyers, and Nixon, who had spent five years in private practice and a similar time as a government lawyer before election to the House of Representatives in 1946. A damning point was made by White House counsel John Dean, a coordinator of the cover-up, who admitted his own part in return for a plea deal.

In four days of evidence to the Senate Select Committee Dean said:

> I prepared a list of who was likely to be indicted as the investigation proceeded ... [M]y first reaction was there certainly are an awful lot of lawyers involved here. So I put a little asterisk beside each lawyer, which was Mitchell, Strachan, Ehrlichman, Dean, Mardian, O'Brien, Parkinson, Colson, Bittman, and Kalmbach .... [H]ow in God's name could so many lawyers get involved in something like this?[116]

---

[111] J Noonan, 'The Purposes of Advocacy and the Limits of Confidentiality' (1966) 64 *Michigan Law Review* 1485.

[112] Freedman (n 110) 'Postscript to the Three Hardest Questions' at 1482.

[113] At the time, Burger was a federal appeals court judge in Washington. He became chief justice three years later. M Schudel, 'Monroe H. Freedman, scholar of legal ethics and civil liberties, dies at 86' *Washington Post* (28 February 2015) www.washingtonpost.com/national/monroe-h-freedman-scholar-of-legal-ethics-and-civil-liberties-dies-at-86/2015/02/28/9e9c562a-beb3-11e4-8668-4e7ba8439ca6_story.html.

[114] ABA, 'Michael Franck Professional Responsibility Award: Past Award Recipients', www.americanbar.org/groups/professional_responsibility/initiatives_awards/awards/aboutthemichaelfranckaward1/mfranck_winner_bios/.

[115] The Freedman Institute, https://freedmaninstitute.hofstra.edu/.

[116] Watergate and Related Activities. Phase I: Watergate Investigation. S. Res. 60. Senate Select Committee on Presidential Campaign Activities, Presidential Campaign Activities of 1972, Book 3 (June 25 & 26,1973) pp 1013, 1054, referring to Exhibit No. 34-47 at p 1312 (cited by K Clarke, 'The Legacy of Watergate for Legal Ethics Instruction' (1999–2000) 51 *Hastings Law Journal* 673, fn 1).

The offences proved against Watergate lawyers included planning the break-in, conducting it, and participating in the cover up. Some were also involved in campaign funding violations revealed by the investigations.[117] Many served prison terms or were disbarred.

Academic writing of the time of the scandal attached great significance to lawyer involvement.[118] Critics suggested that an amoral practitioner culture was encouraged by the adversarial tradition of courtroom advocacy and neutral partisanship, a vindication of the 'hired gun' metaphor. Whether or not this was fair it was undeniable that the lawyers had disregarded public obligations to legality and hence the rule of law. This may have been partly due to misguided loyalty and a disposition to protect those perceived, incorrectly, as clients.

D. The Standard Conception of the Lawyer's Role

A critique of the morality of legal roles began almost immediately. A year after the Watergate denouement, Wasserstrom was critical of the role but unsure of whether it was socially justified. He noted that following Kant's ethical injunction to treat clients as 'ends in themselves' led to nobody else being treated as such.[119] Later critics intensified aspects of his argument. Schwarz suggested that the principle of professionalism, in both criminal and civil proceedings, mandated advocates to 'maximise the likelihood that the client would prevail'[120] and them being 'neither legally, professionally, nor morally accountable for the means used to achieve that end'.[121] In fact, Schwarz argued, non-accountability only applied to lawyers acting as advocates, not in other roles, such as negotiator or counsellor.

In a later article Schwarz honed his consideration of whether arguments for non-accountability could be extended beyond criminal defendants.[122] He argued it should not apply to advocates in civil cases because their role was closer to the role of negotiator or counsellor than to that of criminal advocate. He queried whether '… a legal system [should] morally require a lawyer to assist a client to achieve a lawful but immoral end'.[123] He considered the ability of a lawyer to refuse a client as relevant to their moral accountability for the outcome of representation.[124]

---

[117] John D Erlichman, Spiro T Agnew, Charles W Colson, Herbert W Kalmbach, Richard G Kleindreinst, John N Michell, Egil Krogh Jr, G Gordon Liddy, Robert C Mardian, Harry L Sears, Donald H Segretti, G Bradford Cook. ('The Watergate Lawyers' *ABA Journal*), www.abajournal.com/gallery/watergate/.
[118] See eg JS Auerbach, 'The Legal Profession after Watergate' (1975–1976) 22 *Wayne Law Review* 1287; L Rigertas, 'Post-Watergate: The Legal Profession And Respect For The Interests Of Third Parties' (2102) 16 *Chapman Law Review* 111; MS Ariens, 'The Agony of Modern Legal Ethics, 1970–1985' (2014) 5 *St. Mary's Journal of Legal Malpractice & Ethics* 134; Simon (n 3).
[119] R Wasserstrom, 'Lawyers as Professionals: Some Moral Issues' (1975) 5 *Human Rights* 1.
[120] ML Schwarz, 'The Professional Accountability of Lawyers' (1978) 66 *California Law Review* 669.
[121] ibid.
[122] ML Schwartz, 'The Zeal of the Civil Advocate' (1983) 8(3) *American Bar Foundation Research Journal* 543.
[123] ibid 555.
[124] ibid 545.

In 1978 William Simon proposed that lawyers' ethics in general derived from an 'ideology of advocacy'[125] comprising four principles: neutrality, partisanship, procedural justice, professionalism. These principles required that lawyers accept their clients' objectives regardless of the lawyer's own moral views (principle of *neutrality*), use all lawful means to achieve those objectives (principle of *partisanship*), and, because of an inherent value in judicial proceedings which justified actions without regard for consequences (procedural justice), which are resolved as matters of ethics by lawyers in their collective capacity rather than as individuals.[126]

Simon's last two principles were later collapsed into one as non-accountability, in what came to be known as 'the standard conception of the lawyer's role' ('standard conception').[127] Years of academic criticism focused on these three principles. Regarding neutrality, it was said to be morally outrageous that lawyers represent a position they did not believe in: a black lawyer instructed by the Klu Klux Klan or a pacifist asked to disinherit a son who dodged the draft for the Vietnam War. It was worse that they must act with vigour whatever the morality of the cause.

Examples of dubious tactics encouraged by partisanship were also pilloried. Oppressive discovery involved disclosure of thousands of irrelevant documents to the opponent. Lawyers defending the manufacturer of the Dalkon shield contraceptive against infertility claims devised an intrusive questionnaire into claimants' sexual habits, with the apparent aim of discouraging participation in a class action.[128] Not only were Neutrality, Partisanship and Non-accountability rejected as morally wrong in principle, it was claimed that they had a baleful impact on individual lawyers, the culture of legal practice and society generally.[129]

Simon proposed that lawyers' professional role should be aligned not with neutrality but with common morality. Advocates should be part-time, representing causes they believed in and deciding who to represent. Unpopular clients or causes might have no lawyer but, Simon suggested, that would probably reflect community opinion. In any case, he argued, lack of finance meant many did not anyway.[130] Simon later modified this view, suggesting advocates should temper partisanship according to the morality of a client's situation.[131] What they did for clients then would depend on their sympathy for the client's case. 'Good lawyers', Simon claimed, already sought substantive justice according to their own moral theories.

Following Watergate, Monroe Freedman re-entered discussion of the morality of lawyers with more traditional arguments for the neutral, partisan role. The best way to prevent the state from overpowering the liberty of subjects, he said, was for an independent Bar to challenge government action as zealously and effectively as

---

[125] Simon (n 3) 30.
[126] ibid 38.
[127] Luban (n 1).
[128] D Luban and W Bradley Wendel, 'Philosophical Legal Ethics: An Affectionate History' (2017) 30 *Georgetown Journal of Legal Ethics* 337.
[129] SL Pepper, 'The Lawyer's Amoral Ethical Role: A Defense, A Problem, and Some Possibilities' (1986) 11(4) *Law & Social Inquiry* 613; P Goodrich, 'Law-induced Anxiety: Legists, Anti-Lawyers, and the Boredom of Legality' (2000) 9(1) *Social and Legal Studies* 143.
[130] Simon (n 3) 142.
[131] W Simon, 'Ethical Discretion in Lawyering' (1988) 101 *Harvard Law Review* 1083.

possible.¹³² Others suggested a justification based on the nature of the lawyer and client relationship, which Charles Fried likened to friendship.¹³³ Friends and family stood by those members of the group who broke social norms, he reasoned. It was therefore possible to align the lawyer's role with ordinary morality by recognising that they were simply 'special purpose friends'. This idea provoked a burst of ridicule and parody, payment making lawyers more like prostitutes than friends.¹³⁴

Freedman returned to Fried's point some years later, arguing that interpersonal roles were inevitably affected by familial, social, and professional context: 'One simply cannot be expected, in any rational, practical moral system, to react to every other person in the same way in which one would respond to a spouse, a child, or a close friend.'¹³⁵ A sufficient moral justification, according to Freedman, was the promise lawyers voluntarily gave to serve a client¹³⁶ which covered, expressly or by implication, confidentiality of the client's information. Freedman noted Kant's view that keeping promises was a categorical imperative. This necessarily impinged on any wider social responsibility it would be reasonable to impose on lawyers.

In 1996, William Simon attacked the traditional lawyer's role from a different perspective. This time he challenged the 'Dominant View' that the lawyer's role was constrained by legality¹³⁷ and specifically the idea 'that lawyers should pursue client interests subject only to the clearly defined limits of the "law"'.¹³⁸ Simon suggested that the Dominant View shared with Positivism a strong affinity for categorical judgement. He argued that the Positivist resolved normative conflict by determining the status of competing norms, either in terms of the institution promoting those norms or, if the norms were those of the same institution, whatever criteria were applied to determine priority. He argued that this promoted 'rigid priority of jurisdictional over substantive norms'.¹³⁹

Simon argued there were three arguments for compliance with jurisdictional norms: social order (everyone should obey the law), fairness (if others are, I should), and democracy (law is the product of popular representation and process entitling it to respect). None of these provided, Simon argued, a definitive justification of the Dominant View. Lawyers, Simon argued, were expected to make judgments about legality in circumstances where specific contexts determined the 'right' thing to do. Simon provided two examples where, he suggested, lawyers ran into difficulty.¹⁴⁰

---

¹³² MH Freedman, 'Are There Public Interest Limits on Lawyers' Advocacy' (1977) *The Journal of the Legal Profession* 47 at 54.
¹³³ C Fried, 'The Lawyer as Friend: The Moral Foundations of the Lawyer-Client Relation' (1976) 85 *Yale Law Journal* 1060.
¹³⁴ See EA Dauer and AA Leff, 'Correspondence: The Lawyer as Friend' (1976–77) 86 *Yale Law Journal* 574, and Fried's response at 587.
¹³⁵ A Periman, 'The Beginning of Professor Monroe Freedman's Upcoming Talk in Chicago' (*Legal Ethics Forum*, 23 April 2007) www.legalethicsforum.com/blog/2007/04/the_beginning_o.html.
¹³⁶ ibid.
¹³⁷ WH Simon, 'Should Lawyers Obey the Law' (1996) 38 *William and Mary Law Review* 217 citing, at fn 1, the outline of the dominant view provided by Luban (n 1) 393–403.
¹³⁸ Simon ibid fn 1.
¹³⁹ ibid 220.
¹⁴⁰ ibid.

In Simon's first example a lawyer was faced with clients who needed to falsely claim adultery had occurred to meet legal criteria for divorce. The traditional, Positivist approach could only help the intending divorcees by agitating for a change in the law, a course unhelpful to them in the short-term. A pragmatic lawyer would, Simon argued, help the parties to concoct such claim, even though the 'Dominant View' of ethics would forbid this as suborning perjury. In his second example, a client seeking advice on a tax return asked how many returns were audited, a question directed to exploring illegal evasion. Simon suggested that under the Dominant View the lawyer should hesitate to tell the client that only 5 per cent of returns were audited because it could encourage them to make a false return. The lawyer, he said, had to make a 'contextual judgement' based on an assessment of the client's intention and whether it was lawful or not.[141]

Simon claimed that lawyers with a positivist approach would struggle in his hypothetical situations. They might worry that the advice they could give would assist illegal conduct and therefore be improper. He suggested that such concern would be 'out of step with mainstream views and practices'[142] and 'makes more sense for lawyers than lay people'.[143] While Simon did not say how lawyers should resolve the dilemmas he posed, he suggested that an approach that defined law substantively rather than positively, would 'erase the line between law and morals'.[144] Simon admitted he had no general theory about balancing Positivist and Substantive considerations, but argued that lawyers already compromised the Dominant View in line with a substantive perspective and that 'good lawyers already have their own such theories'.[145]

E. The Rule of Law

A defence against critics of the standard conception was the idea that lawyers had a distinctive 'role morality', based on their place in the adversary system or benefits to the social order.[146] From a moral point of view this was assumed to be a problematic justification since it claimed lawyers legally representing adversaries were absolved of consequences.[147] The tide of academic opinion role was largely negative until the millennium. Within 10 years the framework of analyses of US scholars, notably Daniel Markovitz[148] and W Bradley Wendel,[149] had shifted away from moral

---

[141] ibid 219.
[142] ibid 220.
[143] ibid 251.
[144] ibid 253.
[145] ibid.
[146] R Wasserstrom, 'Roles and Morality' in D Luban (ed), *The Good Lawyer* (Totowa, Rowman and Allanheld, 1984) 26; D Luban, 'The Adversary System Excuse' in Luban (ed), *The Good Lawyer* 83; WH Simon, 'Role Differentiation and Lawyers' Ethics: A Critique of Some Academic Perspectives' (2010) 23 *Georgetown J of Legal Ethics* 987.
[147] But see eg J Andre, 'Role Morality as a Complex Instance of Ordinary Morality' (1991) 28(1) *American Philosophical Quarterly* 73.
[148] D Markovits, *A Modern Legal Ethics: Adversary Advocacy in a Democratic Age* (Princeton University Press, 2008).
[149] Wendel (n 11).

philosophy back to political philosophy and the idea that lawyers' roles supported social institutions such as the rule of law.[150] This was so fundamental to society that some consequential harms were justified, even necessary. Notions of legality offered compromise with the critique of moral philosophers by limiting the scope of what lawyers could do for clients.[151]

Markovitz argued that the role afforded lawyers by the legal system meant that lying (convincing a judge of what they did not believe to be the truth) and cheating (advancing a morally dubious position) were intrinsic,[152] justified by a moral division of labour. Markovitz acknowledged that they were inconsistent with careers aspiring to honesty, playing fair and treating others kindly. The requirement that a lawyer be 'self-effacing' incorporated fidelity to clients into their own personal commitments.[153] By giving voice to the voiceless the lawyer made a virtue of being, quite literally, a mouthpiece or hired gun.[154] Markovitz, therefore, suggested that lawyers' ethical position, or the position of adversary advocates at least, was vindicated by a rounded conception of role.[155]

Wendel suggested that loyalty to clients was a flawed basis on which to justify the lawyer's role because it left the limits of actions on behalf of clients unclear. He argued that fidelity to law was a more defensible underpinning. Lawyers performing their traditional role contributed to a reasonably well-functioning legal system and upheld the values it promoted. This deserved the allegiance of citizens because, among other things it allowed enforcement of their legal entitlements. For Wendel, the lawyer's role was justified by the political legitimacy conferred on democratic law-making within states governed by the rule of law. Lawyers performed their role by working within 'institutional roles and practices that requires moral justifications, but at a higher level of generality'.[156] Echoing the nineteenth century US ethicists, he argued that legal entitlements were 'claims of right' distinguishable from something obtained 'using power, trickery or influence'.

Wendel's general position, that compliance with legality justified the standard conception, was somewhat contradicted by his operational model. This tended to manifest lawyers' fidelity to law but not necessarily the interests of citizens. Wendel claimed lawyers were only entitled to 'protect the legal entitlements of clients, not advance their interests'[157] and that the principle of partisanship should be expressed accordingly.[158] He described neutrality in client selection as an obligation 'for which there can be no moral justification'.[159] He therefore thought that lawyers should be

---

[150] This is less pronounced in the case of Markovitz who focuses on the legitimacy of the legal process (see eg 184).
[151] Not necessarily to the satisfaction of the original critics. See eg responses to Wendel in a journal special edition (2012) 90 *Texas Law Review* 69.
[152] Markovits (n 148).
[153] ibid 165.
[154] ibid 92–96.
[155] ibid 212–13.
[156] Wendel (n 11) 7.
[157] ibid 6 and 49.
[158] ibid 49.
[159] ibid 87.

able to reject clients, reflecting the position in both the US and Canada.[160] But what was the point of legal entitlements if lawyers refused to pursue them?

VI. OTHER CORE JURISDICTIONS

The principle of adversarial trial was accepted in the core common law jurisdictions. In 1992, the High Court of Australia unanimously expressed the view that legal representation in criminal cases, particularly those involving serious crimes, was highly desirable if not necessary to ensure a fair trial.[161] It remained controversial but did not generate the debate it had in America. Academics in core jurisdictions produced material accepting the general applicability of the standard conception and debating its relevance and morality.[162] A variation in the book by Tim Dare equated the standard conception with Sharswood's concept of 'zeal'. He proposed that lawyers owed a limited obligation, 'mere zeal', in most legal work, but 'hyper zeal' in limited spheres such as criminal defence.

VII. DISCUSSION

The lawyer's role was underpinned by social changes affecting conceptions of law. William Simon suggested that the foundations were laid by Thomas Hobbes in Positivist legal theory. In a society of egoistic individuals, the state provided order and space for them to pursue their own ends, governed by rules that were 'artificial, impersonal, objective and rational'.[163] The judge interpreted the sovereign's intention, the lawyer explained to citizens how they would be affected. This was a change in systems of social discipline, the character of which, Foucault argued, depended on three factors: the system's underlying purposes, its social institutions, and the available technology of regulation.[164] In the liberal era social regulation was achieved by sophisticated systems of participation and consent.

Litigation was a natural central focus of social change and the lawyer's role. Early medieval attitudes to litigation were ambivalent. Trial served the dual purpose of providing a legitimate process for resolving disputes and a means of discovering truth. In the late medieval period, lawyers could claim the excuse of role, but not if they had been too partisan. The adversarial trial required them to be both neutral and

---

[160] ibid ch 4 n 70, citing CW Wolfram, *Modern Legal Ethics* (Minneapolis, West publishing Co, 1986) 571 and AC Hutchinson, *Legal Ethics and Professional Responsibility* (Toronto, Irwin Law, 1999) 73.

[161] *Dietrich v The Queen* (1992) 177 CLR 292, cited in A Piper and M Finnane, 'Access To Legal Representation By Criminal Defendants In Victoria 1861–1961 (2017) 40(2) *University of New South Wales Law Journal* 638.

[162] See eg Dare (n 11); A Hutchinson, 'Taking it Personally: Legal Ethics and Client Selection' (1998) 1(2) *Legal Ethics* 168 (Canada); Nicolson and Webb (n 6); C Parker, *Just Lawyers* (Oxford, Oxford University Press, 1999) esp ch 5 (Australia).

[163] Simon (n 3) 40.

[164] M Foucault, *Discipline and Punish: the Birth of the Prison*, 2nd edn (trans A Sheridan) (New York, Random House, 1995).

partisan. Basing conclusions on the available evidence[165] and providing mechanisms for testing it[166] was arguably the best way to resolve conflict. Adversarial advocacy created a distinctly client focused ethos for the lawyer and client relationship, shaped by the unnatural context of the trial.

The individualism of adversarial justice was not an inevitable consequence of transition. It may have reflected the gradual acceptance of liberal (Whiggish) attitudes. Pue suggested that the Victorian state considered advocacy important to the nature of the legal system because it suggested the notion of equality before the law, making 'inseparable the notions of dedication to client, independence of the bar, and constitutional liberty'.[167] By the nineteenth century, the fearless partisan was the Bar's preferred mythology. Nevertheless, Schramm suggested that journalists, barristers, and authors of fiction, those representing the vocabulary of inquiry of criminal investigation, were 'tainted by suggestions of vicarious guilt'.[168] Macaulay's criticisms, and his affectation, not to be drawn on whether the 'doctrine' of the lawyer's obligation to accept a case was 'agreeable to reason and morality',[169] displayed this layman's prejudice.

As Winsberg showed, concern that zealous representation of clients might betray the public interest was deeply rooted in American attitudes to lawyers.[170] This concern was a theme of US literature on the legal profession, exemplified by Anthony Kronman's lament for what he perceived to be the decline of the 'lawyer-statesmen' ideal.[171] Sharswood's articulation of the lawyer's role was a familiar statement of the relationship to the rule of law, being based on a constitutional right to be presumed innocent and to a fair trial, in which a lawyer presented any available defence.[172] The central premise was that justice resulted from the zealous presentation of competing views. The system functioned when lawyers focused on their client's cause, not when they tried to anticipate what 'justice' required.[173]

Although quotations of British barristers, such as Erskine and Brougham and their critics, such as Macaulay, were cited by American critics of the standard conception[174] there was little evidence that they had a decisive influence on American lawyers. Russell Pearce suggested that the American tradition was at least partly rooted in a republican ideal manifested in the nineteenth century in the work of Hoffman and Sharswood, rather than the English Bar. In Sharswood's conception

---

[165] J Auburn, *Legal Professional Privilege: Law and Theory* (Oxford, Hart Publishing Ltd, 2000) 79–80, citing a consensus among many leading legal philosophers and evidence scholars, including John Rawls, Edmund Morgan, Newbold and William Twining.
[166] Wigmore praised cross-examination as a means of getting at the truth.
[167] Pue (n 61) 54.
[168] Schramm (n 48) 301.
[169] Macaulay (n 13) 318.
[170] Winsburg (n 89) 189.
[171] A Kronman, *The Lost Lawyer: Failing Ideals of the Legal Profession* (Cambridge, Massachusetts, The Belknap Press of Harvard University Press, 1994).
[172] Pearce (n 7) 265.
[173] Johnson (n 2) 36; Denti (n 2).
[174] G Postema, 'Moral Responsibility in Professional Ethics' (1980) 55 *NYUL Rev* 63; D Luban, *Legal Ethics and Human Dignity* (Cambridge, Cambridge University Press, 2007) 9; AC Hutchinson *Fighting Fair: Legal Ethics for an Adversarial Age* (Cambridge, Cambridge University Press, 2015) 18.

of the lawyer's role, the rule of law and the protection of property rights were set against adversarial obligations.[175] This balance reflected belief in an organic society in which the state fostered individual virtue and the common good.[176]

During the nineteenth century, Pearce suggested, the idea of democratic virtue was replaced by faith in a virtuous elite comprising a financially secure gentry and professionals such as lawyers. These groups were seen as independent of the marketplace and would make less self-interested political leaders than the merchant classes. This shift in thought was accompanied by moves to make property and contractual rights fixed principles of law controlled by the judiciary. In the late twentieth century, the view that the principles of the standard conception had a malign and unjustifiable influence on lawyers resurfaced.

Luban and Wendel suggested that the seeds of the critique of the lawyer's role lay in the counter-culture of the 1960s and the anti-establishment feelings evoked by the civil rights movement, feminism and anti-Vietnam War sentiment.[177] This 'powerful political mistrust of the Establishment' led to subjection of all kinds of institutions and institutional demands to the test of individual conscience.[178] The standard conception was a straw man for critics of the client-centric social role played by lawyers. It may have excused some lawyers' controlling client choices and avoiding moral accountability. The deluge of criticism, grounded in moral philosophy,[179] drowned out evaluation of the balance between client and public facing norms.

The soul-searching following Watergate was productive but possibly misdirected. Dean's lawyers were said to be corrupted by habits of neutral partisanship. In fact, the problem was that the American system independently encouraged loyalty to the President or the government rather than the Constitution or the People. Why the misbehaviour of government lawyers should cause a moral panic about lawyer and client relations in private practice was unclear, but it fed a narrative which sought to hold lawyers responsible for client actions held to be immoral.

The Reformation led to separation of the state and secular institutions from religion and personal moral conscience. The non-sectarian, civil sphere became one of the primary responsibilities of the state.[180] This created a space in which an intellectual elite, which Koselleck referred to as Critics, became a kind of 'moral judiciary'.[181] Saunders called these 'heirs to religion' who claimed to see through failed practices and institutions to offer new possibilities for the reunification of law and morality.[182] The open society promoted by liberalism undermined its tolerance and pluralism by criticising its institutions, norms and freedoms.[183] Saunders suggested that the Critics

---

[175] Pearce (n 7).
[176] ibid 250.
[177] Luban and Wendel (n 128).
[178] ibid 339.
[179] ibid 337.
[180] D Saunders, *Anti-Lawyers: Religion and the Critics of Law and State* (Abingdon, Routledge, 1997).
[181] Saunders ibid 13, citing R Koselleck, *Critique and Crisis: Enlightenment and the Pathogenesis of Modern Society* (Cambridge, MA, MIT Press, 1988) 82.
[182] Saunders ibid 142.
[183] ibid 6 and see NE Simmonds, 'Book Review: *Anti-Lawyers: Religion and the Critics of Law and State*' (1998) 57(3) *The Cambridge Law Journal* 611 citing Kolakowski and Schumpeter.

proposed remarriage of law and religion, under other names. By uncovering the context of critique, Saunders hoped to reclaim the dignity of the institutions of Law and government which the Critics attacked for ethical failings.[184]

In *The Lost Lawyer*, Anthony Kronman described universities as 'unworldly places'.[185] Critics certainly inhabited the Law School, where legal doctrine initially flourished as a successor of religious doctrine[186] but later careers were built on philosophical critique, such as the moral attack on the standard conception. Simon, for example, cast himself as a critic of both the standard conception and of the Dominant View, Positivism, or legality, its theoretical constraint, on moral grounds. The implication of Saunders' critique, that imagining progress in the conception of lawyers' work was self-indulgent, counterproductive, or wrong, was however also unattractive.

Critics of the standard conception sometimes demonstrated tendencies Saunders attributed to critics as heirs to religion: failing to recognise political reality[187] and encouraging a kind of moral superiority. Rob Rosen noted that lawyers who were not neutral regarding the outcome of clients' cases risked being excessively zealous or self-righteous.[188] As Simon himself recognised, vindicating clients' rights as individuals was a necessary support for liberalism and the rule of law. Significantly, 'ordinary morality' was an illusion in a society of multivariant ethnicities, religions, and interests. The past 300 years produced an acceptable accommodation between lawyers' service to the autonomy of the individual and to legality. The law, not morality, set the framework of legal practice.

VIII. CONCLUSION

Lawyers' roles reflected the moral climate of the age. Early liberalism produced a system, the adversarial trial, and a model of advocacy created and then modified experientially. This provided a means of resolving fundamental clashes of interest to protect citizens. Lawyers received a broadly similar legal education, portrayed by Miller as training in extreme rationality, a neutral position on moral questions, a partisan position on client interests and a dogged proceduralism.[189] They regarded all interactions as potentially adversarial, thought self-interest the best organising principle for life and altruism suspect.[190] Depicted negatively, as concern for procedure over substance,[191] these attitudes were consistent with maintaining liberal individualism and the rule of law.

---

[184] Saunders (n 180) 14.
[185] Kronman (n 171) 315.
[186] Koselleck (n 181) 1.
[187] ibid 13.
[188] RE Rosen, 'On the Social Significance of Critical Lawyering' (2000) 3 *Legal Ethics* 169 at 170.
[189] MC Miller, *The High Priests of American Politics: The Role of Lawyers in American Political institutions* (Knoxville, University of Tennessee Press, 1995) 19.
[190] ibid 26.
[191] ibid 39.

Traditional lawyer morality always attracted criticism. Originally, it was because it involved advocates in obscuring the truth. From the 1970s criticism of the so-called standard conception of the lawyer's role suggested that it had transcended origins in an advocacy profession, the English Bar, to become a universal ethic of lawyers. This was contrary to the origins of the more generic American profession, in an ethic of civic republicanism. Both models supported freedom, but in different ways.[192] The standard conception leaned towards support for individual rights whereas the republican ethic took a broader, institutional view. They struck a different balance in conceiving lawyers' relationship to the rule of law.

---

[192] Pearce (n 7) 250.

Part 3

Profession

The McRuer Report was an extensive inquiry into Canadian civil rights which reported in the late 1960s. One section considered self-governing professions of which there were 22 in Ontario, all with statutory power to license, govern, and control members. The Report stated that a professional calling tended to be:

> one which depends for its pursuit on confidence of two kinds – the personal confidence of the patient or client in the technical competence of the practitioner, and the confidence of the public at large in the integrity and ethical conduct of the profession as a whole; it requires a high standard of technical skill and achievement; it provides a service to members of the public; practitioners are usually employed under a contract for service rather than a contract of service, i.e. they operate as independent practitioners and are not subject to detailed control by those whom they serve; the calling is one in which more than mere technical competence is required for the service of patients or clients and for the protection of the public, i.e. standards of ethical conduct must prevail; confidence is reposed in the practitioner requiring that he does not exploit the intimate details of his patient's or client's life and affairs which are divulged to him.[1]

---

[1] Royal Commission, *Inquiry Into Civil Rights* Ontario Report No 1, Vol 3, at p 1161, cited by WR Flaus, 'Discipline within the New Zealand Legal Profession' (1971) 6 *Victoria U Wellington L Rev* 337, fn 2.

10

Organisation

I. INTRODUCTION

ORGANISATION CAN TAKE many forms, from informal networks to formal institutions. In the case of lawyers, institutional organisation involved settling common identity and presenting it to the world. Beneath the apparent consensus lay sub-groupings, partial membership, and uneven development. These processes produced consistent images across jurisdictions but below the surface lay different purposes. Goals, aspirations, and systems of thought were often shaped by elites in the field of practice. The chronology and processes of adopting law and professionalising lawyers sometimes involved emulating existing institutions, adapting them to local conditions, and re-invention.[1] Was the apparent homogeneity of legal organisations due to inherited tradition or were they inevitable expressions of lawyer roles in the liberal state?

II. THEORY

There are three distinct sociological approaches to analysing lawyer organisations, usually known in the latter stages as professions. The structural approach focused on static characteristics often absent in non-professions.[2] The processual approach focused on the historical stages that occupations went through to become professions.[3] The power approach was concerned with economics, placing emphasis on the work monopolies granted to professions expressly or implicitly by the state.[4]

The eminent sociologist, Emile Durkheim (1858–1917) proposed a theory of structural functionalism, in which society was an organic whole to which units contributed. Secondary institutions such as professions served a general need,

---

[1] A Watson, 'The Evolution of Law: The Roman System of Contracts' (1984) 2 *Law & Hist. Rev* 1; EM Wise, 'The Transplant of Legal Patterns' (1990) 38 *American Journal of Comparative Law Supplement* 1.

[2] E Greenwood, 'Attributes of a Profession' (1957) 2(3) *Social Work* 44; WJ Goode, 'Community within a Community: The Professions' (1957) 22 *American Sociological Review* 194.

[3] T Caplow, *The Sociology of Work* (Minneapolis, University of Minnesota Press, 1954); HL Wilensky, 'The Professionalisation of Work' (1964) 70(2) *American Journal of Sociology* 137.

[4] E Freidson, *Profession of Medicine: A Study of the Sociology of Applied Knowledge* (New York, Harper and Row, 1970); TJ Johnson, *Professions & Power* (London, MacMillan, 1972).

protecting the individual from oppressive action by the state, employers, or other interests.[5] Durkheim's notion that professions served the public good by resisting the drift of the modern state towards domination by markets and state bureaucracy was developed by US sociologists such as Talcott Parsons and Robert K Merton.

The US sociologist, Margatti Safarli Larson, suggested that professional culture in Europe translated medieval notions of craft and community to industrial capitalism.[6] Professional associations were an important vehicle of this transformation because, as Weber suggested, they had 'guardianship' of activity in their sphere. Organisation of lawyers as professions responded to a need for specialised legal knowledge.[7] Weber noted similarities of the processes of priesthood and the new professions of law and medicine emerging in the Middle Ages. Both exerted power, had doctrine (general systematic knowledge), rational training and vocational qualifications.[8]

Weber noted two general meanings of 'profession', one a special kind of occupation and the other an avowal or promise.[9] Indeed, in the translator's notes to *The Protestant Ethic*, Talcott Parsons observed that Weber's word 'beruf' could be read as either 'calling' or 'profession', but not 'vocation'[10] and suggested that this usage deliberately conveyed the idea of a particular attitude to one's work, whatever it involved. Weber had noted roots of public service in Calvinism and the Protestant ideal of 'a life of good works combined into a unified system'.[11]

Weber argued that education and training were more important than economic and social factors in producing rational law.[12] The apprenticeship model produced craftsmen and encouraged formalistic use of law for routine use, while a more rational system would emerge only when specialist schools, such as universities, developed legal theory. Larson pointed to the social control inherent in 'a calling' or vocation.[13] It required a professional socialisation making elite standards part of the individual *subjectivity* of members. The ideology would be consistent with prevalent social ideologies. When the process involved universities, it would promote the values of science in social and economic reform. In this way, she argued, professions turned control of the production of knowledge into control of the production of their own members and then into monopoly provision of the service.

---

[5] E Durkheim, *The Division of Labour in Society* (trans G Simpson) (New York, Free Press, 1893/1933) 14.
[6] MS Larson, *The Rise of Professionalism: A Sociological Analysis* (Berkeley CA, University of California Press, 1977).
[7] G Ritzer, 'Professionalization, Bureaucratization and Rationalization: The Views of Max Weber' (1975) 53(4) *Social Forces* 627, 629.
[8] Ritzer ibid 630 citing M Weber, *Economy and Society: An outline of Interpretative Sociology* (G Roth and W Wittich, eds) (Totowa, New Jersey, Bedminster, 1968) 1164.
[9] DL Bassett, 'Defining the "Public" Profession' (2005) 36(3) *Rutgers Law Journal* 721, 727 citing E Freidson, *Profession of Medicine: A Study of the Sociology of Applied Knowledge* (New York, Harper and Row, 1988) xv.
[10] M Weber, *The Protestant Ethic and the Spirit of Capitalism* (trans T Parsons) (London, George Allen and Unwin Ltd, 1930) nn 11, 194.
[11] Weber (n 8) 117.
[12] Ritzer (n 7) 629 citing Weber (n 8) 776–85.
[13] ibid 227.

III. PROTOTYPES

A. The Bar of England and Wales

The barristers were the modern profession most clearly demonstrating a link with medieval trade guilds.[14] The difference from all other occupations was intensive communal organisation around the London-based Inns of Court based on chambers, collectives of self-employed barristers. In medieval times, the Inns exercised educational functions and regulated entry.[15] Lemmings suggested that, until the eighteenth century the Inns of Court maintained communal, Guild-like ceremonies.[16] In the Tudor period, complex educational activity existed around the appointments of readers and serjeants, a step to becoming a judge. This celebration of merit according to the profession's criteria expressed solidarity and hierarchy and 'consciousness of common devotion to the mysteries of English law'.[17]

The erosion of the Inns' communal features occurred gradually during the 1700s but were compromised long before. In 1606, for example, Coke was quickly sworn as a serjeant so he could become a judge and Chief Justice of the Common Pleas.[18] Prest maintained that it was only in the 1640s that barristers began to be recognised as 'a distinct order of legal practitioners'.[19] This may have led to the rapid disposal of guild like trappings. By 1670, reader rites were abandoned and only ceremonies celebrating success remained. This could have been partly due to the advent of rational and commercial attitudes. It may also have been because the Inns' education for the privileged opened routes into politics.

Following the Civil War, the Inns of Court were a target for abolition or reform,[20] but no action was taken.[21] This may be because many of the 40 barrister members of the Rump Parliament had been students at an Inn.[22] Edmund Ludlow accused lawyers of colluding with Cromwell to prevent restrictions of their privileges.[23] Burrage attributed it to an alliance of the propertied classes and the lawyers in Parliament.[24] Following the Restoration, Charles and then James appointed King's Counsel as benchers to pack Parliament with supporters while conducting vendettas against the Inns to coerce support.

---

[14] Larson (n 6).
[15] During the second half of the 16th century and into the 17th, demand for lawyers expanded; by 1640 apprenticeship lapsed and call to the Bar alone conferred rights of audience (M Burrage, *Revolution and the Making of the Contemporary Legal Profession: England, France and the United States* (Oxford, Oxford University Press, 2006) 388.
[16] D Lemmings, 'Ritual and the Law in Early Modern England' in S Corcoran (ed), *Law and History in Australia* (Adelaide, Adelaide Law Review, 1991) 3.
[17] ibid 5.
[18] ibid 13.
[19] WR Prest, *The Rise Of The Barristers: A Social History Of The English Bar, 1590–1640* (Oxford, Clarendon Press, 1986) 3.
[20] Burrage (n 15) 420–21.
[21] ibid 422–26.
[22] ibid 415.
[23] ibid 356.
[24] ibid 427.

After the Glorious Revolution the Inns' right of self-governance was asserted. Sugarman suggested this 'tacitly affirmed the autonomy of professional, chartered and local bodies as part of England's balanced and unwritten constitution'.[25] They were now perceived to be institutions protected by the 'Lawes and Liberties of this Kingdome' restored by the Bill of Rights.[26] The Bar had apparently achieved a unique constitutional position, independence from the state, while the Inns of Court were an early expression of organised civil society.[27]

In the Hanoverian period the Inn's remaining ceremonials disappeared. The marks of prestige they bestowed were supplanted by offices of the Crown, King's counsel and solicitor or attorney general. These roles took precedence in the Inns of which the postholders were members, producing a new legal elite 'defined by and, in the case of the Law Officers, serving the ends of state power'.[28] The only surviving legal ceremonies of significance involved the judiciary. By the nineteenth century 'the only common sentiment which seemed to encompass all the profession was admiration for the "great men" who had succeeded at the Bar, such as Erskine and Brougham' and found political eminence.[29]

Although educational provision existed at the Inns, it was intermittent and idiosyncratic. With little provision for formal advocacy training, aspiring barristers learned by watching famous advocates perform in court.[30] One institution, pupillage, was of great antiquity but relatively unorganised. Individual barristers provided pupillage to aspirants from at least the 1400s but there was no requirement or regulation.[31]

From 1847, it was customary for pupils to spend a year with a conveyancer or equity draftsman, six months each with a special pleader or common law barrister and a solicitor, before another half-year with a barrister. In 1959, 12 months' pupillage with a qualified pupil supervisor became compulsory and from 1965 pupils were stopped from taking briefs during their first six months. Before 1975, barristers could charge their pupils 100 guineas a year, but this swung around from 2003, when the Bar required that pupils receive a minimum payment from their chambers.

Measures to promote a common education were taken in the mid-1800s. In 1846 a Select Committee of the House of Commons produced a report of over 500 pages

---

[25] D Sugarman, 'Bourgeois Collectivism, Professional Power and the Boundaries of the State: The Private and Public Life of the Law Society 1825 to 1914' (1996) 3(1/2) *International Journal of the Legal Profession* 81, 84.

[26] M Burrage, 'Mrs Thatcher Against the "Little Republics": Ideology, Precedents and Reaction' in TC Halliday and L Karpik (eds), *Lawyers and the Rise of Western Political Liberalism* (Oxford, Clarendon Press, 1997) 125, 150–51.

[27] ibid 154.

[28] Lemmings (n 16) 3.

[29] ibid 15, citing R Cocks, *Foundations of the Modern Bar* (London, Sweet and Maxwell, 1983) 25–29.

[30] These included: Coke, Bacon, Cowper, Yorke, Murray, Burke, Sheridan, Garrow, Brougham, Scarlett, Erskine, Romilly, Copley, Curran, O'Connell, Phillips, Kenealy, Parry, Ballantine, James, Digby-Seymour, Hawkins, Clarke, Holker, Hardinge-Giffard, Russell, Isaacs, Muir, Wrottesley, Carson, Smith, Marshall-Hall, Hastings, Curtis-Benett and Birkett (See A Watson, *Speaking in Court: Developments in Court Advocacy from the Seventeenth to the Twenty-First Century* (London, Palgrave Macmillan, 2019).

[31] G Fetherstonhaugh, 'Pupillage: A Potted History' (*Counsel*, June 2015) www.counselmagazine.co.uk/articles/pupillage-potted-history#:~:text=Regulation%20of%20pupillage%20has%20a%20comparatively%20recent%20history.,for%20practice%20at%20the%20Bar%20only%20since%201959.

criticising legal education in both England and Ireland, saying that there was not much of a public nature worthy of the name and that students were largely left to their own devices.[32] In 1852 the Inns voted to establish a Council of Legal Education, to provide a unified post-graduate education for barristers. This operated out of Lincoln's Inn initially and later in rooms provided in other Inns. In 1967 a purpose-built Inns of Court School of Law opened in Gray's Inn.

A step towards creating an institution for all barristers was taken in 1863, when the Inns joined together to issue Consolidated Regulations. These covered: admission of students, keeping of terms, conditions of Call to the Bar, which granted right to appear in courts, and granting of practising certificates. Formal written law examinations became a pre-requisite of Call.[33] In 1894 the General Council of the Bar, commonly known as the Bar Council, became the main representative body for the Bar.[34]

Criminal legal aid was available to defendants with a defence but without means from 1903 and became more widely available in the 1960s. The number of barristers increased with state funding of cases[35] and routine sentence discounting and charge bargaining and the 'mass production of guilty pleas' placed strains on the system.[36] Neutral and partisan principles were adapted to a framework of due process,[37] placing increased emphasis on barristers' duty to the court and their responsibility for forensic decisions and strategy'.[38] Declining legal aid rates provided little scope for career progression for young barristers, criminal cases being the main source of income for many.[39]

B. The Solicitors

In 1614 an order of the Inns of Court barred attorneys from working alongside barristers. It declared that 'the purpose of the inns was the education of the nobility and gentry' and that 'there ought always to be observed a difference between a Counselor at law which is the principal person next to Sergeants and Judges in the administration of Justice and attorneys and solicitors which are but ministerial

---

[32] *Report from the Select Committee on Legal Education: Report, minutes of evidence, appendix and index* (London, House of Commons, 1846).

[33] Fetherstonhaugh (n 31).

[34] A Senate of the Inns of Court and the Bar existed between 1974 and 1987 but was abandoned after a report by Lord Rawlinson in 1987, which resulted in the creation of the Council of the Inns of Court and General Council of the Bar (Council of the Inns of Court, www.tbtas.org.uk/wp-content/uploads/2013/06/Information-and-Guidance-Pack.pdf).

[35] J Morrison and P Leith, *The Barristers World and the Nature of Law* (Buckingham, Oxford University Press, 1992) 194.

[36] A Ashworth, R Young and M Burton, *Criminal Justice* (Oxford, Oxford University Press, 2010) ch 8.

[37] WH Simon, 'The Ideology of Advocacy: Procedural Justice and Professional Ethics' (1978) *Wisconsin Law Review* 29.

[38] *R v Farooqi* [2013] EWCA Crim 1649, [2014] 1 Cr App R 8, per Lord Judge CJ.

[39] T Smith and E Cape, 'The rise and decline of criminal legal aid in England and Wales' in A Flynn and J Hodgson, *Access to Justice and Legal Aid: Comparative Perspectives on Unmet Legal Need* (London, Bloomsbury, 2017) 63, 77.

persons and of an inferior nature'.[40] In 1633 an ordinance provided that practitioners in the courts of King's Bench and Common Pleas had to serve a Clerk or Attorney of the court for six years or have equivalent education and legal study.[41]

The growing importance of English attorneys and solicitors increased the volume of regulation applied to them. They were loosely supervised by the court until the Attorneys and Solicitors Act 1729 allowed attorneys to practice as solicitors, required both to serve a five-year clerkship before being examined, admitted, and enrolled,[42] and banned unauthorised practice. Legislation in 1750 allowing solicitors to practice as attorneys was probably a significant step towards amalgamating the occupations. A society was formed in 1739, however, which already purported to represent non-barrister lawyers.

The Society of Attorneys, Solicitors, Proctors and others not being Barristers, practising in the Courts of Law and Equity of the United Kingdom, also known as the Gentleman Practisers,[43] represented various London-based lawyer elites. It was sustained by their subscriptions to raise the status of lawyers who were not barristers and, ultimately, to emulate the Bar.[44] The Gentleman Practisers began to define, consolidate, and regulate legal work. In 1740 meetings were held on several Bills to appear before Parliament, including one on summoning juries. The following year a bill affecting Attorneys was revised following resistance from the Society.[45] Within a short time, government consulted the Gentleman Practisers on any proposed legislation within its sphere of interest.[46]

In the early 1800s the Gentleman Practisers sought to establish a more clearly defined identity, planning a headquarters and meeting place incorporating a library and dining club. A prospectus was issued in 1823 for a site in Chancery Lane, in Holborn, Central London, close to the Inns of Court and, it was hoped, next to a proposed Royal Courts of Justice.[47] In 1825, the Gentlemen Practisers became the Incorporated Law Society. By this time the new building was conceived of as a centre of legal science, reflecting the prevailing spirit of scientific exploration and public education, adapting the Bar's perceived ingredients of success to the new age.

The Law Society received a Royal Charter in 1831[48] and came to represent non-barrister lawyers as a single title: solicitor.[49] When completed in 1828, the Law

---

[40] MS Bilder, 'The Lost Lawyers: Early American Legal Literates and Transatlantic Legal Culture' (1999) 11 *Yale Journal of Law and the Humanities* 47 citing CW Brooks, 'Litigants and Attorneys in the King's Bench and Common Pleas' in JH Baker (ed), *Legal Records And The Historian* (London, Royal Historical Society, 1978) 41, 53.
[41] ibid.
[42] AJ Schmidt, 'The Country Attorney in Late Eighteenth-Century England: Benjamin Smith of Horbling' (1990) 8(2) *Law and History Review* 237, 238.
[43] As the Society of Gentleman Practisers in the Courts of Law and Equity (Sugarman (n 25)).
[44] ibid.
[45] *The Records of the Society of Gentleman Practisers in the Courts of Law and Equity* (London, Incorporated Law Society, 1897) iv.
[46] ibid.
[47] The national Archives 'Law Society: Solicitors' Registers of Admission', https://discovery.nationalarchives.gov.uk/details/r/C16438#:~:text=The%20Solicitors%20Act%20of%201860%20enabled%20the%20Society,a%20compulsory%20academic%20year%20was%20required%20for%20clerks.
[48] It was understandably known colloquially as The Law Society but only formally adopted this title in 1903 (P Reeves, 'Case History – A look back to the 18th century to find the origins of the Law Society and the changes over 150 years' (1995) 92 *The Law Society Gazette*).
[49] Sugarman (n 25).

Society Hall contained a large Library, meeting rooms and lecture spaces. Effort was expended on building communities. A registry for articled clerks was opened in 1832, lectures were delivered in the main Hall from 1835. The Solicitors Act 1860 authorised a preliminary examination of solicitors' general education and an intermediate examination in the general principles of law.

In 1903, the Society established a newspaper, the *Law Society Gazette*. It opened its own school of law, which later became the independent College of Law.[50] By 1922, a compulsory academic year was required for clerks. In the 1960s, five-year clerkships began to be phased out and qualification with a law degree and two years served as an articled clerk was introduced.

In 1945 a 'post-war consensus' built on social democracy[51] was influenced by Liberals like William Beveridge and the economist John Maynard Keynes. The Labour government combined state planning and collectivism with civil liberties. In 1948 a generous system of legal aid was launched covering nearly every field of rights enforceable by litigation. In 1949 the Law Society was asked to administer this government scheme,[52] bringing legal advice and assistance, and even representation, within the financial range of most of the population. Legal aid revolutionised solicitors' private practice, with some firms undertaking only legal aid work and specialising in welfare rights. This changed the orientation of the Law Society which became a champion of legal aid.

Declining legal aid rates from the 1990s led law firms to withdraw from legal aid work. In 2012, the Legal Aid, Sentencing and Punishment of Offenders Act 2012 led to many areas of law no longer being covered by legal aid. It remained available for judicial review subject to financial and merits criteria[53] requiring applicants to show that there was no other remedy and that the case had 'the potential to produce a benefit for the individual, a member of the individual's family or the environment'.[54] The preservation of legal aid for actions against the executive did, at least, preserve actions against a main abuser of citizens' rights, while leaving other potential culprits, such as corporations, relatively immune.

IV. LAWYERS IN THE DIASPORA

A. The Common Law Tradition

In early British colonies local administrations sought to follow British traditions, but law and procedure evolved differently from that in the 'home' country. The colonies often had no core of legal personnel. Amateur judges and lawyers misunderstood the principles they were applying and there were long delays involved in sending for and

---

[50] National Archive (n 47).
[51] D Kavanagh, 'Thatcherism and the end of the post-war consensus', www.bbc.co.uk/history/british/modern/thatcherism_01.shtml.
[52] The Solicitors Act 1974, s 46(6).
[53] Public Law Project, 'How to Apply for Legal Aid Funding for Judicial Review' (15 September 2016) https://publiclawproject.org.uk/resources/how-to-apply-for-legal-aid-funding-for-judicial-review/.
[54] Legal Aid, Sentencing and Punishment of Offenders Act 2012, Sch 1, Part 1, para 19(3).

receiving clarification. Even lawyers mistranslated 'traditions'[55] or ignored them on the grounds that the colonial setting demanded something different. Sometimes, after an initial wave of pragmatism, incoming judges and lawyers tried to recreate 'more faithful replicas of the home country'.[56]

The systems of law adopted in the colonies were based on the common law, with the ideology of Magna Carta rights strongly represented, and all used the adversary system. Models of lawyering were influenced by British legal occupations. The Bar, identified particularly with the adversary system, was one model for professional organisation, but its existence in England depended on esoteric conditions. The organisational model provided by the attorneys, based on atomised office space, direct client contact, and selective specialisation, was more flexible and adaptable.

While the transportation of institutions from one geographical location to another was natural it was not inevitable. All the jurisdictions adopted the business lawyer model, but the US and Canada did so while rejecting specialist advocates.[57] Opting for fused professions based on the federalised States was dictated by the size of countries unable to support the kind of centralised Bar operating in England. The fact that Australia and New Zealand recognised distinct advocacy professions despite similar geographical circumstances the American countries may have resulted from their later emergence.

B. The USA

The American colony was the earliest established, but even after independence regional differences, the absence of law schools and bar associations and lack of clarity about what constituted a lawyer made generalisations about lawyer organisation difficult. While the adversarial model of litigation was adopted, colonists were more circumspect regarding substantive law. Roscoe Pound's assertion that English common law was adopted in the period between the Revolution and Civil War[58] was contested. Wise suggested that, not only was the English tradition adapted to local conditions, but French civil law was also influential, particularly in the commercial field.[59]

The evolution of lawyer organisation in America was least obviously influenced by English antecedents. The lack of organisation in colonial America until after the American Revolution reflected a distrust of law and legal roles. Rogers suggested that anti-lawyer feeling resulted from the colonists' Puritan origins, echoing the Puritan Rump Parliament in England: '[o]ur people remembered' that some Inns of Court sold their silver to support the Stuarts.[60]

---

[55] R McQueen and WW Pue, 'Misplaced Traditions: British Lawyers, Colonial Peoples' (1999) 16 *Law in Context: A Socio-Legal Journal* 1.
[56] ibid 3.
[57] C Moore, *The Law Society of Upper Canada and Ontario's Lawyers, 1797–1997* (Toronto, Buffalo, London, University of Toronto Press, 1997).
[58] R Pound, *The Formative Era of American Law* (Boston, Little, Brown & Co, 1938) 94.
[59] Wise (n 1) 11–12.
[60] JG Rogers, 'History of the American Bar Association' (1953) 39(8) *American Bar Association Journal* 659, 662.

Evidence about legal work in the American colonies in the seventeenth century was patchy, but what did exist suggested that in many areas there were few lawyers. Some colonies administered lawyer oaths, but generally lawyers were held in low regard and in some areas actively discouraged.[61] Lawyers provided new reasons for unpopularity. Whig lawyers in New England were active promoters of colonial assemblies, but enemies of wider democracy.[62] Some colluded with local oligarchs to try and establish an American aristocracy. Elsewhere, in the Carolinas in the 1770s for example, lawyer activity precipitated armed uprisings.[63] Most jurisdictions did not operate with lawyers as judges, except perhaps as Chief Justice. Nor were law reports consistently produced.[64]

A study of a relatively small jurisdiction, Rhode Island, in the early days of colonisation suggested that it adopted and adapted English law and institutions.[65] In the seventeenth century Rhode Island invoked all statutes going back to Magna Carta and declared all contrary statutes invalidated.[66] The court records suggested that local advocates had trained as attorneys in England.[67] They appeared in half of the cases in the colony's Court of Trials in that period.[68] Lord Bellomont, on an exploratory expedition in 1699, lamented the dearth of 'legal learning' because there were no barristers in evidence.[69] The colony gradually began to allow a degree of self-regulation, a declaration regarding fees being agreed by Rhode Island lawyers in 1745.[70]

Local conditions led to the recognition of lawyers in some other States. In Maryland, for example, strong commerce, a complex land system and wealthy patrons led to a strong Bar by 1765.[71] One lawyer, Daniel Dulany, an émigré trained at Middle Temple, was so eminent he was consulted by London based lawyers.[72] None of the pre-revolutionary regional centres developed a Bar on the English model and no other systems of training were established. It seemed likely that American lawyers trained in England, particularly in the Inns of Court, imported English conduct norms.[73] It was surprising, however that adversarial principles were apparently adopted quickly, certainly by the date of a notable criminal case in 1770.

The Boston Massacre trials arose when British soldiers guarding the Colonial Administration offices fired on a mob, killing five. Nine soldiers and four civilians were charged with murder. The action resulted in two cases, one against the commanding

---

[61] CR Andrews, *Standards of Conduct for Lawyers: An 800-Year Evolution* (2004) 57 SMU Law Review 1385.
[62] JC Miller, *Origins of the American Revolution* (Little, Brown & Company, Boston, Massachusetts, 1943).
[63] ibid.
[64] C Warren, *A History of the American Bar* (New York, Cambridge University Press, 1911).
[65] Bilder (n 40).
[66] ibid 93.
[67] ibid 71.
[68] ibid 59.
[69] ibid 49.
[70] Andrews (n 61) 1421.
[71] Warren (n 64) 55.
[72] ibid.
[73] Andrews (n 61) citing (at fn 199) LM Friedman, *A History of The American Law* (NY, Simon & Schuster, 1973) 275–76.

officer and the other against the others, including men in the platoon. The future American President John Adams, practising as an attorney, agreed to appear for the defence. He was approached by a loyalist merchant, James Forrest, on behalf of the commander of the guard, Captain Preston, who was accused of giving an order to fire. Forrest told Adams that several attorneys had declined the case, but two had agreed to act if Adams did also.[74] In the earlier trial Preston was acquitted.

Feeling ran high when the trial of the soldiers opened. The jury contained no Bostonians but was selected from the surrounding area. The defence opened by reminding them that the soldiers must be judged based on 'the evidence here in Court produced against them, and by nothing else'. The evidence was that the troops had endured far greater provocation than was usual at that time, that Preston had not given an order to fire and that one soldier, Kilroy, had told a witness before the incident that: 'he would never miss an opportunity, when he had one, to fire on the inhabitants, and that he had wanted to have an opportunity ever since he landed'.[75] Kilroy and another soldier were convicted of manslaughter, but escaped by pleading 'benefit of clergy' and the branding of an 'M' on their thumb, limiting their ability to plead it in future.[76]

The trial was important in dating the transmission of adversary principles to America. The trial process was an odd mixture of different processes. For example, Captain Preston was not allowed to give evidence in his own defence and the punishment of the soldiers was archaic. The insistence on witness evidence was, however, only one example of innovation. Another concerned the standard of proof. John Adams informed the jury that, if they had doubt about the guilt of defendants, they must acquit 'for it is the invariable direction of our English Court of Justice' to lean on the side of mercy. This was said to be the first American case in which the standard of proof required was 'beyond reasonable doubt'.[77] Yet Justice Peter Oliver was recorded as agreeing: 'If upon the whole ye are in any reasonable doubt of their guilt, ye must then, agreeable to the rule of law, declare them innocent.'[78]

It is unclear why Adams invoked and the court accepted a new theory of the standard of proof, if such it was, when it placed a burden on the prosecution calculated at around a 90 per cent probability.[79] 'Reasonable doubt' was associated with the adversarial system.[80] Langbein suggested a version existed earlier in capital cases but that it developed in England at the end of the eighteenth century,[81] after the Boston massacre trial. Even by then, law in the American colonies, was supposedly 'a hazy thing, based

---

[74] D Abrams and D Fisher, *John Adams Under Fire: The Founding Father's Fight for Justice in the Boston Massacre Murder Trial* (Toronto, Hanover Square Press, 2020).

[75] Boston Massacre Historical Society, 'The Summary of the Boston Massacre Trial', www.bostonmassacre.net/trial/trial-summary4.htm.

[76] Benefit was claimed by reciting Psalm.51:1, 'Have mercy upon me, O God, according to thy loving kindness: according unto the multitude of thy tender mercies blot out my transgressions'. It was originally available only to clerics, who could read, but the requirement of reading was abolished in 1705 (ibid).

[77] Abrams and Fisher (n 74).

[78] Boston Massacre Historical Society (n 75).

[79] D Hamer, 'Probabilistic Standards Of Proof, Their Complements And The Errors That Are Expected To Flow From Them' (2004) *University of New England Law Journal* 3.

[80] D Epps, 'The Consequences of Error in Criminal Justice' (2015) 128 *Harvard Law Review* 1065.

[81] JH Langbein, *The Origins of Adversary Criminal Trial* (Oxford, Oxford University Press, 2003) 33.

loosely on the British model'.[82] Quite apart from his argument on the standard of proof, mystery also surrounded the fact that Adams accepted the case at all.

Adams made it clear he was not so much defending the man as the law, supposedly observing 'Counsel ought to be the very last thing an accused person should want in a free country ... the bar ... ought to be independent and impartial at all times and in every circumstance'.[83] He wrote in his diary that the trial had caused him '[a]nxiety, and Obloquy enough' but that agreeing to appear was the:

> most gallant, generous, manly, and disinterested Actions of my whole Life, and one of the best Pieces of Service I ever rendered my Country. Judgement of Death against those Soldiers would have been as foul a Stain upon this Country as the Execution of the Quakers or Witches, anciently. As the Evidence was, the Verdict of the Jury was exactly right.[84]

Adams' co-counsel, Josiah Quincy also resisted pressure to refuse the case. He was chided by his father, who was bitter at having to listen to the criticisms of neighbours. His son wrote to him that until they were proven guilty, the accused were 'entitled by the laws of God and man, to all legal counsel and aid' adding in support of his position his 'attorney's oath and duty'.[85]

The reasons that Adams and Quincy gave for acting echoed the duty of English barristers, but not English attorneys, to accept instructions to represent on a first come first served basis, irrespective of the nature of the case or the conduct, opinions or beliefs of the prospective client.[86] Adams, but apparently few other Boston attorneys, recognised the obligation. This was surprising given the dating of a firm obligation of representation in England to the trial of Tom Paine in 1792.[87] This suggests that attorneys in America were familiar with developments in England almost as they were happening or that they were developing their own adversary principles, perhaps drawing on earlier ideas such as those expressed by Blackstone, published 10 years before the Boston trials.

Where lawyer organisation existed in the pre-revolutionary period, it was a powerful force for change. The Maryland Bar supported resistance to the British authorities in the run up to the American War of Independence.[88] Undoubted regional differences were also found between urban centres and more dispersed communities. Following the American Civil War and westward expansion, many lawyers worked in sparsely populated regions, often as sole practitioners handling all kinds of legal work and crossing lines between litigator, advocate, and business lawyer.

Widespread formation of Bar Associations came late in the nineteenth century. New Hampshire formed a bar association and Massachusetts formed county bar associations after the Revolution, but most areas did not follow their example.[89] When it did begin to happen, it snowballed. One of the earliest State Bars,

---

[82] Abrams and Fisher (n 74).
[83] ibid.
[84] John Adams, Diary entry, 5 March 1773; Boston Massacre Historical Society (n 75).
[85] Abrams and Fisher (n 74).
[86] Bar Code of Conduct 1981, para 601(a) and (b).
[87] See Watson (n 30).
[88] Warren (n 64).
[89] Andrews (n 61) 1421.

New York, was formed in 1870. One of the last States to form a Bar Association, Indiana, did so in 1896. These associations maintained voluntary membership and played a limited role in lawyer regulation. Rogers, albeit from the perspective of the mid-twentieth century, suggested that the slow growth of lawyer organisation was because regulation suggested, despite continuing hostility to lawyers, that they may be necessary.[90]

The American Bar Association (ABA) was founded as a federal body with representation by States.[91] It was conceived in 1878 at a meeting held in Saratoga Springs, New York attended by 100 lawyers from 21 states. The American Civil War had affected local bars badly, Rogers claiming that many 'for the first time welcomed professional discipline and communication when contrasted with the frontier love of independence and suspicion of monopoly in the law'.[92] The ABA campaigned on a range of subjects, many of which were political. In 1911, for example, it opposed a campaign to recall unpopular judges.[93]

Wise suggested that the emergence of law schools drove the process of harmonisation of the various systems of law which evolved in the US.[94] The process began in 1779 with the funding of a professorship at the College of William and Mary in Virginia. In 1900 most States did not demand that lawyers had a college degree but did require periods of apprenticeship. Moves towards a university model of legal education was inspired by a view of law as a science suited to analysis, organisation, and evaluation. The case method associated with the Dean of Harvard Law School in the 1870s, Christopher Langdell, assumed full-time study with access to adequate libraries and Socratic dialogue between teacher and student in the classroom.[95] The ABA was instrumental in the case method gradually replacing other university teaching methods for law.[96]

Rogers claimed that no other Bar association, or other organisation in the world, achieved as much as the ABA in the fields of social welfare, commerce, and finance.[97] It created bodies working across the US to further substantive legal harmony: drafting uniform state laws, particularly for the commercial field and restatements of judicial decisions. One of these, the Association of American Law Schools, was launched in 1900 with around 20 members to instigate law reform. In the 1920s the American Bar Association promoted university education using the case-method as part of its campaign against part-time law schools.[98] This resulted in admission requirements for full-time attendance at an accredited university law school, disadvantaging ethnic minority and working-class students, the main clientele of part-time education, from qualifying as lawyers.

---

[90] Rogers (n 60) suggested that this explains that American preference for electing judges.
[91] ibid.
[92] ibid.
[93] ibid 663.
[94] Wise (n 1) 11–12.
[95] PD Carrington, 'Hail! Langdell!' (1995) 20 *Law and Social Inquiry* 691.
[96] RW Gordon, 'The Case For (and Against) Harvard' (1995) 93 *Michigan Law Review* 1231, 1235.
[97] Rogers (n 60) 665.
[98] JM Law and RJ Wood, 'A History of the Law Faculty' (1996) 35 *Alberta Law Review* 1 at 8 citing JS Auerbach, *Unequal Justice: Lawyers and Social Change in Modern America* (New York: Oxford University Press, 1976) 74–129.

Sunderland identified three phases in the development of the ABA.[99] The initial phase owed much to the work of Simeon F Baldwin, subsequently a Governor of Connecticut and candidate for Senate. He responded to a common aspiration of local bar groups, 'a yearning for social contact or the need for library facilities', but the positive response convinced him of the possibility for a national structure.[100] It was in the second era, 1902–36, which Sunderland called the 'era of expansion', that there was rapid growth in membership. In 1915 a quarterly journal was published, becoming monthly in 1920.

From 1936 the ABA began to evolve into its current form in the era of federation. The third phase of ABA development began in 1936 with the creation of a constitution. This turned the ABA from a 'legal club' to an organisation which could legitimately 'speak for the Bar at large'.[101] It led to strategies to improve the education of lawyers and raise entry standards.[102] It was also part of the institution building process, responding to the democratisation of the Bar and the admission of increasing numbers of entrants from non-professional families.[103]

C. Canada

At the conclusion of the American War of Independence British loyalists migrated to the area then known as Upper Canada, modern day Ontario.[104] The Canadian colony had until that point been administered by a British Governor, based in Quebec, for a largely French population. The law was supposedly English, but a kind of Anglo-French hybrid had developed in the Quebec region extending to Upper Canada. Subjection to French law was unacceptable to the 25,000 mainly British settlers. According to Pue they carried a vision of native law as 'irrational, inconsistent, corrupt ... and civilisation as technology, Christianity, rational social organisation, law, progress and liberty'.[105]

William Osgoode, a young English barrister, became the first chief justice of Upper Canada in 1792. He introduced the Judicature Act 1794, which imported English jurisprudence to the province. The adversary system of justice was adopted, an appeal to acquit a defendant for reasonable doubt being made in 1796.[106] The Act assumed a need for lawyers while restricting competition from incoming barristers from England.[107] Local merchants resisted introducing any lawyers,

---

[99] ER Sunderland, *History of the American Bar Association and Its Work* (Chicago, ABA, 1953).
[100] Rogers (n 60) 662.
[101] ibid 661.
[102] A Marston, 'Guiding The Profession: The 1887 Code Of Ethics Of The Alabama State Bars Association' (1998) 49(2) *Alabama Law Review* 471.
[103] ibid.
[104] Moore (n 57).
[105] WW Pue, 'British Masculinities, Canadian Lawyers: Canadian Legal Education, 1900–1930' (1999) 16 *Law in Context: A Socio-Legal Journal* 80, 83.
[106] B Shapiro, *Probability and Certainty in Seventeenth-Century England: A Study of the Relationships between Natural Science, Religion, History, Law and Literature* (Princeton, NJ, Cambridge University Press, 1983) 171.
[107] Moore (n 57) 32.

arguing that parties continue arguing their own cases, but their motivation was seen as self-interested.[108] Although Osgoode played no further part,[109] a legal profession was soon established in Upper Canada in reaction to an emergency call from government for lawyers to self-regulate.

In 1797 an Act was hurriedly passed authorising practitioners in the province to form a society 'for the better regulating the Practice of Law'.[110] A meeting was called to discuss the Act and the 10 attendees, about two thirds of all the lawyers in Upper Canada at the time, formed the Law Society of Upper Canada (LSUC). Many were under 30 and the six most senior became the Society's benchers, a term borrowed from the English Bar. In its early years the society was not very active; another meeting was not called for two years. The use of the formal terms barristers and solicitors in statutes governing Canadian lawyers was a historical relic, there being no functional difference.[111]

The Act of 1797 bestowed on the main body of Canadian lawyers outside of Quebec the kind of independence gained so painfully by the Inns of Court.[112] The Law Society of Upper Canada agreed three priorities; education, standards and monopoly, the last of which was conferred by the Act. In 1820 the LSUC first exercised disciplinary powers and acquired what was referred as its own 'Inn of Court', Osgoode Hall, in in the city of York, Ontario (now part of Toronto).[113] The aim was to reproduce the Inns of Court at Osgoode Hall and a gentlemanly legal class.[114]

After the LSUC, the next provincial law society to be formed was Nova Scotia in 1825. It was one of seven Canadian Law Societies founded in the 1800s, Quebec having two, the bar of Quebec (1849) and the Chamber of Notaries (1870). Professionalisation was driven by opening the Northwest Territories from 1869.[115] This required settlers who could farm, leading to a large influx of Eastern Europeans. Lawyers scattered through the area were initially unregulated.[116] From 1885 an ordinance recognised current practitioners and provided for admission of new practitioners qualified elsewhere or by a three-year apprenticeship.

The University of Alberta had opened in 1908 and meetings were held with a special committee of the provincial Law Society in 1909 with a view to it administering the Society's examinations. In 1910 a University Act removed an impediment to the University entering arrangements with professional associations. Through the agreement, the Law Society controlled the conduct and content of the examinations, and the University gained a foothold in legal education. The University created a

---

[108] The same merchants were also often judges and bent the rules in their own favour (Moore (n 57) 23).
[109] He became chief justice of Lower Canada in 1794 and returned to England in 1801.
[110] Moore (n 57) 15.
[111] Except in Quebec, which recognised the French distinction between *avocat* and *notaires* (HW Arthurs, R Weisman and FH Zemans, 'The Canadian Legal Profession' (1986) 11(3) *American Bar Foundation Research Journal* 447).
[112] Moore (n 57) 42.
[113] ibid 61.
[114] Pue (n 105) 85.
[115] ibid.
[116] Law and Wood (n 98).

Faculty of Law shortly after.[117] Apprenticeship was, however, the prevailing method of qualification.

In 1913, Dr Ira MacKay presented an argument against the apprenticeship model of training to the Law Society in Calgary. He suggested that the 'system may possibly produce collectors, conveyancers, money lenders, and real estate dealers, but it cannot produce lawyers'.[118] The acquisition of 'legal knowledge scrap by scrap' did not allow a 'consensus of legal opinion and honor' to be forged, resulting in 'apprentices without principles'.[119] MacKay's proposed solution was two years of full-time, university legal education to prepare students for advances in knowledge. This idea captured a mood and Western Canadian lawyers, particularly those from Alberta and Manitoba, led the creation of law schools in the region.

Opening the Northwest Territory was a stimulus to reform movements in Alberta and Manitoba, the two provinces to the south of the new frontier. By the outbreak of World War I, half the population of the Northwest Territories had not been born in Canada. English was not spoken in many areas and local legal regimes proliferated. Widespread strikes in the area in 1919 were blamed on 'foreign' influence, even though the leaders were of British descent. British Canadians' fear of diversity, and the potential for social volatility manifest in the 1919 strike, was seen to call for strong government and the reinforcement of British values, identified by Pue as individualism, social hierarchy, capitalism, self-discipline, and patriarchy.[120] The Canadian Bar Association (CBA), formed in 1896 as a national voluntary association with provincial offices, was at the forefront of this effort.

An early President of the CBA was the Manitoba Lieutenant-Governor, James Aikins, of Winnipeg. In 1919, in a thinly veiled reference to the strike, Aikins inveigled against 'state paternalism' and specifically 'socialism, anarchy, Bolshevism' as 'anathema to "Law"'.[121] The solution was to create lawyers and disseminate law, a common-sense way to provide cohesion to diverse and scattered communities.[122] British colonialists like Aikins aimed to develop, in individuals, respect for the rights of others and the capacity to enjoy their own autonomy. Law and government provided a social and business framework for 'the enlightened conscience and Christian character of the individual'.[123] Law and lawyers, in the hands of a notable colonial administrator, were tools of aggressive moral regulation which assumed the superiority of British ways and British law.[124]

Aikins' notion of Law included the fundamental British principles 'protection of person and property, fair and prompt trial of offences and disputes by a system of

[117] ibid 4.
[118] ibid.
[119] Law and Wood (n 98) citing IA Mackay, 'The Education of a Lawyer' (delivered at the Third Annual Meeting of the Members of the Law Society of Alberta, Calgary, 18, 19 December 1913) and reproduced in (1940–42) 4 *Alberta Law Quarterly* 103 at 110.
[120] Pue (n 105) 90 citing T Loo and C Strange, *Making Good: Law and Moral Regulation in Canada* (Toronto, University of Toronto Press, 1997).
[121] Pue (n 105) 91 citing J Aikins, 'Address of the President' (Canadian Bar Association Presidential Address) (1919) 39 *Canadian Law Times* 537, 539.
[122] Pue (n 105).
[123] ibid 86 citing Aikins, 1919, 543.
[124] Pue (n 105) 83–84.

qualified Judges, of advocates and juries, freedom of religious worship, of speech, of press, of assemblage, government of people by themselves and indeed all those things which pertain to our civilization, a civilization which rests upon Christianity'.[125] Law was infused with Christian principles but the cornerstone of secular rationality, embodying the essence of liberty, the foundation for rational social order and the key to 'progress'.[126] It was the solution to governing geographic immensity and diverse populations.

The growth of university legal education in the period 1914 to 1930 aimed to produce lawyers socialised into the attitudes described in Aikins' speeches. The process assumed pre-selection of suitable individuals, those attuned to the 'mental world of their professional leaders', whose characters could be moulded into 'gentlemen lawyers'.[127] Their task was to carry secular rationality, albeit one 'infused with British Christianness'[128] 'to even the remotest nooks and crannies of the "new" land'.[129] This 'integrative mission' required a 'cultural legal education' delivered to carefully selected full time students using Langdell's case method.

As late as the 1940s, as articulated by MacKay, the value of law offices in remote areas was that they could be a focus of communities built on law. Routines of legal practice disseminated values informally in the wider community. Law was whatever 'legal opinion in the community believes it to be'.[130] It had no meaning beyond that formed by judges, lawyers, and 'the mass of intelligent laymen who direct the organized activities of the state'.[131] Lawyers did not just know law, it mattered what they 'know in their hearts' and law schools could form and promulgate a 'professional consensus of opinion and a professional esprit de corps'.[132]

In 1927 a Conference of Governing Bodies of the Legal Profession in Canada had been formed. This largely operated as an annual conference for law society delegates until it became the Federation of Canadian Law Societies (FCLS) in 1972. A principal aim of the FCLS was to coordinate the policies of the 14 provincial and territorial law societies and to harmonise practice.[133] In 2002 a National Mobility Agreement sought to facilitate inter-provincial recognition of qualification. A full-time CEO was appointed in 2006. In 2010 FCLS implemented a recommendation that the common law societies (excluding Quebec) adopt common requirements for entry to bar admission programs, including an ethics course.[134] This effectively confirmed the regulatory power of the provincial law societies and the CBA as a membership organisation and pressure group.

---

[125] ibid citing J Aikins, 'The President's Address' (1920) 56 *Canada Law Journal* 308, 310.
[126] Pue (n 105) 82–83.
[127] ibid 95.
[128] ibid.
[129] ibid 110.
[130] ibid 96 citing IA MacKay, 'The Education of Lawyer' (1940–42) *Alberta Law Quarterly* 103.
[131] Pue (n 105) 96
[132] ibid 97 citing MacKay, 110–11.
[133] Federation of Canadian Law Societies 'Yesterday and today' Yesterday and Today | Federation of Law Societies of Canada (flsc.ca).
[134] FCLS *Task Force on the Common Law Degree Report* (2009).

D. Australia

The first penal colony was established in Australia in 1788 and free settlers began arriving in small numbers in 1793. A court of civil jurisdiction was established in 1787, but government was by decree of a Governor backed by the military. The largest colony, New South Wales, comprised two modern Australian States, Queensland and Victoria, and New Zealand. New South Wales established a Supreme Court in 1814. In the early years, convicts who had been attorneys in England and unqualified people could present cases. One of these, George Crossly, transported for perjury and described by Kercher as 'a thoroughly dishonest attorney', managed to tie up the courts in litigation and tried to bind the governor to the rule of law.[135]

Another unqualified litigator in the penal colony was 'the next best thing [to a qualified lawyer]: a person in possession of the latest edition of Blackstone'.[136] Blackstone encouraged the view that English Law relevant to the situation of a colony applied there, but that which did not was left behind. In an early property dispute, Magna Carta was invoked to argue that the Governor had no power to make law in the absence of a properly constituted assembly.[137] The argument failed but highlighted the problem with the Blackstone formulation; it did not allow the development of new law contradicting English law.[138] Eventually, the single judge, Jeffrey Hart Bent, denied ex-convicts the right to practice and solicitors had to be lured from England by the promise of a salary.[139] The colonies then changed 'from informal, amateur law that reflected both local needs and some of the formally applicable law of the parent country, to the importation of a stricter legal tradition'.[140]

The Australian colonies were ambivalent about importing the divided profession. In 1824, two English lawyers admitted as barristers in New South Wales applied to exclude attorneys from audience before the court. The court accepted the principle of a divided professions but decided it would continue to hear attorneys.[141] Confirmation of the decision was sought from the UK and an instruction was received in 1834. It stated that only advocates admitted in the UK could be barristers, while attorneys could qualify locally having served five-year articles of clerkship with a licensed lawyer. The instruction also stated that, while attorneys could plead before the court, they would be heard after barristers. In the middle of the nineteenth century some Australian lawyers adopted the English barristers' wigs and gowns to signify superiority to locally qualified lawyers, to claim privileges and to try to secure a more lucrative practice.[142]

---

[135] B Kercher, 'A Convict Conservative: George Crossley and the English Legal Tradition' (1999) 16 *Law in Context: A Socio-Legal Journal* 17, 24–28.
[136] Kercher citing KG Allars, 'George Crossley – an Unusual Attorney' (1958) 44 *Journal of the Royal Australian Historical Society* 261, 283.
[137] Kercher ibid 27.
[138] ibid 24.
[139] F Bartlett and L Haller, 'Australia: Legal Services Regulation in Australia – Innovative Co-regulation' in A Boon (ed), *International Perspectives on the Regulation of Lawyers and Legal Services* (Oxford, Hart Publishing, 2017) 161.
[140] Kercher (n 135) 28.
[141] *Division of the Legal Profession* [1829] NSWSC 34, cited by Bartlett and Haller (n 139) fn 28.
[142] R McQueen, 'Of Wigs and Gowns: A Short History of Legal and Judicial Dress in Australia' (1999) 16 *Law in Context: A Socio-Legal Journal* 31, 56.

Limited democratic elections occurred in New South Wales from 1843, around the same time that transportation of convicts ended. In 1859, the Australian components of New South Wales separated into three administrative States, New South Wales, Victoria and Queensland. New South Wales and Victoria quickly moved to admit practitioners as both barristers and solicitors, allowing a choice of specialisation thereafter. Queensland operated a separate Bar until 2004. Later additions to the current six Australian States, Tasmania, South Australia, and Western Australia began with fused professions but, according to Thornton, an informal and voluntary specialist Bar existed in those States.[143]

The restrictions on former convicts being lawyers meant that the early profession was dominated by colonists qualified as lawyers in England. Their conventions became well-established by the time universities educated lawyers, beginning with Sydney in 1890.[144] The conservatism of Australian lawyers lasted into the twentieth century and there was little interest in a national legal association until the 1920s. Until the 1960s, the courts and the curriculum were dominated by English law.[145]

Attempts at producing a common legal education at national level failed, possibly reflecting an inclination to hold onto traditions. As late as 1942, Sir Owen Dixon declared in relation to the continued relevance of English Law in Australia, 'the first duty of the peoples who share in the possession of the common law is to … hold fast to the conception of the essential unity of the culture which it gives them'.[146] It was not until 1963 that Dixon himself declared that the era he had lauded had ended.[147]

E. New Zealand

New Zealand was part of the foundation colony of New South Wales, along with territories in Australia. Having operated mainly as a harbour for British ships and visitors, it adopted English legislation, common law and constitutional conventions in 1840 and became a self-governing colony in 1852. From 1865 New Zealand exercised limited legislative powers rather than receiving law from Westminster. The Statute of Westminster 1931 removed limitations on the legislative powers of former colonies and in 1947 New Zealand became fully independent.

The first qualified lawyer arrived in New Zealand in 1840.[148] Richard Davies Hanson, an English solicitor, was Land Purchase Officer to the New Zealand

---

[143] M Thornton, 'The Australian Legal Profession: Towards a National Identity' in W Felstiner (ed), *Re-organization and Resistance: Legal Professions Confront a Changing World* (London, Bloomsbury, 200) 133.

[144] The School was formed in 1855, but it did not begin teaching until much later (H Lücke, 'Legal history in Australia: the Development of Australian Legal/historical scholarship' (2010) 34 *Australian Bar Review* 109).

[145] ibid.

[146] ibid 114.

[147] *Parker v R* (1963) 111 CLR 610; [1963] ALR 524 (cited by Lucke 118).

[148] N Cox, *The Effect Of The Lawyers And Conveyancers Act On The Independent Bar* (Aukland, NZ, Aukland District Law Society, 2009), www.researchgate.net/profile/Noel-Cox/publication/46408388_The_Effect_of_the_Lawyers_and_Conveyancers_Act_on_the_Independent_Bar/links/559e1eb508ae76bed0bb6169/The-Effect-of-the-Lawyers-and-Conveyancers-Act-on-the-Independent-Bar.pdf.

Company and, later, the first Crown Prosecutor. In 1841 a Supreme Court Ordinance modelled on the Charters of Justice of older colonies, New South Wales before 1834, Newfoundland, and the West Indies, was passed to control the admission of barristers and solicitors.[149] This had to be re-issued having been refused by the Crown because it did not allow for locally qualified lawyers. Admitted lawyers were allowed to act as solicitors or barristers in recognition of the shortage of both, a situation which persisted. Barristers could choose the designation of 'barrister sole', designating them primarily as courtroom lawyers.

There were voluntary associations of lawyers in Auckland in 1861 and Christchurch in 1868, but they existed only briefly. An Act was passed in 1861 requiring the registration of legal practitioners as having qualified as either a solicitor or barrister in England, although they could practice as both.[150] Judges' rules made in 1864 required barristers and solicitors not admitted overseas and barristers without a degree in arts or law to be examined in general knowledge. The requirements echoed the examinations recommended by an English Parliament Select Committee Report of 1846. All candidates were to be examined in law and those admitted overseas tested on New Zealand law.

The inadequacy of the education provided to those studying for the qualifying examination led to calls for universities to have a role in educating lawyers. The University of New Zealand, created in 1870, ran an LLB from 1875. By 1888 it covered all subjects specified in the rules for admission of barristers. Some coverage was provided by Otago University and Canterbury University. From the mid-1870s university law students could replace the general knowledge examination with other classes.

In 1869 an Act incorporated barristers and solicitors as 'The New Zealand Law Society'.[151] According to its early records, the main purpose of the new body was to institute disciplinary proceedings against practitioners. Nine years later the formation of district societies was permitted.[152] Fourteen were established with the primary function of providing law libraries. The Lawyers and Conveyancers Act 2006 removed the statutory functions of the local law societies, which were to be subsumed within the NZLS. Although all had an option to continue independently, only Auckland chose to do so.[153]

Queen's Counsel were introduced to New Zealand in 1907 and 10 were appointed. By 1963 there were only nine practising, but this number increased with the gradual increase in the numbers of barristers sole. In 1978 there were 84 barristers sole and a further 23 QCs, but by 1996 there were 396 barristers sole and 53 QCs. In 2006 there were a total of 14,999 practising lawyers throughout New Zealand, of whom 1,511,

---

[149] ibid.
[150] P Spiller, 'A History of New Zealand Legal Education: A Study in Ambivalence' (1993) 4 *Legal Education Review* 223.
[151] WR Flaus, 'Discipline within the New Zealand Legal Profession' (1971) 6 *Victoria University of Wellington Law Review* 337.
[152] District Law Societies Act 1878.
[153] S Mize, 'New Zealand: Finding the Balance between Self-Regulation and Government Oversight' in A Boon (ed), *International Perspectives on the Regulation of Lawyers and Legal Services* (Oxford, Hart Publishing, 2017) 116, 123.

including QCs, were barristers sole.[154] The Lawyers and Conveyancers Act 2006 retained the status of the barrister sole, but abolished the title of Queen's Counsel from 31 July 2008, replacing it with Senior Counsel.

In 2009, the Aukland Law Society, the society covering the area where the majority of New Zealand QCs were traditionally located,[155] published a paper by its Public Issues Committee arguing against weakening the independent Bar. It referred to a public discourse around fusion of the legal profession and noted that the 2006 Act, by referring only to lawyers, could be seen as a step towards ending the distinction between barristers and solicitors.[156] It argued that the Act 'could weaken the independent bar, with unforeseen implications in the future of the bar and bench'.[157] Remarkably, the office of QC was reinstated in 2012.[158]

The statutory Conduct and Client Care Rules 2008, made under the 2008 Act, distinguished barristers sole, defined as 'a lawyer who acts only as a barrister and not as a solicitor and who is the holder of a current practising certificate authorising the lawyer to act as a barrister and not as a barrister and solicitor'.[159] It laid out conditions for practice that mirrored those of barristers in England and Wales,[160] including practising from chambers with other barristers sole. It also contained provisions distinguishing the obligations of barristers sole and other kinds of lawyer.[161]

V. DISCUSSION

A. Models

Barristers were the dominant legal profession in England until at least the nineteenth century.[162] Lawyers who were not barristers were generally held in low regard.[163] From the early 1800s the transformation of solicitors into a modern legal profession was a triumph of organisation, but the timing made the English Bar influential on lawyers in the North Americas. Arthurs suggested that, for the Canadian legal profession, 'the real (or imagined) culture of the English bar is the point of reference (not to say reverence)'.[164]

---

[154] Cox (n 148).
[155] NZLS, 'A Rare Honour: Queen's Counsel in New Zealand' (*New Zealand Law Society*, 5 April 2019) www.lawsociety.org.nz/news/lawtalk/issue-927/a-rare-honour-queens-counsel-in-new-zealand/.
[156] Cox (n 148).
[157] ibid 13.
[158] Lawyers and Conveyancers Amendment Act 2012 (2012 No 92), s 6.
[159] Lawyers and Conveyancers Act (Lawyers: Conduct and Client Care) Rules 2008 (Interpretation), s 1(20).
[160] See s 14.
[161] See in particular chs 14 and 15.
[162] See further A Boon, 'The legal professions' new handbooks: narratives, standards and values' (2016) 19(2) *Legal Ethics* 207.
[163] CW Brooks, *Pettyfoggers and Vipers of the Commonwealth: The 'Lower Branch' of the Legal Profession in Early Modern England* (Cambridge, Cambridge University Press, 1986).
[164] HW Arthurs, 'Lawyering in Canada in the 21st Century' (1996) *Windsor Yearbook of Access to Justice* 202 at 223.

Rogers' review of the ABA chose the English Bar in discussing the 'national traits' of lawyers.[165] English writers, Bacon, Fielding, Lamb, Goldsmith, Dickens, were associated with the Inns of Court, while American lawyers were political and practical rather than literary. He claimed (incorrectly) that 'History, philosophy and even belles-lettres are part of the training of European jurists. Our law schools have trained for a craft with little heed to history or general ideas'.[166]

The chronology and processes of professionalisation in the colonies were not predictable or chronological. They typically involved formation of an organising body which, at some point, sought to control the entry, qualification, education, and regulation of members. In America, there was a significant but unorganised body of lawyers long before there was similar in Canada, where professional recognition was rapid and with little foundation in established organisation. People in the US harboured a suspicion of lawyers whereas the Canadian imperialists recognised the framework of law as the essence of a state and good order. English 'law' was an essential element of British identity[167] and 'a very special social tool uniquely capable of transcending the fragmenting and destructive centrifugal forces of religion, class, ethnicity and locality'.[168] Lawyers were not merely people with some legal knowledge but cultural figures operating in the political and economic spheres.[169]

The role of lawyers developed from the common law tradition but took different forms. Common to them were similar ideas about how their collective autonomy and independence was important in representing interests against different kinds of power, including that of the state. Diffusion of responsibility to control power was an extension of the checks and balances underpinning the philosophy of the separation of powers and the rule of law. They also claimed to be analogous to public bodies operating either as or in a spirit of public service. Which of these orientations was emphasised was determined by role.

B. Roles

As with other legal transplants, law and lawyers could have developed locally, resulting from local innovation and selecting ideas from wider sources.[170] Like the rest of the common law world,[171] both America and Canada adopted the adversary system of trial. It was not given that, as fused professions, they would adopt the barristers' obligation to represent all comers. Australia and New Zealand, having begun without barristers, then adopted fully formed versions of English legal roles; a split profession with a cab rank principle for barristers. Despite these different starting points there was remarkable similarity in legal roles across the common law world.

---

[165] Rogers (n 60) 666.
[166] ibid 663.
[167] Pue (n 105) citing SE Merry, 'Law and Colonialism' (1991) 25 *Law and Society Review* 889, 891.
[168] Pue (n 105) citing P Fitzpatrick, *The Mythology of Modern Law* (London, Routledge 1992).
[169] Pue (n 105) 94.
[170] Wise (n 1) 4; A Watson, *Legal Transplants: An Approach to Comparative Literature*, 2nd edn (Athens, Georgia, University of Georgia Press, 1993) 57–60.
[171] Moore (n 57) 37.

Belief in the virtue of the common law may explain the common threads in lawyer roles. By the time lawyer associations began to form, many of the conventions of practice had been either adopted from England or reinvented. Principles from the adversary system were established in the Eastern colonies of America in 1770 and adopted in Upper Canada in the 1790s.[172] The spread of the evidence-based trial may have been due to Blackstone's *Commentaries*, written between 1765–70 and widely distributed between 1765 and 1769.[173]

Blackstone lauded trial by jury[174] arguing that open examination of contradictory witnesses was the best mechanism to sift the facts. Secondly, a jury was necessary because even the best judges would have an unthinking propensity to favour their own class. Thirdly, the tepid mundanity of courts lacking a clash of interests showed that the adversary process was essential to the preservation of Liberty.[175] In American criminal law, both the presumption of innocence and requirement for proof beyond reasonable doubt could be traced to Blackstone,[176] although he did not use the exact terms.

Blackstone's ratio or formulation asserted that 'it is better that ten guilty persons escape than that one innocent suffer'.[177] Elsewhere, he quoted Sir Edward Coke's assertion that 'the evidence to convict a prisoner should be so manifest, as it could not be contradicted'.[178] Rather than these statements lying behind Adams' confident assertions about English justice, it seems plausible that communication between jurisdictions kept American and English thought on similar lines. Thus, lawyers in America and Canada balanced the role of advocate and business lawyer and the values associated with those roles. Those in Australia and New Zealand eventually kept them separate.

C. Independence

Lawyer organisations projected a range of interests, status and exclusivity, and values, independence and public service, that were often interconnected. The historical antecedent for independence was the 'invisible wall' Burrage claimed protected the English Bar from the state after the Glorious Revolution.[179] This was almost a constitutional position, in which the role of barrister, intermediary between citizen and state but independent of both, supported an independent judiciary steeped in these habits and attitudes. The advent of the adversarial system cemented this role in delivering

---

[172] ibid.
[173] S Landsman, 'The Rise of the Contentious Spirit: Adversary Procedure in Eighteenth-Century England' (1990) 75(3) *Cornell Law Review* 591.
[174] *Blackstone's Commentaries on the Laws of England*. Book the Third – Chapter – The Twenty-Third: Trial by Jury, 350.
[175] ibid 379, see also Landsman (n 173).
[176] Epps (n 80).
[177] Sir William Blackstone, *Commentaries On The Laws Of England*, book 4, Chapter 27, 353.
[178] ibid 350, fn t.
[179] Burrage (n 15) 447.

'Magna Carta rights' to all citizens through representative legal advocacy[180] as 'an instrument to constrict the power of the state'.[181]

English solicitors had a very different approach to establishing independence. At stages of its development, the Law Society sought to distance itself from the state by developing a critique of state power. In the late nineteenth century, it cast itself as a counterweight to state authoritarianism[182] and, from the 1880s, campaigned against government bureaucracy.[183] In general, however, it occupied a unique position in civil society which Sugarman characterised as an 'inherent dependence upon and imbrication within the state'.[184]

Lawyers' claims to independence were not protected constitutionally in newly independent colonies, except indirectly, for example, in the US by making judges responsible for overseeing lawyer regulation.[185] The American Bar Association Model Rules claimed institutional independence, stating that 'an independent legal profession is an important force in preserving government under law, for abuse of legal authority is more readily challenged by a profession whose members are not dependent on government for the right to practice'.[186]

Bruce Green argued that, historically, American advocates' independence was expressed in criticising judges, disobeying unlawful court orders and resolving ethical dilemmas for oneself, as a matter of professional conscience.[187] These dimensions of lawyer independence were seen by US nineteenth century courts as equally important to the independence of the judiciary.[188] Green suggested that obligations to independence declined with the rise of advocates' duties to the court, and because lawyers sought judicial protection from government regulation.[189]

Canada manifested a particularly strong commitment to the idea of an independent, self-regulating Bar as part of a constitutional settlement.[190] This appeared to derive, ideologically and legally, either from the common law, or an interpretation of the position of the English Bar. Quoting Thomas Erskine, the Canadian judge, Justice Dickson, proposed that without an independent Bar 'impartial justice, the most valuable part of [our] Constitution can have no existence'.[191] According to Millen, informal support for professional institutional independence was reflected

---

[180] GC Hazard and A Dondi, *Legal Ethics: A Comparative Study* (California, Stanford University Press, 2004) 94.
[181] TC Halliday and L Karpik (eds), *Lawyers and the Rise of Western Political Liberalism* (Oxford, Clarendon Press, 1997) 21.
[182] Sugarman (n 25) 111.
[183] ibid 112.
[184] ibid 104.
[185] BA Green, 'Lawyers' Professional Independence: Overrated or Undervalued?' (2013) 46 *Akron Law Review* 599, 604–7.
[186] ibid 603 quoting *Model Rules of Professional Conduct* preamble 11, 12 (2013).
[187] ibid.
[188] ibid 621–22.
[189] ibid 602.
[190] R Millen, 'The Independence of the Bar: An Unwritten Constitutional Principle' (2005) *Canadian Bar Review* 84.
[191] See 'Remarks by the Right Honourable Brian Dickson, P.C. to the Criminal Lawyers' Association Conference' (1990) 11 *Ontario Criminal Lawyers' Association Newsletter* 9, cited by Millen ibid 113.

in Canadian case law, such as *Canada (Attorney General) v Law Society of BC* (known as *Jabour*) in which Justice Estey described the independence of the Bar from all manifestations of state control as one of the 'hallmarks of a free society'.[192]

In a case brought against the Attorney General of Ontario for failing to supervise lawyers, the court found that government had no right to control the profession.[193] It reasoned that the legal profession preceded Magna Carta and was a fundamental component of the system of government. It stated that the English Inns of Court were self-governing since the fourteenth century, noting the connection between an independent judiciary and public confidence in the legal system.[194] Millen argued that the rationale of this approach made an independent Bar a constitutional requirement in all common law countries.

Bartlett and Haller observed that the Australian bar was 'infused with a spirit of fierce independence',[195] but gave no explanation of this claim. They added that, because the Australian judiciary was drawn from the bar they had an 'intertwined relationship'.[196] Thus, they claimed, the judiciary was historically a voice of caution when government considered reform of the legal profession. When Queen's Counsel were introduced to New Zealand in 1907 it was 50 years after they first appeared in Australia, and 30 years after the last Australian colony introduced them.[197] A specific aim may have been to improve judicial quality.

Since 1914, around half of the New Zealand Bench were appointed from King's or Queen's Counsel, including seven of eight Chief Justices.[198] In response to the Lawyers and Conveyancers Act 2006, the Aukland Law Society argued: 'A strong independent bar is needed for a strong bench. Judges are generally recruited from senior litigators – whether in partnership or barristers sole. The latter are however important as they are both independent and also specialists in their fields, and should form the bedrock of the bench'.[199]

D. Public Service

Legal professions sometimes claimed legal work as a kind of public service. In modern usage public service described government provision for general social benefit, being associated with notions of integrity, impartiality, and accountability. In the 1950s Roscoe Pound, an American founder of sociological jurisprudence, identified professionals as 'a group of men pursuing a learned art as a common calling in a spirit of public service'.[200] Pound treated legal work *as* public service despite it being a

---

[192] *Canada (Attorney General) v Law Society of BC* [1982] 2 SCR 307 at 335 cited by Millen (n 190) 107.
[193] *LaBelle v Law Society of Upper Canada* (2001), 56.R [3d] 413 [C.A.] (cited by Millen (n 190) fn 123.
[194] Millen (n 190) 122.
[195] ibid 167.
[196] ibid.
[197] J Finn, 'A Novel Institution: The First Years of King's Counsel in New Zealand 1907–1915' (1995) *New Zealand Law Journal* 95.
[198] Aukland District Law Society (n 154) 9.
[199] ibid 13.
[200] R Pound, *The Lawyer from Antiquity to Modern Times: With particular reference to The Development of Bar Associations in the United States* (St. Paul, Minnesota, West Publishing, 1953).

means of livelihood. A recent report commissioned by legal services regulators in the UK recommended that education and training was appropriate 'to the public profession of law'.[201] Initial manifestations of public service included contributions to law reform, particularly important in large and diverse countries. Lawyer associations helped to create harmonious laws across State or provincial jurisdictions. Lawyers unified scattered communities, encouraging legality through citizens' understanding of and compliance with law.

Another manifestation of public service was assisting the state and legality by providing 'service to the poor', an obligation present in the Medieval lawyer oaths.[202] One of the earliest recorded addresses to American lawyers by Cotton Mather, a Puritan minister closely identified with the Salem Witch Trials, claimed an obligation to serve the poor.[203] These kinds of obligation were also reflected in institutions such as actions *in forma pauperis* or the 'dock brief', where a lawyer from those present in court was assigned to advise unrepresented persons. In modern times, it became associated with the provision of free legal services supporting citizens' understanding of law and their access to justice.

Given its history, it is unsurprising that the English Law Society identified itself as a profession dedicated to public service rather than independence from the state. In the nineteenth century the administrative machinery of the state was relatively small[204] and the Law Society proved adept at assisting government, which relied on the Law Society well into the twentieth century. The ethos of public service fostered was in tune with the period either side of World War II, when Western countries engaged in social enterprise and welfare programmes, characterised by the American 'New Deal' politics of the 1930s and the welfare state in the UK. In its early incarnation the Law Society was a prototype for public service through law reform. Its identification with legal aid complicated its engagement with a modern manifestation of public service, *pro bono publico* (pro bono).

In Victorian Britain a Poor Man's Lawyers movement was supported by charities based at Mansfield House and Toynbee Hall in East London and received some support from local lawyers. After World War I divorce cases burgeoned and private practitioners, solicitors, and barristers, often provided free assistance. Pro bono work also expanded in the 1990s, but the Law Society, caught between its support for legal aid and the solicitors' firms dependent on it, remained relatively aloof from the organisations promoting it.[205]

Before the millennium, UK legal pro bono was relatively small scale. It was led by legal aid firms and individuals providing voluntary assistance to a rapidly expanding advice centre and law centre movement specialising in welfare rights. In 1996 both

---

[201] JS Webb, J Ching, P Maharg and A Sherr, *Setting Standards: The Future Of Legal Services Education And Training Regulation In England And Wales* (BSB, ILEX Professional Standards, Solicitors Regulation Authority, 2013) para 466.
[202] Andrews (n 61) 1388.
[203] Andrews (n 61) 1423, citing A-H Chroust, *The Rise Of The Legal Profession In America* (Norman, University of Oklahoma Press, 1965).
[204] Sugarman (n 25).
[205] A Boon and A Whyte, 'An Explosion of Legal Philanthropy? The Transformation of Pro Bono Legal Services in England and Wales' in SL Cummings, F De Sa E Silva and LA Trubek, *Global pro bono: Diffusion, Contestation, Learned Lessons* (Cambridge, Cambridge University Press, 2022).

legal professions launched pro bono organisations drawing on voluntary contributions from private practitioners. The Bar's Pro Bono Unit was an initiative of its chairman Peter Goldsmith QC, the future Attorney General, on hearing a speech by future Prime Minister Tony Blair.

The Law Society was reluctant to become involved in pro bono, because small firms were threatened by legal aid cuts. A meeting in 1996 held at the Law Society and opened by its Deputy Vice President, Michael Matthews, suggested mixed views within the professional body. The meeting led to the formation of the Solicitors Pro Bono Group, (described in chapter fifteen 'Corporatocracy') from which the Law Society continued to maintain a distance.

The US had a different history of legal aid, but a similar history of pro bono. The right of impecunious criminal defendants to state funded legal representation was not finally established until 1963[206] and little public provision existed for civil law. There was an early history of philanthropic civil legal assistance schemes, with a charity providing legal assistance to German immigrants established in New York City in 1876.[207] The modern emergence of 'people's lawyers' in the US was connected to various causes; employment rights, pacifism during World War I, civil rights crusades[208] leading to a voluntary network of privately funded organisations with diverse missions.

In 1917 a report by Reginald Heber Smith concluded that the impartiality of justice was illusory because there was no equality before the law between rich and poor.[209] Smith's report led the organised bar to support Legal Aid Societies which often sought to socialise immigrants to American institutions. In the 1930s, Justice Harlan F Stone led an attack on law firms more concerned with supporting businesses than communities. In universities, a legal realist movement recognised the political dimension to legal judgment and posited the capacity of courts to bring about legal reform. This led to a gradual change in the approach of the Legal Aid Society's which had nearly doubled in number by the 1940s.[210]

The use of litigation as a strategy for advancing social rights burgeoned in the 1960s.[211] At the beginning of the period, 400 lawyers were employed by Legal Aid societies. In the early 1960s federal grants set up experimental projects in centres like New York, and a decade later there were over 2,500. The change in approach came because the well-heeled lawyers who supported the societies were no longer needed. The previous approach, providing routine advice and 'reasonable settlement' of claims[212] gave way to campaigns to tackle poverty using litigation as a complement to law reform.

---

[206] *Gideon v Wainwright* 372 U.S. 335. Such support was available in federal cases and felony cases in two-thirds of states.
[207] J Bliss and SA Boutcher, 'Rationalizing Pro Bono: Corporate Social Responsibility and The Reinvention Of Legal Professionalism In Elite American Law Firms' in Cummings, De Sa E Silva and Trubek (n 205) 202)
[208] The American Civil Liberties Union (ACLU) grew from lawyers defending pacifists, see M James, *The People's Lawyers* (New York, Holt, Rinehart and Winston, 1973).
[209] MF Davis, *Brutal Need: Lawyers and the Welfare Rights Movement, 1960–1973* (New Haven, Yale University Press, 1993) 16.
[210] Bliss and Boutcher (n 207) 78.
[211] Davis (n 209) ch 2
[212] ibid 15.

Before 1965 no poverty law cases had been appealed to the Supreme Court in eighty odd years. Between 1965 and 1974, 164 were heard. Some organisations, such as that pioneered by Ed Sparer in New York, worked to exploit weaknesses in welfare administrations and advanced legal arguments based on novel readings of the Constitution, such as the 'right to live', to access basic subsistence.[213] This effort ended in 1970 with the Supreme Court decision in *Dandridge v Williams* (see chapter seven 'Individuality').

Independence also allowed legal organisations like Sparer's to flout conventional lawyer etiquette, using aggressive advocacy and strident assertiveness.[214] In the mid-1960s these strategies were disseminated as part of nationwide programme leading, indirectly, to the establishment of campaign groups such as the National Welfare Rights Organisation.[215] In some of these campaigns, lawyers provided a more conventional role; reassuring clients who feared retribution by the authorities. In this they were sometimes compared to priests.[216]

The modern equivalent of the movements begun in the 1960s were described in collections of essays from international scholars edited by Sarat and Scheingold, describing 'cause lawyers.'[217] Lawyers working at NGOs or in networks of loosely connected individuals advanced specific social causes full time. They differed from ordinary lawyers by refusing to adopt a neutral position on representation and by identifying with the cause rather than their client's interests. In the context of the UK, many legal aid lawyers working in law firms, satisfied these criteria.[218] Even with the decline of legal aid there are indications that this work continued using new sources of finance such as grant and crowd funding.[219]

In parallel with poor people's lawyering, the tradition of pro bono encouraged free advice or representation to poor people as a part-time activity. In the US, poor people's lawyers often graduated from law schools, such as Harvard, Yale and Columbia. Davis speculated that, in the 1970s, large firms actively promoted pro bono to compete for these top graduates leading to increased volume of activity.[220] By 1973, 23 large firms had elements recognisable as pro bono.[221] In this respect, as in in others, there were remarkable similarities between developments of pro bono culture in the US and in the UK.[222]

---

[213] The idea derived from AD Smith, *The Right To Life* (Chapel Hill,: The University of North Carolina Press, 1955).
[214] Davis (n 209) 31.
[215] ibid 45.
[216] ibid 48.
[217] A Sarat and S Scheingold (eds), *Cause Lawyering: Political Commitments and Professional Responsibilities* (New York, Oxford University Press, 1998) and A Sarat and S Scheingold (eds), *Cause Lawyers and the State in a Global Era* (New York, Oxford University Press, 2001).
[218] A Boon, 'Cause Lawyers and the Alternative Ethical Paradigm: Ideology and Transgression (2004) 7(2) *Legal Ethics* 250.
[219] J Kinghan, *Lawyers, Networks and Progressive Social Change: Lawyers Changing Lives* (Oxford, Hart Publishing, 2021) 17.
[220] A law firm memo from 1969 noted a tendency of top graduates from prestige schools to seek public service law jobs (Bliss and Boutcher (n 207) 79).
[221] Bliss and Boutcher (n 207) citing JF Handler, EJ Hollingsworth and HS Erlanger, *Lawyers and The Pursuit Of Legal Rights* (New York, Russell Sage Foundation, 1978).
[222] Boon and Whyte (n 205).

VI. CONCLUSION

The organisation of lawyers involved choices about work roles which dictated different orientations to the values represented in the rule of law. Claims to independence, put at their highest, were claims to a role in constitutional settlements emphasised by lawyer organisations focused on advocacy. This required independence and self-regulation, enabling practitioners to make claims against the state. The other claim, to operate in a spirit of public service, prioritised helping citizens navigate law. This was more likely to be a focus of business lawyers and became more explicitly linked to access to justice and alleviating legal need. Fused professions sought to balance these orientations and regulated accordingly.

11

Regulation

I. INTRODUCTION

IN THE COMMON law world, lawyer organisations negotiated relationships to the state. This formalised self-regulation, the control by the organising body over entry, qualification, education, and regulation of its members. Steps in the transition from external regulation to self-regulation by the professional body included setting standards for assessing performance, acquiring powers to regulate compliance, and establishing enforcement machinery. The outcomes of regulation, publication of standards, conveyed professional ideology to other audiences, clients, the public, the state.[1] Codes of conduct conveyed key characteristics of the professions producing them.[2] This chapter examines the impact on these values of pressure to regulate effectively lawyers' relationship to the rule of law.

II. THEORY

Early analysts of professions were impressed by the high social standards they expressed.[3] Durkheim saw their values as contributing to a more refined common moral ethos, contributing to common understanding, community action, and organic solidarity.[4] Professions were exemplary because their moral codes reinforced social responsibility among a community of interest, a 'restricted group, having its special characteristics ... in the midst of general society'.[5] Talcott Parsons, an American sociologist seen as a successor to Durkheim, suggested that social values might change after disturbances in social systems.

The tendency of groups to develop distinctive modes of thought outside of mainstream culture underpinned the work of French sociologist Pierre Bourdieu, who labelled the internalised norms, skills and dispositions that were passed on as *habitus*.[6]

---

[1] A Abbott, *The System of Professions: An Essay on the Expert Division of Labour* (Chicago, University of Chicago Press, 1988).
[2] HM Vollmer and DL Mills (eds), *Professionalization* (NJ, Prentice-Hall Englewood Cliffs, 1966).
[3] E Durkheim, *Professional Ethics and Civic Morals* (trans C Brookfield) (London, NY, Routledge, 1992),
[4] ibid.
[5] E Durkheim, *The Division of Labour in Society* (G Simpson, trans) (New York, Free Press, 1893/1933) 14.
[6] P Bourdieu, *Outline of a Theory of Practice* (Cambridge, Cambridge University Press, 1977).

Pue and Sugarman noted the dangers of generalisation about legal communities.[7] Analysing the cultural identity of lawyers involved analysing 'the production, transmission and reception of the ideas and practises of lawyers in society over time'.[8] Lawyers conformed to national identity through 'concerns of reputation, social standing and cultural capital'. This potentially created different relationships to the rule of law between lawyers in different jurisdictions.

A motivation to monopolise work tasks, to exclude non-experts, was consistent with Weber's structural approach to occupations.[9] Larsson argued that a principal motivation of professionalisation was translating control of knowledge into closure of markets to outsiders. Andrew Abbott identified the importance of institutionalisation, education, and licensing. Occupations constructed their work so that it was 'impermeable', so that outsiders could not do it.[10] Professionalism worked on three *jurisdictions*, workplace, public and legal, critical to the process of establishing expertise and legitimacy.[11] Rendering group norms as codes of conduct served various purposes depending on which audience was a main recipient of publication.

The final stage of professionalisation, a statutory monopoly, protection by law, and privileges such as self-regulation, required recognition by the state. In the early 1990s Wilkins identified four regulatory systems used in common law jurisdictions.[12] There were disciplinary controls exercised by legal professions under the supervision of the courts, institutional controls operating in the relevant practice forum (for example, a court) legislative controls operated by administrative agencies and liability controls, for example, negligence claims. These tended to operate as different, but complementary ways of controlling lawyer behaviour. To them might be added peer mechanisms of support and control.

III. FROM EXTERNAL REGULATION TO SELF-REGULATION

A. England and Wales

i. Barristers

Lawyers were regulated from the early medieval period by admission oaths, typically sworn before courts, and by statutes. The principal means of enforcement was through the court, where judges dealt with barristers' breaches of discipline until the nineteenth century. These indicated those abuses worth addressing but were probably supplemented by 'received wisdom' about appropriate conduct.[13] This would have

---

[7] W Pue and D Sugarman, *Lawyers and Vampires: Cultural Histories of the Legal Profession* (London, Bloomsbury, 2004).
[8] ibid 13.
[9] E Freidson, *Profession of Medicine: A Study of the Sociology of Applied Knowledge* (New York, Harper and Row, 1970) and see G Ritzer, 'Professionalization, Bureaucratization and Rationalization: The Views of Max Weber' (1975) 53(4) *Social Forces* 627, 630.
[10] Abbott (n 1).
[11] ibid.
[12] D Wilkins, 'Who Should Regulate Lawyers' (1992) 105 *Harvard Law Review* 799.
[13] J Rose, 'The Legal Profession in Medieval England: A History of Regulation' (1998) 48 *Syracuse Law Review* 1.

been more likely in closed institutions like the Inns of Court, where the proximity of practitioners made peer mechanisms effective.[14] This may have emphasised the influence of Whig lawyers, such as Erskine and Brougham, who put the individual client at the centre of the lawyer's universe.

Two ideas were central to the ethic of the English Bar: accepting clients notwithstanding social disapproval of their personality or character or the unpopularity of their cause and doing the best for them, whatever the consequences. In modern times the Bar's representation obligation was expressed in the 'cab rank rule' which Watson dated to the case of Tom Paine.[15] Although the name, and principle, derived from a rule applying to Hackney carriages, the term 'cab rank' was of limited assistance in dating it. Taxi ranks were introduced in London in 1634 and the trade was regulated from the Commonwealth period.[16] The term 'cab' which referred to hansom cabs, introduced in 1834, the period when the Prisoners' Counsel Act was introduced, may have been applied to an earlier practice.

Although the cab rank principle appeared to be of general application, the four Inns of Court dealt with discipline internally rather than by developing a common regulatory institution. Between 1800 and 1860 they disbarred only 10 barristers, usually after conviction of a crime.[17] From the 1850s the Bar was subject to uncoordinated attacks, portrayed as outdated, obstructing reform, and deliberately suppressing the more efficient solicitors.[18] It rode these attacks until scandals between 1859 and 1863 attracted the attention of politicians, lawyers, and media (see chapter five). Pue suggested that five cases, involving eminent members of the Bar including a Lord Chancellor, aspiring Attorney-General, an eminent QC and lawyer member of Parliament, attracted enough attention to transform barristers from 'a relatively open, unregulated status group' into more coordinated, rule-bound body.[19]

Two of the four cases concerned breaches of etiquette regarding the practice, which had become established, that barristers only acted when briefed by attorneys. The case against Charles B Claydon involved a barrister allowing his 'clerk' to prepare a case rather than an attorney.[20] The most serious of several charges against Digby Seymour was that he acted in a matter as 'liquidation of a debt' he owed to the instructing attorney.[21] The benchers of the Inn said this was a threat to 'independence', because the barrister was not being chosen as best for the client but because it suited the attorney's financial interest. The charges against Seymour were found not proven but he was severely censured.

---

[14] CR Andrews, *Standards of Conduct for Lawyers: An 800-Year Evolution* (2004) 57 *SMU Law Review* 1385, 1402

[15] A Watson, *Speaking in Court: Developments in Court Advocacy from the Seventeenth to the Twenty-First Century* (London, Palgrave Macmillan, 2019) (and see M Mclaren, C Ulyatt and C Knowles *The 'Cab Rank Rule': A Fresh View* (London, Bar Standards Board, 2012) 3, n 4).

[16] A rank of horse drawn carriages was operated from 1634 by former sea captain John Baily. (*The Londonist* 'Where was London's first Taxi rank?') https://londonist.com/london/history/where-was-london-s-first-taxi-rank

[17] W Pue, 'Moral Panic at the English Bar: Paternal vs. Commercial Ideologies of Legal Practice in the 1860s' (1990) 15(1) *Law & Social Inquiry* 49, 56.

[18] ibid 58.
[19] ibid 3.
[20] ibid 86.
[21] ibid 96.

Two barristers were disbarred in the early 1860s for matters only marginally connected to the Bar. Old offences came to light during investigations of their background at the point they had been appointed as QCs. The fact that both were Liberal MPs may also have been a factor. One was Seymour, who was confronted with old offences after he had been awarded the QC title. The offences came to light when he applied for the order of the coif and was exposed by the Master of Serjeant's Inn on applying for membership. Seymour later complained to the Benchers that details of his case, which could have only come from the Inn, had been posted around his constituency.

The other MP, Edwin James, was a man of humble origins, about to be appointed Attorney-General, when he suddenly left for New York. The suspicious circumstances, and the fact he was greeted as a celebrity, prompted the benchers of Inner Temple to investigate his dubious financial dealings and disbar him.[22] Pue wondered whether the cause for discipline was political in a narrow and broad sense. Apart from their Party affiliation, both James and Seymour had risen at the Bar outside the usual paths of patronage and represented the 'laissez faire' classes who threatened established patterns of tradition and privilege.[23]

The final disciplinary proceeding called on Charles Rann Kennedy to justify his conduct in the Swinfen will case (see chapter nine 'Morality'). After the case to secure her estate, Patience Swinfen had returned from a holiday to announce she was engaged and would not be paying Kennedy the agreed fee, a third of the value of the bequeathed estate. Kennedy sued in contract for £20,000, but Patience claimed he was barred by the etiquette that barristers only act on instructions from attorneys. The contractual arrangement also broke the law of maintenance and champerty; he had supported the case, unpaid, under arrangements to pay an unspecified sum. This would have been an illegal contingency fee arrangement.

As in the Swinfen will case, Kennedy launched a wide-ranging assault on the system, the market, and its domination by wealthy attorneys' firms. In a pamphlet, he argued that the partisan obligation properly sprang from the employment relationship; the contractual nexus with the lay client made it impossible for a barrister to be:

> a perfectly indifferent person, an assistant of the court, or a minister of justice, rather than a partisan of his client ... An advocate is the client's representative before the court, and the exponent of his case; an assistant of the court thus far, that he brings before it all that may be urged on his client's behalf, but not an assistant of the court in any other sense. If he were a minister of justice, as the Judge is, he should be paid by the public, not by his client.[24]

Kennedy's argument was a bid to establish the commercial mode of practice proposed by the alternative Bar, those without contacts, and was much feared by the established Bar. Kennedy's fee arrangement reflected he claimed, 'laissez-faire principles of political economy'.[25] The ancient fee offences mitigated against justice for the poor and

---

[22] ibid 75.
[23] ibid 100–1.
[24] ibid 105–6 citing CR Kennedy, *Mr Kennedy's Argument in the Common Pleas against the Rule Obtained by the Defendants in Kennedy v. Broun and Wife* (Birmingham, SB Howell, 1862) 29–37.
[25] Pue (n 17) 105.

subsisted alongside a common law right to contract direct, while the etiquette of the Bar was not legally enforceable.

Rejecting Kennedy's arguments, the court recognised the legality of the Bar's etiquette, and Kennedy as a 'threatening renegade'.[26] When the details of his affair with Patience Swinfen was revealed, the press pilloried him. *The Times* accused him avoiding oversight of his fee and of 'unmanly behaviour'.[27] He had openly confronted tradition and disciplinary proceedings were inevitable. The charges laid by Inner Temple claimed his romantic relationship with Patience Swinfen[28] caused him to find attorneys and instruct them rather than the other way round. Concerning payment, barristers' fees were honoraria, not a matter of contract, and attorneys paid them in advance. Kennedy was censured by Inner temple and banned from common buildings for two years.

Hostile press surrounding the five disciplinary cases, crystallised concerns about the Bar and highlighted the need to regulate barristers more effectively. Pue suggested that the public mood changed from criticism of the Bar's paternalism to a kind of 'moral panic' supporting regulation and demanding a modernised professionalism.[29] An 'etiquette' for the Bar was published in 1875[30] but many conventions remained unwritten. It was not until 1894 that the Inns created the General Council of the Bar, which established a collective organisation. The Bar Council, as it was commonly known, became the main representative body[31] and assumed responsibility for disciplinary cases. From 1895, annual statements on professional conduct and etiquette were issued by the General Counsel of the Bar.[32] The outcomes of cases continued to form a substantial part of guidance to conduct well into the twentieth century.[33]

Resistance to produce a code of conduct apparently reflected an attitude that proper conduct was intrinsic to the culture of the Inns of Court. A book on advocacy by Sir Malcolm Hilbery published in 1946, suggested that it could only be learned as an art and not reproduced in a code.[34] The Bar was pressurised to publish a code of conduct by a Royal Commission on Legal Services reporting in 1979.[35] The first *Bar Code of Conduct 1981* (BCC 1981), drew heavily on Hilbery's book, repeating his phrases in rules using the words 'must' and 'must not' frequently. No guidance was provided within the code, which was published in several revisions. There was no statutory authority for the code, but Bar practice in the courts was well-established

---

[26] ibid 108.
[27] ibid 109.
[28] ibid 102.
[29] WW Pue, 'British Masculinities, Canadian Lawyers: Canadian Legal Education, 1900–1930' (1999) 16 *Law Context: A Socio-Legal J* 80, 116.
[30] R Abel, *The Legal Profession in England and Wales* (Oxford, Basil Blackwell, 1988) 133.
[31] A Senate of the Inns of Court and the Bar existed between 1974 and 1987 but was abandoned after a report by Lord Rawlinson.
[32] WW Boulton, *A Guide To Conduct And Etiquette At The Bar Of England And Wales* (London, Butterworth, 1953).
[33] ibid.
[34] The Hon. Sir Malcolm Hilbery, *Duty and Art in Advocacy* (London, Stevens and Sons Ltd, 1946) 7.
[35] *Report of the Royal Commission on Legal Services (Benson Commission), (Final Report)*, Cmnd 7648 (1979), Vol 1, 310.

and reflected in case law. Nevertheless, production of a mandatory code supported the idea that the Bar had some ancient and unwritten authority.

ii. Attorneys and Solicitors

The Attorneys and Solicitors Act 1729 introduced a common oath for attorneys and solicitors appearing in different courts.[36] It was unclear whether this led to the formation of the Society of Attorneys, Solicitors, Proctors and others not being Barristers, practising in the Courts of Law and Equity of the United Kingdom, also known as the Gentleman Practisers, or whether both developments reflected the growing importance of business lawyers. While the Gentleman Practisers aimed to raise the social status of elite non-barristers, their successor organisation, the Law Society, sought to transfer elite standards to the whole membership.

The Law Society unified and regulated the solicitor brand. Initially, bad behaviour was controlled by onerous entry requirements. Prospective members entered five-year articles of clerkship with an established practitioner. They paid a premium to their principle and received no pay. Only the wealthy and most dedicated would survive. Even so, the Law Society set examinations, used its law reform and lobbying activity to gain control over regulating solicitors[37] and even drafted statutes affecting them.[38]

As transaction work involved handling client money the Law Society worked hard to establish solicitors' reputation for financial probity. It initiated court proceedings against dishonest practitioners in 1834.[39] Around the same time it published 'best practice' on issues of etiquette and costs. The government's Petty Bag Office had recorded the names of solicitors in Chancery from the sixteenth century,[40] but passed these duties to the Law Society in 1845. Similar duties were passed over until the Supreme Court of Judicature (Officers) Act 1879 abolished the Petty Bag Office.

Between 1900 and 1905 220 solicitors were declared bankrupt and the Law Society sponsored legislation preventing use of client money for solicitors' purposes.[41] In 1907 they were required to establish separate accounts for holding client and office money.[42] In the 1930s, detailed accounts rules were established, requirements for compulsory indemnity insurance introduced, and a Compensation Fund for victims of dishonesty was established[43] In the 1940s the Law Society acquired power to inspect the accounts

---

[36] Andrews (n 14) 1407.

[37] D Sugarman, 'Bourgeois Collectivism, Professional Power and the Boundaries of the State: The Private and Public Life of the Law Society 1825 to 1914' (1996) 3(1/2) *International Journal of the Legal Profession* 81, 120.

[38] ibid 105 and 114.

[39] The National Archives 'Law Society: Solicitors Registers of Admission', https://discovery.national-archives.gov.uk/details/r/C16438#:~:text=The%20Solicitors%20Act%20of%201860%20enabled%20the%20Society,a%20compulsory%20academic%20year%20was%20required%20for%20clerks.

[40] ibid.

[41] Sugarman (n 37) 110.

[42] National archives (n 39).

[43] Sugarman (n 37) 111.

of practitioners, strike members from the roll of solicitors and levy members for a compensation fund to compensate clients for solicitor fraud. Power to discipline, to set accounts rules, to intervene in the running of law firms and to require that solicitors have liability insurance, were acquired under statutes enacted in the twentieth century.

Many of the powers acquired by the Law Society were consolidated in the Solicitors Act 1974. The creation of a statutory disciplinary tribunal was probably influenced by the report of the Franks Committee in 1957,[44] noting the general principle that tribunals, provided 'cheapness, accessibility, freedom from technicality, expedition and knowledge of their particular subject'.[45] Although those sanctioned by the Solicitors Disciplinary Tribunal (SDT) could appeal to the High Court, it usually endorsed the expertise of the SDT in assessing misconduct.

The rules providing the focus for proceedings before the SDT were the Solicitors Practice Rules (SPR) made under the Solicitors Act 1933, section 1. The first rules, SPR 1936, were relatively brief, comprising four substantive rules on one page. They developed to deal with demarcation of professional boundaries (employed solicitors, not acting as a structural surveyor or valuer), proscriptions (fee sharing, receiving contingency fees, acting for borrower and lender on a private mortgage) and standards (supervision of offices, client care).

The SPR began with broad statements of principle governing solicitors' conduct.[46] After regular updates from 1967,[47] the 1987 version asserted that solicitors were not to do anything to undermine:

(a) the solicitor's independence or integrity;
(b) a person's freedom to instruct a solicitor of his or her choice;
(c) the solicitor's duty to act in the best interests of the client;
(d) the good repute of the solicitor or of the solicitor's profession;
(e) the solicitor's proper standard of work.

These were supplemented in 1990 by a further principle on client care. The dense statements of the SPR appeared unsuitable for dealing with misconduct but were often a basis of disciplinary charges.

In 1960 the Law Society published *A Guide to the Professional Conduct and Etiquette of Solicitors*[48] written by its secretary Sir Thomas Lund. Eight editions, with slightly different names, appeared before 1999.[49] As it developed, *The Guide* merged Lund's narrative with the broad principles of the SPR. Under an editorial committee

---

[44] *Report of the Committee on Administrative Tribunals and Enquiries* (1957) Cmnd. 218.
[45] ibid para 38.
[46] The Law Society *Solicitors' Practice |Rules 1936–2007* (London, The Law Society, undated).
[47] 1967, 1971 and 1975 1987 and 1990 (see further A Boon, 'The legal professions' new handbooks: narratives, standards and values' (2016) 19(2) *Legal Ethics* 207).
[48] T Lund, *A Guide to the Professional Conduct and Etiquette of Solicitors* (London, Law Society, 1960).
[49] It took a new form as *The Guide to the Professional Conduct of Solicitors* (*The Guide*) in 1990. N Taylor (ed), *The Guide to the Professional Conduct of Solicitors*, 7th edn (London, The Law Society, 1993) 2.

the content and guidance proliferated, but the regulatory status of the material was ambiguous. In 1999 the Law Society established a Regulation Review Working Party. Justifying the need for a new code of conduct the Law Society acknowledged that *The Guide* had become 'a mix of mandatory and non-mandatory conduct requirements'.[50] While the paternalistic tone of Lund's original Guide was altered, the 25 sections of detailed and binding practice rules and non-binding guidance was largely a distillation of material in *The Guide* adapted to accommodate new case law.[51]

The *Solicitors Code of Conduct 2007* (SCC 2007) was foregrounded by a list of six principles like those previously used in the SPR. These had been sent by the Law Society Council to the Department of Constitutional Affairs, as a list of 10, as part of the approval process for the new Code of Conduct. The numerous amendments made included the introduction of a completely new first principle: 'You must uphold the rule of law and the proper administration of justice'.[52] This was launched as part of the first unambiguously self-regulating code of conduct for solicitors. It appeared in the same year as the Legal Services Act 2007 (LSA) replaced regulation by professional bodies with 'independent' regulators. The 2007 code survived until 2011.

iii. Independent Regulation

When the Legal Services Act 2007 required regulation of the Bar and solicitors be placed in the hands of independent regulators, the new Bar Standards Board (BSB) and Solicitors Regulation Authority (SRA) began work on new codes of conduct. These appeared as part of regulatory handbooks, the SRA Code of Conduct 2011[53] and the *BSB Handbook 2014*.[54]

The SRA continued to list broad principles as a prelude to the Code of Conduct. This had been recommended for the solicitors by the report leading to the Legal Services Act 2007, prepared by Sir David Clementi, based on his experience of 'Principles Based Regulation' in the financial services sector. The SRA's list of Principles were the six from the Solicitors Code of Conduct 2007, said to represent 'fundamental ethical and professional standards'.[55] The list added 'principles' 7 to 10, concerned with efficient business management and regulatory compliance. The *Bar Handbook 2014* also adopted the solicitors' practice of stating brief and broad principles as a part of their Handbook as 'Core Duties'. The two lists are compared in Table 1.

---

[50] Introduction to the Solicitors Code of Conduct (2007) ix.
[51] *Prince Jefri Bolkiah v KPMG* (a firm) [1999] 2 AC 222 (see further A Boon, *The Ethics and Conduct of Lawyers in England and Wales* (Oxford, Hart Publishing, 2014) 358–62).
[52] Boon (n 47) citing P Camp, 'Countdown to the Code: Taking the plunge' (*Law Society Gazette*, 14 June 2007) 18.
[53] SRA, SRA Handbook 2011 (Version 11, 2015) www.sra.org.uk/solicitors/handbook/code/.
[54] *BSB Handbook 2014*, www.barstandardsboard.org.uk/for-barristers/bsb-handbook-and-code-guidance/the-bsb-handbook.html.
[55] *SRA Handbook* (n 53) Introduction, para 3(a).

Table 1 Comparing the core principles and duties of the legal profession's new codes of conduct in the SRA's 2011 and the Bar's 2014 codes of conduct[56]

SRA Principles[57]	BSB Core Duties[58]
You must: 1. uphold the rule of law and the proper administration of justice; 2. act with integrity; 3. not allow your independence to be compromised; 4. act in the best interests of each client; 5. provide a proper standard of service to your clients; 6. behave in a way that maintains the trust the public places in you and in the provision of legal services; 7. comply with your legal and regulatory obligations and deal with your regulators and ombudsmen in an open, timely and co-operative manner; 8. run your business or carry out your role in the business effectively and in accordance with proper governance and sound financial and risk management principles; 9. run your business or carry out your role in the business in a way that encourages equality of opportunity and respect for diversity; and 10. protect client money and assets.	CD1. You must observe your duty to the court in the administration of justice. CD2. You must act in the best interests of each client. CD3. You must act with honesty and integrity. CD4. You must maintain your independence. CD5. You must not behave in a way which is likely to diminish the trust and confidence which the public places in you or in the profession. CD6. You must keep the affairs of each client confidential. CD7. You must provide a competent standard of work and service to each client. CD8. You must not discriminate unlawfully against any person. CD9. You must be open and co-operative with your regulators. CD10. You must take reasonable steps to manage your practice, or carry out your role within your practice, competently and in such a way as to achieve compliance with your legal and regulatory obligations.

Source: SRA Code of Conduct 2011 and BSB Code of Conduct 2014.

It was notable that despite the very different histories and orientations of the professions, the lists were extremely similar. This raised the issue of how meaningful they were in reflecting what was important in the respective occupations. There were different yet counterintuitive orientations to the rule of law. An example was the requirement of integrity which appeared in the SRA list as Principle 2 and the BSB list as Core Duty 3. In the BSB list, it was with a requirement of honesty, absent from the SRA list.

Integrity was a difficult quality to define, attracting synonyms like 'wholeness' and 'honour' and connoting adherence to the ethical standards of one's profession. It suggested good character, often regarded as integral to professionalism.[59] Historically,

---
[56] Taken from Boon (n 47).
[57] SRA, *SRA Principles 2011* Version 15, www.sra.org.uk/solicitors/handbook/handbookprinciples/.
[58] *BSB Handbook Part:2, The Code of Conduct* (2014) B – The Core Duties.
[59] See generally M Bayles, *Professional Ethics* (Belmont Ca, Wadsworth Publishing, 1981).

attitudes to integrity were very different between the professions. For barristers, the obligation of integrity focused on the duty not to mislead the court and complicated rules around how representation could be provided in all cases while doing so.

The focus of solicitors' integrity was a guarantee of reliability in handling client money. This was reflected Sir Thomas Bingham's statement in *Bolton v The Law Society* that the fundamental purpose of solicitor disciplinary proceedings was 'to maintain the reputation of the solicitors' profession as one in which every member, of whatever standing, may be trusted to the ends of the earth'.[60] In disciplinary tribunals against solicitors a lack of integrity *could* lead to striking off, whereas a finding of dishonesty almost always did.[61]

The absence of honesty from the SRA list was counterintuitive, given that most serious cases of solicitor misconduct involved dishonesty. After a period of uncertainty, in which some English courts suggested that integrity was synonymous with honesty, integrity emerged as a broader concept,[62] involving more than mere honesty. The SRA Standards and Regulations 2019 reduced the SRA's 10 Principles to seven, introduced an obligation of honesty and dropped the four business orientated Principles: providing proper service, being open with regulators, having proper governance and protecting client money.

The SRA provided an explanation of what upholding the rule of law involved in guidance heavily emphasising legality. Published with the 2019 SRA Code online, it quoted the explanation of the duty to 'uphold the rule of law' given by Lord Bingham of Cornhill: 'The core of the existing principle is … that all persons and authorities within the state, whether public or private, should be bound by and entitled to the benefit of laws publicly and prospectively promulgated and publicly administered in the courts'.[63] Addressing the question 'When may a breach [of the rule of law] occur?', examples were: 'Very serious, organised and premeditated offending involving terrorism, violence and/or dishonesty, showing deliberate disregard for the law' or 'a sustained course of serious offending'.[64]

The guidance noted that Principle 1 could be 'engaged by conduct which is not the subject of a criminal conviction'. Examples of this were of actions undermining the administration of justice, such as 'Premeditated actions, intended deliberately to impede or prevent the judicial process or judicial decision-making, or the lawful exercise of enforcement powers …'.[65] One of three such examples was of 'A solicitor who repeatedly brings spurious or hopeless immigration applications knowing, or suspecting, that the true purpose of these was to delay the lawful removal of their clients from the country'.[66] This was rather an odd choice of an example of a lawyer breaching the rule of law.

---

[60] *Bolton v The Law Society* [1994] 1 WLR 512.
[61] *Wingate & Anr v Solicitors Regulation Authority* and *Solicitors Regulation Authority v Malins* [2018] EWCA Civ 366.
[62] *Williams v Solicitors Regulation Authority* [2017] EWHC 1478 (Admin), [2017] 6 WLUK 422.
[63] SRA 'A Guide to the Application of Principle 1', www.sra.org.uk/sra/corporate-strategy/sra-enforcement-strategy/enforcement-practice/guide-application-principle-1/.
[64] ibid.
[65] ibid.
[66] ibid.

Despite the absence of any reference to the rule of law in the BSB Core Duties, it claimed, of its regulatory focus on advocacy and specialist advice, that:

> These legal services have a close relationship to access to justice and the rule of law. Our society is based on a rule of law. Everyone needs to be able to seek expert advice on their legal rights and obligations and to have access to skilled representation in the event of a dispute or litigation. Our system of justice depends on those who provide such services acting fearlessly, independently and competently, so as to further their clients' best interests, subject always to their duty to the Court.[67]

The SRA's definition of supporting the rule of law was the antithesis of that promoted by the Bar. This reflected the different orientation of the professions, the Bar towards the advocacy of rights and the solicitors towards lawful behaviour. Curiously, while the SRA Principles referred to upholding the rule of law the BSB Core Duties made no reference to it at all, despite the Bar's historic contribution to establishing constitutional and human rights.

B. The United States

Regulation of lawyers was generally managed at the level of the colony and later the State. After independence local lawyer organisations were formed and introduced some regulation. New Hampshire, for example, issued rules dealing with admissions and bans on unauthorised practice and champerty.[68] Antagonism to lawyers delayed regulation in some US States. The Indiana Constitution of 1816, for example, specifically forbade it.[69] Virginia vacillated between a ban on lawyers and severe regulation until the end of the seventeenth century.[70] Other States stopped lawyers from receiving fees, barred them from courts or restricted them procedurally or in relation to their charges.[71]

Some States, notably Georgia, Massachusetts, New York, New Jersey, North Carolina, and Virginia, regulated judicial systems in the post-revolutionary period with statutes imposing oaths of office or prescribed disciplinary mechanisms.[72] Bar Association codes formulated by lawyers began to appear towards the end of the nineteenth century. Some became so popular they were adopted by states in legislative form. In 1846 the New York State Constitution mandated codification of State law, directing a three-man Commission to revise and simplify the procedures of State courts of record.[73]

The New York Commission on practice and pleading produced a Code of Procedure enacted in 1848. It became known as the Field Code, after one of the Commissioners. The Field Code prescribed disbarment or suspension of lawyers

---

[67] *BSB Handbook 2018* (Version 3.3), A1: The Bar Standards Board, 11.
[68] Andrews (n 14) 1421.
[69] JG Rogers, 'History of the American Bar Association' (1953) 39(8) *American Bar Association Journal* 659.
[70] Andrews (n 14) 1414.
[71] C Warren, *A History of the American Bar* (New York, Cambridge University Press, 1911) 4.
[72] Andrews (n 14) 1416–17.
[73] MV Coe and LW Morse, 'Chronology of the Development of the David Dudley Field Code' (1942) 27 *Cornell Law Review* 238.

for 'wilful violation'.[74] The formation of the New York State Bar in 1870 followed declining control over admissions, noted corruption scandals and calls for effective regulation.[75] In other States developing regulation of lawyers, State judiciaries typically created Boards covering areas such as education, licensing, or practice. It was not until the mid-twentieth century that membership of State Bar Associations began to become mandatory, and Bar disciplinary processes introduced.[76]

The first modern code of conduct for lawyers was published by the Alabama State Bar in 1887. It was the work of a judge, Thomas Goode Jones, but used essays published by David Hoffman in 1836[77] and George Sharswood in 1854.[78] Both were practitioners turned academics and their books based on lectures on ethics prepared for students.[79] In drafting the Alabama Code, Jones canvassed legal opinion and sent the final draft to the Bar membership for comment. The code was widely circulated[80] and within 20 years of publication 10 other States had adopted something similar.[81] The arrival of the ABA in 1878 assisted with the process of building a wider consensus.

In 1905, shortly after the ABA became the national organisation of attorneys, its president Henry St George Tucker, formed a committee to draft a national code.[82] The Committee looked at all the existing State Bar Codes and concluded that they derived from the Alabama version. Thomas Goode Jones joined the Committee and his draft, also based on the Alabama code, was sent to members with a special print of Sharswood's essay. Over 1,000 letters of comment were received on proposed 'Canons of Ethics', which were adopted in 1908, alongside a model oath of office based on the Field Code. The 1908 Canons were described as a statement of 'fraternal norms' balancing competing duties to the courts, the bar, and the client.[83]

In 1964 30 years into the 'era of federation', ABA President-elect Lewis Powell reviewed the ABA Canons. The proposal for a Model Code of Professional Responsibility ('Model Code'), adopted in August 1969,[84] reflected a feeling that the aspirational tone of the Canons was no longer suitable.[85] The proposed code was a scholarly document, citing authoritative statements on ethics and the Canons, judicial decisions and ABA opinions.[86] Given the federal structure of the ABA, States did not have to adopt the Model code, nor the amendments made annually from 1974.[87]

---

[74] Andrews (n 14) 1425.

[75] G Martin, *Causes and Conflicts: The Centennial History of the Association of the Bar of the City of New York* (New York, Fordham University Press, 1997).

[76] Andrews (n 14) 1452

[77] D Hoffman, *Course of Legal Study: Addressed To Students And The Profession Generally*, 2nd edn (Baltimore, Joseph Neal, 1836).

[78] G Sharswood, *An Essay on Professional Ethics*, 5th edn (Philadelphia, T and JW Johnson, 1907).

[79] See further A Marston, 'Guiding the Profession: The 1887 Code Of Ethics Of The Alabama State Bar Association' (1998) 49(2) *Alabama Law Review* 471.

[80] Andrews (n 14) 1437.

[81] ibid 1439.

[82] ibid 1439.

[83] GC Hazard, 'The Future of Legal Ethics' (1990–1991)100 *Yale LJ* 1239, 1249.

[84] ABA Model Code of Professional Responsibility (August 1969). This was amended by the House of Delegates in February 1970, February 1974, February 1975, August 1976, August 1977, August 1978, February 1979, February 1980, and August 1980.

[85] Andrews (n 14) 1444.

[86] ibid 1445.

[87] ibid 1446.

In 1977, another commission was appointed to review the model code, promote consistency and wider adoption.[88] New Model Rules of Professional Conduct were adopted in August 1983.[89] There were two major revisions, with Ethics 2000 leading to updating, clarification and general tightening up. Since then the ABA made changes to 14 rules in 20 years.[90] In 2000, a version of the Model Rules applied in most States. Provisions of the code were not necessarily accepted as authoritative in judicial decisions.

C. New Zealand

By the late 1850s, nearly 20 years after the arrival of the first lawyer in New Zealand, there was pressure for qualification and admission provisions for locally qualified lawyers. A judicial report in 1859 expressed a need for examinations like those proposed in England.[91] The Law Practitioners Act 1861 allowed Supreme Court judges to regulate the qualification and examination of barristers and solicitors. The result was that solicitors were officers of the court, could be sanctioned by the court and removed from the Roll 'upon reasonable cause'.

The New Zealand Law Society (NZLS), incorporated in 1869, conducted disciplinary proceedings against members for the first 30 years.[92] Barristers were dismissed by their admitting body until the Law Practitioners Act 1908 provided they could be removed by the Supreme Court 'for reasonable cause whensoever and wheresoever the same arises'.[93] The pattern at the turn of the century reflected ambivalence about self-regulation, but in 1928 the Solicitor's Fidelity Guarantee Fund, funded from compulsory subscriptions by practitioners, was created to repay trust fund losses. Local Law Societies began dealing with minor disciplinary matters and campaigned to gain disciplinary powers in 1933.[94]

The campaign for disciplinary powers arose because court processes were cumbersome and gave the public a false impression of the profession. Under the Law Practitioners Amendment Act 1935 the court retained disciplinary oversight, but the legal profession effectively became self-governing. In the Parliamentary debate, the Prime Minister supported proposed self-regulation, observing that it reflected the position of the British legal professions,[95] and expressing pride that New Zealand had a legal profession 'deemed fit to hold its own disciplinary powers'.[96] Flaus characterised the period before 1935 as the 'essentially pragmatic groping of the profession on disciplinary matters'.[97]

[88] ibid 1450.
[89] ibid 1446.
[90] ibid 1448.
[91] P Spiller, 'A History of New Zealand Legal Education: A Study in Ambivalence' (1993) 4 *Legal Education Review* 223.
[92] WR Flaus, 'Discipline within the New Zealand Legal Profession' (1971) 6 *Victoria University Wellington Law Review* 337.
[93] ibid.
[94] ibid 334.
[95] ibid 334–35.
[96] ibid 345.
[97] ibid 339.

The 1935 Act continued a trend towards increasing professional responsibility by instituting a system operated by the profession, establishing procedures and criteria for invoking disciplinary action and providing for appeals to the Supreme Court. The NZLS had no power under the Act to make rules of conduct but could make 'provision that may be desirable or necessary for the effective exercise and performance of the powers and function of the Society':[98] promoting proper conduct, suppressing illegal, dishonourable, or improper practices and preserving and maintaining the integrity and status of the legal profession.[99]

The NZLS standards took the form of circulated rulings on cases of professional misconduct. These were published in newsletters and consolidated by the NZLS Council in 1931. A further compilation entitled *Rules Governing the Conduct of Practitioners* took effect in 1970. Flaus criticised the disciplinary system as providing insufficient guidance, since standards depended on the cases presented and precedents often not well publicised. Standards and rules of procedure varied between law societies and disciplinary rules fell far short of comprehensive guidance on conduct. Disciplinary committees effectively based decisions on broad criteria of whether a respondent was fit and proper.[100]

Since at least 1966 a Prosecutions Advisory Committee advised the NZLS whether misconduct considered for disciplinary proceedings should also be referred to the police for possible criminal prosecution.[101] The profession decided, therefore, whether disciplinary proceedings were sufficient punishment. The secrecy surrounding the outcome of cases heard was criticised from the 1960s, but the profession drew comfort from a general view that there was little benefit and much harm (principally to the respondents) from publicity. This did not explain why guilty decisions should not have been made public.

The Lawyers and Conveyancers Act 2006 represented a significant reform of the legal services sector. It was said to embody a model promoted by the NZLS providing greater independence and accountability.[102] It allowed lawyers to incorporate and created a new profession of conveyancers.[103] It also consolidated regulation in the NZLS, abandoning the structure of local discipline. The NZLS acquired specific regulatory functions:

(a) to control and regulate the practice in New Zealand by barristers and by barristers and solicitors of the profession of the law;
(b) to uphold the fundamental obligations imposed on lawyers who provide regulated services in New Zealand;
(c) to monitor and enforce the provisions of this Act, and of any regulations and rules made under it, that relate to the regulation of lawyers;
(d) to monitor and enforce, throughout the period specified in any order made under section 390, the provisions of this Act, and of any regulations and rules made under it, that relate to the regulation of conveyancers;

---

[98] Law Practitioners Amendment Act 1935, s 121(f).
[99] ibid s 114(1).
[100] Flaus (n 92) 356–57.
[101] ibid 370–71.
[102] 'Lawyers and Conveyancers Bill' (2003) *New Zealand Law Journal* 331, quoting Minister of Justice Phil Goff.
[103] Lawyers and Conveyancers Act 2006, Part 5.

(e) to assist and promote, for the purpose of upholding the rule of law and facilitating the administration of justice in New Zealand, the reform of the law.[104]

The Act also identified a representative function of the NZLS; representing its members and serving their interests.[105]

The main purpose of distinguishing regulatory and representative functions was to allocate different sources to them; practising fees could only be used for regulatory purposes[106] while representative purposes had to be supported by member subscriptions.[107] The NZLS and the Society of Conveyancers were required to have rules addressing a long list of outcomes, including 'standards of professional conduct and client care'.[108] Both also had to have a professional code of conduct[109] made in consultation with the Ministry of Justice and others.[110] The Lawyers and Conveyancers Act (Lawyers: Conduct and Client Care) Rules 2008 (hereafter NZ LCCR 2008) were published to comply with this requirement.[111]

D. Canada

The creation of the Law Society of Upper Canada with an explicit regulatory purpose[112] was forerunner to a strong culture of self-regulation in Canada, perhaps the 'sole remaining case of "unfettered self-regulation" in the common law world'.[113] Ten provinces and three territories ceded broad powers to local law societies and enabling statutes were generally only changed at the instigation of the local law society.[114] The law societies promulgated standards through codes of conduct and conducted disciplinary proceedings.

The Legal Profession Act 1988 of Prince Edward Island was typical of foundational statutes for provincial regulation of lawyers in Canada. It recognised the Law Society as a body corporate and provided a list of statutory objects:

(a) to uphold and protect the public interest in the administration of justice;
(b) to establish standards for the education, professional responsibility and competence of its members and applicants for membership;
(c) to ensure the independence, integrity and honour of the society and its members;

---

[104] ibid s 65.
[105] ibid s 66.
[106] ibid s 73.
[107] ibid s 75.
[108] ibid Part 6, s 94(e).
[109] ibid s 95.
[110] ibid s 100.
[111] Lawyers and Conveyancers Act (Lawyers: Conduct and Client Care) Rules 2008 (SR 2008/214) www.legislation.govt.nz/regulation/public/2008/0214/latest/whole.html#DLM143784.
[112] C Moore, *The Law Society of Upper Canada and Ontario's Lawyers, 1797–1997* (Toronto, Buffalo, London, University of Toronto Press, 1997) 44.
[113] R Dinovitzer and M Dawe, 'Canada: Continuity and Change in a Modern Legal Profession' in R Abel, O Hammerslev, H Sommerlad and U Schultz (eds), *Lawyers in 21st-Century Societies* (Oxford, Hart Publishing, 2020) 80.
[114] N Semple, 'Legal Services Regulation in Canada' in A Boon, *International Perspectives on the Regulation of Lawyers and Legal Services* (Oxford, Hart Publishing 2017) 95.

(d) to regulate the practice of law; and
(e) to uphold and protect the interests of its members.[115]

The Canadian Bar Association produced a Model Code of Conduct for use by Canadian provincial law societies from 1920. The aim was to harmonise conduct rules across the provinces. In 2009, the Federation of Canadian Law Societies (FCLS) published a Model Code of Professional Conduct as a benchmark for harmonising codes of conduct. When the law societies began adopting the FCLS Code the CBA resolved to phase out its own code when the last law society stopped using it.[116] The 2009 code was finally retired in 2019. In 2014 the law societies adopted FLSC National Discipline Standards for handling complaints against lawyers.

E. Australia

Bartlett and Haller suggested that early Australian lawyers did not adopt formal rules from England but adopted 'the cultural practices and professional ethos of their homeland'.[117] In the late 1800s Bar Associations and local law societies began to file complaints about lawyers with courts. The inconvenience of these procedures led to lobbying of provincial government for self-regulatory powers. Disciplinary tribunals began to be established in some States from 1927. There were fewer complaints about barristers, probably because they did not hold client money.[118] There was therefore less pressure on Bar Associations to seek self-regulatory powers and barristers remained under the direct control of the courts. The Law Council of Australia, created in 1933, produced model rules which were adopted in South Australia, Queensland, Victoria, New South Wales and the Australian Capital Territory.[119]

IV. CODES OF CONDUCT

A. Supporting the Rule of Law

Abbott suggested that, in addition to a regulatory function, codes of conduct addressed the different audiences for professional jurisdiction, including the public and government. The rule of law was often referred to in codes of conduct, usually in a preface or preamble. In the New Zealand legislative code, fundamental obligations of lawyers, were stated as:

> to uphold the rule of law and to facilitate the administration of justice in New Zealand:
> to be independent in providing regulated services to clients:

---

[115] Legal Profession Act 1988, s 4, www.princeedwardisland.ca/en/legislation/legal-profession-act.
[116] CBA 'Codes of Professional Conduct', www.cba.org/Publications-Resources/Practice-Tools/Ethics-and-Professional-Responsibility-(1)/Codes-of-Professional-Conduct.
[117] F Bartlett and L Haller, 'Australia: Legal Services Regulation in Australia – Innovative Co-regulation' in Boon (n 114) 161, 166.
[118] ibid.
[119] Law Council of Australia *Australian Solicitors' Conduct Rules* (2011) as updated, www.lawcouncil.asn.au/policy-agenda/regulation-of-the-profession-and-ethics/australian-solicitors-conduct-rules.

to act in accordance with all fiduciary duties and duties of care owed by lawyers to their clients: to protect, subject to overriding duties as officers of the High Court and to duties under any enactment, the interests of clients.[120]

The first obligation in this list combined support for the rule of law and the administration of justice in the same way that the SRA Principles did. The two principles were, however, distinct as explained in the first substantive chapter in the Code of Conduct entitled 'the rule of law and the administration of justice'. They were given different meanings in different jurisdictions. From a Canadian perspective, Millen argued that independent legal professions supported the administration of justice with honesty in litigation while upholding the rule of law involved 'fearless' representation.[121]

There was no mention of the rule of law in the ABA Canons, which spoke only of the need to maintain the system of American justice to a high level of efficiency. This deficit was addressed in a Preamble to the ABA Model Code of Professional Responsibility 1969, which began with an inspirational reference to the rule of law and individual rights:

> The continued existence of a free and democratic society depends upon recognition of the concept that justice is based upon the rule of law grounded in respect for the dignity of the individual and his capacity through reason for enlightened self-government. Law so grounded makes justice possible, for only through such law does the dignity of the individual attain respect and protection. Without it, individual rights become subject to unrestrained power, respect for law is destroyed, and rational self-government is impossible. Lawyers, as guardians of the law, play a vital role in the preservation of society. The fulfilment of this role requires an understanding by lawyers of their relationship with and function in our legal system.

The Model Code of the Canadian Federation of Bars (hereafter FLSC MCPC) also began in reverential terms:

> One of the hallmarks of civilized society is the Rule of Law. Its importance is manifested in every legal activity in which citizens engage, from the sale of real property to the prosecution of murder to international trade. As participants in a justice system that advances the Rule of Law, lawyers hold a unique and privileged position in society. Self-regulatory powers have been granted to the legal profession on the understanding that the profession will exercise those powers in the public interest.[122]

This view of the relationship between lawyers and the rule of law reflected a conception of lawyers as agents of socialisation, described in the previous chapter.

The Model Rules of the New South Wales Bar in Australia, Legal Profession Uniform Conduct (Barristers) Rules 2015 (hereafter LPUCBR 2015) did not refer to the rule of law. Four Principles preceding a model code suggested that 'These Rules are made in the belief that: barristers owe their paramount duty to the administration

---

[120] NZ LCCR 2008 (n 111) Preface.
[121] R Millen, 'The Independence of the Bar: An Unwritten Constitutional Principle' (2005) *Canadian Bar Review* 84.
[122] Federation of Law Societies of Canada *Model Code of Professional Conduct* (as amended 10 October 2014), First para of preface, https://flsc.ca/wp-content/uploads/2014/12/conduct1.pdf.

of justice'.¹²³ The Rules went on to state that: (e) barristers should exercise their forensic judgments and give their advice independently and for the proper administration of justice, notwithstanding any contrary desires of their clients, (f) the provision of advocates for those who need legal representation is better secured if there is a Bar whose members: (i) must accept briefs to appear regardless of their personal beliefs.¹²⁴ A very specific obligation to supporting rights, consistent with the rule of law approach, was expressed in the last clause.

The existence of unexplained references to the rule of law in introductions to codes to conduct were consistent with Abbott's argument that they were intended for non-professional audiences. Inconsistent with this explanation is the relative absence of an explanation of how or why the rule of law intersected with the role of lawyers. The preamble to the ABA Model Rules came closest to providing this. The Canadian extract suggested that the connection was intrinsic in legal roles, whatever form they took. The reason that The Australian Code for the Bar contained no reference to the rule of law possibly lay in a historical absence of such rhetoric in the English Bar. The original Bar Code of Conduct in 1981, despite containing a section on the general purpose of the code, referred merely to 'the interests of justice'.¹²⁵ Like its Australian counterpart, it referred to the need to act for 'any client'.

B. Legalisation

The form of codes of conduct changed over time as their purpose changed. The Alabama State Bar Code of 1887 expressed views of proper conduct but was probably only enforceable when its provisions reflected court rules or statutes.¹²⁶ Novel elements relating to advertising, for example, were probably not supported by State courts.¹²⁷ The ABA Canons (1908) were in the spirit of guidance as 'fraternal norms'.¹²⁸ The framing of codes to have regulatory, and specifically, disciplinary consequences began well into the twentieth century. It occurred in the different jurisdictions at broadly the same time.

The decisive steps in most jurisdictions occurred in the 1920s and 1930s. In sequence, moves towards harmonisation and codification of practice norms were: Canadian Bar Association Model Code 1920; Law Council of Australia Model Rules 1933; Solicitors Practice Rules (England and Wales) 1936; Law Practitioners Amendment Act (New Zealand) 1935; ABA Model Code 1969; Bar Code of Conduct 1981 (England and Wales). While disciplinary powers were acquired with different level of sanction at different times, the creation of these codes were generally with a view to supporting concerted disciplinary action or to support claims for wider disciplinary powers.

---

[123] LPUCBR 2015, para 4(a).
[124] ibid para 4(f).
[125] Code of Conduct of the Bar of England and Wales 1990 Part I – Preliminary, 102.
[126] Andrews (n 14) 1438.
[127] ibid.
[128] Hazard (n 83) 1249.

The ABA Model Code 1969 marked a transition from an ethical framework to a more explicit regulatory one. It had three levels comprising nine high-level Canons, which were discussed and expanded by 'Ethical Considerations'. These were accompanied by disciplinary rules suited to grounding charges and sanctions. While the Model Code was a mix of aspirational ethical principle and rules of conduct, the Model Rules were enforceable regulations.[129] The codes of conduct grew more detailed as they adopted a tougher regulatory focus. The one exception was the codes of the English solicitors which became less detailed following independent regulation in 2007.

The Solicitors Practice Rules were always framed in a mandatory style using the word 'shall' frequently, a format adopted in *The Guide*. The Law Society Compliance and Supervision Committee claimed that the Solicitors' Disciplinary Tribunal and the courts regarded it as authoritative.[130] The SRA's first restructuring of the rule book reduced the volume of the previous code of conduct, replacing rules with Outcomes and Indicative Behaviours. Outcomes stated what solicitors had to achieve, while indicative behaviours were favoured options. This structure was possibly introduced because the SRA was acquiring responsibility for regulating new legal providers, organisations known as Alternative Business Structures, introduced under the LSA 2007 and the format suited institutional audit. Because of the unsuitability of the SRA outcomes for disciplining individual solicitors, reliance on Principles became the norm.[131]

In its consultation on the Code of Conduct 2014 the BSB noted that the SRA's approach had depended on practitioners' interpretation. The BSB doubted the SRA's approach could meet the regulatory objectives described in the Legal Services Act. The BSB Code of Conduct sought to balance the high-level rules represented by its core duties, which provided scope for professional judgement and interpretation, with 'more detailed rules where clients or the public interest would otherwise be at risk'.[132] The code contained core duties, outcomes, rules, and guidance.

In 2019, the SRA Standards and Regulations were introduced comprising a suite of regulatory documents including two codes of conduct in broadly similar terms; one directed at solicitors and the other at employing entities. The new 'standards' were more like rules than the outcomes and indicative behaviours, but the volume of material was further reduced. Some aspects of the Standards were supplemented by online guidance. This was intended to assist solicitors in understanding their obligations, but the SRA stated it 'may have regard to it when exercising our regulatory functions'.[133]

---

[129] ibid 1250, RG Pearce, 'Rediscovering the Republican Origins of the Legal Ethics Codes' (1992) 6(24) *Georgetown Journal of Legal Ethics* 247.
[130] *The Guide* (n 49) 8th edn (1999) 3.
[131] A Boon and A Whyte, 'Lawyer Disciplinary Processes: An Empirical Study of Solicitors' Misconduct Cases in England and Wales in 2015' (2019) 39(3) *Legal Studies* 455.
[132] BSB, *Review of the Code of Conduct: Consultation Paper on the proposed new Code of Conduct for the Bar* (January 2011) para 22, p 7.
[133] SRA Guidance, www.sra.org.uk/solicitors/guidance/.

C. Substance: Client and Public Duties

Since details of the substance of codes of conduct are the subject of the next two chapters, this chapter deals with their origins. Andrews suggested that modern codes were traceable to the oaths sworn by medieval lawyers.[134] These covered both client and public duties. Client duties included competence, diligence, loyalty, confidentiality, reasonable fees and service to the poor.[135] The emphasis of the oaths was, however, on public duties, such as truth and fairness, manifest in rules on pleading, informing courts of falsehoods and requirements for exploring settlement. These implicitly overrode specific duties owed to clients.

An example of a public duty was the duty to the court in the oath sworn by lawyers in the Canton of Geneva. Expressed in modern terms, the swearer promised '[n]ever to employ knowingly, for the purpose of maintaining the causes confided to me, any means contrary to truth, and never to seek to mislead the Judges by any artifice of false statement of fact or law'. In 1839 a book on agency law by Justice Story commended refusing unjust causes and pursuing justice and truth as ancient principles worth emulating.[136] Andrews attributed remarkable similarities between practice norms in England and the US to the medieval oaths. It is proposed to look at the origins of the American norms because they are the basis of the standard conception of the lawyer's role.

Differences in regional standards in the US in the mid-nineteenth century only began to be addressed when lectures by Hoffman and Sharswood[137] were promulgated.[138] The New York Field Code of 1848 echoed the Swiss oath specifying 'duties to respect the courts, to not mislead the courts, to do justice in litigation, to abstain from offensive personality, to not unduly prejudice parties or witnesses, to not incite passion or greed in litigation and to take cases on behalf of the poor and oppressed'.[139] The element of the Field Code not in the Swiss oath was a duty of confidentiality.

Andrews noted that although the Alabama Code 1887 contained 56 rules they covered five of the six themes of the medieval oaths: litigation fairness, loyalty, reasonable fees, confidentiality and service to the poor.[140] The missing theme, competence, was addressed indirectly by several 'best practice' items. Additions to the Alabama Code, reporting lawyer wrongdoing, advertising constraints and seeking settlement, while departing from the common oath template, had appeared in one or more of the earlier English oaths or in 'received wisdom' from the Inns of Court.[141] The most striking addition, confidentiality, was not part of Sharswood's essay. Patterson suggested two possible sources, the Field Code, or the authors of the Alabama Code.

In the Field Code of 1848, the New York legislature enacted a very similar rule on confidentiality to that which later appeared in the Alabama State Code. According to

---

[134] Andrews (n 14) 1385.
[135] ibid 1412–13.
[136] ibid 1433.
[137] See further Marston (n 79).
[138] Andrews (n 14) 1421 and 1432.
[139] ibid 1425.
[140] ibid 1436.
[141] ibid 1437.

Patterson, this was probably Field's own invention since it was not part of the 'oath prescribed to advocates by the laws Geneva', which the Field Code credited as a source.[142] The inspiration may have been a book by Edward O'Brien published in 1842.[143] If so, O'Brien's concept was distorted. He decried discussing client's affairs generally, while envisaging that disclosure might occasionally be required.[144]

The Alabama Code provided that: 'Communications and confidence between client and attorney are the property and secrets of the client[;] … even the death of the client does not absolve the attorney from his obligation of secrecy'.[145] The rise of confidentiality to prominence was attributed by Paterson to Brougham's speech on behalf of Queen Caroline. This was because the preamble to section 791 of the Code of Alabama of 1852 echoed Brougham's language: '[t]o maintain inviolate the confidence, and, at every peril to themselves, to preserve the secrets of their clients'.[146]

Patterson suggested that the obligation of confidence became an absolute moral obligation rather than simply a legal right protected by professional privilege.[147] This established a conflict between loyalty to clients and other possible duties such as a general duty of fairness.[148] Andrews suggested that the ABA Canons were not 'a dramatic shift in either substance or form of existing standards of conduct', but consolidated, updated and nationalised them, making them a focus of future discussion.[149] All but seven of the original 32 ABA Canons were drawn in whole or in part from Sharswood[150] and were presented to the ABA as being based on his work.

The Model Code of Professional Responsibility 1969 developed some of the substance of the canons, such as lawyer competence. The novel addition was a model rule stating that lawyers 'should' devote time to serving the disadvantaged. The 1984 revision of the ABA rule firmed up the commitment, which eventually indicated a yearly aspirational pro bono target of 50 hours. Andrews thought that modern codes offered few genuinely novel additions to the medieval oaths, restrictions on advertising being a notable exception. While this may be true, the rise of confidentiality was potentially seismic. Accommodating it gave different legal occupations rules on similar topics quite different status and inflections. There could also be pressures to add, delete or change rules. This was particularly the case in the US, where substantive changes to the ABA's codes appeared to respond to external pressures.

Post-Watergate criticism of lawyers may have prompted some of the changes attempted in the New Model Rules of Professional Conduct, adopted in August 1983.[151] Early drafts proved controversial and were withdrawn or modified. A draft

---

[142] L Ray Patterson, 'Legal Ethics and the Lawyer's Duty of Loyalty' (1980) 29 *Emory Law Journal* 909, 942 fn 129.

[143] E O'Brien, *The Lawyer: his character and rule of holy life, after the manner of George Herbert's Country parson* (London, William Pickering, 1842).

[144] Patterson (n 142) 941–43.

[145] Marston (n 79) 499.

[146] Patterson (n 142) 941 citing Alabama Code Of Ethics 1887, rule 21.

[147] ibid 935.

[148] ibid 914–15.

[149] Andrews (n 14) 1442.

[150] Pearce (n 129) 243.

[151] Andrews (n 14) 1446.

rule allowing attorneys to breach client confidence to prevent criminal conduct, including fraud, was amended to only allow disclosure to prevent imminent death or substantial bodily injury.[152] The litigation emphasis was reduced by distinguishing the attorney's role as advocate, adviser, intermediary, evaluator and negotiator. The default role, however, remained adversarial.[153]

Changes to the 1983 rules subsequently addressed some of the issues originally canvassed for inclusion and some new issues. Areas addressed by Ethics 2000 was strengthening of the pro bono obligation and lawyers' responsibility to report corporate fraud. In 2002 the ABA amended the new rules to address multi-jurisdictional practice.[154] In 2003, in response to Enron, the rule on confidentiality was adjusted to allow the kind of whistleblowing originally proposed by Ethics 2000.[155] In 2009 a report on possible changes to the ABA Code of Conduct by the Ethics 20/20 Commission recommended rule changes mainly focused on technological change and growth of global legal practice.[156]

D. Enforcement

Enforcement of codes of conduct was through education, normalisation, peer pressure, insurance premiums and so on. More formal paths included the provision of complaint mechanisms or formal misconduct charges. Successful complainants were typically compensated while lawyers found guilty of misconduct faced sanctions including disbarment or striking off. Legalisation ensured these remedies could be more easily pursued by regulatory authorities or disgruntled clients. Complaint and disciplinary processes were sometimes separate, as in England and Wales, or joined, as in the US. This made data from different jurisdictions difficult to compare. Local factors could impact on the particulars of disciplinary prosecutions.

Arthurs observed that until the 1970s the legal profession in Ontario, Canada was dominated by lawyers from elite firms, abetted by leading counsel and members of the local gentry. Discipline operated secretively, allowing firms to police themselves and deal with misconduct outside of professional disciplinary procedures. By the 1990s various factors contributed to more openness and accountability: 'improvement of accounting systems, increases in the sums being dealt with, greater aggressiveness by more sophisticated corporate clients, declining deference towards respected institutions across society'.[157] These factors forced elite firms into the orbit of formal regulation and made the Law Society handle cases transparently.

An environmental factor changing the behaviour of the professional body was the advent of malpractice insurance, which became mandatory in Ontario in the early

---

[152] ibid and fn 464.
[153] ibid 1454.
[154] ibid 1447.
[155] ibid fn 501.
[156] LS Terry, 'Globalization and The ABA Commission on Ethics 20/20: Reflections on Missed Opportunities And The Road Not Taken' (2014) 43 *Hofstra Law Review* 95.
[157] HW Arthurs, 'The Dead Parrot: Does Professional Self-Regulation Exhibit Vital Signs' (1995) 33 *Alberta Law Review* 800, 807.

1970s. Arthurs suggested that the need of the Ontario Law Society to become a self-insurer gave it a stake in reducing the incidence of claims. Rising premiums forced it to make different kinds of intervention leading to adjustments of practice management by law firms, including control systems, specialisation, and in-firm training.

Arthurs' analyses of the academic literature on professional regulation, found disciplinary mechanisms generally portrayed as self-serving, flawed, or unreliable. Following his account of the legalisation of regulation in Ontario, Arthurs suggested that:

> lawyers in Canada are subject to serious discipline for just four reasons: because they have been guilty of theft, fraud, forgery or other some other criminal offence; because they have violated a fiduciary duty imposed on them by law; because they are unable to carry on their practices due to physical or mental disability or serious addiction; or because they have failed to respond to inquiries from their governing body.[158]

The identity of professional regulators therefore did not matter because regulation did not materially affect professional conduct. Rather, he suggested three factors did: 'the personal characteristics of the lawyer, the professional circumstances of his or her practice and the ethical economy of the profession'.[159] The last of these factors determined what attracted the attention of regulators. Activity undermining trust in the profession, such as financial fraud, was a priority whereas ethical behaviour was not. Thus, Arthurs argued, ethical conduct did not need regulation by self-governing professional bodies.

Trends in enforcing professional discipline were replicated elsewhere in the common law world. In England and Wales, cases against elite lawyers were rare, although there was no evidence of regulatory capture of the Law Society. It was, however, under pressure to regulate more effectively, hence the Solicitors Act 1974. The introduction of a mutual scheme of compulsory insurance in 1975 had a significant impact on regulation.[160] The volume of complaints and burden of claims led to the addition of extensive rules on client care to the SPR in the 1990s.

The available evidence suggested that disciplinary cases were low whether mechanisms were self-regulatory or independent. Research on the Solicitors Disciplinary Tribunal in England and Wales showed numbers appearing were consistently below 300, despite the profession more than trebling in size in the years between 1990 and 2015.[161] However, for more than half of that period, prosecution of cases was by the SRA, the regulator installed by government. A feature of these English data comparable with Arthur's conclusions was the very high number of financial misconduct cases and relatively few prosecutions of genuine ethical infractions.

Genuine ethics attracting discipline often arose in exceptional circumstances.[162] This did not mean that professional discipline would be redundant if financial

---

[158] ibid 802.
[159] ibid 803.
[160] A Boon, 'Understanding lawyer default in England and Wales: An analysis of insurance and complaints data' (2017) 24(2) *International Journal of the Legal Profession* 91.
[161] A Boon and A Whyte, 'An Analysis of Solicitors' Disciplinary Processes in England and Wales from 1994 to 2015' (2021) 28(2) *International Journal of the Legal Profession* 129.
[162] See eg *Brett v SRA* [2014] EWHC 2974 (Admin).

misconduct were dealt with in criminal courts. In many cases, it might not meet the threshold for criminal prosecution.[163] Nor was lack of ethics prosecutions evidence of professional norms failing. It could be that most lawyers try to meet standards most of the time. The few ethics misconduct cases that do raise issues of ethics are both informative and salutary. Ethics tends to be for the observant, discipline for the crooked.

V. DISCUSSION

A. Self-regulation

As external regulation morphed into self-regulation the emphasis was on education and entry requirements, but attention to discipline increased during the twentieth century, leading to codes of conduct, more specific standards of behaviour and increased emphasis on ethical education. The English Law Society was exceptional in its use of regulation to cement monopoly, the work of most legal professions being well-established before their attempts to regulate more effectively. The regulatory trajectories of legal professions took different paths. Both the ABA in the US and the CBA in Canada were federal membership organisations[164] and influenced each other. But Canada adopted Langdell's case method, with the aim of producing gentleman lawyers,[165] while some US Law Schools, notably Columbia and Yale, resisted holding to the aim of training generalist lawyer-statesmen.[166]

Pue described the CBA as more gentlemen's club than regulatory body, with an ethos of volunteerism and public service[167] and it gradually lost a regulatory role to the FCLS. Recently, the CBA appeared to resurrect a regulatory claim as 'a powerful, credible [voice] for legislative, regulatory and policy development in many areas of the law' as the 'only national association with a mandate to protect the professional and commercial interests of the legal profession and to promote the rule of law'. The ABA managed to hold on to a regulatory interest with its model rules of conduct.

Andrews suggested that the material for the modern codes reflected the medieval oaths, which balanced two kinds of concern; the need for loyalty in the lawyer client relationship (competence, confidentiality and fees) and public service (service to the poor) reflecting ambivalence about dependence on lawyers.[168] Changes to the modern day merely reflected changes in context.[169] Therefore the public service ideal in post-revolutionary America absorbed litigation fairness.[170] Lawyers' obligation to the rule

---

[163] Boon and Whyte (n 131).
[164] Membership of the CBA was voluntary except in New Brunswick where a deal was struck requiring local lawyers to join, www.cba.org/Our-Work.
[165] Pue (n 29).
[166] RW Gordon, 'The Case For (and Against) Harvard' (1995) 93 *Michigan Law Review* 1231, 1235.
[167] Pue (n 29) 81.
[168] Andrews (n 14) 1455.
[169] ibid 1455.
[170] ibid 1422.

of law balanced client autonomy with the public interest. The themes underwent considerable change of emphasis after the advent of the adversarial system, reflecting the rising importance of representation, client loyalty and concomitant commitments to confidentiality and legal professional privilege. Individualism was represented by adversary principles.

Increased legalisation of disciplinary codes occurred in all the jurisdictions during the twentieth century. The Model Code 1969 represented the ABA's movement from a Weberian 'traditional' institution to a 'bureaucratic' institution regulated by an expedient set of rules.[171] If standards were to be enforced, lawyers wanted precise rules.[172] This led to controversial rethinking of the meaning of traditional duties, generating additional material.[173] The alternative seemed to be to rely on broad and general statements, such as the Principles or Core Duties now used by the legal professions in England. The ABA was sensitive to criticism of its codes and compromised aspects of adversary ethics even though, as Ted Schneyer pointed out, the 'partisan behaviour' cited by critics was often not allowed.[174]

Simon's original critique of neutral partisanship proposed de-professionalisation of advocacy. He later modified this to give lawyers discretion on who they represented and how. Schwarz made similar arguments but was troubled about some clients being unrepresented.[175] He proposed that courts or other authorities should assign lawyers to clients. Nicolson and Webb suggested legal professions have panels of lawyers prepared to represent unpopular clients.[176] None of these suggestions were implemented anywhere. The ABAs response to critics did not always move it further away from traditional conceptions of role. In 1977 it amended the model official oath for admission as an attorney, dropping a promise not to bring 'unjust' causes in case it encouraged prejudgement of cases.[177]

B. The Role of Rules in Regulation

Codes of Conduct became increasingly important in describing desired lawyer conduct, providing a focus for education, practice, and discipline. The tendency to legalise norms attracted criticism, primarily it was argued, because other factors, including moral character, determined ethical conduct.[178] Nicolson suggested detailed codes 'cocoon lawyers from constantly looking to their conscience and sense of right, and from questioning the notions of justice and morality contained within law and

---

[171] Hazard (n 83) 1254–55.
[172] Andrews (n 14) 1457.
[173] ibid 1456.
[174] T Schneyer, 'Moral Philosophy's Standard Misconception of Legal Ethics' (1984) *Wisconsin Law Review* 1529.
[175] ML Schwartz, 'The Zeal of the Civil Advocate' (1983) 8(3) *American Bar Foundation Research Journal* 543, 561.
[176] D Nicolson and J Webb, *Professional Legal Ethics: Critical Interrogations* (Oxford, Oxford University Press, 1999).
[177] Andrews (n 14) 1453.
[178] RL Abel, 'Why Does the ABA Promulgate Ethical Rules?' (1981) 59 *Texas Law Review* 639; D Nicolson, 'Making lawyers moral? Ethical codes and moral character' (2006) *Legal Studies* 601.

legal systems', arguing that socialisation would be more effective.[179] Nicolson argued this would affect guidance to practitioners, proposing a commentary on principles of ethics mainly for educational purposes and pared down rules of conduct.[180]

Disaffection with conduct rules coincided with revival of a tradition in Greek philosophy that only a those of virtuous character make moral decisions.[181] Virtue ethics offered valuable insights into professional roles[182] but harked back to a time of long apprenticeships. In the pressured environment of modern practice, virtue was supported by normative clarity. Economists argued that, for practitioners without the time or inclination for ethical rumination, rules were efficient.[183] Choices were easier with fixed points clarifying the path between competing considerations.[184]

Proponents of fair disciplinary processes argued that regulators, prosecutors, and disciplinary tribunals should operate under clear rules when lawyers faced disciplinary offences.[185] Commenting on the Canadian McRuer Report, Flaus argued that expectation of conduct being known 'intuitively' by members of the profession was rationalisation of lack of clarity.[186] This was important both for procedure and offences. The argument that lawyers offend in unpredictable ways did not justify vague charges. The analogy, open-ended criminal law would be clearly unacceptable.

For the reason identified by McRuer the trend towards lists of Principles invited uncertainty. They were an effective way of projecting group values internally, for educational purposes, and externally, for clarifying public roles, but they could not stand alone, even for these purposes.[187] Their inherent ambiguity raised possibilities for imposing new responsibilities. A specific target was commercial lawyers who, it was proposed, could be sanctioned for failing to control corporate clients under a duty to uphold the rule of law.[188]

Considering the role of the City of London firm, Freshfield's, in the collapse of Lehman Bros. Kershaw and Moorhead suggested SRA Principle 1, requiring 'upholding the rule of law', could make them responsible for the bank's foreseeably unlawful actions.[189] More generally, Loughrey suggested that commercial solicitors might breach Principle 1 by 'setting up schemes that, while strictly legal, undermine the spirit of the law' while, at the same time, breaching Principles 2, 3 and 6.[190]

---

[179] D Nicolson, 'Mapping Professional Ethics: The Form and focus of the codes' (1998) 1(1) *Legal Ethics* 51.
[180] ibid 66–69.
[181] A MacIntyre, *After Virtue* (London, NY, Bloomsbury Academic 2011).
[182] J Oakley and D Cocking, *Virtue Ethics and Professional Roles* (Cambridge, Cambridge University Press, 2001).
[183] Boon (n 160).
[184] ibid.
[185] Flaus (n 92) 377–78 citing The McRuer Report at 1182.
[186] ibid 357.
[187] J Ladd, 'Legalism and Medical Ethics' in A Flores (ed), *Professional Ideals* (Belmont CA, Wadsworth Publishing Co Inc, 1988); W Simon, '*Ethical Discretion in Lawyering*' (1988) 101 *Harvard Law Review* 1083.
[188] D Kershaw and R Moorhead, 'Consequential Responsibility for Client Wrongs: Lehman Brothers and the Regulation of the Legal Profession' (2013) 76 *MLR* 26; J Loughrey, 'Accountability and the Regulation of the Large Law Firm Lawyer' (2014) 77(5) *Modern Law Review* 732.
[189] ibid Kershaw and Moorhead 56–57.
[190] Loughrey (n 188) 758–59.

While control of corporate behaviour was desirable, clearer obligations were required if client rights, as important an aim of the rule of law as legality, were not to be compromised. That was the line the English courts took in deciding that lawyers could not be disciplined for breaches of norms not constituting clear code breaches.[191]

While codes generally became more detailed with the need to enforce, the codes for solicitors in England and Wales became increasingly general. It was not clear whether this trend would be replicated elsewhere. The English Bar regulator, the BSB, went in the other direction. It used outcomes alongside rules to 'explain the reasons for the regulatory scheme and what it is designed to achieve'. Taken from the regulatory objectives defined in the Legal Services Act 2007 its outcomes were said to not be mandatory rules, but 'factors which BSB regulated persons or unregistered barristers should have in mind' when applying Core Duties or Conduct Rules.[192]

The flexibility envisaged in the new English rules came close to operationalising Postema's argument that lawyers fulfilled a 'recourse role; if the answer to an ethical problem was not satisfactorily resolved by rules, they should have recourse to the purpose the role served'.[193]

A recourse role, expanding or contracting in response to the underlying institutional objectives of role, envisaged lawyers having discretion to disobey codes when rules contradicted the objectives of the role.[194] Arguably, this should depend on the lawyer's overriding duty to the rule of law and would have required them to have a thorough and principled understanding of the relationship.

VI. CONCLUSION

The organisation of lawyers in professional associations led to the expression of different relationships to the rule of law. These emphasised the need for independence from the state for advocacy professions and service to the state, public service, for business lawyers. Regulation focused on admission standards and then education, reflecting belief in the importance of character and socialisation. The need to discipline lawyers and, if necessary, remove them from practice, led to more advanced regulatory machinery and standards of professional behaviour. Disciplinary regimes generally became more elaborate and transparent with the need for explicit regulatory focus. Discipline however, usually dealt with dishonest behaviour.

---

[191] *Daphne Evadney Portia O'Connor v Bar Standards Board* [2014] EWHC 4324 (QB).
[192] *BSB Handbook 2017* (v 4.4) General 16.
[193] G Postema, 'Moral Responsibility in Professional Ethics' (1980) 55 *NYUL Rev* 63.
[194] S Kadish and M Kadish, *Discretion to Disobey* (California, Stanford University Press, 1973) 31.

12
Representation

I. INTRODUCTION

THIS CHAPTER EXPLORES the expression of duties to clients in codes of conduct. The framework is provided by the standard conception of the lawyer's role (the standard conception) as the best-known model of client-focused lawyer behaviour. As noted in previous chapters the main principles of the standard conception, neutrality and partisanship, were based on academic analysis of publications of the American Bar Association (hereafter ABA), principally the 1983 Model Rules of professional conduct. This analysis was influential in the international literature, but its correspondence with rules in other jurisdictions was untested. The purpose of this chapter is therefore to see whether these other common law jurisdictions developed obligations to clients in the same way and, to the extent they differ, how differences in conception relate to the rule of law. The third element of the standard conception, accountability, is the subject of the next chapter.

II. THEORY

Codes of conduct, or other expressions of standards of behaviour, potentially served several purposes, from advertisement to regulation, addressed to different audiences. Analysts of professions considered professional culture and ethical codes[1] or regulatory standards and educational programmes[2] as defining characteristics. Other analysts suggested that research into codes should focus on important issues raised in the social science literature on lawyers: the processes of production, the audiences for them, and the functions they performed.[3] One purpose of reading codes is to

---

[1] A Flexner, *Is Social Work a Profession?* (address before the National Conference of Charities and Correction, Baltimore, 17May 1915); E Greenwood, 'Attributes of a Profession' *Social Work* (July 1957) 45.
[2] TJ Johnson. *Professions and Power* (London, Palgrave Macmillan, 1972) 23–35; CO Houle, *Continuing Learning in the Professions* (San Francisco and London, Jossey-Bass, 1980); CW Wolfram, 'Modern Legal Ethics' (St Paul Minnesota, West Publishing Co, 1986); E Schein, *Professional Education: Some New Directions* (New York, McGraw-Hill, 1972) and MD Bayles, *Professional Ethics*, 2nd edn (Belmont, California, Wadsworth Publishing, 1989) 14.
[3] L De Groot-Van Leeuwen and WT De Groot, 'Studying Codes of Conduct: A descriptive framework for Comparative Research' (1998) 1(2) *Legal Ethics* 155.

determine the extent to which they subscribe to a professional 'role morality', distinct from what is considered the ordinary morality of society.[4]

Modern codes of conduct reflected the themes of medieval lawyer's oaths[5] but, by the time extended codes appeared in the twentieth century, these themes were interpreted to reflect Enlightenment thinking about the importance of the individual in society and, particularly their agency. Various scholars speculated that the standard conception may have been inspired by leading members of the English Bar, notably Erskine and Brougham, whose exploits were known in the US. The modern codes of lawyer conduct in different jurisdictions produced differences in broad-brush obligations.

In this volume, the analysis so far suggested that specialist advocacy professions had stronger alignment with the standard conception than more business orientated lawyers such as English solicitors. Professions that did not have an advocacy branch, such as the American attorneys or Canadian lawyers, fell between the two conceptions. As described in chapter nine, academic debates concerning the validity of the lawyer's professional role swung between moral philosophy and political philosophy. Some authors justified the standard conception by its contribution to the rights dimension of the rule of law. Logically, the role of lawyers should be to make operational the Enlightenment aspiration that individual liberty should only be constrained by the proviso that it did not impinge on others' rights.

In 2016 I proposed a model of the legal professional relationships.[6] This placed different kinds of lawyer and client relationship on a spectrum reflecting the client autonomy they allowed and promoted and gave an example in operation. The lowest level of autonomy was present in Paternalism, a traditional approach in which lawyers determined client needs and how to meet them. Next, Participation envisaged lawyers and clients working out ends, and possibly means, together with key-decisions based on lawyers' advice. Next, Autonomy saw the lawyer promoting the client's idea of his own good including their moral choices, an opportunity perhaps confined to the wealthy. Finally, with Empowerment lawyers enable clients to use the law themselves to their own ends, carrying out actions usually performed by lawyers for themselves, a development signalled by the so-called unbundling of legal services.

III. CODES OF CONDUCT AND THE STANDARD CONCEPTION:
COMPARATIVE ANALYSIS

A. Comparing Codes

My limited previous analysis of the regulatory provisions of the ABA code and the different kinds of legal profession in England showed important differences in the

---

[4] D Luban, *Lawyers and Justice: An Ethical Study* (New Jersey, Princeton University Press, 1988); WH Simon, 'Role Differentiation and Lawyers' Ethics: A Critique of Some Academic Perspectives' (2010) 23 *Georgetown Journal of Legal Ethics* 987.
[5] CR Andrews, *Standards of Conduct for Lawyers: An 800-Year Evolution* (2004) 57 *SMU Law Review* 1385.
[6] A Boon, *The Ethics and Conduct of Lawyers in England and Wales*, 3rd edn (Oxford, Hart Publishing, 2014) 300–9.

298 *Representation*

obligations to clients.[7] The analysis conducted for this chapter focused on the second conventional stage of comparative analysis, evaluation of, 'external law', the 'law as actually stated … expressed concretely, in words, action, or orality'.[8] Stage three, evaluating how the internal law operated in cultural context, and the fourth stage, reflection on legal culture formed part of the discussion in the previous two chapters. This showed that professional norms were subject to different kinds of external influence and sometimes changed as a result.

This chapter compares provisions for neutrality and partisanship in the codes of conduct of lawyers. Most of the work was done in 2018 and the codes of conduct or model rules referred to are those operating at that time in England and Wales, the US, Australia, Canada, and New Zealand. Although reference may be made to historical rules for context, the rules used for comparative purposes were the most recent available at the time the analysis was done in 2018 as follows:

Australia: Legal Profession Uniform Conduct (Barristers) Rules 2015 (hereafter LPUC(B)R 2015).[9] Law Council of Australia Australian Solicitors' Conduct Rules 2011 (hereafter LCA ASCR 2011).[10]

Canada: Federation of Law Societies of Canada Model Code of Professional Conduct 2014 (hereafter FLSC MCPC 2014).[11]

England and Wales: Bar Standards Board Code of Conduct 2014 (hereafter BSB CC 2014),[12] Solicitor Regulation Authority Code of Conduct 2011 (hereafter SRA CC 2011).[13]

New Zealand: Lawyers and Conveyancers Act (Lawyers: Conduct and Client Care) Rules 2008 (hereafter NZ LCCR 2008).[14]

United States: ABA Model Rules of Professional Conduct 1983 (hereafter the ABA MRPC 1983).[15]

Both the Bar Standards Board and Solicitors Regulation Authority issued new codes since the analysis, but these are substantively the same in relation to the obligations considered. Where necessary later codes are referred to.

B. Selecting Markers

The first step was to identify the obligation which most closely related to the principles of the client facing principles of the standard conception: neutrality and partisanship.

---

[7] A Boon, 'The legal professions' new handbooks: narratives, standards and values' (2016) 19(2) *Legal Ethics* 207.

[8] EJ Eberle, 'The Methodology of Comparative Law' (2011) 16(1) *Roger Williams University Law Review* 51.

[9] https://legislation.nsw.gov.au/inforce/5a7fbed4-700d-45da-84dc-b6f6b0fb2870/2015-243.pdf.

[10] www.lawcouncil.asn.au/policy-agenda/regulation-of-the-profession-and-ethics/australian-solicitors-conduct-rules#:~:text=The%20Australian%20Solicitors%20Conduct%20Rules%20%28ASCR%29%20were%20collaboratively,professional%20conduct%20rules%20for%20all%20solicitors%20in%20Australia.

[11] https://flsc.ca/national-initiatives/model-code-of-professional-conduct/.

[12] www.barstandardsboard.org.uk/for-barristers/bsb-handbook-and-code-guidance/the-bsb-handbook.html.

[13] www.sra.org.uk/solicitors/standards-regulations/code-conduct-solicitors/.

[14] www.legislation.govt.nz/regulation/public/2008/0214/latest/whole.html#DLM143784.

[15] www.americanbar.org/groups/professional_responsibility/publications/model_rules_of_professional_conduct/.

In each case these were divided into two kinds of obligation. These are referred to as markers, based on Moffett (chapter one), referring to regulation by 'social markers' passed from generation to generation as values and moral codes. The second was to consider the presence and strength of the marker as an indicator of either neutrality or partisanship. This involved considering various factors: the type of provision (rule, guidance or commentary), the form of words used (indicating a strong or weak commitment) and the strength of the obligation (must, should, may).

The framework set out in Figure 1 used key markers for neutrality from the earlier study: (1) a duty to accept consumers as clients,[16] and (2) to accept client objectives including those the lawyer may morally disagree with. The first reflected the rule of law principle that all citizens were equal before the law and that the lawyer's role was to give them voice. The second marker strongly indicated the commitment to support client autonomy, by giving voice to clients' moral perspectives.

Figure 1 Framework for analysing codes commitments to the 'standard conception'

Neutrality	N1: Duty to accept consumers as clients
	N2: Duty to accept client objectives, including those with a moral component
Partisanship	P1: Duty of loyalty (devotion or zeal)
	P2: Duty to use all lawful means

The markers for partisanship were adjusted from the earlier research. The duty of loyalty replaced regard for third party interests, which operated as a negative indictor of client commitments in the previous model. Therefore, the two markers for partisanship were: (1) the way in which the duty of loyalty was manifested, and (2) the nature of the obligation placed on the lawyer (if any) to use all legal means to achieve the client's objective. The first marker expressed the idea that a lawyer really was a citizen's 'champion against all the world'. The second indicated support for client autonomy by using legal methods the client would use if they had legal skills.

A question arising from the choice of rules was whether they were the most appropriate expressions of professions' approaches to client autonomy in the lawyer and client relationship. It was arguable, for example, that a more revealing rule on client autonomy would be sexual relationships between lawyers and clients. Historically, this issue was likely to be addressed from a moralistic perspective rather than as an issue of abuse of power and hence, autonomy. In the mid-1900s Sir Thomas Lund's *A Guide to the Professional Conduct and Etiquette of Solicitors* (Lund's Guide)[17] referred to a disciplinary case where an English solicitor used his position 'to cloak and further an adulterous association' but noted, perhaps regretfully, that 'to be a

---

[16] In this context the term 'consumer' refers to individuals not yet accepted as clients, but owed responsibilities.
[17] T Lund, *A Guide to the Professional Conduct and Etiquette of Solicitors* (London, Law Society, 1960).

co-respondent in a divorce suit is not in itself professional misconduct'.[18] When the issue was reframed as an abuse of power in the 1980s and 1990s research focused on sexual relationships between therapeutic practitioners or teachers and their 'clients'.[19]

The 1990s edition of *The Guide* warned solicitors that it could be a breach of the fiduciary relationship to enter sexual relationships with clients,[20] guidance watered down in the Solicitors' Code of Conduct 2007 (hereafter SCC 2007)[21] and omitted from the SRA CC 2011. The Canadian rules advised against such relations in a commentary on conflicts of interest.[22] The New Zealand rules were unusual in seeking to regulate sexual relations between lawyers and clients. The 1990 rules provided it could be a breach of the relationship of confidence and trust,[23] suggesting that 'A lawyer must not enter into an intimate personal relationship with a client where to do so would or could be inconsistent with the trust and confidence reposed by the client'.[24] Such relationships were banned completely 'where the lawyer is representing the client in any domestic relations matter'.[25]

In 2002 the ABA Model Rules of Professional Conduct (hereafter the ABA MRPC 1983) were amended to implement an Ethics 20/20 proposal to ban 'sexual relations with a client unless a consensual sexual relationship existed between them when the client-lawyer relationship commenced'.[26] A comment on the rule asserted: 'The relationship is almost always unequal; thus, a sexual relationship between lawyer and client can involve unfair exploitation of the lawyer's fiduciary role, in violation of the lawyer's basic ethical obligation not to use the trust of the client to the client's disadvantage'.[27] It went on to indicate a number of risks: impairment of the lawyers' 'exercise of independent professional judgment', the confidentiality of non-privileged communication, and the difficulty of obtaining 'adequate informed consent'. The application of the rule regardless of whether there was prejudice to the client, was criticised for being both underinclusive (not including abusive pre-existing relationships) and over inclusive (for example, not allowing informed consent).[28]

Rules on sexual relationships were informative about professions' sensitivity to issues of power. They did not, however, describe where power formally lay in the lawyer and client relationship and whether lawyers were bound to accept clients' legal objectives in the way clients determined. This, arguably, was the real test of how far legal professions supported individuality and client personal autonomy.

---

[18] ibid 70.
[19] B Pearson and N Piazza, 'Classification of Dual Relationships in the Helping Professions' (1997) 37 *Counselor Education and Supervision* 89.
[20] N Taylor (ed), *The Guide to the Professional Conduct of Solicitors*, 7th edn (London, The Law Society, 1996) r.12.07, Guidance Note 1(b) (hereafter *The Guide*).
[21] Solicitors' Code of Conduct 2007, Guidance to Rule 3 Conflicts of Interest, note 49.
[22] FLSC MCPC 2014 Commentary on 3.4-1, note [11].
[23] *New Zealand Rules of Professional Conduct for Barristers and Solicitors* (Wellington, NZLS, 1990) r 1.01.
[24] ibid r.5.7.
[25] ibid r.5.7.1.
[26] ABA MRPC 1983, r 1.8(j).
[27] ibid Comment 20.
[28] PR Bower and TE Stern, 'Conflict of Interest: The Absolute Ban on Lawyer-Client Sexual Relationships Is Not Absolutely Necessary' (2003) 16 *Georgetown Journal of Legal Ethics* 535.

C. Assessing Role Differentiation

To facilitate comparison it was useful to compare codes of conduct provisions conformity to the standard conception. The following scale was used to allocate a number according to the presence or absence of relevant obligations and the level of obligation imposed, for example, whether mandatory (must), permissive (may) or aspirational (should). The focus of this exercise was the code provision most clearly expressing a specific standard or value. This only considered qualifications of a duty expressed in the relevant provision or section. Other restrictions, the wider constraints of legality, are considered in the next chapter. Numbers allocated in this way were to facilitate discussion rather than definitive judgments on particular codes or provisions.

Table 1 Scale of measurement

9	A1		
8	A2	wide scope, mandatory	High
7	A3	(must), enforceable (rule)	
6	B1		
5	B2	Relevant provision (rule/ outcome); aspirational (should),	Medium
4	B3		
3	C1		
2	C2	relevant provision – narrow scope; permissive (may)	Low
1	C3		
0	D	No relevant provision	

IV. NEUTRALITY INDICATORS IN LAWYERS' CODES OF CONDUCT

A. Neutrality: Accepting Consumers as Clients (N1)

The English barristers' obligation to accept instructions to appear in court was recognised in the Bar Code of Conduct 1981 (hereafter *BCC 1981*) under a rule headed 'Acceptance of instructions and the 'Cab-rank rule', which committed barristers to accepting briefs as presented. A recent incarnation the Bar Standards Board *Code of Conduct* (2014) (hereafter *BSB CC 2014*), stated that:

> if a barrister receives instructions from a professional client to act on the standard Contractual terms of work (or equivalent) and the instructions are appropriate taking into account their experience, seniority and/or field or practice, they must (subject to the exceptions in rC30) accept those instructions irrespective of: The identity of the client; The nature of the case to which the instructions relate; Whether the client is paying privately or is publicly funded; and Any belief or opinion which you may have formed as to the character, reputation, cause, conduct, guilt or innocence of the client.[29]

---

[29] Bar Code of Conduct 1981 (BCC 1981) (London, General Council of the Bar, 1981) para 601(a) and (b).

The exceptions in c.30 were numerous, but not unreasonable, relating to factors such as competence. The cab rank rule was apparently strengthened in BSB CC 2014 by removal of one of the exceptions in c30, refusing briefs when no proper fee was offered, but the intended purpose was that they should not be obliged to accept low legal aid fees.[30] Although approved barristers were able to accept clients without being briefed by solicitors,[31] the cab rank rule only applied when instructions were received for advocacy from professional clients, such as solicitors, accountants, and others. This left the task of 'screening' clients to other professionals and scope to refuse clients seeking other services.

Solicitors were entitled to conduct advocacy in minor courts since the nineteenth century but, they had no equivalent of the cab rank rule.[32] In 1990, legislation ended the Bar's monopoly of higher court advocacy.[33] In the debates preceding enactment there were proposals that all those solicitors gaining higher rights should also be subject to a cab rank rule. At one stage, the Law Society was concerned that the House of Lords might impose one by amendment.[34] The Solicitors Practice Rules 1990 (hereafter SPR 1990) anticipated solicitors gaining the same right of advocacy as barristers[35] an amendment stating '[a]ny solicitors acting as an advocate shall at all times comply with the Law Society's Code for Advocacy'.[36]

The Law Society's concern that a cab rank rule might be imposed proved ill-founded. Nevertheless, a Law Society Code for Advocacy was introduced in 1993. This copied key Bar rules, including that part of the cab rank rule which prohibited refusing instructions on the grounds that 'the conduct, opinions or beliefs of the client are unacceptable to the advocate or to any section of the public'.[37] The advocacy rules were carried into the SCC 2007[38] at which point there was a negligible substantive difference between the professions in relation to advocacy consumers.

The Law Society's Code for Advocacy was dropped with the introduction of the SCC 2007. The essence of a cab rank principle survived in a chapter on Litigation and Advocacy stating that solicitor advocates could not refuse to act because the nature of the case or the conduct, opinions or beliefs of the prospective client were unacceptable to the advocate or to any section of the public.[39] This was not reproduced in codes of conduct in the SRA CC 2011, which referred only to a general duty not

---

[30] BCC 1981, para 604(b). The Bar Council had previously 'deemed' graduated fees for family and criminal legal aid work not proper professional fee for the purpose of the exception and barristers were not obliged to accept that work. Although a rule on adequate fees was retained in Bar Standards Board Code of Conduct 2014 (hereafter BSB CC 2014),[30] the BSB decided that deeming a fee inadequate was a decision that a representative body, rather than a regulatory body, should make.

[31] A scheme called Bar Direct (JA Flood and A Whyte, *Straight There No Detours: Direct Access to Barristers* (London, 2008). University of Westminster School of Law Research Paper No 09-05, https://papers.ssrn.com/sol3/papers.cfm?abstract_id=1321492.

[32] Boon (n 7).

[33] Courts and Legal Services Act 1990.

[34] 'Donaldson advocates general application of cab-rank rule' (1990) (*Law Society Gazette*, 28 February 1987) 3.

[35] Law Society, *Standards and Guidance Committee minutes* (11 July 1990).

[36] SPR 1990, r 16A.

[37] Law Society's Code for Advocacy 1993, para 2.4.2(c).

[38] SCC 2007, r 11.04.

[39] ibid r 11.04(1)(a) and (b).

to discriminate unlawfully when deciding whether to accept clients. Solicitor advocates with higher rights had suddenly become free to refuse those seeking advocacy provided no unlawful discrimination was involved[40] probably defined with reference to protected characteristics defined in statute.[41]

Bartlett and Haller claimed that the adoption of the 'cab rank rule' by Australian barristers was part of the attempted emulation of the English bar.[42] The version in the Code of Conduct of barristers in New South Wales was in very similar terms to those in the Bar Code for England and Wales.[43] Australian model rules for non-barrister lawyers contained no obligatory provisions on accepting clients.

In the US, attorneys' written obligations to accept people as clients were relatively weak. The Canons of Ethics 1908 contained no requirement that attorneys accept anybody, although they did provide that a lawyer 'assigned as counsel for an indigent prisoner ought not to ask to be excused for any trivial reason, and should always exert his best efforts in his behalf'.[44] The Canons also stated that it was 'the right of the lawyer to undertake the defense of a person accused of crime, regardless of his personal opinion as to the guilt of the accused'.[45] This afforded lawyers the privilege of non-accountability rather than obligating them to represent.

In the ABA Model Code of Professional Responsibility 1969 (hereafter ABA MCPR 1969) Canon 2 was headed 'A Lawyer Should Assist the Legal Profession in Fulfilling Its Duty to Make Legal Counsel Available'. Extensive disciplinary rules under this heading provided no concrete obligation to represent. Nor did the Ethical Considerations provide much in the way of formal obligation. The first section merely stated that:

> [t]he need of members of the public for legal services is met only if they recognize their legal problems, appreciate the importance of seeking assistance, and are able to obtain the services of acceptable legal counsel. Hence, important functions of the legal profession are to educate laymen to recognize their problems, to facilitate the process of intelligent selection of lawyers, and to assist in making legal services fully available.[46]

A footnote to the section suggested that it was 'not only the right but the duty of the profession as a whole to utilise such methods as may be developed to bring the services of its members to those who need them, so long as this can be done ethically and with dignity'.[47] It also referred to other authority to similar effect but made no relevant obligatory provisions.

The Model Rules 1983 Rule 1.2, covering the scope of representation, provided that '[a] lawyer's representation of a client, including representation by appointment, does not constitute an endorsement of the client's political, economic, social or moral

---

[40] SRA CC 2011 O.2.1 and IB 2.5.
[41] Equality Act 2010.
[42] F Bartlett and L Haller, 'Australia: Legal Services Regulation in Australia – Innovative Co-regulation' in A Boon (ed), *International Perspectives on the Regulation of Lawyers and Legal Services* (Oxford, Hart Publishing, 2017) 161, 166.
[43] Legal Profession Uniform Conduct (Barristers) Rules 2015, r 17.
[44] ABA Canons of Ethics 1908, Canon 4.
[45] ibid Canon 5.
[46] ABA MCPR 1969, Ethical Consideration 2.1.
[47] See fn 4 referring to *ABA Opinion* 320 (1968).

views or activities'.[48] While excusing lawyers from the moral implications of representation, this provision was, again, not an obligation to represent. Thus, what was supposedly a fundamental principle of the standard conception was not actually a requirement in the US. The vaunted, and much criticised, principle of neutrality was, when it came to client representation, largely rhetorical.

The Canadian Model rules provided that 'A lawyer must make legal services available to the public efficiently …'.[49] Commentary noted that, lawyers have 'a general right to decline a particular representation (except when assigned as counsel by a tribunal)', but it was said to be a right they should exercise 'prudently', particularly where finding representation might prove difficult. Generally, it was said:

> a lawyer should not exercise the right merely because a person seeking legal services or that person's cause is unpopular or notorious, or because powerful interests or allegations of misconduct or malfeasance are involved, or because of the lawyer's private opinion about the guilt of the accused.[50]

New Zealand was exceptional in having a clear and unambiguous rule applying to all lawyers, not just those offering advocacy services. It stated that 'A lawyer as a professional person must be available to the public and must not, without good cause, refuse to accept instructions from any client or prospective client for services within the reserved areas of work that are within the lawyer's fields of practice'.[51] Assuming that morality or character based grounds were not perceived to be a 'good cause' for refusing clients, this rule was arguably the strongest of all the relevant rules, particularly because it was not restricted to lawyers undertaking advocacy.

All the legal professions recognised client selection as an issue. The strongest obligation to represent was that of all lawyers in New Zealand. The next were the barrister occupations, whose 'cab rank rules' were expressed in broad terms but had some limitations on scope. The North American professions presented a strong rhetoric of representation but no obligation, and the Australian and English solicitors recognised only an obligation to obey legal requirements. For these reasons the strength of the various obligations could be expressed as in Figure N1.

Figure N1 The obligation to accept consumers as clients

	US	Bar E&W	Sol E&W	New Zeal.	Aus Sol	Aus Bar	Can	
N1	4	7	0	9	0	7	5	32

B. Neutrality: Accepting Clients' Lawful Objectives (N2)

The cab rank principle only obliged lawyers to accept their client's existing failings, not what they wanted to do. The logic of the rule of law was that lawyers should

---
[48] ABA MRPC 1983, r 1.2(b).
[49] ibid r 4.1-1.
[50] ibid Commentary n [4].
[51] Lawyers and Conveyancers Act (Lawyers: Conduct and Client Care) Rules 2008, r 4.

also try to achieve client objectives because this promoted personal autonomy. This position was seldom clear cut in codes of conduct.

The ABA apparently supported accepting client's lawful objectives. The Disciplinary rules of the Model Code 1969 provided that lawyers '… shall not intentionally … [f]ail to 'seek the lawful objectives of his client through reasonably available means permitted by law and the Disciplinary Rules.'[52] The rule was however, fringed with qualifications and exceptions.

Attorneys could comply with etiquette that mandated concessions to professional opponents. Thus, for example, expecting lawyers to accede to 'reasonable requests of opposing counsel', be 'punctual in fulfilling all professional commitments' and avoid offensive tactics,[53] all contradicted being bound by client preferences for handling a matter. An attorney could also 'exercise his professional judgment to waive or fail to assert a right'.[54]

In the US the moral backlash following Watergate led to some weakening of the obligation to seek a client's lawful objectives. The ABA MRPC 1983 provided that 'a lawyer shall abide by a client's decisions concerning the objectives of representation and … shall consult with the client as to the means by which they are to be pursued'.[55] Although the rules noted that 'lawyers usually deferred to clients regarding such questions as … concern for third persons who might be adversely affected' they noted the possibility of disagreement 'about the means to be used to accomplish the client's objectives'.[56]

After outlining some thoughts on how disagreements might be resolved, the comment on the ABA rule concluded that, if there was 'fundamental disagreement with the client, the lawyer may withdraw from the representation'.[57] Thus, despite the language of obligation, attorneys did not need, ultimately, to accept their clients' objectives; moral compunction was an adequate reason to terminate representation. Hazard and Dondi interpreted the Anglo-American tradition as being that lawyers could refuse to carry out unconscionable though lawful purposes.[58]

The Canadian rules did not deal with client objectives but did talk of 'the need for the client to make fully informed decisions and provide instructions'.[59] They undermined the impression that lawyers were bound by 'instructions' by preventing withdrawal from representation except 'for good cause and on reasonable notice to the client'.[60] The succeeding rule provided that this could occur where there was 'serious loss of confidence between the lawyer and the client' evidenced when '… a lawyer is deceived by his client, the client refuses to accept and act upon the lawyer's advice on a significant point, a client is persistently unreasonable or uncooperative

---

[52] ABA MCPR 1969, DR 7-101.
[53] ibid DR 101-B.
[54] ibid.
[55] ABA MRPC 1983, r 1.2.
[56] ibid Comment 1.2(2).
[57] ibid.
[58] GC Hazard and A Dondi, *Legal Ethics: A Comparative Study* (California, Stanford University Press, 2004) 171.
[59] FLSC MCPC 2014, 3.2-1 Commentary [3].
[60] FLSC MCPC 2014, 3.7-1.

in a material respect, or the lawyer is facing difficulty in obtaining adequate instructions from the client.[61] Lawyers could therefore avoid accepting clients' objectives by giving advice conflicting with them.

In England and Wales, the Bar obligation relevant to accepting clients' lawful objectives was that 'you must promote fearlessly and by all proper and lawful means the *client's* best interests' without regarding consequences to yourself or others.[62] This raised questions of interpretation. The phrase 'all proper and lawful means', was ambiguous, 'proper' possibly provided an excuse for refusing to employ legal means on a client's behalf. Another reason for doubting that the rule promoted autonomy was the phrase 'the client's best interests'. This was potentially paternalistic compared with the ABA obligation, to 'abide by a client's decisions concerning the objectives of representation',[63] which apparently put the client in the driving seat. The Bar formula did not make it clear that the client, not the barrister, was defining their own best interest.

The lawyer identifying client needs and interests fitted the requirements of criminal defence, in which barristers were responsible to the court for the conduct of a trial. In BCC 1981 using 'all proper and lawful means' was qualified by a rule requiring barristers to refuse instructions limiting their ordinary authority or discretion in the conduct of proceedings in Court.[64] The Law Society Code for Advocacy included a version of the Bar rule stating that solicitor advocates were 'personally responsible for the conduct and presentation of their case'[65] but, when the specialist code was dropped, their ordinary codes had no similar provision. The solicitors' rules therefore gave greater scope for clients of solicitor advocates to determine case strategy than clients instructing barristers. This briefly raised solicitors, possibly unintentionally, on the N2 index, making them more libertarian than the Bar. This apparent mistake was abandoned, with the rest of the special rules for advocacy, at the first opportunity.

Historically, English solicitors believed that they were 'acting on a client's instructions', but the scope this gave to client autonomy was unclear. The solicitors used the best interest formula, beginning with Lund's *Guide*. He barely discussed the professional relationship at all and, where he did, he focused on technical issues such as conflicts of interest.[66] Later editions of the Law Society's *Guide* developed Lund's work but continued to obscure the issue of client autonomy and decision-making. The 1974 edition described the solicitor's obligation as doing 'his best for his client in the way that he thinks best for the client'.[67] In the Solicitors Practice Rules 1987, a guidance note stated a 'solicitor must not allow a client to override his professional judgement'.[68] This advice disappeared in the 1990s as *The Guide* began to recognise clients as consumers.

---

[61] ibid 3.7-2 Commentary [1].
[62] BSB 2018, c15.1–c15.3.
[63] ABA MRPC 1983, r 1.2.
[64] BSB CC 2014, r C15.1.
[65] Taylor (n 20) *Law Society's Code for Advocacy* 346, r 7.1(a).
[66] Above n 17, ch 9.
[67] The Law Society, *A Guide To the Professional Conduct of Solicitors* (London, The Law Society, 1974).
[68] SPR 1987, Commentary to principle 6.01, note 5.

From the 1990s, client autonomy fell within the new material on client care.[69] The SPR 1990 was intended to reduce complaints by increasing the information given to clients, particularly on costs and internal complaints procedures. The SCC 2007 was an opportunity to break free from the paternalistic 'best interests' formula. While it was retained, the new code did introduce a requirement to 'identify the client's objectives' and 'agree next steps.'[70] The SRA CC 2011 introduced an Outcome that 'clients are in a position to make informed decisions about the services they need, how their matter will be handled and the options available to them'.[71] This removed the reference to agreeing next steps, which had suggested a client had a say in how their matter was handled. It was consistent with the idea that client gave 'instructions' about outcomes, leaving the means of achieving them to solicitors.

The phraseology in the solicitors' various codes identified processes for the lawyer to follow but were ambiguous on who had the ultimate say on the objectives of representation: 'identifying objectives' did not mean accepting them, 'making informed decisions ... on options' may not include all options and 'agreeing next steps' implied a negotiation rather than an instruction. SRA CC 2011 was therefore no clearer on whether solicitors should accept clients' lawful objectives.

Despite containing several Indicative Behaviours dealing with 'taking instructions'[72] the SRA CC 2011 was unclear about the possibility that solicitors might obtain consent to act against what they perceived to be client's best interests, but in accordance with their wishes. The SRA's Standards 2019 stated solicitors could only act on client instructions[73] and not allow their personal views to affect professional relationships.[74] Neither clearly explained whether clients controlled solicitors' handling of matters or whether 'instructions' were simply confirmation of acting. Online guidance was devoted to client care.

The Australian Bar rules were almost identical to the English rules.[75] There were, however, variations that could have been read in a way that supported client autonomy. In New South Wales, for example, barristers must 'assist the client to understand the issues in the case and the client's possible rights and obligations, sufficiently to permit the client to give proper instructions'.[76] Australian and New Zealand codes also contained rules requiring lawyers to follow 'client instructions'. In Australia, solicitors were obliged to follow 'a client's lawful, proper and competent instructions'.[77]

The preamble to the code for New Zealand lawyers stated that lawyers should 'act competently, in a timely way, and in accordance with instructions received and arrangements made' and 'discuss with you your objectives and how they should best be achieved'. It stated that '[i]n acting for a client, a lawyer must, within the bounds

---

[69] T Williams, 'The Image of a Solicitor' 149 *New Law Journal* 1265.
[70] SCC 2007, r 2.02.1(a) and (c).
[71] SRA CC 2011, O(1.12).
[72] ibid IB 1.25-1.28.
[73] Standards 2019 3.1.
[74] Standards 2019 1.1.
[75] LPUC(B)R 2015, r 35 Duty to the client.
[76] ibid r 37.
[77] LCA ASRC 2011, r 8.1.

of the law and these rules, protect and promote the interests of the client to the exclusion of the interests of third parties'.[78] The New Zealand code suggested a relatively high commitment to client autonomy. Following instructions was probably closer to accepting client objectives than merely protecting clients' best interests, even though agreeing and following 'instructions' may have given lawyers wide areas of discretion. Acting within the bounds of the law and conduct rules, implied an obligation to otherwise pursue all lawful objectives.

Across the various legal professions, the ABA gave most recognition to client autonomy in the primary rule, notwithstanding the numerous qualifications in other places. This was followed by the Bar obligations to use lawful means. Canadian lawyers and the English solicitors' profession were relatively weak on this marker and New Zealand lawyers a little stronger than the Australian solicitors.

Figure N2 The obligation to accept client objectives

	US	Bar E&W	Sol E&W	New Zeal.	Aus	Aus Bar	Can	
N2	7	6	3	6	5	6	3	35

V. PARTISANSHIP INDICATORS IN LAWYERS' CODE OF CONDUCT

A. Partisanship: Duty of Loyalty, Devotion, or Zeal (P1)

The expression of loyalty, which underpinned all lawyer and client relationships, incorporating the duty of confidentiality, had considerable symbolic value. This was illustrated by the fact that 'zealous advocacy' in the ABA rules was a focus for critics of the standard conception. They saw it as an extreme form of partisanship, arguably justified in criminal advocacy, but not other kinds of legal work. English barristers, a profession with a strong emphasis on advocacy, and a history of client *cause celebres* such as Tom Paine or Queen Caroline, might have claimed a need for zeal or some similar phrase. In fact, the obligation to clients, from the BCC 1981 onwards was the more restrained 'fearless': a practising barrister must 'promote and protect fearlessly and by all proper and lawful means his lay client's best interests …'.[79]

Fearless advocacy probably dated from the late 1700s and early 1800s, when barristers displayed fearlessness in challenging vested interests of government or judicial disapproval. It evoked Erskine's stance in *Shipley*, when he refused to be intimated by the judge or Brougham's opening in the trial of Queen Caroline (see chapter six 'Identity'). It was echoed in the Canadian rules, which provided that in adversarial proceedings, the 'lawyer's function as advocate is openly and necessarily partisan'[80] and that they had to 'raise fearlessly every issue, advance every argument and ask

---

[78] NZ LCCR 2008 6.
[79] BCC 1981 r 2.03.
[80] FLSC MCPC 2014, 5.1-1 Commentary [3].

every question'.[81] This was the clear implication of fearlessness, but on its own, it was less descriptive and rather more oblique than zeal. It did not say how advocacy had to be done, merely that the advocate had to carry on with it.

The terminology of zeal did not come into the ABA rules through Brougham. Paterson suggested a hint of Brougham's language in an Alabama Code provision requiring that attorneys were obliged to '... maintain inviolate the confidences, and at every peril to himself, to preserve the secrets of his client'.[82] It was Sharswood's statement that the lawyer owed a client 'warm zeal in the maintenance and defense of his rights', which appeared in the Alabama Code.[83] The ABA Canons of Ethics 1908 conflated the zeal in maintenance of clients' rights (P1), and the use of all legally available means (P2) in Canon 15. This provided that the lawyer owed:

> entire devotion to the interest of the client, warm zeal in the maintenance and defense of his rights and the exertion of his utmost learning and ability, to the end that nothing be taken or be withheld from him, save by the rules of law, legally applied. No fear of judicial disfavor or public unpopularity should restrain him from the full discharge of his duty.

Canon 7 of the Model Code 1969 provided that 'A Lawyer Should Represent a Client Zealously Within the Bounds of the Law'. Ethical Consideration 7.1 again conflated the idea of zealous representation and the use of legally available means. It provided a clear rule of law rationale for the principle of zealous representation while placing a more concrete restriction on it. It explained that:

> The duty of a lawyer, both to his client and to the legal system, is to represent his client zealously within the bounds of the law, which includes Disciplinary Rules and enforceable professional regulations. The professional responsibility of a lawyer derives from his membership in a profession which has the duty of assisting members of the public to secure and protect available legal rights and benefits. In our government of laws and not of men, each member of our society is entitled to have his conduct judged and regulated in accordance with the law; to seek any lawful objective through legally permissible means; and to present for adjudication any lawful claim, issue, or defense.

The conception of the attorney as zealous advocate for clients was an obvious target of academic criticism following the Watergate scandal between 1972 and 1974. The argument that a culture of 'zealous advocacy' infected the work and character of the Watergate lawyers apparently prevailed and the word 'zeal' was removed from the rules in the Model Rules of Professional Conduct 1983, relegated to the preamble and commentary. In the Model Code there were 11 rules in a section headed 'lawyer and client relationship', but none defined the essential quality of that relationship or carried the connotations that 'warm zeal' did. The rules simply required lawyers provide the legal knowledge, skill, thoroughness and preparation reasonably necessary for the representation.[84]

---

[81] ibid 5.1-1 Commentary [1].
[82] L Ray Patterson, 'Legal Ethics and the Lawyer's Duty of Loyalty' (1980) 29 *Emory Law Journal* 909 at 911 citing Alabama State Code 34-3.20 (1975).
[83] RG Pearce, 'Rediscovering the Republican Origins of the Legal Ethics Codes' (1992) 6(24) *Georgetown Journal of Legal Ethics* 246.
[84] ABA MRPC 1983, r 1.1.

The remaining reference to zeal was confined to a Comment on Rule 1.3., which stated that '[a] lawyer shall act with reasonable diligence and promptness in representing a client'.[85] The comment said that a lawyer must 'act with commitment and dedication to the interests of the client and with zeal in advocacy upon the client's behalf'. This limitation of zeal apparently addressed the criticism that it had 'infected' areas of work beyond adversary advocacy. The ABA Model Code 1969 distinguished between the duties owed by advocates and advisers, thus qualifying the nature of the lawyer and client relationship.

The 'Ethical Considerations' attached to the code suggested that, whereas advocates dealt with past conduct and 'must take the facts as he finds them', advisers assisted clients 'in determining the course of future conduct and relationships'.[86] Accordingly, an advocate 'should resolve in favor of his client doubts as to the bounds of the law' whereas an adviser 'should give his professional opinion as to what the ultimate decisions of the courts would likely be as to the applicable law'.[87] Despite the effort to quarantine zeal, many State Bar codes of conduct dropped it as they were revised. When the New York State Bar adopted rules based on the ABA's Model Rules in 2009 it did not include zeal anywhere.[88]

Unsurprisingly, given the orientation of the English solicitors' profession, it never had a partisan commitment to clients. While Lund did not consider the quality of the client relationship[89] later editions of *The Guide*, saw the lawyer's obligation as doing 'his best for his client in the way that he thinks best for the client'.[90] The paternalistic tone was almost calculated to dampen expectations. In later Codes of Conduct, the Principles required solicitors to 'act in the best interests of each client' and the express provisions reflected it. The most relevant Outcome of the SRA CC 2011 was to 'provide services to your clients in a manner which protects their interests in their matter, subject to the proper administration of justice'.[91] The qualification was symptomatic; it made an already anodyne obligation more so.

As regards the P1 obligation in the Old Commonwealth jurisdictions, most of the Codes of Conduct adopted the 'best interests' formula. The Canadian rules stated in commentary on a rule on conflicts of interest that:

> The rule governing conflicts of interest is founded in the duty of loyalty which is grounded in the law governing fiduciaries. The lawyer-client relationship is based on trust. It is a fiduciary relationship and as such, the lawyer has a duty of loyalty to the client. To maintain public confidence in the integrity of the legal profession and the administration of justice, in which lawyers play a key role, it is essential that lawyers respect the duty of loyalty. Arising from the duty of loyalty are other duties, such as a duty to commit to the client's cause, the duty of confidentiality, the duty of candour and the duty to avoid conflicting interests.[92]

---

[85] ibid r 1.3 Diligence.
[86] ibid 'Ethical Considerations' 7.3.
[87] ibid.
[88] LJ Vilardo and VE Doyle III, 'Where Did the Zeal Go?' (2011) 38(1) *Litigation* 1, 4.
[89] Lund (n 17) ch 9.
[90] The Law Society, *A Guide To the Professional Conduct of Solicitors* (London, The Law Society, 1974).
[91] SRA CC 2011, O.1(2).
[92] FLSC MCPC 2014, Commentary on 3.4-1, note 5.

Despite the wordy hedging there was at least commitment to the client's cause.

The New Zealand rule went further by being explicit, stating that '[i]n acting for a client, a lawyer must, within the bounds of the law and these rules, protect and promote the interests of the client to the exclusion of the interests of third parties'.[93] Although stating what was an implicit position in most of the other codes this rule honestly and explicitly excluded third party interests, one of the reasons zealous advocacy attracted criticism in the American literature.

Figure P1 The obligation of loyalty

	US	Bar E&W	Sol E&W	New Zeal.	Aus	Aus Bar	Can	
P1	5	5	4	6	4	5	6	35

B. Partisanship: Using all Lawful Means (P2)

The P2 obligation, to use all lawful means to achieve client goals was subtly different from the P1 obligation, accepting client goals, suggesting a step beyond. This illustrated that obligations in code of conduct potentially overlapped. Accepting client goals could imply obligations to achieve them, whereas using all lawful means to defend client interests was not necessarily the same as using them to achieve client objectives. In the term 'using all lawful means' there may have been explicit or implicit differences in the means available.

The Bar of England and Wales commitment 'to use proper and lawful means on their [clients'] behalf', meant in achieving clients' best interests. This appeared to require that barristers could not quibble about the morality of the means deployed to achieving a client's goals provided they were legal. The qualifier, 'lawful' limited the obligation in terms of law and procedure, such as court and conduct rules. It was also subject to the barrister's operational control of courtroom strategy and procedural compliance.

When the Law Society acquired the facility to confer higher rights of audience on solicitor advocates it adopted the 'proper and lawful means' formula used in the BCC 1981 as part of The Law Society Code for Advocacy 1993.[94] When the advocacy code was absorbed into the SCC 2007, the chapter on litigation and advocacy did not refer to the duty to clients at all. This meant that the general duty '… to act in your client's best interests' applied by default.[95] The solicitors therefore had no obligation to use all legal means to achieve client objectives either in relation to general work or advocacy.

As noted in the previous section, the ABA tended to refer to the use of legally available means in the same context as the requirement to demonstrate zeal. The Canons of Ethics 1908, Canon 5 stated that having undertaken the defence of those

---

[93] NZ LCCR 2008, 6.
[94] N Taylor, *The Guide*, 8th edn, *Law Society's Code of Advocacy* 385.
[95] SCC 2007, r 11, Guidance note 5(b).

accused of crimes 'the lawyer is bound by all fair and honorable means, to present every defense that the law of the land permits, to the end that no person may be deprived of life or liberty, but by due process of law'. In addition to alluding to 'warm zeal' Canon 15 also stated:

> In the judicial forum the client is entitled to the benefit of any and every remedy and defense that is authorized by the law of the land, and he may expect his lawyer to assert every such remedy or defense. But it is steadfastly to be borne in the mind that the great trust of the lawyer is to be performed within and not without the bounds of the law. The office of attorney does not permit, much less does it demand of him for any client, violation of law or any manner of fraud or chicane. He must obey his own conscience and not that of his client.[96]

This formulation was a little ambiguous. It required lawyers to pursue all remedies but, having limited their actions to 'the bounds of the law', it went on to prohibit not only 'fraud or chicane', conflating both with obedience to 'his own conscience'. This was wording going beyond any substantive restriction, making the lawyer the moral arbiter.

In the Model Code, the full Rule 1.2 provision was that 'a lawyer shall abide by a client's decisions concerning the objectives of representation and, as required by Rule 1.4, shall consult with the client as to the means by which they are to be pursued'. This appeared in the Comment on Rule 1.3, which continued the tradition of juxtaposing zeal and the pursuit of client objectives. It stated that attorneys should:

> take whatever lawful and ethical measures are required to vindicate a client's cause or endeavor. A lawyer must also act with commitment and dedication to the interests of the client and with zeal in advocacy upon the client's behalf. A lawyer is not bound, however, to press for every advantage that might be realized for a client. For example, a lawyer may have authority to exercise professional discretion in determining the means by which a matter should be pursued.

The last two sentences qualified the idea that clients set objectives and could determine how they were achieved. The penultimate sentence suggested limitations on attorneys seeking client goals could fall far short of illegality. The final sentence qualified the need to take lawful measures with the phrase 'professional discretion'. The retreat from the idea that lawyers should use all legal means to pursue their client's lawful objectives was almost complete.

In Australia, Canada and New Zealand, the duty to use all lawful means to achieve client objectives was generally explicit for advocacy professions. Australian barristers, for example, had a rule almost identical to that in the English Code for barristers; to pursue 'by all proper and lawful means the client's best interests.'[97] Some codes only imposed P2 obligations in relation to litigation or advocacy. The Canadian code expressed an uncharacteristically strong obligation on P2, stating: 'the lawyer has a duty to the client to raise fearlessly every issue, advance every argument and ask every question, however distasteful, that the lawyer thinks will help the client's case and to endeavour to obtain for the client the benefit of every remedy and defence

---

[96] http://www.minnesotalegalhistoryproject.org/assets/ABA%20Canons%20(1908).pdf
[97] LPUC(B)R 2015, r 35.

authorized by law'.[98] The obligation only applied, however, in relation to 'adversarial proceedings'.[99]

Obligations on lawyers to use all lawful means on behalf of clients tended not to be found outside the sphere of advocacy. The Australian position on non-barristers, that a lawyer must 'follow a client's lawful, proper and competent instructions' would appear to cover both the purpose and means of the representation. In New Zealand, the preface to the legislative code stated that a lawyer must 'discuss with you your objectives and how they should best be achieved'.[100] This left unclear who had the ultimate say on the means of representation. As in other codes of conduct, rhetoric favouring using all lawful means was implicitly subject to a big dose of lawyer discretion.

Figure P2 The obligation to use all lawful means

	US	Bar E&W	Sol E&W	New Zeal.	Aus	Aus Bar	Can	
P2	7	7	2	6	6	7	4	42

VI. CONFORMITY WITH NEUTRAL PARTISANSHIP IN CODES OF CONDUCT

The codes of conduct of lawyers in leading common law jurisdictions manifested varying degrees of formal commitment to principles of neutrality and partisanship. Table 2 allocated scores for those provisions of codes of conduct conforming with markers for neutrality and partisanship. The total at the bottom of each column scored the codes of conduct of solicitors, barrister or lawyer profession in the chosen jurisdictions. The higher the score the more consistent were the key provisions of the code with a differentiated legal 'role morality' aligning lawyers with realising client autonomy, represented by the principles of neutrality and partisanship. Higher scores indicated greater commitment to autonomy and differentiation from ordinary morality. The lowest score, English solicitors, were least differentiated, for example, from ordinary business norms.

Table 2 Code of Conduct scores for consistency with standard conception of the lawyer's role across four markers (out of 10 for each marker)

	US	E&W Bar	E&W sol	New Zeal.	Aus sol	Aus Bar	Can	Total →
N1	4	7	2	9	2	7	5	36
N2	7	6	3	6	5	6	3	36
P1	5	5	4	6	4	5	6	35
P2	7	7	2	6	6	7	4	39
Total↑	23	25	11	27	17	25	18	146

[98] ibid.
[99] FLCS MCPR, r 5.5-1.
[100] Lawyers and Conveyancers Act 2008, Preface.

Codes of conduct appeared to reflect their historic origins and retain time honoured phrases dating from times when lawyers' relationship to clients were more paternalistic. Strong rule of law justifications were often muted. Advocacy professions presented stronger neutrality norms, particularly concerning accepting people as clients. They also expressed strong loyalty norms, requiring lawyers to provide representation up to the limits of the law. English solicitors had weak role-differentiated norms and, like the Canadian Model Code treated clients as customers rather than clients, focusing more on client care and emphasising courteous, thorough, and prompt service[101] rather than relationships promoting client autonomy.

The codes of conduct of the North American legal professions reflected an ambivalent role as advocates and business lawyers. The failure to differentiate led to an unpredictable, mixed bag of obligations. The ABA Code recommended accepting consumers as clients but with no obligation to do so. It expressed strong obligations of loyalty or zeal and acceptance of client objectives then made them subject to lawyers' morals. The Code of Conduct produced under the New Zealand Lawyers and Licensed Conveyancers Act most strongly complied with the standard conception.

Totals at the end of rows showed the score for each marker across the professions. This suggested that P2, the use of all lawful means to assist clients, was a little more strongly expressed across the codes. Despite all the attention it received in the literature, the least strongly represented was N1, the obligation to accept consumers as clients. This was the norm only for advocacy professions, although the New Zealand code applied it to all lawyers.

VII. DISCUSSION

Constitutional government maximised citizens' prospect of liberty by allowing behaviour not impinging on the rights of others. Dicey claimed that the nature of rights was determined by ordinary cases determined in the Common Law Courts and lawyers' roles reflected arrangements most likely to crystallise them. Lawyers were to do for clients what they would do for themselves, if they could, within the limits of the law. The Old Bailey Session papers pointed to the development of a stronger orientation to clients' goals with the advent of the adversary trial system in eighteenth century England.

In England, two iconic principles emerged from the adversary system: the cab rank principle and the obligation of fearless advocacy.[102] The combined effect of these central principles was described by a recent judicial champion of the rule of law, Lord Bingham, as producing a Bar 'fearless in its representation of those who cannot represent themselves, however unpopular or distasteful their case may be'.[103]

---

[101] Service that is '… competent, timely, conscientious, diligent, efficient and civil'. FLSC MCPC 2014, 3.2-1.
[102] BCC 1981, r 2.03.
[103] T Bingham, *The Rule of Law* (London, Penguin, 2011) 93.

This reinforced the role of legal advocates in constraining the state and protecting and expanding the rights of individuals. These goals were mutually reinforcing and contributed to supporting the autonomy of the individual.

The adaptation of the norms of advocacy professions was problematic for the hybrid professions of North America. In the Americas, respect for client autonomy was qualified by vague moral considerations such as honour or integrity. As Codes of Conduct evolved towards the millennium opportunities to shake off paternalism were missed. In fact, the ABA wound down the formal commitment to zealous advocacy, apparently a reaction to the moral critique of the standard conception focused on the word 'zeal'.

Vilardo and Doyle regarded the ABA's change of attitude to 'zealous advocacy' as symptomatic of a systemic shift towards 'compelling the lawyer to be an agent of the legal system and less focused on encouraging and protecting the lawyer's single-minded pursuit of the client's cause'.[104] They attributed this to a persistent but false association of the word 'zeal' with the 'hired gun' image, arguing that the consequences were not purely semantic but reflected in New York adopting a rule requiring lawyer disclosure of false evidence in tribunals.[105] This seemed to mark a transition from the idea that constitutionalism and the rule of law were supported by lawyers being loyal counsellors of citizens.

Professional paternalism may have been expected to erode, with universal suffrage, higher standards of education and consumer society, but conduct rules did not adjust. While lawyers professed loyalty to clients, their professional codes of conduct were often relatively weak in supporting the personal autonomy of citizens, a right to choose. Only the ABA committed lawyers to pursuit of clients' lawful objectives, and this was hedged with qualifications. In other legal professions lawyers' historic paternalistic orientation to clients was reflected in time-honoured phrases without thought for their continuing suitability or relevance.

An example of honouring timeworn phrases was both English professions persistence with the notion of protecting clients' best interests. This was somewhat justified in the case of the Bar because barristers were responsible for how cases were presented in court, so, a laudable objective but not one geared to promote the individual autonomy of the client. The Law Society followed the same formula but without the advocacy justification. In fact, solicitors' norms varied relatively little from 'ordinary morality' and the SRA Codes of Conduct continued with this weak role differentiation. Norms concerned with clients became a little stronger with consumerism, but regimes of 'client care' were perfectly consistent with the paternalistic approach.

The codes of conduct of the antipodean professions used the traditional idea of following 'clients' instructions' rather than lawful objectives or best interests. Being bound by instructions was a traditional notion, arguably a half point between paternalism and client autonomy. 'Following instructions' implied that the lawyer was directed by the client but left an arguable level of discretion in operationalising those instructions. In sum therefore, legal professions' codes of conduct did not necessarily

---

[104] Vilardo and Doyle (n 88).
[105] ibid.

reflect the strong commitment to promoting client autonomy implicit in the standard conception.

It was perhaps significant that the code of conduct most clearly representing the standard conception was the New Zealand Code for Lawyers and Conveyancers enacted in 2008. The New Zealand Law Society claimed that they were 'based to a large extent on the four fundamental obligations of lawyers set out in section.4 of the Act:

> to uphold the rule of law and to facilitate the administration of justice in New Zealand
>
> to be independent in providing regulated services to his or her clients
>
> to act in accordance with all fiduciary duties and duties of care owed by lawyers to their clients
>
> to protect, subject to his or her overriding duties as an officer of the High Court and to his or her duties under any enactment, the interest of his or her clients.

The logical outcome of this approach was production of a lawyer code of conduct working from fundamental principles. This was more likely to be consistent with the rule of law justification, represented in the standard conception, than codes produced by adjusting old codes.

It might be expected that the standard conception of the lawyer's role was more strongly expressed in common law countries, but this was not necessarily the case. The code for Dutch lawyers, for example, observed that 'the advocates' partiality on principle is irreconcilable with looking after interests which conflict with their client's interests'[106] and that 'advocates shall represent the points of view of their clients'.[107] The Dutch provision stating advocates must not 'perform any acts against the apparent wishes of the client'[108] was arguably a stronger assertion of client autonomy than that many in the common law codes.

VIII. CONCLUSION

Analysis of the key provisions of codes of conduct related to the standard conception of the lawyer's role called into question the assumption that they were uniform. Specialist advocacy professions had more consistent markers of neutral partisanship. The score for the Australian Bar was the same as that of the English Bar because its key provisions in this respect were almost identical. Lawyers in the US and New Zealand showed strong conformity with the standard conception despite the relevant codes applying both to advocates and to general practice lawyers. The code of conduct with the strongest conformity to neutral partisanship was that made by the New Zealand Law Society under the Lawyers and Conveyancers Act 2006, while the weakest was the code of solicitors in England and Wales.

---

[106] Netherland Bar Association, The Rules of Conduct of Advocates 1992, Introduction 1.2, www.ccbe.eu/fileadmin/speciality_distribution/public/documents/National_Regulations/DEON_National_CoC/EN_Netherlands_The_Rules_of_Conduct_of_Advocates.pdf.
[107] ibid.
[108] ibid r 9.

13
Incrimination

I. INTRODUCTION

PROMOTING CLIENT AUTONOMY was only part of the private practitioner's responsibility for supporting the rule of law. Corresponding obligations held client rights in tension. The main obligation, to legality itself, was supplemented by duties to the public interest, most clearly manifest as duties to the administration of justice. These obligations carried implications of incrimination, lawyers being guilty of crimes or other wrongdoing when carrying out client instructions. Avoiding illegality, including harm to third party interests, constrained actions for clients. The chapter considers formal commitments to legality in lawyers' codes of conduct. It identifies four rules or provisions as formal markers for duties to the system and for recognising third party interests.

II. THEORY

Tension between client rights and legality was inherent in the legal role, for example, in demands that lawyers have integrity in conducting litigation which were reflected in modern rules of conduct.[1] From the seventeenth century the expanding rights of the individual were subject to the qualification that exercising one's own liberty caused no harm to others. This was connected to the theory of liberal jurists such as Dicey, that citizens could avoid such harm if laws were certain, ascertainable, prospective, and applied to all. But citizens had to know how to comply with law, so lawyers contributed to the culture of legality by informing clients of their legal rights, vindicating them where possible, and dissuading them from illegal actions. This, the principle of dissuasion, was an essential justification of the client's Legal Professional Privilege (LPP) protecting all communication between lawyers and client in the context of litigation or for the purpose of obtaining legal advice.

Some elements of the lawyer's obligations to legality were extensively covered in codes of conduct and the literature, particularly obligations to the administration of justice. Ipp's study of Commonwealth jurisdictions found that such duties tended to comprise four elements: efficient and expeditious conduct of cases; respecting, and

---

[1] CR Andrews, *Standards of Conduct for Lawyers: An 800-Year Evolution* (2004) 57 SMU Law Review 1385.

not abusing, the court process, disclosing certain matters to the court; and not interfering with the administration of justice.[2] A Canadian analysis of the duty suggested three possible principles: (1) using tactics that are legal, honest and respectful to courts and tribunals; (2) acting with integrity and professionalism, while maintaining overarching responsibility to ensure civil conduct; and (3) educating clients about court processes to promote public confidence in the administration of justice.[3] This detailed focus on responsibility to the administration of justice may have justified Nicolson's proposition, based primarily on the English codes, that 'public facing duties' tended to be weakly represented.[4]

III. EVALUATING PUBLIC DUTIES

The framework of legality in codes of conduct was a key component of lawyer regulation. The same codes of conduct used for identifying client duties in the last chapter were used for examining duties to legality in this. Specific obligations related to the rule of law and to the legal system. Some comprised rather abstract behaviour, for example acting with integrity, rather than specific rules. Some rules had both a public face and a private face so, for example, requirements to honour undertakings promoted a public good, probity in business, as well as benefitting third parties.

In the preambles, principles, core duties and other higher-level statements of values in codes of conduct two broad sets of public duties predominated. The first set comprised system values, focused on supporting legality and the administration of justice, and the second, duties to third parties. Following the system used in the last chapter, Figure 1 describes a model of the public-facing duties in codes of conduct with relevant markers.

Figure 1 Public-facing Duties in Codes of Conduct

System duties	S1: Supporting legality/ incl. reporting requirements
	S2: Administration of justice
Third party duties	T1: Fairness
	T2: Avoiding unjustified harm

The first system duty, supporting the rule of law, concerned prohibitions on involvement in or facilitation of illegal client activity. Although this may seem too obvious to need stating, negotiating the line between legitimate advice and counselling illegality was not always easy. Acknowledgement of the issue and providing ways of dealing with it sent signals about the importance professions attached to legality. An ancillary

---

[2] DA Ipp, 'Lawyers' Duties to the Court' (1998) 114 *Law Quarterly Review* 63.
[3] R Bell and C Abela, 'A Lawyer's Duty to the Court' (*Proceedings of a Symposium*, February 2012) www.weirfoulds.com/assets/uploads/11024_10167_CEA-A-Lawyers-Duty-to-the-Court.pdf.
[4] D Nicolson, 'Mapping Professional Ethics: The Form and focus of the codes' (1998) 1(1) *Legal Ethics* 51.

aspect of the marker was responsibility for reporting illegality. Statutory reporting requirements applied for money laundering and terrorism, but beyond these areas lawyers' responsibilities to report illegal client activity was unclear. Addressing this issue would signal a commitment to legality that seriously cut across the idea of loyalty.

The second marker for system duties was commitment to the administration of justice. Examples of this were more prolific, specific, and consistent with the categories identified in the theory section above. Supporting the administration of justice was often bracketed with prohibitions on conduct which were dishonest or otherwise discreditable and likely to diminish public confidence in the legal profession or the administration of justice or otherwise bring the legal profession into disrepute.[5] The various examples of system duties provided well-established constraint on actions for clients.

The other set of duties were owed to identified third parties. The first marker for third party duties was the presence of requirements for fairness or integrity when dealing with others, including opponents or their lawyers. Such requirements were ubiquitous in codes of conduct, but meaningful detail, definition, explanation, or guidance was uncommon. Where it existed it often related to the conduct of litigation, overlapping with obligations to the administration of justice.

The second marker for obligations owed to third parties was avoidance of unnecessary harm. Where it existed this typically involved warning potential victims of client violence or client fraud. Rules allowing or requiring lawyers to take preventative action were potentially controversial because they implied disregard of any legal professional privilege over disclosed information. To fulfil an obligation to disclose, lawyers would implicitly invoke the illegality exception exemplified by *R v Cox & Railton*, but to be effective, they had to do so before the client went on to break the law.

The issue of whether these were the right indicators of legality was examined by looking at the case for pro bono legal services as a marker. There was a case for this based on the argument that accessibility to law promoted legality. The argument was expressed in the preamble to the ABA Model Rules, where it was stated that a lawyer should further public understanding of and confidence in the rule of law and the justice system by facilitating popular participation and support. Lawyers, it was said, should be mindful of the fact that the poor, and not so poor, could not afford adequate legal assistance: 'Therefore, all lawyers should devote professional time and resources and use civic influence to ensure equal access to our system of justice for all those who because of economic or social barriers cannot afford or secure adequate legal counsel'.[6]

The pro bono tradition, while strong in most of the jurisdictions tended not to feature in conduct rules. The ABA Model Rules provided that every practitioner 'should aspire' to provide 50 hours of such work annually.[7] Commentary on a Canadian rule about enhancing the profession 'encouraged ... participating in legal

---

[5] See eg LPUC(B)R 2015, Advocacy rules, 8 General.
[6] ABA MRPC 1983, Preamble – para 6.
[7] ABA MRPC 1983, r 6.1.

aid and community legal services programs or providing legal services on a pro bono basis'.[8] The absence of firm obligation was, however, an unreliable indicator of how much free work professions did. Some jurisdictions had healthy cultures of pro bono work supported outside of formal obligations. This highlighted the possible lack of correspondence between rules and empirical reality. In any event it made pro bono an unreliable, and potentially contentious indictor of commitments to legality.

IV. SYSTEM DUTIES

A. System Duty: Supporting Legality/Including Reporting Requirements (S1)

i. Supporting Legality

Lawyers were potentially involved in two kinds of illegality. The first example was when they were involved in an offence unconnected with clients. Such offences may have been committed outside of the professional role, for example driving offences. Whether or not disciplinary charges were laid depended on the seriousness of the offence and the extent to which it undermined confidence in the profession. For solicitors, any offence involving dishonesty, particularly in financial matters, generally led to striking off, even if it occurred before qualification. Codes of conduct sometimes made this clear. BSB CC 2014, rule c9, having said that barristers must act with honesty and integrity, specified both court proceedings and criminal conduct, other than *minor criminal offences*, or dishonesty as possible breaches of core duties.[9]

The second example of illegality involved clients. Lawyers routinely dealt with clients involved in illegal activity, being instructed to resist pending charges being the essence of the role. All relevant communications were covered by Legal Professional Privilege (LPP) being legal advice or preparation for litigation. Other kinds of situation were more nuanced. For example, if a client mentioned an offence with which they had not been charged, the communication could be covered by LPP if they were seeking advice on what to do or contemplating a criminal charge. If a client made an offhand remark about a past and uncharged offence, they could not claim LPP but could rely only on their lawyer's promise of confidentiality to maintain secrecy.

The difficulty regarding client criminal conduct for lawyers lay in being implicated in illegal client activity not incidental to role performance. Clear rules on this were uncommon, perhaps because rules against illegality were considered unnecessary. Nevertheless, detailing and explaining the expected approach was a sign that codes of conduct were attuned to legality considerations, particularly when reporting requirements would cut across clients' LPP. Those not imposed by legislation, for example in relation to money laundering, were confined to messy exceptions, as demonstrated in *R v Cox and Railton*. Three situations concerning lawyers and client illegality included: (a) being involved in illegality, (b) being consulted on intended illegality, and (c) being involved in illegality beyond the professional role.

---

[8] FLSC MCPC 2014.
[9] BSB CC 2014, gc25.

The situation where a client used a lawyer's services to plan, effect or conceal a criminal act were sometimes dealt with in professional rules. This situation evoked the rationale for LPP, in that it allowed lawyers an opportunity to dissuade clients from illegality.[10] The English solicitors rules, set out in *The Guide* were an example, stating: 'A solicitor must not act, ... where the instructions would involve the solicitor in a breach of the law or a breach of principles of professional conduct, unless the client is prepared to change his or her instructions.'[11] Nothing similar appeared in later codes.

The Model Rules for Canadian lawyers stated that: 'When acting for a client, a lawyer must never knowingly assist in or encourage any dishonesty, fraud, crime or illegal conduct, or instruct the client on how to violate the law and avoid punishment'.[12] Commentary on the rule provided that lawyers suspicious of client motives should 'make reasonable inquiries to obtain information about the client and about the subject matter and objectives' before accepting a retainer. Commentary stated that these steps should 'include verifying who are the legal or beneficial owners of property and business entities, verifying who has the control of business entities, and clarifying the nature and purpose of a complex or unusual transaction where the purpose is not clear. The lawyer should make a record of the results of these inquiries'.[13]

Where rules tackled the issue on advising on illegal plans, they usually allowed latitude to assess the situation. Canadian lawyers were advised that clients could be counselled that minor technical breaches for the purpose of evoking a bona fide test case were permissible provided it was the most effective way of testing the law and 'no injury to a person or violence is involved'.[14] The ABA Model Rules tackled the ramifications of counselling delinquent clients by distinguishing 'good faith efforts' to understand the law:

> A lawyer shall not counsel a client to engage, or assist a client, in conduct that the lawyer knows is criminal or fraudulent, but a lawyer may discuss the legal consequences of any proposed course of conduct with a client and may counsel or assist a client to make a good faith effort to determine the validity, scope, meaning or application of the law.[15]

Commentary on the rule noted that the fact that a client used a lawyer's advice in a criminal or fraudulent course of action did not, of itself, make a lawyer a party to the course of action.[16] It went on to claim '... a critical distinction between presenting an analysis of legal aspects of questionable conduct and recommending the means by which a crime or fraud might be committed with impunity'.

---

[10] See Lady Hale in *Three Rivers District Council & Others v Governor and Company of the Bank of England (No 6)* [2004] UKHL 48, [2005] 1 AC 610 (ch 8 'Legality').
[11] N Taylor (ed), *The Guide to the Professional Conduct of Solicitors*, 7th edn (London, The Law Society, 1993); *The Guide* (1999) 12.02.
[12] FLSC MCPC 2014, r 3.2-7.
[13] Commentary on r 3.2-7, para 3.
[14] ibid para 4.
[15] ABA MRPC 1983, r 1.2(d).
[16] ibid, comment on r 1.2 (paras 9 and 10: Criminal, fraudulent and prohibited transactions), para 9.

Further commentary on Rule 1.2 in the ABA Model rules outlined what lawyers should do on discovering that their client is acting illegally. Providing further assistance was to be avoided and the lawyer was to withdraw representation. Further, the commentary noted, in Rule 4.1, lawyers must not 'fail to disclose a material fact to a third person when disclosure is necessary to avoid assisting a criminal or fraudulent act by a client, unless disclosure is prohibited by Rule 1.6'. Rule 4.1 went on to say that 'withdrawal alone might be insufficient. It may be necessary for the lawyer to give notice of the fact of withdrawal and to disaffirm any opinion, document, affirmation or the like'.[17] The relationship between Rule 4.1. and Rule 1.6, which allowed disclosure to prevent serious physical or financial harm, was potentially confusing. Both seemed to deal with the same problem and the former was broader than the latter.

The New Zealand code also dealt specifically with criminal behaviour. It stated: 'A lawyer must not advise a client to engage in conduct that the lawyer knows to be fraudulent or criminal, nor assist any person in an activity that the lawyer knows is fraudulent or criminal. A lawyer must not knowingly assist in the concealment of fraud or crime'.[18] This did not clarify what the lawyer did with the information although there were reporting requirements for serious crimes (see below). In other jurisdictions, the likelihood was that they simply did not continue to act for the client. In that case, however, it was unclear whether 'not acting' meant not furthering the criminal act, not acting in that matter generally or not acting for that client in any matter.

Although lawyers could not become implicated in client misconduct, express prohibitions were rare. One example occurred in the New Zealand rules, which provided: 'A lawyer must not threaten, expressly or by implication, to make any accusation against a person or to disclose something about any person for any improper purpose'.[19] This rule identified such a precise situation as it appeared to relate to a specific case.

The introduction of statutory reporting requirements with criminal offences attached in relation to money laundering and terrorism, on lawyers and others, suggested that reporting requirements would not otherwise exist. There were typically exemptions where information was obtained in privileged circumstances. Codes of conduct sometimes made confidentiality requirements subject to such laws.[20] Otherwise, being consulted on, or being implicated in, potentially illegal client behaviour raised the issue of whether clients should be reported and, if so, to whom. Nearly all the codes of conduct included some reporting obligation but, except as described below, not related to illegal client activity.

In most instances where general client illegality was considered there was no duty to report the client's intentions. Clear, mandatory reporting duties unconnected with specific contexts were therefore exceptional. The two exceptions were, reporting to

---

[17] ibid para 10.
[18] NZ LCCR 2008, r 2.4.
[19] ibid r 2.7.
[20] See eg SRA, SRA Standards 2019, 6.3.

prevent courts from being misled and reporting to prevent significant third-party harm. In these areas, the policy issues were more balanced in favour of disclosure in the public interest. These specific issues are dealt with as part of the next section; the focus here being systemic harms, damage to the principle of legality protected by the lawyer's role.

A rare example of a reporting duty affecting a lawyer's own clients was provided by the Canadian rules. A lawyer acting for an organisation who discovered ongoing illegality in that entity was to advise the instructing person and the chief legal officer, and possibly the chief executive officer, of the conduct and warn them that it should be stopped.[21] If these individuals ignored the warning the lawyer was required to repeat the process to '… the next highest persons or groups, including ultimately, the board of directors, the board of trustees, or the appropriate committee of the board'.[22]

By limiting the lawyer's obligation to reporting within a client organisation the Canadian code was directed at rogue elements in organisations operating without the knowledge of senior staff. Thus, the rights of the client (the corporation) were not compromised. If the misconduct was more widely spread within the organisation, there was no responsibility to report the client beyond the organisation itself. If the organisation continued the course of conduct the lawyer was required to withdraw from acting in the matter and, '[i]n some but not all cases, withdrawal means resigning from his or her position or relationship with the organization'.[23]

In many codes, an obligation to report other lawyers was expressly or implicitly intended to protect the integrity of the profession. It was generally subject to client's LPP, a succinct example in the New Zealand Code rule providing: 'Subject to the obligation on a lawyer to protect privileged communications, a lawyer who has reasonable grounds to suspect that another lawyer has been guilty of misconduct must make a confidential report to the Law Society at the earliest opportunity'.[24] There might be enough doubt about the possibility of breaching client privilege to justify not making such reports.

The ABA model rule required that the 'appropriate professional authority' be informed of 'a violation of the Rules of Professional Conduct that raises a substantial question as to that lawyer's honesty, trustworthiness or fitness as a lawyer'.[25] It imposed a similar reporting obligation in relation to judges committing breaches of 'applicable rules of judicial conduct'.[26] Some codes of conduct required that lawyers report themselves for misconduct. The Canadian Model Rules, for example, envisaged lawyers reporting matters, misappropriation or misapplication of trust monies and participation in criminal activity related to a lawyer's practice.[27]

---

[21] FLSC MCPR 2015, r 3.2-8.
[22] ibid r 3.2-8, para 5.
[23] ibid.
[24] NZ LCCR 2008, r 2.8.
[25] ABA MRPC 1983, r 8.3 'Integrity of the profession'.
[26] ibid.
[27] FLSC MCPC 2014, r 7.1-3.

324 *Incrimination*

In England and Wales the Bar Standards Board (BSB) required reporting of 'serious misconduct by other barristers or BSB regulated entities or their managers' subject to client confidentiality'.[28] The BSB also required barristers to 'promptly provide all such information to the *Bar Standards Board* as it may, for the purpose of its regulatory functions … and notify it of any material changes to that information'.[29] Managers or owners of BSB regulated entities had to give 'whatever co-operation is necessary'.[30] Guidance to the regulations dealt with the possibility that disclosed documents may include client information subject to LPP. It conceded that, in such circumstances, case law established that LPP overrode the requirement to report serious misconduct by another.[31]

The SRA CC 2011 required that solicitors report themselves and others to the SRA where there was 'serious misconduct by any person or firm authorised by the SRA, or any employee, manager or owner of any such firm'.[32] They also had to report 'any material changes to relevant information about you including serious financial difficulty, action taken against you by another regulator and serious failure to comply with the Principles, rules, outcomes and other requirements of the Handbook'.[33]

The recent SRA Standards 2019 required solicitors to report matters reasonably believed 'capable of amounting to a serious breach of their regulatory arrangements'.[34] SRA Guidance on confidentiality noted that a duty of confidence did not arise where a lawyer was used by a client 'to perpetrate a fraud, and, by analogy, any other crime'[35] but was not clear on whether any reporting duty arose beyond statutory obligations.

There was generally no requirement to report clients' illegal plans or activities beyond the statutory exceptions and those considered below. The Canadian exception provided clear and mandatory guidance on dealing with organisational misconduct. There were however, increasingly, reporting requirements concerning one's own or colleagues' misconduct or other matters of interest to regulators. These requirements reflected attempts to create a general culture of legality among regulated professionals and were consistent with the requirement that English solicitors have compliance officers responsible for monitoring and reporting misconduct and their accountability for failing to do so.

The scoring of S1 obligations reflected both detailed engagement with basic legality issues and the imposition of explicit responsibility, usually in the form of reporting requirements, for dealing with them.

---

[28] BSB CC 2014, c66.
[29] ibid c64.1.
[30] ibid c64.3.
[31] *R (Morgan Grenfell & Co Ltd) v Special Commissioner* [2003] 1 AC 563, referred to in *R (Lumsdon) v Legal Services Board* [2013] EWHC 28 (Admin) at para 73.
[32] SRA CC 2011, O.10.4.
[33] ibid.
[34] SRA Standards 2019, 7.7.
[35] Citing *Gartside v Outram* [1857] 26 LJ Ch (NS) 113.

Table 1 Scoring explicit code of conduct support for legality

	US	E&W Bar	E&W Sols	New Zeal	Aus Sol	Aus Bar	Can
S1	7	6	4	7	2	2	8

B. System Duty: The Administration of Justice (S2)

A duty to the administration of justice was usually central to statements of lawyer duties, possibly ousting duties to clients in terms of priority. In advocacy professions, it concerned behaviour in court, and in generalist legal professions, abuse of the litigation process. Increasing use of written evidence, even in adversarial processes, may have made the duty to the court increasingly similar for advocates and for litigators. The orientation of the professions to advocacy or business did tend to affect which was the focus of codes of conduct.

i. Advocacy

Advocacy professions focused rules on the administration of justice as a duty to the court. This was a legacy of both the medieval oaths and the adversary system, where advocates were made more responsible for what transpired in court, including the evidence presented. As described in Part 2, the Bar eventually settled on a scientific style of advocacy, placing a premium on the organisation of evidence.[36] After scandals in the early and mid-1800s, duties to the court counterbalanced obligations to defend clients by 'all expedient means';[37] counsel could not assert clients' innocence while being aware of their guilt, restrictions were placed on courtroom theatrics,[38] and appeals to emotions were 'disguised as reason'.[39]

The duty to the court was regarded as the obligation to the administration of justice in the BSB Handbook: 'observing your duty to the court in the administration of justice'. The Code of Conduct made it a prior and overriding duty, stating that for barristers it 'overrides any inconsistent obligations which you may have (other than obligations under the criminal law)'.[40] The Australian barrister rules were similar to the English ones, proscribing conduct 'dishonest or otherwise discreditable to a barrister, prejudicial to the administration of justice, or likely to diminish public confidence in the legal profession or the administration of justice or otherwise bring the legal profession into disrepute'.[41]

---

[36] See particularly ch 9.
[37] A Watson, 'Changing Advocacy: Part One' (2001) 165 *Justice of the Peace* 743.
[38] Watson, ibid, attributes this to the arguments of William Forsyth in *Hortensius or the advocate, an historical essay* (1849).
[39] ibid.
[40] BSB 2014 c3.
[41] LPUC(B)R 2015, r 8.

The Australian Solicitors Rules also declared a solicitor's duty to the court and the administration of justice to be paramount and prevailing over any other duty.[42] The preamble to the ABA Model Rules expressed a tripartite focus. A lawyer, as a member of a legal profession, was a representative of clients, an officer of the legal system and a public citizen having special responsibility for the quality of justice.[43]

The dual responsibility placed on advocates by the adversary system, to clients and the courts, meant barristers could not hide behind 'instructions' but were responsible for presentation of cases.[44] This uncomfortable position was expressed in the Australian Solicitors Rules: 'A solicitor representing a client in a matter that is before the court must not act as the mere mouthpiece of the client or of the instructing solicitor (if any) and must exercise the forensic judgments called for during the case independently, after the appropriate consideration of the client's and the instructing solicitor's instructions where applicable.'[45] This left clients responsible only for big decisions, for example whether to plead guilty or settle a claim for damages.

The Bar Code of Conduct stated that barristers must not 'knowingly or recklessly mislead or attempt to mislead the court'.[46] This meant they had to appraise judges of all relevant precedents, including those that were adverse, and not knowingly present misleading evidence. Numerous cases established that this applied to any detail of witness evidence that might be in any way material, including the rank or social status of the witness. Ancillary rules supported the probity of evidence, such as requirements that cross-examination be supported by reasonable instructions and credible information in the lawyer's possession.[47] Although the advocates' duty was not to knowingly mislead the court,[48] ways of 'knowing' consistent with defendant's rights were protected.

Barristers receiving confessions could represent that client on a not guilty plea by making the prosecution prove its case according to law existing at the time the offence was committed. The duty to the court did not, therefore:

> prevent you from putting forward your client's case simply because you do not believe that the facts are as your client states them to be (or as you, on your client's behalf, state them to be), as long as any positive case you put forward accords with your instructions and you do not mislead the court … it is not for you to decide whether your client's case is to be believed.[49]

The duty to the court meant barristers could not present any evidence inconsistent with a private admission of guilt, because that would mislead the court. Therefore, having received a confession, they could not present an alibi. Guidance in the BSB Code of Conduct said they could also draw their client's attention to inconsistencies in their account, suspected, but not known to be untrue and 'indicate that a court may

---

[42] LCA ASCR 2011, r 3.1 (see also NZ LCCR 2008, ch 13.1).
[43] ABA MRPC 1983, para 1.
[44] *R v Farooqi* [2013] EWCA Crim 1649, [2014] 1 Cr App R 8.
[45] LCA ASCR 2011, r 17.1.
[46] BSB CC 2014, c3.1.
[47] NZ LCCR 2008, r 13.10.2.
[48] BSB CC 2014, c3.1 'you must not knowingly or recklessly mislead or attempt to mislead the court'.
[49] ibid gc6.

find a particular piece of evidence difficult to accept'.[50] But, if the witness steadfastly stuck with their account, the court was not misled by the witness being called to confirm their witness statement. In this way, the English Bar struck a balance between clients' rights and legality.

The Canadian rules took a similar line on advocacy, providing:

> Admissions made by the accused to a lawyer may impose strict limitations on the conduct of the defence, and the accused should be made aware of this. For example, if the accused clearly admits to the lawyer the factual and mental elements necessary to constitute the offence, the lawyer, if convinced that the admissions are true and voluntary, may properly take objection to the jurisdiction of the court, the form of the indictment or the admissibility or sufficiency of the evidence, but must not suggest that some other person committed the offence or call any evidence that, by reason of the admissions, the lawyer believes to be false.[51]

Australian barristers were also allowed to represent clients who confessed guilt to them, but wished to maintain a plea of not guilty, provided they did not set up an affirmative case inconsistent with the confession, such as suggesting that someone else committed the offence.[52] The prosecution was 'put to proof' of its case, while the defence argued that there was insufficient evidence for conviction on the offence charged.[53] Australian barristers could not allow clients who had confessed to them to give evidence denying guilt or asserting innocence.[54] One difference from the English rules was that Australian barristers had to counsel clients against breaking court orders and not advise them how to carry out or conceal their intention, but only in exceptional circumstances, threat to another, could they inform the court.[55]

An issue on the borderline of rights and legality concerned perjured testimony not recognised as such by the advocate when it was given, but subsequently found to be so. If clients did not consent to a correction being made, barristers were generally required to cease to act and return instructions, but the English code warned that 'you must not reveal the information to the court'.[56] The other Bars, and even the Australian solicitors, took the same line on discovering that a client or a witness had lied on a material particular or falsified or suppressed material evidence. If clients refused to disclose, lawyers could not inform the court of the lie, falsification, or suppression.[57]

The New Zealand Rules were unusual in putting the duty to the court as high as 'an absolute duty of honesty to the court'.[58] Nevertheless, they also provided that, where material evidence was false, in the absence of a retraction and if the witness was the client, lawyers were only to cease to act for that client.[59] The fact that the US

---

[50] ibid gc7.
[51] FLSC MCPC 2014, r 5.1-1, Commentary note para 10.
[52] LPUC(B)R 2015, r 80(a)-(c).
[53] ibid (d)–(g).
[54] ibid (h).
[55] LPUC(B)R 2015, r 81 (a)-(c).
[56] BSB CC 2014, gC11.
[57] LCA ASCR 2011, rr 20.1.1-20.1.5.
[58] NZ LCCR 2008, 13.1.
[59] NZ LCCR 2008, 13.10.1.

arguably drew on a different tradition was illustrated by greater ambivalence on the issue of testimony discovered to be perjured. This position might have reflected, as Pearce suggested, Sharswood's 'republican belief' that community interests should prevail over client interests.[60]

In drafting the Alabama Code of 1887, Goode Jones extended Sharswood's conception of duty so that lawyers owed courts 'the utmost candor and fairness'.[61] As in England, the Canons and later codes prohibited expression of personal opinion, making arguments contrary to the facts or law, and disrespecting opposing parties and witnesses.[62] There were provisions concerning courtesy and fairness to fellow lawyers and non-clients.[63] Since publishing the Canons, the ABA's struggle with the formal balance between legality and rights centred on reporting untruthful clients to the court.

Of the legal professions that were not specialist advocacy professions, the ABA took a hard line on suspect testimony and client frauds. The Canadian rules took a tough line on misleading,[64] but not on what lawyers should do if the court had been inadvertently misled. The ABA's 1928 Cannons imposed a duty on lawyers to report to an opposing party or his counsel when clients refused to rectify a fraud or deception upon the court or a party.[65] This was replaced in 1953 by an obligation to withdraw from representation, but the duty to inform was reinstated by the 1969 Code of Professional Responsibility.[66] The tightening of obligations to legality in the 1969 code indicated the direction of travel for the ABA.

The 1969 rule mandating representation within the bounds of the law provided that an attorney who discovered that a client had:

> perpetrated a fraud upon a person or tribunal shall promptly call upon his client to rectify the same, and if his client refuses or is unable to do so, he shall reveal the fraud to the affected person or tribunal, except when the information is protected as a privileged communication [and that where a] person other than his client has perpetrated a fraud upon a tribunal shall promptly reveal the fraud to the tribunal.[67]

The exemption for privileged communications was introduced by an amendment in 1974. This complicated matters because most evidence was theoretically privileged until a court decided otherwise. Advocates were therefore in a similar situation to that in *R v Cox and Railton*, having to abrogate privilege before they knew they could.

The ABA MRPC 1983 returned to the requirement of disclosure with amendments following the Ethics 2000 Commission. The rules then provided lawyers should not

---

[60] RG Pearce, 'Rediscovering the Republican Origins of the Legal Ethics Codes' (1992) 6(24) *Georgetown Journal of Legal Ethic*. 246.

[61] A Marston, 'Guiding The Profession: The 1887 Code Of Ethics Of The Alabama State Bar Association' (1998) 49(2) *Alabama Law Review* 471, 499.

[62] Pearce (n 60) 266.

[63] ibid 272-73.

[64] FLSC MCPC 2014, r 5.1-2(e).

[65] VH Kramer, 'Client's Frauds and Their Lawyers' Obligations: A Study in Professional Irresponsibility' (1979) 67 *Georgetown Law Journal* 991.

[66] ibid.

[67] ABA MRPC 1983, DR 7-102 B(1) and(2).

knowingly offer evidence known to be false, but importantly, if they came to know of material evidence that was false, they should 'take reasonable remedial measures, including, if necessary, disclosure to the tribunal'. Further, they provided, '[a] lawyer may refuse to offer evidence, other than the testimony of a defendant in a criminal matter, that the lawyer reasonably believes is false'.[68]

The ABA Model Rules took a stronger line on advocates leading and correcting misleading evidence than the English Bar in two ways. The first required correction of witness testimony found to be false, except 'the testimony of a defendant in a criminal matter'.[69] The second was the obligation to inform tribunals of oral evidence the lawyer *reasonably believed* was false. These duties of disclosure to the tribunal[70] continued to the conclusion of the proceeding, and applied even if information was otherwise protected by Rule 1.6,[71] the rule dealing with confidentiality and its exceptions. A Comment on R.3.3 noted that the advocate's proper course was to remonstrate with the client confidentially, advising on the lawyer's duty of candour, seeking cooperation in withdrawing or correcting the false evidence. Where withdrawal would not undo the effect of false evidence, mandated disclosure would leave the tribunal with a choice of 'ordering a mistrial or perhaps nothing'.[72]

The Australian barristers' rules required correction of misleading statements by the advocate, but not witness evidence, stating barristers 'must take all necessary steps to correct any misleading statement made by the barrister to a court as soon as possible after the barrister becomes aware that the statement was misleading'.[73] This presumably referred to errors made by the barrister rather than corrections of client evidence, to which client privilege could apply. If not, a duty to correct witness evidence would have been inconsistent with the barrister's obligation in *ex parte* proceedings, where clients did not give evidence.[74] There, privileged matters were expressly exempt,[75] but the barrister was required to seek instructions to reveal them and withdraw if this was refused.[76] The Australian solicitors' rules also followed this line, using the same phraseology as the barristers.[77]

The SRA's 2011 rules did not tackle the issue of what to do about evidence later discovered to be false. Oddly, between the 2011 and 2019 codes, the general duty to the was court was moved out of the section on dispute resolution and courts and into a general section on not misleading. Chapter 5 of the 2011 rules comprised five prohibitions: knowingly or recklessly misleading the court; letting others do so; placing yourself in contempt of court; allowing sensitive evidence to be misused; and paying witnesses dependent on their evidence or the outcome of the case. Three positive

---

[68] ibid r 3.3(a)3.
[69] ibid r 3.3a(3).
[70] ibid r 3.3(b).
[71] ABA MCPC 1983, r 3.3(c), Candor to the tribunal, www.americanbar.org/groups/professional_responsibility/publications/model_rules_of_professional_conduct/rule_3_3_candor_toward_the_tribunal/.
[72] ibid comment on r 3.3, para 10.
[73] LPUC(B)R 2015, r 25.
[74] ibid r 27.
[75] ibid r 27(b).
[76] ibid r 28.
[77] LCA ASRC 2011, r 19.2.A.

obligations included informing clients where duties to the court outweighed the solicitor's obligations to them.[78] The equivalent rule in the 2019 Standards stated: 'You draw the court's attention to relevant cases and statutory provisions, or procedural irregularities of which you are aware, and which are likely to have a material effect on the outcome of the proceedings.'[79] This preserved some aspects of the conventional duty to the court, but referred only to 'procedural irregularities' which would not cover incorrect witness evidence. If it was intended to cover witnesses, the rule ignored the issue of client confidentiality and LPP.

ii. Litigation

The medieval codes and the harsh English rules against lawyers financially supporting litigation may have been expected to give rise to strong rules on abuse of process, using courts improperly (for example to intimidate). The Canadian rules proscribed 'abuse of the process of the tribunal by instituting or prosecuting proceedings that, although legal in themselves, are clearly motivated by malice on the part of the client and are brought solely for the purpose of injuring the other party'.[80]

The New Zealand code made similar demands that lawyers not 'obstruct, prevent, pervert, or defeat the course of justice'[81] and provided conventional conduct rules on engagement in proceedings.[82] They stated: 'A lawyer must use legal processes only for proper purposes. A lawyer must not use, or knowingly assist in using, the law or legal processes for the purpose of causing unnecessary embarrassment, distress, or inconvenience to another person's reputation, interests, or occupation'.[83]

General exhortations against abusive litigation were possibly overstated. They risked a chilling effect on litigation generally, contradicting the notion that rights were established incrementally. The ABA 1969 rules addressed this issue. A section on representing a client within the bounds of the law provided that attorneys 'shall not' file actions that 'would serve merely to harass or maliciously injure another, knowingly advance a claim or defense that is unwarranted under existing law, except that he may advance such claim or defense if it can be supported by good faith argument for an extension, modification, or reversal of existing law'.[84]

The SRA Standards 2019 contained no reference to issuing litigation that was an abuse of process. Section 2, dealing with dispute resolution, contained only seven provisions on litigation and advocacy. They mainly addressed corrupt evidence: misusing or tampering with evidence,[85] or influencing its substance, including by 'persuading witnesses to change their evidence'.[86] The advocacy section of the

---

[78] SRA CC 2011, IB 5.5 and 5.5.
[79] SRA Standards 2019, 2.7.
[80] FLSC MCPC 2014, r 5.1-2(a).
[81] NZ LCCR 2008, r 2.2.
[82] See particularly NZ LCCR 2008, r 13.2–13.5.4.
[83] NZ LCCR 2008, r 2.3.
[84] ABA MRPC 1983, DR 7-102.
[85] SRA Standards 2019, 2.1.
[86] ibid 2.2.

Canadian Model Rules contained a provision stating that lawyers 'must not counsel or participate in the concealment, destruction or alteration of incriminating physical evidence'.[87] Commentary to the rule stated that '"evidence" did not depend upon admissibility before a tribunal or upon the existence of criminal charges' and excluded privileged material.[88]

Dedicated advocacy professions were typically not allowed to issue litigation, a task reserved for attorneys in split professions on the English model. The rules of generalist professions tended to focus on litigation, rather than advocacy, although differences between the two areas were less likely to be stark than where rules addressed advocates alone. The same was true of fused professions, the Canadian Model Rules being a good example. A section on advocacy contained a rule against trying to influence the decision or action of a tribunal, other than by open persuasion as an advocate, or allowing anyone else to do so.[89] This tendency, for 'advocacy' to refer also to litigation for fused professions was evident in a list of things that should not happen when lawyers acted as advocates in court proceedings.[90]

The Canadian Model Rules took nearly a whole alphabet to identify advocacy prohibitions. A typical item was influencing 'the course of justice by offering false evidence, misstating facts or law, presenting or relying upon a false or deceptive affidavit, suppressing what ought to be disclosed or otherwise assisting in any fraud, crime or illegal conduct'.[91] While this could be confined to advocacy, examples more accurately applied to the litigator's role: not tampering with juries, not harassing and insulting witnesses and not persuading witnesses to withhold evidence.

The Canadian Model Rules on 'Advocacy' included additional rules of potentially wide application. They stated that lawyers acting as advocate must not 'knowingly assist or permit a client to do anything that the lawyer considers to be dishonest or dishonourable'.[92] The same rule detailed behaviour that was clearly criminal, but it was less clear what was covered by 'dishonourable'. Since the duty to the court covered misleading information, the dishonourable conduct presumably related to the litigation process. It was unclear whether it referred to something underhand or unethical but not quite qualifying as dishonest.

Modern moves towards use of paper evidence potentially elided the distinction between duties to the court in advocacy and litigation. In an English disciplinary case a litigator defended a witness affidavit he knew contained misleading information and then asserted the accuracy of the affidavit to the other side.[93] His defence, that the information was privileged failed on appeal because the court said he could have observed his duty to the court without breaching his client's privilege. One solution

---

[87] FLSC MCPC 2014, r 5.1-2A.

[88] 'It includes documents, electronic information, objects or substances relevant to a crime, criminal investigation or a criminal prosecution. It does not include documents or communications that are solicitor-client privileged or that the lawyer reasonably believes are otherwise available to the authorities' (ibid r 5.1-2A Commentary on r 5.1-2A, para 1).

[89] FLSC MCPR 2015, r 5.1-2(d).

[90] ibid r 5.1-2(a)-(o).

[91] ibid (e).

[92] ibid r 5.1-2(b).

[93] *Brett v Solicitors Regulation Authority* [2014] EWHC 2974 (Admin), [2015] PNLR 2.

was to inform the barrister in the case, who would then have advised how the case could be presented without being misleading. The litigator was suspended because the misleading was reckless rather than intentional, but a later case held that deliberately misleading warranted a near-inevitable striking off.[94]

An area that crossed boundaries between litigation and advocacy was prosecution. The New Zealand statutory rules, the Canadian rules, and the Australian rules for barristers in NSW defined prosecutorial duties. They tended to constrain partisanship, the Canadian rules providing that prosecutors 'must act fairly and dispassionately'.[95] The New Zealand rules provided prosecuting lawyers act fairly and impartially; disclose relevant material to the defence; present the case fairly and with professional detachment; avoid unduly emotive language and inflaming bias or prejudice against an accused; and act in accordance with the ethical obligations of Crown prosecutors.[96] The Australian Bar had rules in similar terms, adding that: 'A prosecutor must not argue any proposition of fact or law which the prosecutor does not believe on reasonable grounds to be capable of contributing to a finding of guilt and also to carry weight.'[97]

All of the codes had extensive obligations to the administration of justice. The provision of clear guidelines on dealing with suspect witness testimony was arguably a strong indication of stances on legality. The English Bar's position, withdrawal from representation, and the ABA's, disclosure to the court, were both consistent with the rule of law and the fair administration of justice. The English position leant more towards rights and the American towards legality, the latter justifying a higher score.

Table 2 Scoring explicit code of conduct support for the administration of justice

	US	E&W Bar	E&W Sols	New Zeal	Aus Sol	Aus Bar	Can	
S2	10	8	5	8	8	8	9	56

V. THIRD PARTY DUTIES

A. Third Party Duty: Fairness (T1)

Lawyers were often under a duty of fairness to others, sometimes expressed as propriety or not taking unfair advantage. The obligations this gave rise to were often unspecific. The fact that they might be owed to a variety of others, litigants, lawyers, witnesses, or court staff, would have justified more detail. This section examines general duties of fairness, before looking at the nature of the duties owed to specific individuals.

---

[94] *Shaw v Solicitors Regulation Authority* [2017] EWHC 2076 (Admin), [2017] 4 WLR 143; Official Transcript Carr J at paras 80, 84–85.
[95] FLSC MCPC 2014, 5.1-3 Commentary note para 1.
[96] NZ LCCR 2008 13.12.
[97] LPUC(B)R 2015, r 86.

i. General Duties of Fairness

Historically, the rules of English solicitors required that 'others' be treated fairly. The Solicitors Code of Conduct 2007 had adopted a rule previously in *The Guide*, not to 'use your position to take unfair advantage of anyone either for your own benefit or for another person's benefit'.[98] Subordinate rules provided examples which were limited in scope; agreeing costs, dealing with unqualified persons and not making unjustifiable claims in letters before action.[99] Later rules prohibited taking 'unfair advantage of third parties in either your professional or personal capacity'.[100] The rules of some other legal professions were a hybrid of a general rule and context, which helped to make the nature of fairness obligations a little clearer.

The English Bar's general core duty to act with honesty and with integrity[101] included requirements not to knowingly or recklessly mislead or attempt to mislead *anyone*.[102] Examples were drafting statements of case, witness statements, affidavits or other documents containing misleading material.[103] Likewise, ABA MRPC, r 4.1A provided guidance on being fair to third parties in general by proscribing 'false statements of material fact or law' made knowingly. Australian solicitors could not knowingly make a false statement to an opponent in relation to a case (including its compromise)[104] and were required to 'take all necessary steps to correct any false statement made by the solicitor to an opponent as soon as possible after the solicitor becomes aware that the statement was false'.[105] Australian barristers were under similar duties; not making misleading statements and correcting those made.[106]

ii. Other Lawyers

The beneficiaries of detailed obligations of fairness were often other lawyers. These may have originally had etiquette requirements introduced to establish genteel or collegial relations. *The Guide* provided for English solicitors once specified duties of 'frankness and good faith' towards other solicitors.[107] These were not retained in later codes but were replaced with general prohibitions on taking unfair advantage or being misleading.[108] The New Zealand rule required that other lawyers be treated with respect and courtesy,[109] but elsewhere the same requirement applied to the lawyer's conduct in relation to 'others, including self-represented persons … when acting in a professional capacity'.[110]

---

[98] SCC 2007, r 10.01.
[99] ibid r 17.03-r 17.05.
[100] SRA CC 2011, O11.1.
[101] BSB CC 2014, CD3.
[102] ibid c8.1.
[103] ibid c9.
[104] LCA ASCR 2011, r 22.1.
[105] ibid r 22.2.
[106] ALPUC(B)R 2015, r 49 (Duty to the opponent) and r 50.
[107] *The Guide* (1999) 19.01.
[108] SRA Standards 2019, 1.1. and 1.4.
[109] NZ LCCR 2008, r 10.1.
[110] ibid r 12.

The Australian solicitors' rules provided that they 'must not take unfair advantage of the obvious error of another solicitor or other person, if to do so would obtain for a client a benefit which has no supportable foundation in law or fact'.[111] The Canadian rules also required lawyers to 'avoid sharp practice [and not to] take advantage of or act without fair warning upon slips, irregularities or mistakes on the part of other lawyers not going to the merits or involving the sacrifice of a client's rights'.[112] They were unusual in requiring courteousness and civility in dealings with others in the course of practice.[113]

iii. Parties in Proceedings

Rules of conduct occasionally protected participants or potential participants in court proceedings. A common area was the improper use of proceedings to embarrass or intimidate. The Australian solicitors' rules covered similar ground in a triumvirate of rules beginning with pre-action processes and progressing to advocacy. They provided that solicitors should not make 'statements grossly exceeding the legitimate assertion of the rights or entitlements of the solicitor's client, and which misleads or intimidates the other person,[114] threaten to institute criminal or disciplinary proceedings if a civil liability to the solicitor's client is not satisfied'[115] or 'use tactics that go beyond legitimate advocacy and which are primarily designed to embarrass or frustrate another person'.[116]

The New Zealand rules provided that 'lawyers engaged in litigation must not attack a person's reputation without good cause in court or in documents filed in court proceedings'.[117] The ABA Model Rule 4.4(a) stated that '[i]n representing a client, a lawyer shall not use means that have no substantial purpose other than to embarrass, delay, or burden a third person, or use methods of obtaining evidence that violate the legal rights of such a person'. They also required lawyers receiving a documents or electronic information 'inadvertently sent shall promptly notify the sender'.[118]

iv. Treatment of Witnesses

The fair treatment of witnesses was not a particular focus of the English Bar rules. Barristers had some latitude provided they did not ask questions 'calculated only to vilify insult or annoy', to impugn a witness they had not cross-examined or make aspersions on their conduct unless 'such allegations go to the matter in issue'.[119]

---

[111] LCA ASCR 2011, r 30.1.
[112] FLSC MCPR 2015, r 7.2-2.
[113] ibid r 7.2-1.
[114] LCA ASCR 2011, r 34.1.1.
[115] ibid r 34.1.2.
[116] ibid r 34.1.3.
[117] NZ LCCR 2008, r 13.8.
[118] ABA MRPC 1983, r 4.4(b).
[119] Bar Code of Conduct 1981, r 610(g) and (h).

The rules also provided that barristers could not 'make statements or ask questions merely to insult, humiliate or annoy a witness or any other person'[120] or 'make a serious allegation against a witness whom you have had an opportunity to cross-examine unless you have given that witness a chance to answer the allegation in cross-examination'.[121] Barristers guilty of seriously offensive or discreditable conduct towards third parties, unlawful victimisation or harassment or abuse of their professional position were potentially in breach of their duties of honesty, integrity, or maintaining independence.[122]

The Canadian conduct rules proscribed lawyers, generally advocates in cross-examination, from offending, threatening, misleading, victimising, harassing, humiliating, intimidating, or embarrassing witnesses in court proceedings. The code for Australian solicitors was unusual in specifying duties toward witnesses who were alleged victims of sexual assault, indecent assault or acts of indecency: not pursuing a line of questioning designed to mislead or confuse the witness or to be unduly annoying, harassing, intimidating, offensive, oppressive, humiliating, or repetitive.[123] They also had to 'take into account any particular vulnerability of the witness in the manner and tone of the questions that the solicitor asks'.[124]

Pearce cited the treatment of witnesses in the ABA Canons of Ethics 1908 as further evidence of the republican orientation of early American ethics.[125] Canon 18 provided witnesses be treated 'with fairness and due consideration', continuing to say that attorneys:

> … should never minister to the malevolence or prejudices of a client in the trial or conduct of a cause. The client cannot be made the keeper of the lawyer's conscience in professional matters. He has no right to demand that his counsel shall abuse the opposite party or indulge in offensive personalities. Improper speech is not excusable on the ground that it is what the client would say if speaking in his own behalf.

The substance, though not the tone of the two sets of rules, were arguably not that different. Both permitted the quite trenchant forms of cross-examination practised by Garrow. English courts moved to mitigate cross-examination of vulnerable witnesses, such as children or rape victims, as have other core jurisdictions.[126] While training took account of these adjustments,[127] the code of conduct was not amended. Whereas all legal professions imposed general duties of fairness, examples often overlapped with duties to the administration of justice.

---

[120] BSB CC 2014, c7.1.
[121] ibid c7.2.
[122] ibid gC25.
[123] LCA ASCR 2011, r 21.8.1.
[124] ibid r 21.8.2.
[125] Pearce (n 60).
[126] A Boon, *The Ethics and Conduct of Lawyers in England and Wales*, 3rd edn (Oxford, Hart Publishing, 2014) 697–702; E Henderson, 'Bigger fish to fry: Should the reform of cross-examination be expanded beyond vulnerable witnesses?' (2015) 19(2) *The International Journal of Evidence & Proof* 83.
[127] A Keane, 'Cross-Examination of Vulnerable Witnesses – Towards a Blueprint for Re-Professionalisation' (2012) 16(2) *The International Journal of Evidence & Proof* 175.

Table 3 Scoring explicit code of conduct support for fairness

	US	E&W Bar	E&W Sols	New Zeal.	Aus Sol	Aus Bar	Can	
T1	7	7	3	4	9	4	2	37

B. Third Party Duty: Preventing Harm to Third Parties (T2)

i. Physical Harm

Provisions allowing disclosure of confidential client information to prevent physical harm to third parties expressed an obligation to legality. The English Bar never had such a rule, but Sir Thomas Lund's book stated that solicitors could inform police of a client's intent to murder.[128] Later editions of the *English solicitors' Guide* provided confidentiality could 'be overridden in exceptional circumstances'[129] including where it was necessary to prevent a client causing serious bodily harm.[130] The SCC 2007 retained this guidance,[131] but it disappeared from SRA CC 2011. The SRA Standards 2019 did not refer to exceptions, although supplementary online guidance outlined the circumstances in which misconduct charges might not follow disclosure.

The SRA guidance warned that any disclosure 'could lead to disciplinary action against you and could also render you liable, in certain circumstances, to a civil action arising out of the misuse of confidential information'.[132] It hinted that regulatory action might not be taken where solicitors reported to prevent client suicide, or the sexual abuse of child clients which they were not authorised to disclose, or child abuse by a client or third party. The guidance also contemplated reporting a client intending 'committing a criminal act that you believe, on reasonable grounds, is likely to result in serious bodily harm'. It went on to warn, however: 'You will need to balance the duty of confidentiality to your client with the public interest in preventing harm to others and will need to consider carefully the information available to you and whether this clearly identifies a proposed victim or is sufficiently detailed or compelling for you to form an opinion that a serious criminal offence will occur'.[133]

Codes of conduct in other jurisdictions were also likely to have rules allowing, but not requiring lawyers to act to avert physical harm to third parties. Australian solicitors were told they 'may' disclose confidential client information 'for the purpose of avoiding the probable commission of a serious criminal offence'[134] or 'of preventing imminent serious physical harm to the client or to another person'.[135] Australian

---

[128] T Lund, *A Guide to the Professional Conduct and Etiquette of Solicitors* (London, Law Society, 1960) 103.
[129] N Taylor, *The Guide*, 8th edn (1999) ch 16, r 16.02.
[130] ibid, Guidance note 3.
[131] SCC 2007 Rule 4, Confidentiality and Disclosure Guidance note 13.
[132] SRA Guidance 'Confidentiality', www.sra.org.uk/solicitors/guidance/confidentiality-client-information/.
[133] ibid.
[134] LCA ASCR 2011, r 9.2.4.
[135] ibid r 9.2.5.

barristers could 'advise the police or other appropriate authorities' if they believed 'on reasonable grounds that there is a risk to any person's safety'.[136]

Rules generally stressed that harm must be future, imminent, and serious. The Canadian rules provided that: 'A lawyer may disclose confidential information, but must not disclose more information than is required, when the lawyer believes on reasonable grounds that there is an imminent risk of death or serious bodily harm, and disclosure is necessary to prevent the death or harm'.[137] There was extensive commentary on the rule.[138] It noted the fundamental importance of loyalty and confidence between lawyer and client, and the guidance on what might constitute serious bodily harm in the leading case in the Supreme Court of Canada.[139] It also indicated factors a lawyer should consider including:

> (a) the likelihood that the potential injury will occur and its imminence; (b) the apparent absence of any other feasible way to prevent the potential injury; and (c) the circumstances under which the lawyer acquired the information of the client's intent or prospective course of action.

The commentary suggested practical steps for responding to situations of threatened harm.

The steps suggested in the Canadian rules included contacting the local law society for ethical advice or seeking a judicial order for disclosure and making a written note setting out '(a) the date and time of the communication in which the disclosure is made; (b) the grounds in support of the lawyer's decision to communicate the information, including the harm intended to be prevented, the identity of the person who prompted communication of the information as well as the identity of the person or group of persons exposed to the harm; and (c) the content of the communication, the method of communication used and the identity of the person to whom the communication was made'.[140]

In the US, the Canons of Ethics 1908 limited the scope of confidentiality to align with privilege but exempted an 'announced intention of a client to commit a crime' and allowed 'such disclosures as may be necessary to prevent the act or protect those against whom it is threatened'.[141] Exceptions to the broad concept of confidentiality in the ABA codes remained both relatively narrow and non-compulsory. The 1969 version provided attorneys 'may' breach confidentiality where there was an intention to commit a crime[142] and the 1983 iteration qualified this by reference to 'imminent death or substantial bodily harm'.[143] In 2003 the ABA House of Delegates approved

---

[136] LPUC(B)R 2015, r 82. Rule 81, which imposed a duty to withdraw if a client threatened to breach a court order, provided that the court should not be advised of reasons unless 'the barrister believes on reasonable grounds that the client's conduct constitutes a threat to any person's safety' (r 81(2)(c)).
[137] FLSC MCPC 2014, r 3.3-3 'Future Harm/Public Safety Exception'.
[138] ibid note paras 1–5.
[139] *Smith v Jones*, [1999] 1 SCR 455, in which the Court observed that serious psychological harm may constitute serious bodily harm if it substantially interferes with the health or well-being of the individual (para 83).
[140] FLSC MCPC 2014, para 5.
[141] ABA Canons of Ethics 1908, Canon 37.
[142] ABA Code of Professional Responsibility 1969, r 1.6.
[143] ABA MRPC 1983, r 1.6.(b)(1).

a modified rule 1(6) so that the harm justifying action could be 'reasonably certain death or substantial bodily injury'.[144]

Comment on the earlier version of the rule suggested that a lawyer could report a client to the authorities who accidentally discharged toxic waste into a town's water supply if there was a 'present and substantial risk' that persons would 'contract a life-threatening or debilitating disease and the lawyer's disclosure was necessary to eliminate the threat or reduce the number of victims'.[145] Although the rule was permissive rather than mandatory, lawyers ignoring such risks may have been at increased risk of common law liability when ignoring such possibilities.

The New Zealand rules were unique in imposing mandatory obligations to protect third parties from harm. They provided that lawyers *must* disclose confidential information where it: 'relates to the anticipated or proposed commission of a crime that is punishable by imprisonment for 3 years or more or the lawyer reasonably believes that disclosure is necessary to prevent a serious risk to the health or safety of any person'.[146] The rule went on to say that disclosure 'must be only to an appropriate person and only to the extent reasonably necessary for the required purpose'.[147]

ii. Financial Harm

The position on the scope of harm exempted from confidentiality requirements was affected by the collapses of large US-based corporations and criticisms of the lawyers involved (see chapter eight 'Legality'). In 2003 the ABA supplemented regulation provided by the Securities Exchange Commission, narrowly accepting an amendment of Rule 1.6 to allow lawyers to reveal confidential information about clients, where necessary:

> (2) to prevent the client from committing a crime or fraud that is reasonably certain to result in substantial injury to the financial interests or property of another and in furtherance of which the client has used or is using the lawyer's services; (3) to prevent, mitigate or rectify substantial injury to the financial interests or property of another that is reasonably certain to result or has resulted from the client's commission of a crime or fraud in furtherance of which the client has used the lawyer's services.[148]

Comment made it clear that disclosure was not required.[149] Further, guidance suggested that the lawyer, in exercising 'the discretion ... may consider such factors as the nature of the lawyer's relationship with the client and with those who might be injured by the client, the lawyer's own involvement in the transaction and factors that may extenuate the conduct in question'.[150]

The New Zealand rules, which as noted above imposed a mandatory obligation to report client actual or intended crimes punishable by imprisonment for three years,

---

[144] ibid r 1.6(a).
[145] ibid Comment on r 1.6, note 6.
[146] NZ LCCR 2008, r 8.2(a) and (b).
[147] ibid r 8.3.
[148] ABA MRPC 1983, r 1.6(b).
[149] ibid comment para 17.
[150] ibid.

applied to financial crime attracting such a punishment. Other rules stated that confidential information about a client's business affairs *may* be disclosed to a third party where it related 'to the anticipated commission of a crime or fraud'[151] or 'the lawyer reasonably believes that the lawyer's services have been used by the client to perpetrate or conceal a crime or fraud and disclosure is required to prevent, mitigate, or rectify substantial injury to the interests, property, or reputation of another person that is reasonably likely to result or has resulted from the client's commission of the crime or fraud'.[152]

The SRA Guidance on confidentiality made no mention of financial harms. One reference to preventing a 'future criminal offence', placed this squarely in the context of physical harm.[153] Therefore, in most but not all the jurisdictions, lawyers had permission to breach confidentiality and client privilege to avert third party harms in specific circumstances. Only the New Zealand rules required disclosure to prevent both serious physical and financial harm. The English professions provided no exemption for lawyers reporting client harms. The SRA promise to look at the circumstances of a breach of confidence when considering misconduct charges represented a theoretically sound way of balancing clients' professional privilege against prevention of third-party harms. The ABA approach, recognising the problem but allowing lawyers to breach privilege at their discretion, could be seen as passing the buck.

Table 4 Scoring explicit code of conduct support for avoiding unjustified harm

	US	E&W Bar	E&W Sols	New Zeal	Aus Sol	Aus Bar	Can	
T2	6	0	4	9	9	8	7	43

VI. DUTIES TO LEGALITY IN THE CODES OF CONDUCT

Public facing duties in lawyers' codes of conduct were divided into two categories concerning duties to legality and the justice system and to individuals particularly affected by the actions of lawyers' clients. As in the previous chapter code provisions were rated on four markers according to the level of attention to the issue, scoring low for mere recognition of issues and high for mandatory rules.

Explicit obligations to legality (S1) were expressed by clear and cogent explanations of how lawyers were supposed to deal with possibly routine but nonetheless difficult cases. Codes which made explicit obligations to dissuade clients from criminal activity showed professions taking legality issues seriously. Taking action when client activity was against the public interest, including reporting where appropriate, was considered in T2. The first row of Table 5 sets out the score allocated to each

[151] ibid r 8.4(b).
[152] ibid r 8.4 (d).
[153] SRA Guidance (n 132).

code in stating legality requirements. As will be seen, the Canadian, US and New Zealand codes were the strongest in imposing requirements and explaining how to handle difficult dilemmas. Both Australian professions and the English solicitors were relatively weak. The total at the end of the row suggested that attention to this marker of legality was in the mid-range for codes of conduct in general.

Table 5 Code of Conduct scores for consistency with rule of law standards

	US	E&W Bar	E&W Sols	New Zeal	Aus Sol	Aus Bar	Can	
S1	7	6	4	7	2	2	8	36
S2	10	8	5	8	8	8	9	56
T1	7	7	3	4	9	4	2	36
T2	6	0	4	9	9	8	7	43
	30	21	16	28	28	22	26	171

The S2 marker, the duty to the administration of justice, was the strongest indicator for legality across the codes. The duty to the court, commonly expressed as a duty not to 'knowingly or recklessly mislead' the court,[154] was part of a broader obligation supporting the administration of justice. The detail of duties to the court often exposed discrepancies between professions. The duties attached to circumstances where courts were misled varied, from the ABA requirement to breach confidence, if necessary, from the general position of the others, withdrawing from representation. While there may have been reservations about the ABA approach on the grounds it prejudiced clients' LPP, it scored highly because it reinforced legality.

The T1 marker, general duties to third parties, was another weak area of public accountability across the codes. Most had vague provisions about being fair to opponents, but specific examples usually protected due process in litigation and had already been covered. Few specific groups were protected by more detailed provisions. Provisions about treatment of other lawyers appeared to be a vestige of etiquette requirements. Other parties and witnesses in proceedings were sometimes protected, particularly in the codes of advocacy professions. The Australian solicitors had relatively strong provisions under this head, including quite clear requirements for handling alleged victims of assaults and sexual offences.

The T2 marker, duties preventing physical or financial harm, was the most variable across the codes. The scope of lawyers' public-facing duties was affected by their duty of confidentiality to clients and by the client's LPP, which vested in the client and was not usually at the lawyer's discretion. Generally, it was only safe to ignore this where a court declared that LPP did not apply, but it was safe to assume this would be the case where clients were threatening to cause third party harm. Rules that required or permitted reporting of clients ignored this difficulty. The SRA's guidance on this was probably the most honest, only promising to consider all the circumstances

---

[154] Bar Code of Conduct 1981, para 302.

before bringing misconduct charges for breaches of client rights to prevent serious physical or psychological harm. Where duties to third parties existed, they tended to be permissive. This was not the case with New Zealand where there was mandatory reporting to prevent both physical and financial harm to third parties.

VII. DISCUSSION

Obligations to legality were a manifestation of the Enlightenment premise that people should have a right to autonomy consistent with the rights of others. Lawyers, people's guide in negotiating law, held these competing objectives in balance. Some authors doubted that lawyers' commitments to legality were meaningfully expressed in lawyers' codes of conduct or criticised the vagueness of public-facing norms.[155] Nicolson concluded that they always gave way to duties to clients which were 'defined with greater clarity and aligned with the economic realities of practice'.[156]

Rules governing lawyers in the US arguably reflected the greatest effort to grapple with the issues, maybe reflecting criticism of the traditional role. This was often from the perspective of morality rather than legality but many who did not approach the issue from a moral standpoint agreed. Pearce had argued that the modern ABA codes gave lawyers wide discretion in how they represented clients. Bassett argued that the ABA's emphasis on clients, and lawyer self-interest, was so pronounced in the ABA codes that the public profession of law was 'more window-dressing than actuality'.[157] She thought that provisions on confidentiality and perjury in the ABA Model Rules deprived the rules themselves of a public focus. She, and others cited academic writing charting the transition of legal practice from 'profession to business' often combined criticism of conduct rules with allegations of the greed, dishonesty, and incivility of US lawyers.

A significant difference between professions arose when an advocate realised after the event that a witness had misled the court. Discussing the ABA's struggles with the issue, Kramer identified the problem as finding the best balance between the competing interests: allowing perjury was unacceptable, requiring full disclosure was 'unacceptably drastic', and compulsory withdrawal from representation was a reasonable compromise. At the time, the prevailing argument was that the goals of society were best served by affirming the lawyer's primary duty to his client and as 'a safe house of nondisclosure for confidential information received from his client'.[158]

The comment to ABA Rule 3.3, noted the possible 'grave consequences' of requiring lawyers to report doubts about evidence. The consequences for clients included betrayal, loss of the case and prosecution for perjury.[159] It justified these by stating that

---

[155] Nicolson (n 4).
[156] ibid 66.
[157] DL Bassett, 'Defining the "Public' Profession' (2005) 36(3) *Rutgers Law Journal* 721, 722.
[158] Kramer (n 65) 1000, citing J Hoffman and ML Small, 'On Learning of a Corporate Client's Fraud-The Lawyer's Dilemma' (1978) 33 *Business Law* 1389, 1404.
[159] ABA MRPC 1983, r 3.3. Comment para 11.

'the alternative is that the lawyer cooperate in deceiving the court, thereby subverting the truth-finding process which the adversary system is designed to implement'. Further, it argued, unless the lawyer had a duty to disclose, the client could reject the advice and insist that the lawyer remained silent: 'Thus the client could in effect coerce the lawyer into being a party to fraud on the court'.

The ABA's explanation of its reporting duty seemed strained. From the description of the adversary system as a 'truth-finding process' to the implication that withdrawal from a case was inadequate to prevent the lawyer being a 'party to fraud', it did not convince. It risked making the same error as the court of first instance in *R v Cox and Railton*; betraying the client when there was still doubt that betrayal was justified. It was, however, system focused, compared with the English professions, which were silent on the issue.

Barristers and solicitors in England and Wales were the only professions in the leading jurisdictions not to have current rules on physical or financial harm, although solicitors had previously done so for significant physical harms. All the other professions had rules, making this the second strongest marker for legality, but only New Zealand *required* breach of confidentiality to prevent offences punishable by imprisonment for three years or more. It did not distinguish between physical, financial, or indeed any other harm. Other codes, such as the ABA MRPC 1983, had detailed provisions on preventing physical harm but only gave lawyers permission to breach confidence. The ABA also allowed lawyers to breach confidentiality to prevent or repair financial harm caused by client activity but did not require them to do so.

When possibly dangerous clients threatened physical harm duties to legality were placed squarely in the balance with duties to clients. The ABA's approach to third party harms was the most scrutinised in the literature. Subin criticised its position, from the Canons onwards, for broadening the cover of confidentiality beyond that required by attorney-client privilege. Since 1969, he noted, the ABA protected nearly all information about clients discovered during representation,[160] manifesting 'hostility to disclosure'.[161] Subin criticised disclosure subject to privilege on the grounds that it applied only in the most extreme circumstances; where the lawyer knew the location of a still living victim and could reveal without implicating his client, a suspect.[162] Neither the current rule, nor the comment, expressly subjected disclosure to prevent client harms to client privilege. The fact that it was permissive, however, probably limited any possible impact.

Generally weak provisions regarding the risk of financial harm were criticised for failing to control the anti-social and risk-taking behaviour of large corporate clients. One of the contentious areas for the scope of privilege was exclusion of documents produced for use in non-adversary processes, such as anti-competition or regulatory investigations. As regards US and the ABA rules, Kramer noted that the application of duties of disclosure of corporate fraud in administrative proceedings varied

---

[160] HI Subin 'The Lawyer as Superego: Disclosure of Client Confidences to Prevent Harm' (1985) 70 *Iowa Law Review* 1091, 1147–59.
[161] ibid 1159.
[162] ibid 1103-6.

significantly between States.¹⁶³ The obligations of lawyers discovering that their client had not made full disclosure in a monopoly investigation by a government agency varied from, at one end of a scale, advising the client to rectify the omission to, at the other, disclosing documents.¹⁶⁴

British academics argued that corporate lawyers should generally bear responsibility for harms their clients caused. In an article on the City of London solicitor firm Linklaters' role in the Lehman Bros debacle, Kershaw and Moorhead argued that misconduct charges should be brought where lawyers actions created a *real, substantial and foreseeable* risk of client action that was unlawful, or probably unlawful.¹⁶⁵ Loughrey noted that the SRA's requirement to uphold the rule of law and administration of justice imposed obligations to the court and to third parties, but other Chapters of its Code of Conduct had minimal relevance to transactional lawyers.¹⁶⁶ Therefore, she argued, the SRA CC 2011 under-regulated by failing to hold lawyers for corporate law firms to account for the main risk represented by their clients.

The scope of possible corporate client wrongdoing was potentially huge. Take, for example, the possibility of reporting client companies undertaking environmentally risky activity. Under the ABA Code reporting may have been allowed under exceptions to confidentiality under T2, where there were serious risks to third party physical or financial health, but they were not clear. Other examples included the documents tobacco companies had withheld showing how the American public were deceived about the health risks of smoking.¹⁶⁷ Imposing responsibility to report such actions were, therefore, hugely consequential. Despite the social harms that could be avoided by imposing clearer responsibility the risks, in terms of the principle of client rights, were well-rehearsed.

When in 2003 the ABA House of Delegates opted to allow breach of client confidence to prevent, mitigate, or rectify client crimes or frauds¹⁶⁸ the American College of Trial Lawyers pointed out difficulties. It claimed that attorneys were bound to be confused by the permissive character of the amendments and ambiguity about when they applied.¹⁶⁹ It noted that attorney-client confidentiality was justified by the ability to give fully informed advice based on knowledge of all relevant facts. The amendments posed issues of notice and timing. What would lawyers tell clients before receiving their confidences? In some circumstances privilege would arise and this resided in the client, not the lawyer. Disclosure would inevitably introduce what the College called 'an adversarial feature into the attorney-client relationship [and raise the question] should the lawyer sacrifice the client to save the lawyer?'.¹⁷⁰

---

¹⁶³ Kramer (n 65) 996.
¹⁶⁴ ibid 997–98.
¹⁶⁵ D Kershaw and R Moorhead, 'Consequential Responsibility for Client Wrongs: Lehman Brothers and the Regulation of the Legal Profession' (2013) 76(1) *Modern Law Review* 26.
¹⁶⁶ J Loughrey, 'Accountability and the Regulation of the Large Law Firm Lawyer' (2014) 77(5) *Modern Law Review* 732.
¹⁶⁷ *United States v Philip Morris Inc (No 1)* [2004] EWCA Civ 330, *Times*, 16 April 2004.
¹⁶⁸ Amendments to Rules 1.6(b)(2), 1.6(b)(3) and 1.13 of the Model Rules of Professional Conduct Proposed by the ABA Task Force on Corporate Responsibility.
¹⁶⁹ American College of Trial Lawyers, 'Amendment of Model Rule 1.6: Progress Or A Step Backward?' (Irvine, Calif., ACTL, 2004) 3.
¹⁷⁰ ibid.

Duties to report possible harms to third parties continued to be contentious. Clear third-party duties set the tone of a profession and off-set counter accusations of selfishness. Ethically, Subin argued, we should have preferred the rights of victims of harm over those of perpetrators.[171] He also acknowledged, however, that mandatory disclosure was problematic and should be reserved for situations where client misconduct threatened the integrity of the legal process.[172] The real-world consequences of such duties included causing lawyers troubled soul searching, the possibility of actions for compensation, and misconduct issues. Whether courts would accept a lawyer's reason for breaching privilege would not usually be testable in advance.

VIII. CONCLUSION

The prevalence of obligations to legality, the other side of lawyers' allegiance to the rule of law, would have diminished neutral partisanship and hence the hired gun image of popular mythology. Lawyers' codes of conduct included provisions asserting legality which balanced duties to clients and, sometimes, negated them altogether. This was problematic when client LPP was prospectively compromised. It was noticeable that the codes of conduct with the clearest obligations to promote client autonomy, the English Bar, attorneys in the US and the New Zealand profession, also had the clearest and strongest obligations to legality. New Zealand had the strongest provisions in both cases. Significant role differentiation was often demonstrated by the balance lawyers were encouraged to achieve between supporting their own client and the harm this caused to the integrity of the justice system and to others.

---

[171] ibid 1159.
[172] ibid 1175.

Part 4

Futures

Here is naught unproven, here is nothing hid:
Step for step and word for word – so the old Kings did!
Step by step, and word by word: who is ruled may read.
Suffer not the old Kings: for we know the breed –
All the right they promise – all the wrong they bring.
Stewards of the Judgment, suffer not this King!

Rudyard Kipling, *The Old Issue* (1899)

14

Professionalism

I. INTRODUCTION

IN THE SECOND half of the twentieth century some governments began to rein in self-regulation by professions, to liberalise their legal services markets. None went as far as England and Wales where successive legislative changes de-professionalised lawyers on the grounds that they were monopolistic and artificially inflated the cost of legal services. The underlying reasons were ideological, characteristic of a wave of reform identified with 'neoliberalism'. The process of undermining professionalism occurred in three main phases; overproducing lawyers, restricting professional monopolies and ending self-regulation. This chapter examines the process in England and Wales, where it was most extreme. It concludes by considering the consequences for the rule of law.

II. THEORY

As noted in Part 2, early sociologists regarded professions as socially beneficial. Durkheim preferred collegial management of occupational expertise to the hierarchical and bureaucratic alternative offered by corporations. In his 'organic' society,[1] professions' norms and values[2] and their commitment to the community interest[3] was a model for civil society. They helped sustain democracy through deliberation, reflection, and critical spirit. In similar vein, Alasdair MacIntyre suggested professions provided moral connections between their social practices and the goods promoted by those practices.[4] Dissatisfaction with professionalised legal services was also recognised, Adam Smith and Max Weber were both concerned that professional organisations could operate as cartels.[5]

---

[1] E Durkheim, *The Division of Labour in Society* (trans G Simpson) (New York, Free Press, 1893/1933) 14.
[2] R Dingwall and P Lewis (eds), *The Sociology of the Professions: Lawyers, Doctors and Others* (London, Macmillan, 1983).
[3] E Durkheim, *Professional Ethics and Civic Morals* (trans C Brookfield) (London, NY, Routledge, 1992); R Pound, *The Lawyer from Antiquity to Modern Times: With particular reference to The Development of Bar Associations in the United States* (St Paul, Minnesota, West Publishing, 1953) 95.
[4] AD MacIntyre, *After Virtue: A Study in Moral Theory* (London, Duckworth, 1985).
[5] C Decker and G Yarrow, *Understanding The Economic Rationale For Legal Services Regulation* (London, Legal Services Board, 2010) www.legalservicesboard.org.uk/Projects/rationalising_scope_of_regulation/pdf/economic_rationale_for_Legal_Services_Regulation_Final.pdf, pp 43–44, para 5.1.

Early British analysis of professions adopted the benevolent evaluation of their social role. In the 1930s, Carr-Saunders and Wilson accepted the power of professional institutions as a counterweight to state power and a cushion against fragmentation of traditional moral order by the division of labour.[6] By the 1970s social groupings and organisations were seen as using available tools to claim power.[7] Lawyers in England and the US were case studies of establishing monopoly by controlling expertise and its production through education.[8] Weber hoped that these strategies might help lawyers resist the 'iron cage' of bureaucracy[9] but by the late 1980s, Harold Perkin identified the decline of professional society. He attributed this to absorption of processes and norms, such as meritocratic selection and sustained education and training, into the commercial mainstream.[10] Alternative means of regulating professional expertise began to be considered.

The English sociologist, Terence Johnson proposed state, consumer, and self-regulation as the main possibilities for regulating expertise-based occupations.[11] From the point of view of cheap consumer services Elliot Freidson identified three economic 'logics' for regulation.[12] The logic of collegial organisation was that people worked for their own satisfaction and the benefit of others, rather than personal financial advantage. Corporate bureaucracy provided efficient management to produce reliable products at reasonable cost. Finally, perfect competition ensured efficient low prices. These possibilities became real in the economic climate of the late twentieth century, a period identified with the rise of the economic, political, and social theory of neoliberalism.

The term neoliberalism was used in the 1800s to describe a society based on the free market.[13] It was revived in the twentieth century by Friedrich Von Hayek, an Austrian academic economist whose tools of analysis were the concepts of wealth, value, exchange, cost, and price.[14] Hayek argued that human activity was based on economic calculation and efficient and productive societies based on economic competition. Price allocated scarce resources through the mechanism of supply and demand, provided the state organised the market economy to ensure that the price system functioned efficiently. This was a two-stage process; the political conditions for a free market must be established and then the state must be reformed to support it.

Hayek specified only one institution essential to the market, the rule of law, using Dicey's notion of a fixed, neutral, universal legal framework. Stable markets would

---

[6] AM Carr-Saunders and PH Wilson, *The Professions* (Oxford, Clarendon Press, 1933).

[7] RM Rich, 'Sociological Paradigms and the Sociology of Law: An Overview' in CE Reasons and R Rich (eds), *The Sociology of Law: A Conflict Perspective* (London, Butterworth & Co, 1978) 148–49.

[8] A Abbott, *The System of Professions: An Essay on the Expert Division of Labour* (Chicago, University of Chicago Press, 1988); MS Larson, *The Rise of Professionalism: A Sociological Analysis* (Berkeley CA, University of California Press, 1977).

[9] M Weber, *Economy and Society* (Totowa, NJ, Bedminster, 1968) 886.

[10] H Perkin, *The Rise of Professional Society: England Since 1880* (London, Routledge, 1989).

[11] TJ Johnson, *Professions and Power* (London and Basingstoke, Macmillan, 1972) 38.

[12] E Freidson, *The Third Logic* (Oxford, Blackwell Publishers, 2001).

[13] In an article by RA Armstrong in the *Modern Review* in 1884 (see K Birch, 'What exactly is neoliberalism' (*The Conversation*, 2 November 2017) http://theconversation.com/what-exactly-is-neoliberalism-84755.

[14] F Von Hayek, *The Road to Serfdom* (Chicago, Illinois, University of Chicago Press, 1944).

result from governments announcing rules in advance and being bound by them. The price mechanism would then allow the maximum liberty to citizens making free choices about their own lives. Hayek argued that individuals should be encouraged to be entrepreneurial, to 'provide for their own needs and service their own ambitions'.[15] Individuals being responsible for their own choices and welfare enabled the state to withdraw from a public sphere dominated by consumerism and private profit.[16]

III. NEOLIBERAL REFORM OF THE LEGAL SERVICES MARKET

A. Decline of Professional Society

Writing in the late 1990s Abel claimed that the professional project of market control had failed in the US and England because legal professions lost control of producing the producers of legal services, practitioners, to universities.[17] Allowing university education as remission from apprenticeship, followed by expansion of tertiary education in the 1960s, over-produced graduates and particularly lawyers. Pressure on professional bodies to accommodate 'surplus production' swelled the legal profession. In England it led to expansion of poor people's law supported by state legal aid. The drain on state welfare was unpopular when government policy was reducing state commitments. Professional requirements, from admission to etiquette, were seen as economically dysfunctional and at odds with open markets.

The second phase of de-professionalisation began in 1985 when a private member's bill, adopted by government, led to legislation creating a new occupation, licensed conveyancer, to undercut solicitors' conveyancing fees.[18] The popularity of the move and the ease with which it passed encouraged attention to barristers' monopoly of advocacy in higher courts.[19] The Courts and Legal Services Act 1990 (CLSA) allowed approved bodies to grant members rights of audience where they had rules of conduct, 'appropriate in the interests of the proper and efficient administration of justice' and effective mechanisms for enforcing them.[20] The Law Society was able to grant rights of audience to solicitors in private practice from 1993 and Legal Executives, Patent Attorneys and Costs Lawyers introduced them later. All required members to take additional qualifications.

The third phase, the end of self-regulation, was achieved when the Legal Services Act 2007 required legal professions to appoint regulatory bodies, the Solicitors Regulation Authority (SRA) and Bar Standards Board (BSB), to operate independently of and without being influenced by the professional body.[21] This regime

---

[15] ibid.
[16] T Lemke, 'The "Birth of Bio-Politics": Michel Foucault's Lecture at the Collège de France on Neo-Liberal Governmentality' (2001) 30(2) *Economy & Society* 190.
[17] R Abel, 'The Decline of Professionalism?' (1986) 49(1) *The Modern Law Review* 1.
[18] Administration of Justice Act 1985.
[19] Solicitors had been able to appear as advocates in lower tier civil cases (County Courts Act 1846) and criminal courts such as magistrates' courts.
[20] Courts and Legal Services Act 1990, s 17.
[21] Legal Services Act 2007, s 29.

was part of a raft of measures affecting the legal services market, ostensibly in the consumer interest, monitored by a new oversight regulator, the Legal Services Board (LSB), accountable to the Ministry of Justice.

B. The Politics of Professionalism

In the first part of the twentieth century, when government policy was dominated by the theories of economist John Maynard Keynes, macro-economic theory promoted desired social ends, such as growth or stable money. The active state was involved in economic regulation, producing the New Deal in the US and the Welfare State in the UK; regimes characterised by public investment in infrastructure, economic stimulus, regulation, unionisation, progressive taxation, and anti-trust (monopoly) regulation. The post-war system economic system lasted until 1971, when the US economy went into deficit causing rapid inflation and a financial crisis.

In the 1980s, key Western nations adopted a policy of international free markets and free trade to tackle de-industrialisation and stagnating economies. This involved 'extending and disseminating market values to all institutions and social action'[22] through policies advocated by Hayek. Through the price mechanism, he reconceived Adam Smith's 'invisible hand of the market' as a mind which computed what individuals could not perceive individually: what is valuable. If people followed their own self-interest, and markets were free and competitive, the price mechanism provided social order.

Hayek recognised no need to provide for a civil sphere, free institutions, religion, press, or protect a strong bourgeoise class. Nor did he recognise rights such as conscience, congregation, or dignity, as basic.[23] He proposed that the only necessary social end was the maintenance of the market. The US President, Ronald Reagan and British Prime Minister, Margaret Thatcher, bonded over their mutual admiration of Hayek. In different ways, they made competition and markets a central plank of their political philosophy, both transforming the state from an entity responsible for public welfare to one concerned with promotion of competition.

Professions were among the targets of neoliberals, who disapproved of state licensure and protected markets for inefficient occupational monopolies.[24] De-professionalisation was overseen by two Prime Ministers and their Lord Chancellors, all of whom were lawyers. The breaking of monopolies was undertaken by Thatcher, a barrister specialising in tax law for five years before she first entered the House of Commons in 1959. She inherited her first Lord Chancellor, Lord Hailsham, a barrister and judge who resisted reform affecting the English Bar.[25] In 1987 he was replaced by Lord Havers, who introduced anodyne reform proposals, and then by

---

[22] W Brown, 'Neo-liberalism and the End of Liberal Democracy' (2003) 7(1) *Theory and Event* 15.
[23] S Metcalf, 'Neoliberalism: The idea that swallowed the world' *The Guardian* (18 August 2017).
[24] M Friedman, *Capitalism and Freedom* (Chicago, University of Chicago Press, 1962) ch 9.
[25] R Abel, *English Lawyers Between Market and State: The Politics of Professionalism* (Oxford, Oxford University Press, 2003) 34.

Lord Mackay, a Scottish barrister with fewer qualms about radical reform ending the Bar's monopoly of advocacy.

The restructuring of the legal services market and end of self-regulation was overseen by the Labour governments of Tony Blair, who became leader of the Labour Party in 1994 and Prime Minister in 1997. Blair and his two Lord Chancellors, Derry Irvine and Charles Falconer, were Scots who attended Oxbridge and met at the Bar. Blair served his pupillage in Lincoln's Inn in Irvine's chambers and practised for a few years before his political career began, culminating in his election to Parliament in 1983. Irvine was Blair's first Lord Chancellor, succeeded in 2003 by Falconer, a friend from Blair's school days and a flatmate while both were at the Bar. Labour accepted neoliberal policies were the only viable national response to fluctuations in world trade and international money markets.[26]

The Labour Party favoured a society based on the notion of rights but encountered a system where the cost of litigation and advocacy were too expensive for ordinary people and legal aid was a drain on state funding. Denial of access to justice was politically difficult, attracting politicians to suggestions that specialist non-lawyers were more effective in handling some work than lawyers[27] and promises that new technologies would replace lawyers with commoditised legal services.[28] These ideas added gloss to alternatives to professionalism, forcing down price through competition, getting more free services out of lawyers, and the use of alternatives to court-based dispute resolution, all policies initiated in the 1990s. While Irvine had mocked Tory attacks on the legal professions, as Lord Chancellor he adopted the same line.[29]

The Labour government's campaigns against the lawyers reflected anger at the large amounts claimed by leading QCs from legal aid, a Law Society press campaign against legal aid cuts, and its lukewarm response to proposals that solicitors should be doing more free work. A more substantive issue was the Law Society's poor handling of complaints against solicitors, a backlog not solved despite several restructurings exciting pressure from the consumer lobby.[30] But in the public sector generally there was increased government willingness to tackle resistance to change through marketisation of sectors, industries and services.

In the 1980s and 1990s new regimes of monitoring, assessment and measuring success at meeting policy goals were introduced in almost all government funded systems. In 2003 the government review of the legal services market by Sir David Clementi considered: 'what regulatory framework would best promote competition, innovation and the public consumer interest in an efficient, effective and independent legal sector'.[31] A graduate in PPE from Oxford and Harvard Business School,

---

[26] J Gray, *False Dawn: The Delusions of Global Capitalism* (London, Granta Publications, 2009).

[27] R Moorhead, 'Contesting Professionalism: Legal Aid and Non-lawyers in England and Wales' (2003) 37 *Law and Society Review* 765.

[28] R Susskind, *The End of Lawyers?: Rethinking the Nature of Legal Services* (Oxford, Oxford University Press, 2008).

[29] Abel (n 25) 70, 296, 320.

[30] S Aulakh and I Kirkpatrick, 'New governance regulation and lawyers: When substantive compliance erodes legal professionalism' (2018) 5 *Journal of Professions and Organization* 167.

[31] Clementi, Sir David Report of the Review of the Regulatory Framework for Legal Services in England and Wales (2004) www.avocatsparis.org/Presence_Internationale/Droit_homme/PDF/Rapport_Clementi.pdf.

Clementi had held several positions in financial sector corporations and was a former deputy director of the Bank of England. Radical proposals were expected.

Writing in 2017, Clementi recounted being told by Lord Falconer in 2003 that previous reviews of the legal profession were not objective, having been conducted by professions with a tendency to think that they were 'very well run', because they were run 'by people like ourselves'.[32] This was only true to the extent that judges had conducted previous important reviews. On this occasion, Clementi received a paper from Falconer's staff which had 'concluded that the regulatory system for lawyers was confusing, that the complaint system needed overhaul, and that the legal profession was full of restrictive practices that worked against the consumer and in favour of the profession'.[33] This was basically what Clementi found.

Clementi's 2005 report questioned the number of consumer complaints bodies, the Law Society's poor record, and the purpose of the Inns of Court.[34] Nevertheless, his report concluded that:

> The current system has produced a strong and independently minded profession, operating in most cases to high standards, able to compete successfully internationally. These strengths would suggest that the failings of the system, identified in the Scoping Study and covered in this Review, should be tackled by reform starting from where we are, rather than from scratch.[35]

In his reflections on his review, Clementi was rather less generous, explaining that he treated the legal professions as restrictive practices expected to justify themselves, stating 'I simply couldn't find a justification for it'.[36] He thought regulation of the financial services sector an aspirational model which the legal profession could learn from. In fact, there was no real evidence of market failure and weak justifications for ending self-regulation, certainly nothing to justify Clementi's assertion that his proposals were an alternative to starting from scratch.

Clementi set the seal on the foregone conclusion of the Legal Service Act 2007, authorising new business forms, corporations called Alternative Business Structures (ABS), which required neither lawyer owners or managers. These, it had been predicted, would be more open to technology to reduce cost.[37] The Act further weakened professional monopolies by designating 'reserved legal activities' which any of the seven frontline regulators of occupations regulated under the Act could apply to regulate. This meant a reserved legal activity traditionally performed by another profession, like advocacy, could potentially be done by all.[38] Legal work not designated reserved activities, including general legal advice, will writing and contractual work not defined as 'reserved instrument activities', could be performed by anybody, regulated or not.

---

[32] 'Sir David Clementi, Author, The Clementi Report' (*Not Just for Lawyers*, 7 January 2017) https://notjustforlawyers.com/sir-david-clementi/.
[33] ibid.
[34] Clementi (n 31) ch 3.
[35] ibid 36.
[36] Clementi (n 32).
[37] Susskind (n 28).
[38] Legal Services Act 2007, s 12.

All the regulators were required to promote eight regulatory objectives of the LSA:[39]

(a) protecting and promoting the public interest;
(b) supporting the constitutional principle of the rule of law;
(c) improving access to justice;
(d) protecting and promoting the interests of consumers;
(e) promoting competition in the provision of services within subsection (2);
(f) encouraging an independent, strong, diverse and effective legal profession;
(g) increasing public understanding of the citizen's legal rights and duties;
(h) promoting and maintaining adherence to the professional principles.[40]

None of these objectives was prioritised or defined by the Act.

C. Professions

The insecure position of the legal professions in the late twentieth century was arguably due to the subjection of Enlightenment institutions to harsh economic analysis. It was also assisted by the complacency of the professions and the opportunistic willingness of some to seize fresh turf. Robertson suggested the Bar had changed little since the seventeenth century.[41] He claimed Bar culture included unflattering vices: 'a genteel interest in money, patronage through old boy networks and political preferment, a social exclusivity and a calculated deference to the wealthy and well-connected'.[42] Burrage saw it as ill-equipped to rebuff assaults on its independence.[43] Before the abolition of the conveyancing monopoly the Law Society had never shown much interest in the 'higher rights of audience',[44] but it almost immediately launched a campaign on advocacy.[45] A committee was formed under Lady Marre to seek a new settlement between the main legal professions.

The Marre Report, published in 1988, was a chance for the professions to agree on reform, but the majority proposed specialist advocacy remain an exclusive activity for barristers, who were equipped to maintain 'the legal and ethical standards which should be observed and not to participate in any deception or sharp practice'.[46] The plea to recognise the Bar's unique *modus operandi* and ethos was, however,

---

[39] ibid s 3(2) and s 28(2).
[40] ibid s 1.1.
[41] G Robertson, *The Tyrannicide Brief: The story of the man who sent Charles I to the scaffold* (London, Chatto & Windus, 2005).
[42] ibid 4.
[43] M Burrage, 'Mrs Thatcher Against the "Little Republics": Ideology, Precedents and Reactions' in TC Halliday and L Karpik (eds), *Lawyers and the Rise of Western Political Liberalism* (Oxford, Clarendon Press, 1997) 125.
[44] D Sugarman, 'Bourgeois collectivism, professional power and the boundaries of the state. The private and public life of the Law Society, 1825 to 1914' (1996) 3(1/2) *International Journal of the Legal Profession* 81, 104.
[45] Burrage (n 43).
[46] Lady Marre CBE, *A Time for Change: Report of the Committee on the Future of the Legal Profession* (London, General Council of the Bar and Council of the Law Society, 1988) 6.1.

viewed with suspicion.[47] In 1989 Lord Mackay published three green papers on legal services.[48] They argued that competition between the professions in all areas of work would increase choice and reduce cost.[49] The Bar responded to the green papers with appeals for recognition of its excellence, independence and special commitment to the administration of justice,[50] but with no explicit constitutional position to defend, it was unable to resist reform.

Slow initial uptake by solicitors of higher rights was attributed to economic, structural, and cultural forces.[51] Firms did not want higher court advocacy or could not afford it in-house. By 2019, however, there were nearly 13,500 self-employed barristers[52] and nearly 7,000 solicitors with higher rights.[53] This put the Bar's basic work, particularly crime, under severe stress. There was pressure to create work arrangements eliminating the requirement of instruction by solicitors. In 2004 barristers were allowed to appear without professional clients in court. They could interview witnesses and take proofs of evidence provided the interests of the lay client and the interests of justice were not prejudiced.[54] In 2005, Bar Direct allowed them to act in an advisory capacity to clients prepared to launch litigation themselves, appearing as their advocates in court.[55]

The Law Society relished the success of its 1990 advocacy campaign. When Mackay announced his reform proposals the Law Society suggested that lawyers should be one profession, with advocacy a specialism selected later.[56] When the judges argued for one regulator for elite advocacy, the Law Society countered it was better resourced for the role.[57] By the time the LSA was mooted, it was presiding over a failing complaints system and facing criticism for poor handling of notable members. In 2003, a former president of the Law Society, the attorney general's pro bono envoy and a member of the Legal Services Board,[58] was accused by a former client of conflict of interest.

The client had discovered that Michael Napier had acted for him against Exxon Mobil while also acting for Esso, a wholly owned subsidiary of Exxon. The complaint

---

[47] A Thornton, 'The Professional Responsibility and Ethics of the English Bar' in R Cranston (ed), *Legal Ethics and Professional Responsibility* (Oxford, Clarendon Press, 1995) 53 at 62.

[48] Notably *The Work and Organisation of the Legal Profession* (Stationery Office Books, 1989) Cm. 570.

[49] ibid para 1.1.

[50] General Council of the Bar, *The Quality of Justice: The Bar's Response* (London, Butterworth, 1989) para 2.3-2.4.

[51] A Boon and J Flood, 'Trials of Strength: The Reconfiguration of Litigation as a Contested Terrain' (1999) 33 *Law and Society Review* 595; M Zander, 'Rights of Audience in the Higher Courts in England and Wales Since the 1990 Act: What Happened?' (1997) 4 *International Journal of the Legal Profession* 167.

[52] Bar Standard Board, 'Statistics on Practising Barristers', www.barstandardsboard.org.uk/news-publications/research-and-statistics/statistics-about-the-bar/practising-barristers.html. There were 3,000 employed barristers not subject to the rule.

[53] SRA 'Number of Practising solicitors with Higher Rights of Audience, www.sra.org.uk/sra/research-publications/regulated-community-statistics/data/higher_rights_of_audience/.

[54] General Council of the Bar of England and Wales, *Code of Conduct of the Bar of England and Wales*, 8th edition (London, GCBEW, 2004) paras 706 and 707.

[55] A Heppinstall, 'Public access to the Bar is good for all' (2005) 155 (7192) *New Law Journal* 1360; L Sinclair, 'Licensed access: opportunity or blind alley?' (2005) 155(7180) *New Law Journal* 895.

[56] Abel (n 25) 34.

[57] 'Judges find "grave breach" of constitution in Green Papers' (1989) 139 *New Law Journal* 707.

[58] A Hirsch and A Luck, 'Law Society "lost control" of investigation into top solicitor' *The Guardian* (24 May 2009) www.theguardian.com/uk/2009/may/24/law-society-investigation-michael-napier.

was made in 2003 and a reprimand issued in 2005. In 2009 a report by the Scottish Law Society, brought in as a neutral arbiter, accused its English equivalent of 'systematic failure' in handling the case. The Law Society had not taken the complaint seriously enough, 'ceased to be objective' and 'failed at the outset … to enable a full and fair consideration of the complaint'.[59] In 2007, the end of self-regulation rendered the Law Society and Bar Council membership organisations with no regulatory role.

D. Judiciary

In its response to the green papers the Bar argued that its advocacy monopoly underpinned independence and was an element of the constitutional independence of the judiciary.[60] This was said to be 'more important now than ever because one of the great constitutional tasks of the courts today is to control misuse of powers by government ministers and departments'.[61] Some judges supported the Bar in this criticism. The Lord Chief Justice described the green papers' proposals as 'sinister'[62] and High Court judges claimed they were 'a grave breach of the doctrine of separation of powers' requiring concurrence of the judiciary.[63]

Abel later assessed resistance to broadening advocacy rights as 'apoplectic hyperbole',[64] but it was temporarily effective in limiting the scope and pace of reform. In the early days of the new advocacy regime there were reports of judicial hostility to solicitor advocates, but this subsided. In 2001 the senior court, the House of Lords, swept away all advocate immunity from actions in negligence.[65] It rejected arguments that immunity supported the rule of law, first by ensuring that barristers observed the cab rank rule, accepting difficult clients, and secondly, that vulnerability to client legal actions would undermine the duty to the court. The public and press seemed indifferent to the weakening of the professions as part of a steady centralisation of state power under the guise of strengthening the market.[66]

Judicial concern about the direction of government policy re-surfaced in 2010, when Lord Neuberger, then Master of the Rolls, warned that the introduction of ABS risked 'a system of unreflective consumer fundamentalism'.[67] He repeated the phrase three years later when, as President of the Supreme Court, he made a speech to the Association of Liberal Lawyers.[68] He foresaw traditional legal values being lost

---

[59] ibid.
[60] General Council of the Bar (n 50) 151.
[61] ibid.
[62] Burrage (n 43) 154.
[63] 'Judges find "grave breach" of constitution in Green Papers' (n 57).
[64] R Abel, 'The Politics of Professionalism: The Transformation of English Lawyers at the End of the Twentieth Century' (1999) 2(2) *Legal Ethics* 131, 132.
[65] *Hall v Simons* [2000] 3 All ER 673 HL.
[66] Burrage (n 43) 157.
[67] 'Edmonds backs BSB as advocacy regulator; MR warns over "consumer fundamentalism"' (*Legal Futures*, 7 November 2010) www.legalfutures.co.uk/regulation/legal-executives/bsb-should-regulate-advocacy-says-edmonds-as-mr-warns-against-consumer-fundamentalism.
[68] 'Neuberger warns against risk of profits before principles in the ABS world' (*Legal Futures*, 22 February 2013) www.legalfutures.co.uk/latest-news/neuberger-warns-risk-profits-principles-abs-world.

to the 'unyielding tentacles of self-interest' represented by external investment. He urged the regulatory bodies to ensure that the rule of law was not overpowered by commercial pressures.

The judiciary had an opportunity to assert the importance of professional independence and the rule of law in a 2016 Supreme Court case turning on interpretation of the competing statutory objectives of the LSA. The Criminal Bar Association sought judicial review of the LSB's decision to approve a scheme to assess criminal advocates. The Quality Assurance Scheme for Advocates (QASA) was a project initiated in the Legal Services Commission following concern about the quality of advocates funded by legal aid. After 2007 the LSB had persuaded the SRA, BSB and ILEX Professional Services to take over the project. Their proposed scheme involved, as part of complex qualification requirements, assessment of advocates' performance in court by presiding judges. The practical consequence for advocates failing either the qualification process or judicial evaluation was that they would not be able to practice as criminal advocates. The Law Society urged the LSB to reject the scheme as disproportionate given lack of any concrete evidence of a failure of standards.[69]

The LSB approved QASA, although it later transpired that its legal director had disagreed with the decision on the grounds that the impact on judicial independence had not been fully considered.[70] The Criminal Bar Association brought a case in the High Court alleging that the scheme undermined the actual or perceived independence of criminal advocates. The 10 grounds included the risk of pressure from judges in criminal trials, the subjectivity of the criteria applied and the lack of any requirement that advocates inform their clients that they were undergoing assessment.

The claimants struggled to raise funding but apparently had a solid case.[71] Criminal defence pitted the citizen against the state, a critical dimension of equality before law. As a solicitor advocate asked, 'is it their [advocates'] job to placate and please the judge, or to fight tooth and nail for their client? i thought i knew the answer to that one …'.[72] The claimants, however, failed at first instance and on appeal to the Court of Appeal. The court stated that:

> The existence of the principle of the independence of advocates is not in doubt. It is a long-established common law principle and one of the cornerstones of a fair and effective system of justice and the rule of law. If clients are not represented by advocates who are independent of the state, the judge and their opponents, they cannot have a fair trial.[73]

---

[69] 'Solicitors make last-ditch bid to halt "unjustified" advocacy quality scheme' (*Legal Futures*, 7 June 2011) www.legalfutures.co.uk/regulation/solicitors-make-last-ditch-bid-to-halt-unjustified-advocacy-quality-scheme.
[70] N Rose, 'Revealed: LSB Legal Director Opposed approval of QASA' (*Legal Futures*, 26 September 2013) www.legalfutures.co.uk/latest-news/revealed-lsb-legal-director-opposed-approval-qasa.
[71] C Baksi, 'Court of Appeal clears advocacy quality challenge' (*Law Society Gazette*, 12 May 2014) www.lawgazette.co.uk/practice/court-of-appeal-clears-advocacy-quality-challenge/5041213.article.
[72] ibid. Comment by Tim Williams.
[73] *The Queen on the Application of Katherine Lumsdon, Rufus Taylor, David Howker QC, Christopher Hewertson v Legal Services Board v General Council of the Bar (acting by the Bar Standards Board), Solicitors Regulation Authority, ILEX Professional Standards, Law Society of England and Wales* [2014] EWCA Civ 1276, [2014] HRLR 29, per the Master of the Rolls at para 14.

The court declared, however, that its role was to consider the proportionality of the decision of the LSB in considering the regulatory objectives of the LSA. These, it was noted, were in no order of priority. It was in the public interest that criminal advocates should be independent but also that they be competent.[74]

Dismissing the appeal, the Court of Appeal decided that the LSB had weighed the priorities appropriately and that it was entitled to conclude that the scheme was a proportionate response to an acknowledged problem, the incompetence of some advocates. It concluded that judicial assessment would not affect advocate performance any more than advocates being under judges' inherent jurisdiction. This missed the point that the judge's inherent jurisdiction was disciplinary rather than aimed at managing incompetence. An appeal to the Supreme Court on a narrow ground also failed.[75]

The Court of Appeal decision ignored the fact that it was unreasonable to expect advocates to stand up to judges when their livelihoods could be threatened. If the legal profession had a role in upholding the rule of law, as the regulatory objectives of the LSA would suggest, QASA compromised it. The fact that the scheme was proposed by a government agency, developed by the legal services regulators, and approved by the judiciary were grounds for concern. They decided that supporting the rule of law was no more important than the interests of consumers. This was inconsistent with the House of Lords' promise that all legislation would be interpreted consistently with the rule of law.[76] Surprisingly, Lord Neuberger saw the possibility that the QASA regime could serve as a sole regulator of advocacy, as an alternative to the BSB.

IV. INDEPENDENT REGULATION

A. Structure

The LSA 2007 made significant changes in the regulatory structure of the legal services market. At the apex of the structure of direct regulation of lawyers was a new agency, the Legal Services Board (LSB). The LSB was a government agency charged with overseeing achievement of the regulatory objectives[77] and accounting to the Ministry of Justice.[78] It had no formal ties to the professional bodies, but was accountable to government competition agencies, initially the Office of Fair Trading and latterly the Competition and Markets Authority, for arrangements preventing, restricting, or distorting competition.[79]

---

[74] ibid para 20.
[75] *R v Legal Services Board* [2015] UKSC 41 (the ground was that Provision of Service Regulations 2009 regulation 14(2)(c) (made under Directive 2006/123/EC on services in the internal market) required a decision that 'the objective pursued cannot be attained by means of a less restrictive measure'.
[76] *R v Secretary of State for the Home Department, ex p Pierson* [1998] AC 539 per Lord Steyn at 581.
[77] Legal Services Act 2007, s 3(2).
[78] The LSB's annual report was required to deal with how, in the Board's opinion, the activities of licensing authorities and licensed bodies have affected the regulatory objectives (Legal Services Act 2007, 110).
[79] Legal Services Act 2007, 57.

The Lord Chancellor appointed the LSB chairman. There had been concerns expressed by the Committee for Standards in Public Life that such appointments often went to political sympathisers.[80] The executive team of the LSB had careers in regulation, with responsibilities for 'consumers' or 'competition' in previous job titles.[81] The majority of LSB members were lay persons, and less than 10 per cent of 30 administrative, regulatory and research staff had a legal qualification. The 'independent regulators' appointed by the professional bodies were also potential regulators of ABS undertaking whatever legal activities the regulator was authorised to regulate. The LSA required that all ABS have designated persons, compliance officers, for conduct and for finance.

The independent regulators for the Bar and the Law Society, the Bar Standards Board (BSB) and the Solicitors Regulation Authority (SRA), assumed responsibility for regulating admissions, practice, and discipline, monitored by the LSB. The system of discipline, including disciplinary tribunals, was retained with misconduct cases investigated and presented by the independent regulators. The only area of regulatory responsibility not transferred to these bodies was complaints, which would all go to a single body. All were constrained only by a section in the LSA requiring that regulatory activity be transparent, accountable, proportionate, consistent and targeted only at cases in which action was needed.[82] The regulatory framework established by the LSA left much to the behaviour of the regulators and their interpretation of the regulatory objectives of the LSA.

B. Independent Regulators and the Professional Bodies

The requirement of the LSA 2007 that regulatory and representative functions be separated was policed by the LSB. Its enthusiasm for this role was demonstrated in 2012 when the BSB asked the LSB to approve a new rule allowing barristers to refuse work from solicitors refusing to accept standard contract terms[83] one of the exceptions to the 'cab rank rule'.[84] The LSB announced an investigation[85] and found that the BSB had used work done by the Bar Council before the LSA. The LSB's 50-page report concluded that the Bar Council had improperly influenced the BSB against the public interest.[86] This also prompted the LSB to commission a report on the cab rank

---

[80] Committee for Standards in Public Life *Striking the Balance* (2016) CM.9327, 8.29-8.30.
[81] A Boon, 'Cocktails of Logics: Reform of Legal Services Regulation in England and Wales' in A Boon (ed), *International Perspectives on the Regulation of Lawyers and Legal Services* (Oxford, Hart Publishing, 2018) 209.
[82] Legal Services Act 2007, s 28(3).
[83] A Boon, *The Ethics and Conduct of Lawyers in England and Wales* (Oxford, Hart Publishing, 2014) 167-68.
[84] Boon, 'Cocktails of Logics' (n 81).
[85] C Baksi, 'Warning over BSB's "cab rank" plans' (*Law Society Gazette*, 26 January 2012); J Hyde, 'Bar Council faces probe over cab rank "interference"' (*Law Society Gazette*, 5 June 2013).
[86] LSB, *Bar Council Investigation Report: Formal investigation into the Bar Council's involvement in the BSB application to the LSB for approval of changes to the Code of Conduct in relation to the 'Cab Rank Rule'* (London, LSB, 2013) para. 3.8, www.legalservicesboard.org.uk/Projects/pdf/LSB_investigation_into_bar_council_influencing_of_the_BSB_(25-11-13).pdf.

rule. Published in 2013[87] it concluded that modern conditions and the exceptions to the rule[88] meant it was a principle but not a meaningful rule. Reports responding to the LSB were commissioned by the Bar Council[89] and by the BSB,[90] both offering detailed and trenchant contradictions. Shortly after, Lord Neuberger's speech calling for respect for the rule of law focused on the importance of the cab-rank rule.[91]

In some matters the interests of the LSB and SRA seemed suspiciously aligned. In 2015 an LSB report to the Ministry of Justice, based on cross-regulator discussions it instigated under Professor Stephen Mayson, claimed it was increasingly clear that residual links between representative bodies and legal regulators were 'a strong impediment to progress' for some.[92] In 2016 the LSB chairman, Sir Michael Pitt, claimed, without evidence, that severing any link would help secure public interest outcomes such as maintaining the rule of law and ensuring access to justice.[93] The LSB suggested boundaries between occupations were eroding, raising issues about links between practitioners and representative bodies. It proposed regulation based on activity rather than professional title, urging that regulatory structures should not entrench increasingly artificial distinctions and impede market innovation. This was effectively a call to abolish legal professions.

The LSB proposed a single regulator of the legal services sector. This would not force fusion of professional groups, which could happen naturally due to pressures of the market. It argued there was a lack of 'full independence' between the professional bodies and their regulators which made governance more complex, distracted senior managers and undermined the credibility of regulation in the public perception.[94] It also claimed that there was confusion in government about which body was responsible for regulatory functions such as money laundering and insolvency regulations.

In 2016 the Parliamentary Justice Committee heard evidence from representatives of the professional bodies and their independent regulators. The SRA chief executive opened the session by identifying independence of regulators from professional bodies as the main issue for the Committee.[95] The Chair of the LSB then wrote to the select committee claiming that 'the current framework does not secure full regulatory

---

[87] J Flood and M Hvvid, *The Cab Rank Rule: Its Meaning and Purpose in the New Legal Services Market*, https://research.legalservicesboard.org.uk/wp-content/media/Cab-Rank-Rule_final-2013.pdf.
[88] Bar Standards Board Code of Conduct 2014.
[89] S Kentridge, *The cab rank rule: A Response to the Report Commissioned by the Legal Services Board*, https://slidelegend.com/the-cab-rank-rule-the-bar-council_59e7c0b81723dd59128078b7.html, p 12.
[90] M Mclaren, C Ulyatt and C Knowles, *The 'cab rank rule': a fresh view*, www.barstandardsboard.org.uk/media/1460590/bsb_cab_rank_rule_paper_28_2_13_v6__final_.pdf.
[91] 'Neuberger warns against risk of profits before principles in the ABS world' (*Legal Futures*, 22 February 2013) www.legalfutures.co.uk/latest-news/neuberger-warns-risk-profits-principles-abs-world.
[92] N Rose, '"Compelling case" for reform of regulation, says LSB, as focus on independence intensifies' (*Legal Futures*, 27 July 2015).legalfutures.co.uk/latest-news/compelling-case-for-reform-of-regulation-says-lsb-as-focus-on-independence-intensifies.
[93] N Rose, 'LSB lays out blueprint for radical reform of regulation' (*Legal Futures*, 12 September 2016) www.legalfutures.co.uk/latest-news/lsb-lays-blueprint-radical-reform-regulation.
[94] Legal Services Board, *A vision for legislative reform of the regulatory framework for legal services in England and Wales* (London, LSB, 2010) para 72, www.legalservicesboard.org.uk/news_publications/LSB_news/PDF/2016/20160909LSB_Vision_For_Legislative_Reform.pdf.
[95] This had also been signalled in the government's announcement of the policy review.

independence'.[96] Days after the LSB chairman accused the Law Society of being 'entirely self-interested', it lost its power to appoint the SRA chair.[97] In 2017[98] the LSB launched another investigation into professional body interference with regulators, this time into whether the Law Society's Business and Oversight Board had exceeded its representative function by monitoring the SRA.[99]

In response to the LSB proposals for radical reform of legal regulation, the chair of the Bar Council, Chantal-Aimée Doerries QC, gave a speech entitled *Barbarians at the Gate: The Attack on Professionalism*.[100] Doerries worried that the LSB's proposals felt like 'an attack on professionalism and professionals'. She focused her fire on one footnote which claimed that the LSB had surveyed the objectives of some of the UK's largest regulators and found that none related to the strength of their sector. She found the comparison of legal regulators to Ofwat (water and sewers) and Ofgem (gas and electricity) 'evidence of the challenges legal professionals face in the 21st century'. She noted that if the sewage providers failed, government could step in but 'if there is no longer a strong independent legal profession, there will be no one to step in to uphold the rule of law.'[101]

C. Regulatory Policy

The BSB generally regulated barristers consistently with traditional regulatory principles but was occasionally driven to make contrary decisions. One was to allow barrister entities conducting litigation, introduced from 2014, a move reflecting demands from barristers wanting to compete with solicitors via 'one stop shops' for litigation and advocacy services. The SRA more closely followed the government's liberalising policy. Three examples illustrate its willingness to eschew the conventions of professionalism and embrace the regulatory logics of competition and corporate bureaucracy. The first related to practice regulation.

As noted in chapter eleven 'Regulation', the SRA Code of Conduct 2011 introduced Outcomes and Indicative Behaviours in place of rules. In response to a consultation the Law Society objected on the grounds that they gave practitioners insufficient guidance, but the consultation response ignored the point. A major revision of the SRA Handbook in 2019 provided a code of conduct for solicitors and a separate code of

---

[96] Letter from Sir Michael Pitt to Robert Neill MP dated 13 July 2016, www.parliament.uk/documents/commons-committees/Justice/correspondence/Letter-dated-13-July-2016-from-Legal-Services-Board.pdf.
[97] S Downey, 'Self-interested Law Society Stripped of Power to Appoint SRA Chair' *Legal Business* (2 May 2014) https://www.legalbusiness.co.uk/blogs/self-interested-law-society-stripped-of-power-to-appoint-sra-chair/.
[98] Letter from Neil Buckley, Chief Executive of the LSB to Paul Tennant, Interim Chief Executive of the Law Society dated 15 February 2017, www.legalservicesboard.org.uk/news_publications/LSB_news/PDF/2017/20170215_NBtoPTNotificationLetter.pdf.
[99] Letter from Neil Buckley, Chief Executive of the LSB to Paul Tennant, Interim Chief Executive of the Law Society dated 20 March 2017, www.legalservicesboard.org.uk/what_we_do/pdf/20170320_NB_To_PT_Letter_re_Scope_Of_Investigation.pdf.
[100] N Hilborne, 'Law Society and Bar Council condemn regulators for "attacks" on profession' (*Legal Futures*, 23 September 2016).
[101] ibid.

conduct for the organisations employing them. Both referred to standards rather than rules, but this was effectively an admission the experiment had not worked.

The second example related to admissions, where the SRA removed undergraduate degree requirements for qualifying as a solicitor. The proposal that entrants had a degree *or equivalent* experience,[102] for example in corporate employment, and then pass a Solicitors Qualifying Examination (SQE),[103] aimed to encourage apprenticeships with future employers. This continued a trend in allowing bespoke, firm sponsored courses which had already fractured the vocational sphere.[104] In theory, the SQE replaced socialisation into professional ideals through a common, liberal education with socialisation into specific organisations.

The third example was revision of the 2019 standards to allow solicitors to work in unregulated businesses, subject to conduct requirements, but without other protections.[105] This carried a risk of scandal most professional regulators would avoid. It was, however, aligned with government competition policies. These allowed so-called 'McKenzie friends, individuals who, since a case in the 1970s, were allowed to assist litigants in person in court proceedings'.[106] Traditionally, they provided quiet advice, but increased litigation in person led to a practice of allowing them to address courts. The 'campaigning agendas' of some McKenzie friends caused criticism,[107] but competition authorities supported continuation of the practice.

D. Regulatory Practice

One of the SRA's responsibilities for practice regulation was to prosecute disciplinary cases before the Solicitors' Disciplinary Tribunal (SDT), which had been established as an independent body by the LSA.[108] The SRA seemed at odds with the SDT from the outset, criticising its use of the criminal standard of proof for solicitors' disciplinary cases rather than the easier to establish civil standard of proof.[109] This was the backdrop for events calling into question the SRA's independence from government.

---

[102] The SQE will 'validate different routes to qualification, including 'earn as you learn' pathways such as apprenticeships', see news release 'SRA announces new solicitors' assessment to guarantee high standards' (25 April 2017) www.politicshome.com/members/article/sra-announces-new-solicitors-assessment-to-guarantee-high-standards.
[103] SRA, *A New Route to Qualification: The Solicitors Qualifying Examination* (2017) www.sra.org.uk/sra/consultations/consultation-listing/solicitors-qualifying-examination/.
[104] See eg Legal Week, 'City LPC: The Elite Mould' (25 October 2004), www.law.com/international-edition/2004/10/25/city-lpc-the-elite-mould/?slreturn=20220304132802 and 'Controversial City LPC consortium splits as firms opt for different providers' (*Law Society Gazette*, 25 March 2004) www.lawgazette.co.uk/news/controversial-city-lpc-consortium-splits-as-firms-opt-for-different-providers/41684.article.
[105] In the sense of removing distinctions (see further GC Hazard and A Dondi, *Legal Ethics: A Comparative Study* (California, Stanford University Press, 2004) 45).
[106] *McKenzie v McKenzie* (1970) 3 WLR 472. This was at the discretion of judges in individual cases.
[107] There have been notable campaigners for fathers' rights refused permission to act as a McKenzie friend on the basis that their agenda takes over the case.
[108] A Boon and A Whyte, 'An Analysis of Solicitors' Disciplinary Processes in England and Wales from 1994 to 2015' (2021) 28(2) *International Journal of the Legal Profession* 129.
[109] A Boon and A Whyte, 'Lawyer Disciplinary Processes: An Empirical Study of Solicitors' Misconduct Cases in England and Wales in 2015' (2019) 39(3) *Legal Studies* 455.

They concerned two cases heard in the Solicitors' Disciplinary Tribunal in 2016 involving lawyers who had sued the British state for abuses of human rights committed by British troops abroad.

The cases arose from events in Iraq after a coalition of countries led by the US deposed the Iraqi dictator, Saddam Hussein. The Southern tip of the country was placed under a multi-national force under British command. While the civilian administration of the area cooperated with the occupation, local militias harassed British troops until they left Iraq in 2009. By 2007 many human rights abuses by troops were recorded. The death of Baha Mousa, a hotel receptionist, was found by a British Inquiry to have resulted from torture involving infliction of serious bodily harm.

In 2008, nearly £3 million was paid to Mousa's family and those of nine others subjected to admitted breaches of the European Convention on Human Rights (ECHR). The case was brought by solicitor Phil Shiner, the principal of a law firm called Public Interest Lawyers (PIL).[110] In 2010 David Cameron's government established the Iraq Historic Allegations Team (IHAT) to review and investigate allegations arising from 2003 to July 2009. Despite replacement of Royal Military Police by Royal Naval Police following judicial review, a former WREN resigned from IHAT in 2012 claiming that its investigations would result in a 'whitewash'.[111] Two firms handled large numbers of claims brought by Iraqis against the Ministry of Defence; PIL and Leigh Day and Co. PIL passed on about 65 per cent of the 3,392 allegations received by IHAT and Leigh Day around 900 claims, many of which were settled by the Ministry of Defence (MoD).

The incident leading to the SDT cases occurred on 14 May 2004, when British troops were ambushed outside Majir Al Kabir in Southern Iraq by a militia called the Mahdi Army. Following the engagement, known as the Battle of Danny Boy, 20 dead insurgents and nine prisoners were taken to Camp Abu Naji (CAN). The prisoners were later taken to Shaibah Logistics Base and released to Iraqi civilian authorities. Removal of dead insurgents from the battlefield was contrary to the Army's practice and local rumours circulated that, when released, the bodies showed signs of torture.

The allegation that live detainees were murdered overnight was made concrete when an Iraqi named Khuder Al Sweady (KAS), instructed PIL to seek damages for the death of his nephew, Hamid Al Sweady. From 2007 Leigh Day assisted in a judicial review claim against the MoD. In 2008 and 2009, Leigh Day were instructed to pursue a claim for the death of the nephew of KAS and by some of the nine detainees for unlawful detention and mistreatment at CAN. The firm assumed the clients were innocent civilians swept up in the wake of the Battle of Danny Boy. Following High Court criticism of the MoD for not disclosing details of an investigation conducted by the Royal Military Police, the Al Sweady Inquiry (ASI) was established and began receiving oral evidence in March 2013.

---

[110] O Bowcott 'Iraq human rights lawyer declared bankrupt' *The Guardian* (18 March 2017).
[111] Louise Thomas claimed that IHAT investigators showed little interest in videos showing abusive interrogations by British soldiers. 'Iraq abuse inquiry little more than a whitewash says official' *The Guardian* (11 October 2012) www.theguardian.com/uk/2012/oct/11/iraq-abuse-inquiry-whitewash-claim.

When the actions were put on hold pending the outcome of the ASI, Leigh Day took counsel's advice on whether it could stop acting for the Danny Boy claimants. In March 2013 they were advised that terminating the retainer would be difficult in the absence of 'really compelling evidence that they have lied to us and/or their cases are utterly hopeless'.[112] In 2012-13, *Al Jedda v UK* effectively created strict liability for civilian detention at army bases. The MoD offered to settle claims. The Al-Sweady claims were included in a list of claims submitted and KAS was offered £40,000 for the unlawful death of his nephew while the detainee claimants were offered £14,500 each. Some claimants wished to pursue higher offers and the decision was made to await conclusion of the ASI.

In November 2013 the MoD withdrew all offers, because the ASI was expected to cast doubt on the Iraqi claims. In 2014 lead counsel for the claimants told the ASI that allegations of deaths at CAN would not be pursued because they were not 'in our professional judgement, properly arguable'.[113] In January 2015 Leigh Day ceased to act for KAS and any of the detainees. The ASI report was published in December 2014. It concluded that the dead Iraqis taken to CAN were insurgents killed in the Battle of Danny Boy, that all detainees taken to CAN were probably combatants, and not innocent bystanders, but that some of the allegations of mistreatment of those detainees was true.[114] It therefore concluded that 'the most serious allegations … have been found to be wholly without foundation and entirely the product of deliberate lies, reckless speculation and ingrained hostility'.[115] In 2016 the SRA initiated proceedings against Phil Shiner[116] and a little later against Leigh Day and Co.

A common element in the charges was the lawyers' media campaign, including a press release claiming that the Majar incident 'is of massive consequence not just for the British Army and the British Government but for the British people'.[117] At a Law Society press conference in February 2008 Shiner made allegations against the soldiers in unqualified terms. He invited a local contact in Iraq, Mazin Younis (MY), to investigate allegations and procure clients. This produced witnesses, including an ambulance driver who alleged that live captives, including Hamid Al-Sweady, were returned dead the next day.[118]

Shiner was accused of breach of *Solicitors Code of Conduct* (2007) rule 7 prohibiting 'unsolicited visits or telephone calls to members of the public'. When the SRA asked to interview MY, he threatened to provide a damaging account unless PIL reinstated his company for translation work, a demand that PS acceded to. Shiner accepted that the facts showed he lacked integrity[119] and had abetted failures of candour to the court.[120] This, the SDT found, 'went to the heart of upholding the rule of law and the

---

[112] SRA v Martyn Jeremy Day, Sapna Malik, Anna Jennifer Crowther and Leigh Day (a firm) (2017) SDT case No. 11502-2016, para 95.
[113] ibid para 96.
[114] ibid paras 99-100.
[115] ibid para 61.
[116] Solicitors Regulation Authority v Philip Shiner (2016) SDT Case No.11510/2016.
[117] ibid para 71.
[118] ibid para 64.12.
[119] ibid para 79.4.
[120] ibid para 90.

administration of justice'.[121] Adjournment on grounds of Shiner's ill health and lack of representation due to impecuniosity were refused. He was struck off in 2017 and ordered to pay the SRA's costs, including an interim payment of £250,000.[122]

The three solicitors named in the proceedings against Leigh Day were Martin Day, who had overall conduct of the claims, Sapna Malik, a partner responsible for day-to-day management, and Anna Crowther, a former trainee who had qualified in 2008. Day was an exceptional product liability specialist recognised by industry guides[123] but he had participated in the Iraqi investigation, meeting clients on a trip to Istanbul in 2008 and working on their witness statements. As with Shiner, the allegations against Day focused on the Law Society press conference in 2008, which he helped organise, and his claim that British soldiers had killed, tortured, and mistreated innocent Iraqi civilians.[124]

The SRA alleged Day had 'endorsed comments made by Shiner ... even if he did not say them'[125] but that he also said of his visit to Iraq: 'Our five clients all say that they were simply in the vicinity of the battle and had absolutely nothing to do with the Mahdi Army ... when eventually they were brought before the Iraqi courts all of them were found not guilty of the charges by the trial judge ... when the shooting started they took cover and once the shooting ended they were swept up by British Army soldiers and beaten, kicked and generally assaulted'.[126] Day detailed horrific mutilations on death certificates issued by Iraqi civilian authorities.

In concluding the press conference Day referred to his and Shiner's combined experience of 60 years interviewing,[127] stating:

> When putting all this together with the supporting evidence of the Iraqi doctors and the death certificates and when comparing this totality of evidence with the coincidences that would need to occur for the British Army's story to be accepted we have to say that on the basis of the evidence currently available we are of the view that our clients' allegations, that the British were responsible for the torture and death of up to 20 Iraqis, may well be true.[128]

Thus, Day conceded '... that the allegations might not be true' but asserted that they found the evidence of their clients compelling.[129]

At the SDT, Mr Dutton, representing the SRA, argued that the Leigh Day had lent professional weight to the assertions of their clients, 'endorsed and adopted' those allegations and that Day had 'aligned himself to the truth of his clients' statements'.[130] Dutton claimed that Day and his partner had not investigated doubts about

---

[121] ibid para 90.21.
[122] O Bowcott, 'Phil Shiner: Iraq human rights lawyer struck off over misconduct' *The Guardian* (2 February 2017) www.theguardian.com/law/2017/feb/02/iraq-human-rights-lawyer-phil-shiner-disqualified-for-professional-misconduct.
[123] Chambers (2017) https://chambers.com/; www.legal500.com/.
[124] For a summary of the case against see O Bowcott, 'Lawyers' clients were part of Iraqi militia, tribunal told' *The Guardian* (25 April 2017).
[125] *SRA v Day, Malik, Crowther and Leigh Day (A Firm)* (n 112) para 141.1.
[126] ibid para 141.3.
[127] ibid para 76.
[128] ibid.
[129] ibid para 76.
[130] ibid para 141.4.

the reliability of the death certificates or the role of KAS. Calls for an inquiry were to generate publicity for the firm.[131] The Solicitors Code of Conduct 2007 Rule 11 required them to exercise professional judgement about statements to the media, to 'consider … the legal position and, for example, whether anything you say might be in contempt of court …' but recklessness 'compromised their duty to act with integrity'.[132]

The key evidence against the Leigh Day lawyers was a document, the 'OMS Detainee List', originally obtained from a journalist at *The Telegraph*, which debunked the claim that the CAN detainees were innocent civilians. The list was issued by the Secretarial Office of Al Sayed Al Shaheed Al Sadr … 'for the British Occupying Forces', setting out, in Arabic, detainee details. It included, in the initial 2004 translation, a column headed 'cell/group' and in a 2007 translation 'name of military unit/company', but neither version referred to the Mahdi Army.

Having been advised by counsel that the OMS list was not privileged, Leigh Day supplied it to the ASI, mistakenly stating it had only been obtained in 2007. In 2013, it was typed up, the word 'militia' added to the heading of the fourth column and details in that column found to be units of the Mahdi Army. The third respondent, then a trainee, had placed the original manuscript translation of the list in the confidential waste bin. Repeated failures to disclose the list were said to be in breach of obligations to uphold the rule of law and proper administration of justice, contrary to SRA Principle 1.01 and Principle 1.06, not behaving in ways diminishing public trust in the profession.

The SRA conceded that Leigh Day was free to act for clients who were reprehensible and was not bound to withdraw when evidence was suspect. It claimed, however, that by April 2008, Day had realised KAS' orchestration of insurgent claimants.[133] In May he was told KAS was a 'senior member' of the Mahdi Army.[134] In emails sent to the respondents and to Richard Hermer QC in March 2013, Day had said it was 'odds on likely' that the ASI would conclude that 'the claims are nonsense … politically or financially motivated … an outrageous slur … and a waste of taxpayers' money for the inquiry to have been held'.[135] Later in March he emailed his partner saying 'the evidence is all pointing in the direction of the clients being lying Bs'.[136] By May, they realised the claims had no foundation and in July, Day emailed her saying 'I am amazed it [the ASI] keeps going!'.[137]

The SRA argued that, at some point, Day should have considered either correcting the record or withdrawing. The respondents argued that guidance on SCC 2007 Rule 11.1 (misleading the court) was that 'Only where it is clear that the client is attempting to put forward false evidence to the court should you stop acting. In other circumstances it would be for the court, and not for you, to assess the truth or otherwise of

---

[131] ibid para 141.14.
[132] ibid para 141.35.
[133] ibid para 143.6.6.
[134] ibid para 143.6.10.
[135] ibid para 143.9.1.
[136] ibid para 143.9.2.
[137] ibid para 143.11.1.

the client's statement'.[138] Richard Hermer QC gave evidence that awareness of the OMS list would not have made any difference to his advice on breach of Article 2; it would not have mattered if a claimant is 'a saint or a member of Al-Qaeda'.[139]

The SDT unanimously found nothing to show lack of integrity and the allegations were dismissed. They were not solicitors of record in the ASI but only for the civil claims, which had been on hold since 2008. In these, the detainees *had* been mistreated and *did have* valid claims, although the courts may have denied them compensation.[140] The claim for KAS was different, but the first time this was seriously doubted was when Patrick O'Connor QC withdrew the contention of deaths in detention in the ASI. Even here, it was sensible for the respondents to await the outcome of the ASI before deciding what to do.

Two of the three person SDT panel found Leigh Day did not need to have ceased acting before January 2015, or to have held a press conference to correct misstatements. Nor had they undermined confidence in the profession. A dissent argued that inaccurate and sensational statements and failing to investigate properly meant Day had failed in his duty to ensure that 'all the statements made were 'correct and balanced' and based on instructions …',[141] compromised his independence and lost sight of his professional obligations.[142]

The extreme rarity of failed cases in the SDT[143] raised an intriguing issue about why Leigh Day was pursued. Light was cast at a preliminary hearing when Patricia Robertson QC, counsel for the Leigh Day respondents, claimed the MoD had pressured the SRA to bring the proceedings.[144] Robertson claimed the MoD was irked when the Al-Sweady inquiry criticised its conduct but not that of Leigh Day, and then tried 'to pass the buck for a very costly public inquiry'. It had been 'very loudly' criticising Leigh Day, hoping to eliminate claims since April 2014, when the SRA began investigating, There had then been a 'change of pace' when defence secretary Sir Michael Fallon criticised 'ambulance-chasing law firms'. The MoD sent a dossier of material on Shiner to the SRA in February 2015 but, as a government body, it should not have influenced the SRA decision on prosecution.

Robertson noted that the decision to investigate and prosecute Leigh Day was taken when government was considering 'streamlining' the SRA. Was it possible, she asked, that it had said: 'you are incredibly inefficient, I can't believe it has taken you this long and frankly if you can't deal with it we will come and reform you?'.[145] As the SRA had clearly followed 'the MoD line', she argued, the tribunal should order disclosure of correspondence between them. The SRA's counsel described Robertson's suspicions

---

[138] Solicitors' Code of Conduct 2007, Guidance para 16.
[139] *SRA v Day, Malik, Crowther and Leigh Day (A Firm)* (n 112) para 143.25.
[140] ibid para 143.35.
[141] ibid para 141.99.
[142] ibid para 141.105.
[143] Boon and Whyte (n 109).
[144] J Hyde, 'MoD leaned on SRA over Iraq war claims, Leigh Day alleges' (*Law Society Gazette*, 10 February 2017) www.lawgazette.co.uk/news/mod-leaned-on-sra-over-iraq-war-claims-leigh-day-alleges/5059808. article.
[145] ibid.

as 'fanciful', but the SDT ordered disclosure. These produced no evidence that prosecution resulted from MoD pressure, but did show that its officials frequently sought details of what was being investigated, suggested lines of inquiry, and requested updates and timeframes for completion.[146] In one email the SRA replied: 'Ministers can rest assured we know how important it is that we do a very good job on this and that public has to have confidence in our investigation and outcome of it.'

The correspondence showed that the SRA chief executive, Paul Philip, had used ministerial interest to both raise its campaign against the SDT and to end the SRA's already tenuous connection to the Law Society. In February 2016, more than a year before the disciplinary proceedings against Leigh Day began, Philip had written to backbench MP Chris Philp explaining progress of the investigation adding: 'I am of course happy to meet up to discuss our regulatory model and wider work.' In April 2016, Philip wrote to defence secretary Sir Michael Fallon, referring to the investigation and suggesting they meet to discuss his complaints about the SDT. Fallon responded, welcoming the opportunity to discuss the 'manner in which the SDT operates'. Philip followed up their meeting, which happened in June 2016, with a letter to Fallon claiming the SDT needed 'root and branch overhaul', adding 'We appreciate your support on this issue.' The same letter referred to the ambition to separate the SRA from the Law Society. Later in the year, Philip wrote advocating regulatory reform to the chair of the Commons Defence Select Committee.

The fact that the Leigh Day clients were tortured was lost in the furore. In 2015, David Cameron, the then Prime Minister, allegedly instigated the clamp down on lawyers representing Iraqis as part of a campaign to change the mood on the issue.[147] Following the referral of Leigh Day to the SRA, Tory MPs complained in the Commons about the 'intolerable burden' on innocent veterans. IHAT dropped 57 outstanding cases. After he was cleared Day gave an interview claiming that misconduct proceedings were politically motivated and expressed 'outrage' that the case should be put in the context 'an industry of vexatious claims'.[148] The accusation that most claims were false was denied by the Army's former Chief Legal Adviser in Iraq, Lt Col Nicholas Mercer, who criticised the government for characterising representatives of Iraqi victims as 'money-grabbing lawyers'.[149]

A bill was introduced in 2017 to protect serving and former military personnel on overseas operations from what the defence secretary Ben Wallace claimed was a '"vexatious" cycle of claims and re-investigations'.[150] It proposed time limits of five years for prosecution and six years for civil claims. Future governments would also 'consider derogating from the European convention on human rights [for] significant

---

[146] J Hyde, 'Yes, minister – SRA's Leigh Day correspondence revealed' (*Law Society Gazette*, 13 December 2018) www.lawgazette.co.uk/news/yes-minister-sras-leigh-day-correspondence-revealed/5068681.article.
[147] M Tran, 'Dozens of inquiries into alleged Iraq war crimes scrapped' *The Guardian* (25 January 2015).
[148] O Bowcott, 'Court case against Iraq war law firm "politically driven"' *The Guardian* (22 June 2017).
[149] Tran (n 147).
[150] O Bowcott, 'Bill sets five-year limit to prosecute UK armed forces who served abroad' *The Guardian* (18 March 2020) www.theguardian.com/uk-news/2020/mar/18/bill-sets-five-year-limit-to-sue-uk-military-veterans-who-served-abroad.

overseas military operations'. In 2019, a speech by the defence secretary promising to protect soldiers from 'lawfare', the use of law to attack a country's defences, was criticised as threatening breach of the rule of law.[151]

The Iraqi war claims exposed the risks of so-called 'independent' regulation to lawyers. PIL, a solicitors' firm only established by Shiner in 1999, quickly folded, but Leigh Day and Co was a more serious proposition, leaders in the fields of human rights and public interest actions. Even so, the cost to Leigh Day could be expected to have a chilling effect on claims against government. The SDT heard from 13 witnesses, considered 12,000 pages of material and examined 250 separate allegations. At the preliminary hearing, it was claimed that Leigh Day had spent £3.9m defending the case to that point. Costs were rarely ordered against the SRA, even on unsuccessful prosecutions. In November 2017 the respondents made an unsuccessful application for the SRA to pay 60 per cent of its costs, at that point exceeding £7 million. The SRA was however ordered to pay the costs of an unsuccessful appeal to the High Court.[152]

V. DISCUSSION

Hayek amplified a division between political liberalism, where institutional arrangements preserved rights, and neoliberalism, which postulated the adequacy of free trade and the rule of law as sole requirements of liberty. Among the trappings of liberal democracy considered inessential were professions authoritative in their areas of expertise. Only 20 years into the neoliberal era, Abel defined professionalism in the past tense, as a historical phase in which occupations exercised substantial control of the market for their services, typically through a professional body.[153] While Clementi's justification for his report referred to the importance of the rule of law, he did not consider professions' role in maintaining it or the consequences of moving lawyers closer to government. Most academic analysis of the post-LSA legal services market followed the same route, assuming 'independent' regulation was achieved in this way.

Short reports by Stephen Mayson reviewing the legal services market perceived the LSA had been a limited success.[154] While different regulators prioritised different regulatory objectives, the LSB was committed to the 'reform and modernise the legal services marketplace in the interests of consumers'.[155] Despite his alignment with these goals Mayson detected 'understandable perceptions from international

---

[151] Editorial, 'Memo to Mordaunt: the rule of law can only be upheld by observing it' *The Guardian* (16 May 2019).

[152] N Rose, 'SRA reveals cost of Leigh Day case and ministers' intense interest' (*Legal Futures*, 18 December 2018) www.legalfutures.co.uk/latest-news/sra-reveals-cost-of-leigh-day-case-and-ministers-interest.

[153] Abel (n 17).

[154] S Mayson, *Independent Review of Legal Services Regulation: Assessment of the Current Regulatory Framework* (London, UCL Centre for Ethics and Law, 2020) www.ucl.ac.uk/ethics-law/publications/2018/sep/independent-review-legal-services-regulation.

[155] ibid 18.

observers and consumers that the regulatory structure in England & Wales is a creature of government and not therefore truly independent'.[156] He suggested that the rule of law was a factor justifying 'sector-specific regulation', alongside 'justice and the interests of UK plc'.[157]

Mayson acknowledged that professional independence was 'important in the context of the rule of law, given that independent legal challenge of government may be required to ensure that government itself acts within the law'.[158] Referencing the CMA's insistence that the issue of regulatory independence was a priority in any market review,[159] Mayson envisaged a context of practice independent of both government and profession. Thus:

> Where a regulatory objective requires an independent legal profession (or, as I might prefer, independent legal advice and representation), independence from government and other representative interests is essential if public confidence in the administration of justice and in legal services is to be achieved.[160]

As one of nine 'significant shortcomings' of the present structure Mayson identified 'the unsatisfactory nature of the separation of regulation and representation'.[161]

A common misconception of government and academics was that lawyers could be 'independent' of the state without connection to a body itself independent of the state. The absence of such institutions created a vacuum, a gap in civil society which could only be filled by the state. The Leigh Day example showed that 'independent regulators' as conceived by the LSA connived with the executive against those they regulated. It showed that lawyers' professional role in acting against the state to expose breaches of the rule of law was not secure. The failed prosecution of the Leigh Day respondents did not prove that the system worked, just that it did on this occasion.

VI. CONCLUSION

The argument for the structural independence of lawyers from the machinery of the state was that they operated both individually and collectively as meaningful constraints on centralised power.[162] In the nineteenth and twentieth centuries, professions were sources of power independent from the state. Group identity instilled and reinforced a disposition to support the rule of law.[163] The marginalisation of legal

---

[156] ibid 17.
[157] S Mayson, *Independent Review of Legal Services Regulation: The Rationale for legal services regulation* (London, UCL Centre for Ethics and Law, 2020) 21.
[158] ibid 17.
[159] ibid 18.
[160] Mayson (n 157) 16.
[161] ibid 22.
[162] See also BZ Tamanaha, *On the Rule of Law: History, Politics, Theory*, (Cambridge, Cambridge University Press, 2004).
[163] D Abrams and MA Hogg, 'Social identification, self-categorization and social influence' (1990) 1(1) *European Review of Social Psychology* 195.

professions in England and Wales towards the end of the twentieth century, would, according to Halliday and Karpik be: 'a good test of the thesis that the independence lost by the bar and judiciary is the gain of executive authority'.[164] In fact, the authority of both government and corporations increased in the period afterwards.

---

[164] TC Halliday and L Karpik, 'Politics Matters' in Halliday and Karpik (eds), *Lawyers and the Rise of Western Political Liberalism* (Oxford, Clarendon Press, 1997) 24.

15
Corporatocracy

I. INTRODUCTION

THE EAST INDIA Company, founded in 1600, was the foundation of nineteenth century British imperialism in India. By the early 1800s it accounted for half of world trade. In the twenty-first century also, modern day commercial power was concentrated in relatively few global corporations.[1] Indeed, this reflected the reality that 'the long-established place occupied by the state in society is now compromised and effectively limited by the reign of the multinational corporation'.[2] Government was subjugated to business interests, forced to accept domination of its policy agendas,[3] organised the state to promote corporate interests and even accept corporate domination of the state.[4] Corporatocracy changed the traditional commitments of some lawyers to the rule of law.

II. THEORY

Between the late 1700s and early 1900s Western political economy was based on classical liberal theory deriving from John Locke, Adam Smith, and David Ricardo. The demands from commercial actors that the state 'leave us alone' '*laissez-nous faire*' led to economies in advanced nations based on property rights, free labour, low taxes, the gold standard, little corporate regulation, no unions, and austerity budgets. By the twentieth century Western governments influenced by John Maynard Keynes' economic theory were more committed to social welfare.[5] From the viewpoint of the 1930s the possibility that Friedrich Von Hayek's ideas would dominate the world economy was implausible.[6]

In the 1930s Hayek was at the London School of Economics and in the shadow of Keynes. In 1938 he met Ludwig von Mises in Paris and was encouraged that someone else saw social democracy, state planning, and the welfare state, as collectivist ventures akin to Nazism and communism. In the 1940s Hayek was at Chicago University, his position supported by wealthy benefactors seeking a small state, low taxes, and minimal

---

[1] S Vitali, JB Glattfelder and S Battiston, 'The Network of Global Corporate Control' (2011) PLoS ONE 6(10): e25995, https://journals.plos.org/plosone/article?id=10.1371/journal.pone.0025995.
[2] HJ Shaw, 'The Rise of Corporatocracy in a Disenchanted Age' (2008) 1(1) *Human Geography* 1.
[3] J Sachs, *The Price of Civilization* (New York, Random House, 2011).
[4] Shaw (n 2).
[5] JM Keynes's *General Theory of Employment, Interest and Money* (1936).
[6] G Monbiot, 'Neoliberalism – the ideology at the root of all our problems' *The Guardian* (15 April 2015).

regulation.[7] He was not held in high regard by his colleagues. Early in his Chicago tenure he was dismissed as a 'stock right-wing man' with a 'stock right-wing sponsor'.[8]

Hayeks' work to justify unequal wealth attracted private sponsors but his principal methodological tool, the price mechanism, could compete for funding with the hard sciences. Individually, he argued, our values were personal, mere opinions, but collectively, the market converted them into prices, or objective facts. Hayek's theory was promoted at other University centres, notably Virginia. During the 1950s and 1960s other members of the Chicago School, Milton Friedman, and Robert Lucas, used it to support anti-welfare economic theories. Friedman argued that economic freedom was essential to political freedom. Government control of the means of production stifled dissent and exchange of ideas.[9] These arguments were supported by an international network of interest groups, like Mont Pelerin Society, sponsored by wealthy donors.[10]

From the 1980s, Hayek's impact arguably matched Keynes. Hayek's predecessors at the Chicago School, such as Frank Knight, Henry Simons and Jacob Viner, acknowledged the importance of reason in identifying and prioritising values. They opposed Roosevelt's New Deal in the 1920s, but distinguished market value from social values.[11] The objective rationale given to human behaviour by Hayek meant values not calculable by price were mere opinions;[12] reason, however rigorous, was subjective or relative. Knight had noted; 'Economic man is the selfish, ruthless object of moral condemnation'[13] but Hayek made economic man both moral and central. Through the influence of successors like Milton Friedman, and adoption by conservative politicians like Reagan and Thatcher, Hayek's use of price to assess value changed public sphere discourse.

Some critics of neoliberalism contended that contraction of public services stripped the state of moral sway, reducing it to 'nothing but authority and obedience'.[14] Others saw neoliberalism as a new mode of regulation. In a lecture series at the Collège de France, Michel Foucault suggested that technologies of governance (power) had to be understood in the context of their underpinning political rationality.[15] Neoliberalism's conception of humans as *homo economicus* comprised two components; their natural attributes and dispositions and their 'investments' in self-maintenance. Through education and training people were the 'entrepreneurs of themselves'.[16] Neoliberalism was a platform for individual, rational choice.

Behaviour in the social sphere was a dimension of the economic domain. Behaviour could be modified by choices. Lemke suggested, for example that the neoliberal did not view crime in moral or normative terms but simply as a form of economic activity. Like everyone else, criminals were individuals making decisions based on rational

---

[7] ibid.
[8] S Metcalf, 'Neoliberalism: The idea that swallowed the world' *The Guardian* (18 August 2017).
[9] M Friedman, *Capitalism and Freedom* (Chicago, University of Chicago Press, 1962).
[10] Monbiot (n 6).
[11] Metcalf (n 8).
[12] ibid.
[13] Metcalf (n 8) citing FH Knight, 'Ethics and the Economic Interpretation' (1922) 36 *The Quarterly Journal of Economics* 454.
[14] Monbiot (n 6).
[15] T Lemke, 'The "Birth of Bio-Politics": Michel Foucault's Lecture at the Collège de France on Neo-Liberal Governmentality' (2001) 30(2) *Economy & Society* 190.
[16] ibid

cost benefit analysis. Controlling rational economic behaviour was simply an issue of managing the economic environment in which it occurred.

The neoliberal emphasis on self-management was consistent with a concept of government common until the eighteenth century. It had embraced different kinds of influences on behaviour, such as attitudes within the family and control of self.[17] Foucault's concept of governmentality suggested that familiar forms of government, such as coercion through law, were typically supplemented by these influences. The balance between the two modes of regulation was fluid. Neoliberalism replaced externally imposed regulatory mechanisms with techniques of self-regulation.[18] Foucault argued that the internalisation of the regulatory environment of the market was a distinct approach to 'governmentality', aiming to regulate conduct through the environment created and the subjectivity of citizens.

Neoliberal governmentality was achieved through definition of problems, concepts to address them, and strategies of intervention. Strategies included agencies, procedures, and legal forms, all of which could be adapted to the market economy.[19] Of Freidson's regulatory logics (see previous chapter), neoliberalism was antithetical to the strategy of professionalism but sought perfect competition, where innovation was encouraged and prices kept low, and encouraged corporate bureaucracy, where efficient management produced reliable products at reasonable cost.[20] Under neoliberalism, corporations were the engine of society.

III. THE RISE OF CORPORATE POWER

Bakan claimed that corporations and corporate capitalism depended on legal foundations and supports 'which taken together represent a massive infusion of state power into society'.[21] Benefits accelerating in the nineteenth century included protecting corporate rights as 'legal persons', validating their legal mandates and shielding their managers, directors and shareholders from legal liability. The development of the world economy after World War II reinforced the impervious condition of the corporation. The worldwide diffusion of deregulation and liberalisation policies by governments, the World Trade Organisation, International Monetary Fund and World Bank created a global marketplace in which multinational corporations were relatively uncontrolled.[22] Three areas in which the rise of the corporation affected society included government, the state, and legal services.

A. The Composition of Government

In the early modern period lawyers were well-represented in legislatures and political leadership within the core common law core and beyond. Argentina's 38 democratically

---

[17] ibid.
[18] ibid.
[19] E Freidson, *Professionalism: The Third Logic* (Oxford, Blackwell Publishers, 2001).
[20] ibid.
[21] J Bakan, 'The Invisible Hand of Law: Private Regulation and the Rule of Law' (2015) 48 *Cornell International Law Journal* 279.
[22] Shaw (n 2).

elected presidents included 23 lawyers. Since 1983, apart from two engineers, all were lawyers.[23] In the nineteenth century, Scandinavian lawyers were in a higher social strata and, being well represented in parliaments, had 'laid the foundations for markets and modern state bureaucracies'.[24] Until the 1970s, Hammerslev noted, legal education provided general training in running a society and introduction to social networks in the upper classes 'with which the legal profession could construct society'.[25]

There were plausible explanations of why the numbers and significance of lawyers in government declined since the 1970s. One was the waning of legal study as a route of aspiration with the relative decay of professionalism and revitalisation of business.[26] Another was the fact that from the 1980s, law enrolled twice as many women as men[27] and despite qualifying as lawyers, women were less likely to go into politics. Business and management both grew in popularity relative to law and enrolled more men than women.

In the UK, the past 50 years saw a steady decline in Parliamentary representation of professions and a steady increase in representatives of business. Table 1 showed that between 1979 and 2015 the UK Parliament had growing numbers of members with business backgrounds while those with professional backgrounds declined. Rounding the percentages up or down, the professions went from 45 per cent to 31 per cent, while business went from 22 per cent to 31 per cent. Those choosing a political route without experiencing another career went from 3 per cent to 17 per cent.

Table 1 Composition of Parliament by occupational group in the House of Commons 1979–2015[28]

Occ grp	1979	1983	1987	1992	1997	2001	2005	2010	2015
professions	278	278	262	258	272	270	242	218	194
business	138	162	161	152	113	107	118	156	192
Manual workers	98	74	73	63	56	33	38	25	19
Misc.	106	115	133	154	188	200	217	222	221
	619	629	629	627	629	630	615	621	626

Source: L Audickas and B Cracknell, *Social Background of MPs 1979–2015* (London, House of Commons Library, 2020).

A drop in the number of lawyers revealed in Table 2 was less dramatic than the fall in professionals overall. It showed that lawyers comprised approximately half of

---

[23] M Böhmer, 'Argentina: The Long Transition of the Legal Profession' in RL Abel, O Hammerslev, U Schultz and H Sommerlad, *Lawyers in 21st-Century Societies, vol. 1: National Reports* (Oxford, Hart Publishing, 2020).

[24] O Hammerslev, 'Denmark, Sweden and Norway: Liberalisation, Differentiation and the Emergence of a Legal Services Market' in Abel, Hammerslev, Schultz and Sommerlad (n 23).

[25] ibid.

[26] Law graduate earnings in the 1970s were less than those in business, engineering and, particularly economics (J Britton, L Dearden, L van der Erve and B Waltmann, *The Impact of undergraduate degree on Lifetime Earnings* (London, Institute of Fiscal Studies, 2020) 21, Fig 13 https://assets.publishing.service.gov.uk/government/uploads/system/uploads/attachment_data/file/869264/The_impact_of_undergraduate_degrees_on_lifetime_earnings_-_online_appendix.pdf.

[27] HESA, 'Who is Studying in HE' (HE enrolments by subject of study, 2019/20), www.hesa.ac.uk/data-and-analysis/students/whos-in-he.

the professions represented in Parliament over the same period, but the numbers of barristers fell from 11 per cent to 6 per cent over the period while solicitors went from 5 per cent to 8 per cent.

Table 2 Composition of Parliament by occupational group in the House of Commons 1979–2015

Occ	1979	1983	1987	1992	1997	2001	2005	2010	2015
Barrister	67	69	57	53	36	33	34	38	38
Solicitor	29	35	31	30	28	35	38	48	51
Politician/political organiser	21	20	34	46	60	66	87	90	107
Publisher/journalist	46	45	42	44	47	50	43	38	34
White Collar	9	21	27	46	72	76	78	84	71

Source: L Audickas and B Cracknell, *Social Background of MPs 1979–2015* (London, House of Commons Library, 2020).

The shift in legislatures toward business graduates and away from lawyers may have had various consequences. It could produce institutions more antagonistic to non-business institutions and values, increase legislation favourable to corporations, and reduce the pool of candidates for Law Officer jobs and, consequently, the quality of those available. Legislative bodies may also have become less insistent on deliberative procedures, less sensitive to procedural abuses and less insistent on the rule of law. These factors were potentially cumulative so that, for example, legislative assemblies would be less likely to respect or support the advice of Law Officers.[29] A more corporate world could lead to the diminution of competing powers, such as government and particularly the judiciary.[30]

B. The Corporatised State

In the US the impact of corporations began to be felt in the 1960s[31] when the enhanced global mobility of ideas, finance, workers, and products[32] encouraged worldwide companies. Global corporations spread American workplace practices. Despite local resistance, traditional employment, secure jobs for life, trade unions and state benefits declined in most countries.[33] In the UK, major supermarkets pressed for the

---

[28] Based on L Audickas and B Cracknell, *Social Background of MPs 1979–2015* (London, House of Commons Library, 2020) https://commonslibrary.parliament.uk/research-briefings/cbp-7483/.
[29] A Kennon 'Legal Advice to Parliament' in A Horne, G Drewry and D Oliver (eds) *Parliament and the Law* (Oxford, Hart, 2013) 121.
[30] G Monbiot 'No 10 and lobby groups set on undermining democracy' *The Guardian* 2nd September 2020.
[31] E Phelps *Mass Flourishing. How grassroots innovation created jobs, challenge, and change (1st edition)*. (Princeton: Princeton University Press, 2013). Chapter 6, section 4: *The New Corporatism*.
[32] Shaw (n 2).
[33] R Sennet *The Corrosion of Character, The Personal Consequences Of Work In the New Capitalism* (London, WW Norton & Co, 1998).

dismantling of Resale Price Maintenance (RPM), which protected small retailers, and, from 1964 onwards, the repeal of the Shops Act 1950 which restricted Sunday trading.[34] By the 1980s, considerable effort had gone into creating a corporatised public sphere.

The US agencies regulated under the Administrative Procedure Act 1946 began to change frameworks in the 1960s to close avenues for the corruption of government by business. These changes were generally seen to be ineffective, partly because of the negative impact of neo-liberalism on the scale, effectiveness, and legitimacy of the administrative state.[35] In the UK, an obvious attempt to reduce the threat proposed by corporations in the 1990s was the production of the Nolan Principles, following allegations of corrupt corporate influence on Parliament (see chapter five 'Institution'). This was evidence of the growing influence of corporate power on state machinery.

Monbiot suggested that research into ways of making Hayek's vision electorally acceptable in the UK was carried out by lobby groups and right-wing thinktanks such as the Institute for Economic Affairs.[36] Madsen Pirie of the Adam Smith Institute claimed to have mapped Margaret Thatcher's rise to power using financial support from wealthy donors. Articles planned with broadsheet leader writers at *The Times* and *The Telegraph*[37] paved the way for Thatcher's premiership between 1979 and 1990. Thatcher clothed her free market philosophy with the revival of the so-called Victorian values of family, community, and hard work. Thatcher claimed: 'There's no such thing as society. There are individual men and women, and there are families. And no government can do anything except through people, and people must look to themselves first'.[38] Rhetoric was accompanied by policies reducing welfare and employment protection, clamping down on trade unions and decreasing higher rate taxation.

In the 1980s free-market programmes were associated with other signature policies: in the US, increased military spending and, in the UK, the sale of public utilities. Thatcher's government began a process of corporatisation, the full or partial privatisation of public institutions on a massive scale. It began with the Housing Act 1980, forcing local councils to sell their housing stock to tenants at discount. This produced £692 million for the government in the first year but diminished the public role of local councils and forced up rents of remaining tenants.[39] Selling assets and responsibilities for energy, water, trains, health, education, roads, and prisons followed. Privatised public services 'enabled corporations to set up tollbooths in front of essential assets' enabling them to collect unearned income, as rent or interest from citizens and government, for their use'.[40] Not only were existing state assets privatised, but future assets were also sold to private capital.

---

[34] Shaw (n 2).
[35] BJ Cook *The Fourth Branch: Reconstructing the Administrative State for the Commercial Republic* (University Press of Kansas, 2021).
[36] Formed in the UK by free traders Anthony Fisher and Oliver Smedley (Monbiot (n 30)).
[37] ibid.
[38] Interview with *Women's Own* magazine (23 September 1987).
[39] A Beckett, 'Right to buy: The housing Crisis that Thatcher built' *The Guardian* (26 August 2015) www.theguardian.com/society/2015/aug/26/right-to-buy-margaret-thatcher-david-cameron-housing-crisis.
[40] Monbiot (n 6).

In 1992, during the premiership of John Major, a scheme called Private Finance Initiative was introduced, using private funding for public projects, deferring the capital costs.[41] The policy continued under the Labour Prime Minister, Tony Blair, rebranded as the Public Private Partnership in the late 1990s, and used to support public assets like hospitals and schools. Overall, the proliferation of private finance policies exacerbated social inequality[42] but the economic benefits were not clearly demonstrated; value for money being difficult to calculate. The costing methodology factored in the transfer of risk from the public sector to the private and yet delivery remained a public obligation. Contract details were often unavailable for public scrutiny because of 'commercial sensitivity'.[43]

Hiding the terms of public and private contracts prevented local consideration or scrutiny of the purpose of the contract and the way it was performed. An example was a PFI contract signed by Sheffield Council with Amey, a subsidiary of the Spanish mega-corporation Ferrovial, in 2012.[44] This covered the felling of 6,000 trees in Sheffield, which many regarded as significant local landmarks. The council asserted that trivial reasons for felling, such as roots cracking paving stones, could not be examined for contractual reasons.

In 2005, the available evidence was that PPP produced generally higher costs overall than public procurement. Meanwhile, staff delivering services under contracts were often paid less than public sector equivalent workers.[45] The risk in the many cases of failure to deliver contractual obligations were not borne by the private contractor but by consumers in increased costs. The absence of information about PPP contracts made scrutiny difficult and democratic accountability unlikely, but the overall conclusion was that these initiatives had resulted in a transfer of wealth from the public to corporations.[46] While there was no democratic mandate for favouritism towards corporations[47] they were able to influence the election of governments likely to continue it.

An example of a global corporation threatening the independence of government was News Corp, a company owned by media tycoon Rupert Murdoch. Because of his extensive interests and power, and the capacity of his media empire to set news agendas, and magnify or suppress scandals, Murdoch was courted by politicians. He was said to be politically neutral, but his media was generally conservative and right wing, favouring politicians supporting his business agendas. His news programming was shown to shape political views, influence voting patterns, and polarise electorates.[48] Murdoch's ownership of a large part of the UK press was assumed to have a disproportionate influence in setting news agendas for other media.

---

[41] J Shaoul, 'The Private Finance Initiative or the Public Funding of Private Profit?' in G Hodge and C Greve (eds), *The Challenge of Public Private Partnerships* (Cheltenham, Edward Elgar, 2005) 190.
[42] ibid 202–3.
[43] ibid 196.
[44] G Monbiot, 'With just one contract, corporate and state power has subverted democracy' *The Guardian* (25 October 2017).
[45] Shaoul (n 41) 201.
[46] ibid 202.
[47] ibid 202–3.
[48] GJ Martin and A Yurukoglu, 'Bias in Cable News: Persuasion and Polarization' *American Economic Review* (2017) 107(9) *American Economic Review* 2565.

The Murdoch press made a rare exception to support the election of the Labour government of Tony Blair in 1997. Blair flew to Australia to convince Murdoch to endorse Labour, but the Murdoch popular title, *The Sun*, quickly shifted back to the Tories when Blair was replaced by Gordon Brown. After the 2010 election the successor Tory government was led by David Cameron. The justice secretary, political veteran Ken Clarke, described a meeting with Rebekkah Brooks, editor of a Murdoch title *News of the World*, shortly after, in which she 'was instructing me on criminal justice policy' and claiming to be running government with Cameron.[49] In the US, Murdoch established a cable television channel, Fox News, which, during Donald Trump's presidency was a source of right-wing bias, misinformation, and propaganda.[50]

C. Legal Services

Towards the end of the twentieth century the contraction of the state and the growth of the private corporate sphere led to massive growth in the numbers and percentages of lawyers working for corporations. This was demonstrated by comparing employment of lawyers in UK national or local government with that of lawyers employed 'in-house' as advisers to corporations. In 1987 the percentage of solicitors in commerce and industry was 18 per cent of all those holding practising certificates and for those in local and national government it was 14 per cent.[51] By 2015 there were 138,000 total practising certificate holders. The percentage in commerce and industry had increased to 13 per cent, while the percentage in government had declined slightly to 3.5 per cent.[52] Thus, national, and local government employed under 3,000 lawyers in 1975 and under 5,000 in 2015, while companies employed only around 1,500 lawyers in 1975 and just over 17,000 in 2015.[53]

A recent empirical study of in-house company lawyers found them to be in a constant battle to establish a form of independence within their organisations, confused by the regulatory framework, and the relevance of rules designed for private practice rather than for them.[54] Their confusion over professional principles led in-house lawyers to seek guidance from their employing organisation, but the authors concluded, these were often only concerned with not breaking criminal law[55] and

---

[49] G Ruddick, 'Clarke suggests Cameron made Sun deal' *The Guardian* (24 November 2017).
[50] J Mayer, 'The making of the Fox News White House' *The New Yorker* (11 March 2019).
[51] P Marks, *Annual Statistical Report 1987* (London, The Law Society, 1987) Table 2.7. These percentages fell by 1997, to 6% in commerce and industry and 4% in government, as the profession expanded from nearly 48,000 to over 71,000. B Cole, *Trends in the Solicitors' Profession: Annual Statistical Report 1997* (London, The Law Society, 1997) Table 2.7.
[52] S King, J Cox and C Roddis, *Trends in the solicitors' profession Annual Statistical Report* (London, The Law Society, 2016) Table 4.1.
[53] Marks (n 51) Table 1.3.
[54] R Moorhead, S Vaughan and C Godinho, *In-house Lawyers Ethics: Institutional Logics, legal Risks and the Tournament of Influence* (Oxford, Hart Publishing, 2019) 226.
[55] ibid 128–29.

took 'untenable positions on the legality of their actions'.[56] More than 50 per cent of in-house lawyers agreed that their employers took actions against their advice on legally important matters.[57]

Analysis of in-house lawyers' values showed weak orientation to professional principles. Allegiance to notions of independence, the rule of law and public trust was less pronounced than that of lawyers in government legal service or private practice.[58] Data collected between 2002 and 2015 also showed that in-house lawyers performed significantly less pro bono work than private practice lawyers.[59] In only two of four yearly data points did more than 20 per cent of in-house lawyers participate, while on all four data points, between 40 and 50 per cent of private practice lawyers participated. The growth of in-house legal services was not the only point of departure from professional legal structures and values.

Sir David Clementi's report on the legal services market recommended legal disciplinary practices (LDPs), allowing different kinds of lawyers to work together, as a step towards allowing the more contentious multi-disciplinary practices, in which lawyers would work with other professionals to provide legal and other professional services to third parties. The draft Legal Services Bill, ostensibly based on Clementi's report, proposed instead Alternative Business Structures (ABS), corporations. The idea was described by Lord Phillips of Worth Maltravers, the Lord Chief Justice, as 'going beyond Clementi in a fairly dramatic way'.[60]

The Joint Committee on the Draft Legal Services Bill expressed concern at the lack of evidence that allowing corporations into the legal services market would improve services to the most vulnerable.[61] The government apparently hoped that national supermarket chains, the likely applicants to be ABS, would undercut lawyers by investing in technology, embracing routinised work practices and overriding the professional desire to perform custom work.[62] A report in 2014 suggested that under 250 ABS had been established[63] but they achieved a significant market share, accounting for a third of all turnovers for personal injury, a significant percentage in mental health, non-litigation (eg, mergers and acquisitions and probate), consumer and social welfare. They did not, however, significantly reduce prices, possibly because they needed lawyers for reserved work and absorbed a regulatory overhead.[64]

---

[56] ibid 145.
[57] ibid 61.
[58] ibid 179.
[59] A Boon and A Whyte, 'An Explosion of Legal Philanthropy? The Transformation of Pro Bono Legal Services in England and Wales' in SL Cummings, F De Sa E Silva and LA Trubek, *Global pro bono: Diffusion, Contestation, Learned Lessons* (Cambridge, Cambridge University Press, 2022).
[60] *Joint Committee on the Draft Legal Services Bill: First report* (UK Parliament, 2006) ch 5 para 250 https://publications.parliament.uk/pa/jt200506/jtselect/jtlegal/232/23204.htm.
[61] ibid para 324.
[62] R Susskind, *The End of Lawyers?: Rethinking the Nature of Legal Services* (Oxford, Oxford University Press, 2008).
[63] SRA Research on Alternative Business Structures (2014) www.sra.org.uk/globalassets/documents/sra/research/abs-quantitative-research-may-2014.pdf?version=4a1ac4.
[64] A Boon, 'Cocktails of Logics – Reform of Legal Services Regulation in England and Wales' in A Boon (ed), *International Perspectives on the Regulation of Lawyers and Legal Services* (Oxford and Portland, Oregon, Hart Publishing, 2017) 209.

As the last chapter showed, the advent of ABS had an impact on the regulatory strategy of the new solicitor regulator, the SRA, which moved towards the logic of corporate bureaucracy. It required all law firms, even sole practices, to adopt roles the LSA specified for ABS, a chief officer for legal practice and a chief officer for finance. In its first code of conduct the SRA adopted Clementi's suggestion of using principle-based regulation to set broad outcomes rather than detailed codes of conduct. These were more suited to guiding the behaviour of organisations than that of individual professionals.[65]

A study of solicitors' firms by Aulakh and Kirkpatrick found that the SRA's regulatory regime encouraged better business management of solicitors' firms and reduced consumer complaints.[66] It also encouraged normative divergence by providing flexible regulatory outcomes. This encouraged firms to align regulation to their own business purposes, fostering distinct local ethics. Individual observance was undermined by a compliance mentality focused on designated officers, management systems and risk management processes, rather than professional responsibility.[67] This was effectively the corporatisation of law work.

IV. LAWYERS AGAINST CORPORATIONS

Large corporations sometimes used law to intimidate opposition. A notable example in the UK was the famous *McLibel* case.[68] As part of a campaign to prevent a McDonald's fast-food outlet opening on their local high street, two environmental activists distributed a few hundred pamphlets outlining alleged company abuses. McDonald's Corporation sued them for corporate libel, spending tens of millions of pounds in litigation lasting 10 years.[69] Legal aid was not available for libel proceedings and the defendants depended on pro bono advice from lawyers, including a future Labour Party leader, the barrister Keir Starmer.[70] The decision largely favoured MacDonald's and Starmer was instructed on an appeal to the European Court of Human Rights. Damages were awarded against the British government for failing to protect the right of the public to criticise corporations. The case, and the subsequent Defamation Act 2013, restricted corporate ability to suppress critics.

In the US, legal actions against corporate critics were known as SLAPPs (strategic lawsuits against public participation).[71] Their primary motive was said to be preventing presentation of arguments in public fora. SLAPPs therefore potentially impeded

---

[65] A Boon, 'Professionalism under the Legal Services Act 2007' (2011) 17(3) *International Journal of the Legal Profession* 195.
[66] S Aulakh and I Kirkpatrick, 'New governance regulation and lawyers: When substantive compliance erodes legal professionalism' (2018) 5 *Journal of Professions and Organization* 167.
[67] ibid.
[68] *McDonald's Corporation v Steel & Morris* [1997] EWHC QB 366.
[69] M Oliver, 'McLibel' *The Guardian* (15 February 2005) www.theguardian.com/news/2005/feb/15/food.foodanddrink.
[70] 'Corrections and clarifications' *The Guardian* (18 January 2020).
[71] GW Pring and P Canan, *SLAPPs: Getting sued for Speaking Out* (Philadelphia, Temple University Press, 1996).

citizen participation in government. By 2016, 29 States had passed legislation preventing corporate defamation SLAPPs[72] but they became increasingly common in Europe. Before her murder for investigative reporting of corruption in awarding government contracts in Malta, the journalist Daphne Caruna Galizia was defending 40 corporate libel suits.[73]

In the US, lawyers were active in creating what was characterised as a new 'human rights industry', holding corporations to account in US courts for their overseas activities.[74] US courts found corporations complicit in state crimes such as genocide[75] in suits filed by private practice cause lawyers or through the pro bono initiatives of corporate law firms.[76] These parallel developments came together in a series of connected cases involving the rights of Indigenous people against oil companies in Ecuador. The litigation showed that lawyers bringing public interest cases against corporations were vulnerable to intimidation by lawsuit.

In 2009, attorneys filed a class-action suit in New York against Texaco on behalf of over 30,000 farmers and Indigenous people of the Lago Agrio region of the Amazon, alleging massive contamination caused by the company's oil drilling.[77] Texaco claimed that it represented 37 per cent of a consortium including the Ecuadorian state oil company and that it had paid $40 million to the Ecuadorian government as a contribution to a clean-up.[78] Texaco admitted the continuing pollution of the region but argued that its liability had ended. Claims were filed in the US on behalf of Indigenous populations affected by a crisis of ill health including birth defects.

Chevron, which had bought Texaco in 2001, claimed that any continuing responsibility was that of the national oil company of Ecuador. Claiming that the Ecuadorian legal system was fair, Chevron sought to transfer the case there and, in 2011, was ordered to pay $18 billion, later reduced to $9.5 billion. Chevron then claimed the judgment was fraudulently obtained and moved its assets out of Ecuador. The claimants' case in Ecuador was handled by a US based attorney, Steven Donziger.

In 2009, Chevron had threatened to demonise Donziger. They hired private investigators and assembled a legal team of hundreds of lawyers from 60 firms. In 2010, a federal court judge, Lewis A Kaplan, ordered that out-takes from a documentary of the litigation, later released as *Crude: The Real Price of Oil*,[79] be disclosed to Chevron, because it showed a court appointed expert attending a claimant meeting. In 2011 Chevron filed racketeering charges under the Racketeer Influenced and

---

[72] AL Roth, 'Upping the Ante: Rethinking Anti-SLAPP Laws in the Age of the Internet' (2016) 2 *Brigham Young University Law Review* 741.
[73] G Phillips, 'How the free press worldwide is under threat' *The Guardian* (26 May 2020).
[74] G Baars, *The Corporation, Law and Capitalism: A Radical Perspective on the Role of Law in the Global Political Economy* (Chicago, Haymarket Books 2020) 360–61.
[75] ibid 363.
[76] ibid 364.
[77] S Lerner, 'How the environmental lawyer who won a massive judgment against Chevron lost everything' (*The Intercept*, 29 January 2020) https://theintercept.com/2020/01/29/chevron-ecuador-lawsuit-steven-donziger/.
[78] NV Binder, 'Making Foreign Judgment law Great Again: The Aftermath of Chevron v. Donziger' (2018) 51 *Suffolk UL Rev* 33, 43.
[79] Later premiered as *Crude: The Real Price of Oil (Dir J Berlinger)*2009 Sundance Festival.

Corrupt Organizations Act 1970 (RICO), legislation originally intended to prevent mafia or other gang infiltration of the business economy.

Kaplan described Chevron as 'a company of considerable importance to our economy that employs thousands all over the world, that supplies a group of commodities, gasoline, heating oil, other fuels, and lubricants on which every one of us depends every single day'.[80] In 2014 he declared the Ecuadorian judgment an 'egregious fraud'. Donziger was accused of inflating the damages claim, tampering with expert reports and paying £500,000 to a trial judge called Zambrano, so that his team could write the judgment.[81] Another Ecuadorian judge, Alberto Guerra, gave evidence that he worked on the final judgment with Zambrano and both were bribed. Donziger was found guilty of racketeering, extortion, wire fraud, money laundering, obstruction of justice, and witness tampering.

The Southern District of New York refused to prosecute Donziger for refusing to surrender his electronic devices, but Kaplan pursued criminal contempt charges himself and appointed a private law firm with recent links to Chevron, Seward & Kissel, to act.[82] In 2020, Donziger was electronically tagged and confined to his apartment for refusing to hand over a mobile phone and computer. He was subsequently disbarred, his bank accounts frozen and his passport seized. He claimed that Chevron were '… trying to totally destroy me'.[83] Kaplan nominated his successor in the case, Lorretta Preska, and in October 2021 she imposed a six-month prison sentence on Donziger for contempt of court.[84]

Chevron's campaign against Donziger divided opinion, not least because of the difficulty of assessing the reported facts. In 2018, however, the Permanent Court of Arbitration in The Hague refused enforcement of the original order against Chevron and referred to the corruption in obtaining it.[85] In 2019 Theodore J Boutrous, Jr, a partner in the law firm of Gibson, Dunn & Crutcher LLP, one of the lead lawyers instructed by Chevron in the Ecuadorian litigation, published an academic article outlining misconduct allegations against Donziger.[86] He suggested the case was part of a pattern of US lawyers bringing fraudulent lawsuits against US companies supported by political smear campaigns. Donziger was said to have secured a public statement in favour of judgment against Chevron from the President of Ecuador. The documentary, *Crude*, was allegedly solicited as part of his campaign.

Kaplan ruled that *Crude* was not covered by journalistic privilege because Donziger had control over the final production. The hours of out-take footage disclosed to

---

[80] Lerner (n 77).
[81] Binder (n 78).
[82] EM O'Hagan, 'In the Chevron court case, ordinary Ecuadorians' voices don't seem to count' *The Guardian* (18 March 2014).
[83] ibid.
[84] E Helmore, 'Lawyer Steven Donziger gets six-month sentence for contempt in Chevron battle' *The Guardian* (1 October 2021) www.theguardian.com/us-news/2021/oct/01/steven-donziger-lawyer-sentenced-contempt-chevron.
[85] J Randazzo, 'Tribunal Condemns Ecuador's $9.5 Billion Ruling Against Chevron' (*Wall Street Journal*, 7 September 2017).
[86] TJ Boutrous, 'The lessons from the Chevron litigation: The defense perspective' (2019) 1(2) *Stanford Journal of Complex Litigation* 219.

Chevron were a 'treasure trove' of damning evidence; signing-up clients on false pretences, making false factual and legal claims and manufacturing evidence.[87] Kaplan's decision to issue an injunction preventing enforcement of the Ecuador decision in the US, and the novel use of the RICO provisions, was upheld on appeal.[88]

Critics of Chevron suggested that they had moved the main witness, the judge Guerra, and his family to the US and paid him an allowance that was more than 20 times his salary. They held over 50 witness preparation meetings with him before the court heard his evidence. They paid more than a million dollars to Guerra, who later admitted lying under oath.[89] In the absence of a jury, Guerra's credibility was assessed by Kaplan alone. A Harvard Law School professor Charles Nesson, who taught evidence, used the Donziger case as an example of asymmetric civil litigation likely to produce an unfair trial.[90]

In 2020, 29 Nobel laureates wrote an open letter alleging that Chevron's action against Donziger constituted 'one of the world's most egregious cases of judicial harassment and defamation'.[91] They noted that environmental activists in many countries were murdered but that Chevron sought 'death by a thousand cuts through the manipulation of a legal system it has managed to stack in its favor'.[92] One of the authors, Jody Williams, said that Chevron were trying to 'show environmentalists, to show activists all over the world that you cannot go up against corporations, you cannot defend what you believe to be true and right'. She added that the signatories did not accept that:[93] 'They believe in the rule of law … They believe in justice.'[94]

Paul Paz y Miño, associate director of Amazon Watch, said that Donziger's experience was 'nothing short of terrifying for any activist challenging corporate power and the oil industry in the US'.[95] Rex Weyler, co-founder of Greenpeace International, argued that climate activists should focus on the Donziger case as part of a larger battle to establish the true economic cost of fossil fuels. The application of RICO to Donziger threatened to hinder enforcement of foreign judgments in American courts and therefore impeded control of environmental damage by US corporations. UN experts based in Geneva provided an opinion that Donziger's two-year house arrest was a breach of human rights that should be remedied by compensation. Amnesty International called for his immediate release.[96]

The cases between Chevron and Donziger could be viewed through many lenses: an uneven struggle against corporate power; the risks of over-identification run by cause

---

[87] ibid 221–22.
[88] *Chevron v Donziger* Nos. 14-0826(L), 14-0832(C), 2016 WL 4173988 (2d Cir. Aug. 8, 2016); 'Cases' (2016) 130 *Harvard Law Review* 745 (and Binder (n 78)).
[89] O'Hagan (n 82).
[90] Lerner (n 77).
[91] ibid.
[92] J Watts, 'Nobel laureates condemn "judicial harassment" of environmental lawyer' *The Guardian* (18 April 2020) www.theguardian.com/world/2020/apr/18/nobel-laureates-condemn-judicial-harassment-of-environmental-lawyer.
[93] ibid.
[94] A Klasfeld, 'Nobel Laureates Condemn Rare Judge-Ordered Prosecution' (*Courthouse News Service*, 16 April 2020) https://www.courthousenews.com/nobel-laureates-condemn-rare-judge-ordered-prosecution/.
[95] Lerner (n 77).
[96] Helmore (n 84).

lawyers; lawyer and client conflict of interest.[97] According to Boustrous, the lawyers' plans for the damages paid little regard to the needs of their clients but prioritised repaying their third-party funders and themselves. Whether the case was primarily an example of claimant lawyer fraud or corporate intimidation, the Donziger case demonstrated the importance of lawyers observing obligations to legality. It was an unfortunate advert for transfer of neutral partisanship to the international sphere.[98] It was certainly an effective deterrent to lawyers considering taking cases against large corporations.

V. CORPORATE LAWYERS

A. Expansion

National modern legal services markets were traditionally served by sole practitioners or relatively small groups of lawyers in firms. Until relatively recently this was even true of elite City of London firms doing corporate work, particularly banking and finance. Under the Companies Act 1948, they were restricted to 20 partners. This cap was removed in 1967, allowing for significant growth in partnership numbers and the size of firms generally.[99] The 1980s privatisation of state assets and the 'Big Bang' de-regulation of financial services in 1986 encouraged an explosion of high-level work.[100] By 1988, Clifford Chance, the largest English firm, had 168 partners, 386 assistant solicitors and 123 articled clerks.[101]

Between 1989 and 1999 the number of solicitors' firms in England and Wales increased from just over 8,000 to just over 8,500.[102] The vast majority of these firms had fewer than 10 partners, but between 1989 and 1999 the number with more than 26 partners increased from 65 to 123. By 1999, 24 had more than 81 partners. These figures underestimated the rate of growth of the largest firms, those concentrated around capital markets in New York and London.[103] Some grew to around a thousand partners, each with thousands of associate solicitors and globally distributed offices. This gave English and American law firms significant advantages in an international market for legal services favouring scale and reputation.

---

[97] For contrasting examples see J Emersberger, 'Manufacturing Disgrace: Reuters Distorts Chevron v Donziger' (*FAIR*, 11 September 2020) https://fair.org/home/manufacturing-disgrace-reuters-distorts-chevron-v-donziger/ and MI Krauss, 'Chevron v Donziger: The Epic Battle for the Rule of Law Hits the Second Circuit' (*Forbes*, 21 April 2015) www.forbes.com/sites/michaelkrauss/2015/04/21/chevron-v-donziger-the-epic-battle-for-the-rule-of-law-hits-the-second-circuit/?sh=739523513602.

[98] V Holmes and S Rice, 'Our common future: The Imperative for a Contextual Ethics in a Connected World' in R Mortensen, F Bartlett and K Tranter, *Alternative Perspectives on Lawyers and Legal Ethics: Reimagining the Profession* (London and New York, Routledge, 2011) 56.

[99] Companies Act 1967, s 120(1)(a).

[100] J Flood, 'Megalaw in the UK: Professionalism or Corporatism? A Preliminary Report' (1989) 64 *Indiana Law Journal* 569.

[101] ibid 574–76.

[102] B Cole, *Trends in the Solicitors' Profession: Annual Statistical report 1999* (London, The Law Society, 2000) Table 3.11.

[103] J Flood, 'Lawyers as sanctifiers: The role of elite law firms in international business transactions' (2007) 14(1) *Indiana Journal of Global Legal Studies* 35.

Large US law firms had experienced a period of exponential growth more than a decade before those in the UK. In 1969 the US already had 20 law firms with 100 lawyers; by 1980 there were 100 such firms.[104] An influential study of the Chicago legal services market found law firms fell into one of two hemispheres, reflecting service to either corporate or individual clients.[105] Later work clarified that the corporate 'hemisphere' was probably larger and that three specialisms, tax, litigation and real estate, crossed hemispheres.[106] While national legal services markets were often varied, there was great analytical and descriptive power in the hemispheric model.

Corporate clients were powerful, savvy, and mobile and their problems large and complex, requiring lawyers to have effective systems and to work in teams. Corporate firms only ever did private work for individuals working within their client corporations.[107] Non-corporate clients presented one-off 'private plight' problems such as personal injury, employment, or divorce. The firms they went to were smaller and geographically spread, with single practitioners handling each matter.

The role of large firm lawyers in relation to the public interest and the rule of law in the US was ambiguous. By virtue of their backgrounds, and the power and status of their firms, they represented a professional elite, yet their position insulated them from ordinary people, ordinary problems, and ordinary law. Their work, solving the legal problems of global corporations in a new, internationalised practice, involved customised work and extreme specialisation in esoteric fields. This made them prime candidates to draft legislation[108] or to be Washington lobbyists, advising clients how to influence legislation and the legislative programme.[109]

B. Values

The values of large law firms in private practice received academic attention in America. Their structures resembled those of their corporate clients more than they did those of other law firms,[110] as did their personnel. Early studies found that elite firms, such as those on Wall Street, appointed graduates from the most prestigious law schools and refused to do the 'dishonourable work' of criminal defence and divorce.[111] Their disdain of private client work suggested that their interests and values would also be distinct from ordinary law firms. These differences, it was

---

[104] RL Nelson, 'Practice and Privilege: Social Change and the Structure of Large Law Firms' 1981 *American Bar Foundation Research Journal* 95.

[105] JP Heinz and EO Laumann, *Chicago Lawyers: Social Structure of the Bar* (New York, Chicago, Russell Sage Foundation, 1982).

[106] JP Heinz, EO Laumann, RL Nelson and E Michelson, 'The Changing Character of Lawyers' Work: Chicago in 1975 and 1995' (1998) 32(4) *Law & Society Review* 751.

[107] ibid.

[108] Nelson (n 104).

[109] MC Miller, *The High Priests of American Politics: The Role of Lawyers in American Political institutions* (Knoxville, University of Tennessee Press, 1995) 44.

[110] Flood (n 100).

[111] EO Smigel, *The Wall Street Lawyer: Professional Organization Man?* (New York, Free Press of Glencoe, 1964) 150.

thought, were 'unlikely to produce a Bar of shared fate and common purpose'.[112] Of their English counterparts, Flood concluded that, unless traditional commitments aligned with the economic realities they faced, large firms would ignore them.[113]

Approaching the millennium, Miller observed that Anglo-American lawyers were distinctive in the size of firm and their devotion to serving capital.[114] Their corporate law firms were criticised for taking a neutral partisan stance in asserting their powerful clients' interests. Academics identified malign consequences where lawyers, typically from large and reputable firms, were accused of precipitating, concealing, or participating in wrongdoing while hiding behind their partisan obligations. This led to involvement in several corporate collapses including liquidation of Lincoln Savings and Loan (1989), but the larger shockwaves were caused by the collapses of Enron Corporation (2001) and Lehman Brothers (2007). Relatively few of the lawyers involved were prosecuted.

Large firms did not necessarily become the rational bureaucracies which Weber predicted would result from large scale. In the early development of large law firms, collegial organisation militated against control by rules or through the authority of leadership. Succession was decided at the highest level, but members controlled their own work and tended to be consulted on issues before decisions affecting the firm were taken.[115] Nelson suggested that methods of control effective in a corporation, including government by rules and the centralised administration of capital, were not necessarily effective in large law firms. They had more fragile authority systems than the corporation, allowing lawyers to have significant client relationships and a voice in the firm.[116]

Some large firms did not move away from professional values. Nelson noted that US large firms had adopted different models of growth, and their choice affected the type of business they operated, who succeeded in it, and what was valued. Although commercialism was on the rise, many firms made decisions for professional rather than financial reasons. There was a feeling of optimism: 'while large-scale bureaucracies may dominate modern society, there are significant and growing professional sectors whose organisational life is dominated by men and tradition rather than by rules and economic rationality'.[117] One test of this was the call for lawyers to undertake pro bono work.

Miller noted that, despite their corporate clientele, members of US corporate law firms were, since the 1960s, involved in 'public interest groups' and advocating liberal causes, including civil and welfare rights.[118] There were many reasons to question whether this would survive the potential stresses of specialisation, competition, workload, and client pressure. With the decline of wider social activism in the 1980s, American large firm pro bono programmes had appeared to decline, but interest was

---

[112] Heinz, Laumann, Nelson and Michelson (n 106) 774.
[113] Flood (n 100) 586.
[114] Miller (n 109) 30–31.
[115] Nelson (n 104) 127.
[116] ibid 136.
[117] ibid 140.
[118] Miller (n 109) 47–48.

reignited around the millennium, particularly in the top 100 firms. This was a surprising direction taken by law firms which regarded rights-based work not as a paying proposition but as free work.

In the UK the 1990s was marked by the growth of the 'justice gap' created by the decline of state funded legal aid. Large corporate law firms were recently but firmly established in the 1990s, when the Labour Party offered a partnership to solve the access to justice crisis. This fitted within Tony Blair's political 'third way', which proposed fusion of neoliberal economic policies with private philanthropy. It included threats to levy large firms to support access to justice.[119] In response to the Labour Party's overtures the Law Society established a pro bono Working Party, but its conclusions, published in 1996, were both self-congratulatory (solicitors do lots of pro bono) and resentful (the state should provide legal aid).[120] In 1997, the new Labour government pursued other solutions, including more radical thinking about regulating the legal services market.

Although the Law Society declined to engage with the pro bono idea, leading figures at the Bar and Law Society reported a campaign of Parliamentary pressure. One of these was Andrew Phillips, founder of Bates Wells and Braithwaite, a commercial firm specialising in charities work and a disgruntled member of the Law Society Working Party.[121] A member of the House of Lords, Phillips was subjected to what he described as a 'drip, drip of denigration of lawyers by government spokesmen'.[122] He convened a meeting in 1996 and a large part of the audience representing large City of London law firms decided to hold a further meeting at one of them. Several committed to financially supporting a new solicitor pro bono organisation to campaign for firm involvement in pro bono. Within a few years, 40 per cent of 130 member firms of the Solicitors Pro Bono Group (SPBG) were in the top 50 firms.[123] Phillips was accompanied at the Law Society by the director of the Professional Firms Group of Business in the Community (BITC), an organisation formed to embed Corporate Social Responsibility in the UK.

C. Corporate Social Responsibility

The interest of large law firms in lawyer in pro bono was part of a wider agenda of Corporate Social Responsibility,[124] the growth of 'soft law' around large companies.[125] Being relatively unregulated at national or international levels, corporations

---

[119] 'Labour Suggests Levy to Support Legal Assistance' (*The Lawyer*, 27 September 1994) 3 and 'Labour Eyes US Pro Bono Model' (*The Lawyer*, 8 November 1994) 2.

[120] A Boon and R Abbey, 'The Provision of Free Legal Services by Solicitors: A Review of the Report of the Law Society's Pro Bono Working Party' (1995) 2(3) *International Journal of the Legal Profession* 261.

[121] A Boon and A Whyte, '"Charity and Beating Begins at Home" The Aetiology of the New Culture of Pro Bono Publico' (1999) 2(2) *Legal Ethics* 169, 177.

[122] A Phillips, 'A want of experience' (*Law Society Gazette*, 28 April 1999).

[123] Boon and Whyte (n 121) 183.

[124] ibid; SL Cummings, 'The Politics of Pro Bono' (2004) 52(1) *UCLA Law Review*.

[125] AB Carroll, 'A History of Corporate Social Responsibility: Concepts and Practices' in A Crane, A McWilliams, D Matten, J Moon and DS Siegel, *The Oxford Handbook of Social Responsibility* (Oxford, Oxford University Press, 2009) 19.

were expected to self-police, identifying the conduct they would observe through voluntary codes. This thinking originated in the US with theories about how to make employees productive. In the 1950s its was articulated as the idea that business organisations should pursue policies and act in ways which were desirable in terms of social objectives and values.[126] Various labels were initially attached to these ideas, but they increasingly became identified as Corporate Social Responsibility (CSR).

In the 1960s CSR concepts proliferated but there was little action on the ground. In the 1970s practical programmes began to accelerate following a report by a committee of business people and academics, the Committee for Economic Development (CED).[127] The report referred to a social contract between business and society involving core, intermediate and peripheral obligations.[128] By 1991, Carroll, who had first proposed a definition of CSR in the 1970s, conceived a pyramid of obligations: economic (be profitable), legal (obey the law), ethical (do what is right, just, fair) and philanthropic (contribute resources to the community, improve the quality of life).[129] As originally conceived, the first three requirements were essential, but philanthropy optional; the 'icing on the cake'.[130] During the late 1980s and 1990s the emphasis on philanthropy as an element of CSR increased markedly.[131]

Moon traced the roots of CSR in the UK to nineteenth century business philanthropy but argued that it took off in the 1980s because of high unemployment, urban decay and social unrest.[132] It was launched following an Anglo-American Conference in 1981 and the formation of Business in the Community (BITC) the same year.[133] At that time, CSR was associated with senior level management and the idea that some executive time should be spent on community activity. It emphasised organisational systems, external links with NGOs and governmental organisations and consultancy. Consequently, Moon suggested, CSR was part of the structure of societal governance of the UK. Carroll argued that corporate altruism was adopted by corporations because it could 'add value to corporate success' and that this depended on the 'business case' for it.[134]

In the 1990s, the business case for CSR was put to large law firms in the UK. BITC's Professional Firms Group aimed to link CSR to the pro bono tradition. This played on the increasing emphasis on local social philanthropy as a key element of CSR. It argued that contributions within organisations should be broadly based and help local communities. The pincer movement, if that is what it was, partially succeeded.

---

[126] ibid 25, citing HR Bowen, *Social Responsibilities of the Businessman* (New York, Harper & Row, 1953) 6.
[127] Committee for Economic Development, *Social Responsibilities of Business Corporations* (New York, CED, 1971).
[128] Carroll (n 125) 29.
[129] AB Carroll, 'The Pyramid of Corporate Social Responsibility: Toward the Moral Management of Organizational Stakeholders' (*Business Horizons* July/August 1991) 5.
[130] ibid.
[131] ibid 37.
[132] J Moon, 'An Explicit Model of Business-Society Relations' in A Habisch, J Jonker, M Wegner, and R Schmidpeter (eds), *Corporate Social Responsibility across Europe* (Berlin, Springer Berlin Heidelberg, 2005) 51.
[133] Boon and Whyte (n 121).
[134] Carroll (n 129) 42.

Although the Law Society was lukewarm in its response to Labour's *pro bono publico* proposals, the Bar and a core of large solicitors' firms responded positively. This may have been because law firms were often under pressure from corporate clients to engage with CSR.[135]

D. Pro Bono Legal Services

Since the 1990s and the rapid decline of legal aid in the UK, lawyers' engagement with issues of access to justice appeared to strengthen. By 2010 a national pro bono centre in Chancery Lane in central London accommodated several pro bono charities and projects making a signal contribution in the provision of pro bono services.[136] Following LASPO 2012, Law Works, an offshoot of the SPBG, sought to preserve legal expertise in areas no longer covered by legal aid by passing on welfare claims expertise into pro bono networks.[137] It provided services in social welfare law, welfare benefits, employment and community care, from bases in London and Bristol and through a web of associated agencies elsewhere. The notional value of solicitors' pro bono roughly tripled over the past 20 years to a current value of around £600 million per annum, roughly one third of the civil legal aid budget.[138]

The ways in which large firms engaged with pro bono were similar in England and the US. Many adopted pro bono policies, appointed pro bono coordinators, often to full-time posts, and set up pro bono committees. Some encouraged employees to do pro bono work and allowed them to count pro bono hours as 'billable hours'. In both countries there was a general increase in the number of lawyer hours worked pro bono, but volume increased with size of firm. Bliss and Boutcher attributed recent increases in the volume of US firms to increased contributions by higher ranked firms, which had routinised and expanded participation.[139] This process had also occurred at large firms in the UK.[140]

There were similarities in the *kind* of pro bono work large law firms did in America and England. The early focus of US firms' efforts on alleviating poverty was attributed to historic conceptions of this as public interest work.[141] Boutcher's earlier work indicated a transition towards advancing civil rights, civil liberties and children and women's rights, rather than environmental, employment or animal rights.[142]

---

[135] Boon and Whyte (n 121).
[136] National pro Bono Centre, *Guide to Pro Bono: Free legal advice in England and Wales*, http://probonoweek.org.uk/wp-content/uploads/2020/08/ProBonoHandBook-2019-npbc.pdf.
[137] Law Works, 'Secondary Specialisation', www.lawworks.org.uk/solicitors-and-volunteers/get-involved/secondary-specialisation.
[138] Boon and Whyte (n 59) 293.
[139] J Bliss and SA Boutcher, 'Rationalizing Pro Bono: Corporate Social Responsibility and The Reinvention Of Legal Professionalism In Elite American Law Firms' in SL Cummings, F De Sa E Silva and LA Trubek, *Global Pro Bono: Diffusion, Contestation, Learned Lessons* (Cambridge, Cambridge University Press, 2021) 77, 82.
[140] Boon and Whyte (n 59).
[141] Bliss and Boutcher (n 139) 87–97.
[142] ibid citing SA Boutcher, 'Lawyering for Social Change: Pro Bono Publico, Cause Lawyering, and the Social Movement Society' (2013) 18 *Mobilization: An International Quarterly* 179.

In the early phase of English corporate pro bono development, solicitors' firms offered community-based 'private plight' legal advice sessions, but this may have evolved to be more strategic. It was clear that, in both countries, the pro bono concept developed so that more senior firm members could advise charities or other community organisations or conduct their property transactions.

It was unclear whether the large firms did more pro bono work from professional responsibility or CSR motivations. In the case of one well known US firm, White and Case, the responsibility to use legal skills for charitable purposes was said to arise from both professionalism and the firm's privileged status.[143] Overall, however, the rationale firms offered shifted away from the professional towards a corporate logic.[144] A similar pattern was found in England and Wales, where analysis of 100 large law firms' websites by Vaughan et al found pro bono within a broader CSR framework[145] grouped as: (i) pro bono and community giving; (ii) diversity and inclusion; and (iii) environmental matters. Many firms made no distinction between pro bono and other categories of CSR and disclosed no data for pro bono work. Therefore, there was no way of distinguishing legal work or 'community giving'.

The close connection between pro bono and CSR suggested that corporate clients had influenced law firms' engagement.[146] This could have affected the kind of work done, making it less likely that politically contentious work or cases threatening corporate clients' broader interests would be done. Large US firms may have responded to client pressure to sign up to the CSR agenda,[147] or to advertise commitment to public service.[148] A respondent in Bliss and Boutcher's research said: 'A leading law firm by today's definition is one that handles high-visibility pro bono cases ... you look for the biggest, splashiest, loudest client relationship, and then you tell everybody in the world you're doing it'.[149]

E. Guantanamo Bay Detention Centre

The Guantanamo Bay Detention Centre was established during the war on terror initiated by George W Bush after the 9/11 terrorist attacks on New York. Built on land leased from Cuba by the US Navy since 1903 the camp held potentially dangerous terrorists outside the jurisdiction of US courts, denying them a venue to invoke human rights. At the height of operations, Guantanamo Bay held 779 prisoners, mainly enemy combatants captured in Afghanistan and Iraq. They were not tried, partly because of lack of evidence or because evidence was tainted by torture. There was a lack of any effective oversight of what happened at the camp and rumours that dubious interrogation methods drifted into torture.[150]

---

[143] Bliss and Boutcher (n 139) 96.
[144] ibid 104.
[145] S Vaughan, L Thomas and A Young, 'Symbolism over substance? Large law firms and corporate social responsibility' (2015) 18(2) *Legal Ethics* 138.
[146] Bliss and Boutcher (n 139) 88, Boon and Whyte (n 121) 187–88.
[147] Bliss and Boutcher ibid 98–100.
[148] ibid 106.
[149] ibid 101.
[150] J Borger, 'Contractor tells of "abusive drift" that resulted in torture' *The Guardian* (23 January 2020).

Pro bono assistance from attorneys representing foreign prisoners held at Guantanamo secured judicial oversight through the jurisdiction of American courts and basic rights for detainees. In 2006, a case involving Salim Hamdan, who claimed he was simply the former driver of Osama Bin Laden, orchestrator of the New York attacks, established that prisoners were entitled to the protection of the Geneva Convention and could not be tried in military tribunals the government had established.[151] Some detainees were returned to countries of origin or elsewhere for trial, while others proved that they were not enemy combatants. This apparently irked members of the executive, and in 2007, the Assistant Secretary of Defense for Detainee Affairs, Charles 'Cully' Stimson, gave an interview to Federal Radio News attacking the lawyers involved.

Stimson professed shock that a freedom of information request revealed that Guantanamo prisoners were represented by lawyers from some of the major law firms in the country.[152] He then named firms[153] continuing, 'when corporate CEOs see that those firms are representing the very terrorists who hit their bottom line back in 2001, those CEOs are going to make those law firms choose between representing terrorists or representing reputable firms, and I think that is going to have major play in the next few weeks. It's going to be fun to watch that play out'. Stimson went on to suggest that some firms may be 'receiving monies from who knows where, and I'd be curious to have them explain that'.[154]

Stimson received little support from the Bush government and a statement distanced the Pentagon from the remarks. He then issued an apology, published in *The Washington Post*, claiming that his comments did not 'reflect my core beliefs ... I believe firmly that a foundational principle of our legal system is that the system works best when both sides are represented by competent legal counsel'.[155] In the meantime, the Attorney General, Alberto Gonzales, had also joined the attacks, blaming lawyers for delays in trying the prisoners, claiming: 'We're challenged every step of the way'.[156]

A *New York Times* editorial responded bluntly to the Attorney General's intervention claiming that there was no truth in the accusation that the lawyers were causing delay and asserting that:

> The cause of the delay in bringing any Guantánamo detainee to trial is Mr. Bush himself. He refused to hold trials at first, then refused to work with Congress on the issue and claimed the power to devise his own slanted court system. Mr. Bush went to Congress only when the Supreme Court struck those courts down. The result was a bill establishing military tribunals for detainees that is a mockery of American justice.[157]

---

[151] *Hamdan v Rumsfeld* 548 U.S. 557 (2006).
[152] 'Top Pentagon Official Calls for Boycott of Law Firms Respresenting Guantanamo Prisoners' (*Democracy Now*, 17 January 2007) (reporting interview with S Oleskey and E Spieler) www.democracy-now.org/2007/1/17/top_pentagon_official_calls_for_boycott.
[153] Pillsbury Winthrop, Jenner & Block, Wilmer Cutler Pickering, Covington & Burling, Sutherland Asbill & Brennan, Paul Weiss Rifkin, Mayer Brown, Weil Gottshal, Pepper Hamilton, Venable, Alston & Bird, Perkins Coie, Hunton & Williams, Fulbright Jaworski.
[154] *Democracy Now* (n 152).
[155] ibid.
[156] ibid.
[157] Editorial, 'Apology not accepted' *New York Times* (9 January 2007) www.nytimes.com/2007/01/19/opinion/19fri2.html.

The editorial reserved even stiffer criticism for Stimson's apology. It found the wording insincere, expressing regret at having 'left the impression' of attacking the integrity of the lawyers, when it clearly had done so. Within a week Stimson had resigned.

A Guantanamo lawyer, Stephen Oleskey, provided context for the controversy in a radio interview. He referred to the relatively few prisoners, around 12, who would be tried under the arrangements the Bush administration had established after *Hamdan*. They were the relatively lucky ones according to Oleskey. Quoting a remark by Justice O'Connor in 2004, the rest were 'sentenced to indefinite life imprisonment without any hearing'. These included six Bosnians, represented by Oleskey, who he claimed were social workers nominated for rendition as terrorists by the US. After a 90-day inquiry, a Bosnian court had found no evidence to justify holding his clients, but the government eventually bowed to US pressure and they had been held at Guantanamo since 20 January 2005.

Olesky explained that there were about 500 '*habeas* counsel', seeking to enforce a basic principle of Anglo-American jurisprudence, inherent in English common law, that the King, or other executive power, cannot hold people indefinitely without charges or a trial. Concerns about the human rights of Guantanamo prisoners were justified. Documents of the Bush administration released to the incoming administration of Barak Obama revealed that advice had been sought at a high level about 'interrogation techniques'[158] including waterboarding, 'walling' (slamming the prisoner head first into a wall while wearing a collar to prevent the neck from being broken), stress positions, sleep deprivation, cramped confinement, and in one case insects placed in a confinement box to exploit a prisoner's phobia.[159]

In 2009, Obama began his presidency promising to close Guantanamo within a year. Opposition from Congress limited reduction in the number of inmates. The process was derailed by the fact that the Bush administration had released prisoners who had gone on to commit terrorist attacks in both Iraq and Afghanistan.[160] There was difficulty finding destinations where detainees could be effectively monitored. At the beginning of Obama's first term there were 242 prisoners, by the end of his second, there were fewer than 40, including five connected with the 9/11 attacks.

In 2017 there was a postscript to the 2007 controversy when US Supreme Court nominee, Neil Gorsuch, was asked in his confirmation hearing about an email he sent in 2006, when employed at the Department of Justice. He had expressed surprise that more had not been made of the fact that '[e]lite law firm pro bono work for terrorists'.[161] He admitted that this was 'not his finest moment', adding, in response to Senator Dick Durbin's assertion that the non-identification of lawyers and their clients was 'critical to the fair administration of justice', that 'I have nothing but admiration for those lawyers'.[162]

---

[158] B Wendel, 'The Torture Memos and the Demands of Legality' (2009) 12(1) *Legal Ethics* 107.
[159] ibid 108.
[160] D Usborne, 'Guantanamo Bay: Why has Obama failed on his promise to close controversial detention Camp?' *The Independent* (16 August 2016) www.independent.co.uk/news/world/americas/guantanamo-bay-closing-why-has-obama-failed-a7194241.html.
[161] T Berenson, 'Neil Gorsuch on Email Slamming Guantanamo Bay Lawyers: 'Not My Finest Moment' (*Time*, 22 March 2017) https://time.com/4710216/neil-gorsuch-confirmation-hearing-email/.
[162] ibid.

VI. DISCUSSION

The corporation was the engine of capitalism. Both were protected by the rule of law. Baars suggested that when lawyers adapted the corporate form from its ecclesiastical origins, it was the lack of materiality that appealed; the corporation had 'no body to kick nor soul to damn'.[163] While corporations were impervious, the individuals within them were insulated from risk or retribution, one of many non-state actors threatening the rule of law.[164] Their disproportionate influence on the global economy presented risks from domination of national governments to corruption of politicians by corporate interests. This justified serious consideration of how to contain them. In fact, Bakan suggested, since the 1980s, corporate regulation lessened without any corresponding reduction in the legal protections of incorporation.[165]

The hold that corporations had over national governments was their ability to move between jurisdictions, locating wherever conditions were most favourable and negotiating terms of domicile. These features posed a threat to balanced government and to legality, both fundamental to the rule of law. They undermined 'the competence, fairness, and democratic legitimacy of the modern state [by substituting] the criteria of willingness-to-pay for criteria based on desert, need, efficiency, and other values'.[166] Controls had not kept pace with the risks they posed and with the de-legalisation of the public sphere. The power to confront corporate power lay with the state, but countries were unwilling to act or actively promoted the corporate form over other institutions.

In England and Wales, corporate power grew while professional power declined. Induction to the discipline of law had included recognition of the need to control the executive. Whereas professions acted as a counterweight to state power, defending the rule of law, corporations were geared to represent the interests of shareholders often against the public interest and sometimes antithetical to the rule of law. The decline of legal aid and lack of judicial review for corporate actions restricted citizen control. Action against corporations might be supported by pro bono lawyers, but for the fact that most lawyers served corporations. Further, changes in regulation threatened unified professional values, such as independence and public service.

Large firm attitudes to pro bono gave a mixed picture of the fate of professional values in a corporate world. Large firm benevolence appeared to be a fragile basis for providing access to justice because lawyer participation depended on firm policies affected by many agendas. Large firm participation had, however, turned relatively small-scale contributions of free legal services into something much more substantial. The Guantanamo representation was a classic rule of law activity which courted executive hostility. It was the kind of community activity advocated by CSR but included

---

[163] Baars (n 74) 46.
[164] M Krygier, 'The Rule of Law: Pasts, Presents and Two Possible Futures' (2016) 12 *Annual Review of Law and Social Science* 199, 221.
[165] Bakan (n 21).
[166] S Rose-Ackerman, 'Corruption: Greed, Culture and the State' (2010) 120 *Yale Law Journal Online* 125, Yale Law & Economics Research Paper No. 409.

actions against arbitrary power. The fact that large firm pro bono was motivated by professional rather than corporate agendas suggested that professional values might survive corporatocracy under certain conditions.

Time has obscured the ways in which, historically, lawyers and legal professions deployed the social capital embedded in law and social relations to promote professional values. As Dezalay and Garth observed: 'The situation becomes taken for granted, which may make it seem as if the power of the law comes from the law itself, but legal capital without social capital was relatively weak'.[167] Situations such as that encountered by the Guantanamo lawyers were a reminder that the social capital of lawyers must sometimes be deployed to support the rule of law. The lawyers involved came under pressure to capitulate, but their assertion of professional responsibility was ultimately vindicated. The situation of Steven Donziger was the tip of an iceberg. Over half of the 357 civil rights defenders murdered in 35 different countries in 2021 were opposing corporations, usually in their abuse of Indigenous land rights.[168] But it also showed that lawyers needed to strictly observe professional values if they were to serve a greater good.

VII. CONCLUSION

Since World War II an emphasis on free markets suggested that states should be geared to operate in the interest of consumers. This inevitably led to them being run in the interests of corporations. Bakan argued that this 'weakens the rule of law and its democratic potential and exacerbates the risk of corporate threats to the public interest'.[169] Traditional counterweights to the state and guarantors of the rule of law, judicial, administrative, and professional, were diminished. The inability of government to control the corporation led to a growth of 'soft law' intended to legitimise corporate global dominance[170] under the umbrella of Corporate Social Responsibility. Corporate law firms adapted *pro bono publico* but might have picked their cases to avoid antagonising a corporate clientele. Some evidence suggested this fear was misconceived, but it was unclear whether lawyers would subscribe to traditional rule of law values with the continued decline of professionalism.

---

[167] Y Dezalay and BG Garth, 'Introduction: Lawyers, law and society' in Y Dezalay and BG Garth (eds), *Lawyers and the Rule of Law in an Era of Globalization* (Abingdon, Routledge, 2011) 4.
[168] K McVeigh, 'They do it with impunity: 357 human rights defenders killed around the globe last year' *The Guardian* (2 March 2022).
[169] Bakan (n 21) 280.
[170] Shaw (n 2).

16
Globalisation

I. INTRODUCTION

GLOBAL TRADE AND technology brought about significant expansion in the range and operation of corporations, creating markets for transnational trade and investment. This process was certainly not new, international trade having existed throughout recorded history.[1] What was new was the beginning of 'world civil society protected by a transnational legal process',[2] and transnational demands for human rights. These trends were mutually supporting yet contradictory, the creation of neoliberal open markets had reduced states' commitment to provide welfare and impinged on the narrative of global rights. This chapter examines the role of lawyers in the globalisation narrative through professions, organisations and individually.

II. THEORY

Boaventura de Sousa Santos saw globalisation as a phase of transnational interaction distinguished from preceding phases, such as modernisation or development.[3] It created a complex social field driven by trade, technology, and migration. There were two distinct processes. Globalised localism was the transfer of the local beyond its national border, as the Hollywood style of acting became localised in European cinema.[4] Localised globalism distorted conditions in the host locality, re-structuring or destroying them to accommodate globalised localisms.[5] These processes tended to be unidirectional; core countries exported localisms and peripheral countries accommodated them.[6]

---

[1] P Frankopan, *The Silk Roads: A New History of the World* (London, NY, Bloomsbury Publishing, 2015).
[2] GA Christenson, 'World Civil Society and the International Rule of Law' (1997) 19 *Human Rights Quarterly* 724.
[3] B de Sousa Santos, *Toward a New Legal Common Sense. Law, Globalization, and Emancipation* (London, Butterworths, 2002); B de Sousa Santos 'Globalizations' (2006) 23 *Theory Culture Society* 393.
[4] Santos (n 3) 396.
[5] ibid 397.
[6] ibid 397.

The core countries, the World's leading economies (the G7), gave globalisation its distinct character. The neoliberal or Washington consensus encompassed four major points of consensus: (1) liberal (or neoliberal) economy; (2) weak states; (3) liberal democracy; and (4) the primacy of the rule of law and the judicial system.[7] Spreading this framework was a kind of cultural imperialism. Results were mixed. Economic development, democracy or human rights could occur when arbitrary power was controlled, but they were not inevitable.[8] State oppression and powerful non-state operators, crime gangs and war lords, could still function despite the appearance of the rule of law.[9] Open economies did not necessarily produce open governments.

Examining reasons for failure of the rule of law, and the sequence of events giving it a chance of success, Ginsburg argued that democratisation preceded establishing independent courts.[10] Levi and Epperley suggested three factors necessary to establish the rule of law: a leader or leaders willing to establish and maintain the principle against opposition and self-interest, a law-abiding bureaucracy and citizen compliance.[11] Principled leaders first obtained the consent of powerful elites to create an institutional design for the future, building in credible constraints on power. The leader showed willingness to abide by the rules of that structure, for example, by stepping down at the end of a prescribed term of office.[12] Those exercising power had to be bound by liberal constitutional principles. North and Weingast suggested that principled leaders were insufficient alone. The rule of law could not be created by introducing democracy or legal institutions unless doorstep conditions, like to control of violence and an open society, were met.

Globalisation increased the possibility of conflict between groups, interests, and ideologies, particularly in the economic, cultural, and legal fields. Santos said globalisation could be resisted at the local level by what he called 'insurgent cosmopolitanism' enabled by easy travel and fast, complex communication. What distinguished insurgent cosmopolitanism from previous connections between global networks, associations, and NGOs was, like, globalisation itself, its scale and intensity. This facilitated resistance to the so-called Washington consensus and the spread of the rule of law. The Chevron case (chapter fifteen 'Corporatocracy') was an example of 'insurgent cosmopolitanism': exploitation of resources by a multi-national corporation, with accompanying ecological destruction, and the transnational mobilisation of legal assistance to protect the environment and assert the rights of Indigenous peoples.[13]

---

[7] ibid 393.
[8] M Krygier, 'The Rule of Law: Pasts, Presents and Two Possible Futures' (2016) 12 *Annual Review of Law and Social Science* 199, 216.
[9] ibid 214.
[10] T Ginsburg, 'The politics of courts in democratization' in JJ Heckman, RL Nelson and L Cabatingan (eds), *Global Perspectives on the Rule of Law* (London and NY, Routledge, 2010) 175.
[11] M Levi and B Epperly, 'Principled Principals in the Founding Moments of the Rule of Law' in Heckman et al ibid 192, 208.
[12] ibid 202.
[13] Santos (n 3) 397.

III. A GLOBAL ORDER OF THE RULE OF LAW?

A. The Washington Consensus

The ineffectiveness of international organisations was blamed for the economic depression of the 1930s, the rise of Nazi Germany, and the catastrophe of World War II. The creation of the United Nations (UN) in 1948 began the process of filling this vacuum, beginning with the Nuremberg trials.[14] In the economic sphere the mission of the UN was to create a stable world built on good international relations. Its main strategies were to promote trade and good governance efforts. UN institutions worked alongside more narrowly based organisations designed to complement post-war reconstruction.

The leadership of the UN in the economic sphere was assisted by a network of complementary organisations. From 1948 the Organisation for European Economic Co-operation (OEEC) administered US aid to Europe. In 1961 it was succeeded by the Organisation for Economic Co-operation and Development (OECD), currently an intergovernmental initiative of 37 countries dedicated to promoting democracy and the market economy. Organisations such as the UN Commission on International Trade Law (UNCITRAL), created in 1966, led development of international trade, removing legal obstacles and modernising and harmonising law.[15]

The post-war economic order confirmed by the Bretton Woods Agreement in 1944 was a compromise between the leading British and American Treasury Departments championing the theories of their chief economists, John Maynard Keynes and Harry Dexter White. The Western post-war economic system abandoned the gold standard, pegging currencies to the American dollar backed by three quarters of the world gold supply. The World Bank aided reconstruction by lending to European governments, and the International Monetary Fund (IMF) assisted member countries with economic problems such as balance of payments deficits. From the 1970s the European focus of the World Bank broadened from economic governance to 'good governance' generally. This was to assist a wider range of countries to reduce corruption and money laundering.

In 1989, John Williamson, a senior fellow at the Peterson Institute for International Economics, described policies addressing financial crises in South America as the 'Washington consensus'.[16] The Washington consensus described a basket of 10 policies,[17] the core comprising 'disciplined macroeconomic policies, the use of

---

[14] G Baars, *The Corporation, Law and Capitalism: A Radical Perspective on the Role of Law in the Global Political Economy* (Chicago, Haymarket Books 2020) 199.

[15] United Nations Commission on International Trade Law, www.uncitral.org.

[16] The consensus represented was that of American institutions including Congress, senior members of the administration, the international financial institutions, government economic agencies, the Federal Reserve Board and think tanks (J Williamson, 'A Short History of the Washington Consensus' A paper for the conference *From the Washington Consensus towards a new Global Governance* Barcelona, 24–25 September 2004, www.piie.com/publications/papers/williamson0904-2.pdf.

[17] Fiscal Discipline, Reordering Public Expenditure Priorities to support infrastructure, basic health and education, Tax Reform, Liberalising Interest Rates, Competitive Exchange Rate, Trade Liberalisation, Liberalisation of Inward Foreign Direct Investment, Privatisation, Deregulation and Expanding Property Rights, ibid.

markets, and trade liberalization'.[18] Some years later, Williamson agreed with a conference discussant who had proposed that agreement about the list was 'far short of consensus but runs far wider than Washington'.[19] In the years when George W Bush's 'war on terror' led to intervention in Iraq, the term 'Washington consensus' became in Williamson's words, 'a propaganda gift to the old left'.[20]

Williamson later identified two unintended meanings attached to the Washington consensus. One identified it with neoliberalism, which Williamson refuted, the only neoliberal policy on his list being sale of state assets. Another confusion was between the Washington consensus and policies applied by the international financial institutions established at Bretton Woods, the World Bank and the IMF. Here, Williamson was inclined to accept some overlap.

From the 1990s the World Bank began looking beyond economic factors when considering aid applications.[21] Five dimensions of 'good governance' identified:

Voice and accountability, which includes civil liberties and political stability;

Government effectiveness, which includes the quality of policy making and public service delivery;

The lack of regulatory burden;

The rule of law, which includes protection of property rights; and

Independence of the judiciary; and control of corruption.[22]

The European Bank of Reconstruction and Development joined the World Bank in only lending money to countries committed to promoting the rule of law. Their campaigns addressed policy challenges from the liberalisation of the old Soviet empire to the threat to South American States from narco-trafficking.[23] The breadth of ambition acted as a brake on spreading 'thick' versions of the rule of law.

In 2000 the UN General Assembly set millennial development goals including access to justice.[24] In relaunching these goals for the period post-2015, Western countries wanted to make the rule of law an explicit goal. Although consensus could not be reached the rule of law was promoted as a prerequisite of market reform.[25] Research for the World Bank suggested that aid could only promote governance and rule of law reform in countries with sound economic management and robust government institutions.[26] Aid supported ongoing reform but could not 'buy' it.

---

[18] Williamson (n 16) 13.
[19] ibid 4.
[20] ibid 6.
[21] C Santiso, 'Good Governance and Aid Effectiveness: The World Bank and Conditionality' (2001) 7(1) *The Georgetown Public Policy Review* 1.
[22] D Kaufmann, A Kraay and P Zoido-Lobaton, *Governance Matters* Policy Research Working Paper 2196 (Washington, The World Bank, 1999) cited by Santiosi at 5.
[23] T Carothers, 'Rule of law temptations' in Heckman, Nelson and Cabatingan (n 10) 17.
[24] J Beqiraj and L McNamara, *The Rule of Law and Access to Justice in the Post-2015 Development Agenda: Moving Forward but Stepping Back* (Bingham Centre Working Paper 2014/04) (Bingham Centre for the Rule of Law, BIICL, London, August 2014).
[25] Santiso (n 21) 113.
[26] See generally Santiso (n 21) 9–10, citing C Burnside and D Dollar, *Aid, the Incentive Regime, and Poverty Reduction* Policy Research Working Paper 1937 (Washington, DC, The World Bank, 1998).

Updating the prescriptions of the Washington consensus to address the problems of South America in 2004, Williamson noted the importance of institution building to address the endemic problems found there: 'archaic judiciaries, rigid civil service bureaucracies, old fashioned political systems, teachers' unions focused exclusively on producer interests, and weak financial infrastructures'.[27] A key omission from the Washington consensus was promoting equity. Therefore, Williamson argued, future prescriptions must include education, enabling those in poverty to develop human capital and hope for the future.

B. Measuring the Rule of Law

Tom Bingham observed that '[n]o one would choose to do business ... involving large sums of money, in a country where parties' rights and obligations were undecided'.[28] The significance of the rule of law in international finance and trade broadened the perspective of conventional rule of law scholars and led organisations to devise measures of effectiveness focused on institutions.

The World Justice Project (WJP)[29] ranked nations according to detailed lists of factors (Table 1) reflecting the risk they posed for foreign investment.[30]

Table 1 Factors in WJP Rule of Law Index

Limits on the power of state, its agents and others	Public interest, public protection, dispute and grievance settlement
Factor 1: Constraint on Government Powers	Factor 5: Order and Security
Factor 2: Absence of Corruption	Factor 6: Regulatory Enforcement
Factor 3: Open Government	Factor 7: Civil Justice
Factor 4: Fundamental rights	Factor 8: Criminal Justice

Source: World Justice Project *Rule of Law Index 2015* (https://worldjusticeproject.org/sites/default/files/roli_2015_0.pdf).

The four WJP principles focused on formal legality were:

> The government and its officials and agents as well as individuals and private entities are accountable under the law.
>
> The laws are clear, publicised, stable, and just; are applied evenly; and protect fundamental rights, including the security of persons and property.
>
> The process by which the laws are enacted, administered, and enforced is accessible, fair, and efficient.

---

[27] Williamson (n 16) 11.

[28] T Bingham, *The Rule of Law* (London, Allen Lane, 2010) 38.

[29] It was established in 2006 as a presidential initiative of the American Bar Association (ABA) and became an independent non-profit organisation in 2009.

[30] R Barro, 'Democracy and the Rule of Law' in B de Mesquita and H Root (eds), *Governing for Prosperity* (New Haven, Yale University Press, 2000); 'Rule of Law' *Stanford Encyclopaedia of Philosophy*, https://plato.stanford.edu/entries/rule-of-law/.

Justice is delivered timely by competent, ethical, and independent representatives and neutrals who are of sufficient number, have adequate resources, and reflect the makeup of the communities they serve.[31]

The WJP framework indicators aimed to be widely recognised and to strike a balance between 'thin' or minimalist conceptions of the rule of law focused on formal, procedural rules, and a 'thick' conception including substantive characteristics: self-government and fundamental rights and freedoms.[32] Substantive characteristics included sufficient material to guarantee core human rights under international law. The absence of such measures from the WJP would, it was thought, suggest 'rule by law', not a 'rule of law system'.

In some ways, the WJP Index was very broad brush. It assessed countries rather than jurisdictions, so the three jurisdictions of the UK had only one score. It also compared countries within geographic and income bands, so each jurisdiction's score was only comparable with those in their geographical region. Nevertheless, the WJP index gave an impression of countries' performance on rule of law criteria and areas of weakness. Its data collection was ambitious. Using 44 indicators, each of which could receive a score up to 1, the WJP collected data from over 100 countries, 100,000 households, 2,400 expert surveys, and three settlement and grievance mechanisms (factors 5, 6, 7, and 8 of the Index). Rankings of the leading countries appear in Table 2.

Table 2 World Justice Project Rule of Law Index Rankings 2017–18

Denmark	0.89	1	Estonia	0.80	12	Spain	0.70	23
Norway	0.89	2	Singapore	0.80	13	Costa Rica	0.68	24
Finland	0.87	3	Japan	0.79	14	Poland	0.67	25
Sweden	0.86	4	Belgium	0.77	15	Slovenia	0.67	26
Netherlands	0.85	5	Hong Kong SAR, China	0.77	16	Chile	0.67	27
Germany	0.83	6	Czech Republic	0.74	17	St. Kitts & Nevis	0.66	28
New Zealand	0.83	7	France	0.74	18	Romania	0.65	29
Austria	0.81	8	United States	0.73	19	Barbados	0.65	30
Canada	0.81	9	Republic of Korea	0.72	20	Italy	0.65	31
Australia	0.81	10	Portugal	0.72	21	United Arab Emirates	0.65	32
United Kingdom	0.81å	11	Uruguay	0.71	22	St. Lucia	0.63	33

Source: World Justice Project *Rule of Law Index 2017–18* (https://worldjusticeproject.org/our-work/research-and-data/wjp-rule-law-index-2017%E2%80%932018).

---

[31] ibid.
[32] World Justice Project *Rule of Law Index 2015*, 10, https://worldjusticeproject.org/sites/default/files/roli_2015_0.pdf.

Based on the WJP criteria, Scandinavian countries led the world rankings. The UK, and other common law countries were at the bottom of the top 10 and the US at 19. Although the US was the worst performer on access to justice in this group, Australia, an innovator in legal services reform, was not far behind. Most countries scored well on due process measures, but the US and Japan were somewhat behind the others.

C. The Spread of the Rule of Law

Efforts since World War II to create a world order of the rule of law partially succeeded. The result was a patchwork of countries with levels of engagement that were new or a legacy of empire. The policies of the International Monetary Fund and World Bank sometimes backfired, producing 'authoritarian, despotic, paramilitaristic, and/or corrupt state forms and agents within civil society'.[33] The rule of law was synonymous with the imposition of Western values and Islamic regimes based on Sharia law might not satisfy requirements such as the accountability of government, equal political rights, and access to justice.[34] In Pakistan, however, an independent Islamic state since 1947, lawyers engaged in street protests in support of an independent judiciary.[35] In Africa, the infrastructure of the rule of law was often vulnerable.

The former British colony of Rhodesia, Zimbabwe since 1980, was ruled by the party built on the revolutionary faction, ZANU PF, which won general elections under Robert Mugabe. Karekwaivanane described how the 2000 election victory of a new party, the Movement for Democratic change, led ZANU PF to conduct an aggressive campaign to hold onto power. The Zimbabwean Law Society actively supported human rights, the rule of law and judicial independence through public statements, legal challenges, and street protests.[36] Mugabe survived years of protest until he was deposed by the Army in 2017. In elections in 2018 his successor in ZANU-PF, Emmerson Mnangagwa, survived an opposition appeal to the Constitutional Court based on election fraud.

Some recent examples of the introduction of the rule of law were more successful. After World War II the US changed the Japanese system of government, introducing a Constitution embodying liberalism, the separation of powers and human rights. The Constitution survived until the present day and the US and Japan remained allies, their relationship developing and intensifying during the Cold War period.[37] Successful operation of the rule of law could be an important factor in international relationships.

---

[33] W Brown, 'Neo-liberalism and the End of Liberal Democracy' (2003) 7(1) *Theory and Event* 15.

[34] T Kuran, 'The rule of law in Islamic thought and practice' in Heckman, Nelson and Cabatingan (n 10) 71.

[35] J Waldron, 'The rule of law and the importance of procedure' (2011) 50 *Nomos* 3, 5.

[36] GH Karekwaivanane, 'Zimbabwe: Legal Practitioners, Politics and Transformation since 1980' in R Abel, O Hammerslev, U Schultz and H Sommerlad (eds), *Lawyers in 21st-Century Societies, vol. 1: National Reports* (Oxford, Hart Publishing, 2020) ch 27.

[37] S Yoshimi (trans D Buist), 'America as desire and violence: Americanization in postwar Japan and Asia during the Cold War' (2003) 4(3) *Inter-Asia Cultural Studies* 433.

Other attempts to embed the rule of law were less enduring. Governments publicly justified interventions by the US and its allies in Afghanistan and Iraq by claiming the continuing threats posed either by terrorists (Afghanistan) or weapons of mass destruction (Iraq). Wendy Brown argued that a subtext was that these countries required and deserved 'liberation' from tyrants and that imposing democracy was protecting of 'our way of life'. She suggested that the interests really defended were the neo-liberal order and the access of global corporations to new markets, illustrated by the appointment of Halliburton by Vice President Cheney to restructure Iraq. It was probably more of a geopolitical strategy to maintain some control of an important region both economically and politically.[38]

D. Alternatives to the Rule of Law

In the period immediately after World War II, a new world order of the rule of law met notable opposition from a handful of states, most notably the Soviet Union. Under the Tsars, Russia had moved from monarchical autocracy to a Communist one-party state[39] and had no rule of law tradition.[40] In the late 1980s Mikhail Gorbachev embarked on a programme of liberalising reforms including limited democracy and greater openness. As some Soviet states declared independence in the late 1980s, Gorbachev narrowly survived a coup engineered by the security services. The 1991 collapse of the Soviet empire and, with it, communism in Eastern Europe, left Russia with the choice of embracing democracy and the rule of law.

The first president of Russia in 1999, Boris Yeltsin, appeared to be a 'principled principal' capable of establishing a rule of law regime. He was a liberal committed to economic reform, but his terms in office were marred by mismanagement and an attempted coup. Yeltsin was succeeded in 1999 by a nominated successor, Vladimir Putin, a former law graduate, intelligence agent and head of the Federal Security Service (FSB). Under Putin, Russia was nominally a democracy but gradually became an autocratic state. His power lay in his ability to tap into popular sentiments and conform to expectations of leadership.[41]

As the Russian regime became more oppressive, it forced a flourishing community of NGOs into increased dependence on government,[42] suppressed critics, free media, and political opposition. Its institutions were vague echoes of Western models and processes but did not promote the rule of law. Its economy was weak because of extortion and bribery, and its elites used open access order countries, particularly in Western Europe, to store their wealth.[43] Under Putin the external measures of

---

[38] Frankopan (n 1) chs 25–26.
[39] Krygier (n 8) 208.
[40] Carothers (n 23) 21.
[41] L Baglione, 'Post-Soviet Russia at Twenty-Five: Understanding the Dynamics and Consequences of Its Authoritarianism' (2016) 48(4) *Polity* 580.
[42] BR Weingast, 'Why Developing Countries Prove So Resistant to the Rule of Law' in Heckman et al (n 10) 42.
[43] S Tisdall, 'Putin, a criminal and incompetent president, is an enemy of his people' *The Observer* (19 January 2020).

civil and political rights in Russia declined consistently. By 2006, over 22 per cent of all cases before the European Court of Human Rights were from Russia[44] and in 2019 this had risen to nearly 34 per cent (15,000 of 44,500 applications).[45] This was a marked contrast with other European countries: France (506); Germany (182); UK (109).

Repressive domestically, Russia became openly antagonistic to the international rule of law. It attacked former citizens abroad and political opponents at home, publicly denying attempted assassinations, but using manufactured poisons only accessible to state operatives. One victim was Putin's main critic Alexei Navalny, who was poisoned with a nerve agent in August 2020. He received medical care in Germany but was arrested on his return to Russia and sentenced to a prison camp for breaking parole. Russia ignored an ECHR finding that there was a credible threat to Navalny's life in jail.[46] Russia under Putin also seemed intent on retrieving as much of the Soviet empire as possible annexing the Crimea in 2014, supporting the independence claims of two other areas of the Ukraine and then invading the country in 2022.

In the 1990s, the dissolution of the Soviet Union allowed countries formerly satellites of Russia to explore new constitutional arrangements. Some did so but quickly lapsed into autocracy. Bozóki described how, in Hungary, the 'negotiated revolution' of 1989 established liberal constitutional arrangements, a representative assembly, opposition and independent constitutional courts.[47] Hungarians embraced democracy and the EU but were disappointed when they failed to deliver prosperity. In 2010 Victor Orban was re-elected promising a new 'social contract' based on 'the pillars of our common future: work, home, family, health and order'.[48]

By the 2014 election the Hungarian state had become centralised and politicised, a multi-party democracy 'within a rigged political, judicial and media system'.[49] Members of the former regime and political opponents were targeted by retroactive legislation and attacked in government campaigns. The media was controlled, government contracts handed to cronies and government employees dismissed at will.[50] In 2018 Orban was re-elected after a campaign of intimidation and xenophobia.[51]

The world's largest democracy, India, became a 'Hindu supremacist' state after the election of Narendra Modi in 2014.[52] His campaign had criticised opponents' alleged corruption while he offered probity, efficiency, and welfare.[53] Promising to

---

[44] European Court of Human Rights, *Survey of Activities 2006* (Strasbourg, Registry of the European Court of Human Rights, 2007).

[45] The next highest were Turkey (over 9,000) and Ukraine (nearly 9,000). European Court of Human Rights, *Annual Report 2019* (Strasbourg, Council of Europe, 2020) 128.

[46] A Roth, 'Navalny bound for prison after appeal rejected' *The Observer* (21 February 2021).

[47] A Bozóki, 'The Illusion of Inclusion: Configurations of Populism in Hungary' in M Kopecek and P Wcislik (eds), *Thinking Through Transition: Liberal Democracy, Authoritarian Pasts, and Intellectual History in East Central Europe after 1989* (Budapest, New York, Central European University Press, 2015) 275, 304.

[48] ibid 305.

[49] ibid 310.

[50] ibid 306–7.

[51] J Rankin, 'Hungary: Anger at Tory vote against sanctions' *The Guardian* (26 June 2018).

[52] P Mishra, 'The custodians of democracy failed to see it rotting away' *The Guardian* (20 September 2019).

[53] T Khaitan, 'Killing a Constitution with a Thousand Cuts: Executive Aggrandizement and Party-state Fusion in India' (2020) 14(1) *Law & Ethics of Human Rights* 49.

disregard procedures impeding development, the government centralised power and incrementally weakened institutions constraining the executive.[54] The slide towards autocracy led to pressure on the Supreme Court, which had been an effective counterweight to the executive since the 1990s. Consequently, it became 'timid, tentative, fragmented and vulnerable, wary of hurting the central executive which has grown mighty in strength'.[55] After Modi's re-election in 2019, the process of rolling back the rule of law became more overt.

Amartya Sen claimed that the situation in India was symptomatic of the world facing a 'pandemic of autocracy', for which different countries claimed different justifications. Turkey and Egypt defined terrorism to embrace dissent, in the Philippines it included drug trafficking, in Hungary immigration, in Poland gay lifestyles, in India, sedition, the label incorrectly given to anti-government protest, and, in Brazil, corruption.[56] In the European zone Italy (Berluscone), Belarus (Lukashenka), and Croatia (Tudman) became more autocratic.[57] The mixture of autocracy and democracy justified Bozóki's description of these countries as illiberal democracies.[58] The 2018 WJP Index suggested a decline of fundamental human rights in two-thirds of 113 countries surveyed was attributable to the surge in populism, authoritarian nationalism and a retreat from international legal obligations.'[59] This was a 'backlash against a globalising economy' posing an existential threat to the rule of law.

IV. COMPROMISING THE RULE OF LAW

A. Insurgent Cosmopolitanism

One of the apparent consequences of globalisation, illustrating Santos' notion of insurgent cosmopolitanism, was an upsurge in terrorist attacks conducted in countries identified with the rule of law. Terrorism was defined as violent attack on civilians with a view to attracting attention, inducing fear, and influencing 'political decisions or the polity as such'.[60] Since World War II it occurred in different parts of the world with apparently different causes. In post-colonial contexts such as India, Malaysia and Algeria it reacted to attempts to re-establish empire, in Europe it was associated with anti-capitalism and in Latin America it occurred in weak states following the collapse of socialism.[61] Since the 1970s Islamic terrorism emanating from the Middle

---

[54] ibid.
[55] M Sebastian, 'How Has the Supreme Court Fared During the Modi years?' (*The Wire*, 12 April 2019) https://thewire.in/law/supreme-court-modi-years.
[56] A Sen, 'India Once stood for liberty. Now despotism has taken over' *The Guardian* (27 October 2020).
[57] Bozóki (n 47) 308.
[58] ibid 311.
[59] W Bordell and J Robins, '"Crisis for rights" as world retreats from rule of law' *The Guardian* (31 January 2018).
[60] E Zimmermann, 'Globalization and Terrorism' (2011) 27 *European Journal of Political Economy* S152, S153.
[61] B Krug and P Reinmoeller, *The Hidden Costs of Ubiquity: Globalisation and Terrorism* Erasmus Report Series Research In Management (Rotterdam, Research Institute of Management, 2003).

East predominated.⁶² This variety was attributable to the threat globalisation posed to Muslim identity and the desire for social control, expressed as the need to protect holy sites.⁶³ Other explicit links between globalisation and terrorism occurred in Afghanistan, the Philippines and Columbia.⁶⁴

One theory linking globalisation and terrorism was that the global system weakened with the addition of new areas, while protesters in those areas became stronger, relative to their weak economic position, by the acquisition of new technologies and opportunities for transport.⁶⁵ Terrorists often wanted to block development because their interests lay in other areas, for example religious fundamentalism or criminal activity. Their targets often included local elites and the incomers they collaborated with. Terrorist activity was also linked to immigration. Incoming minorities weakened the state and contributed to economic and social inequality.⁶⁶ The attainment of high education levels by incomers, and failure to integrate them socially, led some to provide terrorist leadership. Thus, terrorist perpetrators often came from newly globalised areas to the old, or globalising, areas where victims were located.

The combination of immigration and terrorism resulted in countries seeking to export the rule of law globally, compromising it domestically. Cases involved extraordinary or irregular rendition and transferring suspects out of jurisdiction so they could be interrogated under torture. Challenges to state actions often evoked hostile reactions from the executive, requiring legal institutions to defend the lawyers concerned. In the US a postscript to the involvement of large firm lawyers in asserting the rights of prisoners at Guantanamo Bay occurred in 2010, when the Attorney General, Eric Holder, confirmed that nine Department of Justice lawyers ((DoJ lawyers) had represented detainees or were engaged in advocacy on their behalf.⁶⁷ The lawyers were criticised in some media for undermining the US during a time of war, and online by right wing groups labelling them the 'Al Qaeda 7'. They were defended by the liberal press, which suggested that the attacks were really attempts to smear President Barak Obama⁶⁸ or to deflect attention from the policy of detention.⁶⁹ They were also supported by parts of the legal community which might have been anticipated to be antagonistic to them. These asserted a constitutional obligation to act for the unpopular.

Many establishment lawyers, including Bush's former Solicitor General Ted Olson and Attorney General Michael Mukasey, signed an open letter condemning the attacks

---

⁶² In 2009 half of all terror attacks were by Sunni Muslim extremists associated with 90 groups. The Taliban and then Al-Shabaab caused the most fatalities (Zimmermann (n 60) S153).

⁶³ FM Moghaddam, *How globalization spurs terrorism: The lopsided benefits of 'one world' and why that fuels violence* (Praeger Security International, 2008).

⁶⁴ ibid.

⁶⁵ Zimmermann (n 60) S154.

⁶⁶ ibid S155.

⁶⁷ HF Madbak, 'Guantanamo Lawyers under attack' (*nysbar.com*, 18 March 2010) http://nysbar.com/blogs/ExecutiveDetention/2010/03/guantanamo_lawyers_under_attac_1.html.

⁶⁸ E Robinson, '"Al-Qaeda 7" smear campaign is an assault on American values' (*Washington Post*, 9 March 2010) www.washingtonpost.com/wp-dyn/content/article/2010/03/08/AR2010030803122.html.

⁶⁹ Editorial, 'Are You or Have You Ever Been a Lawyer? *New York Times* (7 March 2010) www.nytimes.com/2010/03/08/opinion/08mon1.html.

on the DoJ lawyers.[70] A letter from the Brooking Institution in 2010 provided similar support from lawyers located in military and state defence institutions.[71] The New York State Bar Association President, Michael E Getnick, wrote that the 'right to counsel is an essential, constitutionally mandated component of due process and the rule of law. To attack those who fulfilled that constitutional imperative is to threaten the independence of the bar, while at the same time manipulating the outcome of future cases by attempting to deprive defendants of certain counsel'.[72]

B. The Reaction to Terrorist Threats in the UK

In 1996 the European Court of Human Rights found the UK in breach of the EU Convention on Human Rights Article 3 in deporting a Sikh separatist to India, where he faced torture.[73] The UK was also found in breach of Article 5(4) which provided that anyone 'deprived of his liberty by arrest or detention shall be entitled to take proceedings by which the lawfulness of his detention shall be decided speedily by a court and his release ordered if the detention is not lawful'. The government then created the Special Immigration Appeals Commission (SIAC) to hear appeals against deportation, or deprivation of citizenship, when national security matters were in issue.[74] The Act provided that the tribunal should apply principles of judicial review in reaching decisions.[75]

In 2001 terrorists flew aeroplanes into two UN buildings in New York. Osama Bin Laden, who planned the attacks, threatened similar action against the UK. Despite having only introduced anti-terrorism legislation in the previous year, The British government enacted the Anti-terrorism, Crime and Security Act 2001,[76] described by one academic as the most draconian peacetime legislation for 100 years.[77] Part 4 of the Act, dealing with Immigration and Asylum, allowed indefinite detention of non-nationals suspected of terrorism, but whose deportation was prevented, for example, by the risk that their human rights would be abused in destination countries.[78]

---

[70] Signatories included 'Kenneth W. Starr; Larry Thompson, the former Deputy Attorney General under John Ashcroft; Peter Keisler, a former Acting Attorney General during President Bush's second term; and Bradford Berenson, the former Associate White House Counsel during President Bush's first term'.

[71] Signatories included Frank Jimenez, the former General Counsel of the Navy and former Principal Deputy General Counsel of the Department of Defense; Suzanne E. Spaulding, the former Executive Director of the National Commission on Terrorism; Daniel Dell'Orto, the former Principal Deputy General Counsel and former Acting General Counsel of the Department of Defense; and Matthew Waxman, the former Deputy Assistant Secretary of Defense for Detainee Affairs.

[72] Madbak (n 67).

[73] *Chahal v UK* (1996) 23 EHRR 413.

[74] Special Immigration Appeals Commission Act 1997. These procedures applied to people outside the European Economic Area The member countries of the EEA comprised those in the European Union and the European Free Trade Area.

[75] ibid ss 2B-2D (as amended).

[76] Anti-terrorism, Crime and Security Act 2001.

[77] A Tomkins, 'Legislating Against Terror: The Anti-Terrorism, Crime and Security Act 2001' (2002) *Public Law* 205.

[78] Anti-terrorism, Crime and Security Act 2001, s 23.

Numerous renditions from countries to the US included two Libyan families from Bangkok to Tripoli in 2004 approved by former Labour Foreign Secretary Jack Straw.[79] Such incidents were, apparently, relatively rare but later regretted or attributed to extraordinary circumstances.[80] When the Crime and Security Act 2001 was passed the Home Secretary, David Blunkett, invoked Article 15 of the European Convention on Human Rights, (time of war or other public emergency threatening the life of the nation) to derogate from some aspects of Article 5 (the right to liberty).[81] Detainees could apply for bail or appeal against certification as an international terrorist by the Home Secretary to SIAC.

In *A and others v Secretary of State for the Home Department*,[82] nine detained foreign nationals, none with criminal records or facing charges, challenged their detention as terrorist suspects.[83] The House of Lords held that their detention was unlawful under the Human Rights Act because it discriminated against non-nationals. The majority found the detentions to be a violation of a multi-lateral convention of the UN General Assembly to which the UK had been a signatory since 1968[84] and 'so inconsistent with the United Kingdom's other obligations under international law within the meaning of article 15 of the European Convention (on Human Rights)'.[85]

The House of Lords held that the Immigration Act 1971 and the Convention Article 5(1) meant that foreign nationals could only be detained pending deportation.[86] Article 15(1), allowing derogation for a 'public emergency threatening the life of the nation', had to be strictly required by the situation and consistent with international law obligations.[87] The court therefore considered whether detention of non-nationals was incompatible with the Convention because it was disproportionate and discriminatory. The government, represented by the Attorney-General, sought to establish that the situation justified derogation from Article 5.

The Attorney General argued that courts should not intrude on the policy of a democratically elected government. Lord Bingham accepted courts should not intervene in the political job of government, but accepted the argument of the NGO, Liberty, an intervenor in the case, that a spectrum of 'relative institutional competence' was political at one end and legal at the other. Bingham conceded that the case was towards the political end of the spectrum but rejected the Attorney General's argument[88] that courts could not assess the threat.[89]

---

[79] R Syal and I Cobain, 'Labour call for Straw to face MPs over role in Libyan renditions' *The Guardian* (12 May 2018).

[80] Hansard, *Detainee Mistreatment and Rendition* (2 July 2018), Column 25, https://hansard.parliament.uk/Commons/2018-07-02/debates/5FDC06A8-00A0-40C3-9153-8867E07164A1/DetaineeMistreatmentAndRendition.

[81] The Human Rights Act 1998 (Designated Derogation) Order 2001 on 11 November 2001.

[82] *Appellant A and Others v Secretary of State for the Home Department* [2004] UKHL 56 (the extracts cited are from 'Case Law' (2005) 17 *International Journal of Refugee Law* 117, and the detailed references are to page numbers of the journal.

[83] Anti-terrorism, Crime and Security Act 2001, s 23.

[84] *International Covenant on Civil and Political Rights* (1966) (ICCPR), Article 26.

[85] Per Lord Bingham, with whom Lords Hope, Scott, Rodgers and Nicholls agreed.

[86] *Appellant A and Others* (n 82) 120.

[87] ibid 122.

[88] The Attorney General drew attention to the dangers identified by R Ekins in 'Judicial Supremacy and the Rule of Law' (2003) 119 *Law Quarterly Review* 127.

[89] *Appellant A and Others* (n 82) 138.

The function of independent judges to interpret and apply the law was, Lord Bingham said, 'universally recognised as a cardinal feature of the modern democratic state, a cornerstone of the rule of law itself' and the 1998 Act gave 'the courts a very specific, wholly democratic, mandate, in the words of Professor Jowell, delineating the boundaries of a rights-based democracy'.[90] Bingham did not accept that the 'more purely political' a question was, the less likely it was to be an appropriate matter for judicial decision, nor that courts should defer to political authorities.[91]

Lord Hoffmann found that the power of detention claimed by government was incompatible with the Constitution and an ancient liberty: freedom from arbitrary arrest and detention. The power the Home Secretary claimed to detain people indefinitely without charge or trial was 'antithetical to the instincts and traditions of the people of the United Kingdom'.[92] Hoffmann did not believe that derogation from Article 5 was justified by the 'exigencies of the situation', observing that '[t]errorist violence, serious as it is, does not threaten our institutions of government or our existence as a civil community'.[93]

Baroness Hale disagreed with the Attorney General's suggestion that different categories of person warranted different treatment.[94] Difference had to be objectively justified, serve a legitimate aim and be proportionate:

> Democracy values each person equally. In most respects, this means that the will of the majority must prevail. But valuing each person equally also means that the will of the majority cannot prevail if it is inconsistent with the equal rights of minorities. As Thomas Jefferson said in his inaugural address: 'Though the will of the majority is in all cases to prevail, that will to be rightful must be reasonable … The minority possess their equal rights, which equal law must protect, and to violate would be oppression.'[95]

The suspected international terrorist was a minority because they were 'foreign' rather than 'black', 'disabled', 'female', 'gay', but this did not justify them being treated differently.[96]

Adopting a similar approach to Lord Atkin's dissent in Liversidge v Anderson, the House of Lords balanced national security and individual liberty, holding, eight to one, that indefinite detention of foreign terror suspects was incompatible with the European Convention on Human Rights and the Human Rights Act 1988. Following the House of Lords' decision, the government repealed the legislation and introduced control orders, including house arrest and other restrictions, applicable to British citizens and non-nationals and not therefore discriminatory.[97] These were replaced in 2011 by more flexible tracking orders (TPIM notices).[98]

---

[90] Citing J Jowell, 'Judicial Deference: servility, civility or institutional capacity?' (2003) *Public Law* 592, 597.
[91] *Appellant A and Others* (n 82) Lord Bingham, 132.
[92] ibid 163.
[93] ibid 166.
[94] ibid, Lady Hale at 236.
[95] ibid 237.
[96] ibid 238.
[97] Prevention of Terrorism Act 2005.
[98] Terrorism Prevention and Investigation Measures Act 2011.

C. Lawyers and Special Procedures

SIAC's capacity to certify a person as an international terrorist was removed in 2005, but it retained jurisdiction over immigration and citizenship cases deemed security sensitive by the Home Secretary.[99] Under SIAC's founding legislation the Lord Chancellor made rules of procedure. These had to include the right to legal representation while securing 'that information is not disclosed contrary to the public interest' and that parts of proceedings could take part in the applicant's absence.[100] In order to achieve these aims private practitioners, usually barristers, were designated 'special advocates' to represent appellants' interests.

Special advocates were security vetted by the authorities. Their role was governed by two manuals, one of which could only be viewed by someone who had been vetted. The open manual provided special advocates did not 'act for' the appellant, but in their best interests.[101] They were constrained by procedural restrictions including a 'closed material procedure' (CMP) designed to preserve security sensitive information. In some cases, special advocates acted without instructions or, sometimes, without consent of 'clients'. In others, they interviewed clients at the start of the case before they had seen any 'closed' evidence against them. Having later seen the evidence they were no longer allowed to communicate with the detainee.

Although the special advocates' role differed from the conventional role of barristers, suitable candidates were nominated by the professional body. The cadre of special advocates was small, around 13, and in the early years of SIAC they performed well.[102] After the decision in *A and Others* a senior member of the special advocate panel resigned, declaring the 2001 Act an 'odious blot on the legal landscape' and its detention provisions a 'defiance of the rule of law'.[103] Using barristers appeared to 'legitimise the system' despite restrictions limiting their traditional role.[104] In 2004–5 the House of Commons Constitutional Affairs Committee investigated the work of SIAC.[105] The Attorney General acknowledged that he had received a deputation of eight special advocates and promised improvements to the system. The Committee heard evidence that government lawyers, not private practitioners, should be special advocates.

In 2008 Binyam Mohamed, a British resident, sought disclosure of documents relating to his detention at Guantanamo Bay.[106] The Court of Appeal decided there

---

[99] Special Immigration Appeals Commission Act 1997, s 2 (as amended).
[100] ibid s 5(2) and s 5(3).
[101] A Boon and S Nash, 'Special Advocacy: Political Expediency and Legal Roles in Modern Judicial Systems' (2006) 9 *Legal Ethics* 101, 114 citing *Open Manual* para 7.
[102] ibid 106.
[103] ibid 106, citing I MacDonald, 'Police State?' (*Counsel*, March 2005) 16.
[104] ibid 122.
[105] House of Commons Constitutional Affairs Committee *The Operation of the Special Immigration Appeals Commission and the Use of Special Advocates 2004–5* (HC 323-1) para 55.
[106] *R (Binyam Mohamed) v Secretary of State for Foreign and Commonwealth Affairs* [2010] EWCA Civ 65 and see a note of the decision J Pobjoy, 'Torture, Executive Accountability and the Rule of Law' (Human Rights Law Centre, 10 February 2010) www.hrlc.org.au/human-rights-case-summaries/mohamed-v-secretary-of-state-for-foreign-commonwealth-affairs-2010-ewca-civ-65-10-feb-2010.

was no valid reason for non-disclosure, Lord Neuberger implying he would have accepted the minister's national security veto but for a decision of a US court that the appellant had been tortured. In 2011 three other foreign nationals formerly resident in the UK sued the British government in respect of their ill-treatment by foreign authorities at various locations including Guantanamo Bay.[107] They claimed damages for false imprisonment, trespass to the person, conspiracy to injure, torture and breach of the Human Rights Act 1998. The security services argued for the use of a CMP on grounds of national security.

Nine justices of the Supreme Court held that a CMP would not be acceptable in ordinary civil cases, including judicial review, there being 'certain features of a common law trial which are fundamental to our system of justice', such as the principles of 'open justice' and 'natural justice' only changeable by Parliament.[108] Following the Supreme Court decision, the government legislated to extend the CMP to civil proceedings.[109] Concerns about the proposed legislation were highlighted in a Parliamentary briefing note[110] stating 57 Special Advocates responding to a consultation on extending CMPs had called for more research on alternative systems. Their concerns included appellants being denied lawyers of their choice, the fact that the US was more open about sensitive material, and that regimes in four other countries described in an Appendix to the Green Paper were less restrictive than the UK.

In April 2012, a Parliamentary Joint Committee on Human Rights (JCHR) published a report critical of the government proposals.[111] The Lord Chancellor and Justice Secretary had admitted at a session in March that 'the evidence of the special advocates most unsettled me. I was surprised by their strong reaction. It's important we take on board their strong strictures'.[112] The Committee agreed with the special advocates, that the CMP was 'inherently unfair'[113] and using the law of Public Interest Immunity (PII) was preferable. It declared that '[t]he rule of law requires that decisions about the disclosure of material in legal proceedings be taken by judges not ministers'.[114]

The JCHR rejected the argument that the proposed measures were necessary to maintain the security relationship with the US, claiming that:

> ... proposals for reform which are intended to provide the US with a cast-iron guarantee that any intelligence they share can never be disclosed in a UK court cannot be justified. Such an aim is incompatible with the Government's commitment to the rule of law. The Committee also considers that the Government should proactively address the apparent misperception of US officials that UK courts cannot be trusted to ensure that national security-sensitive material is not disclosed.[115]

---

[107] *Al Rawi and others (Respondents) v The Security Service and others* (Appellants) [2011] UKSC 34.
[108] ibid per Lord Dyson para 9.
[109] Justice and Security Act 2013, s 6.
[110] A Home, 'Special Advocates and Closed Materials Procedures' (House of Commons Library, 25 June 2012) 10, https://researchbriefings.files.parliament.uk/documents/SN06285/SN06285.pdf.
[111] Parliamentary Joint Committee on Human Rights (JCHR) 4 April 2012.
[112] Page 9 citing leader, 'Ken Clarke unsettled by criticism of secret courts plan' *The Guardian* (6 March 2012).
[113] ibid p 10.
[114] ibid.
[115] Home (n 110).

The government made some changes to the Bill. CMPs were to be used only in cases involving national security rather than when ministers thought the public interest was involved.[116] Courts could declare the suitability of a CMP in proceedings,[117] needing to be satisfied that the Secretary of State had considered a claim for public interest immunity in relation to the material.[118] The House of Lords Constitution Committee noted that government retained a central role in deciding what evidence was available to parties in proceedings against it.[119]

D. The Incremental Erosion of Rights

The adjustment of normal court processes was not the only measure affecting lawyers the UK government took to counteract terrorism. They included statutory reporting requirements regarding clients suspected of terrorist or money-laundering activity, and provisions against tipping off clients when reports were made. The Regulation of Investigatory Powers Act 2000 (RIPA)[120] extended the powers of public bodies conducting surveillance and investigation and interception of communications[121] for national security, crime detection, prevention of disorder, public safety, protecting public health, or in the interests of the economic well-being of the UK.[122]

The interception of communications between lawyers and clients was endorsed by the European Court of Human Rights[123] but concerned senior judges.[124] In *Re McE* Lord Phillips dissented from a House of Lords decision allowing covert surveillance of defendants and their lawyers[125] arguing that such powers should only 'be granted by a statute that adequately defined those circumstances and who was to ascertain that they existed'.[126] Subsequently, statutory instruments limited authorisation to circumstances deemed 'exceptional and compelling', such as threats to national security or to life or limb,[127] but this did not rule out authorities 'fishing' for information.[128]

On the second reading of the Bill in 2011, the Home Secretary presented a proposed Protection of Freedoms Act as 'a chance to roll back the creeping intrusion of the state into our everyday lives, and to return individual freedoms to the heart of our legislation'. The Bar Council proposed amendments to the Bill aimed at preventing

---

[116] ibid 11–12.
[117] Justice and Security Act 2013, s 6(1).
[118] ibid s 6(7).
[119] Home (n 110) 12, citing House of Lords Constitution Committee, Press Release: Committee raise concerns with 'closed trial' proposals in Justice and Security Bill, 15 June 2012.
[120] Regulation of Investigatory Powers Act 2000.
[121] This was originally limited to public bodies such as local authorities but was extended to a wide range of other bodies. ibid Sch 1.
[122] ibid s 5(3).
[123] *Öcalan v Turkey* (2005) 41 E.H.R.R. 45.
[124] See eg Lord Nicholls in *Three Rivers District Council & Others v Governor and Company of the Bank of England (No. 6)* [2004] UKHL 48, [2005] 1 AC 610.
[125] *Re McE* [2009] 1 AC 908.
[126] ibid para 41.
[127] SI 2010/123 and SI 2010/461.
[128] N Griffin and G Nardell, 'R.I.P. Legal Professional Privilege' (*Counsel*, May 2012) 30.

the targeting of legally privileged information and setting out what should happen when it was obtained. These were rejected at report stage in the House of Lords.[129]

In May 2013, Edward Snowden, a contractor with the US National Security Agency, used his access to state held information to send thousands of stolen documents to *The Guardian*, and other liberal newspapers around the world, which used them in news items. The papers revealed the scale of government intrusion in private communications and the cooperation of the British government in spying on its own citizens. Snowden faced espionage charges in the US and fled to Russia. Journalists at *The Guardian* and *The Washington Post* were awarded the 2014 Pulitzer prize for public service for articles based on these data. In 2020 a US court found that the data released by Snowden had been collected in breach of the Constitution but allowed its use in a case against terrorists.[130]

In August 2013, detectives from the Metropolitan Police detained and interrogated David Miranda for nine hours at London Heathrow Airport. He was the spouse of the *The Guardian* journalist who had received the Snowden documents and was carrying encrypted Snowden documents. Border control points had been advised that publishing the Snowden files was a terrorist act because it was 'for the purpose of promoting a political or ideological cause'.[131]

Miranda's claim against the police was dismissed by the Court of Appeal because publication could be terrorism 'if it endangered life and the publisher intended it to have that effect'.[132] It held that the arrest did not breach the right to receive and impart information and ideas without interference by public authority. The court went on to say that use of the stop power for journalistic material was incompatible with the European Convention on Human Rights Article 10 because it was not 'prescribed by law' as required by Article 10(2) and was not subject to adequate legal safeguards to avoid arbitrary exercise.[133]

The Court of Appeal granted a certificate of incompatibility requiring Parliament to consider safeguards, such as judicial or other independent and impartial scrutiny. Several free speech organisations had intervened in the litigation. The director of English Pen greeted the decision as 'a significant victory for press freedom, remedying a very worrying gap in the law for safeguarding journalistic material and sources'.[134] Four years after the police held Miranda at Heathrow their criminal investigation had still not concluded. A spokesperson for the National Union of Journalists urged that the police investigation should halt immediately: 'Journalism is not a crime.'[135]

In 2015 a balanced *Newsweek* article reviewed the security position in the UK in the light of the Miranda case. It noted that in 2011 Home Secretary Theresa May

---

[129] ibid.
[130] *United States v Moalin* No. 13-50572 (9th Cir. 2020).
[131] R Gallagher, 'U.K. Police Investigation Of Snowden Leak Journalists Enters Fourth Year' (*The Intercept*, 29 November 2017) https://theintercept.com/2017/11/29/met-police-snowden-leaks-operation-curable/.
[132] *David Miranda v Secretary of State for the Home Department, the Commissioner of Police for the Metropolis and three interveners* ([2014] EWHC 255 (Admin), paras 38–56.
[133] ibid paras 94–117.
[134] O Bowcott, 'Terrorism Act incompatible with human rights, court rules in David Miranda case' *The Guardian* (19 January 2016), www.theguardian.com/world/2016/jan/19/terrorism-act-incompatible-with-human-rights-court-rules-in-david-miranda-case.
[135] Gallagher (n 131).

had appointed barrister David Anderson to review classified government documents and terrorism legislation and recommend changes.[136] Anderson concluded that the Miranda case showed 'the definition of terrorism was edging into dangerous territory' and needed fundamental review. While there was no argument that police should have power to seize stolen security material, holding Miranda for nine hours was intimidatory.

E. Migration

The last area to test state commitments to the rule of law concerns treatment of migrants. Actions included appeals against refusal of asylum and mistreatment in detention. These areas were complicated by fear of 'home grown' terrorists. In 2015 the Counter-terrorism and Security Act 2015 placed a duty on public bodies,[137] listed in Schedule 3 to the Act, to have 'due regard to the need to prevent people from being drawn into terrorism'.[138] It issued guidance advising[139] that extremism potentially leading to terrorism can be identified as: 'vocal or active opposition to fundamental British values, including democracy, the rule of law, individual liberty and mutual respect and tolerance of different faiths and beliefs'.[140] In 2015, Theresa May, while Home Secretary, referred to the rule of law as one of three key values underlying society.[141] She was, however, also an advocate of the UK leaving the European Convention on Human Rights, because she argued it hindered deportations.[142]

In October, May made a speech to the Conservative Party Conference proposing a 'deal', to reduce the numbers of people 'who wrongly claim asylum in Britain' in return for more generous help to 'the most vulnerable people in the world's most dangerous places'.[143] She continued 'my message to the immigration campaigners and human rights lawyers is this: you can play your part in making this happen – or you can try to frustrate it. But if you choose to frustrate it, you will have to live with the knowledge that you are depriving people in genuine need of the sanctuary our country can offer. There are people who need our help, and there are people who are abusing our goodwill – and I know whose side I'm on'.[144]

The Bar's in-house journal observed that May's 'deal' assumed that barristers could refuse clients or enter deals with government which would impede their

---

[136] LM Goodman, 'David Miranda and the Human-Rights Black Hole' (*Newsweek Magazine*, 1 July 2015) www.newsweek.com/2015/01/16/edward-snowdens-helpers-296988.html.
[137] The sectors identified in Schedule 3 were schools, local authorities and the healthcare sector.
[138] Counter-terrorism and Security Act 2015, s 26.
[139] Guidance was issued under s 29.
[140] Revised Prevent Duty Guidance: for England and Wales, www.gov.uk/government/publications/prevent-duty-guidance/revised-prevent-duty-guidance-for-england-and-wales.
[141] With democracy and religious tolerance. See J May, 'Government will promote "British values", Theresa May says' (*Politics Home*, 13 May 2015) www.politicshome.com/news/uk/social-affairs/politics/news/69579/government-will-promote-british-values-theresa-may-says.
[142] BBC News, 'Theresa May: Tories to consider leaving European Convention on Human Rights' (9 March 2013) www.bbc.co.uk/news/uk-politics-21726612.
[143] 'Theresa May's speech to the Tory Party conference' *Independent* (6 October 2015) www.independent.co.uk/news/uk/politics/theresa-may-s-speech-to-the-conservative-party-conference-in-full-a6681901.html.
[144] ibid.

independence, or act as filters of the merits of claims. Presentation of cases for adjudication on their merits did not play a role in maintenance of the rule of law. This revealed ignorance, it claimed, 'of the Bar as a staunchly independent profession and essential actor in ensuring the observance of the rule of law'.[145]

In September 2017 the Home Office declined a request by lawyers for Samim Bigzad, a former Afghan translator for the Americans, to delay his deportation to Kabul, where the Taliban would try to kill him. While he was on the plane Morris J made an order that he be returned. Two applications by the Home Office to vary the order were dismissed by other judges and five days later the Court of Appeal also held against the Home Office. Charles Faulkner, the former Lord Chancellor, thought that the Home Secretary, Amber Rudd, must have confused herself with a sixteenth century monarch.[146] When a similar thing happened in 1991, he said, the court which ruled against the then Home Secretary, Kenneth Baker, observed that failure to comply meant that the executive obeyed law 'as a matter of grace, not as a matter of necessity, a proposition which would reverse the result of the Civil War'.[147]

In 2020 the issue of lawyers preventing deportations featured in an apparently concerted government campaign. In August 2020 the permanent secretary of the Home Office conceded that a promotional video on Twitter should not have claimed that 'activist lawyers' were frustrating attempts to deport migrants with no right to remain.[148] Yet, on 3 September, the Home Secretary Priti Patel, again claimed that activist lawyers were preventing deportations. Early in September a man carrying a large knife, confederate flag and far right literature was arrested at a firm specialising in immigration law.[149] He was later charged with terrorist offences having threatened to kill an immigration solicitor.[150]

At the Conservative Party Conference on 4 October 2020 Patel condemned' the traffickers, the do-gooders, the lefty lawyers, the Labour Party' who are 'defending the broken [asylum] system'. On the same day, *The Mail on Sunday* and *Mail Online* reported that the firm at which the September attack had taken place had 'pocketed' £55 million in legal aid 'from taxpayers' in the previous three years.[151] The article reported an unsubstantiated innuendo that the firm's staff had solicited work at a migrant camp in Calais. The firm issued a rebuttal.[152] In his own conference speech,

---

[145] L Hoyano, 'No Deal' (*Counsel*, June 2016) www.counselmagazine.co.uk/articles/no-deal.
[146] C Falconer, 'The law is for ministers too' *The Guardian* (19 September 2017).
[147] ibid.
[148] J Grierson, 'Home Office wrong to refer to "activist lawyers" top official admits' *The Guardian* (28 August 2020).
[149] M Townsend, 'Lawyers claim knife attack at law firm was inspired by Priti Patel's rhetoric' *The Guardian* (10 October 2020).
[150] BBC News, 'Man charged with right-wing terror plot to kill immigration solicitor' (23 October 2020) www.bbc.co.uk/news/uk-england-london-54661222.
[151] S Howes, 'Revealed: Taxpayers foot 55 million bill for lawyer for blocking deportation flights of channel migrants' *Mail on Sunday* (4 October 2020).
[152] Duncan Lewis solicitors, 'Attacks on Duncan Lewis Solicitors and legal aid undermine the rule of law and an individual's constitutional right to access to justice' (7 October 2020) www.duncanlewis.co.uk/news/_Attacks_on_Duncan_Lewis_Solicitors_and_legal_aid_undermine_the_rule_of_law_and_an_individual%E2%80%99s_constitutional_right_to_access_to_justice_(7_October_2020).html.

the Prime Minister, Boris Johnson, claimed that 'the entire criminal justice system was being hamstrung by lefty human rights lawyers'.[153]

Patel was accused of endangering lawyers and court staff.[154] The president of the Law Society stated 'the fact that a lawyer represents an asylum seeker does not make them a lefty lawyer … it simply makes them a lawyer' and, referring to the increased risk of attacks on lawyers, called on ministers to be 'unequivocal in their support for the rule of law'.[155] The chair of the Bar Council, Amanda Pinto, criticised the politicisation of lawyers 'for simply doing their job in the public interest'.[156] She added 'It is not the job of lawyers to limit parliament's own laws in a way that the government of the day finds most favourable to its political agenda. The law, not politics, is what matters to a profession that upholds the rule of law.'[157]

Criticism of the government's position was not confined to the professional bodies. Pinto pointed out that Patel's Cabinet colleague, Lord Chancellor Robert Buckland, had said only a few days previously: 'It is wholly wrong for any professional to be threatened, harassed or worse, attacked simply for doing their job – we must call it out and deal with it. And make the point that those who attack people providing a professional service will be subject to that very same rule of law.'[158] The former Tory Lord Chancellor, David Gauke, raised concerns with the Home Secretary about Patel's language, asserting that 'violence or abuse against lawyers is unacceptable'.[159]

V. THE GLOBALISATION OF LAWYERING

Dezalay and Garth described the rule of law as a 'global language' helping the spread of capitalism.[160] They suggested that it evolved by lawyers investing social and legal capital to translate social relations into law and state governance. Expecting the rule of law to flourish in developing countries failed to recognise the relationship between law and social relations.[161] This led to attempts to introduce democracy, or legal institutions, or NGOs, which often failed.[162] These strategies missed the importance of investing social and legal capital to translate social relations into law and state

---

[153] Townsend (n 149).
[154] A Woodcock, 'Priti Patel accused of putting lawyers at risk by branding them "lefty do-gooders"' *Independent* (6 October 2020) www.independent.co.uk/news/uk/politics/priti-patel-immigration-lawyers-migrants-law-society-bar-council-b832856.html.
[155] J Slingo, 'Lawyers at risk of physical attack after Patel speech, says Law Society' (*Law Society Gazette*, 5 October 2020).
[156] 'PM is asked to withdraw attack on "lefty lawyers"' *The Guardian* (10 October 2020).
[157] Bar Council, 'Bar Council condemns attempts to paint lawyers as lefties' (Press Release, 5 October 2020) www.barcouncil.org.uk/resource/bar-council-condemns-the-government-s-attempt-to-paint-lawyers-as-lefties.html.
[158] ibid.
[159] D Gauke, 'Why we need lawyers – "lefty" or otherwise' *The Guardian* (21 October 2020).
[160] Y Dezalay and BG Garth, 'Introduction: Lawyers, law and society' in Y Dezalay and BG Garth (eds), *Lawyers and the Rule of Law in an Era of Globalization* (Abingdon, Routledge, 2011).
[161] ibid 2.
[162] ibid 3.

governance.[163] Lawyers had to repeat the historic processes of building the rule of law in each new context. Steps included establishing independent legal professions, promulgating legal norms by lawyers working on the ground, and gathering support from global legal institutions.

A. Legal Professions

Lawyers were controlled in many jurisdictions by self-regulating professional associations. The American Bar Association Legal Profession Reform Index (LPRI) provided resources to strengthen emergent legal professions' claims to independence based on criteria developed by the United Nations and Council of Europe. The LPRI criteria of independent professions specified that '[p]rofessional associations of lawyers are self-governing, democratic, and independent from state authorities',[164] that they should 'promote the interests and independence of the profession, establish professional standards, and provide educational and other opportunities to their members'.[165] It specified that '[p]rofessional associations of lawyers … are actively involved in the country's law reform process'.[166]

In 2016 the IBA reported on performance of three regulatory functions, admission, practice regulation and discipline,[167] in 233 jurisdictions, representing 158 countries. The function was allocated to an entity with primary responsibility: professions, courts, independent agency, or government agency.[168] This revealed regional patterns. Professions conducting all three functions were found in Europe, some former African colonies and Canada.[169] State nominated bodies did so in some Western states[170] and a government lawyer or legal body acted in West Africa and parts of the Caribbean.[171] Professional associations played a nominal role, if any, in Gulf states[172] and Central and East Asia.[173] Courts registered and disciplined practitioners in much of South America and the Caribbean, and some US States.

Table 3 provides a revelatory picture of regulatory autonomy. Self-regulation was the most, and government regulation the least, popular mode. Having an independent regulator was the next most popular model, but true independence from government was difficult to assess, as the example of England and Wales showed.

---

[163] ibid.
[164] American Bar Association Legal Profession Reform Index, Factor 21.
[165] ibid Factor 22.
[166] ibid Factor 24.
[167] A Boon, 'The Regulation of Lawyers and Legal Services' in A Boon (ed), *International Perspectives on the Regulation of Lawyers and Legal Services* (Oxford, Hart Publishing, 2018) 1, 15.
[168] International Bar Association, *Directory of Regulators of the Legal Professions* (IBA 2016) www.ibanet.org/IBA_Regulation_Directory_Home.
[169] Canadian regulation is conducted by independent provincial and territorial law societies under statute.
[170] See eg England and Wales, a number of US States, Canada, and parts of Australia.
[171] See eg parts of West Africa, the Gambia and Ghana, and parts of the Caribbean, Belize and Jamaica.
[172] See eg Saudi Arabia, Qatar, Oman and the UAE.
[173] See eg Tajikistan, Kyrgyzstan, Taiwan, People's Republic of China and Vietnam.

Table 3 Regulation of admission, practice and discipline by jurisdiction[174]

Regulator	Admission		Practice		Discipline	
National or local bars	N 71 (32%) L 22 (10%) Total 93	42%	N 114 (52%) L 17 (8%) Total 131	60%	N 100 (46%) L 16 (7%) Total 116	53%
Independent regulatory authorities	58	26%	24	11%	51	24%
Courts	27	12%	42	19%	27	12%
Government	16	7%	14	6%	13	6%
Mixed or shared responsibility	29	13%	8	4%	9	4%
	223	100%	219	100%	217	100%

Source: International Bar Association, *Directory of Regulators of the Legal Professions* (IBA 2016).

B. Global Law Firms

The impact of globalisation on international legal work was demonstrated by the growth of international law firms.[175] The US firm, Baker & McKenzie, was a trailblazer in 1988 with 1,400 lawyers in 44 offices around the world.[176] The English firm Clifford Chance was second only to Baker and Mackenzie in the number of overseas offices.[177] The rapid domestic growth of English firms had made them creative and entrepreneurial[178] and they had other advantages, such as historic overseas connections with Hong Kong, where British lawyers were automatically admitted to the local bar.[179] Large law firms spread and reinforced the lawyer norms of the core jurisdictions in host countries, spreading out from centres of high 'network connectivity' where financial, legal, and other services were concentrated.[180]

Legal services focused on international centres of finance (London, New York, Hong Kong and Tokyo), dispute resolution (the International Criminal Court or centres of arbitration in London and Paris) and multi-national government (Brussels,

---

[174] Based on International Bar Association *Directory of Regulators* (n 168).
[175] Defined as such when 40% or more of their lawyers are working outside their home country (The American Lawyer, 'Methodology' (*The American Lawyer*, 20 September 2011) www.law.com/jsp/tal/PubArticleFriendlyTAL.jsp?id=1202516515870).
[176] J Flood, 'Megalaw in the UK: Professionalism or Corporatism? A Preliminary Report' (1989) 64 *Indiana Law Journal* 569.
[177] ibid 578.
[178] ibid 584.
[179] ibid 582.
[180] J Faulconbridge, J Beaverstock, D Muzio and PJ Taylor, 'Global law Firms: Globalization and Organizational Spaces of Cross-Border Legal Work' (2008) 28 *Northwestern Journal of International Law and Business* 455 at 474–77.

Luxembourg and Strasbourg).[181] The main centres were London and New York.[182] In 2006, 75 per cent of the 100 leading world firms by turnover were from the US and 17 per cent from the UK.[183] Overseas offices were staffed by attorneys or solicitors combined with lawyers from the host country.[184] Some countries, such as Japan, were late in getting large firms, restricting their international reach,[185] but there were new challenges from firms close to emerging centres in Europe, India and China.

C. International Lawyer Associations

The growth of international legal business increased the prominence of international lawyer organisations, notably the International Bar Association (IBA), inspired by creation of the United Nations and based in New York from 1947.[186] The IBA's original 34 national bar associations grew to a membership of over 200. Its aims included establishing the rule of law worldwide, promoting information exchange between legal associations, supporting the independence of the judiciary, promoting the right of lawyers to practice their profession without interference, and supporting the human rights of lawyers worldwide.

A Standing Committee on Human Rights and the Just Rule of Law was added to the IBA's subject sections in the 1980s. In 1992 it launched a programme to investigate and observe trials in circumstances where the independence of judges and lawyers was threatened. It supported the development of associations for lawyers in countries where there was no tradition of an independent Bar. The first IBA International Code of Ethics was published in 1954 and the last version in 1988.[187] The IBA also published General Principles of Ethics,[188] comprising 10 principles and commentary, describing the lawyer as a trusted adviser who aims also to '... further the development of the law, and to defend liberty, justice and the rule of law'.[189]

The Council of the Bars and Law Societies of Europe (CCBE) originally represented legal associations of the European Economic Community and then Member

---

[181] RL Abel, 'Transnational Legal Practice' (1993–95) 44 *Case Western Reserve Law Review* 737 at 743.
[182] P Taylor, G Catalano and D Walker, 'Measurement of the World City Network' (2002) 39 *Urban Studies* 2367.
[183] 'The Lawyer reveals Global 100' (*The Lawyer*, 30 October 2006) www.thelawyer.com/the-lawyer-reveals-global-100/.
[184] In 2011 there were nearly 6,000 solicitors from England and Wales based overseas. The largest concentrations were in Hong Kong (15% of the total), the United Arab Emirates (13%) and Singapore (9%). TheCityUK, 'Legal Services February 2011' Table 5 Distribution of Solicitors Overseas, 4, www.thecityuk.com/assets/Uploads/Legal-Services-2011.pdf.
[185] KW Chan, 'The Emergence of Large Law Firms in Japan: Impact on Legal Professional Ethics' (2008) 11 *Legal Ethics* 154.
[186] www.ibanet.org/About_the_IBA/About_the_IBA.aspx.
[187] International Bar Association, *International Code of Ethics* (1988).
[188] International Bar Association, *International Principles on Conduct for the Legal Profession* (adopted 28 May 2011) www.ibanet.org/resources.
[189] International Bar Association, *Commentary on the International Principles on Conduct for the Legal Profession*.

States of the European Union. It promoted their interests in relation to three main objects:[190]

> promoting the rule of law, the administration of justice and substantive developments in the law at a European and international level.
>
> acting as an intermediary body between the European legal professions and the institutions of the European Union and the European Economic Area.
>
> monitoring defence of the rule of law and the protection of fundamental and human rights and freedoms.

In 1979 the CCBE intervened in a European Court of Justice case concerning whether legal professional privilege covered communication with in-house counsel.[191] It subsequently maintained a permanent delegation to EU courts and consulted on the implications of EU Directives for affected legal professions.

The CCBE published two documents coordinating European legal professions' approaches to ethics: a charter and a code of conduct. The Charter of Core Principles of the European Legal Profession ('the Charter'), adopted in 2006, contained common rules of European legal professions, providing a model for emerging bar associations, a source of education for lawyers, decision-makers and the public. The common core principles were:

(a) The independence of the lawyer, and the freedom of the lawyer to pursue the client's case.
(b) The right and duty of the lawyer to keep clients' matters confidential and to respect professional secrecy.
(c) Avoidance of conflicts of interest, whether between different clients or between the client and the lawyer.
(d) The dignity and honour of the legal profession, and the integrity and good repute of the individual lawyer.
(e) Loyalty to the client.
(f) Fair treatment of clients in relation to fees.
(g) The lawyer's professional competence.
(h) Respect towards professional colleagues.
(i) Respect for the rule of law and the fair administration of justice, and
(j) The self-regulation of the legal profession.[192]

The CCBE's Code of Conduct for European Lawyers aimed to bind Member States and their bars and law societies engaged in cross border activity. It was adopted as

---

[190] *Statutes of the Council of the Bars and Law Societies of Europe* (adopted November 2013) www.ccbe.eu/fileadmin/user_upload/document/statuts/statutes_en.pdf.
[191] *Australian Mining & Smelting Europe Ltd v Commission of the European Communities (AM & S)* (155/79) [1982] ECR 1575.
[192] Council of Bars and Law Societies of Europe, *Charter of Core Principles of the European Legal Profession Code of Conduct for European Lawyers* (November 2013). www.ccbe.eu/NTCdocument/EN_CCBE_CoCpdf1_1382973057.pdf.

part of the Solicitors' Overseas Practice Rules 1990.[193] In 2013, the code comprised five sections and a preamble which stated:

In a society founded on respect for the rule of law the lawyer fulfils a special role ... Respect for the lawyer's professional function is an essential condition for the rule of law and democracy in society. A lawyer's function therefore lays on him or her a variety of legal and moral obligations (sometimes appearing to be in conflict with each other) towards:

- the client;
- the courts and other authorities before whom the lawyer pleads the client's cause or acts on the client's behalf;
- the legal profession in general and each fellow member of it in particular;
- the public for whom the existence of a free and independent profession, bound together by respect for rules made by the profession itself, is an essential means of safeguarding human rights in face of the power of the state and other interests in society.[194]

The CCBE code contained three substantive sections: 'Relations with Clients', 'Relations with Courts' and 'Relations Between Lawyers'. Reflecting the consensus of over 30 legal professions it was expressed at a high level of generality, and its contradictions highlighted the difficulty of finding commonality.[195]

VI. DISCUSSION

Principe argued that nations committed to the rule of law valued individuals and their importance while those ignoring it produced elitist societies in which 'race, gender, wealth, and power are the values most important to the regime'.[196] The attractiveness of liberalism as a political philosophy lay in the balance between the spread of commerce and the protection of rights. The moral and economic values it supported contrasted favourably with those of autocratic, aristocratic, or theocratic regimes, but unattractive features included the latitude it gave to exploit and despoil the planet.

The process of globalisation did not abate international tensions between regimes supporting the rule of law and those opposing it. Powerful countries, such as Russia, stood outside the emerging world order, their ruling elites reluctant to submit to the rule of law, arguing that the international framework of law was antithetical to their countries' national geopolitical interests. China's relatively recent emergence as a world economic power in the capitalist system was not matched by progress on the rule of law. Breaches included persecution of Uighur Muslims, oppression of its newly acquired citizens in Hong Kong, and suppression of dissent and criticism, manifest in the disappearance or prosecution of citizens, including lawyers, for

---

[193] Adoption of the CCBE Code of Conduct 2006 (posted December 2013) www.ccbe.eu/NTCdocument/Status_of_the_CCBE_C1_1386165089.pdf.
[194] CCBE, *Charter of Core Principles of the European* (November 2013) (n 192).
[195] See A Boon, *Lawyers' Ethics and Professional Responsibility* (Oxford, Hart Publishing, 2016) 404.
[196] ML Principe, 'Albert Venn Dicey and the Principles of the Rule of Law: Is Justice Blind? A Comparative Analysis of the United States and Great Britain' (2000) 22 *Loyola of Los Angeles International & Comparative Law Review* 357, 371.

asserting rights.[197] A retreat from the rule of law was evident in many states in which it had been reasonably well established.

A litmus test for the rule of law was the independence of judges.[198] North and Weingast suggested that, in natural states, the corruption of judiciaries inhibited contract enforcement and dispute resolution, undermining economic integrity and the rule of law.[199] Legislatures could not rely on courts for support when checking the executive and administration and external investors could not be certain that transparent rules applied.[200] It was therefore necessary for progression to greater legality that courts could demonstrate independence, draw attention to issues, expose corruption in the regime and provide a focal point for action.[201] The reverse was also true. An initial sign of the drift of states from the rule of law towards autocracy, in Turkey, Poland, Hungary, and India, included removal of large numbers of judges.

In the core common law jurisdictions, independent judiciaries were built on independent legal professions, from which they acquired attitudes of independence and drew support. While the World Justice Project, originally an initiative of the ABA, made no mention of independent professional associations of lawyers in its four 'universal principles' of the rule of law, the LPRI maintained a stronger focus. The IBA and CCBE provided rhetorical support to the need for independent legal professions and the absence of meaningful and autonomous professional organisation was symptomatic of autocracy. For example, although Russian advocates were an autonomous profession compared with other Russian lawyers, they are under pressure from state agencies and judges to cooperate with the authorities and had limited opportunities to investigate cases or present evidence and arguments in court.[202]

In core jurisdictions the rule of law was supposedly a transcendent value in legal services regulation; a higher goal to be served.[203] The CCBE Code claimed that membership of liberal professions played an important role in guaranteeing lawyers' independence': 'self-regulation of the profession is vital in buttressing the independence of the individual lawyer'.[204] The commentary to the CCBE Charter claimed state control of professions threatened the rule of law.[205] A report by the UN Special Rapporteur on the independence of judges and lawyers[206] noted the difficulty of

---

[197] Chinese Human Rights Defenders, 'New Wave of Persecution Against Chinese Human Rights Lawyers Must Sound the Alarm' (6 December 2021) www.nchrd.org/2021/12/new-wave-of-persecution-against-chinese-human-rights-lawyers-must-sound-the-alarm/.
[198] 'Commonwealth principles on the accountability of the relationship between the three branches of government' (2004) 96(1) *Commonwealth Legal Education* 7, Principle IV.
[199] Weingast (n 42) 35.
[200] Ginsburg (n 10) 178.
[201] ibid.
[202] E Moiseeva and T Bocharov, 'A Professional Portrait of Russian Advocates: Challenges of the Market and Boundary Work' in R Abel, O Hammerslev, U Schultz and H Sommerlad (eds), *Lawyers in 21st-Century Societies, vol. 1: National Reports* (Oxford, Hart Publishing, 2020) ch 16.
[203] N Semple, *Justicia's Legions* (Cheltenham, Edward Elgar, 2015) 193–95.
[204] Council of Bars and Law Societies of Europe, *Charter of Core Principles* (n 194) Commentary on Principle J.
[205] ibid at 10.
[206] L Despouy, *Report of the Special Rapporteur on the independence of judges and lawyers: Substantive topics and issues identified by the Special Rapporteur* (Geneva, United Nations Human Rights Council, 2004) www.ohchr.org/EN/Issues/Judiciary/Pages/Annual.aspx.

establishing independence when national democratic institutions were at risk. There was often no foundation of basic rights, freedom from arbitrary arrest or detention and torture, freedom of opinion and expression, freedom of peaceful assembly and association, as a platform for challenge.[207]

The IBA Taskforce on the independence of the legal profession warned of the risk to the rule of law in Western countries posed by measures to counter organised crime and terrorism. The IBA Task Force cited the Snowden case was one of several examples of threats to rule of law principles in the UK. They included judicial bribery,[208] investigatory powers legislation[209] and regulation impinging on Legal Professional Privilege.[210] Government documents declassified in November 2014 revealed that the GCHQ, MI5 and MI6 had interfered with the privileged communications of lawyers, journalists and others handling confidential information.[211] This material was used in at least one legal case.[212] The core common law jurisdictions were not secure in their adherence to the rule of law.

Arguments for codes of conduct for lawyers working across international borders was a recurring theme of debates about globalised lawyering.[213] While both the IBA and CCBE codes arguably reflected an Anglo-American conception of the lawyer, balancing the neutral and partisan role with legality, it was probably the most robust and widely accepted model for the internationalisation of lawyer norms.[214] The UN Special Rapporteur noted that it was important that groups claiming independence in the international sphere respected the duties attached to their roles.[215] The lack of an international body capable of policing international practice and prosecuting misconduct was a problem in establishing such a regime, as was the issue of deciding relevant rules.

VII. CONCLUSION

Globalisation had unpredictable impacts on the rule of law, facilitating proliferation of legal norms through international organisations but provoking resistance to its

---

[207] ibid para 11.

[208] International Bar Association, *The Independence of the Legal Profession: Threats to Bastion of a Free and Democratic Society* (*Report of the IBA Presidential Task Force*, 2016) fn 31, www.ibanet.org/MediaHandler?id=6E688709-2CC3-4F2B-8C8B-3F341705E438&.pdf&context=bWF-zdGVyfGFzc2V0c3wzMTQxNzd8YXBwbGljYXRpb24vcGRmfGg4NC9oZGUvODc5NzEyNT-M0NTMxMC82RTY4ODcwOS0yQ0MzLTRGMkItOEM4Qi0zRjM0MTcwNUU0MzgucGRmf-Dk2OTg0ZjU1ZWE5OTJlM2ViZTc2MWEwMGE3Zjc4ZDQwOTYwMWYxMDU4OTNlMDc4-YTJlODU0Y2I3OTBhZWQzY2U.

[209] ibid fn 67.

[210] ibid fn 69.

[211] O Bowcott, 'Security services spy on lawyers' *The Guardian* (7 November 2014).

[212] IBA (n 208) fn 119.

[213] RL Abel, 'Transnational Legal Practice' (1993–5) 44 *Case Western Reserve Law Review* 737; A Boon and J Flood, 'The Globalisation of Professional Ethics?: The Significance of Lawyers' International Codes of Conduct' (1999) 2(1) *Legal Ethics* 29; C Whelan, 'Ethics Beyond the Horizon: Why Regulate the Global Practice of Law' (2001) 34 *Vanderbilt Journal of Transnational Law* 931.

[214] Boon and Flood (n 213).

[215] ibid para 39.

liberalising tendencies. Increasing awareness of the interconnectedness of world relations placed liberal countries in increasing opposition to autocracies, most notably Russia and China. Establishing the rule of law ran into difficulty even in countries willing to embrace it. Although the establishment of independent legal professions and judges was a symptom of the rule of law rather than the cause, they played a critical role in embedding it. The Anglo-American conception of the lawyer's role, in which lawyers' roles placed them on the side of the citizen and at a remove from the state was arguably the most viable model. It was an example of globalised localism because it promoted a Western notion of law and lawyering, but it also provided tools for counterhegemonic struggle.

17

Democracy

I. INTRODUCTION

BROAD-BASED ELECTORATES REALISED the Enlightenment ideal of the will of the People, legitimised sovereign assemblies and supported the idea that citizens held rulers to account in the public realm.[1] Electing representatives and holding them to account was accompanied by a raft of other democratic conventions: transparent election practices, peaceful handover of power and legislators following their conscience. The solid links between democracy and the rule of law, always dependent on socio economic conditions and state structures,[2] was threatened in 2016 by the UK referendum on leaving the European Union (Brexit) and the election of Donald Trump in the US.[3] Both were labelled 'populist' events, engaging degrees of nativism, xenophobic nationalism, and opposition to liberalism. This chapter focuses on the role of judges and government lawyers in resisting moves characteristic of populist governments, to instal a new order.[4]

II. THEORY

Modern interpretations of Aristotle suggested that he favoured democracy[5] as a system of government most likely to serve the common interest.[6] His proposed constitutional arrangements promoted the freedom and self-regulation of citizens through daily involvement in politics. The aim was to foster 'an ongoing ethical, social, and political practice on the part of the same citizens that constitution governs, with a view to the future'.[7]

---

[1] MJC Vile, *Constitutionalism and the Separation of Powers*, 2nd edn (Minneapolis, Liberty Fund, 1998) 346–47.
[2] PC Schmitter and TL Karl, 'What democracy is … and is not' (1991) 2(3) *Journal of Democracy* 75.
[3] C Mudde, 'How populism became the concept that defines our age' *The Guardian* (22 November 2018).
[4] A Bozóki, 'The Illusion of Inclusion: Configurations of Populism in Hungary' in M Kopecek and P Wcislik (eds), *Thinking Through Transition: Liberal Democracy, Authoritarian Pasts, and Intellectual History in East Central Europe after 1989* (Budapest, New York, Central European University Press, 2015) 275, 311.
[5] J Frank, *A Democracy of Distinction: Aristotle and the Work of Politics* (Chicago, Chicago University Press, 2005).
[6] M Krygier, 'The Rule of Law: Pasts, Presents and Two Possible Futures' (2016) 12 *Annual Review of Law and Social Science* 199, 205 citing Aristotle, *The Politics* (Cambridge, Cambridge University Press, 1988) §1287a, 18–21.
[7] J Frank, 'Aristotle on Constitutionalism and the Rule of Law' (2007) 8(1) *Theoretical Inquiries in Law* 37, 41.

So understood, the constitution disciplines the power of the people, the power of those who govern, and the power of law itself. But it does so not by standing over and against a citizenry, or its rulers, or the polity, for the source of its disciplinary power does not lie outside those it regulates. Instead, the constitution is itself a practice of self-discipline.[8]

Democracy was not a licence for citizens to do what they wanted but implied restraint consistent with this responsibility.

Aristotle envisaged participatory citizenship to involve law making and execution of law by a group of notables, a quite different proposition from modern ideas of democracy.[9] Stephen Holmes suggested that the liberal ideal of collective self-rule derived from Enlightenment thinking about government based on consent.[10] In medieval Europe, Niccolò Machiavelli (1469–1527) revived interest in republicanism based on popular sovereignty. Rousseau proposed that executive power should be balanced by the People, envisaging a right to participate rather than to be represented. Other political theorists were less in favour of democracy.

Both Montesquieu and Locke feared that broad-based electorates would lead to the tyranny of the majority and the abuse of minorities.[11] Montesquieu regarded the experiment with Cromwell's Commonwealth 'a very droll spectacle', since English 'efforts towards the establishment of democracy' resulted in them having 'recourse to the very government which they had so wantonly proscribed'.[12] He regarded democracy as unnatural, at risk of corruption from a 'spirit of inequality' springing from self-interest. The People would want to perform the functions of government themselves but be unconcerned with the public good. He proposed constitutional mechanisms to prevent direct government by the people.

Neither Dicey nor Bagehot grounded the sovereignty of Parliament in the electorate. Dicey was particularly opposed to the direct democracy of the referendum. He anticipated two problems in his *Introduction to the Theory of the Constitution*. The first was whether 'the anti-reforming press [would] exhaust itself in malignant falsehoods calculated to deceive the people'. The second was that 'the people, it is said, are too stupid to be entrusted with the referendum; the questions must never be put before them with such clearness that they may understand the true issues submitted to their arbitrament'.[13]

While Tamanaha placed participatory democracy at the 'thick' end of formal arrangements contributing to the rule of law,[14] constitutional theory recognised

---

[8] ibid 49.
[9] S Fosdyke, 'Reviewed Work: *A Democracy of Distinction: Aristotle and the Work of Politics* by Jill Frank' (2006) 101(2) *Classical Philology* 171.
[10] It excluded the consent of women and non-whites by omission or on discriminatory criteria (C Pateman, *The Sexual Contract* (Stanford, Stanford University Press, 1988); C Mills, *The Racial Contract* (Ithaca, Cornell University Press, 1997)).
[11] S Holmes, *Passions and Constraint: On the Theory of Liberal Democracy* (Chicago, Chicago University Press, 1995) 29.
[12] Montesquieu, *The Spirit of the Law Book III*: The Principles of the Three kinds of Government, Book III: The Principle of Democracy.
[13] AV Dicey, *Introduction To The Study Of The Law Of The Constitution*, 3rd edn (London, Macmillan, 1889) cxiii.
[14] B Tamanaha, *On the rule of Law: History, Politics, Theory* (Cambridge, Cambridge University Press, 2004) 10.

the danger of populism posed by democracy. In Athens it was associated with Demagoguery, manipulation of a mob[15] with appeals to desires and prejudices rather than reason or morality. The demagogues' characteristics were lust for power and low regard for conventional politics or institutions. They ignored process and were prone to corruption: rigging elections, appointing cronies to high positions, and improperly awarding public benefits. Their dispositions and tactics included lying, attacking potential critics, and eroding constraints on power. These characteristics appealed to voters drawn to populists.

The fears of both classical and Enlightenment scholars were joined in the twentieth century. Populism was a term 'widely used and widely contested' in political literature[16] to describe three traditions: ideology, style, and strategy. Each used different definitions, sources of evidence and investigatory methods.[17] While distinct in theory, in practice, they often overlapped. A common ideological element was a binary, moral opposition between 'the People' and an establishment represented by an oligarchy, professional political elite or simply a status quo.[18] In terms of style, personalistic political leadership was able to 'create' such a cleavage, making populism more a form of expression than an ideology.[19] Overriding institutions or norms involved resort to the popular will, an 'us and them' antagonism.

Populism was consistent with ideologies on the extreme right or left, including socialism, communism, nationalism and, indeed, neoliberalism.[20] Left-wing forms were prevalent in South America and right-wing forms in the US and Europe.[21] Right-wing populism played to a nativist impulse: nostalgia for an imagined past, the preservation of inherent privileges and the exclusion of groups external to national identity. There was a tendency to whip up anger, demonise outsiders, such as migrants, or elites, like judges, frustrating the popular will. Frank Wilhoit argued that conservatism shared features with right wing populism, needing 'in-groups whom the law protects but does not bind, alongside out-groups whom the law binds but does not protect'.[22]

III. THE UNITED KINGDOM

A. The 'Brexit' Referendum

In *The Spirit of Laws* (1748) Montesquieu advised that moderation was the guiding principle of government: monarchs ruled according to law while despots did not.

---

[15] M Signer, *Demagogue: The Fight to Save Democracy from Its Worst Enemies* (New York, Palgrave Macmillan, 2009) 33.
[16] N Gidron and B Bonikowski, 'Varieties of Populism: literature review and research agenda' (Cambridge MA, Wetherhead Centre for International Affairs, Harvard University, 2013).
[17] ibid as described there in more detail in Table 1 at 17.
[18] Bozóki (n 4).
[19] Gidron and Bonikowski (n 16).
[20] ibid 277.
[21] ibid and see Hans-Georg Betz, *Radical Right-Wing Populism in Western Europe* (Basingstoke, Hants, Palgrave Macmillan, 1994).
[22] Goodreads, 'Frank Wilhoit', www.goodreads.com/author/quotes/20632851.Frank_Wilhoit.

Moderate government was rare because it was much more difficult to achieve than despotism.[23] A negative impact of the Reform Act 1832 was reducing the control the mixed/balanced Constitution gave to monarch and Lords and the harmony gained by having large numbers of aristos in Parliament.[24] Constitutional structures constraining popular will were justified by deontological conceptions of individual rights advocated by Kant. They were protected by separation of powers and a legislative process which was deliberative,[25] protecting minority rights through the exercise of conscience.

The robustness and resilience of the UK's constitutional arrangements were tested when a referendum approved Britain leaving the European Union (Brexit), a trading block and political union it had first joined in 1973. This overlapped with a long period of de-industrialisation and relative economic decline, worse outside major metropolitan centres which had not regenerated. Economic problems were exacerbated by the financial crisis of 2008, leading to government austerity. The EU was a populist target because its institutions were remote and largely overseas. Margaret Thatcher, generally a supporter of trading agreements with Europe, was resistant to plans for ever closer political union of EU countries.

In 1993 a small number of 'Eurosceptic' Tories formed a pressure group, the European Research group (ERG), to coordinate right of centre politicians in Europe. Their main targets were the regulatory infrastructure and rights, employment and environmental protection demanded by the EU. From its early days, the ERG co-operated with the newly formed United Kingdom Independence Party (UKIP) which was committed to leaving the EU. UKIP opposed the principle of free movement of labour, co-opting an anti-immigration rhetoric which oscillated according to public opinion, party leadership and the party in government.[26] Support for UKIP grew, notably in elections to the European Parliament. In the 2015 general election it polled 12.5 per cent of the total vote and held onto one of two Parliamentary seats gained by Tory defections. The Tory Prime Minister, David Cameron, spooked by the damage the issue was doing inside and outside the party, promised a referendum.

The Vote Remain campaign, led by Cameron, focused on the economic advantages of frictionless trade with the EU customs area and predicted dire economic consequences of departure. The Vote Leave campaign focused on political sovereignty, the saving of EU contributions, and escape from EU regulation and free movement. The Referendum on 23 June 2016 resulted in narrow victory for Vote Leave. After the referendum defeat, Cameron resigned and was succeeded by Theresa May. She vowed to follow the outcome of the referendum but was confronted by a Parliament with widely different views of what the result demanded and how it was to be achieved.

---

[23] C-L Montesquieu (trans/ed AM Cohler, BC Miller and HS Stone), *The Spirit of the Laws*, t. (Cambridge, Cambridge University Press, 1992) 63, cited by Krygier (n 6) 206.
[24] Vile (n 1) 109 and 242.
[25] Holmes (n 11).
[26] Gidron and Bonikowski (n 16) citing T Bale, S van Kessel and P Taggart, 'Thrown Around With Abandon? Popular Understandings of Populism as Conveyed by the Print Media: A UK case study' (2013) 46(2) *Acta Politica* 111.

B. Notice of Withdrawal

May announced that she did not need the consent of Parliament to invoke Article 52, which would start the clock ticking on the two-year withdrawal period. A citizen, Gina Miller, sought judicial review, arguing that Brexit would directly impact citizens' substantive legal rights under UK domestic law and therefore required the consent of Parliament. In *Miller v Secretary of State for Exiting the European Union*, a Divisional Court of the High Court declared that Article 52 could not be invoked under Crown prerogative powers and *would* require the consent of Parliament. It cited the authority of *The Case of Proclamations*: 'the King by his proclamation or other ways cannot change any part of the common law, or statute law, or the customs of the realm' and that 'the King hath no prerogative, but that which the law of the land allows him'. The decision was unsuccessfully challenged in the Court of Appeal.[27]

On 4 January 2016 the *Daily Mail* front page pictured the three Court of Appeal judges who affirmed the right of Parliament under the headline 'Enemies of the People', identifying one as 'openly' homosexual. Liz Truss, a non-lawyer Lord Chancellor, was criticised for her silence on the issue and her failure, despite the Constitutional Reform Act 2005, to uphold the independence of the judiciary. The Lord Chief Justice, Lord Thomas of Cwmgiedd, said that circuit judges had reported having defendants taunt them and there was harassment online.[28] He told the House of Lords Constitution Select Committee that Truss was 'completely and utterly wrong to say she could not criticise the media'.[29]

In January 2017 a majority of eight of the 11 sitting justices of the UK Supreme Court confirmed that invoking Article 50(2) required the consent of Parliament.[30] The issue was put succinctly by Lord Hughes as a choice between two rules.[31] The first was that the 'executive cannot change law made by Act of Parliament, nor the common law' and the second that 'the making and unmaking of treaties is a matter of foreign relations within the competence of the government'. The majority decision that Rule 1 applied[32] changed the course of the Brexit process, forcing the government to promise Parliament a 'meaningful vote' on any exit agreement. The Labour Party favoured remaining in a customs union, other parties wanted a second referendum, and the ERG wanted a clean break.

C. Getting Brexit Done

May decided to present a take it or leave it package at the end of negotiations, but this failed to build cross party support for her relatively moderate draft agreement.

---

[27] *R (on the application of Miller) v Secretary of State for Exiting the European Union* Divisional Court, Queen's Bench Division 3 November 2016 [2016] EWHC 2768 (Admin) [2016] HRLR 23.

[28] C Davies, 'Judges tell of fears for safety as hostility rises' *The Guardian* (27 February 2017).

[29] O Bowcott, 'Lord chief justice attacks Truss for failure to defend the judiciary' *The Guardian* (23 March 2017).

[30] *R (on the application of Miller and another) (Respondents) v Secretary of State for Exiting the European Union (Appellant) REFERENCE by the Attorney General for Northern Ireland – In the matter of an application by Agnew and others for Judicial Review REFERENCE by the Court of Appeal (Northern Ireland) – In the matter of an application by Raymond McCord for Judicial Review* [2017] UKSC 5.

[31] ibid para 277.

[32] ibid para 36.

She was defeated three times by a coalition of MPs hoping for different things. This included the ERG comprising 100 MPs, less than a third of the Parliamentary party, which hoped for a 'no-deal' outcome.[33] May resigned in July 2019 following bad results for the Tories in elections to the European Parliament. Boris Johnson, a leading member of the Leave campaign, was elected party leader by the first Tory Party members' vote. He vowed to leave the EU by a revised deadline of 30 October 2019 if agreement was not reached.

At the end of August, Johnson requested that the Queen prorogue Parliament for approximately a month from early September. Government ministers claimed that this was normal and within the scope of executive power, but the real motive was apparently to stop Parliament intervening to prevent a 'no-deal Brexit' on 30 October. When it was announced in the Commons, the Speaker of the House of Commons, John Bercow, responded that the prorogation was 'not typical. It is not standard. It is one of the longest for decades, and it represents, not just in the minds of many colleagues but for huge numbers of people outside, an act of Executive fiat'.[34]

The prorogation was challenged in Scotland and England, where the courts reached different conclusions. The English High Court decided that the reason for prorogation was a point of political contention and therefore not justiciable. In September 2019, the combined appeals came before the Supreme Court. No member of the government swore any affidavit as to the intention behind the prorogation. For the claimants, David Pannick QC alleged that the prorogation was for the 'improper purpose' of denying Parliament the opportunity to review government policy and negotiating strategy with the EU.[35] Although Pannick was interrupted by questions from Lords Carnwath and Reed, the minority judges in the Article 50, case, they then agreed with the other justices of the Supreme Court; there was no evidence 'that there was any reason – let alone a good reason – for the prorogation'.

Citing the *Case of Proclamations*, and *Entick v Carrington*, the Supreme Court declared that the issue was justiciable, and that the prerogative power was subject to Parliamentary sovereignty. It was therefore held illegal, null, and had no effect. The unanimous decision was unsurprising constitutionally. On the contrary, it would have been surprising if the court had upheld the right of the government, the executive power, to deny the supremacy of the legislative power. The EU hailed the decision as a victory for the rule of law.[36]

During the prorogation litigation, Tories, including government ministers, joined the press in accusing the 'unelected judiciary' of thwarting the public will. Senior Tories and ministers made unfounded claims that the case raised constitutional issues

---

[33] In 2018 the Information commissioner ordered Steve Baker, a former leader of the ERG and by then the Minister for Exiting the EU, to reveal an email 'briefing a smaller and more senior group'. It was to 21 people some of whom were not MPs (P Geoghegan and J Corderoy 'Key members of Jacob-Rees Mogg's pro-Brexit MP lobby group finally revealed' (Open Democracy, 1 May 2019) www.opendemocracy.net/en/dark-money-investigations/key-members-of-jacob-rees-moggs-pro-brexit-mp-lobby-group-finally-revealed/.

[34] F Davis, 'Decision of the Supreme court on the prorogation of Parliament' (House of Commons Library, 24 September 2019) https://commonslibrary.parliament.uk/decision-of-the-supreme-court-on-the-prorogation-of-parliament/.

[35] *The Guardian* (18 September 2019) 8–9.

[36] D Boffey and J Rankin, 'Relief that rule of law is "alive and kicking" in Britain' *The Guardian* (25 September 2019).

about supremacy (Iain Duncan Smith), that 'many people ... are saying the judges are biased' (Business Minister, Kwasi Kwarteng of the Scottish case),[37] that unelected judges had thwarted the will of the British public (Dominic Raab, future Foreign Secretary), that the decision was a 'constitutional coup' (Jacob Rees-Mogg, future leader of the House of Commons) and that it 'was wrong' of the court to pronounce on a political question (Boris Johnson).[38]

Having failed to leave the EU by stealth, Johnson apparently decided that a general election was the only solution. He was blocked by the Fixed Term Parliaments Act 2011 which provided for elections at five-year intervals and earlier only if two-thirds of the House of Commons agreed or there was a motion of no-confidence and an alternative government could not be formed.[39] This meant an election would not occur until 2022. When Parliament reconvened the day after the Supreme Court decision a petitioner in the Scottish action, Scottish National Party MP Joanna Cherry, asked what legal advice the Attorney General, Geoffrey Cox QC had given on prorogation. Cox responded with what Bercow later called an 'unstoppable rant', booming: 'This Parliament is a dead Parliament. It should no longer sit ... This Parliament is a disgrace.'[40] It was subsequently leaked that Cox had advised that prorogation was legal.[41]

Later in September Bercow gave Members of Parliament time to promote amendments to the European Withdrawal Act (No 2) 2019 (also called the 'Benn Act' because it was introduced by the opposition MP Hilary Benn) to limit the chances of a 'no deal' Brexit and to require the government to seek a further extension if no agreement was reached by 30 October. The Act passed with the help of 21 Tory rebels. They had the whip removed, preventing them standing as Tory MPs at future elections. Johnson said he would rather be 'dead in a ditch' than seek an extension and wrote to Tory Party members saying he was only bound by the Act, 'in theory'.

Ways of avoiding the Benn Act were apparently mooted, but Robert Buckland, the Lord Chancellor, confirmed he had spoken to Johnson, regarding 'the importance of the rule of law, which I as Lord Chancellor have taken an oath to uphold'.[42] In October a Scottish court of session declined to make an order that Johnson comply with the Benn Act because Government counsel Richard Keen QC gave an undertaking the government would comply. The court considered it unthinkable that the government would not honour that undertaking.[43]

Johnson's proposed exit agreement, essentially May's negotiated agreement with changes relating to customs arrangements in Northern Ireland, failed to get

---

[37] A Mohdin, 'Minister heavily criticised over judicial bias claim' *The Guardian* (13 September 2019).
[38] The secret barrister, 'Against the law – why judges are under attack' *The Guardian* (22 August 2020) www.theguardian.com/books/2020/aug/22/against-the-law-why-judges-are-under-attack-by-the-secret-barrister.
[39] Fixed-term Parliaments Act 2011, s 1(2) and ss 1(3) and 2(1)(b).
[40] 'Attorney general tells MPs "this Parliament is a disgrace"' (*bbc.co.uk*, 25 September 2019) www.bbc.co.uk/news/av/uk-politics-49827307; M Kettle, 'Johnson's gambit now is to turn his humiliation into rocket fuel' *The Guardian* (26 September 2019).
[41] H Stewart, P Walker and R Mason, 'He misled the Queen, the people and Parliament' *The Guardian* (25 September 2019).
[42] H Stewart, R Syal and L O'Carroll, 'PM heads to Dublin amid fears of more resignations' *The Guardian* (9 September 2019).
[43] O Bowcott, 'Minister refuses to say in court whether parliament could be prorogued again' *The Guardian* (18 September 2019).

a majority in the Commons. Ditching a line in the political declaration to Theresa May's agreement proposing that the UK would 'consider' aligning with European Union rules in future trade talks was important in securing the support of the ERG.[44] A further extension was then requested and granted by the EU to 31 January 2020. After goading in the House of Commons, the opposition parties agreed to an election to be held in December 2019. Johnson fought it on the promise to exit the EU on the terms of his agreement defeated in October.

The result of the election was a Tory majority of 80 seats. The UK duly left the EU in January 2020. The aftermath of Brexit was a more right-wing Tory Parliamentary Party. The 21 MPs from whom the whip was removed were leading moderates including two former Lord Chancellors and an Attorney-General.[45] Although some MPs were later reinstated the government, now dominated by members of the ERG, was relatively extreme. Turning its attention to the impediments it perceived had hindered the Brexit process it rapidly demonstrated the tendency of populist government to undermine constraints on power and conventions supporting legality.

D. Weakening Executive Constraints

Boris Johnson's term as an elected Prime Minister began with plans to weaken constraints on executive power. Dominic Cummings, the Brexit mastermind credited with the referendum slogan (Take Back Control) and election slogan (Get Brexit Done) was appointed special adviser. He had previously declared an agenda of restructuring the civil service. Another target was the British Broadcasting Corporation (BBC) which, as Director of New Frontiers Foundation in 2004, Cummings had declared a 'mortal enemy', outlining plans to discredit it and allow a right-wing competitor or replacement like the American Fox News.[46]

Antagonism was common to a faction in the Tory party which saw the BBC as a hostile institution, peddler of a liberal version of the world, and insufficiently supportive of Brexit.[47] In fact, it was the BBC editorial commitment to 'scrutinise arguments, question consensus and hold power to account', which appeared to be the problem for some, but not all.[48] In 2016 a white paper proposing changes to the BBC board had been seen to threaten the independence of the BBC, hailed as 'a declaration

---

[44] L O'Carroll, 'How is Boris Johnson's Brexit deal different from Theresa May's?' *The Guardian* (17 October 2019) www.theguardian.com/politics/2019/oct/17/how-is-boris-johnson-brexit-deal-different-from-theresa-may.
[45] BBC News, 'Who were the Tory rebels who defied Boris Johnson?' www.bbc.co.uk/news/uk-politics-49563357.
[46] R Mason, 'Dominic Cummings thinktank called for "end of BBC in current form"' *The Guardian* (20 January 2021) www.theguardian.com/politics/2020/jan/21/dominic-cummings-thinktank-called-for-end-of-bbc-in-current-form.
[47] N Cohen, 'The last thing troubled civil service needs is your advice' *The Guardian* (18 April 2021) www.theguardian.com/commentisfree/2021/apr/18/dominic-cummings-the-last-thing-the-troubled-civil-service-needs-is-your-advice.
[48] A Beckett, 'The BBC is finding out the hard way you can't do "balance" with this government' *The Guardian* (18 November 2021) www.theguardian.com/commentisfree/2021/nov/19/bbc-balance-boris-johnson.

of war on pluralism and independence',[49] and caused a storm in the Tory party.[50] A stronger faction shared Margaret Thatcher's opposition to the BBC funding model, a licence fee paid by television owners. There had been a tendency of Tory governments to roll up complaints about BBC political coverage with the issue of the licence fee.

The lawyers responsible for protecting the rule of law within government were the Lord Chancellor, Robert Buckland QC, and Attorney-General, Suella Braverman. Buckland, a former solicitor-general, had supported remaining in the EU, a rarity in the Cabinet. But his first major policy declaration, that 'those suspected of serious crimes to be granted anonymity but only if they had a reputation to protect',[51] was the antithesis of equality before the law. Braverman, a former chair of the ERG, was, in her early career at the Bar, briefed by the Home Office to defend claims of unlawful detention in immigration cases. She had written in *Conservative Home* that human rights had been 'stretched beyond recognition' and that 'elected decision-makers' needed to 'take back control' from unelected, unaccountable judges.[52]

One of Cummings' first acts in post was to appoint what he called 'weirdos and misfits with odd skills' to replace civil servants as government advisers.[53] This was followed by the civil service cuts affecting the 'Arms' Length Bodies' scrutinising government.[54] The Johnson government renewed the aim of removing the licence fee and appointed Richard Sharp as BBC Chairman.[55] Sharp, a former banker, Conservative party donor and adviser to the Chancellor of the Exchequer, was said to be 'open minded' about the licence fee.[56] In 2022 the government's Culture Secretary announced the freezing of BBC funding, adding that the people who worked at the BBC had a 'certain political bias'.[57]

The Tories had made two manifesto commitments likely to lead to the weakening of checks on executive power. The first was to repeal the Fixed Terms Parliament Act. The government ignored concerns expressed by parliamentary committees to return to the 'tried and tested system' of allowing the Prime Minister to choose an election date.[58] The second was to establish a commission to review the constitution, rights,

---

[49] M Kettle, 'At times like this we need to rethink our US infatuation' *The Guardian* (1 October 2020).

[50] J Martinson, 'BBC white paper could spark revolt among Tory MPs' *The Guardian* (11 May 2016).

[51] F Elliott, J Ames and R Ford, 'Boris Johnson snubs Robert Buckland's call for sex offenders to remain anonymous' *The Times* (1 August 2019) www.thetimes.co.uk/article/suspects-in-sex-crimes-should-be-anonymous-5q9c3lvxj.

[52] D Trilling, 'For the panto authoritarians, overt cruelty is a winning hand' *The Guardian* (18 February 2020).

[53] R Syal, 'Dominic Cummings role provokes alarm in civil service' *The Guardian* (25 July 2022) www.theguardian.com/politics/2019/jul/25/dominic-cummings-role-provokes-alarm-inside-civil-service.

[54] J Elgott, 'Radical shake-up of civil service comms to be in place by April 2022' *The Guardian* (16 March 2021) www.theguardian.com/politics/2021/mar/16/radical-shake-up-of-civil-service-comms-to-be-in-place-by-april-2022.

[55] S Noah, 'Boris Johnson's "attacks" on the BBC are "dangerous" says David Dimbleby' *The Independent* (26 September 2020).

[56] A Bland, 'Next BBC chair says it may be worth looking again at licence fee' *The Guardian* (14 January 2021) www.theguardian.com/media/2021/jan/14/next-bbc-chair-may-be-worth-looking-again-licence-fee-richard-sharp.

[57] A Rajan, 'Nadine Dorries: BBC licence fee announcement will be the last' (*BBC News*, 16 January 2022) www.bbc.co.uk/news/entertainment-arts-60014514.

[58] House of Commons Library, 'Fixed term Parliaments Act 2011' (24 December 2020) https://commonslibrary.parliament.uk/research-briefings/sn06111/.

and democracy, in which it was assumed the main target was the judiciary, or at least, judicial review. In July 2020 Lord Chancellor Buckland told Parliament that judicial review was 'an essential part of our democratic constitution – protecting citizens from an overbearing state' but identified a need to 'ensure this precious check on government power ... is not abused or used to conduct politics by another means'.[59]

Buckland said that the review would consider 'whether certain executive decisions should be decided on by judges' and 'which grounds and remedies should be available in claims brought against the government'. In December 2020 Buckland explained to the Commons Public Administration and Constitutional Affairs Committee that the constitutional review would be conducted through workstreams working on 'the relationship between our domestic courts and the European Court of Human Rights in Strasbourg, and the impact of the Human Rights Act 1998 on the relationship between the judiciary, the Executive and the legislature'.[60]

Defending the independence of the workstreams to the Committee Buckland said the review of Administrative Law was chaired by Edward Faulks, 'a former minister but now an independent peer'. Faulks had previously criticised courts' incursions into 'political territory' and had declared the Human Rights Act 'a promotional tool for left-wing campaigners'.[61] Asked about the involvement of other political parties in the constitutional review, Buckland claimed that the government had won an election and was now going about its manifesto commitments with 'great care and deliberation'.[62] Buckland justified a partisan political review of a central constitutional institution by claiming that the presence of an academic, Professor Carol Harlow, on the Administrative Law workstream of five members provided 'balance'.[63]

The first question from committee member David Jones sought clarification of the government's claim that constitutional review was necessary 'to restore trust in our institutions and in how our democracy operates'. Buckland provided evasive and irrelevant answers, none of which related to the judiciary, and failed to justify the claim of lost trust.[64] Sacked at the end of 2021, he was replaced as Lord Chancellor by Dominic Raab, who left City law firm Linklaters soon after qualifying as a solicitor. As someone who criticised the Supreme Court decision in *Miller* as frustrating the will of the people[65] and was antipathetic to the European Court of Human Rights,[66] Raab was an unlikely defender of the rule of law. Even the Tory Brexit

---

[59] 'Government launches independent panel to look at judicial review' (31 July 2010) www.gov.uk/government/news/government-launches-independent-panel-to-look-at-judicial-review.
[60] Public Administration and Constitutional Affairs Committee meeting on 20 December 2020, Q90, https://committees.parliament.uk/oralevidence/1369/default/.
[61] The secret barrister (n 38).
[62] Public Administration and Constitutional Affairs Committee (n 60) Q94.
[63] ibid Q93.
[64] ibid Q96–102.
[65] P Dominiczak, C Hope and K McCann, 'Judges vs the people: Government Ministers resigned to losing appeal against High Court ruling' *The Telegraph* (3 November 2016) (www.telegraph.co.uk/news/2016/11/03/the-plot-to-stop-brexit-the-judges-versus-the-people/.
[66] E Malnick, 'Dominic Raab: I'll overhaul Human Rights Act to stop Strasbourg dictating to us' *The Telegraph* (16 October 2021) www.telegraph.co.uk/politics/2021/10/16/dominic-raab-sets-plans-overhaul-human-rights-act-reform-judicial/.

stalwart David Davis promised to resist Raab's proposed changes to judicial review,[67] which he said were sacrificing the balance between individual liberty and the rule of law 'on the altar of power'.[68]

E. Legality

In September 2020, the government admitted to Parliament that it intended to legislate to remedy problems created by the customs arrangements in Northern Ireland. The proposed United Kingdom Internal Markets Bill breached the Withdrawal Agreement with the EU. The minister, Brandon Lewis presenting the Bill to the Commons, admitted it breached international law[69] to a general incredulity. Two former Tory Attorney-Generals, Geoffrey Cox and Jeremy Wright, abstained from voting on the second reading of the Bill.[70]

Invited to speak at the Annual Meeting of the Bar Council, Suella Braverman was grilled about the Internal Markets Bill. Asked whether she thought that ministers would be breaking the ministerial code by pursuing it she replied that the code was not legally enforceable or, alternatively, that the Cabinet Secretary had said that the Act would not breach the code. She was asked, probably rhetorically, why she had appointed three committed Brexiteers, two academics and a barrister qualified for one year, rather than Treasury Counsel Sir James Eadie, to advise on the legality of deliberately breaching the Withdrawal Agreement.[71]

The government was also accused of corrupt procurement, patronage, and lobbying typical of politicised systems with weak rule of law.[72] Johnson became Prime Minister amid accusations that, as London Mayor, he provided grants and business opportunities to an entrepreneur he was having an affair with. An investigation released after the election found no evidence of his approval of grants, but that the council officers making them did so because they were aware of the affair.[73] The review concluded Johnson had breached Nolan principles by failing to disclose a conflict of interest but found no evidence of criminal conduct. An investigation by the London Assembly continued.[74]

---

[67] N Bano, 'Dominic Raab's Judicial Review Plans are Another Power Grab' (*Tribune*, 5 January 2022) https://tribunemag.co.uk/2022/01/judicial-review-conservative-party-legislation-dominic-raab-boris-johnson.

[68] D Davis, 'Our right to challenge the state is in peril' *The Guardian* (26 October 2021).

[69] J Elgot, R Syall and D Boffey, 'We are breaking law with Brexit Bill, minister admits' *The Guardian* (9 September 2020).

[70] J Elgot and P Walker, 'Johnson seeks to calm Tory rebels as more say they can't back bill that breaches law' *The Guardian* (16 September 2020).

[71] M Savage and T Helm, 'Top Lawyers slam minister for wrecking UK's reputation' *The Observer* (13 September 2020); O Bowcott, 'Braverman put on spot over advisers' *The Guardian* (16 September 2020).

[72] ibid.

[73] Independent Office for Police Conduct, 'No criminal investigation of Boris Johnson for misconduct in public office while Mayor of London' (21 May 2020) www.policeconduct.gov.uk/news/no-criminal-investigation-boris-johnson-misconduct-public-office-while-mayor-london.

[74] BBC News, 'The investigations into Boris Johnson and the government' (5 November 2021) www.bbc.co.uk/news/uk-politics-56926219?at_campaign=KARANGA&at_medium=RSS.

Since 2015–16[75] only 22 MPs had been referred to the Parliamentary Standards Committee[76] and three of the referrals, all upheld, involved Boris Johnson. Typical of these was a finding in 2018–19 that he had registered, late, nine payments totalling over £50,000 resulting from 'an over-casual attitude towards obeying the rules of the House and a lack of effective organisation within Mr Johnson's office'.[77] Johnson faced two possible new investigations by the Parliamentary Standards Commissioner, Kathryn Stone, the undeclared use of a colleague's property in the Caribbean and funding of the decoration of his government residence.[78]

Favouritism and procurement allegations arose after the COVID-19 pandemic struck in early 2020. Public health measures were introduced in March and rules introduced imposing strict lockdowns for infected persons, including restrictions on travel and large fines for breaches. New regulations, some involving the possibility of long jail terms for breaking restrictions on social distancing, were implemented without Parliamentary scrutiny.[79] Police forces sometimes interpreted the restrictions, and their powers, in a draconian way.[80] Jonathan Sumption, the former Law Lord expressed concern at the way people had been 'terrorised into surrendering basic freedoms which are fundamental to our existence'.[81] There was concern that those in government did not follow the rules they had made.

Johnson's chief adviser, Dominic Cummings, travelled from London to his parents in Durham having contracted COVID-19. He then visited a local tourist spot to 'test his eyesight' for the drive back to London. Resignations followed in other cases, but Johnson reviewed the facts and declared Cummings had 'done nothing wrong'.[82] Public confidence in the government's ability to handle the pandemic fell as did willingness to follow government rules and guidelines.[83] In December 2021, there was another furore when it was rumoured that several Christmas 'parties' had been held in government offices, including Downing Street, in breach of COVID-19 regulations.[84] 'Party-gate' was a threat to the principle of equality before the law

---

[75] Including 2021–22, only partially completed at time of writing.

[76] Their offences typically involved failure to register financial interests or use of Parliamentary facilities for private purposes (UK Parliament, 'Allegations Reported to the Standards Committee' www.parliament.uk/mps-lords-and-offices/standards-and-financial-interests/parliamentary-commissioner-for-standards/complaints-and-investigations/allegations-reported-to-the-standards-committee/).

[77] UK Parliament Committee of Standards, *Boris Johnson: Report 2018–19* https://publications.parliament.uk/pa/cm201719/cmselect/cmstandards/1797/179703.htm#_idTextAnchor000.

[78] P Walker, 'Johnson will not declare Spanish holiday in MPs' register, says No 10' *The Guardian* (5 November 2021) www.theguardian.com/politics/2021/nov/05/boris-johnson-will-not-declare-spanish-holiday-in-mps-register-says-no-10.

[79] J Elgot, 'Trust in law "is at risk if ministers bypass MPs"' *The Guardian* (19 February 2020).

[80] V Dodd and L O'Carroll, 'Police warned against "overreach" in use of virus lockdown powers' *The Guardian* (31 March 2020).

[81] O Bowcott, 'Former law lord accuses ministers of abuse of power over Covid-19' *The Guardian* (8 October 2020).

[82] M Weaver, 'Cummings "should have resigned in May", say Barnard Castle witnesses' *The Guardian* (13 November 2020).

[83] D Fancourt, A Steptoe and L Wright, 'The Cummings effect: Politics, trust and behaviours during the COVID-19 pandemic' (*The Lancet*, 15 August 2020) www.thelancet.com/pdfs/journals/lancet/PIIS0140-6736(20)31690-1.pdf.

[84] L Kuenssberg, 'Downing Street party: No 10 staff joked about party amid lockdown restrictions' (*BBC News*, 8 December 2021) www.bbc.co.uk/news/uk-politics-59572149?at_medium=RSS&at_campaign=KARANGA.

because it suggested that the executive ignored its own regulations while preventing citizens being with dying relatives. It was a potential threat to the Prime Minister if he misled the House of Commons, in responses to questions, by claiming no rules were broken.

After significant criticism Johnson announced that an investigation of the events would be conducted by respected civil servant Sue Gray. Just as it was to be delivered a police investigation was announced and only the gist of the report was made public. By February 2022, around 20 Tory MPs had submitted letters of no-confidence in the Prime Minister, short of the 54 needed to trigger a vote. Others were said to be calculating whether Johnson remained an electoral asset before deciding whether to lodge letters. The liberal press was in no doubt that the seeds of the debacle were laid in the populist insurgency of Brexit.[85]

In June 2021 the first of several actions for judicial review of the award of government contracts was heard. It challenged the decision by Michael Gove, then Minister for the Cabinet Office, to award a £500,000 market research contract to Public First, run by friends of Dominic Cummings, without tender. The government refused to limit its costs of the action, putting the future of the claimant, the Good Law Project, at risk should it lose the case. The High Court held that the award had given rise to a real danger of apparent bias and was unlawful,[86] a decision overturned by a Court of Appeal decision that Cummings' involvement was justified by the exigencies of emergency.[87]

Other challenges to lack of due process concerned provision of personal protective equipment for medical workers. Government claimed early shortages justified the award of £10.5 billion worth of contracts, without open tendering, to parties connected to government, but with no previous experience of public health procurement.[88] Many examples of favouritism emerged, such as a contract for the supply of glass vials by the landlord of the Health Minister's local pub.

There was a resurgence of allegations of MPs improperly using influence for personal gain. Nolan had recommended that former Cabinet ministers should normally wait three months before taking up outside employment, but in cases where a longer period was considered necessary, the Advisory Committee on Business Appointments should require a maximum of two years.[89] In 2018, following resigning as Prime Minister, and as an MP shortly after, Cameron became adviser to Greensill Capital, a company specialising in 'supply chain financing'.[90] The founder and CEO Lex Greensill had, according to his business cards, been appointed 'senior adviser to the Prime Minister's office' during Cameron's premiership.[91]

---

[85] J Freedland, "Partygate' has shown how Brexit corrupted Conservatism' *The Guardian* (22 January 2022).

[86] D Conn, '"Apparent bias": Gove acted unlawfully, judge rules' *The Guardian* (23 June 2021).

[87] *R (On the application of the Good Law Project) v Minister for the Cabinet Office and Public First* (2021) EWCA 1569 (TTC) 89.

[88] D Conn, 'Government spends £60 million on challenge' *The Guardian* (11 February 2021).

[89] Lord Nolan (Chair), *Standards in Public Life: First Report of the Committee for Standards in Public Life* (London, HMSO, 1995) (cm 2850-1) para 33, Recommendation 22.

[90] The business involved scheduling payments for clients, in this case government, for a fee.

[91] H Stewart and R Syal, 'Labour urges inquiry into David Cameron links to Greensill Capital' *The Guardian* (31 March 2021) www.theguardian.com/politics/2021/mar/31/labour-urges-inquiry-into-david-cameron-links-to-greensill-capital.

During the COVID-19 pandemic Cameron lobbied the Chancellor of the Exchequer and other ministers to secure government grants for Greensill Capital.[92] These were ultimately refused and the Company collapsed. It was revealed that Cameron was paid £7 million in his advisory role and might have received £70 million from stock options if the company had survived and been floated on the stock exchange.[93] A House of Commons Treasury Committee report found Cameron had broken no rules, but that the rules needed strengthening, and that he had shown a 'significant lack of judgement' in his lobbying effort.[94]

A scandal involving a leading Brexit MP, Tory Owen Paterson, was more notable for the use of the Tory Parliamentary majority to try and save him. Paterson was found by the parliamentary commissioner for standards to have been guilty of multiple counts of paid advocacy on behalf of two companies paying him more than £100,000 a year for consultancy since 2016. The Committee on Standards in Public Life rejected Paterson's allegations against the Standards Commissioner, Kathryn Stone, of a flawed investigation and his defence to the charges, essentially that he had declared his interests. The Committee found he had 'repeatedly used his position as a Member to promote the companies by whom he was paid', an egregious case of paid advocacy[95] for which it imposed a 30-day suspension.[96]

On 3 November 2021, the government whipped a vote on a motion to review the Paterson case and the standards system generally. The resolution referred Paterson's case to a new committee to be constituted with a Tory majority and a Tory chair. Some Tories voted with the government but were unhappy to have been whipped on the issue. Others abstained. A junior minister was sacked as a result. Lord Evans, a crossbench peer and former director general of the Security Service, and chair of the Committee on Standards in Public Life, criticised 'an 'extraordinary proposal' which was an attack on standards.[97] He said 'The political system in this country does not belong to one party or even to one government … It is a common good that we have all inherited from our forebears and that we all have a responsibility to preserve and to improve.'[98]

The vote excited criticism from Tory supporters and normally supportive media.[99] The *Daily Mail* led with the headline 'Shameless MPs sink back into sleaze'.[100] The

---

[92] K Makortoff, 'David Cameron texted Rishi Sunak to get Covid loans for Greensill, says report' *The Guardian* (21 March 2021) www.theguardian.com/politics/2021/mar/21/david-cameron-texted-rishi-sunak-to-get-covid-loans-for-greensill-says-report.
[93] ibid and A Allegretti, 'Cameron faces calls to explain Greensill role amid claims he earned £7m' *The Guardian* (11 August 2021).
[94] House of Commons Treasury Committee, *Lessons from Greensill Capital* 6th Report of 2021-22, 142.
[95] UK Parliament, *Report of the Committee on Standards* 'Owen Paterson' (26 October 2021) https://publications.parliament.uk/pa/cm5802/cmselect/cmstandards/797/79703.htm, paras 111 and 212.
[96] ibid.
[97] R Booth, 'Standards chair attacks Tory efforts to dismantle anti-sleaze system' *The Guardian* (4 November 2021) www.theguardian.com/politics/2021/nov/04/standards-committee-chair-attacks-tory-dismantling-anti-sleaze-system.
[98] ibid.
[99] A Allegretti, 'Boris Johnson makes U-turn over anti-sleaze regime for MPs' *The Guardian* (4 November 2021) www.theguardian.com/politics/2021/nov/04/boris-johnson-makes-u-turn-over-anti-sleaze-regime-for-mps-owen-paterson.
[100] *Daily Mail* (4 November 2021).

next day the government announced that the plan would not be pursued and Paterson resigned his seat.[101] Johnson admitted to the Tory 1922 Committee of backbenchers: 'On a clear road I crashed the car into a ditch'.[102] The business secretary Kwasi Kwarteng apologised for having, in the wake of the vote, queried the future of the Standards Commissioner and suggesting that it was up to her to 'consider her position'.[103]

Scandals were not limited to the pandemic. In November 2020, the Prime Minister's adviser on the ministerial code, senior civil servant Sir Alex Allen, resigned after Johnson rejected his advice, which was not published in full, that Home Secretary Priti Patel's bullying of civil servants breached the ministerial code.[104] Even the *Daily Mail* was critical, noting it was the first time a minister had not left their post following a serious breach of the code.[105] It observed that Johnson's request for MPs to 'form a square around the Pritster' suggested he did not understand the gravity of the situation.

Allegations also surrounded the Housing Secretary, Robert Jenrick, who, having sat next to the developer Richard Desmond at a Tory Party fundraiser, approved a local development plan which had been rejected by the relevant local council, the government's planning inspectorate and his own departmental civil servants. The approval was granted just in time for Desmond to avoid a £45 million levy and he had then made a £12,000 contribution to the Tory party.[106]

The final area in which the government was accused on corruption was in appointments, where it failed to observe the Nolan Principles of standards in public life or the various codes that had been created since. Nolan had accepted a government commitment that all appointments to Quango Boards be made on merit.[107] The process was that ministers should make appointments, but candidates should have been assessed as suitable by an independent advisory panel[108] and subject to review by an independent Public Appointments Commissioner.[109] The government appeared to prefer the suggestion of one of the newer thinktanks, Policy Exchange, which called for reversing the tradition of meritorious and apolitical appointment to public jobs and appointment of leaders of public bodies with 'culture and values' aligned with government.

---

[101] ITV News, 'Ministers U-turn on standards overhaul amid outrage over Owen Paterson case' (4 November 2021) www.itv.com/news/2021-11-04/ministers-u-turn-on-standards-overhaul-amid-outrage-over-owen-paterson-case.

[102] K Ferguson and N Clarke, 'Tory Cold Shoulder' *The Sun* (17 November 2021) www.thesun.co.uk/news/16769437/boris-johnson-apologised-sleaze-scandals-angry-tory-mps/.

[103] BBC News, 'Minister Kwasi Kwarteng sorry for upset caused by Standards Commissioner remarks' (15 November 2021) www.bbc.co.uk/news/uk-politics-59298861?at_medium=RSS&at_campaign=KARANGA.

[104] H Stewart and S Murphy, 'Fury as PM tells Tories to back "bully" Patel' *The Guardian* (21 November 2020).

[105] S Glover, 'Now we know: It's Boris Johnson and his gang against the world' *Daily Mail* (20 November 2020) www.dailymail.co.uk/debate/article-8971663/STEPHEN-GLOVER-know-Boris-Johnson-gang-against-world.html.

[106] Mail Online, www.dailymail.co.uk/news/article-8467707/Officials-begged-Robert-Jenrick-kill-Richard-Desmonds-controversial-1bn-property-deal.html.

[107] Nolan (n 89) para 35 and Recommendation 30.

[108] ibid Recommendation 34.

[109] ibid Recommendation 32.

Jobs as adviser or running government programmes were given to 25 of 94 Conservatives MPs leaving Parliament in the previous two general elections.[110] Some key public appointments were rejected during screening of suitable candidates, but the candidates were appointed anyway. In one such case, the person appointed head of the Charity Commission had been rejected by a Parliamentary Committee on grounds of inexperience and partiality.[111] In February 2022 the High Court heard a case claiming that, at the height of the COVID-19 pandemic the Health Minister had appointed leaders to critical public health roles who had neither had any medical or administrative background. The court held that he had not complied with the public sector equality duty in making appointments to the National Institute for Health Protection and NHS Test and Trace.[112]

A rather extreme example of government's attempt to make a political appointment to a sensitive public role was its effort to install Paul Dacre, former editor of the *Daily Mail* and critic of the BBC, as the head of the media regulator Ofcom. Dacre had previously accused the BBC of bias, amounting to 'a kind of cultural Marxism', and not reflecting the views of the population.[113] An independent panel found him unsuitable, but the government attempted to reconstitute it and change the appointment criteria.[114]

IV. THE USA

A. The 2016 Election

Early primaries in the 2016 campaign for election of the US Presidency suggested that Democrat Hilary Clinton and Republican Donald Trump would be their party's candidates. Clinton's candidacy was overshadowed by an announcement on 10 July 2015 that the Federal Bureau of Investigation was looking into her use of a personal email server, rather than an official government account, while she was Secretary of State to the previous president, Barak Obama.[115] This may have exposed classified information to hacking and was in breach of a non-disclosure agreement she had signed on entering office.

Before the election, in May 2016, a policy adviser to the Trump team told an Australian diplomat that the Russians had offered them compromising material on

---

[110] Cohen (n 47).

[111] K Weakley, 'MPs formally reject Commission chair but Minister gives backing' (*Civil Society News*, 25 February 2018) www.civilsociety.co.uk/news/mps-want-to-force-minister-to-explain-charity-commission-chair-appointment.html.

[112] J Grierson, 'Hancock ignored equality duty over pandemic jobs' *The Guardian* (16 February 2022).

[113] O Gibson, 'Dacre attacks BBC 'cultural Marxism' *The Guardian* (23 January 2007) https://www.theguardian.com/media/2007/jan/23/dailymail.bbc.

[114] H Goodwin, 'No 10 can't find anyone willing to interview Paul Dacre for Ofcom job' (*London Economic*, 31 August 2021) www.thelondoneconomic.com/politics/no-10-cant-find-anyone-willing-to-interview-paul-dacre-for-ofcom-job-288168/.

[115] A Zurcher, 'Hilary Clinton emails – What's it all about?' (*BBC News*, 6 November 2016) www.bbc.co.uk/news/world-us-canada-31806907.

Clinton.[116] On 9 June, Trump's son, Donald Junior, his son in law, Jared Kushner, and campaign adviser, Paul Manafort, met a Russian lawyer regarding the offer. When Clinton's emails began appearing online in July 2016 the Australian government reported their diplomat's conversation to the US authorities. At about the same time the FBI received a dossier by a former British intelligence agent, Christopher Steele, detailing alleged links between Trump and Russia. At the end of July, the FBI began investigating a possible conspiracy between the Trump campaign and Russia to interfere in the election.

James Comey, Director of the FBI, a lifelong Republican, former government lawyer, and public prosecutor, oversaw the Clinton email and Russian interference investigation. In July 2016 it was announced that Clinton had breached protocols and hindered government oversight of her communications but that this did not warrant criminal prosecution. Then, a fortnight before election day, Comey announced the discovery of new emails and publicly re-opened the inquiry. Two days before polling commenced, he again confirmed that no criminal charges were warranted. Comey was later criticised for revealing the Clinton investigation and concealing the Russia investigation, swinging the election result in Trump's favour.

Trump was inaugurated on 20 January 2017. He was quickly at odds with Sally Yates, acting Attorney-General, an Obama appointee who had stayed on to ensure a smooth a transition and enjoyed bipartisan support.[117] At the beginning of 2017 Trump declared a preference for Christian migrants to the US, a week later signing an executive order banning refugees, immigrants and travellers from seven Muslim-majority countries, including Syria. The US code stated that if 'the president finds the entry of any aliens or class of aliens … would be detrimental to the interests of the United States, he may by proclamation … suspend the entry of all aliens or any class of aliens as immigrants or non-immigrants, or impose on the entry of aliens any restrictions he may deem to be appropriate'.[118] Hundreds of US diplomats signed a petition opposing the ban.[119]

Actions were brought in four States citing provisions proscribing discrimination in providing an 'immigrant visa because of the person's race, sex, nationality, place of birth or place of residence'. Judges held that travellers from the named countries beginning their journey with appropriate documentation before the order was signed should not be deported.[120] The attorney-generals of Washington and New York sought declarations that the executive order was invalid. There were reports that agents at some airports were trying to enforce the ban in defiance of the judicial

---

[116] S LaFraniere, M Mazzetti and M Apuzzo, *New York Times* (30 December 2017) www.nytimes.com/2017/12/30/us/politics/how-fbi-russia-investigation-began-george-papadopoulos.html.

[117] Johnny Isakson, the Republican Senator of Georgia, greeted Yates' appointment at the justice department in 2015 with a speech identifying her as: 'an equal opportunity prosecutor. She's prosecuted Democrats, Republicans, independents, Olympic park bombers, anybody that violated the public trust, any abuse of power'. D Smith, B Jacobs and S Ackerman, 'Sally Yates fired by Trump after acting US attorney general defied travel ban' *The Guardian* (31 January 2017) www.theguardian.com/us-news/2017/jan/30/justice-department-trump-immigration-acting-attorney-general-sally-yates.

[118] A Yuhas, 'Trump's immigration ban: which cases are in play and what happens next?' *The Guardian* (30 January 2017) www.theguardian.com/us-news/2017/jan/30/trump-travel-ban-explainer-muslim-immigration-aclu.

[119] Smith, Jacobs and Ackerman (n 117).

[120] Yuhas (n 118).

decisions while others were helping lawyers to access detainees. Yates instructed Justice Department officials not to enforce the order.[121] Her letter stated:

> I am responsible for ensuring that the positions we take in court remain consistent with this institution's solemn obligation to always seek justice and stand for what is right … At present I am not convinced that the defense of the executive order is consistent with these responsibilities nor am I convinced that the executive order is lawful.[122]

In the wake of Yates' sacking some media accused her of failing to protect American citizens, following a statement from the White House press secretary's office accusing her of being 'weak on illegal immigration' and that 'tougher vetting for individuals travelling from seven dangerous places is not extreme. It is reasonable and necessary to protect our country'.[123] Republican Senator Ted Cruz said Yates had refused to carry out her constitutional duty to enforce and defend the law, adding that she 'put brazen partisan interests above fidelity to law'.[124]

Liberal critics lauded Yates and criticised Trump. David Strauss, a professor at the University of Chicago School of Law, opined that government 'should not be a personal fiefdom of the person who happens to be in the White House' adding that Trump's order 'expresses a kind of contempt for law'.[125] Democrat Zac Petkanas, a senior adviser to the Democratic National Committee, contrasted 'heroic patriot' Yates and 'this tyrannical presidency'.[126] Patrick Leahy, the senior Democrat on the Senate judiciary committee, said: 'She was fired for recognising that her oath is to the Constitution and not to President Trump'. Yates' sacking was compared to the 1973 'Saturday night massacre' when the attorney general, Elliot Richardson, resigned after Richard Nixon ordered the sacking of the special Watergate prosecutor, Archibald Cox.[127]

Another notable lawyer sacked during the early stages of Trump's presidency was Preet Bharara, another Obama appointee. Bharara was the US Attorney General for the southern district of New York (Manhattan), the jurisdiction established by George Washington to prosecute serious white-collar crime and corruption. Clear outs of previous appointees were not unusual, but Trump had asked Bharara to stay on after his election. Bharara became uncomfortable after phone calls from Trump to 'shoot the breeze'.[128] The day before his dismissal, Bharara had failed to respond to a phone call from Trump because he detected the threat to his independence.[129] He joined a list of 46 other US Attorney Generals forced to resign. Trump's personal attorney claimed credit for the dismissal, having allegedly told Trump in Spring 2017 'this guy is going to get you'.[130]

---

[121] Smith, Jacobs and Ackerman (n 117).
[122] ibid.
[123] ibid.
[124] ibid.
[125] Yuhas (n 118).
[126] Smith, Jacobs and Ackerman (n 117).
[127] ibid.
[128] A Buncombe, 'Donald Trump's lawyer boasted about getting prosecutor fired: "He will get you"' *Independent* (13 June 2017).
[129] E Pilkington, 'Donald Trump doesn't want to be investigated, so he's undermining people's faith in the rule of law' *The Guardian Review* (16 March 2019).
[130] ibid.

B. The Russia Investigations

In January 2017 Comey met Trump privately to update him on the Russia investigation. Comey claimed that Trump opened discussion of directorship of the FBI and twice asked for a declaration of 'loyalty'. Comey claimed that he later regretted his offer of 'honest loyalty'. In February, at the end of a meeting on other matters Trump was said to have asked Comey to consider 'letting go' Michael T Flynn over the Russia inquiry. Flynn, a former senior officer in the US Army who had acted as an adviser to the Trump election campaign, was sworn in as National Security Adviser in January 2017 but resigned after he was found to have lied in his security vetting about meetings with senior Russian diplomats. With hindsight, Comey suggested he was uncertain whether Trump was just talking about letting go of Flynn or of the Russia investigation in general.

In early May 2017 Comey gave evidence to a Senate Committee about the ongoing investigation into Russian interference in the 2016 election. Trump was said to have been alarmed by the scope of the investigation and, on 8 May 2017 he asked Attorney General Jeff Sessions and Deputy Attorney General Rod Rosenstein to set out a case against Comey. The next day Rosenstein wrote outlining criticisms of Comey's handling of the Clinton email case. Trump fired Comey on 10 May 2017, four years into his 10-year term as Director of the FBI, citing handling of Clinton's case as the official explanation.

On 17 May 2017 Robert Mueller, a former private practitioner and government lawyer and a former FBI Director, was appointed as special counsel to the Justice Department to investigate the allegations of Russian interference. In June, the *Washington Post* announced that Mueller was investigating Trump for obstruction of justice. Trump asked for evidence that could be used to remove Mueller, then instructed White House counsel to have Mueller sacked, then ordered him to lie about having given the order.[131] Later in the month Trump refrained from sacking Mueller only when White House Counsel Don McGhan threatened to resign if he did.[132] During Mueller's investigation, five of six of Trump's associates facing criminal charges pleaded guilty. Minor criminal charges were pending against Michael T Flynn until he agreed to assist the Mueller Inquiry. Trump pardoned him on 25 November 2020.

Comey's deputy, a Republican, career lawyer and Obama appointee, Andrew McCabe, became acting director of the FBI. He quickly authorised the investigation of Trump for obstructing the Russian investigation and became the target of Trump tweets. One taunted him that he could be fired before his imminent retirement.[133]

---

[131] J Freedland, 'Trump's great advantage: he will always play dirty' *The Guardian* (20 April 2019).

[132] MS Schmidt and M Haberman, 'Trump Ordered Mueller Fired, but Backed Off When White House Counsel Threatened to Quit' *New York Times* (25 January 2018) www.nytimes.com/2018/01/25/us/politics/trump-mueller-special-counsel-russia.html.

[133] G Price, 'All the times Trump attacked Andrew McCabe before the Deputy Director stepped down' (*Newsweek*, 29 January 2018) www.yahoo.com/news/times-trump-attacked-andrew-mccabe-181954593.html?guce_referrer=aHR0cHM6Ly93d3cuYmluZy5jb20v&guce_referrer_sig=AQAAAB2D KZFUGRcPbqZwo77utps77ilD0O4rEBXAMBfg-XaT-0k3Axtn5YsAR0Anm1wJZ69Vy0xJNkUtmQcV4 a7tdGWej2GCKmoDzNLrYt7aBlHekuqCJv6fAMy0hc7gpRfY22BKJyM_Go4OA_okBe7oOL_JU_BAE bc9MF0wkS6JrV5Z&guccounter=2. McCabe was replaced by Christopher A Wray.

He was in fact dismissed the day before retiring for alleged leaks. The White House counsellor, Kellyanne Conway, cited the failure to prosecute McCabe as an example of Trump being a victim of a politicised justice system.[134]

Mueller delivered his report to Attorney General William Barr in March 2019. Barr had promised that executive privilege would not be exercised over any of the report, but it was printed with significant redacted material. The first volume concluded that there had been significant Russian interference in the 2016 election. Although the Trump campaign had welcomed this and had colluded with the Russians in the hope of using the information, there was insufficient evidence of an agreement to obtain it, which was required for conspiracy charges.[135] Mueller found that many of those connected to the Trump campaign had personal connections to the Russian government and were prosecuted for lying about those contacts.

The second volume of the Mueller report listed 10 occasions Trump may have obstructed justice in connection with the inquiry. In July 2019, Mueller testified to a Congressional committee that his view had been that a sitting president could only face charges for crimes, including obstruction of justice, after they left office.[136] Impeachment for high crimes and misdemeanours was a matter for Congress.

C. Impeachments

Trump faced his first impeachment in December 2019, although not in connection with links with Russia. In September 2019 a report concluded that he had tried to get the Ukrainian government to investigate the business activity of Joe Biden, Trump's probable rival in the 2020 election, who had business interests in Ukraine. Trump threatened to withhold military aid, already voted by Congress, until Ukraine launched an investigation. The House of Representatives passed only the third ever motion of impeachment on grounds of abuse of power and obstruction of justice. The motion was defeated by a Republican majority in the Senate.

The months leading to the election suggested that a coup attempt might happen.[137] Lord Darroch of Kew, an ambassador to the US at the beginning of Trump's term, predicted in September that Trump would focus on postal voting to call an adverse election result into question.[138] As the polling results went against him, Trump claimed that the election was being 'stolen'. He litigated the electoral outcome in several states but produced no evidence of fraud. By mid-November legal challenges

---

[134] E Pilkington, 'Trump aide says president is victim of a politicised justice system' *The Guardian* (17 February 2020).

[135] R Wolffe, 'Of course Trump's campaign colluded with the Russians but unfortunately that's not a crime' *The Guardian* (18 April 2019) www.theguardian.com/commentisfree/2019/apr/18/trump-collusion-russia-mueller-barr.

[136] J Thomsen, 'Mueller: Trump could be charged with obstruction of justice after leaving office' (*The Hill*, 24 July 2017) https://thehill.com/policy/national-security/454502-mueller-trump-could-be-charged-with-obstruction-of-justice-after.

[137] J Borger, 'Trump's Last Stand' *The Observer* (10 January 2021); R Solnit, 'Trump built an army to enforce his reality. This was inevitable' *The Guardian* (8 January 2021).

[138] J Borger, 'Very volatile: genuine risk of US election violence former ambassador warns' *The Guardian* (16 September 2020).

had been dismissed as 'groundless'.[139] In early December Attorney-General William Barr announced that there had been no evidence found of significant election fraud. A New Yorker comment noted 'At long last, the country's chief law-enforcement officer has defended American democracy'.[140] Trump announced that Barr would step down on 23 December.

Biden polled 7 million votes more than Trump but the vagaries of the electoral system made it worth Trump trying to bully and cajole a Republican returning officer in Georgia 'to find' him 11,000 votes.[141] Acting attorney general, Jeffrey Rosen, successor to William Barr, had refused Trump's order to instruct the Republican leadership in Georgia to overturn his electoral defeat there.[142] Justice Department lawyers had apparently resolved to resign en masse if Rosen was fired and Trump loyalist Jeffrey Clark installed. It was a reasonable speculation that the pretext of a rigged election might lead to other action. This made sense of Trump's response in a candidate debate, when Biden invited him to condemn the Proud Boys, a right ring, nationalist organisation which policed his rallies, and Trump had responded: 'Proud Boys – stand back and stand by'.[143]

On the night of 6 January 2021 Vice President Mike Pense was to formalise the decision of the electoral college at the Capitol. Trump tried to persuade Pense to refuse. He called for supporters to attend a rally outside the White House, promising 'it will be "wild"'. He made a speech urging them to protest against the 'stolen election', saying 'You'll never take back our country with weakness. You have to show strength, and you have to be strong' and 'If you don't fight like hell you're not going to have a country anymore'.[144] A large crowd marched the short distance to the Capitol Building. Four died when a mob stormed the building. William Barr declared Trump's incitement of the crowd a betrayal of his office.

Trump's second impeachment hearing in the Senate, in February 2021, took place after he left office. The charge was the high crime and misdemeanour of incitement of insurrection. The weekend before the hearing, five lawyers resigned from his defence team. There were reported disagreements because Trump insisted that the defence be based on the 'stolen' election, but the official reason for their departure was failure to agree fees.[145] Two new lawyers were appointed; Fox News contributor David Schoen

---

[139] A Feinberg, 'Most respectable lawyers have quit Trump's lawsuits. The ones who haven't are getting desperate and dangerous' *The Independent* (19 November 2020) www.independent.co.uk/voices/trump-lawyers-rudy-giuliani-sidney-powell-desperate-b1724470.html.

[140] D Rhode, 'William Barr's break with Donald Trump' (*The New Yorker*, 5 December 2020) www.newyorker.com/news/daily-comment/william-barrs-break-with-donald-trump.

[141] Q Scanlan, 'Trump demands Georgia secretary of state "find" enough votes to hand him win' (*ABC News*, 4 January 2021) https://abcnews.go.com/Politics/trump-demands-georgia-secretary-state-find-votes-hand/story?id=75027350.

[142] M Pengelly, 'Trump "plotted to sack attorney general" in desperate attempt to reverse election result' *The Guardian* (24 January 2021).

[143] US News Today, https://eu.usatoday.com/story/news/politics/elections/2020/09/29/trump-debate-white-supremacists-stand-back-stand-by/3583339001/.

[144] T McCarthy, 'Impeachment trial: Trump lawyers claim "fight like hell" speech did not incite riot' *The Guardian* (2 February 2021) www.theguardian.com/us-news/2021/feb/02/trump-capitol-riot-powder-keg-impeachment-prosecutors.

[145] ibid.

and former county prosecutor Bruce Castor. Listening to the impeachment hearing at one of his golf clubs, Trump was reported to be frustrated that the prosecution came over powerfully and that his defence team were not pursuing the stolen election thesis.[146]

Senate voted to impeach Trump by 57–43, not the required two-thirds majority of 67. Only seven Republicans joined Democrat senators. Shortly after voting not to impeach, the leading Republican, Mitch McConnell, told reporters that Trump was 'practically and morally responsible' for the events of 6 January.[147] This assessment created a serious constitutional precedent for, as a CNN television journalist observed: 'If Trump's actions are not impeachable, then nothing is, and we may as well strike that provision from the constitution'.[148] It was of course, impossible to know what was in Trump's mind, but the evidence was consistent with an attempted coup d'état. Joe Biden hailed his inauguration as the triumph of democracy[149] but this was a misconception. It depended on resolute defence of the Capitol on 6 January, the mobilisation of the National Guard and Republicans like Pense facilitating a transition of power. This was a triumph of the rule of law. Democracy was the problem.

V. DISCUSSION

Phelps suggested that the 1960s marked the end of a period of social development and emancipation, a 'mass flourishing', underway since the 1820s.[150] The Rawlsian utopia of post-war liberal democracy gave way to right-wing values labelled neoliberalism. Maclean argued that this resulted from the fortune spent by Charles Koch sponsoring James McGill Buchanan[151] to produce public choice theory, the freedom of the very rich to exploit wealth. Buchanan recognised the need to reduce demand for tax by building a 'counter intelligentsia' spearheading the de-construction of public services and social benefits built by democracy. The rule of law was protection for what Monbiot claimed was the aim of the right ring think-tanks: despotic government.[152]

In 2003, left-wing academic Wendy Brown suggested that, in the US, the 'neoliberal evisceration of a non-market morality' encouraged evaluation of government on criteria of expedience.[153] This was not fascist or totalitarian in character but led

---

[146] A Gabbatt, 'Donald Trump "frustrated with lawyers" as he watches impeachment trial on TV' *The Guardian* (10 February 2021) www.theguardian.com/us-news/2021/feb/10/trump-watching-impeachment-trial-tv-mar-a-lago.

[147] A Holpuch, 'McConnell "Spoke out of two sides of his mouth"' *The Guardian* (15 February 2021).

[148] V Bekiempis, 'Trump's acquittal shows paltry punch of impeachment process' *The Guardian* (14 February 2021).

[149] I Bremner, 'Democracy Barely Prevailed: But Biden's Inauguration Should Still Give Us New Hope' (*Time*, 20 January 2021).

[150] E Phelps, *Mass Flourishing: How grassroots innovation created jobs, challenge, and change*, 1st edn (Princeton, Princeton University Press, 2013).

[151] N MacLean, *Democracy in Chains: The Deep History of the Radical Right's Stealth Plan for America* (for a summary see G Monbiot, 'A despot in disguise: one man's mission to rip up democracy' *The Guardian* (19 July 2017)).

[152] G Monbiot, 'Neoliberalism – the ideology at the root of all our problems' *The Guardian* (15 April 2015).

[153] W Brown, 'Neo-liberalism and the End of Liberal Democracy' (2003) 7(1) *Theory and Event* 15.

to the gradual erosion of 'significant features of constitutional and representative democracy':

> civil liberties equally distributed and protected; a press and other journalistic media minimally free from corporate ownership on one side and state control on the other; uncorrupted and unbought elections; quality public education oriented, *inter alia*, to producing the literacies relevant to informed and active citizenship; government openness, honesty and accountability; a judiciary modestly insulated from political and commercial influence; separation of church and state; and a foreign policy guided at least in part by the rationale of protecting these domestic values.[154]

The retreat of liberalism and the growth of populism was evident in both the US and UK. Campaigns to 'Leave' the EU and 'Get Brexit done' were populist moments comparable to Donald Trump's success in the US presidential election.[155] The governments they elected demonstrated similar tendencies to erode the rule of law.

Demagogic tendencies were evident in Trump's 'tweets' commenting on events, picking fights with opponents, calling for 'retribution' for slights, denying 'fake news', and even announcing policy.[156] He employed 'dog whistle politics', meanings lying not in what was said but in the interpretations of followers. The message was more important than the truth and 'alternative facts' were sufficient for supporters.[157] Trump's political stance was economic protectionism, but he campaigned on building a wall between the US and Mexico to keep out migrants and imprisoning Clinton over the email affair. His rallies featured audience chants around these policies ('USA'; 'Build that Wall'; 'Lock Her Up'). Trump promised to 'drain the swamp', a stock phrase in American politics to refer to restricting lobbyists but widely interpreted to mean dismantling the Washington liberal establishment.[158]

Trump's term in office was marked by inappropriate appointments to senior offices of state and a revolving door of advisers and lobbyists.[159] He appointed a climate change denier with oil industry connections to head up the Environmental Protection Agency. When he was forced to resign in an ethics scandal he was replaced by a former coal lobbyist. Trump's Attorney General, Jeff Sessions, was the first senator to endorse Trump as Republican candidate for president, making him, according the Shugerman's classification (see chapter four 'Execution'), a politico and an insider. At his confirmation hearing he denied communications with Russians during the 2016 election campaign, but evidence emerged of two meetings with its ambassador in 2016. The lapse was somewhat recovered when Sessions resisted pressure to

---

[154] ibid.

[155] J Henley, 'Populism: Movements here to stay, but they can be beaten' *The Guardian* (26 September 2017).

[156] For example, after a satirical sketch of Trump featuring Alec Baldwin on the US TV programme 'Saturday Night Live' (K Lyons, 'President calls for retribution after Baldwin sketch' *The Guardian* (19 February 2019)).

[157] The phrase is attributed to Kellyanne Conway, Counsellor to President Trump, defending his claims to have attracted the largest ever crowd to an inauguration at a Meet the Press interview on 22 January 2017.

[158] J Traub, 'Can the left save liberalism from Trump?' *New York Times* (17 October 2019) www.nytimes.com/2019/10/17/opinion/liberalism-trump.html.

[159] I Johnston, 'Climate change denier Scott Pruitt's appointment to EPA would be 'unprecedented assault' on its work' *Independent* (7 February 2017) www.independent.co.uk/climate-change/news/climate-change-denier-scott-pruitt-epa-appointment-unprecedented-assault-environment-protection-agency-donald-trump-global-warming-a7566946.html.

investigation into Russian interference on grounds of conflict of ...p sacked him.

...p also tried to undermine the traditional political balance of the Supreme C...t, the importance of which had been evident in the 2000 Presidential election. Nominations to the electoral college had been finely balanced between the Republican candidate George W Bush and the Democrat, Al Gore.[160] The Presidency hung on the outcome in Florida, with the difference only hundreds of votes. After frequent arguments the Florida Supreme Court ordered a full recount, but Bush appealed to the US Supreme Court. It initially pushed the case back to Florida but, forced to decide the appeal, it held that there were flaws in the process but no time to resolve them. It declared the process closed, with Bush ahead.[161] This began a practice of both sides having teams of lawyers ready to contest close results and turned attention to the composition of the court.

The Supreme Court justices had historically represented conservative, moderate or liberal tendencies in their political leanings and their decisions over time reflected these propensities.[162] In *Bush v Gore* the Supreme Court had divided exactly along political lines, with five conservative judges backing Bush and four liberals backing Gore. In March 2016 Obama had nominated Merrick Garland to replace recently deceased Antonin Scalia, a legal conservative appointment of Ronald Reagan. The Republican majority in the Senate refused Garland a hearing on the grounds that there could be an election within a year and the appointment should be that of the incoming President.

During his term, Trump appointed conservatives Neil Gorsuch and Brett Kavanaugh[163] creating a conservative majority in the Supreme Court of 5 to 4.[164] After the death of the liberal justice, Ruth Bader Ginsburg in September 2020, only six weeks before the 2020 presidential election, Trump nominated arch conservative, Amey Coney Barratt. She was confirmed by the Senate on 27 October, a week before the beginning of the election. The political balance of the court was then six conservatives, including three Trump appointees, and three liberals.

Packing the Supreme Court with ultra-conservatives apparently anticipated ballot litigation.[165] A politically skewed Supreme court might help Trump as it had Bush, but the result was not close enough to raise an issue. Legal challenges in many States failed but still Trump refused to formally concede the election. This was probably because he knew that support for him would continue despite his attempt to overthrow the Constitution and rule of law. Research showed that the top three factors

---

[160] L Kennedy, 'How the 2000 Election came down to a Supreme Court decision' (*History*, 24 September 2020).history.com/news/2000-election-bush-gore-votes-supreme-court.

[161] *Bush v Gore* 531 U.S. 98 (2000).

[162] JA Segal and HJ Spaeth, *The Supreme Court and the Attitudinal Model Revisited* (Cambridge, Cambridge University Press, 2002).

[163] There were strong objections, on the grounds of partisanship, to Kavanaugh's appointment to the Washington Appeals court in 2006. At the nomination hearings for the Supreme Court three women made plausible accusations of sexual misconduct in his earlier life.

[164] Axios, 'The political leanings of the Supreme Court Justices' (1 June 2019 www.axios.com/supreme-court-justices-ideology-52ed3cad-fcff-4467-a336-8bec2e6e36d4.html.

[165] Kettle (n 49).

in support for Trump in 2016 were Republican Party loyalty, feelings of cultural displacement and support for deporting illegal immigrants,[166] factors not dependent on integrity in office.

The *Bush v Gore* decision hardened political lines in the US. Brown lamented that 'the scandal' was accepted as 'business as usual'.[167] She saw a more troubling turn in politics: 'deception, hypocrisies, interlocking directorates, featherbedding, or corruption' did not affect the way people voted.[168] This reflected the growing polarisation of the electorate, a coarsening of political sensibilities, and the normalisation of extreme views, fuelled by electronic communications and media expansion to accommodate vehicles like Fox News. The polarised political environment led Republican politicians to twice refuse to impeach a President who had clearly acted contrary to established rule of law principles and contributed to the storming of the Capitol.

The Brexit crisis created a populist moment led by a figure superficially different to Trump. As Mayor of London, Boris Johnson had criticised Trump, but in June 2018, as Home Secretary, he expressed increasing admiration for the 'method in his madness'.[169] He invited an audience to 'Imagine Trump doing Brexit … There'd be all sorts of breakdowns, all sorts of chaos. Everyone would think he'd gone mad. But actually, you might get somewhere. It's a very, very good thought'.[170] The following month, Johnson met Stephen K Bannon, Trump's former chief strategist and controversial alt-right figure. Bannon was 'on a crusade to install right-wing nationalist governments across Europe' and declared Johnson to be 'very impressive … It is like Donald Trump. People dismissed him'.[171] Trump welcomed Johnson's election, calling him 'Britain Trump'.

Moffett suggested that the Brexit vote was a classic example of the clash of patriotic and nationalistic viewpoints.[172] The EU could not supplant nationalistic loyalties because of its changing membership, movable borders and historic schisms: 'The EU offered no grand foundation story, no venerable symbols or traditions'.[173] Those voting for Brexit 'saw an economic and peacekeeping tool as a threat to their national identity'.[174] Their economic interests and social welfare were not served by leaving the EU, but they were persuaded by nationalist and anti-immigration sentiments. This constellation of motives was ambiguously captured in the campaign slogan: 'take back control'.

---

[166] D Cox, R Lienesch and RP Jones, *Beyond Economics: Fears of Cultural Displacement Pushed the White Working Class to Trump* (Washington DC, PRRI/The Atlantic, 2017) www.prri.org/research/white-working-class-attitudes-economy-trade-immigration-election-donald-trump/.
[167] Brown (n 153).
[168] ibid.
[169] K de Freytas-Tamura, 'Boris Johnson, a "Burqa Storm" and Perhaps Some Populist Calculations' *New York Times* (8 August 2018) www.nytimes.com/2018/08/08/world/europe/boris-johnson-trump-burqa.html?.
[170] BBC News (8 June 2018) www.bbc.co.uk/news/av/uk-politics-44410514.
[171] de Freytas-Tamura (n 169).
[172] MW Moffett, *The Human Swarm: How Our Societies Arise, Thrive and Fall* (London, Head of Zeus Ltd, 2019) 350.
[173] ibid 350.
[174] ibid.

The Leave referendum campaign used a poster suggesting that Turkey would gain EU membership. On 16 June 2016 a pro-EU Labour MP, Joe Cox, was murdered by a mentally disturbed white supremacist shouting: 'This is for Britain', 'keep Britain independent', and 'Put Britain first'.[175] During the campaign, Cameron was shocked to find the press against him. A member of his team suggested that Remain would have won comfortably with it.[176] Researchers found, however, that the attraction of the Leave campaign was deeper than Brexit: supporters admired Trump and hated 'scroungers, political correctness and urban liberals, especially if they're from London'.[177] This appeared to be part of a Europe wide swing to the right[178] forcing centrist parties to adopt anti-immigrant policies.[179] It had become a part of Tory Party campaigning before Brexit.

In 2015 David Cameron's speech commemorating Magna Carta claimed that scrapping the Human Rights Act would restore its legacy.[180] Theresa May made a speech at the 2016 Conservative conference in which she claimed that 'if you believe you are a citizen of the world, you are a citizen of nowhere', a statement foregrounded by references to remote politicians, global elites and ordinary people, which echoed the populist appeals of dictators.[181] In the run up to his leadership bid, Boris Johnson wrote a piece in the *Daily Telegraph* ostensibly criticising Denmark for banning the Islamic burqa, but observing that women wearing them looked like letterboxes or bank robbers. Sayeeda Warsi, a former chair of the Tory party, claimed that this was a 'dog whistle' to anti-Islamic rank and file members who would determine the Tory leadership election.[182]

Threats to the rule of law posed by the US and British governments were similar, albeit posed as threats to democracy.[183] There was a pattern of illiberalism on immigration, including proposed suspensions of process rights,[184] and offshore processing of asylum claims, in both the US and Britain.[185] There were similar attacks on independent media. In the UK this included the BBC, one of few trusted sources of information, threatening the polarisation of media evident in the US.[186]

---

[175] I Cobain and M Taylor, 'Far-right terrorist Thomas Mair jailed for life for Jo Cox murder' *The Guardian* (23 November 2016) www.theguardian.com/uk-news/2016/nov/23/thomas-mair-found-guilty-of-jo-cox-murder.

[176] G Younge, 'The Tories can't win without the rightwing press on their side' *The Guardian* (15 November 2019).

[177] A Becket, 'Will Labour ever rebuild its red wall?' *The Guardian* (12 September 2020).

[178] M Rooduijn, 'One in six Europeans now vote for the far right' *The Guardian* (3 March 2020).

[179] B O'Connor, 'Trump's useful thugs' *The Guardian* (21 January 2021).

[180] J Stone, 'Scrapping the human rights act will restore magna Carta legacy claims David Cameron' *Independent* (15 June 2015).

[181] R Merrick, 'Theresa May speech "could have been taken out of Mein Kampff" Vince cable says' *The Independent* (5 July 2017).

[182] de Freytas-Tamura (n 169).

[183] M Kettle, 'Like Trump, Johnson is dismantling democracy' *The Guardian* (4 February 2022).

[184] J Swaine, 'Trump demands suspension of legal process at borders' *The Guardian* (25 June 2018).

[185] L O'Carroll, 'Priti Patel to reveal proposals for offshore centres for asylum seekers' *The Guardian* (5 July 2021) www.theguardian.com/uk-news/2021/jul/05/priti-patel-to-reveal-proposals-for-offshore-centres-for-asylum-seekers.

[186] J Freedland, 'Without the BBC we would be facing a post-truth dystopia' *The Guardian* (25 June 2010).

VI. CONCLUSION

Democracy and equality before law encouraged a condition of legality and voluntary compliance.[187] The failure of the post-war liberal consensus resulted in a small number of rich winners, an army of losers, and a surge of nativism and militant parochialism which threatened the rule of law. Vile cited historical examples of countries with separation of constitutional powers succumbing to tyranny.[188] In Brexit Britain and Trump's America, majorities may have expected some undermining of democratic liberalism by the people they elected, but it was unpredictable whether they would continue to do so when faced with the consequences.[189] The rule of law was an impediment to executive control in both Britain and America[190] but government lawyers, judges, and other guardians of the rule of law were tested by political assaults on liberal institutions. Too often, lawyers ignored or minimised threats, and those that tried to act were removed. Clear breaches of the rule of law were ignored by elected representatives. This was a warning that constitutions required stronger mechanisms to counter erosion of the rule of law.[191]

---

[187] M Levi and B Epperly, 'Principled Principals in the Founding Moments of the Rule of Law' in JJ Heckman, RL Nelson and L Cabatingan (eds), *Global Perspectives on the Rule of Law* (London and NY, Routledge, 2010) 192, 208.
[188] The Welmar Republic, Republican Spain, the Kingdom of Italy and many South American countries (Vile (n 1) 340).
[189] A Rawnsley, 'Tories are wrong to think that they will never face a day of reckoning for sleaze' *The Observer* (25 April 2021).
[190] T Carothers, 'Rule of law temptations' in JJ Heckman, RL Nelson and L Cabatingan (eds), *Global Perspectives on the Rule of Law* (London and NY, Routledge, 2010) 17, 26.
[191] ibid.

18

Epilogue

I. INTRODUCTION

THE LEGACY OF the European Enlightenment was liberal political systems controlling the state and maximising the autonomy of the individual, producing societies governed by consent. The liberal tradition assumed conditions, core practices and institutions: personal security, constitutional government, elections, free speech, tolerance of other religions and cultures and a free market.[1] Wendy Brown elaborated these features to include a press free of corporate or state ownership, public education 'producing the literacies relevant to informed and active citizenship', judiciaries 'insulated from political and commercial influence, separation of church and state and foreign policy consistent with such values'.[2] These arrangements had the dual purpose of preserving and enhancing personal and collective liberty and promoting legality with minimum coercive force. This chapter reviews conclusions regarding lawyers' engagement with the rule of law and considers threats currently confronting it and possibilities for the future.

II. LAWYERS AND THE RULE OF LAW

Dicey's proposed elements of the rule of law suggested that it operated as a constraint on centralised power, the royal prerogative[3] and, latterly, on arbitrary action by the executive.[4] Its operation was supported by different kinds of lawyers, a strong, independent judiciary, government lawyers controlling the executive, and private practice lawyers constructing a legal role around formal legality,[5] as advocates for mechanisms such as judicial review[6] and for rights such legal professional privilege. These activities

---

[1] S Holmes, *Passions and Constraint: On the Theory of Liberal Democracy* (Chicago, Chicago University Press, 1995) 13–14.
[2] W Brown, 'Neo-liberalism and the End of Liberal Democracy' (2003) 7(1) *Theory and Event* 15.
[3] *The Case of Proclamations* (1611) 12 Co Rep 74, [1610] 77 ER 1352, [1610] EWHC KB J2277.
[4] See also BZ Tamanaha, *On the Rule of Law: History, Politics, Theory* (Cambridge, Cambridge University Press, 2004).
[5] TC Halliday and L Karpik, 'Politics Matters' in Halliday and Karpik (eds), *Lawyers and the Rise of Western Political Liberalism* (Oxford, Clarendon Press, 1997) 24.
[6] A Street, *Judicial Review and the Rule of Law: Who is in Control?* (London, The Constitution Society, 2013).

supported the claims of the professions to institutional independence from the state and afforded them roles in civil society as champions of the rule of law. Sociologists saw professions as a force for moral order and a bulwark against government excess.[7]

Lawyers' support for the rule of law, as judges, government lawyers, or private practitioners, drew on distinct dispositions and obligations which overlapped. The most notable was independence. Halliday and Karpik thought judicial independence was harder to sustain without independent professions[8] and Semple thought that drawing judiciaries from professional practitioners instilled judicial independence from the state and reinforced the separation of powers.[9] Responsibility of judges and other lawyers for maintaining the rule of law was mutual[10] and symbiotic.[11] Courts relied on government lawyers and those in private practice to present cases responsibly and effectively using arguments that allowed them to declare law.[12] Despite commonalities, the different legal roles emphasised different relationships to the rule of law. These tended to be cumulative, so that experience of practice contributed to government focused roles. Tasks relevant to the rule of law were roughly as follows:

A. Private Practice

- Translating economic, social, and political needs into legal principles.
- Supporting the autonomy, agency, and rights of individuals.
- Insisting on a role as neutral partisans.
- Communicating legal values in advising clients.
- Promoting legality, particularly in interactions with clients.
- Promoting procedural regularity, particularly in criminal cases.
- Rejecting pressure for 'substantive justice'.
- Resisting and protesting constitutional breaches undermining the rule of law.
- Conceiving of and advancing new substantive rights.
- Upholding the administration of justice.
- Advocating the rule of law in circumstances where it did not exist or was under threat.
- Educating clients and public in the meaning of and importance of the rule of law.

---

[7] AM Carr-Saunders and PH Wilson, *The Professions* (Oxford, Clarendon Press, 1933).
[8] Halliday and Karpik (n 5) 21.
[9] N Semple, *Legal Services Regulation at the Crossroads: Justitia's Legions* (Cheltenham, Edward Elgar Publishing, 2015) 223.
[10] T Bingham, *The Rule of Law* (London, Allen Lane 2010) 93.
[11] *IBA Report of the IBA Presidential Task Force on the Independence of the Legal Profession*, (draft, 2016).
[12] GC Hazard and A Dondi, *Legal Ethics: A Comparative Study* (Stanford, Stanford University Press, 2004).

B. Government Lawyers

- Conceiving constitutions, systems and principles supporting the rule of law.
- Acting consistently with the rule of law.
- Drafting legislation complying with the rule of law.
- Supporting and reinforcing the separation of powers in government.
- Advising government on the legality of its actions.
- Monitoring compliance with the rule of law.
- Resisting arbitrary use of power.

C. Judges

- Interpreting statutory and common law.
- Maintaining independence, including from other government functions.
- Upholding constitutional norms.
- Requiring executive compliance with law.
- Upholding citizens' civil rights.
- Recognising the validity of new rights.

The skills common to the tasks included creating, interpreting, and communicating law. The attitudes included independence, neutrality, and fairness. These propensities meant that lawyers were sensitive to the need for fair procedures, individual rights, and equality of treatment.

III. DECLINE OF THE RULE OF LAW

Holmes claimed that liberalism presented 'a clearly defined set of principles and institutional choices endorsed by specific politicians, publicists, and popular movements.'[13] Ideal-typical liberal attitudes; were against clericalism, militarism, hereditary monopoly and for scientific progress, freedom of movement and equality of economic opportunity.[14] The rule of law protected minorities with rights which were functional in encouraging observance of law.[15] Substantive fairness, including principles of equality described a rule of law recognising dignity, equality, and human rights, ensured the rule *of* law rather than rule *by* law. Liberal ideas, including reverence of science and reason, were however challenged by modern conditions and quite opposite attitudes.

---

[13] S Holmes, *Passions and Constraint: On the Theory of Liberal Democracy* (Chicago, University of Chicago Press, 1995) 13.
[14] ibid.
[15] P Gowder, *The Rule of Law in the Real World* (Cambridge, Cambridge University Press, 2016).

The information age led, perversely, to the prevalence of misinformation, a decline of reason in public discourse, and an increased tendency to autocratic leaders and governments. Electorates' acceptance of false claims, accusations of witch-hunts, fake news and rigged elections reflected a paranoid culture which saw conspiracy everywhere and was resistant to reason. There was growing hostility to journalism contradicting the 'alternative narratives' of authoritarian power. In Hungary, Viktor Orban used the COVID-19 pandemic to rule by decree, with lengthy jail terms for those spreading 'false' information.[16] In July 2021 it was revealed that many authoritarian governments were clients of a spyware company which had successfully infected the smart phones of rivals, opponents, and critics.[17]

The opportunities presented by new technologies, for disinformation, distortion, and targeted messaging, predicted a world in which it would become harder for truth to prevail. Autocrats had strong incentives to attack reliable sources of information. In Turkey and Egypt journalistic criticism was treated as dissent. In the Czech Republic the president, Milos Zeman, held up a rifle with 'at journalists' written on it.[18] Physical and other attacks on journalists weakened investigation and led to self-censorship.[19] The assault on truth was not limited to failed or illiberal democracies. Amal Clooney, the UK barrister appointed by the Foreign Secretary as special envoy for media freedom, while seeking support for a report for the IBA's International Law Institute campaign for journalists,[20] criticised President Trump as a source of anti-journalist rhetoric.

During his period in office, Trump ignored or condoned despots' abuse of the truth and of their own citizens. In a photo-call before a meeting at the G20 summit in Osaka in 2019, Trump joked with Putin about getting rid of journalists, 26 of whom had been murdered in Russia during Putin's presidency.[21] An extreme case of the murder of a journalist was that of the US-based *Washington Post* Journalist, Jamal Khashoggi, a Saudi Arabian dissident, at its consulate in Istanbul in October 2018.[22] The group photo of the world leaders at the G20 showed Trump and the Saudi prince, Mohammed bin Salman, strongly suspected of ordering Khashoggi's murder, centre-front, shaking hands.

George Orwell and Hannah Arendt identified cultures of pervasive lying at the heart of the totalitarianism, whereby 'the destruction of epistemological foundations creates a crisis of knowledge'.[23] Sen noted that a casualty of autocracy was often Kant's 'freedom to make public use of one's reason on all matters.'[24] Polarised political cultures, which validated 'alternative narratives' meant that conduct once considered political suicide was no longer so. The last two US presidents to be impeached both

---

[16] Editorial, 'Viktor Orban's power grab is a further step towards autocracy' *The Guardian* (20 March 2020).

[17] G Monbiot, 'Pegasus is just the latest tool autocrats use to stay in power' *The Guardian* (28 July 2021).

[18] G Phillips, 'How the free press worldwide is under threat' *The Guardian* (26 May 2020).

[19] ibid.

[20] P Wintour, 'Landscape for rights to media freedom "pretty bleak", warns Clooney' *The Guardian* (17 February 2020).

[21] J Borger, 'Trump and Putin joke about getting rid of reporters' *The Guardian* (29 June 2019).

[22] H Cengiz, 'We ignore Jamal's murder at our peril' *The Guardian* (2 October 2019).

[23] S Churchwell, 'I WON THE ELECTION' *The Guardian Review* (21 November 2020).

[24] A Sen, 'India Once stood for liberty. Now despotism has taken over' *The Guardian* (27 October 2020).

escaped for political reasons. Senate votes in the 1998 impeachment of President Bill Clinton for lying under oath and obstructing justice, largely followed party lines, but senators were also affected by public opinion and the desire to appear 'dignified'.[25]

In the Trump impeachments Republican Senators voted to acquit for partisan reasons, from fear of de-selection, fear of violence from extremists, or because he still enjoyed voter support.[26] After the assault on the Capitol, Trump's approval rating remained high with Republican voters. A survey in February 2021 found that 79 per cent of them still viewed him favourably, two-thirds agreed that President Joe Biden's election win was illegitimate, and a majority supported the use of force to stop the decline of 'the American way of life'.[27] Almost a third sympathised with the QAnon conspiracy theory that Trump was battling a global child sex-trafficking ring. Only 11 million, around three per cent of the US population, watched Trump's second impeachment hearing and Fox News ratings plummeted when they were on.[28]

The information society was closely associated with populist governments. Overall, they potentially supported aspects of the rule of law, mobilising marginalised sections of society, promoting democratic engagement, and sometimes narrowing the gap between rich and poor.[29] This was probably because of the impact of left-wing populist parties, Syriza in Greece and Podemos in Spain. European experience suggested, however, that populist parties at opposite ends of the political spectrum parties often shared policies, such as opposition to the European Union.[30] Whatever their outlook, populist government nearly always resulted in a decline in the rule of law:[31] declining quality of elections and press freedom, loosening of constraints on executive power and corruption.

The weakening of standards commonly accompanying populist governments undermined 'the competence, fairness, and democratic legitimacy of the modern state', substituting 'the criteria of willingness-to-pay for criteria based on desert, need, efficiency, and other values'.[32] Numerous examples included Hungary, where the EU Commission found 50 per cent of public procurement contracts were awarded where there was only one tender.[33] One of many different measures of state corruption, the Corruption Perception Index (CPI) measured levels of corrupt practices in state public sectors: 'bribery, the use of public office for private gain, and the diversion of public funds'.[34] On a scoring system where 100 was 'very clean' and leading nations

---

[25] J Turley, 'Reflections on Murder, Misdemeanours, and Madison' (1999) 28 *Hofstra Law Review* 439.
[26] 'Trump's Legacy' (*The Economist*, 9–15 January 2021) 9.
[27] DA Cox, *After the ballots are counted: Conspiracies, political violence, and American exceptionalism* (Washington DC, American Enterprise Institute, Survey Centre on American Life, 2021) www.aei.org/research-products/report/after-the-ballots-are-counted-conspiracies-political-violence-and-american-exceptionalism/.
[28] D Smith, 'Trump's Republican base will not be shaken despite the Senate's rebuke' *The Observer* (14 February 2021).
[29] P Lewis, S Clarke and C Barr, 'Populist presidents linked to reduced inequality' *The Guardian* (7 March 2019).
[30] C Mudde, 'How populism became the concept that defines our age' *The Guardian* (22 November 2018).
[31] Team Populism, https://populism.byu.edu/.
[32] S Rose-Ackerman, 'Corruption: Greed, Culture and the State' (26 July 2010) 120 *Yale Law Journal Online* 125–40, 2010; Yale Law & Economics Research Paper No. 409.
[33] T Garton Ash, 'Hungary is dismantling democracy. The EU must act' *The Guardian* (20 June 2019).
[34] This collated and standardised data from 12 independent sources such as the World Bank and World Economic Forum, www.transparency.org/en/cpi/2021.

scored over 80, Hungary was in decline, slipping 12 points between 2012 and 2021 to a score of 43 and ranked 73rd of 180 countries. Considering everything, this was moderately good. Russia, for example, had a score of 29 and was placed 136th.

Increased corruption was not limited to autocratic states. The scores of the UK and US declined during periods of populist government. The UK had reached a high score of 82 in 2017 but slipped to 78, 11th place, in 2021. The US slipped from a high of 76 in 2017 to 67, and 27th place, in 2020. Among the core countries, New Zealand was one of three countries with a first-place score of 88 on the CPI. On another survey, the 2021 Global Corruption Index, showed corruption levels based on 40 criteria.[35] Most of the core jurisdictions had reasonably low levels with New Zealand 3rd, Australia 7th, the UK 10th, Canada 16th and the US 35th. It could however, take up to five years for corruption to impact on scores.

Populist government could lead to 'elective dictatorship', slide into autocracy, or seizure of power by force. Both the US and the UK had demonstrated some vulnerability which needed to be guarded against, but how? Constitutional approaches to protecting the rule of law involved better controlling power, possibly by reviewing the separation of powers. Controlling the executive could involve adjustment of vertical, horizontal, and diagonal accountability mechanisms.[36] The vertical mechanism was electoral accountability, the horizontal the separation of powers, including fourth branch institutions such as the civil service, and diagonal, answering to the media, the academy, and civil society. Making the executive more accountable suggested strengthening state capacity[37] while institutional ways to protect the rule of law involved assigning specific responsibilities to existing agencies or creating new ones.

Institutional accountability required regulatory institutions to monitor, maintain credible constraints, and impose appropriate sanctions. Existing agencies might have been empowered to determine breaches of the rule of law and require remedies, whereas new agencies could have addressed specific problems exposed by populism. They could assist diagonal accountability by improving and preserving reliable sources of information, preventing presentation of factual distortions as 'news', and creating informed electorates resistant to misinformation. Reviewing horizontal accountability in the light of recent experience in the UK suggested a need for a stronger separation of electoral and executive roles, perhaps by introducing a Presidential system, written Constitution, and Constitutional Court as counterweights to abuse of executive power.

Procedural adjustments would have ensured that government was less prone to corruption in relation to public appointments and accountability mechanisms. Simple changes of procedure, such as greater use of anonymity, might improve processes in some contexts. A former Republican senator, Jeff Flake, estimated that 35 Republican senators would have voted for the first impeachment of Donald Trump had the ballot been secret.[38] In that case, numbers would probably have increased for the second

---

[35] Global Corruption Index, https://risk-indexes.com/global-corruption-index/.

[36] T Khaitan, 'Killing a Constitution with a Thousand Cuts: Executive Aggrandizement and Party-state Fusion in India' (2020) 14(1) *Law & Ethics of Human Rights* 49.

[37] Rose-Ackerman (n 32).

[38] Editorial, 'Republicans have offered up the soul of the party to keep Trump in power' *The Guardian* (3 February 2020).

(insurrection) impeachment. Procedural adjustments in the UK would have required a system implementing the principle that merit match reward in public appointments.[39] They might have included review of the Prime Minister's responsibility for acting on breaches of the Ministerial Code, a clear conflict of interest replaceable by independent judicial or administrative mechanisms.

Developing constitutional government by trial and error had advantages of flexibility but populism exposed chronic weaknesses. These were demonstrated by the storming of the Capitol in the US, the Queen's agreement to an illegal prorogation of the UK Parliament, and the Owen Paterson episode, where reluctant MPs voted to suspend Parliamentary anti-corruption procedures. These events were warnings of the vulnerability of the rule of law. Better ways to safeguard it included constitutional solutions, revising the separation of the power to make, execute, and decide law, institutional solutions, the creation of counterbalancing agencies, and procedural solutions, the revision or creation of process attuned to rule of law issues. To these could be added improvements to the culture of government. Each involved or potentially involved lawyers.

IV. JUDICIARIES

Judiciaries were a main line of defence against encroachment of the state on the rule of law. In the constitutional tradition of the UK, courts checked executive rather than legislative power but this approach was not immutable. Following Enlightenment reasoning, weakening the rule of law by changing the Constitution would depend on the consent of the People, but two models of consent potentially conflicted.[40] The first, majoritarianism, suggested an elected party had wide legislative discretion to change existing law, including the rights inherent in constitutional law. The second, following the logic of Dicey's formulation of the rule of law, was that the underlying principles of liberal democracy could not be changed, even with the consent of the people.

The theory that a majority government could make fundamental constitutional changes was unconvincing. Majority parties were often elected on a minority of electoral votes. In 2016 Trump won the US presidency on a 55 per cent turnout, and despite polling nearly 3 million fewer votes than Clinton. In Hungary, Fidesz won 66 per cent of Parliamentary seats on 44 per cent of the vote.[41] In 2019 the British Conservative Party won a majority of 84 seats with 43.6 per cent of just over a 67 per cent turnout of eligible voters.[42] The next two parties, Labour and Liberal Democrat, had a slightly higher share of the popular vote. Election victory was therefore a weak mandate for constitutional change. The 'first past the post' electoral system encouraged majoritarianism and increased the risk that illiberal government would threaten liberal democracy.

---

[39] Lord Nolan (Chair), *Standards in Public Life: First Report of the Committee for Standards in Public Life* (London, HMSO, 1995) para 91.
[40] L Mosesson, 'Dr. Bonham in Woolf's clothing? Sovereignty and the rule of law today' (2007) *Mountbatten Yearbook of Legal Studies* 5.
[41] Garton Ash (n 33).
[42] BBC News, 'Results', www.bbc.co.uk/news/election/2019/results.

Dicey spent time in America studying the political system. He wrote that systematic party discipline risked individual interests corrupting public service.[43] This was demonstrated in the Trump impeachment trials, where the majority of Republican senators vetoed conviction. Dicey had also predicted: 'The evil is very apparent in England and will become more so'.[44] Several factors contributed to the UK's electoral system being a threat to thick versions of the rule of law: the strength of the party system, the disadvantage of smaller parties, the limited power of the House of Lords to change bills[45] and the fact that royal assent to legislation was, by convention, a formality.[46] The ability of governments with strong majorities to do more or less what they wanted, to the detriment of what may be the majority of the population, was called 'elective dictatorship' by a Tory Lord Chancellor, Lord Hailsham.[47]

The second understanding of consent assumed fundamental constitutional principles, such as democracy or the Rule of Law, could not be changed by majority governments.[48] This was the case in Canada where the Supreme Court found in a key Canadian constitutional case 'democracy in any real sense of the word cannot exist without the rule of law'.[49] 'Thick' conceptions of the rule of law might include *all* established Human Rights or merely a core of constitutional rights. Thicker conceptions of democracy would require an extraordinary constitutional mechanism to change the constitutional order. Despite their weak democratic mandate, the UK government elected in 2019 embarked on a programme of what could be seen as 'illiberal' legislation. These included measures interpretable as a retreat from the rule of law, for example, restrictions on rights of protest,[50] on the right to vote,[51] and on the human rights of those in detention.[52]

If the majoritarian view of consent were accepted, 'the people' posed a threat to the rule of law when they agreed to it being undermined to deprive others, not considering the potentially corrosive impact on their own rights. One analysis of why this happened suggested that populist leaders 'forgave' electors their petty corruption, including prejudices, in return for them forgiving politicians grand corruption.[53]

---

[43] AV Dicey, *Introduction to the Study of Law of the Constitution* (Boston, Adamant Media Corporation, 2005) foreword, xv.
[44] ibid.
[45] As a result of the Parliament Acts 1911 and the Salisbury Convention.
[46] G Monbiot, 'The UK is a democracy in name only' *The Guardian* (4 June 2020).
[47] Richard Dimbleby Lecture (BBC, 1976).
[48] Mosesson (n 40).
[49] *Reference concerning certain questions on the Secession of Quebec* (1998) 161 DLR (4th) 385, 416.
[50] UK Parliament, 'Police, Crime, Sentencing and Courts Bill' (15 March 2021) https://committees.parliament.uk/committee/93/human-rights-joint-committee/news/152774/police-crime-sentencing-and-courts-bill/.
[51] The Conservative chair of the Commons Public Administration and Constitutional Affairs Committee said that the Committee was unconvinced that measures to prevent voter fraud were justified evidence of by a problem, while the change would lead to a projected drop of 2.3% in voting, mainly by electors opposing the government (PA Media, 'MPs urge halt to elections bill as "voter ID may hit turnout"' *The Guardian* (13 December 2021) 14).
[52] Even before the independent report it commissioned, the government announced its intention to introduce a right for judges to overrule the ECHR (R Syal, 'Alarm at overhaul of human rights law' *The Guardian* (14 December 2021) 1).
[53] M Stephenson, 'Petty Corruption, Grand Corruption, and the Politics of Absolution' (*The Global Anticorruption Blog*, 2 January 2018) https://globalanticorruptionblog.com/2018/01/02/petty-corruption-grand-corruption-and-the-politics-of-absolution/.

Thus, in Italy, Berlusconi's psychological manipulation of electors was labelled the 'politics of absolution'.[54] Populist governments invariably slid quickly into impropriety and corruption, possibly due to the absence of integrity in populist leaders[55] or because of corner cutting, to get things done.[56]

The notion of Parliamentary sovereignty assumed government was so trustworthy that constitutional guarantees were unnecessary. It assumed a peaceful handover of power by a losing party in an election, that supporters would accept the legitimacy of rule by the majority party, and that some legislation 'would be politically impossible to adopt'.[57] The inviolability of the first two of these assumptions was challenged by events in the US. The transition from illiberal democracy to increasingly authoritarian government threatened rights, civil, human, electoral, with irreversible change. The short-term authoritarian impulse of a majority could jeopardise the rights of the minority and, with that, their own long-term rights. It was arguable that, at the very least, government should have supermajorities to legislate against the rule of law.[58]

The advent of populism raised the question of whether the judicial role should formally encompass control of the executive and, in extraordinary circumstances, the legislature. Sir Edward Coke, and more recently Lord Woolf, envisaged that the judiciary might intervene when 'the political side of the constitution has failed conspicuously'.[59] In the extreme circumstance that a court declared an Act of Parliament unconstitutional, for example because it abolished fundamental constitutional rights, there would be a crisis. This was an argument for identifying such circumstances and installing institutions of impeccable impartiality, such a Constitutional Court, with appointment procedures insulated from politics.

In 1957 Gower wrote that the role of politics in selecting British judges had been eradicated over the previous 25 years.[60] A remaining criticism was that the judiciary was drawn from an elite section of society, entrants to the Bar. Greater fairness was achieved in the process when the Constitutional Reform Act 2005 created an independent Judicial Appointments Commission procedure. This was partially successful,[61] with solicitors being appointed to senior judicial roles, but the change potentially changed the character of the judiciary. Of the five appointed deputy High Court judges in 2017[62] one was in government, an adviser to the Ministry of Justice and Deputy Prime Minister, and others had corporate law backgrounds. These histories

---

[54] ibid.
[55] V White, C Foster-Gilbert and J Sinclair, *Integrity in Public Life* (Haus Publishing, 2019)
[56] Nolan (Chair) (n 39) para 85.
[57] M Elliott, 'United Kingdom: Parliamentary sovereignty under pressure' (2004) 2(1) *International Journal of Constitutional Law* 545.
[58] Editorial, 'There is no law in Britain against cabinet knavery. Maybe there should be' *The Guardian* (24 January 2022).
[59] Mosesson (n 40) 19.
[60] LCB Gower and L Price, 'The Profession and Practice of the Law in England and America' (1957) 20(4) *The Modern Law Review* 317, 338.
[61] The first female judge of the senior court, Baroness Hale, and subsequent appointees, Lady Black and Lady Arden, were former barristers, although Hale also had an academic career (but see L Barnes and K Malleson, 'The Legal Profession as Gatekeeper to the Judiciary: Design Faults in Measures to Enhance Diversity' (2011) 74(2) *Modern Law Review* 245).
[62] M Fouzder, 'Five solicitors sworn in as High Court judges' (*Law Society Gazette*, 23 October 2020) www.lawgazette.co.uk/news/solicitors-sworn-in-as-high-court-judges/5106126.article.

were unlikely to instil values, such as holding power to account, traditionally associated with judicial appointees. If this trend continued the judiciary would become more government and corporation oriented and less infused with the barristers' ethos of individual rights.

Selection remained a problem in the US where judges were often elected on a party ticket and the Supreme Court was predicted to divide on political lines over abortion laws. Judicial appointments processes were used by Trump in an overtly politicised way to undermine the traditional independence of the Supreme Court. The judicial role was also threatened by intimidation, including by online mobs. James Robart, a Seattle judge who ruled against Trump's Muslim travel ban 'received a million hostile emails and death threats deemed so credible he had to be given 24-hour protection'.[63] Such developments might only be dealt with by reinforcing respect for the rule of law.

V. GOVERNMENT LAWYERS

The open society of liberal aspiration depended on 'government openness, honesty and accountability'.[64] The independence of lawyers lay at the heart of constitutionalism in core jurisdictions. Years before his own term as Attorney-General to President Trump between 2017–18, Jeff Sessions asked, at Sally Yates' confirmation hearings, how she would respond to a president proposing unlawful action. She responded: 'Senator I believe the Attorney-General or the deputy attorney general has an obligation to follow the law and the Constitution, and to give their independent legal advice to the president'.[65] Sessions apparently approved of her answer, possibly why, despite his reputation as a maverick hardliner, he did not last long in post.

The ethics of providing legal advice to the executive, the key role of senior government lawyers, was tested by the government of President Bush Jr which asked about the legality of torturing terrorist suspects. Wendell argued that there were some situations, the 'ticking-bomb example' where critics of torture must concede a case for it.[66] This did not, he argued, make it ethical for lawyers to advise that there were circumstances where it would be legal. While a 'good president' might authorise torture in extreme circumstance '[i]t is the job of a lawyer to say that some action is not lawful, even if it is something the client (whether an individual, private entity, or the government) very much wants to do'.[67] Another ethical dilemma faced by government lawyers was whether to give inaccurate legal advice to prevent government action they believed to be wrong.

Bob Woodward, veteran journalist of Watergate, reported the case of an official who had acted to thwart a Trump policy he disagreed with.[68] Gary Cohn, Trump's

---

[63] J Freedland, 'Just societies need referees. We abuse them at our peril' *The Guardian* (13 April 2019).
[64] ibid.
[65] D Smith, B Jacobs and S Ackerman, 'Sally Yates fired by Trump after acting US attorney general defied travel ban' *The Guardian* (31 January 2017) www.theguardian.com/us-news/2017/jan/30/justice-department-trump-immigration-acting-attorney-general-sally-yates.
[66] B Wendel, 'The Torture Memos and the Demands of Legality' (2009) 12(1) *Legal Ethics* 107, 120.
[67] ibid 122.
[68] B Woodward, *Fear: Trump in the White House* (New York: Simon & Schuster, 2018).

economic adviser, had removed documents authorising withdrawal from the NAFTA trade agreement, which were waiting on Trump's desk for signature. If Cohn thought this served the national interest, was it the right thing to do? Braun subjected his action to the test set by Saint Thomas Aquinas for resisting unjust rulers; was the law just and had the community affected by it participated in its formulation.[69] Applying this test, Braun concluded, thwarting the NAFTA treaty withdrawal was wrong because it frustrated action implicitly approved by the electorate. Some hypotheticals were less easily answered: should lawyers present presidents with legal impediments to launching nuclear missiles, as Trump threatened against North Korea and Iran, even if there were none?[70]

In the UK, as in other jurisdictions, the lawyers permeating government had distinct responsibilities for the rule of law. The law officers' role included advising on constitutional issues (for example, observance of separation of powers), observance of rights (for example, Attorney General prosecution decision), and the requirements of legality (advice to executive).[71] Lawyers based in ministerial departments advised politicians on legislation while Parliamentary Counsel scanned legislation for rule of law issues such as comprehensibility, retroactivity and equal application.[72] They guarded against their authority as legal experts being used for political purposes.[73] Their roles made government lawyers suitable monitors of rule of law infractions and corruption. Government policy and practice might also require them to act contrary to the rule of law, for example by endorsing a policy denying valid rights against government.

In 2017 a New Zealand QC noted the impact of declining legal aid in that country on access to justice, human rights, equality before the law and, hence, the rule of law.[74] She said few lawyers still did legal aid because of low rates, bureaucracy, and punitive recovery mechanisms. Those that did confronted a system in which institutional defendants, including government, exploited claimant helplessness, initially denying all claims, and then making offers impossible to refuse to those with legal help so as not to establish a precedent.[75] Such tactics were presumably dictated by government policies, suggesting the need for more autonomous structures acting consistently with the rule of law.

If government lawyers were the frontline in determining standards of government, their orientation needed to be clear. Dotan suggested two models, a 'single client model', in which instructing government officials or departments were treated as ordinary clients, or a 'public interest model'.[76] This echoed Appleby's distinction,

---

[69] CN Braun, 'The Morality of Resisting Trump' Academia Letter www.academia.edu/45003512/The_Morality_of_Resisting_Trump.
[70] S Tisdall, 'America needs to get a grip on democracy, for all our sakes' *The Guardian* (7 August 2018).
[71] JLJ Edwards, *The Attorney General, Politics and the Public Interest* (London, Sweet and Maxwell, 1984) 215.
[72] O Heald, 'The role of the Law Officers' (Speech by Solicitor General Oliver Heald QC MP to Kent Law School 18 October 2012) www.gov.uk/government/speeches/the-role-of-the-law-officers.
[73] G Barzilai and D Nachmias, 'Governmental Lawyering in the Political Sphere: Advocating the Leviathan' (1998) 3(2) *Israel Studies* 30, 43.
[74] F Joychild, 'Continuing the Conversation ... The fading star of the rule of law' https://eveningreport.nz/2015/03/24/frances-joychild-qc-on-the-fading-star-of-the-rule-of-law/.
[75] ibid; DP Currie, 'Positive and Negative Constitutional Rights' (1986) 53 *U Chi L Rev* 864, 882–83.
[76] Y Dotan, *Lawyering for the Rule of Law: Government Power and the Rise of Judicial Power in Israel* (Cambridge, Cambridge University Press, 2014) 5 (and see various contributors to (2015) 11(1) *Jerusalem Review of Legal Studies*.

based on the Australian Solicitor General, between 'the autonomous expert', who acted as a structural safeguard against illegality and the 'team member', who did not.[77] The English approach adopted the client model, Heald, claiming government lawyers, like the 'best lawyers ... help their clients walk the line, to achieve what they want, the property bought, the contract agreed, the deal done, all within the law'.[78] Weak independence was encouraged by exclusion from inner circles of policy and decision making, attending Cabinet 'as needed'. Stricter institutional separation, like the Solicitor General's Office in New Zealand, may have contributed to that country's superior record on corruption.

Dotan's account of the Office of the Attorney General in Israel showed that institutional separation could achieve better protection for the rule of law but also indicated negative aspects of such independence.[79] A legacy of the British mandate in Palestine was that the Israeli Supreme Court sat as a High Court of Justice (HCJ) to handle claims against the government. From the 1980s, the HCJ broadened the category of eligible judicial review claimants, creating constitutional rights in relation to religion, citizenship, and territory, often in contradiction of parliamentary sovereignty. The government was represented in these cases by lawyers from the Office of the Attorney General based in a High Court of Justice Department (HCJD). Contrary to what one might expect, the HCJD increasingly fell under the control of the HCJ rather than the executive.

Supported by successive Attorney Generals, the HCJD developed independence from government and institutional loyalty to the rule of law. This had the effect of enhancing the independence of the Office of the Attorney General. When the HCJ was constitutionally most active, the HCJD attracted Israel's brightest law students. Ties between HCJ and HCJD became closer when lawyers from the department moved to the bench. The result was replication of judicial values in a key part of the executive. Lawyers in the HCJD began to conceive of their duty to be to the rule of law and their task as anticipating the Court, which was the physical manifestation of it. Consequently, the lawyers took on more of the tasks of court administration and, in a small number of crucial cases, they sided with the Court against the government.

In Israel, the experience of constituting lawyers as independent agencies reinforced the rule of law. It demonstrated, as Vile predicted, that institutions would develop as autonomous centres of power to counterbalance and control state power.[80] They encouraged development of a consensus about the best way to do the job leading to the emergence of new procedures. People within them would be influenced by colleagues evolving in the same milieu and develop their own values and traditions.[81] These might include clear procedures for responding to circumstances where an administration embarked on an illegal course of action. Apart from law officer departments, other agencies might be empowered to defend the rule of law.

---

[77] G Appleby, *The Role of the Solicitor-General: Negotiating Law Politics and the Interest* (Oxford, Hart Publishing, 2018) 17.
[78] Heald (n 72).
[79] Dotan (n 76) and see I Ravid, 'Sleeping with the Enemy? On Government Lawyers and their Role in Promoting Social Change: the Israeli Example' (2014) 50(1) *Stanford Journal of International Law* 185.
[80] MJC Vile, *Constitutionalism and the Separation of Powers*, 2nd edn (Minneapolis, Liberty Fund, 1998).
[81] ibid 17.

Cook suggested that administrative institutions in the US were designed to accommodate professional classes, including lawyers.[82] Over the past 40 years the strengthening of these agencies sought to manage the interface between the state and the expanding power of finance capitalism and large corporations by insulating the sectors from politics, regulating them tightly and creating an expert administrative establishment dedicated to the public interest. The administrative state became more bureaucratic, centralised, and professionalised. Cook argued that it performed such important checks on the other state powers that should be recognised as a fourth constitutional branch.[83] The British state had gone in the opposite direction, weakening administrative control, and using special advisers rather than administrative specialists in the Civil Service.

Although the importance of administration could be recognised by separating executive power into the formulation and the carrying out of law, Cook argued it would be better to empower the administrative state to promote the public interest. This might involve increased responsibility for enacting laws but would focus on improving the calibre (including expertise), security and resources of the administrative class.[84] The recruitment of more high-level government lawyers protecting the rule of law in government would have enhanced independence and protected against executive overreach, particularly when it was clear that the lawyers' primary duty was to the rule of law.

There were various ways in which government lawyers could be assisted in supporting the rule of law, including non-political posts, appointment for a fixed term, or removal only for good cause. All would increase security and lessen political pressure.[85] A further step would be to separate the tasks of law officers so that, for example, the person advising government was not the one controlling prosecutions or piloting legislation. Standards could be developed for these different legal activities of government and systems of monitoring and evaluation established. Institutional protections assume the professional independence of those whose autonomy and independence was to be protected, hence the importance of the background of appointees.

The common denominator in lawyers' commitment to the rule of law was the virtue of independence instilled by professional socialisation and practice. Drawing parallels with private professional roles was common in discussions of government lawyers, for example Heald's reference to 'helping clients walk the line'. Further, Jones observed that Law Officer advice was 'given with complete detachment and independence, as is the case with counsel's advice to any client'.[86] In a written submission to the Chilcott Inquiry Tony Blair refuted suggestions he pressured Lord Goldsmith to change his advice on the Iraq War by stating that it would have been 'wholly pointless … He is a British barrister through and through'.[87] Blair, ironically, recognised professional identification as a foundation of the independence of government lawyers

---

[82] BJ Cook, *The Fourth Branch: Reconstructing the Administrative State for the Commercial Republic* (University Press of Kansas, 2021).
[83] ibid.
[84] ibid.
[85] Book review by E Barendt (1985) 34 *International and Comparative Law Quarterly* 413.
[86] E Jones, 'The Office of Attorney-General' (1969) 27 *Cambridge Law Journal* 43, 47.
[87] 4 News, 'Iraq inquiry focuses on Blair-Goldsmith relationship' (21 January 2011) www.channel4.com/news/iraq-inquiry-focuses-on-blair-goldsmith-relationship.

VI. PRIVATE PRACTICE

In common law jurisdictions lawyers in judiciaries and governments were drawn from private professions. This ensured they were trained to be neutral about clients and their interests, had experience of acting for citizens, and developed habits of independence. They identified with institutions and professions, other than those of government. In the late twentieth century England and Wales ended the self-regulating system which had operated for hundreds of years, calling into question lawyers' roles and the way they represented and engaged with the rule of law. This had ramifications for other aspects of legal professionalism also under threat: bifurcated work roles, the adversary system, LPP and professional institutions.

A. Roles

Taking English lawyers as an example, Larson suggested that ideal conditions of professionalism included provision of an important, universal service independent of the demands of the markets and of sponsoring elites. Remarkable procedural consistency in the litigation systems of Western countries saw claims instigated by petitioners, with assistance of lawyers, and eventually brought before judges.[88] Rule of law requirements did not generally require that disputing parties had advocates,[89] despite their key role in establishing rights. In England, the bifurcated profession separated advocacy from other kinds of work, including managing litigation conducted by more business orientated lawyers. Barristers were distinguished by sole practitioner status and general accessibility. They were selected by other professionals for specific circumstances, the availability of a core of specialist advocates not necessarily 'in-house'. Gower saw the '*corps d'elite* of specialist advocates' as producing higher quality, and higher cost in cases where it was not needed.[90]

Sole practice insulated barristers from organisational pressure and justified claims to a distinctive form of independence. They could appear for prosecution or defence in successive cases or against barristers from the same chambers. The separation from clients and courts meant they were under no pressure to act unprofessionally. Barristers adopted a position of neutrality in terms of clients 'however unpopular or distasteful their case may be',[91] distinct from business lawyers. Their code of conduct was almost entirely devoted to the balance between duties to client and the court. Detailed protocols explained the mechanics of maintaining this balance.

Since the 1990s the English Bar was threatened by competition. It had advantages in this struggle, including autonomous work, low office overheads, high levels of skill, and specialisation in a defined field. Inefficient or uneconomic aspects, being accompanied in court by a solicitor, applied only in more complex cases. Barristers were,

---

[88] Hazard and Dondi (n 12) 63–64.
[89] ibid 92.
[90] Gower and Price (n 60) 319.
[91] Bingham (n 10).

however, disadvantaged by competing with solicitors' firms who could direct their clients to in-house advocacy services. The histories and orientations of the different kinds of lawyer suggested distinct advantages in specialist advocacy for preserving the rule of law. While the economics of practice would determine the future of a distinct advocacy professions, there were strong arguments for preserving them, or at least not abolishing them.[92]

B. The Adversary System

Critics suggested that the adversary system was a historical upstart[93] which struck the wrong balance between individualistic and communitarian values[94] and produced a flawed system of adjudication.[95] In the US, critics of the system's expense and fairness, like Sward,[96] pointed to 'significant failures in the system that we are trying to adjust for'.[97] She argued that the adversary search for truth was too costly and unreliable and the fact that litigants ceded control to lawyers was 'hardly consistent with either individual dignity or an individualistic ethic'.[98] She argued for favouring community interests over individual will,[99] a move to a more inquisitorial system, as in Continental Europe, employing a generalised search for the truth compared with the adversaries' versions of the facts.[100] It was arguable that such a system could employ much better protections than those available in the 1730s.[101]

While the adversary system was an accident of history it remained an efficient way of recognising the varied interests of judges, lawyers, defendants, and jurors, in litigation. As it developed, it incorporated principles of natural justice, as recently explained in the UK Supreme Court:

> A party has a right to know the case against him and the evidence on which it is based. He is entitled to have the opportunity to respond to any such evidence and to any submissions made by the other side. The other side may not advance contentions or adduce evidence of which he is kept in ignorance ... Another aspect of the principle of natural justice is that the parties should be given an opportunity to call their own witnesses and to cross-examine the opposing witnesses.[102]

---

[92] R Kerridge and G Davies, 'Reform of the Legal Profession: An Alternative "Way Ahead"' (1999) 62(6) *Modern Law Review* 807.
[93] JH Langbein, 'The Criminal Trial Before the Lawyers' (1978) 45 *Chicago Law Review* 263, 316
[94] EE Sward, 'Values, Ideology, and the Evolution of the Adversary System' (1989) 64(2) *Indiana Law Journal* 301.
[95] S Landsman, 'The Rise of the Contentious Spirit: Adversary Procedure in Eighteenth-Century England' (1990) 75(3) *Cornell Law Review* 498, 502, 604–5.
[96] FEA Sander and SB Goldberg, 'Fitting the Forum to the Fuss: A User-Friendly Guide to Selecting an ADR Procedure' (1994) 10(1) *Negotiation Journal* 49.
[97] Sward (n 94) 301, 302.
[98] ibid 318–19.
[99] ibid 311.
[100] J Auburn, *Legal Professional Privilege: Law and Theory* (Oxford, Hart Publishing, 2000) 84.
[101] The emphasis on private prosecution kept the judge from proper investigation (Langbein (n 93) 314).
[102] *Al Rawi and others (Respondents) v The Security Service and others* (Appellants) [2011] UKSC 34, paras 12–13.

In a similar vein, Article 6 of the European Convention on Human Rights provided that a fair trial involved 'a fair and public hearing within a reasonable time by an independent and impartial tribunal established by law'.[103] This applied to cases involving the determination of civil rights and obligations or criminal charges.[104]

Article 6 specified aspects of adversary procedure, such as the defendant knowing the nature and cause of the accusation, having time and facilities to prepare a defence, being able to defend themselves, and being able to examine witnesses against them.[105] For criminal proceedings only, there was a right to present a defence '... in person or through legal assistance of his own choosing or, if he has not sufficient means to pay for legal assistance, to be given it free when the interests of justice so require'.[106]

The ECtHR suggested that features of adversarial trials should also be present in civil proceedings involving civil rights. Applicants needed to show that their complaint involved breach of a civil right, which was not always clear from the nature of the matter. In one case the ECtHR held that a decision by the Law Society to reprimand and fine a solicitor was not a matter of civil rights[107] but in other areas, for example employment rights of civil servants, a complex case law developed. Pension rights were defined as civil rights, so that applicants could claim adversarial process. They were entitled to know what evidence was presented in their case and could comment on it.[108]

A 'justice gap' caused by the expense of litigation had caused government to try and reduce reliance on lawyers. It tried to create an alternative advice sector,[109] alternative dispute resolution processes, unregulated services,[110] 'online courts', and remove routine cases from the court system. This was not possible in all cases. According to the ECtHR the fair trial requirements of Article 6 meant that free assistance should still be given in civil cases where complex arguments were involved and where litigants were unable to represent themselves without assistance.[111] Government guidance that legal aid would 'be granted only in rare and extreme cases' in an eligible category of case was held unlawful.[112]

---

[103] European Convention on Human Rights (1953) Article 6(1).
[104] ibid.
[105] ibid Article 6(3)(a)–(d).
[106] ibid Article 6(3)c.
[107] *R (on the application of Thompson) v Law Society* [2004] EWCA Civ 167, [2004] 2 All ER 113, *Times*, 1 April 2004.
[108] An employee of a state part-owned enterprise appealed from a decision regarding his pension. The Portuguese Supreme Court dismissed the appeal having considered it in private with a member of the Attorney General's department. The applicant did not see an opinion of the Attorney General prepared in advance of that meeting. The ECtHR held that he should have had that right in adversarial proceedings (*Lobo Machado v Portugal* (1996) 23 EHRR 79).
[109] These included a Community Legal Service, which failed in much the same way as public provision since. In 2109 it was revealed that half of law centres in England and Wales had closed in the previous six years due to cuts in legal aid and local authority funding (O Bowcott, 'Half of legal advice centres have closed in past six years' *The Guardian* (15 July 2019)).
[110] A Boon, 'Cocktails of Logics – Reform of Legal Services Regulation in England and Wales' in A Boon (ed), *International Perspectives on the Regulation of Lawyers and Legal Services* (Oxford, Hart Publishing, 2017).
[111] Lexis Library, 'Article 6: Right to a fair trial' [III Hum 928].
[112] The case involved immigration cases under s 10 of the Legal Aid, Sentencing and Punishment of Offenders Act 2012: *G v Director of Legal Aid Casework (British Red Cross Society intervening)* [2014] EWCA Civ 1622, [2015] 1 WLR 2247.

The adversarial trial demanded a higher level of formality than inquisitorial processes and was more consistent with legal values and rule of law principles.[113] Landsman observed that 'the association between contentious methods, procedural fairness, and political liberty in English history warranted the most careful scrutiny of modern proposals designed to curtail adversarial methods', arguing 'these "threaten the bedrock" of the court system'.[114] Some modifications of criminal processes used elsewhere were worth investigating[115] but both Article 6 and the practice of the ECtHR suggested continental systems accepted adversary principles in conceiving of 'fair trial'.

C. Confidence and Privilege

Courts in core jurisdictions had generally increased the sanctity of communications between lawyers and clients. In the UK, in *Three Rivers*, Lord Scott said that the right of citizens to Legal Professional Privilege (LPP) was unique among confidential communications[116] and fundamental to a condition of liberty.[117] Those between 'doctor and patient, accountant and client, husband and wife, parent and child, priest and penitent' only received legal protection subject to a test of public interest.[118] This posed problems for clients of multi-disciplinary organisations in which advice may or may not be covered by privilege.[119] Recent legislative policy was to extend LPP to those providing different kinds of legal services,[120] possibly leading to a different kind of confusion.

LPP cut across ordinary peoples' conception of justice[121] apparently making the sanctity of lawyer and client communications a higher priority than truth.[122] The risk of weakening the protections of individuals in conflict with the state[123] was expressed poetically in a case in 1846:

> Truth, like all other good things, may be loved unwisely – may be pursued too keenly – may cost too much. And surely the meanness and the mischief of prying into a man's confidential communications with his legal adviser, the general evil of infusing reserve and

---

[113] R Cotterrell, *Law's Community: Legal Theory in Sociological Perspective* (Oxford, Clarendon Press, 1995) 156.
[114] Landsman (n 95) 503.
[115] In modern Germany, for example, the judge meets the jury and prepares a joint statement of findings (Langbein (n 93) 289).
[116] Some jurisdictions provide professions, for example journalism, with privilege but often only relating to civil proceedings (Auburn (n 100) 60).
[117] *Three Rivers District Council & Others v Governor and Company of the Bank of England (No. 6)* [2004] UKHL 48, [2005] 1 AC 610.
[118] Lord Scott in *Three Rivers* (n 117) para 28.
[119] Auburn (n 100) 134.
[120] In England and Wales for example it was first extended by the Courts and Legal Services Act 1990, s 63 to members of a body approved to provide advocacy, conveyancing or probate services.
[121] S Mize, 'New Zealand: Finding the Balance between Self-Regulation and Government Oversight' in A Boon (ed), *International Perspectives on the Regulation of Lawyers and Legal Services* (Oxford, Hart Publishing, 2017) 116.
[122] Auburn (n 100) 81 citing Knight-Bruce VC in *Pearse v Pearse* 1 De G & Sm 12.
[123] ibid Auburn 62.

dissimulation, uneasiness, and suspicion and fear, into those communications which must take place, and which, unless in a condition of perfect security, must take place uselessly or worse, are too great a price to pay for truth itself.[124]

Because of the wide-reaching implications of LPP it was vulnerable to being restricted. In *Three Rivers* Lord Rodger of Earlsferry speculated that civil procedure reforms in England and Wales, and Scotland could reduce the adversary nature of litigation and the case for litigation privilege.[125] This made the wide scope given advice privilege in *Three Rivers* additionally important.

In 2016 a Law Society seminar discussed executive antagonism to LPP, apparently fuelled by suspicion of the financial services sector and professional advisers following the 2008 economic crisis.[126] The Work and Pensions Select Committee had accused lawyers of 'laziness' for not waiving privilege in the investigation into the collapse of the high street chain British Home Stores. Elsewhere, the Serious Fraud Office and the Financial Conduct Authority had claimed that solicitors had blocked investigations by asserting privilege. There were threats to lawyer and client communication posed by technological developments, bulk interception, acquisition, and equipment interference, to be regulated by the Investigatory Powers Bill. The resolve of the meeting to defend LPP was important given government's increased propensity to create legislative exceptions.

D. Legal Professions

Many judges and academics argued that independent legal professions and the rule of law were linked. Lord Bingham claimed an independent legal profession was 'scarcely less important' than an independent judiciary to maintaining the rule of law.[127] Hazard and Dondi argued that holding the state to account demanded 'a legal profession sufficiently autonomous to invoke the authority of an independent judiciary'.[128] Semple suggested that independence made it more likely that lawyers would create 'legal tools' and deploy zealous advocacy against the state.[129] Monroe Freedman believed 'there is only one way to keep the law "trustworthy" – only one way to keep the bureaucrats honest, and to make the law work, that is, by making sure that there is an independent Bar, prepared to challenge government action and to do so as zealously and effectively as possible'.[130] The Australian judge, Kirby J, went further, asserting that: 'Where there is no independent legal profession there can be no independent judiciary, no rule of law, no justice, no democracy and no freedom'.[131]

---

[124] Knight Bruce V-C in *Pearse v Pearse* (n 122) 28–29 (cited by Lord Carswell in *Three Rivers* at para 112).
[125] *Three Rivers* (n 117) para 52.
[126] Is legal professional privilege under threat? A roundtable discussion at the Law Society (28 October 2016) www.lawsociety.org.uk/communities/the-city/articles/is-legal-professional-privilege-under-threat/.
[127] Bingham (n 10) 92.
[128] Hazard and Dondi (n 12) 1 and 29.
[129] Semple (n 9) 219–28.
[130] MH Freedman, 'Are There Public Interest Limits on Lawyers' Advocacy' (1977) *The Journal of the Legal Profession* 47 at 54.
[131] International Bar Association, *The Independence of the Legal Profession: Threats to Bastion of a Free and Democratic Society* (Report of the IBA Presidential Task Force, 2016) citing The Hon Michael Kirby

There were theoretical justifications of independent self-regulation. The private interest rationale was that representation, supported by lawyer and client privilege, provided access to law and protected rights. The public interest lay in accountable agents operating the court system, serving both clients and the administration of justice.[132] Legal professions' independence from the state was manifest in their constitution as self-regulating bodies. Burrage traced the idea to the Glorious Revolution and the constitutional settlement guaranteeing autonomy to the Inns of Court.[133] Professional independence, he claimed, was embedded in 'widely shared ideals and aspirations' in the 'deep structures' of English life.[134] This allowed leading practitioners to govern some occupations and define the public interest in their area of jurisdiction.[135] Unless there was a clear public interest in interfering in this sphere, government would do so only when invited.[136]

Concrete constitutional supports for the autonomy of professional bodies were elusive in the UK, but Millen suggested there was evidence for them in the North American jurisdictions.[137] The Canadian Supreme Court had claimed power to strike down legislation inconsistent with unwritten but foundational principles of the Constitution Act 1867, although this was implicit rather than express.[138] Selecting superior court judges from provincial bars[139] was originally a way of limiting royal influence.[140] Because judicial independence was fundamental to the rule of law, Millen argued, an independent bar had to exist by 'necessary implication'.[141] Secondly, Canadian courts regarded the adversary system as inviolable, being superior to inquisitorial approaches in exposing flaws in investigatory procedures.[142] These factors made threats to professional independence justiciable issues.[143]

AC CMG, Australia, www.ibanet.org/MediaHandler?id=6E688709-2CC3-4F2B-8C8B-3F341705E438&.pdf&context=bWFzdGVyfGFzc2V0c3wzMTQxNzd8YXBwbGljYXRpb24vcGRmfGg4NC9oZGUvODc5NzEyNTM0NTMxMC82RTY4ODcwOS0yQ0MzLTRGMkItOEM4Qi0zRjM0MTcwNU-U0MzgucGRmfDk2OTg0ZjU1ZWE5OTJlM2ViZTc2MWEwMGE3Zjc4ZDQwOTYwMWYxMDU4OTNlMDc4YTJlODU0Y2I3BhZWQzY2U.

[132] R Millen, 'The Independence of the Bar: An Unwritten Constitutional Principle' (2005) *Canadian Bar Review* 84; Boon, 'Cocktails' (n 110) and Semple (n 9).

[133] M Burrage, 'Mrs Thatcher Against the 'Little Republics': ideology, Precedents and Reaction' in Halliday and Karpik (n 5) 125.

[134] ibid 153.
[135] ibid 154.
[136] ibid 154.

[137] See generally Millen (n 132) citing *In Re McConnell* (370 U.S. 230 at 236 (1962)) at fn 40, where the US Supreme Court held that a vigorous, independent bar is indispensable to the system of justice and *Legal Services Corporation v Velaquez* (531 U.S. 533 (2001)) where legally aided attorneys were allowed to challenge welfare decisions despite legislation limiting their appearance in such cases.

[138] *Babcock v Canada (Attorney General)* [2002] 3 SCR 3 at 29 (cited by Millen (n 132) fn 24).
[139] Constitution Act 1867, ss 97–98.
[140] W Lederman, 'The Independence of the Judiciary' (1956) 34 *Canadian Bar Review* 769 at 776–78 cited by Millen (n 132).

[141] In *Mackin v New Brunswick* [2002] 1 SCR 405, a statute was declared invalid because it impaired judicial independence (Millen (n 132) fn 25) but see *British Columbia v Mangat* [2001] 3 SCR where the Court of Appeal held that a statute could allow non-lawyers to 'practice law' in a specific area (immigration). This overturned a first instance decision that to allow practice of law by non-lawyers was ultra vires Parliament.

[142] Vancouver Sun case exposed failing in an original investigative hearing.

[143] In *Wilder v Ontario (Securities Commission)*, the court decided that the Securities Commission proposed proceedings, which could lead to a reprimand for a lawyer, did not interfere with the independence of the bar or undermine the Rule of Law (Millen (n 132) 124–25).

Finally, Millen argued, international obligations were an aid to interpreting the Canadian Constitution and these supported independent professions.[144]

Among the international consensus supporting independent professions in Canada were, Millen argued, the Latimer House Guidelines for the Commonwealth. These promoted good governance, the rule of law and human rights, stating that 'an independent, organized legal profession is an essential component in the protection of the rule of law'.[145] Canada had accepted other international instruments supporting independent judiciaries and legal professions, such as the Vienna Declaration and Programme of Action 1993[146] and the UN Basic Principles on the Role of Lawyers.[147] The Supreme Court of Canada had cited the United Nations Universal Declaration on the Independence of Justice 1983 in support of the independence of the judiciary.[148]

The argument that self-regulating legal professions were integral to the Canadian Constitution rested on the idea that allowing state agencies to socialise lawyers would inevitably detract from the oppositional orientation needed to challenge the state. The McRuer Report had suggested that the delegation of legislative and judicial functions to self-governing professions should survive because it promoted the public interest, not because it was traditionally so.[149] It suggested that justification should be the subject of 'realistic analysis of why the legal profession should be self-governing' based on description and assessment of the system in theory and in practice. It decided that the Canadian profession passed this test, advising that a single tribunal to hear disciplinary cases for all self-governing professions undermined the basic rationale for self-government.

Few of the core common law jurisdictions met Canada's purist approach to preserving independent professions. Most claimed co-regulatory arrangements, meaning that government were involved in some aspects of the key regulatory processes of admissions, practice regulation or discipline.[150] Canada appeared to have the strongest self-regulation and least intrusive state involvement. Its concession to co-regulatory ideals was recommending that lay members be appointed to oversee exercise of disciplinary power in the public interest.[151] In the US, judicial oversight of powers delegated to the legal profession aligned the judiciary and profession in controlling the executive. In Australia and New Zealand there was partial

---

[144] Millen (n 132).

[145] ibid fn 105.

[146] Asserting the importance of independent judiciaries and legal professions in realising human rights and sustaining democracy and sustainable development.

[147] Adopted by the Eighth United Nations Congress, it stated that adequate protection of the human rights and fundamental freedoms 'requires that all persons have effective access to legal services provided by an independent legal profession'.

[148] States that the independence of legal professions and lawyers are an essential guarantee of human rights so that persons have effective access to independent lawyers so as 'to protect and establish their economic, social and cultural as well as civil and political rights'.

[149] F Schindeler, 'Hon. J. C. McRuer, Royal Commission Inquiry into Civil Rights: Report No. 1. Toronto: Queen's Printer, 1968, Pp. Lix, 1331' (1969) 2 *Canadian Journal of Political Science* 131.

[150] D Buckingham, 'Disciplining Lawyers in New Zealand: Re-Pinning the Badge of Professionalism' (2012) 15 *Legal Ethics* 57.

[151] WR Flaus, 'Discipline within the New Zealand Legal Profession' (1971) 6 *Victoria University Wellington Law Review* 337, 377–78 and citing Mcruer (n 149) 1186.

involvement of government agencies although, as in most of the core jurisdictions, there was pressure to adapt traditional modes of regulation.

Mize described the New Zealand approach as co-regulatory, with government appointing a Legal Complaints Review Officer and administering the Disciplinary Tribunal.[152] In 2009 the Bazley Report concluded a review of legal aid by urging government to institute 'independent' (government) regulation if unverified cases of abuse were not stamped out in three years.[153] Australia had a relatively successful experience of co-regulation, particularly in some states, but also a degree of de-regulation and breaking down of professional demarcation.[154] In Australia the Mutual Recognition Act 1992 facilitated free movement of lawyers between states.[155] This encouraged admission of all lawyers as 'legal practitioners' with specialisation occurring later.[156] Observers were often suspicious of government attempts to encroach on lawyer regulation. McQueen, for example, saw pressure on Australian barristers to abandon traditional wigs and gowns as part of an effort to undermine the independence of courts.[157]

In England and Wales, the Legal Services Act 2007 established regulation by agencies said to be independent but in fact controlled by government via an oversight regulator. The structure and focus of regulation shifted from professional independence to promoting the 'missing voices' of consumers.[158] The shift also raised questions about the role of professional associations without regulatory powers. The North American professional bodies coped without a direct regulatory role, but membership of the ABA was never compulsory for practising attorneys. In 1953, the ABA had 50,000 members, a quarter of practitioners,[159] but this rose to half by the 1980s before falling back to 20 per cent in 2018.[160] Small memberships often affected the representativeness and legitimacy of professional organisations. Rogers observed that until the 1950s, Presidents of the ABA were well known as advocates or specialists but thereafter were usually heads of larger firms.[161]

---

[152] Mize (n 121) 125.
[153] ibid 127 citing M Bazley, *Transforming the Legal Aid System: Final Report and Recommendations* (Ministry of Justice, 2009), www.beehive.govt.nz/sites/default/files/Legal%20AidReview.pdf, p (i).
[154] M Thornton, 'The Australian Legal Profession: Towards a National Identity' in WLF Felstiner (ed), *Reorganisation and Resistance: Legal Professions Confront a Changing World* (Oxford, Hart Publishing, 2005) 133.
[155] ibid 134.
[156] ibid.
[157] R McQueen, 'Of Wigs and Gowns: A Short History of Legal and Judicial Dress in Australia' (1999) 16 *Law in Context: A Socio-Legal Journal* 31, 56.
[158] F Vibert, 'Independent Agencies: No Fixed Boundaries' 7, https://www.lse.ac.uk/accounting/assets/CARR/documents/Regulatory-Agencies-under-Challenge/CARR-DP81-Frank-Vibert.pdf; A Boon, 'Professionalism under the Legal Services Act 2007' (2011) 17(3) *International Journal of the Legal Profession* 195; Semple (n 9) 4.
[159] JG Rogers, 'History of the American Bar Association' (1953) 39(8) *American Bar Association Journal* 659, 666.
[160] Of 400,000 members only 185,000 had paid dues (MH Stanzione, 'New ABA Membership Strategy Aims to Reverse Slide' https://news.bloomberglaw.com/business-and-practice/abas-new-membership-model-logo-go-into-effect.
[161] Rogers (n 159) 666.

The fact that membership of professional organisations often fell when it became voluntary negatively affected their revenue, capacity, and authority. Weakened professional bodies might still perform a useful role in supporting members and the public. They could perform functions not performed by other groups, such as promoting legal reform and the specification of citizens' rights,[162] providing 'principled principals' to institutions, and educating about the rule of law.[163] Their role in civil society, as bulwarks against erosion of the rule of law was, however, vulnerable to their marginalisation by the state. There was also a clear risk that government regulators would compromise professional independence for consumerist policies, trade it for institutional favours, and undermine professional bodies.

Government's task in neutralizing legal professions in England and Wales was assisted by misunderstanding of the complexities of what was done. Academics from other core jurisdictions thought the English arrangements had become more co-regulatory.[164] Rhode and Wooley, for example, perceived that 'there are structures within which the profession shares authority with, and is accountable to, non-lawyer regulators'.[165] In fact, the profession had no regulatory authority left to share. This confusion was shared with journalists. Years after self-regulation ended, the perception that lawyer self-interest had a malign impact on the service economy persisted.[166] Almost no one considered the impact of the decline of legal professions in securing the rule of law.[167] An exception was the International Bar Association (IBA), which continued to draw attention to the connection between lawyer independence from government and the rule of law.

In 2016 an IBA Taskforce report drew on publications, responses from member organisations and experts to produce a schema comprising 10 'indicators of independence'.[168] An edited version of the indicators and threats appears as Appendix II.[169] The fifth indicator on the IBA list, effective independent regulation of legal professions, referred to institutions impinging on self-regulation funded by the executive and staffed by government employees.[170] The line between impinging and not impinging was fine, the taskforce accepting the legitimacy of co-regulatory models

---

[162] BR Weingast, 'Why Developing Countries Prove So Resistant to the Rule of Law' in JJ Heckman, RL Nelson and L Cabatingan (eds), *Global Perspectives on the Rule of Law* (London and NY, Routledge, 2010) 46.

[163] M Levi and B Epperly, 'Principled Principals in the Founding Moments of the Rule of Law' in Heckman et al ibid 18.

[164] J Maute, 'Global continental shifts to a new governance paradigm in lawyer regulation and consumer protection: riding the wave' in R Mortensen, F Bartlett and K Tranter, *Alternative Perspectives on Lawyers and Legal Ethics* (London, Routledge, 2010) 21; D Rhode and A Wooley, 'Comparative Perspectives on Lawyer Regulation: An Agenda for Reform in the United States and Canada' (2012) 80 *Fordham Law Review* 2761.

[165] Rhode and Wooley ibid 2762.

[166] S Jenkins, 'From militant doctors to angry lawyers, professionals are the new union barons' *The Guardian* (19 November 2015).

[167] But see D Sciulli, 'Continental Sociology of Professions Today: Conceptual Contributions' (2005) 53 *Current Sociology* 915.

[168] *IBA Report* (n 11) paras 40–42.

[169] Since it is promulgated by a lobbyist for legal professionalism, it may be debated whether the indicators are essential. Nevertheless, meeting several of the indicators could be a warning sign that a legal profession is prevented from supporting the rule of law.

[170] *IBA Report* (n 11) 26.

and acknowledging that '[s]ome degree of external influence (in the form of governmental regulation, for example) need not diminish independence, as long as it does not interfere with a profession's ability to uphold the Rule of Law'.[171]

The IBA Task Force report suggested 38 threats to independence, several of which applied in the UK. These included judicial bribery,[172] introduction of a further investigatory powers bill[173] and regulation of company tax activities impinging on LPP.[174] Several further examples occurred since the report including, for example, failure to protect judges from the national press.[175] Threats described in this book are listed below with the item in the IBA list (see Appendix II) indicated in brackets:

- The Leigh Day proceedings (3.C. Arbitrary disbarment or targeted disciplinary proceedings and 7.A. Violence, harassment and intimidation of lawyers representing unpopular clients).
- Anti-money laundering and terrorist legislation (4.A. Legislation requiring lawyers to breach the principle of lawyer-client confidentiality, 4.C. Existence of tipping-off prohibitions).
- Increasing government control of profession (5.A. Regulatory framework in which regulators are predominantly or exclusively made up of government-appointed members).
- Curtailing self-regulation (5.C. Legislation reducing self-regulatory powers of legal profession).
- Statutory authority to interfere with lawyer client communication (8.C. Surveillance of private communications between lawyer and client or confiscation of private and confidential work product in the context of legal advice, representation, or court proceedings).
- Political attacks on lawyers helping asylum seekers and detainees (9.B. Frequent public attacks against the profession by prominent political figures).
- Physical and social media attacks on lawyers (9.C. Negative public opinion of the legal profession and judges, and a general tendency by the public to associate lawyers with their clients, corruption, dishonesty and greed).
- The growth of unregulated services (10.A. The rise of unregulated alternative ownership models, where ownership rests in the hands of non-lawyers or other unregulated professionals; 10.B. The proliferation of new categories of unregulated legal professionals providing legal services).

While some may have disagreed that independent and authoritative legal professions were essential to maintaining the rule of law, the link between the decline of legal professionalism and the rule of law demanded more attention than it received in the 15 years since the end of self-regulation.

---

[171] ibid 8.
[172] ibid fn 31.
[173] ibid fn 67.
[174] ibid fn 69.
[175] A breach of Indicator 1.C. Protection of judiciary from criticism.

VII. CONCLUSION

This book argued that the rule of law is about societies governed by law with minimal coercion. Creating such societies involved the consent of the governed, secured by striking a balance between a general condition of legality and the rights of the individual. This realised the promise of the European Enlightenment that the individual be given as much freedom as possible not impinging on the rights of others. Lawyers were the most important promoters of this idea of the rule of law[176] and its vital defenders.[177] Their engagements in common law countries under the rule of law were similar: resisting autocracy, establishing the separation of powers,[178] committing to formal legality, developing justice systems protecting fundamental rights,[179] controlling corruption, and restricting arbitrary action by government.[180]

The role of lawyers generally was to protect the rights of citizens, primarily against encroachment by the state. By claiming procedural justice for clients, lawyers assumed a role supporting rights to individuality. A collection of rights recognised by the state included clients' LPP, part of a core of constitutional rights protecting liberty, and the principle of judicial review of executive action, which reinforced these rights.[181] This emphasis prevented lawyers putting third party interests above client interests except where clients threatened legality. They were deflected from excessive partisanship by the principle of legality, manifest as responsibility for the integrity of the legal system and legal institutions. Lawyers were also responsible for assisting the public in understanding the social significance of the web of obligations created by law, crucial in societies based on individual freedom.

Training for and working in private practice was ideal preparation for lawyers working in public roles as judges or government lawyers. It instilled attitudes of neutrality, consciousness of the importance of procedural fairness, and orientation to clients. These orientations allowed lawyers in the public sphere to hold in balance rights of citizens and obligations to legality, the essence of the rule of law. Most importantly, their identity as lawyers, a different caste from politicians, enabled them to counsel government and place the rule of law above loyalty to it. This disposition was reinforced by membership of legal professions, forces for moral order and bulwarks against government excess.[182] The tendency of government to breach the rule of law suggests the need to strengthen institutional support for government lawyers.

Legal professions helped lawyers uphold the rule of law. They provided the reference point of a body of peers sustaining norms distinct from the mainstream, induction into common professional values, and moral support in resisting

---

[176] C Michelon, *The Anxiety of the Jurist: Legality, Exchange and Judgement* (Oxford, Routledge, 2013) 24–25.
[177] ibid.
[178] See generally TC Halliday and L Karpik, *Lawyers and the Rise of Western Political Liberalism*, (Oxford, Clarendon Press, 1997).
[179] Halliday and Karpik (n 5) 15, 21 and 30.
[180] N MacCormick, 'The Ethics of Legalism' (1989) 2(2) *Ratio Juris* 184.
[181] Street (n 6).
[182] AM Carr-Saunders and PH Wilson, *The Professions* (Oxford, Clarendon Press, 1933).

employment pressure.[183] Lawyers, whether in practice or government, were part of a common tradition and aware of the judgement of lawyers past and present.[184] Professions bound different kinds of lawyers, representing different dimensions of the rule of law. The relationship was often symbiotic. Lawyers made arguments for judges to evaluate, and professions were more able than either judges or government lawyers to comment and campaign on political issues, particularly those concerning the rule of law.[185]

Analysts agreed that the rule of law was, historically, established in fits and starts.[186] At the edges, the conception of rights for example, it adapted to context. Recent trends saw the authority of legal professions diminish under pressure from consumerism, the power of corporations increased, and the rule of law weakened by populism. The long-term impact of these changes and responses to them were unclear. The Law Society of England and Wales website membership page declared that it was 'The voice of solicitors, driving excellence and safeguarding the rule of law'.[187] But while legal professions could claim to be champions of the rule of law it was probably doubtful that educational, institutional, and procedural changes could replace professional identity and solidarity as underpinning their historically unique role.[188] The future of government, lawyers and the rule of law remain all to play for.

---

[183] MC Miller, *The High Priests of American Politics: The Role of Lawyers in American Political institutions* (Knoxville, University of Tennessee Press, 1995) 25.

[184] ibid 29.

[185] As in Pakistan in 2007, for example, when lawyers demonstrated on behalf of the deposed Chief Justice of the Supreme Court and against the military regime of General Pervez Musharaf (see A Boon, *Lawyers' Ethics and Professional Responsibility* (Oxford, Hart Publishing, 2016) 278–80; T Ginsburg, 'The politics of courts in democratization' in Heckman et al (n 162) 175, 186–88).

[186] T Carothers, 'Rule of Law Temptations' in Heckman et al (n 162) 17, 21.

[187] The Law Society, www.lawsociety.org.uk/membership/.

[188] A Dieng, 'Role of Judges and Lawyers in Defending the Rule of Law' (1997) 21(2) *Fordham International Law Journal* 550, 553.

Appendices

APPENDIX I: THE WORLD JUSTICE PROJECT RULE OF LAW INDEX

Factor 1 Constraints on Government Powers	1.1 Government powers are effectively limited by the legislature
	1.2 Government powers are effectively limited by the judiciary
	1.3 Government powers are effectively limited by independent auditing and review
	1.4 Government officials are sanctioned for misconduct
	1.5 Government powers are subject to nongovernmental checks
	1.6 Transition of power is subject to the law
Factor 2 Absence of Corruption	2.1 Government officials in the executive branch do not use public office for private gain
	2.2 Government officials in the judicial branch do not use public office for private gain
	2.3 Government officials in the police and military do not use public office for private gain
	2.4 Government officials in the legislative branch do not use public office for private gain
Factor 3 Open Government	3.1 Publicized laws and government data
	3.2 Right to information
	3.3 Civic participation
	3.4 Complaint mechanisms
Factor 4 Fundamental Rights	4.1 Equal treatment and absence of discrimination
	4.2 The right to life and security of the person is effectively guaranteed
	4.3. Due process of the law and rights of the accused
	4.4 Freedom of opinion and expression is effectively guaranteed
	4.5 Freedom of belief and religion is effectively guaranteed
	4.6 Freedom from arbitrary interference with privacy is effectively guaranteed
	4.7 Freedom of assembly and association is effectively guaranteed
	4.8 Fundamental labor rights are effectively guaranteed

(continued)

(Continued)

Factor 5 Order & Security	5.1 Crime is effectively controlled 5.2 Civil conflict is effectively limited 5.3 People do not resort to violence to redress personal grievances
Factor 6 Regulatory Enforcement	6.1 Government regulations are effectively enforced 6.2 Government regulations are applied and enforced without improper influence 6.3 Administrative proceedings are conducted without unreasonable delay 6.4 Due process is respected in administrative proceedings 6.5 The government does not expropriate without lawful process and adequate compensation
Factor 7 Civil Justice	7.1 People can access and afford civil justice 7.2 Civil justice is free of discrimination 7.3 Civil justice is free of corruption 7.4 Civil justice is free of improper government influence 7.5 Civil justice is not subject to unreasonable delay 7.6 Civil justice is effectively enforced 7.7 Alternative dispute resolution mechanisms are accessible, impartial, and effective
Factor 8 Criminal Justice	8.1 Criminal investigation system is effective 8.2 Criminal adjudication system is timely and effective 8.3 Correctional system is effective in reducing criminal behavior Criminal justice system is impartial 8.4 Criminal justice system is free of corruption 8.5 Criminal justice system is free of improper government influence 8.6 Due process of the law and rights of the accused

APPENDIX II: EDITED VERSION OF THE IBA TASKFORCE INDICATORS FOR INDEPENDENT LEGAL PROFESSIONS AND COMMON THREATS TO ACHIEVING INDICATOR

Indicator 1: Constitutional guarantees of judicial independence

A. No constitutional recognition of role of judiciary in preserving the rule of law

B. Controls on judicial independence

C. Protection of judiciary from criticism

Indicator 2: The freedom to associate through independent bar associations and organizations

A. Restrictions on rights of lawyers to join independent non-governmental organizations

B. Restrictions on the structure, aim and scope of permissible activities by non-governmental organizations

Indicator 3: Clear and transparent rules on admission to the Bar, disciplinary proceedings, and disbarment

A. Vague regulations on admission or disciplinary proceedings and disbarment.

B. Lack of publicly available information on the process of disbarment and disciplinary proceedings or disciplinary orders.

C. Arbitrary disbarment or targeted disciplinary proceedings.

Indicator 4: Protection of legal professional privilege/professional secrecy – the scope of protection, and procedural guarantees.

A. Legislation requiring lawyers to breach the principle of lawyer-client confidentiality

B. Criminal sanctions against lawyers who fail to disclose confidential client information

C. Existence of tipping-off prohibitions

Indicator 5: Effective independent regulation of the profession.

A. Regulatory framework in which regulators are predominantly or exclusively made up of government-appointed members

B. Regulatory framework is funded by the executive

C. Legislation reducing self-regulatory powers of legal profession

Indicator 6: Comprehensive legal education and professional training.

A. Lack of financial resources for education and training

B. Absence of adequate admission standards

C. Corruption in obtaining educational or professional qualifications or securing admission

Indicator 7: Freedom of choice in representation, including freedom from fear of prosecution in controversial or unpopular cases.

A. Violence, harassment and intimidation of lawyers representing unpopular clients

B. Legislative attempts to limit freedoms of expression and association

C. Arbitrary arrests and detention of lawyers

Indicator 8: Ability to uphold the Rule of Law in situations of heightened national security concerns.

A. Vague and imprecise anti-terrorism legislation which undermines basic human rights

B. Harassment and intimidation of lawyers during anti-terrorism investigations

C. Surveillance of private communications between lawyer and client or confiscation of private and confidential work product in the context of legal advice, representation, or court proceedings.

Indicator 9: Ability to respond to political/media/community pressure in times of war/terror/emergency

A. Negative political, societal or media propaganda in times of war, terror or emergency.

B. Frequent public attacks against the profession by prominent political figures.

C. Negative public opinion of the legal profession, and a general tendency by the public to associate lawyers with their clients, corruption, dishonesty and greed.

Indicator 10: Ability to adapt and react to business practices and quasi-legal practices without undermining exercise of independent judgment in the best interest of the client.

A. The rise of unregulated alternative ownership models, where ownership rests in the hands of non-lawyers or other unregulated professionals.

B. The proliferation of new categories of unregulated legal professionals providing legal services.

Bibliography

BOOKS, CHAPTERS, AND ACADEMIC JOURNAL ARTICLES

Abel, RL, 'Why Does the ABA Promulgate Ethical Rules? (1981) 59 *Texas Law Review* 639.
Abel, RL, 'The Decline of Professionalism?' (1986) 49(1) *Modern Law Review* 1.
Abel, RL, *The Legal Profession in England and Wales* (Oxford, Basil Blackwell, 1988).
Abel, RL, 'Transnational Legal Practice' (1993–95) 44 *Case Western Reserve Law Review* 737.
Abel, RL, 'The Politics of Professionalism: The Transformation of English Lawyers at the End of the Twentieth Century' (1999) 2(2) *Legal Ethics* 131.
Abel, RL, *English Lawyers Between Market and State: The Politics of Professionalism* (Oxford, Oxford University Press, 2003).
Abbott, A, *The System of Professions: An Essay on the Expert Division of Labour* (Chicago, University of Chicago Press, 1988).
Abrams, D and Fisher, D, *John Adams Under Fire: The Founding Father's Fight for Justice in the Boston Massacre Murder Trial* (Toronto, Hanover Square Press, 2020).
Abrams, D and Hogg, MA, 'Social identification, self-categorization and social influence' (1990) 1(1) *European Review of Social Psychology* 195.
Acemoglu, D and Robinson, JA, *Why Nations Fail: The Origins of Power, Prosperity, and Poverty* (UK, Crown Business, 2013).
Ackroyd, P, *A History of England Volume I: Foundation* (London, Macmillan, 2011).
Ackroyd, P, *A History of England Volume III: Civil War* (London, Pan, 2015).
Ackroyd, P, *The History of England Volume V: Dominion* (London, Macmillan, 2018).
Albrow, M, 'Legal Positivism and Bourgeois Materialism: Max Weber's View of the Sociology of Law' (1975) 2 *British Journal of Law and Society* 14.
Allan TRS, *Law Liberty and Justice: The Legal Foundations of British Constitutionalism* (Oxford, Oxford University Press, 1993).
Allen, G, *The Last Prime Minister: Being Honest About the UK Presidency* (London, House of Commons, 2003), (2002) 56(2) *Parliamentary Affairs* 359.
Andre, J, 'Role Morality as a Complex Instance of Ordinary Morality' (1991) 28(1) *American Philosophical Quarterly* 73.
Andrews, CR, *Standards of Conduct for Lawyers: An 800-Year Evolution* (2004) 57 SMU Law Review 1385.
Appleby, G, *The Role of the Solicitor-General: Negotiating Law Politics and the Interest* (Oxford, Hart Publishing, 2018).
Ariens, MS, 'Lost and Found: David Hoffman and the History of American Legal Ethics' (2014) 67 *Arkansas Law Review* 571.
Ariens, MS, 'The Agony of Modern Legal Ethics, 1970–1985' (2014) 5 *St. Mary's Journal of Legal Malpractice & Ethics* 134.
Arlidge, A and Judge, I, *Magna Carta Uncovered* (Oxford, Hart Publishing, 2014).
Aristotle, *The Politics* (Cambridge, Cambridge University Press, 1988).
Arthurs, HW, 'The Dead Parrot: Does Professional Self-Regulation Exhibit Vital Signs?' (1995) 33 *Alberta Law Review* 800.
Arthurs, HW, 'Lawyering in Canada in the 21st Century' (1996) *Windsor Yearbook of Access to Justice* 202.
Arthurs, HW, Weisman, R and Zemans, FH, 'The Canadian Legal Profession' (1986) 11(3) *American Bar Foundation Research Journal* 447.
Ashcraft, R and Goldsmith, MM, 'Locke, Revolution Principles, and the Formation of Whig Ideology' (1983) 26(4) *The Historical Journal* 773.
Ashworth, A, Young, R and Burton, M, *Criminal Justice* (Oxford, Oxford University Press, 2010).

Auburn, J, *Legal professional privilege: Law and Theory* (Oxford, Hart Publishing Ltd, 2001).
Auerbach, JS, 'The Legal Profession after Watergate' (1975–1976) 22 *Wayne Law Review* 1287.
Auerbach, JS, *Unequal Justice: Lawyers and Social Change in Modern America* (New York, Oxford University Press, 1976).
Aulakh, S and Kirkpatrick, I, 'New governance regulation and lawyers: When substantive compliance erodes legal professionalism' (2018) 5 *Journal of Professions and Organization* 167.
Baars, G, *The Corporation, Law and Capitalism* (Leiden, Boston, Brill Nijhoff, 2019).
Babington, T, *Critical and Historical Essays, Vol. 2* [1832]. Lord Bacon (July 1837) 280, https://oll.libertyfund.org/title/macaulay-critical-and-historical-essays-vol-2.
Bacon, F, *Essays, Civil and Moral XX Of Counsel The Harvard Classics, 1909–14.* www.bartleby.com/3/1/20.html.
Bagehot, W, *The English Constitution* (London, Chapman and Hall, 1867).
Baglione, L, 'Post-Soviet Russia at Twenty-Five: Understanding the Dynamics and Consequences of Its Authoritarianism' (2016) 48(4) *Polity* 580.
Bailyn, B, *The Ideological Origins of the American Revolution* (Cambridge, The Belknap Press of Harvard University Press, 1967).
Bakan, J, 'The Invisible Hand of Law: Private Regulation and the Rule of Law' (2015) 48 *Cornell International Law Journal* 279.
Baker, J, 'Law Reporting in England 1550–1650' (2017) 45(3) *International Journal of Legal Information* 209.
Baker, JH, 'Solicitors and the Law of Maintenance 1590-1640' (1973) 32 *Cambridge Law Journal* 56.
Baker, JH, *The Legal Profession and the Common Law: Historical Essays* (London and Ronceverte, The Hambledon Press, 1986).
Baker, JH, *An Introduction to English Legal History* (London, Butterworths, 2002).
Bale, T, van Kessel, S and Taggart, P, 'Thrown Around with Abandon? Popular Understandings of Populism as Conveyed by the Print Media: A UK case study' (2013) 46(2) *Acta Politica* 111.
Barendt, E, (1985) 34 *International and Comparative Law Quarterly* 413.
Barnhizer, D and Barnhizer, D, *Hypocrisy and Myth: The Hidden Order of the Rule of Law* (Lake Mary, Florida, Vanderplas Publishing 2009).
Barmes, L and Malleson, K, 'The Legal Profession as Gatekeeper to the Judiciary: Design Faults in Measures to Enhance Diversity' (2011) 74(2) *Modern Law Review* 245.
Barro, R, 'Democracy and the Rule of Law' in B de Mesquita and H Root (eds), *Governing for Prosperity* (New Haven, Yale University Press, 2000).
Bartlett, F and Haller, L, 'Australia: Legal Services Regulation in Australia – Innovative Co-regulation' in A Boon (ed), *International Perspectives on the Regulation of Lawyers and Legal Services* (Oxford, Hart Publishing, 2017) 161.
Barzilai, G and Nachmias, D, 'Governmental Lawyering in the Political Sphere: Advocating the Leviathan' (1998) 3(2) *Israel Studies* 30.
Bassett, DL, 'Defining the "Public" Profession' (2005) 36(3) *Rutgers Law Journal* 721.
Bayles, M, *Professional Ethics* (Belmont Ca, Wadsworth Publishing, 1981).
Beard, AS, 'From Hero to Villain: The Corresponding Evolutions of Model Ethical Codes and the Portrayal of Lawyers in Film' (2010) 55 *New York Law School Law Review* 961.
Beattie, JM, 'Scales of Justice: Defense Counsel and the English Criminal Trial in the Eighteenth and Nineteenth Centuries' (1991) 9(2) *Law and History Review* 221.
Beck, G, 'Immanuel Kant's Theory of Rights' (2006) 19(4) *Ratio Juris* 371.
Bennet, T, 'Privacy and Incrementalism' in A Koltay and P Wragg (eds), *Comparative Privacy and Defamation* (Cheltenham, Edward Elgar, 2020) 24.
Berghian, A-M, 'Fundamental Human Rights and Liberties: Concept and Classification' (2007) 10 *Annales Universitatis Apulensis Series Jurisprudentia* at para 38.
Berlin, I, 'Two Concepts of Liberty' in *Four Essays on Liberty* (London, Oxford University Press, 1969) 118.
Biddle, BJ, *Role Theory: Expectations, Identities and Behaviors* (New York and London, Academic Press, 1979).
Bilder, MS, 'The Lost Lawyers: Early American Legal Literates and Transatlantic Legal Culture' (1999) 11 *Yale Journal of Law and the Humanities* 47.

Binder, NV, 'Making Foreign Judgment law Great Again: The Aftermath of Chevron v. Donziger' (2018) 51 *Suffolk UL Rev* 33.
Bingham, T, 'The Rule of Law and the Sovereignty of Parliament?' (2008) 19(2) *King's Law Journal* 223.
Bingham, T, 'The Case of Liversidge v. Anderson: The Rule of Law Amid the Clash of Arms' (2009) 43(1) *The International Lawyer* 33.
Bingham, T, *The Rule of Law* (London, Penguin, 2011).
Blackstone, W, *Blackstone's Commentaries on the Laws of England* (1765-1770). The Online Library of Liberty, http://files.libertyfund.org/files/2140/Blackstone_1387-01_EBk_v6.0.pdf and https://avalon.law.yale.edu/subject_menus/blackstone.asp.
Bliss, J and Boutcher, SA, 'Rationalizing Pro Bono: Corporate Social Responsibility and The Reinvention Of Legal Professionalism In Elite American Law Firms' in SL Cummings, F De Sa E Silva and LA Trubek *Global pro Bono: Causes, Context and Contestation* (Cambridge, England, Cambridge University Press, 2022) 77.
Bogdanor, V, *The New British Constitution* (Oxford, Hart Publishing, 2009).
Böhmer, M, 'Argentina: The Long Transition of the Legal Profession' in RL Abel, O Hammerslev, U Schultz and H Sommerlad, *Lawyers in 21st-Century Societies, vol. 1: National Reports.* (Oxford, Hart Publishing, 2020).
Boon, A, 'Cause Lawyers and the Alternative Ethical Paradigm: Ideology and Transgression (2004) 7(2) *Legal Ethics* 250.
Boon, A, 'Professionalism under the Legal Services Act 2007' (2011) 17(3) *International Journal of the Legal Profession* 195.
Boon, A, *The Ethics and Conduct of Lawyers in England and Wales* (Oxford, Hart Publishing, 2014).
Boon, A, *Lawyers' Ethics and Professional Responsibility* (Hart, Oxford Publishing, 2015).
Boon, A, 'The legal professions' new handbooks: narratives, standards, and values' (2016) 19(2) *Legal Ethics* 207.
Boon, A, 'Understanding lawyer default in England and Wales: An analysis of insurance and complaints data' (2017) 24(2) *International Journal of the Legal Profession* 91.
Boon, A, 'The Regulation of Lawyers and Legal Services' in A Boon (ed), *International Perspectives on the Regulation of Lawyers and Legal Services* (Oxford, Hart Publishing, 2018) 1.
Boon, A, 'Cocktails of Logics: Reform of Legal Services Regulation in England and Wales' in A Boon (ed), *International Perspectives on the Regulation of Lawyers and Legal Services* (Oxford, Hart Publishing, 2018) 209.
Boon, A and Abbey, R, 'The Provision of Free Legal Services by Solicitors: A Review of the Report of the Law Society's Pro Bono Working Party' (1995) 2(3) *International Journal of the Legal Profession* 261.
Boon, A and Flood, J, 'Trials of Strength: The Reconfiguration of Litigation as a Contested Terrain' (1999) 33 *Law and Society Review* 595.
Boon, A and Flood, J 'The Globalisation of Professional Ethics?: The Significance of Lawyers' International Codes of Conduct' (1999) 2(1) *Legal Ethics* 29.
Boon, A and Nash, S, 'Special Advocacy: Political Expediency and Legal Roles in Modern Judicial Systems' (2006) 9 *Legal Ethics* 101.
Boon, A and Whyte, A, '"Charity and Beating Begins at Home" The Aetiology of the New Culture of Pro Bono Publico' (1999) 2(2) *Legal Ethics* 169.
Boon, A and Whyte, A, 'Lawyer Disciplinary Processes: An Empirical Study of Solicitors' Misconduct Cases in England and Wales in 2015' (2019) 39(3) *Legal Studies* 455.
Boon, A and Whyte, A, 'An Analysis of Solicitors' Disciplinary Processes in England and Wales from 1994 to 2015' (2021) 28(2) *International Journal of the Legal Profession* 129.
Boon, A and Whyte, A, 'An Explosion of Legal Philanthropy? The Transformation of Pro Bono Legal Services in England and Wales' in SL Cummings, F De Sa E Silva and LA Trubek, *Global pro bono: Causes, Contexts, and Contestation* (Cambridge, Cambridge University Press, 2022).
Boucher, D and Kelly, P, 'The Social Contract and Its Critics' in D Boucher and P Kelly (eds), *The Social Contract from Hobbes to Rawls* (London and New York, Routledge, 1994).
Boulton, WW, *A Guide To Conduct And Etiquette At The Bar Of England And Wales* (London, Butterworths, 1953).
Bourdieu, P, *Outline of a Theory of Practice* (Cambridge, Cambridge University Press, 1977).

Boutrous TJ, 'The lessons from the Chevron litigation: The defense perspective' (2019) 1(2) *Stanford Journal of Complex Litigation* 219.
Boutcher, SA, 'Lawyering for Social Change: Pro Bono Publico, Cause Lawyering, and the Social Movement Society' (2013) 18 *Mobilization: An International Quarterly* 179.
Bowen, HR, *Social Responsibilities of the Businessman* (New York, Harper & Row, 1953).
Bower, PR and Stern, TE, 'Conflict of Interest: The Absolute Ban on Lawyer-Client Sexual Relationships Is Not Absolutely Necessary' (2003) 16 *Georgetown Journal of Legal Ethics* 535.
Boyer, AD, *Sir Edward Coke and the Elizabethan Age* (Stanford, Stanford University Press, 2003).
Bozóki, A, 'The Illusion of Inclusion: Configurations of Populism in Hungary' in M Kopecek and P Wcislik (eds), *Thinking Through Transition: Liberal Democracy, Authoritarian Pasts, and Intellectual History in East Central Europe after 1989* (Budapest, New York, Central European University Press, 2015) 275.
Braddick, MJ, *God's Fury, England's Fire: A New History of the English Civil Wars* (London, Penguin, 2009).
Braddick, MJ, *The Common Freedom of the People: John Lilburne and the English Revolution* (Oxford, Oxford University Press, 2018).
Bradley, AW and Ewing, KD, *Constitutional and Administrative Law: Volume 1* (London, Longman, 2002) 96.
Brincat, SK, 'Death to Tyrants': The Political Philosophy of Tyrannicide – Part I' (2008) 4(2) *Journal of International Political Theory* 212.
Brooke, H, 'The History of Judicial Independence in England and Wales' (2015) *European Human Rights Law Review* 446.
Brooks, CW, 'Litigants and Attorneys in the King's Bench and Common Pleas' in JH Baker (ed), *Legal Records And The Historian* (London, Royal Historical Society, 1978) 41, 53.
Brooks, CW, *Pettyfoggers and Vipers of the Commonwealth: The 'Lower Branch' of the Legal Profession in Early Modern England* (Cambridge, Cambridge University Press, 1986).
Brougham, H, *The Life And Times Of Henry Lord Brougham, Written By Himself* (1871) (Cambridge, Cambridge University Press, 2015).
Brown, D, *Bury My Heart at Wounded Knee: An Indian History of the American West* (London, Vintage Books, 1991).
Brown, RC, 'The Law of England During the Period of The Commonwealth' (1931) 6(6) *Indiana Law Journal* 359.
Brown, W, 'Neo-liberalism and the End of Liberal Democracy' (2003) 7(1) *Theory and Event* 15.
Buckingham, D, Disciplining Lawyers in New Zealand: Re-Pinning the Badge of Professionalism' (2012) 15 *Legal Ethics* 57.
Burrage, M, 'Mrs Thatcher Against the 'Little Republics': Ideology, Precedents and Reactions' in TC Halliday and L Karpik (eds), *Lawyers and the Rise of Western Political Liberalism* (Oxford, Clarendon Press, 1997) 137.
Burrage, M, *Revolution and the Making of the Contemporary Legal Profession: England France and the United States* (Oxford, Oxford University Press, 2006).
Cahill O'Callaghan, R, *Values in the Supreme court: Decisions, Division and Diversity* (Oxford, Hart Publishing, 2020).
Campbell, J, *The Lives of the Lord Chancellors and Keepers of the Great Seal of England: From the Earliest Times Till the Reign of George IV* Volume I (Philadelphia, Lea and Blanchard, 1847).
Caplow, T, *The Sociology of Work* (Minneapolis, University of Minnesota Press, 1954).
Carbado, DW, 'Black Rights, Gay Rights, Civil Rights' (2000) 47 *UCLA L Rev* 1467.
Carothers, T, 'Rule of law temptations' in JJ Heckman, RL Nelson and L Cabatingan (eds), *Global Perspectives on the Rule of Law* (London and NY, Routledge, 2010) 17.
Carrington, PD, 'Hail! Langdell!' (1995) 20 *Law and Social Inquiry* 691.
Carroll, AB, 'The Pyramid of Corporate Social Responsibility: Toward the Moral Management of Organizational Stakeholders' (1991) *Business Horizons* 5.
Carroll, AB, 'A History of Corporate Social Responsibility: Concepts and Practices' in A Crane, A McWilliams, D Matten, J Moon and DS Siegel, *The Oxford Handbook of Social Responsibility* (Oxford, Oxford University Press, 2009) 19.
Carr-Saunders, AM and Wilson, PH, *The Professions* (Oxford, Clarendon Press, 1933).
Casper, G, 'An Essay in Separation of Powers: Some Early Versions and Practices' (1989) *William and Mary Law Review* 211.

Chan, KW, 'The Emergence of Large Law Firms in Japan: Impact on Legal Professional Ethics' (2008) 11 *Legal Ethics* 154.
Christenson, GA, 'World Civil Society and the International Rule of Law' (1997) 19 *Human Rights Quarterly* 724.
Chroust, A-H, *The Rise Of The Legal Profession In America* (Norman, University of Oklahoma Press, 1965).
Cladis, MS, *A Communitarian Defence of Liberalism: Emile Durkheim and Contemporary Social Theory* (Stanford, Stanford University Press, 1992).
Clarke, K, 'The Legacy of Watergate for Legal Ethics Instruction' (1999–2000) 51 *Hastings Law Journal* 673.
Cocks, R, *Foundations of the Modern Bar* (London, Sweet and Maxwell, 1983).
Coe, MV and Morse, LW, 'Chronology of the Development of the David Dudley Field Code' (1942) 27 *Cornell Law Review* 238.
Cole, GDH, *The Life of William Cobbett* (London, Routledge, 1924).
Collins, D, 'The Role of Solicitor General in Contemporary New Zealand' in P Keyser and G Appleby (eds), *Public Sentinels: A Comparative Study of Australian Solicitors-General* (London, Taylor and Francis, 2016) 171.
Cook, BJ, *The Fourth Branch: Reconstructing the Administrative State for the Commercial Republic* (University Press of Kansas, 2021).
Cotterrell, R, *Law's Community: Legal Theory in Sociological Perspective*, (Oxford, Clarendon Press, 1995) 156.
Cummings, SL, 'The Politics of Pro Bono' (2004) 52(1) *UCLA Law Review* 1.
Currie, DP, 'Positive and Negative Constitutional Rights' (1986) 53 *U Chi L Rev* 864.
Cust, R, 'News and Politics in Early Seventeenth-Century England' (1986) 112(1) *Past & Present* 60.
Dare, T, 'Lawyers, Ethics and To Kill a Mockingbird' (2001) 25(1) *Philosophy and Literature* 127.
Dare, T, *The Counsel of Rogues? A Defence of the Standard Conception of the Lawyer's Role* (Farnham, Ashgate Publishing Ltd, 2009).
Dauer, EA and Leff, AA, 'Correspondence: The Lawyer as Friend' (1976–77) 86 *Yale Law Journal* 574.
Davies, S, 'Atticus Finch Alive or dead? A Socio-legal Question' (2019) 36(1) *Law in Context* 36.
Davis, MF, *Brutal Need: Lawyers and the Welfare Rights Movement, 1960–1973* (New Haven, Yale University Press, 1993) 16.
De Groot-Van Leeuwen, L and De Groot, WT, 'Studying Codes of Conduct: A descriptive framework for Comparative Research' (1998) 1(2) *Legal Ethics* 155.
DeLong, M, 'To Save a House Divided: Lincoln's Suspension of Habeas Corpus' (1996) *Senior Research Projects* 118, https://knowledge.e.southern.edu/senior_research/118/.
Denti, V, 'Public Lawyers, Political Trials and the Neutrality of the Legal Profession' (1981) 1 *Israel Law Review* 20.
de Sousa Santos, B, *Toward a New Legal Common Sense. Law, Globalization, and Emancipation* (London, Butterworths, 2002).
de Sousa Santos, B, 'Globalizations' (2006) 23 *Theory Culture Society* 393.
de Tocqueville, A, *Democracy in America* (trans H Reeve) (Penn State Electronic Classics Serie, 1831) 266, http://seas3.elte.hu/coursematerial/LojkoMiklos/Alexis-de-Tocqueville-Democracy-in-America.pdf.
Devlin, P, *Trial by Jury* (Stevens, London, 1956).
Devlin, P, *The Judge* (Oxford, Oxford University Press, 1979).
Dezalay, Y and Garth, BG, 'Introduction: Lawyers, law and society' in Y Dezalay and BG Garth (eds), *Lawyers and the Rule of Law in an Era of Globalization* (Abingdon, Routledge, 2011) 4.
Dicey, AV, *Introduction to the study of law of the constitution* (Boston, Adamant Media Corporation, 2005).
Diehm, JW, 'The Government Duty to Seek Justice in Civil Cases' (2000) 9 *Widener Journal of Public Law* 289.
Dieng, A, 'The Role of Judges and Lawyers in Defending the Rule of Law' (1997) 21(2) *Fordham International Law Journal* 550.
Dingwall, R and Lewis, P (eds), *The Sociology of the Professions: Lawyers, Doctors and Others* (London, Macmillan, 1983).
Dinovitzer, R and Dawe, M, 'Canada: Continuity and Change in a Modern Legal Profession' in R Abel, O Hammerslev, H Sommerlad and U Schultz (eds), *Lawyers in 21st-Century Societies* (Oxford, Hart Publishing, 2020) 65, 80.

Dittmar, JE, 'Information technology and economic change: the impact of the printing press' (2011) 126(3) *The Quarterly Journal of Economics* 1133.
Dolding, L and Mullender, R, 'Tort Law, Incrementalism, and the House of Lords' (1996) 47(1) *Northern Ireland Legal Quarterly* 12.
Dotan, Y, *Lawyering for the Rule of Law: Government Power and the Rise of Judicial Power in Israel* (Cambridge, Cambridge University Press, 2014).
Drewry, G, 'The GCHQ Case – A Failure of Government Communications' (1985) 38(4) *Parliamentary Affairs* 371.
Duke, W, 'Lawyers in Literature' (1929) *Juridical Review* 41.
Duman, D, 'The English Bar in the Georgian Era' in WR Prest (ed), *Lawyers in Early Modern Europe and America* (London, Croom Helm, 1981) 86.
Durkheim, E, *The Division of Labour in Society* (trans G Simpson) (New York, Free Press, 1893/1933).
Durkheim, E, *Professional Ethics and Civic Morals* (trans C Brookfield) (London, NY, Routledge, 1992).
Dworkin, R, 'Political judges and the rule of law' (1978) 64 *Proceedings of the British Academy* 259.
Eberle, EJ, 'The Methodology of Comparative Law' (2011) 16(1) *Roger Williams University Law Review* 51.
Economides, K and O'Leary M, 'The Moral of the Story: Toward and Understanding of Ethics in Organisations and Legal Practice' (2009) 10 *Legal Ethics* 5.
Edwards, JLJ, *The Attorney General, Politics and the Public Interest* (London, Sweet and Maxwell,1984).
Ekins, R, 'Judicial Supremacy and the Rule of Law' (2003) 119 *Law Quarterly Review* 127.
Elliott, M, 'United Kingdom: Parliamentary sovereignty under pressure' (2004) 2(1) *International Journal of Constitutional Law* 545.
Ellis, W (trans), *Aristotle's Politics: A Treatise On Government* (London, George Routledge and Sons, 1895).
Eltis, D, *Economic Growth and the Ending of the Transatlantic Slave Trade* (New York, Oxford University Press, 1987).
Emlyn, S, *A complete collection of state-trials and proceedings for high-treason: and other crimes and misdemeanors; from the reign of King Richard II. to the reign of King George II* (London, John Walthoe, 1730).
Epps, D, 'The Consequences of Error in Criminal Justice' (2015) 128 *Harvard Law Review* 1065.
Fancourt, D, Steptoe, A and Wright, L, 'The Cummings effect: Politics, trust and behaviours during the COVID-19 pandemic' (*The Lancet*, 15 August 2020) www.thelancet.com/pdfs/journals/lancet/PIIS0140-6736(20)31690-1.pdf.
Faulconbridge, J, Beaverstock, J, Muzio, D and Taylor, PJ, 'Global law Firms: Globalization and Organizational Spaces of Cross-Border Legal Work' (2008) 28 *Northwestern Journal of International Law and Business* 455.
Faulkner, R, 'Faith of Our Modern Fathers: Bacon's Progressive Hope and Locke's Liberal Christianity' in DA Gish and DP Klinghard (eds), *Resistance to Tyrants, Obedience to God: Reason, Religion and Republicanism, at America's Founding* (Lanham US, Lexington Books, 2013) 38.
Finn, JE and Finn, JD, *Constitutions in crisis: political violence and the rule of law* (Oxford, Oxford University Press on Demand, 1991).
Finn, J, 'A Novel Institution: The First Years of King's Counsel in New Zealand 1907–1915' (1995) *New Zealand Law Journal* 95.
Firth, CH (ed), *Memoirs of Edmond Ludlow Lieutenant-General of the Horse in the Army of the Commonwealth of England, 1625–1672* (Oxford, Clarendon Press, 1894).
Fitzpatrick, P, *The Mythology of Modern Law* (London, Routledge 1992).
Flaus, WR, 'Discipline within the New Zealand Legal Profession' (1971) 6 *Victoria University of Wellington Law Review* 337.
Flood, J, 'Megalaw in the UK: Professionalism or Corporatism? A Preliminary Report' (1989) 64 *Indiana Law Journal* 569.
Flood, J, 'Lawyers as Sanctifiers: The Role of Elite Law Firms in International Business Transactions' (2007) 14(1) *Indiana Journal of Global Legal Studies* 35.
Fosdyke, S, 'Reviewed Work: *A Democracy of Distinction: Aristotle and the Work of Politics* by Jill Frank' (2006) 101(2) *Classical Philology* 171.
Foucault, M, *Discipline and Punish: The Birth of the Prison*, 2nd edn (trans A Sheridan) (New York, Random House, 1995).

Foxley, R, *The Levellers: Radical Political Thought in the English Revolution* (Manchester, Manchester University Press, 2013).
Frank, J, *A Democracy of Distinction: Aristotle and the Work of Politics* (Chicago, Chicago University Press, 2005).
Frank, J, 'Aristotle on Constitutionalism and the Rule of Law' (2007) 8(1) *Theoretical Inquiries in Law* 37.
Frankopan, P, *The Silk Roads: A New History of the World* (London, Bloomsbury, 2015).
Freedman, MH, 'Professional Responsibility of the Criminal Defense Lawyer: The Three Hardest Questions' (1966) 64 *Michigan Law Review* 1469.
Freedman, MH, 'Atticus Finch – Right and Wrong' (1994) 45 *Alabama Law Review* 473.
Freedman, MH, 'Henry Lord Brougham And Zeal' (2006) 34(4) *Hofstra Law Review* 1319.
Freedman, MH, 'Henry Lord Brougham – Advocating At The Edge for Human Rights' (2007) 36 *Hofstra Law Review* 311.
Freedman, MH, 'Henry Lord Brougham & Resolute Lawyering' (2010–11) 37 *The Advocates' Quarterly* 403.
Freedman, MH, 'Are There Public Interest Limits on Lawyers' Advocacy' (1977) *The Journal of the Legal Profession* 47.
Fried, C, 'The Lawyer as Friend: The Moral Foundations of the Lawyer-Client Relation' (1976) 85 *Yale Law Journal* 1060.
Friedman, L, 'Lawyers in Cross-Cultural Perspective' in RL Abel and PSC Lewis (eds), *Lawyers in Society: Volume 3: Comparative Theories* (Berkeley, University of California Press, 1989).
Friedman, M, *Capitalism and Freedom* (Chicago, University of Chicago Press, 1962).
Freidson, E, *Profession of Medicine: A Study of the Sociology of Applied Knowledge* (New York, Harper and Row, 1970).
Freidson, E, *The Third Logic* (Oxford, Blackwell Publishers, 2001).
Fukuyama, F, *The End of History and the Last Man* (New York, Free Press, 1992).
Fukuyama F, 'Women and the Evolution of World Politics' (1998) 77(5) *Foreign Affairs* 24.
Fukuyama, F, *Origins of Political Order: From Prehuman Times to The French Revolution* (New York, Farrar, Straus, and Giroux, 2011).
Fuller, LL, 'Positivism and Fidelity to Law – A Reply to Professor Hart' (1958) 71(4) *Harvard Law Review* 630.
Fuller, LL, *The Morality of Law* (New Haven, Yale University Press 1969).
Gellner, E, *Conditions of Liberty: Civil Society and Its Rivals* (Toronto, Hamish Hamilton/Penguin, 1994).
Gibson, JL and Caldeira, GA, 'Has legal realism damaged the legitimacy of the U.S. Supreme Court?' 45 *Law & Society Review* 195.
Gidron, N and Bonikowski, B, 'Varieties of Populism: literature review and research agenda' (Cambridge MA, Wetherhead Centre for International Affairs, Harvard University, 2013).
Ginsburg, T, 'The Politics of Courts in Democratisation' in JJ Heckman, RL Nelson and L Cabatingan (eds), *Global Perspectives on the Rule of Law* (London and New York, Routledge, 2010) 175.
Gippini-Fournier, E, 'Legal Professional Privilege in Competition Proceedings before the European Commission: Beyond the Cursory Glance' (2005) 28 *Fordham International Law Journal* 967.
Gladden, E, *Civil Services in the United Kingdom 1855–1970* (London, Frank Cass, 1967).
Goode, WJ, 'Community within a Community: The Professions' (1957) 22 *American Sociological Review* 194.
Goodrich, P, 'Law-induced Anxiety: Legists, Anti-Lawyers, and the Boredom of Legality' (2000) 9(1) *Social and Legal Studies* 143.
Gordon, RW, 'The Case For (and Against) Harvard' (1995) 93 *Michigan Law Review* 1231.
Gordon, RW, 'A Collective Failure of Nerve: The Bar's Response to Kay Scholer' (1998) 23 *Law and Social Inquiry* 315.
Gordon, RW, 'The Role of Lawyers in Producing the Rule of Law: Some Theoretical Reflections' (2010) 11 *Theoretical Inquiries in Law* 441.
Gowder, P, *The Rule of Law in the Real World* (Cambridge, Cambridge University Press, 2016).
Gower, LCB and Price, L, 'The Profession and Practice of the Law in England and America' (1957) 20(4) *The Modern Law Review* 317.
Graves, MAR, *Elizabethan Parliaments 1559–1661*, 2nd edn (London, NY, Routledge, 1996).
Gray, J, *False Dawn: The Delusions of Global Capitalism* (London, Granta Publications, 2009).

Green, BA, 'Must Government Lawyers "Seek Justice" in Civil Litigation?' (2000) 9 *Widener Journal of Public Law* 235.
Green, BA, 'Lawyers' Professional Independence: Overrated or Undervalued?' (2013) 46 *Akron Law Review* 599.
Greenwood, E, 'Attributes of a Profession' (1957) 2(3) *Social Work* 44.
Greve, MS and Parrish, AC, 'Administrative Law without Congress' (2015) 22 *George Mason Law Review* 501.
Griffiths, CC, 'The Prisoners' Counsel Act 1836: Doctrine, Advocacy and the Criminal Trial' (2014) 4(2) *Law, Crime and History* 28, 40.
Habermas, J, *Between Facts and Norms* (trans W Rehg) (Oxford, Polity Press/Blackwell, 1996).
Hall, MR, 'Guilty but Civilly Disobedient: Reconciling Civil Disobedience and the Rule of Law' (2007) 28(5) *Cardozo Law Review* 2083.
Halliday, TC and Karpik, L, 'Politics Matter: A Comparative Theory of Lawyers in the Making of Political Liberalism' in TC Halliday and L Karpik (eds), *Lawyers and the Rise of Western Political Liberalism* (Oxford, Clarendon Press, 1997) 15.
Hallpike, CR, *The Principles of Social Evolution* (Oxford, Clarendon Press, 1986).
Hamer, D, 'Probabilistic Standards of Proof, Their Complements and The Errors That Are Expected to Flow from Them' (2004) *University of New England Law Journal* 3.
Hammerslev, O, 'Denmark, Sweden and Norway: Liberalisation, Differentiation and the Emergence of a Legal Services Market' in R Abel, O Hammerslev, U Schultz and H Sommerlad (eds), *Lawyers in 21st-Century Societies, vol. 1: National Reports* (Oxford, Hart Publishing, 2020) 175.
Handler, JF, Hollingsworth, EJ and Erlanger, HS, *Lawyers and the pursuit of legal rights* (New York, Academic Press, 1978).
Harari, YN, *Sapiens: A Brief History of Humankind'* (Israel, Dvir Publishing House Ltd, 2011).
Harris, R, 'Law, finance and the first corporations' in JJ Heckman, RL Nelson and L Cabatingan (eds), *Global Perspectives on the Rule of Law* (London and New York, Routledge, 2010) 145.
Hart, HLA, 'Positivism and the Separation of Law and Morals' (1958) 71(4) *Harvard Law Review* 593.
Hart, HLA, 'Bentham and the Demystification of the Law' (1973) 36(1) *The Modern Law Review* 2.
Hart, HLA, *The Concept Of Law* (Oxford, Clarendon Press, 1994).
Hayek, FA, *The Political Ideal of the Rule of Law* (Cairo, National Bank of Egypt, 1955).
Hazard, GC, 'The Future of Legal Ethics' (1991)100 *Yale Law Journal* 1239.
Hazard, GC and Dondi, A, *Legal Ethics: A Comparative Study* (Stanford, Stanford University Press, 2004).
Heinz, JP and Laumann, EO, *Chicago Lawyers: Social Structure of the Bar* (New York, Chicago, Russell Sage Foundation, 1982).
Heinz, JP, Laumann, EO, Nelson, RL and Michelson, E, 'The Changing Character of Lawyers' Work: Chicago in 1975 and 1995' (1998) 32(4) *Law & Society Review* 751.
Henderson, E, 'Bigger fish to fry: Should the reform of cross-examination be expanded beyond vulnerable witnesses?' (2015) 19(2) *The International Journal of Evidence & Proof* 83.
Heuston, RFV and Goodhart, A, *The Lives of the Lord Chancellors: 1940–1970* (Oxford, Clarendon Press, 1987).
Hewart, G, *The New Despotism* (London, Ernest Benn Limited, 1929).
Hilbery, M, *Duty and Art in Advocacy* (London, Stevens and Sons Ltd, 1946).
Hill, C, *The Century of Revolution, 1603–1714* (London and NY, Routledge, 1961).
Hobbes, T, *Leviathan or the Matter, Forme and Power of a Common-wealth Ecclesiastical and Civill*, www.gutenberg.org/files/3207/3207-h/3207-h.htm#link2H_4_0306.
Hodgson GM, '1688 and all that: property rights the glorious revolution and the rise of British capitalism' (2017) 13(1) *Journal of Institutional Economics* 79.
Hoeflich, M, 'Legal Ethics in the Nineteenth Century: The "Other Tradition"' (1998) 47 *University of Kansas Law Review* 793.
Hoffman, D, *Course of Legal Study: Addressed to Students And The Profession Generally* (Baltimore, Joseph Neal, 1836).
Hoffman, J and Small, ML, 'On Learning of a Corporate Client's Fraud-The Lawyer's Dilemma' (1978) 33 *Business Law* 1389.
Holdsworth, WS, *A History of English Law* Vol VI (Methuen, 1924) (1937 reprint).
Holmes, S, *Passions and Constraint: On the Theory of Liberal Democracy* (Chicago, University of Chicago Press, 1995).

Holmes, V and Rice, S, 'Our common future: The Imperative for a Contextual Ethics in a Connected World' in R Mortensen, F Bartlett and K Tranter, *Alternative Perspectives on Lawyers and Legal Ethics: Reimagining the Profession* (London and New York, Routledge, 2011) 56.
Horton, S, 'The Public Service Ethos in the British Civil Service: An Historical Institutional Analysis' (2006) 21(1) *Public Policy and Administration* 32.
Hostettler, J, *Sir Edward Coke: A Force for Freedom* (Chichester, Barry Rose Law Publishers, 1997).
Hostettler, J *Thomas Erskine and Trial by Jury* (Hook, Hants, Waterside Press Ltd, 2010).
Houle, CO, *Continuing Learning in the Professions* (San Francisco and London, Jossey-Bass, 1980).
Huguenard, AH, 'Dr. Johnson on the Law and Lawyers' (1933) 8 *Notre Dame Law Review* 195.
Hutchinson, AC, 'Taking it Personally: Legal Ethics and Client Selection' (1998) 1(2) *Legal Ethics* 168.
Hutchinson, AC, *Legal Ethics and Professional Responsibility* (Toronto, Irwin Law, 1999).
Hutchinson, AC, *Fighting Fair: Legal Ethics for an Adversarial Age* (Cambridge, Cambridge University Press, 2015).
Ipp, DA, 'Lawyers' Duties to the Court' (1998) 114 *Law Quarterly Review* 63.
Israel, JI, *Radical Enlightenment: Philosophy and the Making of Modernity, 1650–1750* (Oxford, England, Oxford University Press, 2001).
Johnson, TJ, *Professions & Power*, (London, MacMillan, 1972).
Jones, E, 'The Office of Attorney-General' (1969) 27 *Cambridge Law Journal* 43.
Jordan, D and Walsh, M, *The King's Revenge: Charles II and the Greatest Manhunt in British History* (London, Little, Brown Book Group, 2013).
Jowell, J, 'Judicial Deference: servility, civility or institutional capacity?' (2003) *Public Law* 592.
Kadish, S and Kadish, M, *Discretion to Disobey* (Stanford, Stanford University Press, 1973) 31.
Kanetake, M, 'The Interfaces Between the National and International Rule of Law: A Framework Paper' in M Kanetake and N Nollkaemper (eds), *The Rule of Law at the National and International Levels* (Oxford, Hart Publishing, 2016) 11.
Karekwaivanane, GH, 'Zimbabwe: Legal Practitioners, Politics and Transformation since 1980' in R Abel, O Hammerslev, U Schultz and H Sommerlad (eds), *Lawyers in 21st-Century Societies, vol. 1: National Reports* (Oxford, Hart Publishing, 2020) 547.
Keane, A, 'Cross-Examination of Vulnerable Witnesses – Towards a Blueprint for Re-Professionalisation' (2012) 16(2) *The International Journal of Evidence & Proof* 175.
Keith, LC, 'The United States Supreme Court and Judicial Review of Congress, 1803–2001' (2007) 90:4 *Judicature* 166.
Kercher, B, 'A Convict Conservative: George Crossley and the English Legal Tradition' (1999) 16 *Law in Context: A Socio-Legal Journal* 17.
Kerridge, R and Davies, G, 'Reform of the Legal Profession: An Alternative "Way Ahead"' (1999) 62(6) *Modern Law Review* 807.
Kershaw, D and Moorhead, R, 'Consequential Responsibility for Client Wrongs: Lehman Brothers and the Regulation of the Legal Profession' (2013) 76 *Modern Law Review* 26.
Keynes, JM, *General Theory of Employment, Interest and Money* (London, Palgrave Macmillan, 1936).
Khaitan, T, 'Killing a Constitution with a Thousand Cuts: Executive Aggrandizement and Party-state Fusion in India' (2020) 14(1) *Law & Ethics of Human Rights* 49.
King, A and Allen, N, '"Off With Their Heads": British Prime Ministers and the Power to Dismiss' (2010) 40(2) *British Journal of Political Science* 249.
Kinghan, J, *Lawyers, Networks and Progressive Social Change: Lawyers Changing Lives* (Oxford, Hart Publishing, 2021) 17.
Knight, FH, 'Ethics and the Economic Interpretation' (1922) 36 *The Quarterly Journal of Economics* 454.
Koselleck, R, *Critique and Crisis: Enlightenment and the Pathogenesis of Modern Society* (Oxford, Berg, 1988).
Kramer, VH, 'Client's Frauds and Their Lawyers' Obligations: A Study in Professional Irresponsibility' (1979) 67 *Georgetown Law Journal* 991.
Kronman, A, *The Lost Lawyer: Failing Ideals of the Legal Profession* (Cambridge, Massachusetts, The Belknap Press of Harvard University Press, 1994).
Krygier, M, 'The Rule of Law: Pasts, Presents and Two Possible Futures' (2016) 12 *Annual Review of Law and Social Science* 199.
Kuran, T, 'The rule of law in Islamic thought and practice: a historical perspective' in JJ Heckman, RL Nelson and L Cabatingan (eds), *Global Perspectives on the Rule of Law* (London and New York, Routledge, 2010) 71.

Ladd, J, 'Legalism and Medical Ethics' in A Flores (ed), *Professional Ideals* (Belmont CA, Wadsworth Publishing Co Inc, 1988).
Landsman, S, 'A brief survey on the development of the adversary system' (1983) 44(3) *Ohio State Law Journal* 713.
Landsman, S, 'The Rise of the Contentious Spirit: Adversary Procedure in Eighteenth-Century England' (1990) 75(3) *Cornell Law Review* 498.
Langbein, JH, 'The Criminal Trial Before the Lawyers' (1978) 45 *Chicago Law Review* 263.
Langbein, JH, 'Shaping the Eighteenth-Century Criminal Trial: A View from the Ryder Sources' (1983) 50 *University of Chicago Law Review* 1.
Langbein, JH, *The Origins of Adversary Criminal Trial* (Oxford, 2003).
Langevoort, DC, 'What Was Kaye Scholer Thinking?' (1998) 23 *Law and Social Inquiry* 297.
Larson, MS, *The Rise of Professionalism: A Sociological Analysis* (Berkeley CA, University of California Press, 1977).
Laslett, P (ed), 'Introduction' *Locke: Two Treatises of Government* (Cambridge, Cambridge University Press, 1960) 34.
Lauterpacht, H, *An International Bill of the Rights of Man* (New York, Columbia University Press, 1945).
Law, JM and Wood, RJ, 'A History of the Law Faculty' (1996) 35 *Alberta Law Review* 1
Laws, J, 'The Rule of Law Today' in J Jowell and D Oliver (eds), *The Changing Constitution*, 5th edn (Oxford, Oxford University Press, 2000).
Laws, J, 'The Rule of Law: The Presumption of Liberty and Justice' (2017) 22(4) *Judicial Review* 365.
Lawson, G, *An Examination of the Political Part of Mr Hobbs in his Leviathan* (London, 1657).
Lederman, W, 'The Independence of the Judiciary' (1956) 34 *Canadian Bar Review* 769.
Lemke, T, 'The "Birth of Bio-Politics": Michel Foucault's Lecture at the Collège de France on Neo-Liberal Governmentality' (2001) 30(2) *Economy & Society* 190.
Lemmings, D, 'Ritual and the Law in Early Modern England' in S Corcoran (ed), *Law and History in Australia* (Adelaide, Adelaide Law Review, 1991) 3.
Lemmings, D, 'Criminal trial procedure in eighteenth-century England: The impact of lawyers' (2005) 26(1) *Journal of Legal History* 73.
Levi, M and Epperly, B, 'Principled Principals in the Founding Moments of the Rule of Law' in JJ Heckman, RL Nelson and L Cabatingan (eds), *Global Perspectives on the Rule of Law* (London and New York, Routledge, 2010) 192.
Levinson, S, 'Popular Sovereignty and the United States Constitution: Tensions in the Ackermanian Program' (2014) 123 *Yale Law Journal* 2644.
Lindell GJ, 'Why is Australia's Constitution Binding? – The Reasons in 1900 and Now, and the Effect of Independence' (1986) 16(1) *Federal Law Review* 29.
Lishlansky, MA, *Parliamentary Selection: Social and Political Choice in Early Modern England* (Cambridge, Cambridge University Press, 1986).
Locke, J, *Two Treatises of Government In the Former, The False Principles, and Foundation of Sir Robert Filmer, and His Followers, Are Detected and Overthrown. The Latter Is an Essay Concerning The True Original, Extent, and End of Civil Government* (London, Awnsham Churchill, 1690) and *Second Treatise of Government* (Indianapolis, Hackett, 1980).
Locke, J, *An Essay Concerning Human Understanding* (London, 1690) b10, bk. IV, ch. XV, § 5.
Loesch, MC, 'Motive Testimony and a Civil Disobedience Justification' (1991) 5 *Notre Dame Journal of Law, Ethics & Public Policy* 1069.
Lounsbury, RR, 'Lawyers in the Constitutional Convention' (1927) 13 *ABA Journal* 720.
Loo, T and Strange, C, *Making Good: Law and Moral Regulation in Canada* (Toronto, University of Toronto Press, 1997).
Loughrey, J, 'Accountability and the Regulation of the Large Law Firm Lawyer' (2014) 77(5) *Modern Law Review* 732.
Lovat-Fraser, JA, *Erskine.* (Cambridge, Cambridge University Press, 1932).
Lovell, GI, 'The Myth of the Myth of Rights' (2012) 59 *Studies in Law, Politics and Society* 1.
Luban, D, 'The Adversary System Excuse' in D Luban (ed), *The Good Lawyer* (Totowa: Rowman and Allanheld, 1984) 83.
Luban, D, *Lawyers and Justice: An Ethical Study* (New Jersey, Princeton University Press, 1988).
Luban, D, *Legal Ethics and Human Dignity* (Cambridge, Cambridge University Press, 2007).

Luban, D and Bradley, WW, 'Philosophical Legal Ethics: An Affectionate History' (2017) 30 *Georgetown Journal of Legal Ethics* 337.
Lücke, H, 'Legal history in Australia: the Development of Australian Legal/historical scholarship' (2010) 34 *Australian Bar Review* 109.
Lund, T, *A Guide to the Professional Conduct and Etiquette of Solicitors* (London, Law Society, 1960).
MacCormick, N, 'The Ethics of Legalism' (1989) 2(2) *Ratio Juris* 184.
MacIntyre, A, 'Theories of Natural law in the Culture of Advanced Modernity' in EB McLean (ed), *Common Truths: New Perspectives on Natural Law* (Wilmington, Del, ISI books, 2000).
MacIntyre, A, *After Virtue* (London, NY, Bloomsbury Academic 2011).
Macpherson, CB, *The Political Theory of Possessive Individualism: Hobbes to Locke* (Oxford, Oxford University Press, 1962).
Macrossan, J Saunders, K, Berns, S, Sheehan, C and McConnel, K, *Griffith, the law, and the Australian Constitution* (Brisbane, Royal Historical Society of Queensland, 1998).
Markovits, D, *A Modern Legal Ethics: Adversary Advocacy in a Democratic Age* (Princeton University Press, 2008).
Marshall, B, 'The Protest Movement and the Law' (1965) 51(5) *Virginia Law Review* 785.
Marston, A, 'Guiding The Profession: The 1887 Code Of Ethics Of The Alabama State Bar Association' (1998) 49(2) *Alabama Law Review* 471.
Martin, G, *Causes and Conflicts: The Centennial History of the Association of the Bar of the City of New York* (New York, NY, Fordham University Press, 1997).
Martin, GJ and Yurukoglu, A, 'Bias in Cable News: Persuasion and Polarization' (2017) 107(9) *American Economic Review* 2565.
Marx, K, *The Grundrisse* Notebook 4, 1857–22 January 1858 (1857).
Marx, K, *Capital* (Hamburg, Verlag von Otto Meisner, 1867).
Maute, J, 'Global continental shifts to a new governance paradigm in lawyer regulation and consumer protection: riding the wave' in R Mortensen, F Bartlett and K Tranter, *Alternative Perspectives on Lawyers and Legal Ethics* (London, Routledge, 2010) 21.
McCann, MW, 'Law and social movements: Contemporary perspectives' (2006) 2 *Annual Review of Law and Social Science* 17.
McGovney, DO, 'The British Origin of Judicial Review of Legislation' (1944) 93(1) *University of Pennsylvania Law Review* 1.
McNaughton, JT, *Evidence in Trials at Common Law* (Boston, Little, Brown & Co, 1961).
McQueen, R, 'Of Wigs and Gowns: A Short History of Legal and Judicial Dress in Australia' (1999) 16 *Law in Context: A Socio-Legal Journal* 31.
McQueen, R and Pue, WW, 'Misplaced Traditions: British Lawyers, Colonial Peoples' (1999) 16 *Law in Context: A Socio-Legal Journal* 1.
Merry, SE, 'Law and Colonialism' (1991) 25 *Law and Society Review* 889.
Michelon, C, *The Anxiety of the Jurist: Legality, Exchange and Judgement* (Oxford, Routledge, 2013).
Miles, AS, 'Blackstone and his American Legacy' (2000) 5(2) *Australia & New Zealand Journal of Law and Education* 1327.
Millen, R, 'The Independence of the Bar: An Unwritten Constitutional Principle' (2005) *Canadian Bar Review* 84.
Miller, JC, *Origins of the American Revolution* (Little, Brown & Company, Boston, Massachusetts, 1943).
Miller, MC, *The High Priests of American Politics: The Role of Lawyers in American Political institutions* (Knoxville, University of Tennessee Press, 1995).
Mills, C, *The Racial Contract* (Cornell University Press, 1997).
Mize, S, 'New Zealand: Finding the Balance between Self-Regulation and Government Oversight' in A Boon (ed), *International Perspectives on the Regulation of Lawyers and Legal Services* (Oxford, Hart Publishing, 2017) 116.
Moffett, MW, *The Human Swarm: How Our Societies Arise, Thrive and Fall* (London, Head of Zeus Ltd, 2019).
Moiseeva, E and Bocharov, T, 'A Professional Portrait of Russian Advocates: Challenges of the Market and Boundary Work' in R Abel, O Hammerslev, U Schultz and H Sommerlad (eds), *Lawyers in 21st-Century Societies, vol. 1: National Reports* (Oxford, Hart Publishing, 2020) 331.
Montagu, B, *A review of The Works of Francis Bacon, Lord Chancellor of England: A new Edition* (London, 1825–1834).

Montesquieu, CL, *The Spirit of the Laws* (transl/ed AM Cohler, BC Miller, HS Stone) (Cambridge, Cambridge University Press, 1992).
Moon, J, 'An Explicit Model of Business-Society Relations' in A Habisch, J Jonker, M Wegner, and R Schmidpeter (eds), *Corporate Social Responsibility across Europe* (Berlin, Springer Berlin Heidelberg, 2005) 51.
Moore, C, *The Law Society of Upper Canada and Ontario's Lawyers, 1797–1997* (Toronto, Buffalo, London, University of Toronto Press, 1997).
Moorhead, R, 'Contesting Professionalism: Legal Aid and Non-lawyers in England and Wales' (2003) 37 *Law and Society Review* 765.
Moorhead, R and Cahill-O'Callaghan, R, 'False Friends? Testing commercial lawyers on the claim that zealous advocacy is founded in benevolence towards clients rather than lawyers' personal interest' (2016) 19(1) *Legal Ethics* 30.
Moorhead, R, Vaughan, S and Godinho, C, *In-house Lawyers Ethics: Institutional Logics, legal Risks and the Tournament of Influence* (Oxford, Hart Publishing, 2019).
Morris, G, 'Devils down under: Perceptions of Lawyer's Ethics in New Zealand Fiction' (2013) *Victoria University Wellington Law Review* 609.
Morrison, J and Leith, P, *The Barristers World and the Nature of Law* (Buckingham, Oxford University Press, 1992).
Morrow, J, *History of Political Thought* (Palgrave, London, 1998).
Mosesson, L, 'Dr Bonham in Woolf's Clothing: Sovereignty and the Rule of Law Today' (2007) *Mountbatten Yearbook of Legal Studies* 5.
Murphy, AR, *Liberty Conscience and Toleration: The Political Thought of William Penn* (Oxford, Oxford University Press, 2016).
Nelson, RL, 'Practice and Privilege: Social Change and the Structure of Large Law Firms' 1981 *American Bar Foundation Research Journal* 95.
Nicol, D, *The Constitutional Protection of Capitalism* (Oxford, Hart Publishing, 2010).
Nicolson, D, 'Mapping Professional Ethics: The Form and focus of the codes' (1998) 1(1) *Legal Ethics* 51.
Nicolson, D, 'Making lawyers moral? Ethical codes and moral character' (2006) *Legal Studies* 601.
Nicolson, D and Webb, J, *Professional Legal Ethics: Critical Interrogations* (Oxford, Oxford University Press, 1999).
Noonan, JT, 'The Purposes of Advocacy and the Limits of Confidentiality' (1966) 64 *Michigan Law Review* 1485.
North, DC, Wallis, JJ and Weingast, BR, *Violence and Social Orders: A Conceptual Framework for Understanding Recorded Human History* (Cambridge, Cambridge University Press, 1989).
North, DC and Weingast, BR, 'Constitutions and Commitment: The Evolution of Institutions Governing Public Choice in Seventeenth-Century England' (1989) 49(4) *Journal of Economic History* 803.
Norton-Kyshe, JW, *The law and privileges relating to the Attorney-General and Solicitor-General of England: with a history from the earliest periods, and a series of King's Attorneys and Attorneys and Solicitors-General from the reign of Henry III. to the 60th of Queen Victoria* (London, Stevens and Haynes, 1897) 18–19.
Nye, JS, 'Corruption and Political Development: A Cost-Benefit Analysis' (1967) 61(2) *American Political Science Review* 417.
Oakley, J and Cocking, D, *Virtue Ethics and Professional Roles* (Cambridge, Cambridge University Press, 2001).
O'Brien, E, *The Lawyer: his character and rule of holy life, after the manner of George Herbert's Country parson* (London, William Pickering, 1842).
O'Connor, DJ, *Aquinas and Natural Law* (London, Macmillan International Higher Education, 1967).
Olmstead, CE, *History of Religion in the United States* (Englewood Cliffs, NJ, Prentice-Hall, 1960).
Pannick, D, *Advocates* (Oxford, Oxford University Press, 1992).
Parker, C, *Just Lawyers* (Oxford, Oxford University Press, 1999).
Pateman, C, *The Sexual Contract* (Stanford: Stanford University Press, 1988).
Patterson LR, 'Legal Ethics and the Lawyer's Duty of Loyalty' (1980) 29 *Emory Law Journal* 909
Pearce, RG, 'Rediscovering the Republican Origins of the Legal Ethics Codes' (1992) 6(24) *Georgetown Journal of Legal Ethics* 241.
Pearson, B and Piazza, N, 'Classification of Dual Relationships in the Helping Professions' (1997) 37 *Counselor Education and Supervision* 89.

Pepper, SL, 'The Lawyer's Amoral Ethical Role: A Defense, A Problem, and Some Possibilities' (1986) 11(4) *Law & Social Inquiry* 613.
Perkin, H, *The Rise of Professional Society: England Since 1880* (London, Routledge, 1989).
Phelps, E, *Mass Flourishing. How grassroots innovation created jobs, challenge, and change*, 1st edn (Princeton, Princeton University Press, 2013).
Pincus, S and Wolfram, A, 'A Proactive State? The Land Bank, Investment and Party Politics in the 1690s' in P Gauci (ed), *Regulating the British Economy, 1660–1850* (Abingdon, Routledge, 2016).
Pinker, S, *The Better Angels of Our Nature: The Decline of Violence in History and Its Causes* (London, Viking Books, 2011).
Piper, A and Finnane, M, 'Access To Legal Representation By Criminal Defendants In Victoria 1861–1961 (2017) 40(2) *University of New South Wales Law Journal* 638.
Postema, G, 'Moral Responsibility in Professional Ethics' (1980) 55 *New York University Law Review* 63.
Pound, R, *The Formative Era of American Law* (Boston, Little, Brown & Co, 1938).
Pound, R, *The Lawyer from Antiquity to Modern Times: With particular reference to The Development of Bar Associations in the United States* (St. Paul, Minnesota, West Publishing, 1953).
Prest, WR, *The Rise Of The Barristers: A Social History Of The English Bar, 1590–1640* (Oxford, Clarendon Press, 1986).
Principe, ML, 'Albert Venn Dicey and the Principles of the Rule of Law: Is Justice Blind? A Comparative Analysis of the United States and Great Britain' (2000) 22 *Loyola of Los Angeles International & Comparative Law Review* 357.
Pring, GW and Canan, P, *SLAPPs: Getting sued for Speaking Out* (Philadelphia, Temple University Press, 1996).
Pue, WW, 'Moral Panic at the English Bar: Paternal vs. Commercial Ideologies of Legal Practice in the 1860s' (1990) 15(1) *Law & Social Inquiry* 49.
Pue, WW, 'Lawyers and Political Liberalism in Eighteenth and Nineteenth Century England' in in TC Halliday and L Karpik (eds), *Lawyers and the Rise of Western Political Liberalism* (Oxford, Clarendon Press, 1997) 167.
Pue, WW, 'British Masculinities, Canadian Lawyers: Canadian Legal Education, 1900–1930' (1999) 16 *Law in Context: A Socio-Legal Journal* 80.
Pue, WW and Sugarman, D, *Lawyers and Vampires: Cultural Histories of the Legal Profession* (London, Bloomsbury, 2004).
Putnam, RD, Leonardi, R and Nanetti, RY, *Making Democracy Work: Civic Traditions in Modern Italy* (Princeton, Princeton University Press, 1994).
Qvortrup, M, *The Political Philosophy of Jean-Jacques Rousseau: The Impossibility of Reason* (Manchester, Manchester University Press, 2003).
Raab, D, *The Assault on Liberty: What Went Wrong With Rights?* (London, Fourth Estate, 2009).
Rahe, PA, 'An Inky Wretch: The Outrageous Genius of Marchamont Nedham' *The National Interest* 70 (2002–2003) 55.
Ravid, I, 'Sleeping with the Enemy? On Government Lawyers and their Role in Promoting Social Change: the Israeli Example' (2014) 50(1) *Stanford Journal of International* Law 185.
Rawlinson, P, *A Price Too High* (London, Orion Publishing Co, 1989).
Rawls, J, *A Theory of Justice* (Cambridge, MA, Harvard University Press, 1971).
Rawls, J, *Political Liberalism* (New York: Columbia University Press, 1996).
Raz, J, *The Authority of Law: Essays on Law and Morality* (Oxford, Clarendon Press, 1979).
Reid, J, 'The Judge as Lawmaker' (1972–73) *Journal of the Society of the Public Teachers of Law* 22.
Rhode, D, *In the Interests of Justice* (New York, Oxford University Press, 2000).
Rhode, D and Paton, P, 'Lawyers, Ethics and Enron' (2002–3) 8 *Stanford Journal of Law Business and Finance* 9.
Rhode, D and Wooley, A, 'Comparative Perspectives on Lawyer Regulation: An Agenda for Reform in the United States and Canada' (2012) 80 *Fordham Law Review* 2761.
Rich, RM, 'Sociological Paradigms and the Sociology of Law: An Overview' in CE Reasons and R Rich (eds), *The Sociology of Law: A Conflict Perspective* (London, Butterworth & Co, 1978).
Rigertas, L, 'Post-Watergate: The Legal Profession and Respect For The Interests Of Third Parties' (2102) 16 *Chapman Law Review* 111.
Rigg, JM, 'Scott, John (1751–1838)' Dictionary of National Biography, 1885–1900 Vol 51 in L Stephen and S Lee (eds), *Dictionary of National Biography*: from the earliest times to 1900 (London, Oxford University Press, 1949).

Ritzer, G, 'Professionalization, Bureaucratization and Rationalization: The Views of Max Weber' (1975) 53(4) *Social Forces* 627.
Roberts, A, *Ancestors: The Pre-history of Britain in Seven Burials* (London and New York, Simon and Schuster, 2021).
Robertson, G, *Crimes Against Humanity: The Struggle for Global Justice*, 2nd edn (London, Penguin Books, 2002).
Robertson, G, *The Tyrannicide Brief: The story of the man who sent Charles I to the scaffold* (London, Chatto & Windus, 2005).
Roberston, G, *Stephen Ward was Innocent OK?: The Case for Overturning his Conviction.* (London, Biteback Publishing, 2013).
Rodes, RE, 'Government Lawyers' (2000) 9 *Widener Journal of Public Law* 281.
Rogers, JG, 'History of the American Bar Association' (1953) 39(8) *American Bar Association Journal* 659.
Rogers, S, 'The Ethics of Advocacy' (1899) 15 *Law Quarterly Review* 259.
Rose, J, 'The Legal Profession in Medieval England: A History of Regulation' (1998) 48 *Syracuse Law Review* 1.
Rose, J, 'The Ambidextrous Lawyer: Conflict of Interest and the Medieval and Early Modern Legal Profession' (2000) 7 *University of Chicago School of Law Roundtable* 137.
Rose-Ackerman, S, 'Corruption: Greed, Culture and the State' (2010) 120 *Yale Law Journal Online* 125.
Rosen, RE, 'On the Social Significance of Critical Lawyering' (2000) 3 *Legal Ethics* 169.
Roth, AL, 'Upping the Ante: Rethinking Anti-SLAPP Laws in the Age of the Internet' (2016) 2 *Brigham Young University Law Review* 741.
Rousseau, JJ, *On the Social Contract, or, Principles of Political Rights* (1762) in *Jean-Jacques Rousseau: The Basic Political Writings* (trans DA Cress) (Cambridge, MA, Hackett Publishing Company, 1987).
Rousseau, JJ, *The Discourse on the Origin and Foundations of Inequality Among Men* Rousseau, in *Jean-Jacques Rousseau: The Basic Political Writings* (trans DA Cress) (Cambridge, MA, Hackett Publishing Company, 1987).
Rudé, G, *Revolutionary Europe: 1783–1815* (Oxford, Blackwell, 1964).
Sachs, J, *The Price of Civilization* (New York, Random House, 2011).
Sahni, BP, 'A Legal Analysis of the British East India Company' (2013) 54(4) *Acta Juridica Hungarica* 317.
Sandell, J, *Liberalism and the limitations of justice* (Cambridge, Cambridge University Press).
Sander, FEA and Goldberg, SB, 'Fitting the Forum to the Fuss: A User-Friendly Guide to Selecting an ADR Procedure' (1994) 10(1) *Negotiation Journal* 49.
Sands, P, *East West Street* (London, Wiedenfeld and Nicolson, 2016).
Santiso, C, 'Good Governance and Aid Effectiveness: The World Bank and Conditionality' (2001) 7(1) *The Georgetown Public Policy Review* 1.
Sarat, A and Scheingold, S (eds), *Cause Lawyering: Political Commitments and Professional Responsibilities* (New York, Oxford University Press, 1998).
Sarat, A and Scheingold, S (eds), *Cause Lawyers and the State in a Global Era* (New York, Oxford University Press, 2001).
Saunders, D, *Anti-Lawyers: Religion and the Critics of Law and State* (Abingdon, Routledge, 1997).
Schein, E, *Professional Education: Some New Directions* (New York, McGraw-Hill, 1972).
Scheingold, S, *The Politics of Rights: Lawyers, Public Policy and Political Change* (Ann Arbor, University of Michigan Press, 2004).
Schindeler, F, 'Hon. J. C. McRuer, Royal Commission Inquiry into Civil Rights: Report No. 1. Toronto: Queen's Printer, 1968, Pp. Lix, 1331' (1969) 2 *Canadian Journal of Political Science* 131. Royal Commission – *Inquiry Into Civil Rights*. Ontario Report No. 1, Volume 3.
Schleifer, JT, *The Making of Tocqueville's Democracy In America*, 2nd edn (Indianapolis, Liberty Fund, 1980) https://oll.libertyfund.org/title/pierson-the-making-of-tocqueville-s-democracy-in-america.
Schmidt, AJ, 'The Country Attorney in Late Eighteenth-Century England: Benjamin Smith of Horbling' (1990) 8(2) *Law and History Review* 237.
Schmitter, PC and Karl, TL, 'What democracy is … and is not' 2(3) *Journal of Democracy* 75.
Schneyer, T, 'Moral Philosophy's Standard Misconception of Legal Ethics' (1984) *Wisconsin Law Review* 1529.
Schouls, PA, 'John Locke And William III: A Dutchman's Rule In England Curtailed By An Englishman To Whom The Dutch Had Extended Political Asylum' (1985) 6(2) *Canadian Journal Of Netherlandic Studies* 60, https://caans-acaen.ca/Journal/issues_online/Issue_VI_ii_1985/Schouls.pdf.

Schramm, J-M, '"The Anatomy of A Barrister's Tongue": Rhetoric, Satire, And The Victorian Bar In England' (2004) 32 *Victorian Literature and Culture* 285.

Schudson, M, 'Public, Private, and Professional Lives: The Correspondence of David Dudley Field and Samuel Bowles' (1977) 21 *American Journal of Legal History* 191.

Schwartz, ML, 'The Professionalism and Accountability of Lawyers' (1978) *California Law Review* 669.

Schwartz, ML, 'The Zeal of the Civil Advocate' (1983) 8(3) *American Bar Foundation Research Journal* 543.

Sciulli, D, 'Continental Sociology of Professions Today: Conceptual Contributions' (2005) 53 *Current Sociology* 915.

Sciulli, D, *Professions in Civil Society and the State: Invariant Foundations and Consequences* (Leiden and Boston, Brill Publishing, 2009).

Sedley, S, 'When Judges Sleep' (1993) 15(11) *London Review of Books*.

Sedley, S, *Lions Under the Throne: Essays on the History of English Public Law* (Cambridge, Cambridge University Press, 2015).

Segal, JA and Spaeth, HJ, *The Supreme Court and the Attitudinal Model Revisited* (Cambridge, Cambridge University Press, 2002).

Selznick, P, 'The sociology of law' in DL Sillis and RK Merton (eds), *The International Encyclopedia of the Social Sciences, Vol. 9* (New York, Macmillan 1968) 52.

Semple, N, *Justicia's Legions* (Cheltenham, Edward Elgar, 2015).

Semple, N, 'Legal Services Regulation in Canada' in A Boon, *International Perspectives on the Regulation of Lawyers and Legal Services* (Oxford, Hart Publishing, 2017) 95.

Sennet, R, *The Corrosion of Character, The Personal Consequences of Work in the New Capitalism* (London, WW Norton & Co, 1998).

Shaoul, J, 'The Private Finance Initiative or the Public Funding of Private Profit?' in G Hodge and C Greve (eds), *The Challenge of Public Private Partnerships* (Cheltenham, Edward Elgar, 2005) 190.

Shapiro, B, *Probability and Certainty in Seventeenth-Century England: A Study of the Relationships between Natural Science, Religion, History, Law and Literature* (Princeton, Cambridge University Press, 1983).

Shapiro, B, '"To a Moral Certainty": Theories of Knowledge and Anglo-American Juries 1600–1850' (1986) 38(1) *Hastings Law Journal* 153.

Sharswood, G, An Essay on Professional Ethics, 5th edn (Philadelphia, T and JW Johnson, 1907).

Shaw, HJ, 'The Rise of Corporatocracy in a Disenchanted Age' (2008) 1(1) *Human Geography* 1.

Shawcross, H, *The Office of the Attorney General* (Law Society, 1953) 3.

Shugerman, JH, 'Professionals, Politicos, and Crony Attorneys General: A Historical Sketch of the U.S. Attorney General as a Case for Structural Independence' (2019) 87 *Fordham L Rev* 1965.

Siedentop, L, *Inventing the Individual: The Origins of Western Liberalism* (Allen Lane, 2014).

Signer, M, *Demagogue: The Fight to Save Democracy from Its Worst Enemies* (New York, Palgrave Macmillan, 2009).

Simmonds, NE, 'Book Review: *Anti-Lawyers: Religion and the Critics of Law and State*' (1998) 57(3) *The Cambridge Law Journal* 611.

Simon WH, 'The Ideology of Advocacy: Procedural Justice and Professional Ethics' (1978) *Wisconsin Law Review* 29.

Simon, WH, 'Ethical Discretion in Lawyering' (1988) 101 *Harvard Law Review* 1083.

Simon, WH, 'Should Lawyers Obey the Law' (1996) 38 *William and Mary Law Review* 217.

Simon, WH, 'The Kaye Scholer Affair: The Lawyer's Duty of Candor and the Bar's Temptations of Evasion and Apology' (1998) 23 *Law and Social Inquiry* 243.

Simon, WH, 'Role Differentiation and Lawyers' Ethics: A Critique of Some Academic Perspectives' (2010) 23 *Georgetown J of Legal Ethics* 987.

Simpson, AWB, *In the Highest Degree Odious: Detention without Trial in Wartime Britain* (New York, Clarendon Press of Oxford University Press, 1992).

Smigel, EO, *The Wall Street Lawyer: Professional Organization Man?* (New York, Free Press of Glencoe, 1964).

Smith, AD, *The Right To Life* (Chapel Hill: The University of North Carolina Press, 1955).

Smith, T and Cape, E, 'The rise and decline of criminal legal aid in England and Wales' in A Flynn and J Hodgson, *Access to Justice and Legal Aid: Comparative Perspectives on Unmet Legal Need* (London, Bloomsbury, 2017) 63.

Solaiman, SM, 'The Enron collapse and criminal liabilities of auditors and lawyers for defective prospectuses in the United States, Australia and Canada: A Review' (2006–7) 26(8) *Journal of Law and Commerce* 81.

Spaulding, NW, 'The Myth of Civic Republicanism: Interrogating the Ideology of Antebellum Legal Ethics' (2003) 71 *Fordham Law Review* 1397.
Spiller, P, 'A History of New Zealand Legal Education: A Study in Ambivalence' (1993) 4 *Legal Education Review* 223.
Spinoza, B, *Tractatus Theologico-Politicus* (Hamburg, Henricus Künraht, 1670).
Stephens, JER, 'The Growth of Jury Trial in England' 10:3 (1896) *Harvard Law Review* 150.
Stimpson, SC, *The American Revolution in the Law: Anglo-American Jurisprudence before John Marshall* (Princeton, Princeton University Press, 1990).
Stryker, LP, *For the Defense: Thomas Erskine, the most enlightened liberal of his times, 1750–1823* (New York, Doubleday, 1949).
Stumpf, SE, 'Austin's Theory of the Separation of Law and Morals' (1960–1961) 14 *Vanderbilt Law Review* 117.
Subin, HI, 'The Lawyer as Superego: Disclosure of Client Confidences to Prevent Harm' (1985) 70 *Iowa Law Review* 1091.
Sugarman, D, 'Bourgeois Collectivism, Professional Power and the Boundaries of the State: The Private and Public Life of the Law Society 1825 to 1914' (1996) 3(1/2) *International Journal of the Legal Profession* 81.
Sunderland, ER, *History of the American Bar Association and Its Work* (Chicago, ABA, 1953).
Susskind, R, *The end of lawyers?: rethinking the nature of legal services* (Oxford, Oxford University Press, 2008).
Sward, EE, 'Values, Ideology, and the Evolution of the Adversary System' (1989) 64(2) *Indiana Law Journal* 301.
Tamanaha, BZ, *On the Rule of Law: History, Politics, Theory*, (Cambridge, Cambridge University Press, 2004).
Taylor, N (ed), *The Guide to the Professional Conduct of Solicitors*, 8th edn (London, The Law Society, 1999).
Taylor, P, Catalano, G and Walker, D, 'Measurement of the World City Network' (2002) 39 *Urban Studies* 2367.
Taylor, T, *The Anatomy of the Nuremberg Trials* (New York, Bloomsbury, 1992).
Terry, LS, 'Globalization and The ABA Commission on Ethics 20/20: Reflections on Missed Opportunities And The Road Not Taken' (2014) 43 *Hofstra Law Review* 95.
Thornbury, W, 'The Bank of England' in *Old and New London: Volume 1* (London, 1878) 453, 455. British History Online www.british-history.ac.uk/old-new-london/vol1/pp453-473.
Thornton, A, 'The Professional Responsibility and Ethics of the English Bar' in R Cranston (ed), *Legal Ethics and Professional Responsibility* (Oxford, Clarendon Press, 1995).
Thornton, M, 'The Australian Legal Profession: Towards a National Identity' in W Felstiner (ed), *Re-organization and Resistance: Legal Professions Confront a Changing World* (London, Bloomsbury, 200) 133.
Thrush, A and Ferris, JP, *The History of Parliament: The House of Commons 1604–1629* (Cambridge, Cambridge University Press, 2010).
Timberlake, EW, 'The Lawyer as an Officer of the Court' (1925) 11(4) *Virginia Law Review* 263.
Tomkins, A, 'Legislating Against Terror: The Anti-Terrorism, Crime and Security Act 2001' (2002) *Public Law* 205.
Tomkins, A and Scott, P (eds), *Entick v Carrington: 250 Years of the Rule of Law* (Oxford and Oregon, Hart Publishing, 2015).
Trubek DM, 'Max Weber on Law and the Rise of Capitalism' (1972) 3 *Wisconsin Law Review* 720.
Turner, RV, *King John: England's Evil King?* (Stroud, History Press, 2009).
Unger, R, *Law in Modern Society* (New York, Free Press, 1976).
Van Hoecke, M, 'Methodology of Comparative Legal Research' (2015) *Law and Method* www.bjutijdschriften.nl/tijdschrift/lawandmethod/2015/12/RENM-D-14-00001.
Van Kley, DK, *The Religious Origins of the French Revolution: From Calvin to the Civil Constitution: 1560–1791* (New Haven and London, Yale University Press, 1996).
Vaughan, S, Thomas, L and Young, A, 'Symbolism over substance? Large law firms and corporate social responsibility' (2015) 18(2) *Legal Ethics* 138.
Vilardo, LJ and Doyle, VE, 'Where Did the Zeal Go?' (2011) 38(1) *Litigation* 1.

Vile, MJC, *Constitutionalism and the Separation of Powers*, 2nd edn (Minneapolis, Liberty Fund, 1998).
Vitali, S, Glattfelder, JB and Battiston, S, 'The Network of Global Corporate Control' (2011) PLoS ONE 6(10): e25995, https://journals.plos.org/plosone/article?id=10.1371/journal.pone.0025995.
Vollmer, HM and Mills, DL (eds), *Professionalization* (Prentice-Hall Englewood Cliffs, N.J. 1966).
Von Hayek, F, *The Road to Serfdom* (Chicago, University of Chicago Press, 1944).
Wade, N, *A Troublesome Inheritance* (New York, Penguin Books, 2014).
Wald, E, 'Lawyers and Corporate Scandals' (2004) 7 *Legal Ethics* 54.
Waldron, J, 'The rule of law and the importance of procedure' (2011) 50 *Nomos* 3.
Wall, M, *Warriors and Kings: The 1500-year Battle for Celtic England* (Glocs, Amberely, 2017).
Warren, C, *A History of the American Bar* (New York, Cambridge University Press, 1911).
Wasserstrom, R, 'Lawyers as Professionals: Some Moral Issues' (1975) 5 *Human Rights* 1.
Watson, A, 'The Evolution of Law: The Roman System of Contracts' (1984) 2 *Law & History Review* 1.
Watson, A, *Legal Transplants: An Approach to Comparative Literature*, 2nd edn (Athens, Georgia, University of Georgia Press, 1993).
Watson, A, *Speaking in Court: Developments in Court Advocacy from the Seventeenth to the Twenty First Centuries* (Gewerbestrasse, Switzerland, Palgrave MacMillan, 2019).
Weber, M, *The Protestant Ethic and the Spirit of Capitalism* (trans T Parsons) (London, George Allen and Unwin Ltd, 1930).
Weber, M, *The Protestant Ethic and the Spirit of Capitalism* (trans. T Parsons) (London, Butler and Tanner, 1930).
Weber, M, *Economy and Society: An outline of Interpretative Sociology* (G Roth and W Wittich (eds)) (Totowa, New Jersey, Bedminster, 1968) and 2nd edn (Berkeley, University of California Press, 1978) https://archive.org/details/MaxWeberEconomyAndSociety/mode/2up.
Weiner, M, *Culture and the Decline of the Industrial Spirit 1850–1980* (Cambridge, Cambridge University Press, 1981).
Weingast, BR, 'Why Developing Countries Prove So Resistant to the Rule of Law' in JJ Heckman, RL Nelson and L Cabatingan (eds), *Global Perspectives on the Rule of Law* (London and New York, Routledge, 2010) 28.
Wendel, WB, 'The Torture Memos and the Demands of Legality' (2009) 12(1) *Legal Ethics* 107.
Wendel, WB, *Lawyers and Fidelity to Law* (Princeton University Press, 2010).
Whelan, C, 'Ethics Beyond the Horizon: Why Regulate the Global Practice of Law' (2001) 34 *Vanderbilt Journal of Transnational Law* 931.
White, V, Foster-Gilbert, C and Sinclair, J, *Integrity in Public Life* (London, Haus Publishing, 2019).
Wilensky, HL, 'The Professionalisation of Work' (1964) 70(2) *American Journal of Sociology* 137.
Wilkins, D, 'Who Should Regulate Lawyers' (1992) 105 *Harvard Law Review* 799.
Winsberg, S, 'Attorney "mal-practices": an invisible ethical problem in the early American republic' (2016) 19(2) *Legal Ethics* 187.
Wise, EM, 'The Transplant of Legal Patterns' (1990) 38 *American Journal of Comparative Law Supplement* 1.
Wolfram, CW, 'Modern Legal Ethics' (St. Paul Minnesota, West Publishing Co., 1986).
Wood, GV and Adams, JQ, *Heir to the Fathers: John Quincy Adams and the Spirit of Constitutional Government* (Lanham Maryland, Lexington Books, 2004).
Woodhouse, D, *The Office of Lord Chancellor* (London, Bloomsbury, 2001).
Woodward, B, *Fear: Trump in the White House* (New York, Simon & Schuster, 2018).
Wooley, A, 'Reconceiving the Standard Conception of the Prosecutor's Role (2017) 95(3) *Canadian Bar Review* 795.
Woolf, T, 'Droit Public – English Style' *Public Law* (1995) 57.
Yoshimi, S and Buist, D (trans), 'America as desire and violence: Americanization in postwar Japan and Asia during the Cold War (2003) 4(3) *Inter-Asia Cultural Studies* 433.
Zacharias, FC, 'Rethinking Confidentiality' (1989) 74 *Iowa LR* 351, R Cranston (ed), *Legal Ethics and Professional Responsibility* (Oxford, Clarendon Press, 1995).
Zander, M, 'Rights of Audience in the Higher Courts in England and Wales Since the 1990 Act: What Happened?' (1997) 4 *International Journal of the Legal Profession* 167.
Zimmermann, E, 'Globalization and Terrorism' (2011) 27 *European Journal of Political Economy* S152, S153.

REPORTS

Government and Parliamentary Committee Reports

House of Commons

Constitutional Affairs Committee, *The Operation of the Special Immigration Appeals Commission and the Use of Special Advocates: 7th Report of 2004–5* (London, HC323-1, 2005).
Constitutional Affairs Committee, *Constitutional Role of the Attorney General: 5th Report of 2006–7* (London, HC306, 2007).
Public Administration Select Committee, *Public Service Ethos: 7th Report of 2001–2* (London, HC263-I, 2002)
Treasury Committee, *Lessons from Greensill Capital: 6th Report of 2021–22* ((London, HC151, 2022).

House of Lords

Select Committee on the Constitution, *First Report of Session 2001–02: Reviewing the Constitution: Terms of Reference and Method of Working* (HL Paper 11, 2002) https://publications.parliament.uk/pa/ld200102/ldselect/ldconst/11/1102.htm.
Select Committee on the Constitution, *Fifth Report of Session 2005–06: Constitutional Reform Act 2005* (HL Paper 83, 2006). https://publications.parliament.uk/pa/ld200506/ldselect/ldconst/83/83.pdf.
Select Committee on the Constitution, *Sixth Report of Session 2014–15: The Office of Lord Chancellor* (HL Paper 75, 2015) https://publications.parliament.uk/pa/ld201415/ldselect/ldconst/75/75.pdf.
Select Committee on the Constitution, *Sixth Report of Session 2006–07: Relations between the Executive, the Judiciary and Parliament* (HL Paper 151, 2007) https://publications.parliament.uk/pa/ld200607/ldselect/ldconst/151/15103.htm#a8.

Government

Lord Chancellor's Department, *The Work and Organisation of the Legal Profession* (Stationery Office Books, 1989) Cm. 570.
Ministry of Justice, *Judicial Review: Proposals for further reform: The Government Response* (2014) Cm. 8811. https://consult.justice.gov.uk/digital-communications/judicial-review/results/judicial-review---proposals-for-further-reform-government-response.pdf.
Ministry of Justice, *The Governance of Britain* (2007) Cm 7170. https://assets.publishing.service.gov.uk/government/uploads/system/uploads/attachment_data/file/228834/7170.pdf.
Ministry of Justice, *Human Rights Act Reform: A Modern Bill of Rights* (London, HMSO, 2021) CP 588.

Standards Committee

Standards in Public Life: First Report of the Committee for Standards in Public Life (London, HMSO, 1995) Cm 2850-1.
Report on the conduct of Mrs Natalie Elphicke, Sir Roger Gale, Adam Holloway, Bob Stewart, Theresa Villiers 21st July 2021. https://committees.parliament.uk/committee/290/committee-on-standards/news/156736/committee-on-standards-publishes-report-on-the-conduct-of-mrs-natalie-elphicke-sir-roger-gale-adam-holloway-bob-stewart-theresa-villiers/.
Report on the conduct of Boris Johnson 6 December 2018. https://publications.parliament.uk/pa/cm201719/cmselect/cmstandards/1797/179703.htm#_idTextAnchor000.
Report on the conduct of Owen Paterson 26 October 2021. https://publications.parliament.uk/pa/cm5802/cmselect/cmstandards/797/79703.htm.

US

Final Report of Attorney General's Committee on Administrative Procedure (Senate Document No. 8, 77th Congress, First Session, 1941) Library of Congress Web Archives.
Attorney General's Manual on the Administrative Procedure Act U.S. Department of Justice (1947).

Other

Audickas, L and Cracknell, B, *Social Background of MPs 1979–2015* (London, House of Commons Library, 2020) https://commonslibrary.parliament.uk/research-briefings/cbp-7483/.
Bar Standard Board, 'Statistics on Practising Barristers' www.barstandardsboard.org.uk/news-publications/research-and-statistics/statistics-about-the-bar/practising-barristers.html.
Bazley, M, *Transforming the Legal Aid System: Final Report and Recommendations* (New Zealand, Ministry of Justice, 2009) www.beehive.govt.nz/sites/default/files/Legal%20AidReview.pdf, p (i))
Beqiraj, J and McNamara, L, *The Rule of Law and Access to Justice in the Post-2015 Development Agenda: Moving Forward but Stepping Back* (Bingham Centre Working Paper 2014/04), Bingham Centre for the Rule of Law, BIICL, London, August 2014.
Britton, J, Dearden, L, van der Erve, L and Waltmann, B, *The Impact of undergraduate degree on Lifetime Earnings* (London, Institute of Fiscal Studies, 2020) 21, Fig. 13, https://assets.publishing.service.gov.uk/government/uploads/system/uploads/attachment_data/file/869264/The_impact_of_undergraduate_degrees_on_lifetime_earnings_-_online_appendix.pdf.
Burnside, C and Dollar, D, *Aid, the Incentive Regime, and Poverty Reduction* Policy Research Working Paper 1937 (Washington, DC, The World Bank, 1998).
Clementi, D, *Review of the Regulatory Framework for Legal Services in England and Wales* (2004) www.avocatsparis.org/Presence_Internationale/Droit_homme/PDF/Rapport_Clementi.pdf.
Cole, B, *Trends in the Solicitors' Profession: Annual Statistical Report 1997* (London, The Law Society, 1997).
Cole, B, *Trends in the Solicitors' Profession: Annual Statistical report 1999* (London, The Law Society, 2000).
Committee for Economic Development, *Social Responsibilities of Business Corporations* (New York, CED, 1971).
Cox, D, Lienesch, R, and Jones, RP, *Beyond Economics: Fears of Cultural Displacement Pushed the White Working Class to Trump* (Washington DC, PRRI/The Atlantic, 2017) www.prri.org/research/white-working-class-attitudes-economy-trade-immigration-election-donald-trump/.
Cox, DA, *After the ballots are counted: Conspiracies, political violence, and American exceptionalism* (Washington DC, American Enterprise Institute, Survey Centre on American Life, 2021) www.aei.org/research-products/report/after-the-ballots-are-counted-conspiracies-political-violence-and-american-exceptionalism/.
Cox, N, *The Effect of The Lawyers and Conveyancers Act on The Independent Bar* (Aukland, NZ, Aukland District Law Society, 2009) www.researchgate.net/profile/Noel-Cox/publication/46408388_The_Effect_of_the_Lawyers_and_Conveyancers_Act_on_the_Independent_Bar/links/559e1eb508ae76bed0bb6169/The-Effect-of-the-Lawyers-and-Conveyancers-Act-on-the-Independent-Bar.pdf.
Decker, C and Yarrow, G, *Understanding the Economic Rationale For Legal Services Regulation* (London, Legal Services Board, 2010).
Democracy Now, 'Top Pentagon Official Calls for Boycott of Law Firms Respresenting Guantanamo Prisoners' (17 January 2007) (reporting interview with S Oleskey and E Spieler) www.democracynow.org/2007/1/17/top_pentagon_official_calls_for_boycott.
Editorial, 'Apology not accepted' *New York Times* (9 January 2007) www.nytimes.com/2007/01/19/opinion/19fri2.html.
Despouy, L, *Report of the Special Rapporteur on the independence of judges and lawyers: ubstantive topics and issues identified by the Special Rapporteur* (Geneva, Switzerland, United Nations Human Rights Council, 2004) www.ohchr.org/en/special-procedures/sr-independence-of-judges-and-lawyers/annual-thematic-reports.
Donald, A, Gordon, J and Leach, P, *The UK and the European Court of Human Rights* Equality and Human Rights Commission Research report 83 (Manchester, Equality and Human Rights Commission, 2012) www.equalityhumanrights.com/sites/default/files/83._european_court_of_human_rights.pdf.

European Court of Human Rights, *Survey of Activities 2006* (Strasbourg, Registry of the European Court of Human Rights, 2007).

Flood, J and Hvvid, M, *The Cab Rank Rule: Its Meaning and Purpose in the New Legal Services Market* (London, Legal Services Board, 2013) https://legalservicesboard.org.uk/reports/the-cab-rank-rule-its-meaning-and-purpose-in-the-new-legal-services-market.

Flood, JA and Whyte, A, *Straight There No Detours: Direct Access to Barristers* (London, 2008). University of Westminster School of Law Research Paper No. 09-05, https://papers.ssrn.com/sol3/papers.cfm?abstract_id=1321492.

General Council of the Bar, *The Quality of Justice: The Bar's Response* (London, Butterworth, 1989).

Higher Education Statics Agency, '"Who is Studying in HE" HE enrolments by subject of study 2019/20' www.hesa.ac.uk/data-and-analysis/students/whos-in-he.

International Bar Association, *The Independence of the Legal Profession: Threats to Bastion of a Free and Democratic Society* (Report of the IBA Presidential Task Force, 2016) www.ibanet.org/MediaHandler?id=6E688709-2CC3-4F2B-8C8B-3F341705E438&.pdf&context=bWFzdGVyfGFzc2V0c3wzMTQxNzd8YXBwbGljYXRpb24vcGRmGg4NC9oZGUvODc5NzEyNTM0NTMxMC82RTY4ODcwOS0yQ0MzLTRGMkItOEM4Qi0zRjM0MTcwNUU0MzgucGRmFDk2OTg0 gOZjU1ZWE5OTJlM2ViZTc2MWEwMGE3Zjc4ZDQwOTYwMWYxMDU4OTNlMDc4YTJlODU0Y2I3OTBhZWQzY2U.

Kaufmann, D, Kraay, A and Zoido-Lobaton, P, *Governance Matters* Policy Research Working Paper 2196 (Washington, The World Bank, 1999).

Kentridge, S, *The cab rank rule: A Response to the Report Commissioned by the Legal Services Board* (London, Bar Standards Board, 2013) https://slidelegend.com/the-cab-rank-rule-the-bar-council_59e7c0b81723dd59128078b7.html.

King, S, Cox, J and Roddis, C, *Trends in the solicitors' profession Annual Statistical Report* (London, The Law Society, 2016).

Krug, B and Reinmoeller, P, *The Hidden Costs of Ubiquity: Globalisation and Terrorism* Erasmus Report Series Research in Management (Rotterdam, Research Institute of Management, 2003).

Legal Services Board, *A vision for legislative reform of the regulatory framework for legal services in England and Wales* (London, LSB, 2010) www.legalservicesboard.org.uk/news_publications/LSB_news/PDF/2016/20160909LSB_Vision_For_Legislative_Reform.pdf.

Legal Services Board, *Bar Council Investigation Report: Formal investigation into the Bar Council's involvement in the BSB application to the LSB for approval of changes to the Code of Conduct in relation to the 'Cab Rank Rule'* (London, LSB, 2013) para 3.8. www.legalservicesboard.org.uk/Projects/pdf/LSB_investigation_into_bar_council_influencing_of_the_BSB_(25-11-13).pdf.

Marks, P, *Annual Statistical Report 1987* (London, The Law Society, 1987).

Marre, M, CBE, *A Time for Change: Report of the Committee on the Future of the Legal Profession* (London, General Council of the Bar and Council of the Law Society, 1988).

Mayson, S, *Independent Review of Legal Services Regulation: Assessment of the Current Regulatory Framework* (London, UCL Centre for Ethics and Law, 2020) www.ucl.ac.uk/ethics-law/publications/2018/sep/independent-review-legal-services-regulation.

Mayson, S, *Independent Review of Legal Services Regulation: The Rationale for legal services regulation* (London, UCL Centre for Ethics and Law, 2020).

McLaren, M, Ulyatt, C and Knowles, C, *The 'Cab Rank Rule': A Fresh View* (London, Bar Standards Board, 2012).

Moghaddam, FM, *How globalization spurs terrorism: The lopsided benefits of 'one world' and why that fuels violence* (Praeger Security International, 2008).

Morris, SD, *Forms of Corruption* (2011) 9(2) *CESifo DICE Report* 10.

Northcote, SH and Trevelyan, CE, *Investigation and report into The Organisation of the Permanent Civil Service* (1853) www.politicsweb.co.za/news-and-analysis/the-northcotetrevelyan-report.

Solicitors Regulation Authority, *A New Route to Qualification: The Solicitors Qualifying Examination* (2017) www.sra.org.uk/sra/consultations/consultation-listing/solicitors-qualifying-examination/.

Solicitors Regulation Authority *Research on Alternative Business Structures* (London, SRA, 2014) www.sra.org.uk/globalassets/documents/sra/research/abs-quantitative-research-may-2014.pdf?version=4a1ac4.

Street, A, *Judicial Review and the Rule of Law: Who's in Control?* (London, Constitution Society, 2013).

Webb, JS, Ching, J, Maharg, P and Sherr, A, *Setting Standards: The Future of Legal Services Education And Training Regulation In England And Wales* (BSB, ILEX Professional Standards, Solicitors Regulation Authority, 2013).

World Economic Forum, *The Future Role of Civil Society* (Geneva, 2013) www3.weforum.org/docs/WEF_FutureRoleCivilSociety_Report_2013.pdf.

World Justice Project *Rule of Law Index 2015* https://worldjusticeproject.org/rule-of-law-index/.

NEWSPAPER AND MAGAZINE ARTICLES

Allegretti, A, 'Cameron faces calls to explain Greensill role amid claims he earned £7m' *The Guardian* (11 August 2021).

Allegretti, A, 'Boris Johnson makes U-turn over anti-sleaze regime for MPs' *The Guardian* (4 November 2021) www.theguardian.com/politics/2021/nov/04/boris-johnson-makes-u-turn-over-anti-sleaze-regime-for-mps-owen-paterson.

Allegretti, A and Gayle, D, 'Shapps vows "loophole" will be closed as Tories rage at Colston acquittal' *The Guardian* (7 January 2022).

Anderson, S, 'Did Nelson really back the slave trade?' *Eastern Daily Press* (21 October 2020) www.edp24.co.uk/lifestyle/heritage/lord-nelson-slave-trade-simon-taylor-letter-doctored-6408146.

Baksi, C, 'Warning over BSB's 'cab rank' plans' (*Law Society Gazette*, 26 January 2012).

Baksi, C, 'Court of Appeal clears advocacy quality challenge' (*Law Society Gazette*, 12 May 2014) www.lawgazette.co.uk/practice/court-of-appeal-clears-advocacy-quality-challenge/5041213.article.

Bano, N, 'Dominic Raab's Judicial Review Plans are Another Power Grab' (*Tribune*, 5 January 2022) https://tribunemag.co.uk/2022/01/judicial-review-conservative-party-legislation-dominic-raab-boris-johnson.

Becket, A, 'Will Labour ever rebuild its red wall?' *The Guardian* (12 September 2020).

Beckett, A, 'The BBC is finding out the hard way you can't do "balance" with this government' *The Guardian* (18 November 2021) www.theguardian.com/commentisfree/2021/nov/19/bbc-balance-boris-johnson.

Beckett, A, 'Right to buy: The housing Crisis that Thatcher built' *The Guardian* (26 August 2015) www.theguardian.com/society/2015/aug/26/right-to-buy-margaret-thatcher-david-cameron-housing-crisis.

Bekiempis, V, 'Trump's acquittal shows paltry punch of impeachment process' *The Guardian* (14 February 2021).

Berenson, T, 'Neil Gorsuch on Email Slamming Guantanamo Bay Lawyers: "Not My Finest Moment"' (*Time*, 22 March 2017) https://time.com/4710216/neil-gorsuch-confirmation-hearing-email/.

Bland, A, 'Next BBC chair says it may be worth looking again at licence fee' *The Guardian* (14 January 2021) www.theguardian.com/media/2021/jan/14/next-bbc-chair-may-be-worth-looking-again-licence-fee-richard-sharp.

Boffey, D and Rankin, J, 'Relief that rule of law is "alive and kicking" in Britain' *The Guardian* (25 September 2019).

Booth, R, 'Standards chair attacks Tory efforts to dismantle anti-sleaze system' *The Guardian* (4 November 2021) www.theguardian.com/politics/2021/nov/04/standards-committee-chair-attacks-tory-dismantling-anti-sleaze-system.

Bordell, W and Robins, J, '"Crisis for rights" as world retreats from rule of law' *The Guardian* (31 January 2018).

Borger, J, 'Trump and Putin joke about getting rid of reporters' *The Guardian* (29 June 2019).

Borger, J, 'Contractor tells of 'abusive drift' that resulted in torture' *The Guardian* (23 January 2020).

Borger, J, 'Very volatile: genuine risk of US election violence former ambassador warns' *The Guardian* (16 September 2020).

Borger, J, 'Trump's Last Stand' *The Observer* (10 January 2021).

Bowcott, O, 'Judge defends court role over terror suspects' *The Guardian* (5 March 2013).

Bowcott, O, 'Security services spy on lawyers' *The Guardian* (7 November 2014).

Bowcott, O. 'Downing Street under pressure on plans to restrict judicial review access' *The Guardian* (26 November 2014) www.theguardian.com/politics/2014/nov/26/downing-street-under-pressure-plans-restrict-judicial-review-access.

Bowcott, O, 'Khan will reverse curbs on judicial review' *The Guardian* (2 March 2015).

Bowcott, O, 'Terrorism Act incompatible with human rights, court rules in David Miranda case' *The Guardian* (19 January 2016) www.theguardian.com/world/2016/jan/19/terrorism-act-incompatible-with-human-rights-court-rules-in-david-miranda-case.

Bowcott, O, 'Phil Shiner: Iraq human rights lawyer struck off over misconduct' *The Guardian* (2 February 2017) www.theguardian.com/law/2017/feb/02/iraq-human-rights-lawyer-phil-shiner-disqualified-for-professional-misconduct.
Bowcott, O, 'Iraq human rights lawyer declared bankrupt' *The Guardian* (18 March 2017).
Bowcott, O, 'Lord chief justice attacks Truss for failure to defend the judiciary' *The Guardian* (23 March 2017).
Bowcott, O, 'Court case against Iraq war law firm "politically driven"' *The Guardian* (22 June 2017).
Bowcott, O, 'Half of legal advice centres have closed in past six years' *The Guardian* (15 July 2019).
Bowcott, O, 'Minister refuses to say in court whether parliament could be prorogued again' *The Guardian* (18 September 2019).
Bowcott, O, 'Bill sets five-year limit to prosecute UK armed forces who served abroad' *The Guardian* (18 March 2020) www.theguardian.com/uk-news/2020/mar/18/bill-sets-five-year-limit-to-sue-uk-military-veterans-who-served-abroad.
Bowcott, O, 'Braverman put on spot over advisers' *The Guardian* (16 September 2020).
Bowcott, O, 'Former law lord accuses ministers of abuse of power over Covid-19' *The Guardian* (8 October 2020).
Bremner, I, 'Democracy Barely Prevailed: But Biden's Inauguration Should Still Give Us New Hope' (*Time*, 20 January 2021).
Buncombe, A, 'Donald Trump's lawyer boasted about getting prosecutor fired: "He will get you"' *The Independent* (13 June 2017).
Camp, P, 'Countdown to the Code: Taking the plunge' (*Law Society Gazette*, 14 June 2007).
Cengiz, H, 'We ignore Jamal's murder at our peril' *The Guardian* (2 October 2019).
Churchwell, S, 'I WON THE ELECTION' *The Guardian Review* (21 November 2020).
Cobain, I and Taylor, M, 'Far-right terrorist Thomas Mair jailed for life for Jo Cox murder' *The Guardian* (23 November 2016) www.theguardian.com/uk-news/2016/nov/23/thomas-mair-found-guilty-of-jo-cox-murder.
Cohen, N, 'The last thing troubled civil service needs is your advice' *The Guardian* (18 April 2021) www.theguardian.com/commentisfree/2021/apr/18/dominic-cummings-the-last-thing-the-troubled-civil-service-needs-is-your-advice.
Conn, D, '"Apparent bias": Gove acted unlawfully, judge rules' *The Guardian* (23 June 2021).
Conn, D, 'Government spends £60 million on challenge' *The Guardian* (11 February 2021).
Conn, D, 'Hillsborough: why has the trial collapsed and what happens next?' *The Guardian* (26 May 2021) www.theguardian.com/football/2021/may/26/hillsborough-why-has-the-trial-collapsed-and-what-happens-next.
Conn, D, '"Apparent bias": Gove acted unlawfully, judge rules' *The Guardian* (19 June 2021).
Davies, C, 'Judges tell of fears for safety as hostility rises' *The Guardian* (27 February 2017).
Davis, D, 'Our right to challenge the state is in peril' *The Guardian* (26 October 2021).
Davies, G, 'Tory MPs set to be suspended for trying to influence trial of ex-MP Charlie Elphicke' *The Telegraph* (21 July 2021) www.telegraph.co.uk/news/2021/07/21/tory-mps-set-suspended-trying-influence-trial-ex-mp-charlie/.
de Freytas-Tamura, K, 'Boris Johnson, a "Burqa Storm" and Perhaps Some Populist Calculations' *New York Times* (8 August 2018) www.nytimes.com/2018/08/08/world/europe/boris-johnson-trump-burqa.html?.
Dodd, V and O'Carroll, L, 'Police warned against "overreach" in use of virus lockdown powers' *The Guardian* (31 March 2020).
Dominiczak, P, Hope, C and McCann, K, 'Judges vs the people: Government Ministers resigned to losing appeal against High Court ruling' *The Telegraph* (3 November 2016) (www.telegraph.co.uk/news/2016/11/03/the-plot-to-stop-brexit-the-judges-versus-the-people/.
Dyer, C and Wintour, P, 'Woolf leads judges' attack on Ministers' *The Guardian* (4 March 2004).
Dyke, T, 'Why Cameron has got it wrong on judicial review reform' (*The Lawyer*, 29 January 2013).
Editorial, 'Are You or Have You Ever Been a Lawyer? *New York Times* (7 March 2010) www.nytimes.com/2010/03/08/opinion/08mon1.html.
Editorial, 'Memo to Mordaunt: the rule of law can only be upheld by observing it' *The Guardian* (16 May 2019).

Editorial, 'Republicans have offered up the soul of the party to keep Trump in power' *The Guardian* (3 February 2020).
Editorial, 'Viktor Orban's power grab is a further step towards autocracy' *The Guardian* (20 March 2020).
Editorial, 'There is no law in Britain against cabinet knavery. Maybe there should be' *The Guardian* (24 January 2022).
Elgot, J, 'Trust in law "is at risk if ministers bypass MPs"' *The Guardian* (19 February 2020).
Elgott, J, 'Radical shake-up of civil service comms to be in place by April 2022' *The Guardian* (16 March 2021) www.theguardian.com/politics/2021/mar/16/radical-shake-up-of-civil-service-comms-to-be-in-place-by-april-2022.
Elgot, J, Syall, R and Boffey, D, 'We are breaking law with Brexit Bill, minister admits' The *Guardian* (9 September 2020).
Elgot, J and Walker, P, 'Johnson seeks to calm Tory rebels as more say they can't back bill that breaches law' *The Guardian* (16 September 2020).
Elliott, F, 'Britain's top judge forced out by bullying Blunkett' *The Independent* (31 October 2004).
Elliott, F, Ames, J and Ford, R, 'Boris Johnson snubs Robert Buckland's call for sex offenders to remain anonymous' *The Times* (1 August 2019) www.thetimes.co.uk/article/suspects-in-sex-crimes-should-be-anonymous-5q9c3lvxj.
Elliott, L and Treanor, J, 'Five years on from Lehman: "We had almost no control"' *The Guardian* (13 September 2013).
Falconer, C, 'The law is for ministers too' *The Guardian* (19 September 2017).
Fetherstonhaugh, G, 'Pupillage: A Potted History' (*Counsel*, June 2015) www.counselmagazine.co.uk/articles/pupillage-potted-history#:~:text=Regulation%20of%20pupillage%20has%20a%20comparatively%20recent%20history.,for%20practice%20at%20the%20Bar%20only%20since%201959.
Feinberg, C, 'Most respectable lawyers have quit Trump's lawsuits. The ones who haven't are getting desperate and dangerous' *The Independent* (19 November 2020) www.independent.co.uk/voices/trump-lawyers-rudy-giuliani-sidney-powell-desperate-b1724470.html.
Ferguson, K and Clarke, N, 'Tory Cold Shoulder' *The Sun* (17 November 2021) www.thesun.co.uk/news/16769437/boris-johnson-apologised-sleaze-scandals-angry-tory-mps/.
Fouzder, M, 'Five solicitors sworn in as High Court judges' (*Law Society Gazette*, 23 October 2020) www.lawgazette.co.uk/news/solicitors-sworn-in-as-high-court-judges/5106126.article.
Freedland, J, 'Without the BBC we would be facing a post-truth dystopia' *The Guardian* (25 June 2010).
Freedland, J 'Just societies need referees. We abuse them at our peril' *The Guardian* (13 April 2019).
Freedland, J, 'Trump's great advantage: he will always play dirty' *The Guardian* (20 April 2019).
Freedland, J, '"Partygate" has shown how Brexit corrupted Conservatism' *The Guardian* (22 January 2022).
Gabbatt, A, 'Donald Trump "frustrated with lawyers" as he watches impeachment trial on TV' *The Guardian* (10 February 2021) www.theguardian.com/us-news/2021/feb/10/trump-watching-impeachment-trial-tv-mar-a-lago.
Garton Ash, T, 'Hungary is dismantling democracy. The EU must act' *The Guardian* (20 June 2019).
Gauke, D, 'Why we need lawyers – "lefty" or otherwise' *The Guardian* (21 October 2020).
Gayle, D, 'Colston's firm enslaved more Africans than any other, Olusoga tells court' *The Guardian* (17 December 2021).
Gayle, D, '"Be on the right side of history," jury in Colston statue trial is urged' *The Guardian* (5 January 2022).
Gibb, F, 'Woolf rejects Blunkett criticism' *The Times* (22 May 2003).
Gibson, O, 'Dacre attacks BBC "cultural Marxism"' *The Guardian* (23 January 2007) www.theguardian.com/media/2007/jan/23/dailymail.bbc.
Glover, S, 'Now we know: It's Boris Johnson and his gang against the world' *Daily Mail* (20 November 2020) www.dailymail.co.uk/debate/article-8971663/STEPHEN-GLOVER-know-Boris-Johnson-gang-against-world.html.
Goodman, LM, 'David Miranda and the Human-Rights Black Hole' (*Newsweek Magazine*, 1 July 2015) www.newsweek.com/2015/01/16/edward-snowdens-helpers-296988.html.
Grierson, J, 'Home Office wrong to refer to "activist lawyers" top official admits' *The Guardian* (28 August 2020).
Grierson, J, 'Hancock ignored equality duty over pandemic jobs' *The Guardian* (16 February 2022).

Griffin, N and Nardell, G, 'R.I.P. Legal Professional Privilege' (*Counsel*, May 2012) 30.
Helmore, E, 'Lawyer Steven Donziger gets six-month sentence for contempt in Chevron battle' *The Guardian* (1 October 2021) www.theguardian.com/us-news/2021/oct/01/steven-donziger-lawyer-sentenced-contempt-chevron.
Henley, J, 'Populism: Movements here to stay, but they can be beaten' *The Guardian* (26 September 2017).
Heppinstall, A, 'Public access to the Bar is good for all' (2005) 155(7192) *New Law Journal* 1360.
Hilborne, N, 'Law Society and Bar Council condemn regulators for "attacks" on profession' (*Legal Futures*, 23 September 2016).
Hirsch, A, 'Toppling statues? Here's why Nelson's column should be next' *The Guardian* (22 August 2017) www.theguardian.com/commentisfree/2017/aug/22/toppling-statues-nelsons-column-should-be-next-slavery.
Hirsch, A and Luck, A, 'Law Society "lost control" of investigation into top solicitor' *The Guardian* (24 May 2009) www.theguardian.com/uk/2009/may/24/law-society-investigation-michael-napier.
Holpuch, A, 'McConnell "Spoke out of two sides of his mouth"' *The Guardian* (15 February 2021).
Howes, S, 'Revealed: Taxpayers foot 55 million bill for lawyer for blocking deportation flights of channel migrants' *Mail on Sunday* (4 October 2020).
Hoyano, L, 'No Deal' (*Counsel*, June 2016) www.counselmagazine.co.uk/articles/no-deal.
Hyde, J, 'Bar Council faces probe over cab rank "interference"' (*Law Society Gazette*, 5 June 2013).
Hyde, J, 'Legal background is ticket to seat in new parliament' (*Law Society Gazette*, 21 May 2015) www.lawgazette.co.uk/news/legal-background-is-ticket-to-seat-in-new-parliament/5048967.article.
Hyde, J, 'MoD leaned on SRA over Iraq war claims, Leigh Day alleges' (*Law Society Gazette*, 10 February 2017).
Hyde, J, 'Yes, minister – SRA's Leigh Day correspondence revealed' (*Law Society Gazette* 13 December 2018) www.lawgazette.co.uk/news/yes-minister-sras-leigh-day-correspondence-revealed/5068681.article.
Jeffrey, S, 'Lord Goldsmith's legal advice and the Iraq war' *The Guardian* (27 April 2005) www.theguardian.com/world/2005/apr/27/iraq.iraq2.
Jenkins, S, 'From militant doctors to angry lawyers, professionals are the new union barons' *The Guardian* (19 November 2015).
Johnston, I, 'Climate change denier Scott Pruitt's appointment to EPA would be 'unprecedented assault' on its work' *The Independent* (7 February 2017) www.independent.co.uk/climate-change/news/climate-change-denier-scott-pruitt-epa-appointment-unprecedented-assault-environment-protection-agency-donald-trump-global-warming-a7566946.html.
Kettle, M, 'Johnson's gambit now is to turn his humiliation into rocket fuel' *The Guardian* (26 September 2019).
Kettle, M, 'At times like this we need to rethink our US infatuation' *The Guardian* (1 October 2020).
Kettle, M, 'Like Trump, Johnson is dismantling democracy' *The Guardian* (4 February 2022).
Klasfeld, A, 'Nobel Laureates Condemn Rare Judge-Ordered Prosecution' (*Courthouse News Service*, 16 April 2020) www.courthousenews.com/nobel-laureates-condemn-rare-judge-ordered-prosecution/.
Krauss, MI, 'Chevron v Donziger: The Epic Battle for the Rule of Law Hits the Second Circuit' (*Forbes*, 21 April 2015) www.forbes.com/sites/michaelkrauss/2015/04/21/chevron-v-donziger-the-epic-battle-for-the-rule-of-law-hits-the-second-circuit/?sh=739523513602.
LaFraniere, S, Mazzetti, M and Apuzzo, M, 'How the Russia Inquiry Began: A Campaign Aide, Drinks and Talk of Political Dirt' *The New York Times* (30 December 2017) www.nytimes.com/2017/12/30/us/politics/how-fbi-russia-investigation-began-george-papadopoulos.html.
Leigh, D, 'Obituary: Clive Ponting' *The Guardian* (6 August 2020) www.theguardian.com/politics/2020/aug/06/clive-ponting-obituary.
Lerner, S, 'How the environmental lawyer who won a massive judgment against Chevron lost everything' (*The Intercept*, 29 January 2020) https://theintercept.com/2020/01/29/chevron-ecuador-lawsuit-steven-donziger/.
Lewis, P, Clarke, S and Barr, C, 'Populist presidents linked to reduced inequality' *The Guardian* (7 March 2019).
Lyons, K, 'President calls for retribution after Baldwin sketch' *The Guardian* (19 February 2019).
MacDonald, I, 'Police State?' (*Counsel*, March 2005).
Makortoff, K, 'David Cameron texted Rishi Sunak to get Covid loans for Greensill, says report' *The Guardian* (21 March 2021) www.theguardian.com/politics/2021/mar/21/david-cameron-texted-rishi-sunak-to-get-covid-loans-for-greensill-says-report.

Malik, N, 'When petitions and pleas are ignored, protest is essential' *The Guardian* (15 June 2020).

Malnick, E, 'Dominic Raab: I'll overhaul Human Rights Act to stop Strasbourg dictating to us' *The Telegraph* (16 October 2021) https://www.telegraph.co.uk/politics/2021/10/16/dominic-raab-sets-plans-overhaul-human-rights-act-reform-judicial/.

Martinson, J, 'BBC white paper could spark revolt among Tory MPs' *The Guardian* (11 May 2016).

Mason, R, 'Dominic Cummings thinktank called for 'end of BBC in current form' *The Guardian* (20 January 2021) www.theguardian.com/politics/2020/jan/21/dominic-cummings-thinktank-called-for-end-of-bbc-in-current-form.

Mayer, J, 'The making of the Fox News White House' (*The New Yorker*, 11 March 2019).

McCarthy, T, 'Impeachment trial: Trump lawyers claim "fight like hell" speech did not incite riot' *The Guardian* (2 February 2021) www.theguardian.com/us-news/2021/feb/02/trump-capitol-riot-powder-keg-impeachment-prosecutors.

McSmith, A, 'Tony Blair showed "little appetite" to ensure Iraq War was legal, Chilcot report says' *The Independent* (6 July 2016) www.independent.co.uk/news/uk/politics/chilcot-report-lord-goldsmith-legal-advice-iraq-war-tony-blair-verdict-latest-news-a7122756.html.

McVeigh, K, 'They do it with impunity: 357 human rights defenders killed around the globe last year' *The Guardian* (2 March 2022).

Media, PA, 'MPs urge halt to elections bill as "voter ID may hit turnout"' *The Guardian* (13 December 2021).

Merrick, R, 'Theresa May speech "could have been taken out of Mein Kampff" Vince cable says' *The Independent* (5 July 2017).

Metcalf, S, 'Neoliberalism: The idea that swallowed the world' *The Guardian* (18 August 2017).

Mishra, P, 'The custodians of democracy failed to see it rotting away' *The Guardian* (20 September 2019).

Mohdin, A, 'Minister heavily criticised over judicial bias claim' *The Guardian* (13 September 2019).

Monbiot, G, 'Neoliberalism – the ideology at the root of all our problems' *The Guardian* (15 April 2015).

Monbiot, G, 'A despot in disguise: one man's mission to rip up democracy' *The Guardian* (19 July 2017).

Monbiot, G, 'With just one contract, corporate and state power has subverted democracy' *The Guardian* (25 October 2017).

Monbiot, G, 'Pegasus is just the latest tool autocrats use to stay in power' *The Guardian* (28 July 2021).

Monbiot, G, 'The UK is a democracy in name only' *The Guardian* (4 June 2020).

Monbiot, G, 'No 10 and lobby groups set on undermining democracy' *The Guardian* (2 September 2020).

Mudde, C, 'How populism became the concept that defines our age' *The Guardian* (22 November 2018).

Noah, S, 'Boris Johnson's "attacks" on the BBC are "dangerous" says David Dimbleby' *The Independent* (26 September 2020).

O'Carroll, L, 'How is Boris Johnson's Brexit deal different from Theresa May's?' *The Guardian* (17 October 2019) www.theguardian.com/politics/2019/oct/17/how-is-boris-johnson-brexit-deal-different-from-theresa-may.

O'Carroll, L, 'Priti Patel to reveal proposals for offshore centres for asylum seekers' *The Guardian* (5 July 2021) www.theguardian.com/uk-news/2021/jul/05/priti-patel-to-reveal-proposals-for-offshore-centres-for-asylum-seekers.

O'Connor, B, 'Trump's useful thugs' *The Guardian* (21 January 2021).

O'Hagan, EM, 'In the Chevron court case, ordinary Ecuadorians' voices don't seem to count' *The Guardian* (18 March 2014).

Oliver, M, 'McLibel' *The Guardian* (15 February 2005) www.theguardian.com/news/2005/feb/15/food.foodanddrink.

Olusoga, D, 'The toppling of Edward Colston's statue is not an attack on history. It is history' *The Guardian* (8 June 2020) www.theguardian.com/commentisfree/2020/jun/08/edward-colston-statue-history-slave-trader-bristol-protest.

Olusoga, D, 'A year on, the battered and graffitied Colston is finally a potent memorial to our past' *The Guardian* (6 June 2021) https://amp.theguardian.com/commentisfree/2021/jun/06/year-on-battered-graffitied-colston-finally-potent-memorial-to-our-past.

Pengelly, M, 'Trump "plotted to sack attorney general" in desperate attempt to reverse election result' *The Guardian* (24 January 2021).

Phillips, A, 'A want of experience' (*Law Society Gazette*, 28 April 1999).

Phillips, G, 'How the free press worldwide is under threat' *The Guardian* (26 May 2020).

Pilkington, E, 'Donald Trump doesn't want to be investigated, so he's undermining people's faith in the rule of law' *The Guardian Review* (16 March 2019).

Pilkington, E, 'Trump aide says president is victim of a politicised justice system' *The Guardian* (17 February 2020).
Price, G, 'All the times Trump attacked Andrew McCabe before the Deputy Director stepped down' (*Newsweek*, 29 January 2018) www.yahoo.com/news/times-trump-attacked-andrew-mccabe-181954593. html?guccounter=1&guce_referrer=aHR0cHM6Ly93d3cuYmluZy5jb20v&guce_referrer_sig=AQ AAAB2DKZFUGRcPbqZwo77utps77ilD0O4rEBXAMBfg-XaT-0k3Axtn5YsAR0Anm1wJZ69Vy0 xJNkUtmQcV4a7tdGWej2GCKmoDzNLrYt7aBlHekuqCJv6fAMy0hc7gpRfY22BKJyM_Go4OA_ okBe7oOL_JU_BAEbc9MF0wkS6JrV5Z.
Randazzo, J, 'Tribunal Condemns Ecuador's $9.5 Billion Ruling Against Chevron' (*Wall Street Journal*, 7 September 2017).
Rankin, J, 'Hungary: Anger at Tory vote against sanctions' *The Guardian* (26 June 2018).
Rawnsley, A, 'Tories are wrong to think that they will never face a day of reckoning for sleaze' *The Observer* (25 April 2021).
Reeves, P, 'Case History – A look back to the 18th century to find the origins of the Law Society and the changes over 150 years' (1995) 92 *The Law Society Gazette*.
Rhode, D, 'William Barr's break with Donald Trump' (*The New Yorker*, 5 December 2020) www.newyorker. com/news/daily-comment/william-barrs-break-with-donald-trump.
Robinson, E, '"Al-Qaeda 7" smear campaign is an assault on American values' *Washington Post* (9 March 2010) www.washingtonpost.com/wp-dyn/content/article/2010/03/08/AR2010030803122.html.
Rooduijn, M, 'One in six Europeans now vote for the far right' *The Guardian* (3 March 2020).
Roth, A, 'Navalny bound for prison after appeal rejected' *The Observer* (21 February 2021).
Roth, A, 'Obituary: Lord Nolan' *The Guardian* (26 January 2007) www.theguardian.com/news/2007/ jan/26/guardianobituaries.obituaries.
Ruck, J, 'Confederate statures removed across Southern US States' *The Guardian* (15 August 2017) www. theguardian.com/us-news/gallery/2017/aug/15/confederate-statues-removed-across-southern-us-states-in-pictures.
Ruddick, G, 'Clarke suggests Cameron made Sun deal' *The Guardian* (24 November 2017).
Savage, M and Helm, T, 'Top Lawyers slam minister for wrecking UK's reputation' *The Observer* (13 September 2020).
Schmidt, MS and Haberman, M, 'Trump Ordered Mueller Fired, but Backed Off When White House Counsel Threatened to Quit' *New York Times* (25 January 2018) www.nytimes.com/2018/01/25/us/ politics/trump-mueller-special-counsel-russia.html.
Schudel, M, 'Monroe H. Freedman, scholar of legal ethics and civil liberties, dies at 86' *Washington Post* (28 February 2015) www.washingtonpost.com/national/monroe-h-freedman-scholar-of-legal-ethics-and-civil-liberties-dies-at-86/2015/02/28/9e9c562a-beb3-11e4-8668-4e7ba8439ca6_story.html.
Secret barrister, 'Against the law- why judges are under attack' *The Guardian* (22 August 2020) www. theguardian.com/books/2020/aug/22/against-the-law-why-judges-are-under-attack-by-the-secret-barrister.
Sen, A 'India Once stood for liberty. Now despotism has taken over' *The Guardian* (27 October 2020).
Siddique, H and Syal, R, 'Raab to claim overhaul of human rights law will counter "political correctness"' *The Guardian* (14 December 2021) www.theguardian.com/law/2021/dec/14/raab-to-claim-overhaul-human-rights-law-counter-political-correctness.
Sinclair, L, 'Licensed access: opportunity or blind alley?' (2005) 155(7180) *New Law Journal* 895.
Slack, J, 'Enemies of the People' *Daily Mail* (4 November 2016).
Slingo, J, 'Lawyers at risk of physical attack after Patel speech, says Law Society' (*Law Society Gazette*, 5 October 2020).
Smith, D, 'Trump's Republican base will not be shaken despite the Senate's rebuke' *The Observer* (14 February 2021).
Smith, D, Jacobs, B and Ackerman, S, 'Sally Yates fired by Trump after acting US attorney general defied travel ban' *The Guardian* (31 January 2017) www.theguardian.com/us-news/2017/jan/30/justice-department-trump-immigration-acting-attorney-general-sally-yates.
Solnit, R, 'Trump built an army to enforce his reality. This was inevitable' *The Guardian* (8 January 2021).
Stewart, H and Murphy, S, 'Fury as PM tells Tories to back "bully" Patel' *The Guardian* (21 November 2020).
Stewart, H, Syal, R and O'Carroll, L, 'PM heads to Dublin amid fears of more resignations' *The Guardian* (9 September 2019).

Stewart, H and Syal, R, 'Labour urges inquiry into David Cameron links to Greensill Capital' *The Guardian* (31 March 2021) www.theguardian.com/politics/2021/mar/31/labour-urges-inquiry-into-david-cameron-links-to-greensill-capital.

Stewart, H, Walker, P and Mason, R, 'He misled the Queen, the people and Parliament' *The Guardian* (25 September 2019).

Stone, J, 'Scrapping the human rights act will restore magna Carta legacy claims David Cameron' *Independent* (15 June 2015).

Swaine, J, 'Trump demands suspension of legal process at borders' *The Guardian* (25 June 2018).

Syal, R, 'Alarm at overhaul of human rights law' *The Guardian* (14 December 2021).

Syal, R, 'Dominic Cummings role provokes alarm in civil service' *The Guardian* (25 July 2022) www.theguardian.com/politics/2019/jul/25/dominic-cummings-role-provokes-alarm-inside-civil-service.

Syal, R and Cobain, I, 'Labour call for Straw to face MPs over role in Libyan renditions' *The Guardian* (12 May 2018).

Syal, R and Siddique, H, 'Dominic Raab's paper seen as fulfilment of quest to destroy Human Rights Act' *The Guardian* (14 December 2021) www.theguardian.com/politics/2021/dec/14/dominic-raabs-paper-seen-as-fulfilment-of-quest-to-destroy-human-rights-act?s=08.

Taylor, D, 'Top judge attacks Blunkett' *Evening Standard* (17 May 2002).

Tisdall, S, 'Putin, a criminal and incompetent president, is an enemy of his people' *The Observer* (19 January 2020).

Tisdall, S, 'America needs to get a grip on democracy, for all our sakes' *The Guardian* (7 August 2018).

Townsend, M, 'Lawyers claim knife attack at law firm was inspired by Priti Patel's rhetoric' *The Guardian* (10 October 2020).

Tran, M, 'Dozens of inquiries into alleged Iraq war crimes scrapped' *The Guardian* (25 January 2015).

Traub, J, 'Can the left save liberalism from Trump?' *New York Times* (17 October 2019) www.nytimes.com/2019/10/17/opinion/liberalism-trump.html.

Trilling, D, 'For the panto authoritarians, overt cruelty is a winning hand' *The Guardian* (18 February 2020).

Turley, J, 'Reflections on Murder, Misdemeanours, and Madison' (1999) 28 *Hofstra Law Review* 439.

Usborne, D, 'Guantanomo Bay: Why has Obama failed on his promise to close controversial detention Camp?' *The Independent* (16 August 2016) www.independent.co.uk/news/world/americas/guantanamo-bay-closing-why-has-obama-failed-a7194241.html.

Walker, P, 'Johnson will not declare Spanish holiday in MPs' register, says No 10' *The Guardian* (5 November 2021) www.theguardian.com/politics/2021/nov/05/boris-johnson-will-not-declare-spanish-holiday-in-mps-register-says-no-10.

Wall, T, 'How Bristol dumped its hated slaver in the docks, and a nation searched its soul' *The Guardian* (14 June 2020).

Watts, J, 'Nobel laureates condemn "judicial harassment" of environmental lawyer' *The Guardian* (18 April 2020) www.theguardian.com/world/2020/apr/18/nobel-laureates-condemn-judicial-harassment-of-environmental-lawyer.

Weaver, M, 'Cummings "should have resigned in May", say Barnard Castle witnesses' *The Guardian* (13 November 2020).

Wintour, P, 'Landscape for rights to media freedom "pretty bleak", warns Clooney' *The Guardian* (17 February 2020).

Wintour, P and Bowcott, O, 'David Cameron plans broad clampdown on judicial review rights' *The Guardian* (19 November 2012).

Wolffe, R, 'Of course Trump's campaign colluded with the Russians but unfortunately that's not a crime' *The Guardian* (18 April 2019) www.theguardian.com/commentisfree/2019/apr/18/trump-collusion-russia-mueller-barr.

Woodcock, A, 'Priti Patel accused of putting lawyers at risk by branding them "lefty do-gooders"' *The Independent* (6 October 2020) www.independent.co.uk/news/uk/politics/priti-patel-immigration-lawyers-migrants-law-society-bar-council-b832856.html.

Younge, G, 'The Tories can't win without the rightwing press on their side' *The Guardian* (15 November 2019).

Yuhas, A, 'Trump's immigration ban: which cases are in play and what happens next?' *The Guardian* (30 January 2017) www.theguardian.com/us-news/2017/jan/30/trump-travel-ban-explainer-muslim-immigration-aclu.

ONLINE RESOURCES: NEWS, BLOGS, WEBSITES

Afrati, A, 'The Stanford Affair: Another Bad Day for Proskauer's Tom Sjoblom' (*Wall Street Journal Law Blog*, 27 August 2009) www.wsj.com/articles/BL-LB-18063.

American College of Trial Lawyers, 'Amendment of Model Rule 1.6: Progress Or A Step Backward?' (Irvine, Calif., ACTL, 2004).

The Arraignment And Tryall Of Robert Earl Of Essex And Henry Earl Of Southampton At Westminster The 19th Of February, 1600. And In The 43 Year of The Reign Of Queen Elizabeth, https://quod.lib.umich.edu/e/eebo/A25875.0001.001/1:2?rgn=div1;view=fulltext.

Axios, 'The political leanings of the Supreme Court Justices' (1 June 2019) www.axios.com/supreme-court-justices-ideology-52ed3cad-fcff-4467-a336-8bec2e6e36d4.html.

BBC News, 'Theresa May: Tories to consider leaving European Convention on Human Rights' (9 March 2013) www.bbc.co.uk/news/uk-politics-21726612.

BBC News, 'Who were the Tory rebels who defied Boris Johnson?' (5 September 2019) www.bbc.co.uk/news/uk-politics-49563357.

BBC News, 'Geoffrey Cox tells MPs: "This Parliament is a disgrace"' (25 September 2019) https://www.bbc.co.uk/news/av/uk-politics-49827307.

BBC News 'Results' (undated) www.bbc.co.uk/news/election/2019/results.

BBC News, 'Man charged with right-wing terror plot to kill immigration solicitor' (23 October 2020) www.bbc.co.uk/news/uk-england-london-54661222.

BBC News, 'The investigations into Boris Johnson and the government' (5 November 2021) www.bbc.co.uk/news/uk-politics-56926219?at_campaign=KARANGA&at_medium=RSS.

BBC News, 'Minister Kwasi Kwarteng sorry for upset caused by Standards Commissioner remarks' (15 November 2021) www.bbc.co.uk/news/uk-politics-59298861?at_medium=RSS&at_campaign=KARANGA.

Bell, R and Abela, C, 'A Lawyer's Duty to the Court' *Proceedings of a Symposium* (February 2012) www.weirfoulds.com/assets/uploads/11024_10167_CEA-A-Lawyers-Duty-to-the-Court.pdf.

Blick, A and Jones, G, 'The Institution of Prime Minister' UK Government https://history.blog.gov.uk/2012/01/01/the-institution-of-prime-minister/.

Boston Massacre Historical Society, 'The Summary of the Boston Massacre Trial' www.bostonmassacre.net/trial/trial-summary4.htm.

Braun, CN, 'The Morality of Resisting Trump' Academia Letter www.academia.edu/45003512/The_Morality_of_Resisting_Trump.

Burke, E, *Reflections on the Revolution in France* (1790) www.bl.uk/collection-items/reflections-on-the-revolution-in-france-by-edmund-burke.

Cassese, A, *Affirmation of the Principles of International Law recognized by the Charter of the Nürnberg Tribunal General Assembly resolution 95 (I)* https://legal.un.org/avl/ha/ga_95-I/ga_95-I.html.

Chevron v Donziger Nos. 14-0826(L), 14-0832(C), 2016 WL 4173988 (2d Cir. Aug. 8, 2016) 'Cases' (2016) 130 *Harvard Law Review* 745.

Corruption Perceptions Index 2021, www.transparency.org/en/cpi/2021.

Davis, F, 'Decision of the Supreme court on the prorogation of Parliament' (House of Commons Library, 24 September 2019) https://commonslibrary.parliament.uk/decision-of-the-supreme-court-on-the-prorogation-of-parliament/.

'Donald Trump tells Proud Boys to "stand back and stand by" at debate' *USA News Today* https://eu.usatoday.com/story/news/politics/elections/2020/09/29/trump-debate-white-supremacists-stand-back-stand-by/3583339001/.

Downey, S, 'Self-interested Law Society Stripped of Power to Appoint SRA Chair' (*Legal Business*, 2 May 2014) www.legalbusiness.co.uk/index.php/lb-blog-view/2337-self-interested-law-society-stripped-of-power-to-appoint-sra-chairman.

Duncan Lewis solicitors, 'Attacks on Duncan Lewis Solicitors and legal aid undermine the rule of law and an individual's constitutional right to access to justice' (7 October 2020) www.duncanlewis.co.uk/news/_Attacks_on_Duncan_Lewis_Solicitors_and_legal_aid_undermine_the_rule_of_law_and_an_individual%E2%80%99s_constitutional_right_to_access_to_justice_(7_October_2020).html.

Eighteenth Century Collections Online, *The trial of Thomas Paine: for a libel, contained in The second part of rights of man, before Lord Kenyon, and a special jury, at Guildhall, December 18. With the speeches of the Attorney General and Mr. Erskine, at large* https://quod.lib.umich.edu/e/ecco/004809446.0001.000/1:2?rgn=div1;view=fulltext.

Emersberger, J, 'Manufacturing Disgrace: Reuters Distorts Chevron v Donziger' (FAIR, 11 September 2020) https://fair.org/home/manufacturing-disgrace-reuters-distorts-chevron-v-donziger/.

'Federalist Papers: Primary Documents in American History' *Library of Congress* https://guides.loc.gov/federalist-papers/full-text#:~:text=The%20Federalist%20Papers%20were%20written%20and%20published%20to,explain%20particular%20provisions%20of%20the%20Constitution%20in%20detail.

Flexner, A, *Is Social Work a Profession?* (address at the National Conference of Charities and Correction, Baltimore, 17 May 1915) The Adoption History Project, https://pages.uoregon.edu/adoption/archive/FlexnerISWAP.htm.

4 News, 'Iraq inquiry focuses on Blair-Goldsmith relationship' (21 January 2011) www.channel4.com/news/iraq-inquiry-focuses-on-blair-goldsmith-relationship.

Gallagher, R, 'U.K. Police Investigation Of Snowden Leak Journalists Enters Fourth Year' (*The Intercept*, 29 November 2017) https://theintercept.com/2017/11/29/met-police-snowden-leaks-operation-curable/.

Gardiner, S, Morrison, D and Robinson, S, (2021) 'Integrity in Public Life: Reflections on a Duty of Candour' *Public Integrity* www.tandfonline.com/doi/full/10.1080/10999922.2021.1903165.

Geoghegan, P and Corderoy, J, 'Key members of Jacob-Rees Mogg's pro-Brexit MP lobby group finally revealed' (*Open Democracy*, 1 May 2019) www.opendemocracy.net/en/dark-money-investigations/key-members-of-jacob-rees-moggs-pro-brexit-mp-lobby-group-finally-revealed/.

Global Corruption Index, https://risk-indexes.com/global-corruption-index/.

Goodwin, H, 'No 10 can't find anyone willing to interview Paul Dacre for Ofcom job' (*London Economic*, 31 August 2021) www.thelondoneconomic.com/politics/no-10-cant-find-anyone-willing-to-interview-paul-dacre-for-ofcom-job-288168/.

Hallpike, CR, 'A Response to Yuval Harari's *Sapiens: A Brief History of Humankind*' (*New English Review*) www.hallpike.com/wp-content/uploads/a-review-of-sapiens.pdf.

Heald, O, 'The role of the Law Officers' Speech by Solicitor General Oliver Heald QC MP to Kent Law School (18 October 2012) www.gov.uk/government/speeches/the-role-of-the-law-officers.

Home, A, 'Special Advocates and Closed Materials Procedures' (House of Common Library, 25 June 2012) p 10 https://researchbriefings.files.parliament.uk/documents/SN06285/SN06285.pdf.

House of Common Library, 'Fixed term Parliaments Act 2011' (24 December 2020) https://commonslibrary.parliament.uk/research-briefings/sn06111/.

House of Common Library, 'Lord Chancellor's Oath and the Rule of Law' (13 October 2020) https://commonslibrary.parliament.uk/research-briefings/cdp-2020-0107/.

Howell, TB (compiler), *A Complete Collection of State Trials and Proceedings for High treason and Other Crimes and Misdemeanours from the Earliest Period to the Year 1783*, Volume IV (24: Charles I, 1649: Trial of Charles the First) (London) 995. https://babel.hathitrust.org/cgi/pt?id=hvd.hxj2f4;view=1up;seq=512.

Independent Office for Police Conduct, 'No criminal investigation of Boris Johnson for misconduct in public office while Mayor of London' (21 May 2020) www.policeconduct.gov.uk/news/no-criminal-investigation-boris-johnson-misconduct-public-office-while-mayor-london.

International Bar Association, *Directory of Regulators of the Legal Professions* (IBA 2016) www.ibanet.org/IBA_Regulation_Directory_Home.

ITV News, 'Ministers U-turn on standards overhaul amid outrage over Owen Paterson case' (4 November 2021) www.itv.com/news/2021-11-04/ministers-u-turn-on-standards-overhaul-amid-outrage-over-owen-paterson-case.

Joychild, F, 'Continuing the Conversation … The fading star of the rule of law' https://eveningreport.nz/2015/03/24/frances-joychild-qc-on-the-fading-star-of-the-rule-of-law/.

Kavanagh, D, 'Thatcherism and the end of the post-war consensus' www.bbc.co.uk/history/british/modern/thatcherism_01.shtml.

Kennedy, L, 'How the 2000 Election came down to a Supreme Court decision' (*History*, 24 September 2020) www.history.com/news/2000-election-bush-gore-votes-supreme-court.

Kuenssberg, L, 'Downing Street party: No 10 staff joked about party amid lockdown restrictions' (*BBC News*) www.bbc.co.uk/news/uk-politics-59572149?at_medium=RSS&at_campaign=KARANGA.

Law Society, 'Is legal professional privilege under threat? A roundtable discussion at the Law Society' (28 October 2016).

Law Works, 'Secondary Specialisation' www.lawworks.org.uk/solicitors-and-volunteers/get-involved/secondary-specialisation.

Legal Futures, 'Edmonds backs BSB as advocacy regulator; MR warns over "consumer fundamentalism"' www.legalfutures.co.uk/regulation/legal-executives/bsb-should-regulate-advocacy-says-edmonds-as-mr-warns-against-consumer-fundamentalism.

Legal Futures, 'Neuberger warns against risk of profits before principles in the ABS world' (22 February 2013) www.legalfutures.co.uk/latest-news/neuberger-warns-risk-profits-principles-abs-world.

Legal Futures, 'Solicitors make last-ditch bid to halt "unjustified" advocacy quality scheme' (7 June 2011) www.legalfutures.co.uk/regulation/solicitors-make-last-ditch-bid-to-halt-unjustified-advocacy-quality-scheme.

Littleboy, C and Kelly, R, 'Pepper v Hart' Parliament and Constitution Centre, Standard Note: SN/PC/392 (House of Commons Library, 2005) https://researchbriefings.files.parliament.uk/documents/SN00392/SN00392.pdf.

Locke, J, 'Letter Concerning Toleration' (1689) *American History* www.let.rug.nl/usa/documents/1651-1700/john-locke-letter-concerning-toleration-1689.php.

Madbak, HF, 'Guantanamo Lawyers under attack' http://nysbar.com/blogs/ExecutiveDetention/2010/03/guantanamo_lawyers_under_attac_1.html.

Mail Online, 'Officials "begged" Robert Jenrick to kill Richard Desmond's controversial £1bn property deal' www.dailymail.co.uk/news/article-8467707/Officials-begged-Robert-Jenrick-kill-Richard-Desmonds-controversial-1bn-property-deal.html.

Malcom, N, 'Hobbs and Spinoza' in JH Burn (ed), *Cambridge Histories Online* (Cambridge University Press, 2008) www.johnjthrasher.com/wp-content/uploads/2014/01/Hobbes-and-Spinoza-Noel-Malcolm.pdf.

May, J, 'Government will promote "British values", Theresa May says' (*Politics Home*, 13 May 2015) www.holyrood.com/news/view,may-uk-government-will-promote-british-values_11521.htm.

National Pro Bono Centre Guide to Pro Bono: Free legal advice in England and Wales http://probonoweek.org.uk/wp-content/uploads/2020/08/ProBonoHandBook-2019-npbc.pdf.

O'Donnell, G, 'Public Inquiries' (19 March 2010) https://assets.publishing.service.gov.uk/government/uploads/system/uploads/attachment_data/file/60808/cabinet-secretary-advice-judicial.pdf.

Pobjoy, J, 'Torture, Executive Accountability and the Rule of Law' (*Human Rights Law Centre*, 10 February 2010) www.hrlc.org.au/human-rights-case-summaries/mohamed-v-secretary-of-state-for-foreign-commonwealth-affairs-2010-ewca-civ-65-10-feb-2010.

Public Law Project, 'How to Apply for Legal Aid Funding for Judicial Review' (15 September 2016) https://publiclawproject.org.uk/resources/how-to-apply-for-legal-aid-funding-for-judicial-review/.

Rajan, A, 'Nadine Dorries: BBC licence fee announcement will be the last' (*BBC News*, 16 January 2022) www.bbc.co.uk/news/entertainment-arts-60014514.

The Records of the Society of Gentleman Practisers in the Courts of Law and Equity (London, Incorporated Law Society, 1897). *Internet Archive* https://archive.org/details/cu31924021686344.

Revised Prevent Duty Guidance: for England and Wales, www.gov.uk/government/publications/prevent-duty-guidance/revised-prevent-duty-guidance-for-england-and-wales.

Robert H Jackson: Opening Statement Nuremberg Trials (1945) *The Supreme Court* www.thirteen.org/wnet/supremecourt/personality/print/sources_document12.html.

Rose, N, 'Revealed: LSB Legal Director Opposed approval of QASA' (*Legal Futures*, 26 September 2013) www.legalfutures.co.uk/latest-news/revealed-lsb-legal-director-opposed-approval-qasa.

Rose, N, 'LSB lays out blueprint for radical reform of regulation' (*Legal Futures*, 12 September 2016) www.legalfutures.co.uk/latest-news/lsb-lays-blueprint-radical-reform-regulation.

Rose, N, 'SRA reveals cost of Leigh Day case and ministers' intense interest' (*Legal Futures*, 18 December 2018) www.legalfutures.co.uk/latest-news/sra-reveals-cost-of-leigh-day-case-and-ministers-interest.

Rose, N, '"Compelling case" for reform of regulation, says LSB, as focus on independence intensifies' (*Legal Futures*, 27 July 2015) www.legalfutures.co.uk/latest-news/compelling-case-for-reform-of-regulation-says-lsb-as-focus-on-independence-intensifies.

'Rule of Law' (*Stanford Encyclopaedia of Philosophy*) https://plato.stanford.edu/entries/rule-of-law/.

Scanlan, Q, 'Trump demands Georgia secretary of state "find" enough votes to hand him win' (*ABC News*) https://abcnews.go.com/Politics/trump-demands-georgia-secretary-state-find-votes-hand/story?id=75027350.

Sebastian, M, 'How Has the Supreme Court Fared During the Modi years?' (*The Wire*, 12 April 2019) https://thewire.in/law/supreme-court-modi-years.

Stanzione, MH, 'New ABA Membership Strategy Aims to Reverse Slide' https://news.bloomberglaw.com/business-and-practice/abas-new-membership-model-logo-go-into-effect.

Stephenson, M, 'Petty Corruption, Grand Corruption, and the Politics of Absolution' *The Global Anticorruption Blog* https://globalanticorruptionblog.com/2018/01/02/petty-corruption-grand-corruption-and-the-politics-of-absolution/.

Thomsen, J, 'Mueller: Trump could be charged with obstruction of justice after leaving office' (*The Hill*, 24 July 2017) https://thehill.com/policy/national-security/454502-mueller-trump-could-be-charged-with-obstruction-of-justice-after.

UK Government, 'Government launches independent panel to look at judicial review' (31 July 2010) www.gov.uk/government/news/government-launches-independent-panel-to-look-at-judicial-review.

UK Parliament, 'Allegations Reported to the Standards Committee' www.parliament.uk/mps-lords-and-offices/standards-and-financial-interests/parliamentary-commissioner-for-standards/complaints-and-investigations/allegations-reported-to-the-standards-committee/.

Vibert, F, 'Independent Agencies: No Fixed Boundaries' www.lse.ac.uk/accounting/assets/CARR/documents/Regulatory-Agencies-under-Challenge/CARR-DP81-Frank-Vibert.pdf.

Weakley, K, 'MPs formally reject Commission chair but Minister gives backing' (*Civil Society News*, 25 February 2018) www.civilsociety.co.uk/news/mps-want-to-force-minister-to-explain-charity-commission-chair-appointment.html.

Whitman, JQ, 'What Are the Origins of Reasonable Doubt?' (*History News Network*, George Mason University, 25 February 2008) https://openyls.law.yale.edu/bitstream/handle/20.500.13051/185/0-Whitman__Origins_of_Reasonable_Doubt1.pdf?sequence=2&isAllowed=y.

Williamson, J, 'A Short History of the Washington Consensus' A paper for the conference *From the Washington Consensus towards a new Global Governance* Barcelona, 24–25 September 2004) www.piie.com/publications/papers/williamson0904-2.pdf.

Zurcher, A, 'Hilary Clinton emails – What's it all about?' (*BBC News*, 6 November 2016) www.bbc.co.uk/news/world-us-canada-31806907.

Index

Please *see* entries for particular countries for entries relating to that country rather than subject headings

ABA *see* American Bar Association (ABA)
absolutism/autocracy *see also* **tyranny or despotism**
   authoritarianism 25, 263, 404
   decline of the rule of law 454
   Divine Right of monarchs to rule/absolutism 30–1, 33–4, 36–8
   European Union 404
   Glorious Revolution 47–8
   law as what sovereign commands 10
   populism 456
   totalitarianism 454–5
abuse of power 10, 25, 30, 123, 130, 456
abuse of process 54, 325, 330–2
accept consumers as clients, duty to 299, 301–8, 311
accountability
   anonymity 456–7
   civil proceedings 228
   civil service 120–1
   civil society 112
   corporatised state 377
   decline of the rule of law 456–7
   definition of the rule of law 2
   diagonal (media, academy, and civil society) 456
   horizontal (separation of powers) 456
   institutional accountability 107, 456
   lawyers for clients, of 48
   morality 212–13, 215, 228, 235
   Nuremberg Military Tribunal (NMT) 173
   open access order 24
   prosecutions 217
   public service 264
   vertical (electoral accountability) 456
accused, rights of the 138, 154
ad hoc criminal tribunals, establishment of 178
administration 118–23 *see also* **civil service**
   administrative state 108, 118–19, 129
   agencies 129
   control, weakening administrative 463
   institutions 118–23, 129
   public inquiries 122–3

administration of justice, duty to the 325–32
   advocacy 325–30
   barristers 325, 332
   codes of conduct 340
   incrimination 325–32, 340
   litigation process, abuse of the 325, 330–2
   non-interference 318
   public duties 319
   solicitors 343
   system duties 325–32
adversary system 3, 138–45
   18th century 138–41, 145, 154, 226
   19th century 221–2, 234
   accused, rights of the 138
   advocacy 140, 314, 325
   barristers
      cab rank rule 219, 234, 271, 314
      celebrities, barristers as 140–1
      identity and mythology of the Bar 140–1, 154
   cab rank rule 219, 234, 271, 314
   capitalism 154, 157–8
   civil proceedings 139, 466
   colonies 248
   common law 156–8, 233
   courtroom, lawyers as controlling the 141
   criminal trials 138–40, 466
   criticism 465
   cross-examination 140, 143–4
   ethics of representation 218–20
   evidence 142–3, 157–8
   fair hearing, right to a 466–7
   formalities 467
   identity 138–45, 154–8
   ideology 229, 234, 236
   independence of the legal profession 262–3
   independent and impartial tribunals 466
   individualism 234, 236, 465
   inquisitorial system 465, 467
   juries, role of 139, 145, 154, 157, 220
   justice gap 466
   lawyer and client relationship 141–2
   legal aid 466
   Legal Professional Privilege 197, 468

legality 185–6
moral crisis 218–22, 231, 233–6
natural justice 465
Old Bailey Session Papers (OBSP) 138–40, 144, 156
partisanship 220–1, 228, 233–4
political issues 221
Prisoners Counsel Act 1836 152, 155–6, 218–19, 221, 271
private practice 465–7
process 142–3, 154–5, 158, 467
prosecution, involvement of lawyers in 139
records of State Trials 138–9
social change 154
standard conception of the lawyer's role 233
thief-takers
  criminal process, interference in the 139
  rewards 139, 144–5
transformation 138–41
treason 218
trial strategy 144–5
advice to government 460–1
Attorney General (AG) 85, 88–90, 92–4, 104–5
bills, on 89
confidentiality 88, 89, 104
independence 93–4
Iraq War 2003 88–9, 92
law officers 88–90
publication 88–90
senior government lawyers 95–6, 103
Solicitor General 97
advocacy 325–30
17th century 126
administration of justice, duty to 325–30
adversary system 220–1, 325
Attorney General 86
attorneys 152
autonomy 315
barristers 139–40, 302, 349, 351, 353–5, 465
behaviour in court 325
Common Pleas 136–7
fearless advocacy, obligation of 148, 308–9, 314
immunity 355
independence of the legal profession 268, 295, 356–7
law officers 85, 86, 88
McKenzie friends 361
monopoly of barristers 137, 302, 349, 351, 353–5, 465
morality 229, 234, 236
nature of advocacy 140
neoliberalism 349, 351–7
procedural justice 229

public interest 357
Quality Assurance Scheme for Advocates (QASA) 356
scientific style 325
separation from other work 464
Solicitor General 97
solicitors 302–3, 306, 311, 465
Afghanistan 390, 392, 402, 405
Al Sweady Inquiry 362–3, 366
Alternative Business Structures (ABSs) 287, 358, 379–80
alternatives to the rule of law 402–4
American Bar Association (ABA) 252–3, 261, 280 *see also* **Canons of Ethics (ABA); Model Rules of Professional Conduct 1983 (MRPC) (ABA)**
accept clients, duty to 303
Canons of Ethics 4, 280, 285, 287, 289, 303, 328
code of conduct 280–1, 286–7, 289–90, 293, 297–8
Model Code of Professional Responsibility 280, 286, 289, 293, 303
morality 4, 227
New Model Rules of Professional Conduct (ABA) 281, 286, 289–90
number of members 471
politics, participation in 128
role of lawyers 20
self-regulation 292–3
American Civil War
Confederate soldiers, erection of statues to 187
habeas corpus, suspension of 163
legal profession 248, 251–2
legality 186
American Revolution 29, 48, 56
Articles of Confederation 56
Declaration of Independence 48, 51, 75, 172, 182
Federalist Papers 56
French Revolution, as influencing the 48
ideological foundations 56–7
legal profession 248, 251
republicanism 56
separation of powers 56–7
society based on law 9
anti-establishment attitudes 146–51, 155, 235
Argentina 93, 120, 373–4
aristocracy 14–16, 31, 54
Aristotle 11, 29–30, 119, 125, 160, 424–5
Assize courts 136–7
associations *see* **professional associations**
Attorney General (AG) 84–6
accountability 86

advice to government   86, 88–90, 92–4, 104–5
  confidentiality   88
  independence   93–4
  Iraq war of 2003   88–9, 92
  publication   88–90
Attorney General's Office   87
BAE systems litigation, SFO discontinuance of   92–3
bills, advice on   89
Cabinet, advice to the   89
cash for honours prosecutions   92–3
civil servants   121
common law jurisdictions   97–101
complexity of role   92–3
confidentiality of advice   89, 104
criminal proceedings   87
Crown litigation   88
departments, advice to government   89
Director of Public Prosecutions   87
fair trials   88
Government legal department   88
guardian of the rule of law, as   92, 94, 103
hierarchy of officers   87
independence   86, 89–90, 93–4, 103–5
junior counsel, panel of   121
legal qualifications, need for   92–3
lenient sentences to Court of Appeal, referrals to   87, 88
managerial role   87
media, contempt of court trials involving the   88
ministerial functions   94
nolle prosequi, terminating proceedings through   87
oath   94
origins of role   84
points of law in criminal cases to Court of Appeal, referral of   87
political bias   92–4, 103
prerogative powers   86
proportionality and predictability of law   87
prosecutions, consent to   87, 92–3, 103
public confidence   94
public interest   86, 88, 92–4
publication of advice   88–90
separation of legal and ministerial functions   94
Solicitor General   87, 97
whistleblowing   104
attorneys   136, 152–4, 245–6, 274–6
Austin, John   10–11, 107
Australia *see also* **Australia, legal profession in**
  common law   6
  Constitution   74
  corruption   456
  government/executive   74
  measurement of the rule of law   401
  separation of powers   74
Australia, legal profession in   257–8 *see also* **Legal Profession Uniform Conduct (Barristers) Rules 2015 (LPUC(B)R) (Australia)**
  18th century   257
  19th century   258, 284
  administration of justice, duty to   326
  adversary system   233, 326
  advocacy   332, 334, 340
  Attorney General   100–1
  attorneys   257
  autonomy of clients   307
  barristers   257–8, 261–2, 284, 285–6, 303, 312, 329, 336–7, 471
  British model   257–8, 261, 284, 286, 303, 312, 316
  cab rank rule   261, 303, 304
  colonialism   257–8, 264
  co-regulation   471
  discipline   284
  education and training   258
  English law, relevance of   258
  fairness   333–4
  free movement between states   471
  government lawyers   462
  independence   264, 471
  judiciary   264
  Law Council of Australia model rules   284, 286
  lawful objectives, accepting clients'   307
  Legal Professional Privilege   190, 196, 198, 203, 329
  legalisation   286
  Magna Carta   257
  Model Rules of NSW Bar   285–6, 303, 332
  morality   233
  Mutual Recognition Act 1992   471
  neutrality   303
  organisation of profession   257–8
  prosecutorial duties   332
  regulation   284, 470–1
  self-regulation   284
  Solicitor General   100
  solicitors   258, 262, 284, 298, 326, 334, 336–7
  Solicitors Rules
    clients, duty to   326
    correction of misleading statements   329
    duty to the court   326
    fairness   334
    physical harm, prevention of   336–7
    witnesses, treatment of   335
  specialist advocates   248, 257, 262
  transportation   257–8

autocracy *see* absolutism/autocracy; tyranny or despotism
authoritarianism   25, 263, 404
autonomy of clients   7, 297, 299, 305, 315, 344

Bagehot, William   59–60, 425
Bank of England, establishment of   108
Bar of England and Wales   243–5 *see also* **Bar Code of Conduct (BCC) 1981 (England and Wales); BSB Code of Conduct BSB CC) 2014 (England and Wales); cab rank rule; Inns of Court**
   17th century   152
   18th century   154
   19th century   271, 325
   access   464
   administration of justice, duty to   325, 332
   advocacy
      adversary system   139–40
      monopoly   137, 302, 349, 351, 353–5, 465
      separation from other work   464
      solicitors   302, 465
   Bar Council   245, 306, 355, 358–60
   Bar Direct   354
   Bar Handbook 2014   276, 325
   Bar Standards Board (BSB)   276–7, 295, 358, 349–50, 357, 360
   best interests of client   306, 311, 315
   business lawyers   152
   celebrities, barristers as   140–1, 147–8, 155–6, 272
   ceremonies   243–4
   chambers   243
   communal features, erosion of   243
   competition   464–5
   Consolidated Regulations   245
   Core Duties   277, 279, 295
   co-regulation   472
   Council of Legal Education (CLE)   245
   criminal legal aid, introduction of   245
   culture   353
   discipline   270–3, 290
   education and training   243–5
   entry, regulation of   243
   etiquette, breaches of   271–3
   fees   302
   financial harm, prevention of   342
   honesty   277, 333
   identity   140–1, 147–8, 154–6
   immigration   413–14
   independence   147–8, 262, 271, 354–5, 464
   integrity   277–8, 333
   lawful objectives, accepting clients'   306
   Legal Professional Privilege   324
   Legal Services Act 2007   287, 295, 349–50
   legality   332
   loyalty, devotion, or zeal, duty of   306
   medieval trade guilds, link with   243
   merit   243
   minimum payments for pupils   244
   mislead, duty not to   326–7, 333
   monopoly in advocacy   137, 302, 349, 351, 353–5, 465
   mythology of the Bar   140–1
   neutralisation   472
   neutrality   245, 298, 301–2, 306, 313–14, 464
   one stop shops   360
   organisation   243–5, 248, 250
   partisanship   245, 272–3, 298, 308, 313–15
   peer mechanisms   271
   politics, as entrance into   243
   physical harm, prevention of   342
   Pro Bono Unit   266
   professional conduct   273
   professionalism   273, 277
   public service   266
   pupillage   244
   readers, appointment of   243
   reform   243, 271
   regulation   270–4, 276, 360
   rule of law, upholding the   279
   Rump Parliament   243, 248
   scientific style of advocacy   325
   screening clients   302
   self-employment   243
   self-governance   244
   separation of powers   355
   serjeants, appointment of   243
   sole practitioners   464
   solicitors   302–3, 306, 313–14, 465
   SRA Principles, comparison with   277–8
   standard conception of the lawyer's role   297
   suspect witness testimony   332
   terrorism cases, special advocates in   409
   withdrawal from representation   332
Bar Code of Conduct (BCC) 1981 (England and Wales)
   accepting consumers as clients   301
   all lawful means to achieve client's objective, use of   311
   lawful objectives, accepting clients'   306
   legalisation   286
   loyalty, devotion, or zeal, duty of   308
   neutrality   306
   resistance   273–4, 286
barristers *see* **Bar of England and Wales**
BBC, attacks on   431–2, 449
BCC *see* **Bar Code of Conduct (BCC) 1981 (England and Wales)**
behaviour modification   136, 372–3

Bentham, Jeremy   8, 11, 16, 125, 163, 218
best interests of clients   212, 222, 306, 311, 315
Big Bang de-regulation of financial services in City of London   153–4, 384
Bill of Rights 1689   76, 127, 162, 168, 170, 177
Blackstone, William   8, 10–11, 56–7, 62, 108–11, 124–5, 156, 161–3, 166–7, 171, 183, 193, 226, 251, 257, 262
Boston massacre   249–51
Bretton Woods Agreement 1944   397
Brexit
  consent of Parliament   102, 428
  COVID-19   436
  democracy   424, 426–32, 436, 446, 448–9
  European Research Group (ERG)   427–9, 431–2
  'getting Brexit done'   428–31
  global financial crisis 2008   427
  immigration   448–9
  independence of the judiciary   428
  Internal Markets Bill as breaching international law   434
  legality   434
  media, attitude of the   449
  no deal outcome   429–30
  Northern Ireland protocol   430–1, 434
  notice of withdrawal from EU   428
  Parliamentary sovereignty   429
  patriotism and nationalism, clash between   448
  populism   424, 431, 436, 446, 448
  proroguing of Parliament, litigation on   429–30
  referendum   426–7, 448–9
  slogans   431, 446, 448
  UKIP   427
  Withdrawal Agreement   434
Brougham, Henry   148–51, 155, 156, 197, 208, 219–20, 223–4, 226, 234, 244, 271, 289, 297, 308–9
BSB Code of Conduct (BSB CC) 2014 (England and Wales)
  autonomy of clients   344
  client and court, balance between duties to   464
  confessions, receiving   326–7
  cross-examination, fairness in   334–5
  lawful objectives, accepting clients'   306
  legalisation   287
  misleading or attempting to mislead the court   326–7
  neutrality   298, 301–2, 306, 313–14
  partisanship   298, 308, 313–15
  reporting requirements   324
  witnesses, treatment of   334–5

Business in the Community (BITC)   387, 388
business lawyers   152–4
  attorneys   152–3
  barristers   152
  corporations   153
  identity   126, 152–4, 158
  land, dealing in   135, 153
  solicitors   152, 152–3, 158

cab rank rule   251, 301–2
  adversary system   219, 234, 271, 314
  fees   302
  morality   215
  regulation   358–9
  screening clients   302
  solicitors   302–3
Cabinet
  Attorney General's advice   89
  Cabinet Manual   77–8, 89, 97, 104
  composition   55–6
  establishment   55–6
  government/executive   60
  increase in power   55–6
  Lord Chancellor   83
Calvinism   17–18, 33, 37, 106, 242
Canada *see also* Canada, legal profession in
  British North America Act 1867   73
  common law   6, 248
  Constitution   73
  corruption   456
  democracy   458
  McRuer Report   239, 294, 470
  Minister of Justice   97
  Minister of Public Safety   97
  separation of powers   73–4
  Supreme Court   73–4
  United States   98
Canada, legal profession in   253–6 *see also* FCLS Model Code of Professional Conduct (Canada)
  18th century   253–4, 262
  19th century   255
  accept clients, duty to   304
  accountability   290
  adversary system   253, 261–2, 469
  advocacy   327, 330–2
  apprenticeship model   255
  autonomy of clients   315
  best interests of clients   310–11
  British model and values   253–6, 260–1, 263, 327
  Canadian Bar Association (CBA)   255–6, 284, 285, 286, 292
  Canadian Federation of Bars Model Code   285–6

Index   515

Christianity 255–6
codes of conduct 284, 285–6, 290–1, 294, 297
colonialism 253–5, 261
common law 263, 283, 470
Constitution
  independence 469–70
  international obligations 470
co-regulation 470
discipline 284, 290–1, 470
education and training 254–6
Federation of Canadian Law Societies (FCLS) 256, 284, 285, 292
French law 253
fusion 248, 254, 261
independence 254, 263–4, 283, 469–70
insurance for malpractice 290–1
integrity 318
judges, independence of 469–70
  UN Basic Principles on the Role of Lawyers 470
  UN Universal Declaration on the Independence of Justice 1983 470
  Vienna Declaration and Programme of Action 1993 470
Latimer House Guidelines for the Commonwealth 470
Law Society of Upper Canada (LSUC) 254–5, 283
lawful objectives, accepting clients' 305–6, 308
Legal Professional Privilege 198, 203–4
legality 318
legislation, striking down 469
Magna Carta 264
misleading the court 328
Model Codes of Conduct 284, 285, 286
money laundering 204
monopolies 254
morality 233
native law 253
organisation of profession 253–6
Osgoode Hall 254
partisanship 308–9, 312–13
professional calling, characteristics of 239
professionalism 318
provincial law societies 254–6, 283–4, 337
public confidence, educating clients to maintain 318
public interest 470
regulation 256, 283–4, 291–2
secular rationality 256
self-regulation 283, 292, 470
sexual relationships 300
socialisation, lawyers as agents of 285
specialist advocates, rejection of 248, 254, 261

standard conception of the lawyer's role 297
standard of proof 253
supporting the rule of law 285
tactics 318
university model 254–6
canon law 108
Canons of Ethics (ABA) 280, 285–7
  accept clients, duty to 303
  all lawful means to achieve client's objective, use of 311–12
  candour and fairness, duties of 328
  confidentiality 289, 337–8
  cross-examination 335
  fraud by clients 328
  legalisation 286–7
  loyalty, devotion, or zeal, duty of 309, 312
  physical harm, prevention of 337–8
  supporting the rule of law 285
  suspect testimony 328
  third party harms, prevention of 342
  withdrawal from representation 328
  witnesses, treatment of 335
capitalism
  adversary system 154, 157–8
  corporatocracy 373, 393
  enclosure process 153
  globalisation 22, 415
  government lawyers 463
  professions 17–19
  solicitors 157–8
cartels 347
cash for honours prosecutions 92–3
cash for questions scandal 114
celebrities, lawyers as 140–1, 145–52
  18th century 145–52
  anti-establishment, as 146–51, 155
  barristers 140–1, 147–8, 155–6, 272
  criminal trials as spectacles 155
  culture, embedding in 150–2
  high office 150–2
  identity 140–1, 145–52, 155
  jury trials 145–7, 156–7
  loyalty, devotion, or zeal, duty of 308
  neutral partisans 146–50
  Prisoners Counsel Act 1836 152, 155–6
  reputation 145–6, 155–6
  Tories in public life, mistrust of 155–6
  Whigs 150–1, 152, 155–6
chancery specialists 152
checks and balances 53, 80, 261
Chicago School 371–2
Chilcott Inquiry into the Iraq War 2003 90, 463
China 420–1
Christianity/Church see also **Protestantism**
  Calvinism 17–18, 33, 37, 106, 242

capitalism 17–19
Catholicism 17, 31
   emancipation 113, 168
   mendicant orders 160
colonialism 171
Divine Right of monarchs to rule/
     absolutism 30–1, 33–4, 36–8
God's law 10–11
professional priesthood, rise of the 135
Puritanism 17–18, 33, 37
rationalisation 135
Reformation 32–3, 235
religious freedom 162, 168–70
royal authority, passive obedience to 113
separation of church and state 110, 160,
   235–6, 451
citizenship 171–3, 182–3
civil and political rights 110
civil disobedience 186–7, 207
civil liberties 162–6 *see also* **rights and liberties**
   Bill of Rights 1689 162, 184
   emergency, executive power in times of 163–5
   executive decisions, need for justification
     of 163–6
   negative liberty 162
   presumption of innocence 162–3
   silence, right to 162–3
   tyranny 162
civil proceedings 139, 228, 466
civil rights movements 182, 235
civil service 119–22, 129–30
   accountability 120–1
   Civil Service Commission 119
   code of ethics 120, 130
   Crimea War 119
   cuts 432
   examination, entry by 119
   expansion of the state 120
   Fulton Report 120
   government department standing counsel 121
   Government Legal Department 121
   law officers 121
   loyalty to the government 120
   Northcote Report 119
   open competition 119
   Oxbridge candidates 119–20
   partisanship 120
   patronage 119
   policy role 120–1
   private sector values 120
   public service ethos 119–20, 130
   scandals 120
   separation of powers 119
   special advisers 120
   Treasury Counsel (Treasury Devil) 121–2

   Treasury solicitors 121
   Trevelyan Report 119
   whistleblowing 130
civil society 107–8, 109–13, 129–31
   18th century 109–11
   abuse of power 130
   accountability of the state 112
   corruption 131
   courts, influence on 135
   definition 112
   diversity 131
   Enlightenment 10, 107–8
   expertise of the state, counterbalancing
     the 112
   free press 110
   identity 154
   Levellers 109–10
   news books 109–10
   NGOs 112–13
   The North Briton 111
   pamphlets and tracts, publication of 109–12
   Parliamentary proceedings, monopoly to
     print 111–12
   political focus, requirement for a 112
   Political Register 112
   printing presses 109–12
   professional associations, membership of 19,
     472
   Representation of the People Act 1832 112
   seditious libel 111
   solicitors 263
civil war *see* **American Civil War**; **English civil**
   wars
class actions 136
Clementi Report 276, 351–2, 379–80
client autonomy *see* **autonomy of clients**
clients
   accept consumers as clients, duty to 299,
     301–8, 311
   accountability of lawyers 48
   all lawful means to achieve client's objective,
     use of 299, 311–13, 315–16
   autonomy 7, 297, 299, 305, 315, 344
   best interests of clients 212, 222, 306, 311,
     315
   client care 291
   client money 274–5
   confidence 207–9
   corporate clients and financial harm 205–6,
     210
   court, balance between duties to client
     and 464
   dangerous clients 204–5, 209–10, 342
   factual account, obligation to accept
     client's 142

government lawyers   462
illegal activity of clients   189, 231, 318–21, 343
lawyer-client relationship   141–2, 190–1
loyalty to clients   141–2
morality   225–7, 235–6, 299
objectives
   accepting client's lawful objectives   299, 301–8, 311
   all means to achieve client's objective, use of   299, 311–13, 315–16
   moral disagreement with objectives   299
public duties   288–90
screening   302
third parties, prevention of harms to   204–6, 209–11, 213, 319, 323, 336–9, 340–2, 344
closed material procedure (CMP)   409–11
codes of conduct   284–92 *see also* Bar Code of Conduct (BCC) 1981 (England and Wales); BSB Code of Conduct (BSB CC) 2014 (England and Wales); Canons of Ethics (ABA); FCLS Model Code of Professional Conduct (Canada); Lawyers: Conduct and Client Care Rules (LCCR) (New Zealand); Legal Profession Uniform Conduct (Barristers) Rules 2015 (LPUC(B)R) (Australia); Model Rules of Professional Conduct 1983 (MRPC) (ABA); SRA Code of Conduct 2011
administration of justice   340
best interests of clients   315
Canton of Geneva, oaths sworn by lawyers in the   288–9
civil service   120, 130
clients, duties to   288–90, 296–314
comparative analysis   297–301
complaint mechanisms   290
confidentiality   288–9
Council of the Bars and Law Societies of Europe (CCBE)   419–20, 421
criticism   293–4
cultures and norms   19–20
differentiation of roles, assessment of   301
discipline   286, 290, 294
enforcement   290–2
Greek philosophy   294
incrimination   339–44
International Bar Association (IBA)   418–19
key characteristics of professions   269
Legal Services Act 2007   3
legalisation   286–7, 290
legality   317, 325, 339–41
Ministerial Code, breaches of the   61, 117–18, 438, 457

misconduct charges   290
neutrality   296, 298–9, 301–14
oaths   288–9, 292–3, 297
origins   288–9
Parliament   116–18
partisanship   298–300, 308–14
paternalism   297, 314–15
public duties   288–90, 318–20
regulation   284–94
reporting requirements   322
sanctions   290
solicitors   276, 299, 302, 307, 311, 333, 336, 365–6
standard conception of the lawyer's role   297–301, 316
substance   288–90
supporting the rule of law   284–6
Coke, Edward   29, 33–9, 48–51, 56, 65–6, 71–2, 216–17, 223, 243, 262, 459
colonialism and empire
adversary system   248
British model   248
Christianity   171
colonial lawyers   128
independence of the legal profession   263
land   167
Magna Carta   248
natural law   171
organisation of profession   247–61
State of Nature   161
Colston statue in Bristol, pulling down of   187–9
Committee of Privileges   116
common law systems
adversary system   156–8, 233, 248
attorneys   152
barristers   273
changes in law through judicial interpretation   136
client confidence   207–8
confidentiality   191–2
constitutional government   11, 57
core jurisdictions   6
courts   34, 36, 49, 137
custom   34
human rights   161, 182
inalienable rights   10
judges   50, 61–2, 64–7, 69, 123–4
law as what sovereign commands   10
Legal Professional Privilege   191, 193–4, 198
Lord Chancellor   82–3
organisation of profession   247–8, 261–2
Parliament, supremacy of common law to   66
precedent   34
prerogative courts   34, 50
private practice   464

regulation 270, 289
revolutions 34, 36, 49–50
senior government lawyers 97–101
Solicitor General 97
sovereign power, constraints on 11
Common Pleas 34, 36, 49, 136–7
communitarianism 465
comparative analysis
  codes of conduct 297–301
  standard conception of the lawyer's role 297–301
competition 24, 119, 350–1, 357, 360, 369, 464–5
Competition and Markets Authority (CMA) 357, 369
compromising the rule of law 404–15
confessions 326–7
confidences 189–204 *see also* confidentiality; Legal Professional Privilege (LPP)
  counselling role 189, 198, 204, 208, 211, 318, 321
  crime, fraud, or iniquity exception 201–4
  integrity 189–90
  lawyer and client relationship 190–1
  private practice 467–8
  privilege in 190–1
  legality 189–204
confidentiality 190–3
  Attorney General's advice to government 88, 89, 104
  codes of conduct 288–9
  common law 191–2
  journalists' sources 191–2
  Legal Professional Privilege 186, 201, 204, 208–9, 317, 320, 330, 340, 422, 467–8
  loyalty, devotion, or zeal, duty of 308
  public interest 190, 191
  reasonable expectation of confidence 191
  solicitors 158, 324, 339
consent and legality 13, 186–9
  civil disobedience 186–9
  freedom of speech 186
  minority interests, protection of 186
  obedience, habits of 186
  protest, right to 186–9
  rebellion 186–7
  statue controversies 187–9
conspiracy theories 454
constitutional government 53–80
  abuse of power 54
  aristocracy 54
  balanced constitution 53, 57–8
  Bill of Rights 1689 76
  Cabinet
    Cabinet Manual 77–8
    composition 55–6

establishment 55–6
  increase in power 55–6
  power 55–6
common law 11
consent 457–8
constitutional documents 76
constitutional monarchy 55
Constitutional Reform Act 2005 76–8, 90–7
constitutionalism 64, 130
devolution 77
diffusing power 58–9
Enlightenment 9–10, 457
European Union membership 77
Fixed-Term Parliaments Act 2011 77
foreign jurisdictions 72–5
forms 55–8
functions 58–64
  diffusing power 58–9
  separating the three functions of law 59–64
Human Rights Act 1998 77
judges 64–72
Magna Carta 56, 76
majoritarianism 457
mixed government 53, 55–6
monarch, influence of the 57–8
Parliament Acts of 1911 and 1949 76
parliamentary sovereignty 1–2, 55, 58
power 53–6, 60–1
Protestantism 17
separation of powers 10, 53–5, 57–64, 72–80, 130
sovereign power 53–4
theory 53–5
written constitution, proposal for 77–8
Constitutional Reform Act 2005 2, 90–7
  Lord Chancellor 84, 90–2
  government/executive 76–8, 90–7
  independence of the judiciary 428
  judiciary 428, 459–60
  law officers 90, 92–4, 102
  legislature, control of 68
  senior government lawyers 92–7, 102, 104
  Supreme Court 62–3
contingency fees 214
Cook, John 29, 42–6, 48–9, 176
Corn Laws 170
corporate lawyers 384–92
  19th century 153
  attorneys 153
  Big Bang 384
  City of London firms 384
  corporate social responsibility 387–9
  expansion 384–5
  Guantanamo Bay Detention Centre 390–2, 393–4, 405–6

hemispheric model   385
increase in number of law firms   384–5
international market   384
justice gap   387
legal aid cuts   387, 389, 393
neoliberalism   387
neutral partisanship   386
partners, abolition of limits on   384
pro bono legal services   386–7, 389–90, 394
rational bureaucracies   386
social capital   394
solicitors   152–3
values   385–7, 393
corporate social responsibility (CSR)   387–9
business case   388–9
Committee for Economic Development (CED)   388
definition   388
Law Society   389
pro bono work   387, 389, 390, 393–4
social contract   388
soft law   387, 394
corporatised state   375–8
accountability   377
corrupt corporate influence on Parliament   376
free market   376–7
lobby groups   376
media ownership   377–8
neoliberalism   376
Private Finance Initiative (PFI)   377
Public Private Partnerships (PPPs)   377
public utilities, sale of   376
resale price maintenance (RPM)   375–6
right-wing think tanks   376
Sunday trading   376
Victorian values   376
corporatocracy   8, 371–94
19th century   373
Alternative Business Structures (ABSs)   379–80
canon law   108
capitalism   373, 393
corporate bureaucracy   373, 380
corporations, definition of   108–9
defamation   381, 383
deregulation   373
free market   394
government, composition of   373–5, 393
governmentality   373
in-house lawyers   378–9
invention of corporations   107–8
Joint Stock Companies Act 1844   109
judiciary   459–60
laissez-nous faire   371
lawyers against corporations   380–4

legal disciplinary practices (LDPs)   379
Legal Professional Privilege   194–7, 200, 210
legal services   378–80
liberalisation   373
Limited Liability Act 1855   109
multinationals   371, 373, 381–4, 393, 396
neoliberalism   372–3
number of lawyers in corporations   378
Parliamentary representation   374–5
political leadership   373–4
power, rise of corporate   373–80, 393
privilege   210
professionalism   374
self-regulation   373
social values   372
SRA Code of Conduct   380
theory   371–3
corruption
administrative state   119
corporate influence on Parliament   376
Corruption Perception Index (CPI)   455–6
COVID-19   113, 435–6
decline of the rule of law   455–7
democracy   434–8, 457
elective dictatorships   131, 456
government/executive   113–14
grand corruption   113–14
media   131
ministers   119
morality   213
Parliament   113–15
petty corruption   113–15
planning   438
populism   455–6, 458–9
public appointments   456
public inquiries   122–3
public procurement   434–6
senior government lawyers   461
violence, control of   24
cosmopolitanism   396, 404–6
costs   274, 307, 347
Council of Europe (CoE)   178–81
Council of the Bars and Law Societies of Europe (CCBE)   418–22
charter   419, 421
Code of Conduct for European Lawyers   419–20, 421
Solicitors' Overseas Practice Rules 1990   420
counselling role   189, 198, 204, 208, 211, 318, 321
Court of Chancery   34
COVID-19
Brexit   436
corruption   113, 435–6
democracy   435–7, 439

equality before the law   435–6
favouritism in PPE procurement   436
judicial review   436
lobbying   437
lockdown rules, government not
    following   435–6
Parliamentary scrutiny, lack of   435
Party-gate   435–6
procurement, corruption in   435–6
public appointments, political motivation
    for   439
crime *see also* **corruption; criminal trials;
    terrorism**
crime, fraud, or iniquity exception to
    confidences   201–4
crimes against humanity   175
genocide   174–6, 178
illegal activity of clients   189, 231, 318–21,
    343
war crimes   175, 177–8
Crimea War   119
criminal trials *see also* **prosecutions**
18th century   137, 139–40, 144–5, 155
ad hoc criminal tribunals, establishment of
    178
adversary system   138–40
Attorney General   87
barristers, advocacy by   139–40
confessions   326–7
defence counsel, control of   144–5
fair hearing, right to a   466
felonies, no defence in court for   137
identity   137–8, 152, 155–6
International Criminal Court (ICC)
    178
judges
    18th century   137–8, 156
    bias   138
    enforcers of criminal law, as   137
    protecting the defendant, role in   138, 156
Justices of the Peace   137
legal aid   245
legal representation   137–40, 152, 155–6
political defendants   138
Prisoners Counsel Act 1836   152, 155–6
records of State Trials   138–9
rewards, impact of   144–5
speak for themselves, requirement that
    defendants   137
spectacles, as   155
speed of trials   139–40
strategy   144–5
thief-takers   139
treason cases   138, 217–18
witnesses   137

cross-examination   140–1, 143–4, 334–5
culture
    celebrities, lawyers as   150–1
    codes of conduct   19–20
    counter-culture of 1960s   235
    identity   269–70
    language   184
    organisation of profession   242
    polarised political cultures   454–5
    religious freedom   162, 168–9
    rights   158, 162, 168–70, 184
    study, right to   183
custom   31
customary international law   176, 178

dangerous clients   204–5, 209–10, 342
De Tocqueville, Alexis   8, 14–16, 49, 81, 128,
    207–8
decline of the rule of law   453–7
    abuse of power   456
    accountability mechanisms   456–7
    corruption   455–7
    illiberal democracies   454
    impeachments   455
    journalists, attacks on   454
    misinformation   454
    polarised political cultures   454–5
    populism   455–6
    totalitarianism   454–5
defence counsel, role of   144–5
defendants, rights of   138, 154
definition of the rule of law   2, 12, 25
democracy   8, 424–50
    aristocratic government   14–16
    Brexit   424, 426–31, 434, 436, 446, 448–9
    corruption   434–8, 457
    COVID-19 crisis   435–7, 439
    elections, transparency of   424
    Enlightenment   424, 426
    equality before the law   450
    globalisation   396, 402, 415–16
    government/executive constraints,
        weakening   431–4, 449–50
        BBC, attacks on   431–2, 449
        civil service cuts   432
        European Court of Human Rights
            and domestic courts, relationship
            between   433–4
        Fixed-Term Parliaments Act 2011   430,
            432–3
        Human Rights Act 1998   433
        judicial review, attacks on   432–4
        trust   433
    Human Rights Act 1998, repealing the   449
    illiberal democracies   404, 449, 454, 457

individual rights   427
legality   14, 434–9, 450, 457
legislature   59
liberal democracy   22–4, 396, 457–8
majoritarianism   458
mediating institutions, lawyers as   14–16
minorities, abuse of   425
morality   230
nativism   450
neoliberalism   445–6
Parliamentary sovereignty   425
participatory citizenship   425
popular sovereignty   425
populism   425–6, 431, 436, 446, 448–9
professionalism   347
public choice theory   445
public services and social benefits, deconstruction of   445
referendums   424–5
separation of powers   427, 450
theory   424–6
thick conceptions   458
think tanks, aims of right-wing   445
tyranny of the majority   14–15, 425
United Kingdom   426–39, 448–9, 458
despotism *see* **tyranny or despotism**
devolution   77
diaspora, lawyers in the   247–60
Dicey, Albert Venn   1–2, 11, 13, 58, 60, 65, 77–8, 118, 159, 185, 314, 317, 348–9, 425, 451, 457–8
Director of Public Prosecutions (DPP)   87
discipline
barristers   270–3, 290
codes of conduct   286, 290, 294
Franks Committee   275
legality   320
Parliament   115–116
regulation   270, 295, 416–17
solicitors   275, 278, 290–2, 299, 358, 361–8
dishonesty   202–4, 232, 277–8, 320, 333
dissuasion, principle of   208, 211, 317, 321, 339
Divine Right of monarchs to rule/ absolutism   30–1, 33–4, 36–8
doorstep conditions to meeting rule of law   24
Draft Code of Crimes against the Peace and Security of Mankind **(ILC)**   178
Durkheim, Émile   106–7, 241–2, 269, 347

East India Company   371
economic rights   162, 166–8, 182–3
education and training
apprenticeship   242
Attorney General   92–3
barristers   49, 243–5

law degrees   247
Lord Chancellor   91
monopolies   348
organisation of profession   242
private practice   464
professionalism   348
public service   265
regulation   270, 295
self-regulation   292
solicitors
 advocacy   349
 apprenticeships   361
 articled clerks   246–7, 274
 Solicitors Qualifying Examination (SQE)   361
universities/law schools   236, 247, 349
elections *see also* **franchise, extension of the**
accountability   456
elective dictatorships   456, 458
electoral and executive roles, separation of   456
first past the post   457
free elections   131
minority of votes, majority parties elected on a   457
transparency   424
elites   24, 31, 54, 459
emergency, executive power in times of   163–5
habeas corpus, suspension of   163
World War II, restrictions in UK during   163–6
empire *see* **colonialism and empire**
enclosure process   153
Enlightenment
abuse of power, checks on   25
balanced constitution   53
citizenship   171
civil society   10, 107–8
constitutional government, model of   9–10, 457
democracy   424, 426
government/executive   8–9
inalienable rights   10
individual rights   474
institutions   107–8
legacy   451
legality   341
liberalism   451
literature   8–9
mixed government   53
morality   213
natural law   30
Nuremberg Military Tribunal (NMT)   175, 183
private practice   14

religion   10, 160
separation of powers   53–4
social contract   9
English civil wars   41–4
  Commonwealth, creation of a   44
  Cook, John, role of   29, 42–3
  execution of Charles I   44, 45
  Grand Remonstrance   40, 109
  identity   135
  journalism   110
  Parliament   29, 34, 35–44, 48, 51
  prison, commitment of parliamentarians to   51
  ship money   39
  trial of Charles I   41–2, 48
  tyranny, accusation of   42–4
  war crimes   42
English revolutions   31–52 *see also* **English civil wars; Glorious Revolution**
  accountability of lawyers for who they represent   48
  arbitrariness   52
  Anglo-Saxons   31
  Catholicism, imposition of   31
  Celtic insurrections   31
  Coke, Edward, role of   29, 33–9, 50–1
  common law   34, 36, 49–50
  custom of the community embodying law of God, as   31
  Divine Right of monarchs to rule/absolutism   30–1, 33–4, 36–8
  Inns of Court   49, 50–1
  institutional constraints   34–5
  Magna Carta   31–2, 35, 37–8, 50–1, 52
  Normans   31–3
  Parliament, role of   29, 34, 35–41, 48, 50–1
  Reformation   32–3
  Restoration   44–6
  tyranny   29–31
Enron, collapse of   205, 386
equality   2, 435–6
  arms, of   189
  before the law   13, 64, 106, 299, 435–6, 450
  COVID-19   435–6
  institutionalised inequality   159
  justice   136
  neutrality   299
  political rights   168
equity   82–3
Erskine May, Thomas   59, 114, 118, 127
ethics *see* **morality**
ethnicities   23, 171, 182
etiquette   271–6
European Enlightenment *see* **Enlightenment**

European Union (EU) *see also* **Brexit**
  autocracies   404
  Charter of Fundamental Rights of the EU   178
  membership   77
  Parliamentary sovereignty   66–7
  populist opposition   455
evidence   124, 142–3, 158
executions   138, 145, 156
executive *see* **government/executive**
expertise, control of   112, 120, 347–8

fairness   136, 319, 332–6
  cross-examination   334–5
  fair hearing, right to a   88, 234, 466–7
  general duties   333
  morality   230–1, 234
  other lawyers, to   333–4
  parties in proceedings   334
  procedural fairness   2, 65, 125–6, 130, 176, 229
  rights and liberties   184
  solicitors   333
  substantive fairness   65, 453
  third party duties   219, 332–6
  witnesses, treatment of   334–5
fake news   454
FCLS Model Code of Professional Conduct (Canada)   284, 285, 292
  abuse of process   330–1
  accept clients, duty to   304
  advocacy prohibitions   331
  all lawful means to achieve client's objective, use of   311–12
  confessions   327
  confidentiality   337
  counselling   321
  customers, clients as   314
  disclosure   337
  fairness   334, 335
  illegality, assistance in   321
  lawful objectives, accepting clients'   305–6, 308
  legality, duty to   340
  loyalty, devotion, or zeal, duty of   308–11
  misleading the court   328
  neutrality   298, 304, 305–6, 313–14
  other lawyers, fairness towards   334
  partisanship   298, 313–14
  physical harm, prevention of   337
  reporting requirements   323
  self-reporting for misconduct   323
  sexual relationships   300
  withdrawal from representation   323
  witnesses, treatment of   335

Federation of Canadian Law Societies (FCLS)
    see FCLS Model Code of Professional
    Conduct (Canada)
feudalism   32–3, 107
fictions   3, 25
films, lawyers in   4
financial harm, prevention of   205–6, 338–9,
    340–2
Fixed-Term Parliaments Act 2011   77, 430,
    432–3
formalism   125
Fox News   378
France
    Canadian lawyers   253
    constitutional government   54, 56, 76
    Declaration of the Rights of Man and the
        Citizen   171, 177
    French Revolution   10, 29, 48, 147, 151
    litigation   214–15
    political trials   151
    precedent   208
    taxes   48
franchise, extension of the
    equal access to voting rights   168
    Reform Act 1832   168, 427
    Representation of the People Act 1832
        112
    rights and liberties   168
    rotten boroughs, abolition of   112
    Whig supremacy   113
    women   168
free market   348–9, 350, 376–7, 394
freedom see liberty
Freedom Association   112
freedom of speech   3–4, 38, 131, 177, 184, 186,
    412
Fuller, Lon   11, 126
futures   6, 7, 21–5

G7   396
genocide, crime of   174–6, 178
Germany   125 see also Nazi Germany
global financial crisis 2008   206, 427
globalisation   8, 23–4, 395–423
    alternatives to the rule of law   402–4
    authoritarian nationalism   404
    capitalism   22, 415
    compromising the rule of law   404–15
    core countries   396
    democracy   396, 402, 415–16
    global law firms   417–18
    global order   397–404
    human rights   395
    illiberal democracies   404
    independence of the judiciary   418, 421–2
    independence of the legal profession   416,
        418, 421–3
    international lawyer associations   418–20,
        421–2
    international organisations   397–8, 423
    lawyering   415–20
    legal professions   416–17, 421–3
    liberal democracy   396
    localism   395, 423
    measurement of the rule of law   399–401, 404
    migration   413–15
    multinationals, exploitation of resources
        in   381–4, 396
    neoliberalism   395–6
    populism   404
    social relations   415
    spread of the rule of law   401–2
    terrorist attacks   404–13
    theory   395–6
    unification, process of   22
    Washington Consensus   397–9
Glorious Revolution   29, 46–8, 262
    absolute monarchy, end of   47–8
    barristers   244
    Catholic emancipation   46
    civil society   110
    constitutional monarchy   47–8
    independence of the legal profession   262, 469
    institutions   107
    landed gentry, interests of   153
    prosecutions, accountability for   217
    William of Orange, invitation to   46–7
government/executive   8–14 see also Cabinet;
        constitutional government; government
    lawyers; law officers of the Crown; ministers
    aristocracy   14–16
    BBC, attacks on   431–2, 449
    civil liberties   163–6
    civil service cuts   432
    composition   373–5, 393
    Constitutional Reform Act 2005   90–7, 102
    conventions   60–1
    corruption   113–14
    COVID-19 lockdown rules, government not
        following   435–6
    democracy   431–4, 449–50
    electoral and executive roles, separation
        of   456
    emergency, executive power in times of   163–5
    Enlightenment   8–9
    European Court of Human Rights and
        domestic courts, relationship
        between   433–4
    Human Rights Act 1998   69
    illegality   70

independence of the legal profession as bulwark against excess   452
judicial review   68–72, 432–4
judiciary   64–72, 154, 459–60
  control functions   65–72
  credulousness to assurances   128
  power, checks on   154, 457, 459
  subversion of the rule of law   127–8
  justification for decisions   163–6
  legality and order   10–11
  legislative function   59–60
  liberty   9–10, 69
  literature   8–14
  Lord Chancellor   84
  majoritarianism   60
  ministers   60–1
  natural justice   72
  one person, power invested in   54
  Parliament   69, 113–14
  preparation of legislation   60
  Prime Minister   60–1, 83
  rationality   70–2
  removal by the People   9
  rule by law   13–14
  rule of law   11–14
  separation of powers   54, 60–1
  social contract   9
  sovereign power of the People, distinguished from   9
  theory   81–2
  trust   433, 459
  weakening constraints   431–4, 449–50
government lawyers   460–3 *see also* **Attorney General (AG); law officers of the Crown; Lord Chancellor; senior government lawyers**
  advisory role   460–1
  civil service   121
  development of role   7
  Government Legal Department   121
  independence   452, 460, 462–3
  institutional separation   462–3
  list of tasks relevant to rule of law   453
  prosecutions   130, 139
  public interest model   461–3
  public prosecutors, obligations of   130
  single client model   461–2
  socialisation and practice   463
  standards   461–2
  supporting the rule of law   460–3
  values and traditions   462
Guantanamo Bay Detention Centre   390–2, 393–4
  habeas corpus   392
  pro bono work   391–2, 405–6

terrorism   405–6, 409–10
torture   390, 392
guilds, medieval trade   243

habeas corpus   38–9, 83, 111, 163–4, 172, 392
Habermas, Jürgen   130, 135–6
harm, prevention of *see* third parties, prevention of client harms to
Hart, HLA   11, 125–6, 163, 185–6
Hayek, Friedrich von   348–50, 371–2, 376
Hillsborough inquiry (Taylor inquiry)   122–3
Hobbes, Thomas   8–11, 21–2, 30, 53–4, 59, 80, 107, 161, 168, 183, 185, 233
honesty   202–4, 232, 277–8, 320, 333
House of Lords
  appeals   62
  British Constitution   57
  Charles I, prosecution of   41
  electoral reform   168
  Human Rights Act 1998   68
  impeachment   40
  Lord Chancellor   90, 92, 94–5, 102
  petitions   61
  Protectorate, abolition during the   44
  speakers   84
  Star Chamber   169
  Supreme Court   68, 78
human rights *see also* civil liberties; rights and liberties
Humanitarian revolution   22
Hungary
  corruption in public procurement   455
  COVID-19   113
  democracy   403
  European Union   403
  majority party elected on minority vote   457
  terrorism   404

identity   135–58
  19th century   157–8
  adversary system   138–45, 154–8
  barristers   147–8, 155–6
  business lawyers   135, 152–4, 158
  celebrity   140–1, 145–52, 155
  changes in society   135–6
  common law systems   136
  culture   269–70
  fair dispute resolution   136
  historical groupings   135
  justice   136, 154
  litigation   135, 136–8, 152, 155–6
  nationality   270
  rational system of formally elaborated law, lawyers as playing role in creating a   135

shared social values 136
social change 158
split profession in UK 154
theory 135–6
illegal activity of clients 189, 231, 318–21, 343
illiberal democracies 404, 449, 454, 457
immigration 405, 413–15, 448–9
immunity 355
impeachment 443–5, 455, 456, 458
  decline of the rule of law 455
  English civil wars 40, 48
  polarised political cultures 454–5
incrimination 317–44
  administration of justice 325–32, 340
  codes of conduct 318–20, 339–44
  dissuasion, principle of 208, 211, 317, 321, 339
  Legal Professional Privilege 317, 340
  pro bono services 319–20
  public duties, evaluating 318–20
  public interest 317
  system duties 320–32
  theory 317–18
  third party duties 317, 332–9, 340
independence *see* **independence of the judiciary; independence of the legal profession; independent regulation in England and Wales**
independence of the judiciary
  Act of Settlement 1702 156
  administrative state 118
  Brexit 428
  definition of the rule of law 2
  globalisation 418, 421–2
  government/executive 130
  independent and impartial tribunals 466
  liberalism 451
  Lord Chancellor 91–2
  neoliberalism 355–6
  neutrality 141
  Parliament 117
  procedural protections for clients 156
  separation of powers 80, 452
  UN Basic Principles on the Role of Lawyers 470
  UN Universal Declaration on the Independence of Justice 1983 470
  Vienna Declaration and Programme of Action 1993 470
independence of the legal profession 262–4, 468–9
  adversarial system 262–3
  advocacy 268, 295, 356–7
  Attorney General 86, 89–90, 93–4, 103–5
  barristers 147–8, 262, 271, 464

  cause lawyers 267
  colonialism 263
  co-regulation 472–3
  corporatocracy 378–9
  decline of legal professions 472–3
  globalisation 416, 418, 421–3
  Glorious Revolution 262, 469
  government excess, bulwark against 452
  government lawyers 452, 460, 462–3
  indicators 472–3
  Inns of Court 49
  Legal Professional Privilege 473
  organisation of profession 262–4, 267–8
  private practice 464
  public interest 469
  self-regulation 469, 472
  solicitors 262, 275, 287, 361–2, 471
  threats to independence, list of 473
independent regulation in England and Wales 276, 357–70
  Alternative Business Structures (ASB) 358
  barristers and one stop shops 360
  Bar Council 358–60
  Bar Standards Board (BSB) 358, 360
  cab rank rule 358–9
  competition 357, 360, 369
  corporate bureaucracy 360
  Iraq War, claims arising from the 361–8
  Law Society 360, 367
  Legal Services Act 2007 357–8
  Legal Services Board (LSB) 357–60, 368–9
  McKenzie friends as advocates, use of 361
  Mayson Report 359, 368–9
  policy 360–1
  practice 361–8
  professional bodies 358–60
  professionalism 357–70
  public interest 359, 368
  regulatory policy 360–1
  regulatory practice 361–8
  Solicitors Code of Conduct 2007 365–6
  Solicitors' Disciplinary Tribunal (SDT) 361–8
  Solicitors Regulation Authority (SRA) 358–68, 369
  structure 357–8
India 403–4, 421
indigenous people, rights of 167, 172, 175, 396
individuality 7, 159–84 *see also* **rights and liberties**
  agency 159
  Christianity 159–60
  citizenship 171–3
  classical societies 159–60
  hierarchy 159
  inequality, institutionalised 159

international order   171–81
justice   160–1
legitimacy of the state   161
marginalised societies   159
martyrdom   159
national law   160
Nuremberg Military Tribunal (NMT)   173–6, 178, 183–4
private/public sphere   159
rationality   160
religion   159–60
Roman social structure   160
slaves   159
theory   159–61
tyranny   161
universalism   177–81
women   159
Industrial Revolution   109, 154, 157–8
in-house lawyers   378–9
inhuman or degrading treatment   406
innocent until proven guilty   154
Inns of Court   243–5, 248, 271
discipline   271
education and training   49
independence   49
reform   352
revolutions   49, 50–1
royal authority, challenging   49, 50–1
inquiries *see* **public inquiries**
inquisitorial system   195, 197, 465, 467
institutions   106–31
17th century   131
18th century   131
accountability   107
administration   118–23, 129
churches   106
civil service   119–22, 129–30
civil society   107–8, 109–13, 129, 130–1
corporations   107–8, 131
corruption   131
Enlightenment   107–8
equality before the law   106
feudalism   107
framework for the rule of law   131
institutionalisation   270
jurisdictional differences   128–9
justice   123–8
legality   129, 131
mediating institutions   107
open access order   108–9, 130–1
Parliament   113–18
professions   107
public consultation on proposed legislation   131

theory   106–8
utilitarianism   107
instrumentalism   190, 194
insurgent cosmopolitanism   396, 404–6
integrity   189–90, 277–8, 333
interception of communications   411
International Bar Association (IBA)   418, 421–2
Code of Ethics   418
General Principles of Ethics   418
Human Rights and the Just Rule of Law, Standing Committee on   418
independence of the judiciary and lawyers   418, 422
model of common law lawyers   7
Taskforce Indicators for Independent Legal Professions and Common Threats   472–3
International Criminal Court (ICC)   178
international financial centres   417
international financial institutions (IFIs), policies of   398
International Monetary Fund (IMF)   373, 397, 401
interpretation
gap-filling   126
judiciary   64–5
justice   126–7
ministerial statements   127
Pepper v Hart   127
Iraq 2003, invasion of   361–8, 402
Al Sweady Inquiry   362–3, 366
Attorney General's advice to government   88–9, 92
claims arising out the invasion   361–8
Israel, role of Attorney-General in   462

Japan   401, 418
Johnson, Boris   415, 429–36, 438, 448–9
journalists
attacks on   454
sources, protection of   191–2
stop power for journalistic material, use of   412–13
judicial review   59, 68–72, 247, 432–4, 436
judiciaries   64–72, 457–60 *see also* **independence of the judiciary**; **Lord Chancellor**
Act of Settlement 1701   110
activism   79
administrative state   119
appeals   62
appointments   90, 459–60
backgrounds   459–60
common law   50, 61–2, 64–7, 69, 123–4
Constitutional Reform Act 2005   459–60
constitutional rights   64

control function   65–72
corporation-oriented, becoming more   459–60
declarations of incompatibility   68
development of role   7
elites   459
equality before the law   64
good behaviour, appointment during   61–2
government/executive   64–72, 154, 459–60
  control functions   65–72
  credulousness as a response to   128
  power, checks on   154, 457, 459
  subversion of the rule of law   127–8
government-oriented, becoming more   459–60
House of Lords   62–3, 78
Human Rights Act 1998   68
individual rights, protection of   55
interpretative role   61–5
judgments, petitions to overturn   61
Judicial Appointments Commission   90, 459
juries   55, 62
law-making   130
legislative power, checks on   65–8, 457
Lord Chancellor   63, 84, 90–2
Lord Chief Justice   63, 72, 82
neoliberalism   355–7
Parliamentary sovereignty   64–8, 181
politics   61, 127, 459–60
populism   458–9
removal   62
remuneration   61–2, 80, 124
rights and liberties   182
security of tenure   62
separation of powers   54–5, 61–4, 78–80
social change   130
solicitors   459
subversion of the rule of law   127–8
Supreme Court (UK)   63, 66–7
trust   63
jury trials
  17th century   124
  advantages   262
  adversary system   139, 145, 154, 157, 220
  bloody code   156–7
  celebrities, lawyers as   145–7, 156–7
  executions   145, 156
  incorrect verdicts, jury's fear of   157
  judicial functions   55
  justice   124–5
  moral certainty instruction   157
  nullification   169–70, 207
  perverse verdicts   145, 169–70
  role   139, 145, 154, 157
  selection of jurors   139
  social changes   139

  witnesses
    jurors as   139
    questioning   137
justice   123–8
  17th century   124
  common law judges during Protectorate   123–4
  courts as tools of the monarch   123
  definition of the rule of law   2
  equality   136
  evidence
    17th century   124
    mathematical theory of knowledge   124
    moral theory of knowledge   124
    physical theory of knowledge   124
    Protestant theologians and naturalists   124
  fact and law, distinctions between   123
  formalism, rise of   125
  gap   386, 466
  good, competing notions of the   136
  identity   136, 154
  impartiality   136
  individuality   160–1
  institutions   123–8
  interpretation   126–7
  judicial credulousness to executive assurances   128
  judicial subversion of the rule of law   127–8
  jury trial, right to   124–5
  legal aid cuts   387, 389, 393
  legal positivism   125–6, 130
  liberal conceptions   136
  liberty   13
  natural justice   72, 465
  popular idea of justice   5
  primary goods, allocation of   13
  procedural justice   125–6, 130
  purposive interpretation   126
  Rump Parliament   124
  superstition to reason, changes from   123
  trial, definition of   124
  veil of ignorance   13
Justice (civil society organisation)   113
Justices of the Peace   137

Kant, Immanuel   8, 13, 69, 125, 136, 160–1, 183–4, 228, 230, 427, 454

laissez-nous faire   371
land
  business lawyers   135, 153
  colonised land   167
  economic rights   166–7
  landed gentry, interests of   153
  Magna Carta   31

monopolies   153
Normans, allocation by   32
perpetuity   31
transfers   135, 153
Latimer House Guidelines for the Commonwealth   470
law centre movement   265
law firms
  Alternative Business Structures (ABSs)   287, 358, 379–80
  City of London firms   384
  elite global firms   153–4, 417–18
  increase in number of law firms   384–5
  international financial centres   417
  legal disciplinary practices (LDPs)   379
  London   417–18
  New York   418
  partners, abolition of limits on   384
Law of Nature   30–1, 54, 66
law officers of the Crown   81–2, 84–90 *see also* Attorney General (AG); government lawyers
  advice to government   88–90
  advocacy role   85, 86
  civil servants   86–90, 92–4, 103–5, 121
  Cabinet, membership of the   89
  Constitutional Reform Act 2005   90, 92–4, 102
  Crown litigation   88
  fees earned from private practice   88
  foreign jurisdictions   97–101
  guardians of the rule of law, as   92, 94
  history   84–6
  House of Commons Constitutional Affairs Committee   92–4
  independence   89
  investigation, prosecution and advocacy   88
  managerial role   86, 87
  Parliament   85, 87–8
  private practice, combining role with   88
  prosecution decisions   86
  public interest litigation   88
  reduction in pool of candidates for office   375
  responsibilities   86–90
  Scotland, Advocate General in   86
  Solicitor General   84–5, 87, 92
law reports   50
lawful means to achieve client's objective, use of all   299, 311
Laws, John   2, 59, 66, 69–70, 72, 122
Law Society   246–7, 263, 475
  accounts, inspection of   274–5
  advocacy rights   353
  Code for Advocacy   302–3, 306, 311
  complaints handling   351, 354–5
  conveyancing monopoly   353
  corporate social responsibility (CSR)   389
  discipline   291
  Guide to the Professional Conduct and Etiquette of Solicitors   275–6, 287
  independence   262
  law reform   265
  Law Society Gazette   247
  legal aid   265–6
  pro bono work   266, 387
  public service   265
  regulation   292, 360, 367
  self-regulation   292
  Solicitors Regulation Authority (SRA)   360, 367
  standards   274
  state authoritarianism, as counterweight to   263
lawyers   133, 451–3, 474 *see also* attorneys; barristers; government lawyers; law firms; legal profession; legal representation in court; senior government lawyers; solicitors (England and Wales); standard conception of the lawyer's role
  activist lawyers   414
  aristocracy, lawyers as   15–16
  attorneys   136, 152–4, 245–6, 274–6
  authority of lawyers, decline in   25
  business lawyers   152–4
  celebrities   140–1, 145–52
  centralised power, constraints on   451
  client and lawyer relationship   141–2
  colonial lawyers   128
  control of the courtroom   141
  corporate lawyers   384–92
  counselling role   189, 198, 204, 208, 211, 318, 321
  criticism of lawyer's role   212, 216–18
  diaspora, lawyers in the   247–60
  films, portrayal in   4
  globalisation   415–20
  hostility   221, 248–9, 252, 279
  jargon for mystification, use of   16
  judges   453
  list of tasks relevant to rule of law   453
  Lord Chancellor   91, 102
  mediating institutions, lawyers as   14–16
  MPs, as   113
  mystique of lawyers   16
  over-production   349
  Parliament, influence on   114
  politicisation   415
  priesthood, lawyers as a   242
  private practice   14–16, 452, 464–73
  public inquiries, lawyers as chair of   122
  recourse role, lawyers as having a   295

rule of law as rule of lawyers   25
serjeants   136–7, 243
social role   213
special procedures   409–11
supporting the rule of law   279, 284–6, 343, 460–3, 474–5
tasks relevant to the rule of law   452–4
Lawyers: Conduct and Client Care Rules (LCCR) (New Zealand) 2008
  abuse of process   330, 332
  all lawful means to achieve client's objective, use of   312–13, 315–16
  autonomy of clients   308
  confessions   327–8
  confidentiality   338–9, 342
  criminal behaviour   322
  financial harm, prevention of   338–9, 341
  illegality, assistance in   322
  instructions, following clients'   307, 315–16
  Legal Professional Privilege   323
  legality, duty of   340, 344
  neutrality   298, 316
  other lawyers with respect, treating   323, 333
  parties in proceedings, respecting   334
  partisanship   298, 311–13, 315–16, 316
  physical harm, prevention of   338–9, 341
  regulatory functions   282–3
  reporting requirements   323
  sexual relationships   300
  standard conception of lawyers' role   314
legal aid
  adversary system   466
  cause lawyers   267
  cuts   247, 266, 351, 387, 389, 393
  criminal legal aid   245
  judicial review   247
  neoliberalism   349, 351
  over-production in lawyers   349
  public service   265
  QCs, amounts claimed by   351
  rare and extreme cases, grant in   466
  solicitors   247, 265–7
legal disciplinary practices (LDPs)   379
legal positivism   125–6, 130, 185–6, 206–7, 233, 236
legal profession *see also* **Australia, legal profession in; Canada, legal profession in; independence of the legal profession; law firms; lawyers; New Zealand, legal profession in**
  autonomy   469–70
  decline of legal professions   472–3
  neutralisation   472
  private practice   14–16, 468–73
  regulatory functions   416–17
  split profession in UK   154, 464

Legal Profession Uniform Conduct (Barristers) Rules 2015 (LPUC(B)R) (Australia)   285–6
  adversary system   326
  all lawful means to achieve client's objective, use of   312–13
  cab rank rule   303, 304
  confessions   327
  correction of misleading statements   329
  court, duty to the   326
  dishonesty   325
  false statements   333
  instructions, following clients'   315–16
  lawful objectives, accepting clients'   307
  neutrality   298, 303, 304, 307, 313–14
  other lawyers, fairness towards   334
  parties in proceedings, respect for   334
  partisanship   298, 313–16
  witnesses, duties towards   335
Legal Professional Privilege (LPP)   186, 193–204
  16th century   158
  adversarial system   197, 468
  advice privilege   193–6, 197–202, 210
    adversarial system   468
    common law   198
    confidentiality   201, 204
    corporations   200, 210
    crime, fraud, or iniquity exception   201–3
    Law Reform Committee   199
    legality   197–200
    limitations   199
    litigation privilege   196, 199
    public interest   200–1
    reporting requirements for suspected terrorism, money laundering or tipping off   204
    scope   194, 198–9
  barristers   324
  common law   191, 193–4, 198
  confidentiality   186, 201, 204, 208–9, 317, 320, 330, 340, 422, 467–8
  constitutional principle, as   194, 474
  corporations   194–7, 200, 205, 210
  crime exception   201–4
  disclosure   191, 209
  dishonest conduct   202–4
  dissuasion, principle of   317, 321
  exceptions   201–4
  executive antagonism   468
  fraud exception   201–4
  Human Rights Act 1998   194
  incrimination   317, 340
  independence of lawyers   473
  individuals   194, 467–8
  iniquity exception   201–4

instrumentalism   190, 194
legality   186, 193–200, 321
litigation privilege   193–5, 196–7
   adversarial proceedings   197, 468
   advice privilege   196, 199
   contemplation, where litigation is in reasonable   196–7
   corporations   197
   dual purposes   196
   inquisitorial proceedings   195, 197
   legality   196–7
   progress, litigation in   196
   sole or dominant purpose test   196–7
loss of privilege   191
money laundering, reporting   204, 210
multi-disciplinary organisations   467
national security   422
origins   193
private practice   467–8
public interest   186, 196
quality of confidence   190
restrictive view   194, 198
rights   194, 210
rule of evidence, as   194
rule of law   200–1
search warrants, validity of   194
social benefits   190
solicitors   158
terrorism, reporting   210
third parties   191
waiver   468
wide scope   194, 198–9
legal representation in court
   18th century   139
   Barebones Parliament   124
   criminal trials   137–40, 152, 155–6
   ethics of representation   218–20
   obligation of representation   215
   Prisoners Counsel Act 1836   152
   treason   138
Legal Services Act 2007 (England and Wales)
   adversarial justice system   3
   barristers   287, 295
   neoliberalism   352–6
   regulation   2–3, 349–50, 357–8
   rule of law, inclusion of mention of the   2–3
   solicitors   276, 287, 471
Legal Services Board (LSB)   350, 356–60, 368–9
legality   2, 6, 185–211 *see also* **incrimination**
   administration of justice, non-interference with the   318
   adversarialism   185–6
   Brexit   434
   civil disobedience   207
   client confidence   207–9

   codes of conduct   317, 322, 325, 339–41
   confidences   189–204
   consent   13, 186–9
   corporate privilege   210
   democracy   14, 434–9, 450, 457
   discipline   320
   disclosure of certain matters to the court   318
   dishonesty, offences involving   320
   dissuasion, duty of   208, 211, 317, 321, 339
   efficient and expeditious conduct of cases   317
   equality before the law   13
   favouritism   435, 436
   formal legality   13–14, 64
   general, prospective, and clear, law as   13
   government/executive   10–11
   illegality
      consultation   320
      involvement in   320–1
      professional role, being involved beyond the   320
   individual rights   474
   inner morality of law   11
   institutions   129, 131
   legal observance   206–7
   Legal Professional Privilege   186, 193–201, 320–1
   lobbying   434, 437
   morality   213, 218, 230–1, 236
   natural law   185
   Parliamentary sovereignty   65–8
   partisanship   474
   personal morality   185
   positivism   185–6, 206–7
   public appointments, politically motivated   438–9, 457
   public interest   339
   public service   265
   regulation   318
   reporting   211, 320, 322–4
   respect for the court process   317–18
   retrospectivity   185
   senior government lawyers   461
   social contract   11, 185
   solicitors   324, 343
   striking off   320
   supporting legality   320–5
   theory   185–6
   third parties, prevention of client harms to   204–6, 211, 323, 342
legislature *see also* **Parliament**
   Constitutional Reform Act 2005   68
   democracy   59
   dignified role of the monarch   59
   government/executive   59–50
   Human Rights Act 1998   68

judiciary 65–8, 457
  legality, principle of 67–8
  Lord Chancellor 84
  Parliament sovereignty 58
  separation of powers 59–60, 76–7
legitimate expectations 2
Lehman Brothers, collapse of 206, 210, 294, 343, 386
Lemkin, Rafael 174–5
Levellers 109–10
liberal democracy 22–4, 396, 457–8
liberalism 136, 154, 175, 235–6, 451, 453 *see also* illiberal democracies
liberty *see* rights and liberties
licensed conveyancers 349
literature 8–25
litigation process 135, 136–8 *see also* **criminal trials**
  13th century 136
  17th century 137
  abuse of process 54, 325, 330–2
  access to lawyers 215
  accountability 215
  Assize courts 136–7
  attorneys 136
  common law courts 137
  elite pleaders 136
  encouragement of litigation 214
  groups 136–7
  identity 135, 136–8
  lawyers, controlling 214–15
  litigation privilege 193–5, 196–7, 199
  London practice 136
  maintenance, champerty, barratry, crimes and torts 214
  oaths 214–15
  officers of the court, lawyers as 214
  public interest 214
  representation, lawyer's obligation of 215
  serjeants 136–7
litigation process, abuse of the 325, 330–2
Lloyd's of London 153
lobbying 115, 376, 434, 437
localism 395, 423
Locke, John 8–9, 31, 46–7, 51, 54, 80, 106–7, 110, 124, 157, 160, 371, 425
Lord Chief Justice (LCJ) 63, 72, 82
Lord Chancellor
  advice to government 95–6, 105
  alternative source of power and authority, as 83
  Attorney General 97
  Cabinet 83, 97
  Chancery 82, 84
  Commissioners of the Seal 82
  common law courts 82–3
  Constitutional Reform Act 2005 84, 90–2, 94–5, 104
  court system, responsibility for the 91–2
  development 82
  equity 82–3
  government/executive 81–4
  guardian of the rule of law, as 91–2, 95–7, 102–3
  habeas corpus 83
  House of Commons, as a member of the 90
  House of Lords
    as member of the 90
    Select Committee on the Constitution 94–7, 102–4
  independence of the judiciary 91–2, 95–7
  Judicial Appointments Commission 90
  judicial functions 63, 84, 90–1
  judiciary, responsibility for the 91–2
  jurisdiction 82–3
  lawyer, Lord Chancellor as a 91, 102
  legislature, functions of 84
  literature 82
  Ministerial Code 97
  Ministry of Justice 90–1
  monarchy, threats to 83
  monitoring and compliance role 95–6, 103, 105
  oaths 91–2, 95
  politics, detachment from 84
  Prime Minister, as 83
  Privy Councillor, as 82
  qualifications 91
  role 81–4
  Royal Seal, as custodian of the 82–3
  Secretary of State for Justice, combined with 94–6
  senior government lawyers 81–2, 94–7, 102–3
  separation of powers 63, 78, 90–1
loyalty, devotion, or zeal, duty of
  18th century 308–9
  19th century 308–9
  adversary system 141–2
  barristers 306
  celebrities, lawyers as 308
  confidentiality 308
  fearless advocacy 308–9
  hired gun, lawyers as 315
  morality 228, 232, 233, 236
  partisanship 299, 308–11, 313–14
  solicitors 310
Lund's *Guide* 299–300, 306, 310, 333, 336
lying and cheating 232, 454–5

Machiavelli, Niccolò   30, 425
McKenzie friends   361
McLibel case   380
Magna Carta   56, 257, 264
   colonies   248
   customary rights of the barons   31
   elite privileges   31
   emergency, executive power in times of   164
   Human Rights Act 1998   449
   inheritance   31
   land ownership, perpetuity of   31
   organisation of profession   248
   Parliament   37–8
   prerogative powers   35, 76
   revolutions   31–2, 35, 37–8, 50–1, 52
   separation of powers   75
   social rights   170
   taxes   32, 50–1
   Universal Declaration of Human Rights   177
majoritarianism
   consent   457–8
   democracy, changes to   458
   first past the post   457
   government/executive   60
   illiberal governments   457
   minority of votes, majority parties elected on a   457
   populism   458–9
   rights and liberties   160–1
   supermajorities to legislate against rule of law, requirement for   459
   tyranny of the majority   14–15, 425
marginalised societies   159
martyrdom   159
Marxism   12, 153
measurement of the rule of law   399–401, 404
media/press
   accountability   456
   BBC, attacks on   431–2, 449
   Brexit   449
   civil society   131
   contempt of court   88, 192
   corruption   131
   fake news   454
   free press   110
   independence   451
   institutions   131
   journalists
      attacks on   454
      sources, protection of   191–2
      stop power for journalistic material, use of   412–13
   ownership   377–8
   pamphlets and tracts, publication of   109–12
   Parliamentary proceedings, monopoly to print   111–12
   politics   377
   printing presses   109–12
members of parliament (MPs)
   consultancies, MPs with paid   115
   lawyers, as   113
   Nolan Committee   114–18, 436
      outside employment   436
      Principles   376, 434, 438
   outside employment, MPs taking   115, 436
   outside interests, declarations of   115
   paid advocacy by MPs   437–8
   register of financial interests   116
   scandals   114–16
migration   405, 413–15, 448–9
Mill, John Stuart   8, 18–19
Millennium Development Goals (MDGs)   398
ministers
   administrative state   119
   Attorney General, ministerial functions of the   94
   Cabinet Secretary on misconduct, advice from   118
   collective ministerial responsibility   60–1, 104, 117
   corruption   119
   individual ministerial responsibility   60–1
   Ministerial Code, breaches of the   61, 117–18, 438, 457
   Nolan Committee   117
   Parliament   117–18
   powers   119
   resignations   60–1, 117
   separation of powers   60–1
   statements in interpretation, use of   127
minorities   186, 425
mislead, duty not to   326–7, 329–30, 333
Model Rules of Professional Conduct 1983 (MRPC) (ABA)
   accept clients, duty to   303–4
   administration of justice, duty to the   326, 332
   all lawful means to achieve client's objective, use of   311–12
   autonomy of clients   344
   candour, duty of   329
   confidentiality   338–9, 340, 341, 342
   consumers, clients as   314
   correction of testimony found to be false   329
   counselling   321
   criticism   341
   disclosure   328–9, 341, 342–4
   Ethics 2000 Commission   281, 290, 328–9
   Ethics 20/20   290, 300, 309–10
   fairness   333, 334

financial harm, prevention of 338, 342–3
fraud, disclosure in cases of corporate 342–3
greed, dishonesty and incivility 341
illegality, assistance in 321–4
independence 263
lawful objectives, accepting clients' 305, 308
Legal Professional Privilege 328
legality, duty of 340, 341
loyalty, devotion, or zeal, duty of 308–11, 312, 314–15
misleading the court 341
neutrality 298, 303–4, 305, 313–14
parties in proceedings, fairness to 334
partisanship 298, 308, 311–15
perjury 341–2
pro bono services 319
reporting requirements 323, 341–3
self-reporting for misconduct 323
sexual relationships 300
supporting the rule of law 286
third parties, disclosure to 322
withdrawal from representation 322, 341–2
monarchy 29–31
  Church of England 113
  constitutional monarchy 55, 113
  constraints 11
  consulted, to encourage and to warn, right to be 58
  courts as tools of the monarch 123
  despotism 55
  Divine Right of monarchs to rule/absolutism 30–1, 33–4, 36–8
  executive/government, influence on 57–8
  Inns of Court 49, 50–1
  Lord Chancellor 83
  Parliament, dignified role of the monarch in 59
  power 10–11, 34, 50, 53–6, 154
  separation of powers 54–5
  sovereign power 54
money laundering 204, 210, 319–20, 322
monopolies
  advocacy 137, 302, 349, 351, 353–5, 465
  education and training 348
  expertise, control of 347–8
  land transfers 153
  neoliberalism 349, 350, 352–3
  organisation of profession 242
  Parliamentary proceedings, monopoly to print 111–12
  professionalism 347–8
  regulation 270
  reserved legal activities 352
  solicitors 292

Montesquieu, Charles-Louis 8–10, 54–5, 58, 62, 76, 161, 425–7
morality 3–4, 212–37
  accountability 212–13, 215, 228, 235
  adversarialism, moral crisis of 218–22, 231, 233–6
  advocacy, ideology of 229, 234, 236
  anti-establishment feelings 235
  best interests of clients 212, 222
  bureaucracy of the legal system 213
  civic republicanism 213
  civil proceedings 228
  civil rights movements 235
  civil society 10
  client focus 225–7, 235–6
  codes of conduct 297
  conflicts of interest 234
  corruption 213
  counter-culture of 1960s 235
  criticism of lawyer's role 212, 216–18
  emotional detachment 212
  fairness 230–1, 234
  hired guns, lawyers as 213, 228
  honesty 232
  illegal conduct, assisting 231
  individualism 106
  inner morality of law 11
  juries, role of 157
  jurisdictional norms, compliance with 230–1
  law and morality, no connection between 11
  legality 213, 218, 230–1, 236
  legitimacy 232, 233
  liberalism 235–6
  litigation lawyers, controlling 214–15
  loyalty 228, 232
  lying and cheating 232
  marginalised societies 159
  neutrality 212, 215, 216, 228–30, 232–6, 299
  non-accountability 212, 215, 228–9, 235
  objectives of clients 299
  open society 235–6
  partisanship 212, 215, 228–30, 232–5
  personal morality 185
  positivism 230–1, 233, 236
  presumption of innocence 234
  procedural justice 229
  professionalism, principle of 228–9
  prosecutors 216–18
  public interest 213, 234
  public opprobrium 212
  rule of law, role in relation to 231–7
  separation of Church and state 235–6
  social order 230–1
  social role of lawyers 213

Index   535

standard conception of the lawyer's role
    212–13, 228–31, 233, 236–7
  theory   212–13
  third party harms   213
  universities/law schools   236
  Watergate   227–30, 235
  zeal, conception of   233, 234, 236
multinationals   371, 373, 393

nationalism   23, 448
nativism   426, 450
natural justice   72, 465
natural law   30, 51, 160, 171, 185
natural rights   183–4
nature, law of   30–1, 54, 66
nature, state of see State of Nature
Nazi Germany
  legal positivism   126, 207
  Nuremberg Military Tribunal (NMT)   173–6,
    178, 183–4
negative liberty   162
neoliberalism   347–8, 349–57
  advocacy   349, 351–7
  Alternative Business Structures (ASB)   352,
    355–6
  barristers
    advocacy monopoly, ending of   349, 351,
      353–5
    Bar Council   355
    Bar Direct   354
    Bar Standards Board (BSB)   349–50, 357
    cab rank rule   355
    culture   353
    independence   354–5
    separation of powers   355
  Clementi Report   351–2
  competition, promotion of   350–1
  complaints handling   351–2
  corporate lawyers   387
  corporatised state   376
  corporatocracy   372–3
  decline of professional society   349–50
  de-professionalisation   349–51
  free market   348–9, 350
  globalisation   395–6
  judiciary   355–7
  Law Society
    advocacy rights   353
    complaints handling   351, 354–5
    conveyancing monopoly   353
  legal aid   349, 351
  Legal Services Act 2007   352–6
  Legal Services Board (LSB)   350, 356–7
  licensed conveyancers, introduction of   349
  macroeconomics   350

  marketization   351
  Marre Report   353–4
  monopolies   349, 350, 352–3
  neoliberalism, definition of   348
  over-production of lawyers   349
  politics of professionalism   350–3
  public interest   357
  public investment   350
  reform of legal services market in England and
    Wales   347–8, 349–57
  regulation   352–3
  rule of law, definition of   348–9
  self-regulation, ending   349–51, 355
  separation of powers   355
  solicitors, rights of audience of   349, 354
  Solicitors Regulation Authority (SRA)   349–50
  state, withdrawal of the   349
  universities   349
  welfare   349–50, 395
neutrality   298–9, 301–8
  17th century   216
  19th century   216
  accept consumers as clients, duty to   299, 301–4
  autonomy of clients   299, 305
  barristers   245, 298, 301–2, 306, 313–14, 464
  celebrities, lawyers as   146–50
  codes of conduct   298–9, 301–8
  corporate lawyers   386
  equality before the law   299
  indicators   301–8
  judges   141
  lawful objectives, accepting clients'   304–8
  morality   212, 215, 216, 228–30, 232–6, 299
  partisanship   146–50, 212, 228–30, 232–5,
    313–16, 344, 386
  private practice   464, 474
  social markers   298–9
  solicitors   298, 302–3, 307, 313–14
  standard conception of the lawyer's role   299
Netherlands   316
News Corp   378
New Zealand see also New Zealand, legal
    profession in
  Bill of Rights 1689   75
  Bill of Rights 1990   74–5
  Cabinet Manual   75
  common law   6
  Constitution Act   74
  corruption   456
  separation of powers   74–5
New Zealand, legal profession in   258–60
    see also Lawyers: Conduct and Client
    Care Rules (LCCR) (New Zealand)
  19th century   258–9, 281
  accountability   282

admission provisions 281
all lawful means to achieve client's objective, use of 312–13
associations 259–60
Attorney General as a political appointment 101
Auckland Law Society 259–60, 264
autonomy of clients 308, 344
barristers 259–60, 261–2, 281–3
British model 258–60, 262, 281
cab rank rule 261
colonialism 258
Conduct and Client Care Rules 2008 260
co-regulation 471
corruption 462
discipline 281–2, 471
disclosure 338
education and training 259
English law 258–9
fairness 333, 334
fusion 260, 261–2
government lawyers 461–2
independence 264, 282
judiciary
  appointment of the 264
  regulation 281
lawful objectives, accepting clients' 307–8
Lawyers and Conveyancers Act 2006 259–60, 264, 282, 316
legal aid cuts 461
Legal Complaints Review Officer, appointment of 471
Legal Professional Privilege 194, 196, 203
neutrality 298
New Zealand Law Society (NZLS) 259, 281–3, 316
organisation of profession 258–60
partisanship 298, 311, 312–13
prosecutions 282, 332
qualifications 281
Queen's Counsel/Senior Counsel 259–60, 264
regulation 281–3, 470–1
reporting requirements for serious crime 322
Rules Governing the Conduct of Practitioners 282
self-regulation 281
sexual relationships 300
Society of Conveyancers 283
Solicitor General 101
solicitors 259–60, 281, 283
specialist advocates 248, 261–2
standards 282–3
Statute of Westminster 1931 258
supporting the rule of law 284–5
university model 259

Nolan Committee on standards in public life 114–18, 436
  outside employment 436
  Principles 376, 434, 438
non-governmental organisations (NGOs) 112–13
Normans 31–3
Northern Ireland
  Brexit and NI protocol 430–1, 434
  Troubles 186
Nuremberg Military Tribunal (NMT) 173–6, 183–4
  accountability 173
  crimes against humanity 175
  customary international law 176
  Enlightenment 175, 183
  genocide, crime of 174–6, 178
    Genocide Convention 1948, adoption of 176
    Native Americans, claims by 175
  International Criminal Court (ICC) 178
  legitimacy 176
  London Charter 173, 175–6
  natural rights 183–4
  procedural fairness 176
  UN 397
  war crimes 175, 178

oaths
  Attorney General 94
  Canton of Geneva, oaths sworn by lawyers in the 288–9
  codes of conduct 288–9, 292–3, 297
  litigation 214–15
  Lord Chancellor 91–2
  medieval lawyers 225, 265, 270, 288–9, 292, 297, 325
  solicitors 274
  witnesses 137
objectives of clients
  accepting client's lawful objectives 299, 301–8, 311
  all means to achieve client's objective, use of 299, 311–13, 315–16
  moral disagreement with objectives 299
Old Bailey Session Papers (OBSP) 138–40, 144, 152, 156
open access order 108–9, 130–1
Organisation for Economic Co-operation and Development (OECD) 397
organisation of profession 241–68
  apprenticeship model 242
  associations 242
  Bar of England and Wales 243–5, 248, 260
  callings 242

colonies   247–61
common law tradition   247–8, 261–2
culture   242
diaspora, lawyers in the   247–60
diffusion of responsibility   261
economics   241
education and training   242
historical stages   241
independence   262–4, 267–8
models   260–1
monopolies   242
oppression, professions as protection from   242
power approach   241
priesthood, similarities to   242
processual approach   241
profession, definition of   242
prototypes   243–7
  Bar of England and Wales   243–5, 248, 260
  solicitors   245–7, 260
public service   264–7, 268
roles   261–2
separation of power   261
social contract   242
socialisation   242
sociological approaches   241
solicitors   245–7, 260
static characteristics   241
structural approach   241
structural functionalism   241–2
subjectivity of members   242
theory   241–2
vocations   242
outsiders   23

Paine, Thomas   9, 48, 56, 147–8, 155, 219, 251, 271, 308
Pakistan   401
Parliament   113–18 *see also* **House of Lords; legislature**
  abuse of power   123
  Barebones Parliament   124
  Brexit   102, 428–9
  cash for questions scandal   114
  Church of England's passive obedience to royal authority   113
  codes of conduct   116–18
  collective ministerial responsibility   117
  Committee of Privileges   116
  common law, supremacy of   66
  conflicts of interest   116
  consultancies, MPs with paid   115
  corporate influence on Parliament   376
  corporatocracy   374–5
  corruption   113–15

COVID-19 measures, lack of scrutiny of   435
discipline   115–16
employment outside Parliament   115
English civil wars   38–44, 51
executive/government power   55, 113–14
freedom of speech   38
independence from monarchy   35
influence of lawyers   114
institutions   113–18
judiciary   50, 61–2, 65–9, 117
law officers   85, 87–8
legality, principle of   67
lobbying work   115
Long Parliament   40, 44–6
Magna Carta   37–8
ministers
  Cabinet Secretary on misconduct, advice from   118
  Ministerial Code   117–18
  Nolan Committee   117
  resignation   117
MPs as lawyers   113
Nolan Committee on standards in public life   114–17
outside interests, declarations of   115
Parliamentary Commissioner for Standards   116–17
Parliamentary Standards Committee, referrals to   435
party system   458
political parties   113
prerogative powers   39, 50–1
print Parliamentary proceedings, monopoly to   111–12
proroguing of Parliament, litigation on   429–30
register of financial interests   116
revolutions   29, 34, 35–41, 48
Rump Parliament   44, 124, 243, 248
scandals   114–16
separation of powers   116–17
sovereignty   55, 58, 65–9, 425
  Brexit   429
  British Constitution   1–2
  EU law   66–7
  interpretation   64
  judicial invention, as   181
  legality, principle of   67
  ministers   119
  trust in government   459
  veto   55
standards   114–16
trade union sponsorship   115
Parliament Acts of 1911 and 1949   76
Parliamentary Counsel   461
parties in proceedings, fairness to   334

partisanship 298–300, 308–13
  19th century 234
  adversary system 233–4
  all means to achieve client's objective, use of 299, 311–13
  autonomy 299
  barristers 245, 272–3, 298, 308, 313–15
  celebrities, lawyers as 146–50
  civil service 120
  codes of conduct 298–300, 308–14
  corporate lawyers 386
  indicators 308–13
  legality 474
  loyalty, devotion, or zeal, duty of 299, 308–11
  Lund's *Guide* 299–300
  morality 212, 215, 228–30, 232–5
  neutrality 313–16, 344
    adversary system 233–4
    celebrities, lawyers as 146–50
    codes of conduct 313–14
    corporate lawyers 386
    morality 212, 215, 228–30, 232–5
  prosecutions 216–18
  social markers 298–9
  solicitors 298, 310, 313–15
  tactics 229
paternalism 310, 314–15
patriotism 23, 448
patronage 119, 434
phone hacking scandal 122
physical harm, preventing 336–9, 342
Plato 29–30, 119
polarisation 454–5
politics 22–3 *see also* Whigs
  adversary system 221
  Attorney General 92–4, 103
  barristers 243
  civil and political rights 110
  civil society 112
  judiciary 61, 127, 459–60
  lawyers 128–9, 415
  leadership 373–4
  liberalism 154
  Lord Chancellor 84
  media ownership 377
  personalistic political leadership 426
  polarised political cultures 454–5
  political parties 60, 113, 166, 433
    emergence 46
    judiciary 127
  political rights 162, 168, 184
  professionalism 350–3
  public appointments, politically motivated 438–9, 457, 459
  trials 34, 151

Poor Man's Lawyers movement in Victorian Britain 265
Popish Plot 138
populism
  accountability 456
  appointments to public office, politicisation of 459
  autocracy 456
  binary, moral opposition between people and establishment 426
  Brexit 424, 431, 436, 446, 448
  constitutional courts 459
  corruption 455–6, 458–9
  decline of the rule of law 455–6
  demagoguery 426
  elective dictatorships 456
  EU, opposition to the 455
  extreme right or left 426
  globalisation 404
  ideology, style and strategy 426
  judiciary 458–9
  nativism 426
  personalistic political leadership 426
  popular sovereignty 425
  seizure of power by force 456
positivism 125–6, 130, 185–6, 206–7, 233, 236
poverty 171, 399
pre-agrarian societies 21–2
precedent 34, 207–8
prerogative courts 34, 50
prerogative powers 35–6, 39, 50–1, 72, 76, 86
press *see* media/press
presumption of innocence 154, 162–3, 234
Prime Minister 60–1, 83
Prisoners Counsel Act 1836 152, 155–6
  adversary system 152, 155–6, 218–19, 221, 271
  legal representation in criminal trials, right to 152
Private Finance Initiative (PFI) 377
private practice 14–16, 464–73
  adversary system 465–7
  common law countries 464
  confidence 467–8
  development of role 7
  education and training 474
  Enlightenment 14
  independence of the lawyers 464
  law officers 88
  legal professions 468–73
  literature 14–16
  neutrality 464, 474
  privilege 467–8
  professionalism, threats to 464
  roles 25, 464–5

self-regulation   464
social order   6
private property, right to   166–8
private/public sphere   159
privilege *see* **Legal Professional Privilege (LPP)**
pro bono work
  barristers   266
  Chancery Lane, national centre in   389
  corporate lawyers   386–7, 389–90, 394
  Guantanamo Bay Detention Centre   391–2, 405–6
  incrimination   319–20
  Law Works   389
  legal aid cuts   389
  poverty   389–90
  private plight work   390
  public duties   319–20
  public service   265–6
  solicitors   266
procedural propriety/fairness   2, 65, 125–6, 130, 176, 229
professional associations *see also* **American Bar Association (ABA); International Bar Association (IBA); Inns of Court; Law Society**
  Auckland Law Society   259–60, 264
  Bar Council   245, 306, 355, 358–60
  Canadian Bar Association (CBA)   255–6, 284, 285, 286, 292
  civil society   19, 472
  Council of the Bars and Law Societies of Europe (CCBE)   418–20, 421
  cultures and norms   19
  globalisation   397–8, 423
  international lawyer associations   418–20, 421–2
  New Zealand Law Society (NZLS)   259, 281–3, 316
  organisation   242
  public service   265
  regulation   358–60, 416
  self-regulation   269, 416
  size of membership   471
  solicitors   471
professionalism in England and Wales   347–70
  barristers   273, 277
  cartels   347
  civil society   347
  corporatocracy   374
  costs   347
  democracy   347
  de-professionalisation   347, 473
  education and training   348
  expertise, controlling   348
  independent regulation   357–70

monopolies   347–8
morality   228–9
neoliberal reform of legal services market   347–8, 349–57, 368
norms and values   347
overproducing lawyers   349
politics   350–3
private practice   464
regulation   348
social role   347–8
state power, counter-weight to   348
theory   347–9
professions   17–20, 239 *see also* **organisation of profession; professional associations; professionalism**
  capitalism   17–19
  codes of conduct   8, 19–20
  culture   19–20
  de-professionalisation   349–51
  exclusions   20
  historical context   8
  institutions   107
  key characteristics   269
  Legal Profession Reform Index (LPRI)   416, 421
  legality   20
  literature   17–20
  moral neutrality   20
  neoliberalism   349–51
  norms of practice, adoption and articulation of   6
  occupational role theory   19–20
  professionalization   8, 19
  rationality   17–19
  roles   19–20, 25
  standard conception of lawyers' role   20
property rights   162
proportionality   2, 72, 87
prosecutions
  18th century   139
  accountability   217 why the gap?
  Attorney General, consent of   87, 92–3, 103
  cash for honours prosecutions   92–3
  Director of Public Prosecutions (DPP)   87
  government departments, prosecutions by   139
  involvement of lawyers in   139
  law officers   86–8, 92–3, 103
  partisanship   216–18
  public prosecutors, obligations of   130
  solicitors   291–2
  state involvement   139
Protectorate   44, 123
protest, right to   186–9

Protestantism
    American Revolution 56
    Bill of Rights 1689 47, 168
    capitalism 17–19
    Elizabethan Settlement of 1559 33
    natural law 160
    oaths in House of Commons 40
    organisation of profession 242
    Reformation 32–3, 235
    theologians and naturalists 124
    Whigs 46, 113
public appointments
    corruption 456
    culture and values 438
    judiciary 73, 90, 447–8, 459–60
    politically motivated appointments 73, 438–9, 447–8, 457, 459–60
public choice theory 445
Public Private Partnerships (PPPs) 377
public inquiries 122–3
    Cabinet Secretary memorandum 122
    chairs, lawyers as 122
    corruption 122–3
    Hillsborough inquiry (Taylor inquiry) 122–3
    Inquiries Act 2005 122
    phone hacking scandal 122
    statutory inquiries 122
public interest
    advocacy 357
    Attorney General 86, 88, 92–4
    confidentiality 190, 191
    government lawyers 461–3
    incrimination 317
    independence of the legal profession 469
    Legal Professional Privilege 186, 196, 200–1
    legality 339
    litigation 88, 214
    morality 213, 234
    neoliberalism 357
    Public Interest Immunity (PII) 410–11
    regulation 360–1
    third parties, prevention of harm to 323
Public Law Project 113
public/private sphere 159
public procurement, corruption in 434–6
public service 264–7, 318–20
    accountability 264
    associations of lawyers 265
    civil service, ethos of 119–20, 130
    clients 288–90
    divorce cases, free assistance in 265
    education and training 265
    impartiality 264
    integrity 264
    law centre movement 265
    law reform, contributions to 265
    legal aid firms 265
    legality 265
    organisation of profession 264–7, 268
    pro bono work 265–6
    regulation 288–90, 292
    welfare rights 265
public utilities, sale of 376
Pufendorf, Samuel von 107, 160–1, 166
Puritanism 17–18, 33, 37

Quality Assurance Scheme for Advocates (QASA) 356

rationality 2, 17–19, 24, 70–2
Rawls, John 13, 136, 183, 445
rebellions 186–7 see also revolution
reciprocity 23
records of State Trials 138–9
Reform Act 1832 168, 427
Reformation 32–3, 235
regulation 269–95 see also independent regulation in England and Wales; self-regulation
    barristers 270–4, 472
    client and public duties 288–90, 292
    closure of markets 270
    codes of conduct 284–94
    common law 270, 289
    co-regulation 472–3
    cultural identity 269–70
    deregulation 373
    discipline 270, 295
    education and training 270, 295
    enforcement 270
    habitus 269
    institutionalisation 270
    insurance 291
    Legal Services Act 2007 2–3, 349–50
    legality 318
    legislative controls 270
    licensing 270
    medieval period 270
    monopolies 270
    national identity 270
    neoliberalism 349–51, 355
    peer mechanisms 271
    professionalism 269, 348
    recourse role, lawyers as having a 295
    rules, role of 293–5
    self-regulation 270–84, 292–3
    social values 269
    socialisation 294–5
    solicitors 274–9, 471–2
    standards 269

theory 269–70
United States 279–81
Regulation of Investigatory Powers Act 2000 411
religion *see also* **Christianity/Church**
  authority, rejection of 160
  Enlightenment 160
  freedom 162, 168–70, 182
  law as replacing religion 25
  natural law 160
  rationality 2
  scepticism 160
  Sharia law 401
  state and religion, separation of 160
  toleration 131
  wealth, legitimacy of the pursuit of 17
rendition 407
reporting requirements
  barristers 324
  codes of conduct 322
  legality 211, 320, 322–4
  money laundering 204, 319–20, 322
  self-reporting 324
  solicitors 324
  terrorism 204, 319, 322, 411
  third parties, harm to 206, 344
representation 296–316 *see also* **advocacy**; **codes of conduct**; **legal representation in court**
republic, law of a 54–5
reputation 145–6, 155–6, 274
resale price maintenance (RPM) 375–6
Restoration 31, 44–6, 55, 61–2, 243
retrospectivity 185
revolution 29–52 *see also* **American Revolution**; **English revolutions**
  French Revolution 10, 29, 48, 147, 151
  monarchies, establishment of constitutional orders in place of 29
  theory 29–31
  tyranny/despotism 29–30, 51
rights and liberties 9, 14, 160–71
  17th century 182
  Act of Settlement 1702 161
  arbitrary power 11
  basic rights 162
  Charter of Fundamental Rights of the EU 178
  civil liberties 162–6, 184
  common law 161, 182
  creations, rights to 184
  cultural rights 162, 168–70, 184
  democracy 427, 433–4
  discretion authority of government 11
  economic rights 162, 166–8
  enforcement 182
  European Court of Human Rights 178–81
    domestic courts, relationship with 433–4
    hostility 179–81
    individual petitions 178
    judiciary 68
    leaving 413
  fairness 184
  freedom of speech 3–4, 38, 131, 177, 184, 186, 412
  globalisation 395
  Human Rights Act 1998 68, 77
    Bill of Rights, replacement with 181
    legislature, control of 67
    repeal, proposals for 449
    terrorism 407–8, 410
  identity 154
  inalienable rights 10
  incremental erosion of rights 411–13
  indigenous people, rights of 167, 172, 175, 396
  individual, and the 9–10
  inhuman or degrading treatment 406
  International Bill of Rights 177–8
  judiciary 55, 68–9
  justice 13, 182
  laws of nature 9
  left alone, right to be 161
  legal liberty 184
  legality 474
  legislature, control of 67
  liberty and security, right to 406–8
  majority, claims of the 160–1
  mythic quality of rights 182–3
  negative liberty 161–2
  political rights 110, 162, 168, 184
  positive liberty 161–2, 183
  property rights 162
  protest, right to 186–9
  reciprocal freedom 184
  religious freedom 162, 168–70, 182
  sexual rights 184
  social movements 182
  social rights 162, 170–1
  State of Nature 30–1, 161
  subordination of individuals 9
  supremacy of regular law 11
  terrorism 407–8, 410
  Universal Declaration of Human Rights 162, 177–8
  universal rights 171, 173
  welfare rights 161, 170–1, 183, 247, 265, 386
Rousseau, Jean-Jacques 8–9, 21–2, 171, 425
rule by law 13–14, 453
Rump Parliament 44, 124, 243, 248

rural areas, attorneys in 153
Russia 402–3, 420–1
  advocates, autonomy of 421
  authoritarianism 402–3
  corruption 455
  Crimea, annexation of 403
  European Court of Human Rights (ECtHR) 403
  NGOs 402
  repression 403
  Soviet Union, collapse of 402–3
  Ukraine, invasion of 403
  United States, Russia investigations in 440, 442–3, 446–7

Scandinavia 374, 401
scientific inquiry, revolution in 8
Scotland, Advocate General in 86
seditious libel 111
self-interest 5–6
self-regulation 270–84, 292–3
  admission 416–17
  autonomy 416–17
  corporatocracy 373
  discipline 416–17
  education and entry requirements 292
  independence of the legal profession 469, 472
  liberalisation 347
  private practice 464
  professional associations 269, 416
  professionalism 347, 473
  solicitors 276, 472
senior government lawyers 94–101 see also Attorney General (AG); Lord Chancellor
  advisory role 95–6, 103
  Cabinet Manual 97, 104
  common law jurisdictions, in other 97–101
  Constitutional Reform Act 2005 92–7, 102, 104
  corruption 461
  diffused responsibility, notion of 104–5
  guardians of the rule of law, as 95–7, 103–5, 461
  legality 461
  Lord Chief Justice 72
  other common law jurisdictions, in 97–101
  Parliamentary Counsel 461
  Solicitor General 81, 84–5, 87, 97–101
separation of church and state 110, 160, 235–6, 451
separation of powers 53–4, 57–64, 76–9
  abuse of powers 10
  accountability 456
  civil service 119
  common law courts 79
  Constitutional Reform Act 2005 78
  decline of the rule of law 456
  democracy 427, 450
  diffusing power 58–9
  elites 54
  Enlightenment 54
  foreign jurisdictions 72–5
  government/executive 10, 53–4, 57–64, 80, 130
  horizontal diffusion 58
  House of Lords 62–3
  judiciary 54–5, 61–4, 78–80
  judicial review 79
  juries 55, 62
  legislative function 58–60, 76–7, 116–17
  Lord Chancellor 63, 90–1
  monarchies 54–5
  nature, law of 54
  neoliberalism 355
  organisation of profession 261
  procedural justice 130
  republic, law of a 54–5
  vertical diffusion 58
serjeants 136–7, 243
sexual relationships 299–300
silence, right to 48, 162–3
SLAPPs (strategic lawsuits against public participation) 380–3
slave trade
  abolition 113
  citizenship 172–3, 182–3
  economic rights 167–8, 182–3
  habeas corpus 172
  marginalised societies 159
  political bias 183
  Somerset case 172
  Whig supremacy 113
Smith, Adam 8, 110, 347, 350, 371
social capital 394
social change 130, 154, 158
social contract 30–1, 51
  coercive force, society not governed by 9
  corporate social responsibility (CSR) 9
  Enlightenment 9
  free and equal society 9
  government/executive 9
  legality 11, 185
  liberty 30–1
  organisation of profession 242
  State of Nature 30–1
social movements 182, 235
social organisation 21
social rights 162, 170–1
soft law 387, 394

Solicitor General (SG)   81, 84–5, 87, 97–101
solicitors (England and Wales)   245–7 *see also* Law Society; SRA Code of Conduct 2011
  16th century   274
  17th century   152
  18th century   153, 274
  abuse of process   330–1
  accounts, rules on   274–5
  administration of justice, duty to the   343
  admissions   361
  advocacy   302–3, 306, 311, 349, 354, 465
  agencies   471
  all lawful means to achieve client's objective, use of   311
  Alternative Business Structures (ABSs)   287, 358, 379–80
  apprenticeships   361
  articled clerks   247, 274
  Attorneys and Solicitors Act 1729   274
  attorneys, distinguished from   245–6
  audience, rights of   311
  autonomy of clients   306
  bankruptcy   274–5
  best practice   274
  Big Bang de-regulation of financial services in City of London   153–4
  business lawyers   152–3, 158
  cab rank rule   302–3
  capitalism   157–8
  cause lawyers   267
  Chancery Lane   246
  chancery specialists, as   152
  civil society   263
  clerkships   246–7, 274
  client care   291
  client money   274–5
  compensation fund   274
  confidentiality   158, 324, 339
  consumers, clients as   306–7
  conveyancing monopoly   349, 353
  co-regulation   472
  corporate law   152–3
  costs   274, 307
  differentiated roles   314–15
  discipline   275, 278, 290–2, 358
    Franks Committee   275
    Solicitors Disciplinary Tribunal (SDT)   275, 291, 361–8
  dishonesty   277–8
  education and training   246–7, 274, 349
  elite global firms   153–4
  entry requirements   274
  etiquette   274–6
  fairness   333

  financial harm, prevention of   339, 342
  Gentlemen Practisers   246, 274
  independence   262, 275, 287, 361–2, 471
  insurance   291
  integrity   277–8
  judiciary   459
  law centre movement   265
  law degrees   247
  law reform   265
  lawful objectives, accepting clients'   306
  legal aid   247, 265–7
  Legal Professional Privilege   158, 330
  Legal Services Act 2007   276, 287, 471
  Legal Services Board (LSB)   359
  legality   324, 343
  Lund's *Guide*   299–300, 306, 310, 333, 336
  monopolies   292, 349, 353
  neoliberalism   349, 354
  neutralisation of legal profession   472
  neutrality   302–3, 306, 313–14
  oaths   274
  organisation of profession   245–7, 260
  Petty Bag Office   274
  physical harm, prevention of   342
  pro bono work   266
  professional associations   471
  prosecutions   291–2
  qualifications   247
  regulation   274–9, 291, 471–2
  reputation for financial probity   274
  rule of law, upholding the   279, 343
  self-regulation   276, 472
  sexual relationships   299–300
  socialisation   361
  Solicitors Act 1974   275, 291
  Solicitors Code of Conduct (SCC) 2007
    advocacy   302, 311
    best interests of clients   307
    fairness   333
    misleading the court   365
    physical harm, prevention of   336
    principles   276
    regulation   365–6
    sexual relationships   299
  Solicitors Disciplinary Tribunal (SDT)   275, 291, 361–8
  Solicitors' Overseas Practice Rules 1990   420
  Solicitors Practice Rules 1936   275, 286
  Solicitors Practice Rules 1987   275
  Solicitors Practice Rules 1990   275–6, 286–7
    cab rank rule   302–3
    client care   291
    lawful objectives, accepting clients'   307
    Outcomes and Indicative Behaviours   287

Solicitors Pro Bono Group   266
Solicitors Qualifying Examination (SQE)   361
Solicitors Regulation Authority (SRA)   276–8
   Alternative Business Structures (ABSs)   379–80
   confidentiality   324, 339, 340–1
   Legal Services Board (LSB)   359
   neoliberalism   349–50
   principles   277–8, 285, 287, 294–5
   regulation   358–68, 369
   Standards and Regulations   287, 324
SRA Standards 2019
   abuse of process   330–1
   correction of misleading statements   329–30
   disclosure   336
   instructions, acting on client's   307
   Outcomes and Indicative Behaviours   287
   physical harm, prevention of   336
   reporting requirements   324
   unregulated businesses, work in   361
   standards   274, 324, 330–1
   state authoritarianism   263
   supervision   246–7
   unregulated businesses, work in   361
sorcerers or shamans, lawyers as   16, 19, 25
sovereign power
   aristocracy   54
   executive/government   53–5, 459
   forms   53–4
   Parliament   181, 459
   people/popular   9, 57, 425
Soviet Union, collapse of   402–3
special advisers (SPADS)   120
special advocates   409–11
Special Immigration Appeals Commission (SIAC)   406, 409
SRA Code of Conduct 2011   276, 287
   advocacy   302–3
   all lawful means to achieve client's objective, use of   311
   cab rank rule   302–3
   corporatocracy   380
   correction of misleading statements   329–30
   disclosure   336
   discrimination   302–3
   illegality, risk of   343
   lawful objectives, accepting clients'   307
   loyalty, devotion, or zeal, duty of   310
   neutrality   298, 302–3, 307, 313–14
   Outcomes and Indicative Behaviours   310, 360–1
   partisanship   298, 310, 313–15
   paternalism   310
   physical harm, prevention of   336

   principles and duties   276–7
   reporting requirements   324
   self-reporting   324
standard conception of the lawyer's role   20, 297–301
   barristers   297
   codes of conduct   297–301, 316
   comparative analysis   297–301
   morality   212–13, 228–31, 233, 236–7
   neutrality   299
Star Chamber   34, 40, 163
State of Nature   8–9, 30–1, 161, 166
statues, pulling down
   Colston statue in Bristol, pulling down of   187–9
   Confederate soldiers, erection of statues to   187
   Nelson, statue of   187
   slavery, associations with   187–9
substantive rule of law, model of   11, 13–14
Sunday trading   376
supporting the rule of law   279, 284–6, 343, 460–3, 474–5
surveillance   411
Switzerland
   Canton of Geneva, oaths sworn by lawyers in the   288–9
   litigation   214–15
system duties   320–32

tactics   229
taxes   32, 48, 50–1, 76
Taylor Inquiry   123
television programmes   4–6
terrorism   404–13
   Anti-terrorism, Crime and Security Act 2001   406–7
   barristers as special advocates   409
   closed material procedure (CMP)   409–11
   deportation   406–7
   detention   405–9
   freedom of expression   412
   Guantanamo Bay   405–6, 409–10
   Human Rights Act 1998   407–8, 410
   immigration   405
   incremental erosion of rights   411–13
   inhuman or degrading treatment   406
   insurgent cosmopolitanism   404–5
   interception of communications   411
   journalistic material, use of stop power for   412–13
   liberty and security, right to   406–8
   Islamic terrorism   404–5
   Legal Professional Privilege   210
   migration   413

Protection of Freedoms Act   411–12
Public Interest Immunity (PII)   410–11
  reaction to threats to UK   406–8
Regulation of Investigatory Powers Act 2000
    411
rendition   407
reporting requirements   204, 210, 319, 322,
    411
special advocates   409–11
Special Immigration Appeals Commission
    (SIAC)   406, 409
special procedures and lawyers   409–11
surveillance   411
terrorism, definition of   413
tipping off   411
TPIM notices   408
whistleblowing   412
thick conceptions of the rule of law   458
thief-takers
  criminal process, interference in the   139
  rewards   139, 144–5
think tanks   376, 445
third parties *see* third parties, prevention of client
    harms to; third party duties
third parties, prevention of client harms
    to   204–6
  barristers   342
  corporate clients and financial harm   205–6,
    210
  dangerous clients   204–5, 209–10, 342
  financial harm, prevention of   205–6, 338–9,
    340–2
  legality   204–6, 211, 323, 342
  morality   213
  physical harm   336–9, 342
  public interest   209, 323
  reporting requirements   323, 344
  warnings   205, 209, 319
third party duties   317, 332–9
  fairness   319, 332–6
  financial harm   338–9
  harm, preventing unnecessary   319, 336–9
  incrimination   317, 332–9, 340
  integrity   319
  physical harm, preventing   336–9
  public duties   318, 319
tipping off   204, 411
Tories   46–7, 108, 113, 155, 378, 427, 429, 432,
    437–8
torture   390, 392
totalitarianism   454–5
trade unions   71–2, 79, 112, 115, 166, 375–6
training *see* education and training
treason cases   138, 217–18
Treasury Counsel (Treasury Devil)   121–2

Treasury Solicitor's Department   121
Trump, Donald   378, 424, 439–50, 454–61
trust   24, 63, 189–90, 433
tyranny or despotism   29–30 *see also*
        absolutism/autocracy
  abuse of power   30
  civil liberties   162
  English civil wars   42–4
  justifications for replacing rulers   51
  monarchy   55
  natural law   52
  resignation to tyranny   30
  resistance   30
  social contract   51
  tyranny of the majority   14–15, 425
  unnecessary laws as tyranny   161

Ukraine, invasion of   403
UN Commission on International Trade
    (UNCITRAL)   397
United Nations (UN)   397
United States *see also* American Revolution;
        United States, legal profession in;
        Watergate
    scandal
  abortion law   171, 460
  administrative agencies   129–30, 376
  Administrative Procedure Act 1946   376
  adversary system   224–6, 465
  Afghanistan, intervention in   402
  American Civil War   163, 186–7, 248, 251–2
  Articles of Confederation   75
  Bill of Rights   57, 177
  Canada   98
  capitalism   463
  citizenship   171–3, 182–3
  civic republicanism   237
  client focus   225–7, 235
  Committee of Detail   75
  Committee of Style   75
  common law   57
  confidentiality   226
  Congress   57
  Constitution
    Bill of Rights   57, 177
    citizenship   171
    constitutional government   54, 56–7, 75–6
    criticism   75–6
    drafting   56
    ideological origins   57
    law reports   50
    legal representation in Congress
        128–9
    senior government lawyers   102
    Supreme Court   72–3

Constitutional Conventions 75
corporate social responsibility (CSR) 388, 390
corporatised state 375–6
corporatocracy 380–4, 394
Declaration of Independence 48, 51, 75, 172, 182
demagoguery 446
democracy 439–46
  election in 2016 424, 439–41
    cultural displacement, feelings of 448
    email servers of Hillary Clinton, investigations into 439–40, 442
    illegal immigration 448
    loyalty to Republican Party 448
    popular vote, Trump's loss of the 457
    populism 446
    Russia investigations 440, 446–7
  election in 2020 443–4, 455
    fraud, allegations of 443–4, 447–8, 455
    insurrection at the Capitol Building 444, 455
    postal voting 443–4
fake news 446
formalism, rise of 125
genocide of Native Americans 175
Guantanamo Bay Detention Centre 390–2, 393–4, 405–6, 409–10
human rights 381–4
illiberalism 449, 459
immigration 448, 449
impeachments 443–5, 455, 456, 458
  abuse of power 443
  anonymity 456–7
  incitement to insurrection 444–5
  obstruction of justice 443
  party discipline 458
insurrection at the Capitol Building 444–5, 455
Iraq, invasion of 402
journalists, executive's attack on 454
majoritarianism, risks of 459
malpractice actions 225–6
manifest destiny 172
measurement of the rule of law 401
media 378, 449
morality 212, 223–35
Muslim countries, ban on refugees, immigrants and travellers from seven 440–1, 460
Native Americans 167, 172, 175
neoliberalism 445–6
neutrality 224
New Deal 129, 265, 350, 372
organisation of profession 248–53
partisanship 98–100, 101–2
polarisation 448, 449
politician lawyers 128–9

popular sovereignty 57
populism 424, 446, 456
postal voting 443–4
poverty 171
public appointments, politicisation of 446
public interest 223, 463
QAnon conspiracy theory 455
regulation 279–81
republican ideal 223–6
Russia investigations 440, 442–3, 446–7
  executive privilege 443
  Mueller investigation 442–3, 447
  obstruction 443
  redactions 443
Sarbanes-Oxley Act 205–6
Securities and Exchange Commission (SEC) 205–6
Selma civil rights march 186–7
Senate 57
separation of powers 57, 72–3, 75–6
slave trade 168, 172–3, 182–3
  Amistad case 172–3, 182–3
  Dred Scott case 167–8, 182–3
  emancipation claims 167–8
  political bias 183
social rights 170–1
terrorism 410–11
UK, relationship with the 410–11
Universal Declaration of Human Rights 177–8
Virginia Plan 75
voting rights 168
welfare, constitutional rights to 170–1
workplace practices 375–6
United States, legal profession in 248–53 *see also* **American Bar Association (ABA); Canons of Ethics (ABA)**
  17th century 248–9, 262
  18th century 249–51, 279
  19th century 251–3, 266
  abuse of process 330
  accept clients, duty to 303
  accountability 303
  adversary model 248–50, 261–2, 290, 292, 343
  Alabama Code of 1887 280, 286, 288–9, 309, 328
  American Civil War 248, 251–2
  American Revolution 248, 251
  anti-lawyer feelings 248–9, 252, 279
  attorney-client privilege 190–1
  attorney fraud actions 225
  Attorney Generals
    Cabinet 98–100, 101–2
    independence 98–100

resignation of 441
separation from executive, proposal for 102
autonomy of clients 308, 315
bar associations, formation of 251–2, 261, 279, 471
Bar, development of a 249–51
Boston massacre 249–51
British model 248–51, 262, 297–8
cab rank model 251
candour, duty of 328
civil legal assistance schemes 266
client and public duties 292–3
codes of conduct 279–81
  best practice 288
  changes 289–90
  client and public duties 288–91
  English codes, comparison with 297–8
  Field Code (New York) 279–80, 288–9
  legalisation 286
  multi-jurisdictional practices 290
  oaths 288–9, 293
  standard conception of the lawyer's role 297
  supporting the rule of law 285
colonialism 248–9, 262, 279
common law 248
confidentiality 289–90, 343
democratisation of bar 253
discipline 279–80, 286, 305, 343
disclosure/discovery 191, 332
education and training 249, 252–3, 260, 280
  ethnic minority and working class students 252–3
  law schools, emergence of 252
  university model 252
executive, control of 470
fairness 328
Field Code (New York) 279–80, 288–9
French civil law 248
fusion 248, 261
global law firms 418
government lawyers 460–1
Guantanamo Bay Detention Centre 390–2, 393–4, 405–6
illegality, participating in 386
increase in number of law firms 385
independence 251, 263, 267, 287
independent and impartial tribunals 251
law schools, emergence of 252
lawful objectives, accepting clients' 305, 308
Legal Aid Societies 266
legal realism 266
Legal Professional Privilege 196, 198, 203
legality 332

licensing 280
Magna Carta 249
mediating institutions, lawyers as 14–15
Model Code of Professional Responsibility 1969 (ABA) 280–1, 285, 289, 303
  abuse of process 330
  lawful objectives, accepting clients' 305
  legality 328
  loyalty, devotion, or zeal, duty of 310
  withdraw from representation, obligation to 328
  multi-jurisdictional practices 290
National Welfare Rights Organisation 267
New Model Rules of Professional Conduct (ABA) 281, 286, 289–90
non-accountability 303
oaths 288–9, 293
partisanship 293, 308–11, 312, 314–15
people's lawyers, emergence of 266
poverty cases 266–7, 389
President 76
presumption of innocence 262
pro bono work 266–7, 290, 389–92
public interest 293, 381–5, 386–7
public service 265–6, 292–3
Puritanism 248
regional differences 249
regulation 252, 263, 279–81, 287, 292
Rhode Island 249
self-interest of lawyers 225–6
self-regulation 292–3
senior government lawyers 98–100, 101
SLAPPs (strategic lawsuits against public participation) 380–3
social activism 266–7, 386–7
Solicitor General 98
specialist advocates, rejection of 248, 261
standard conception of the lawyer's role 212–13, 228–31, 236–7, 297, 308, 315
standard of proof 250–1, 262
Supreme Court
  abortion law 460
  Bush v Gore recount case, impact of 447–8
  ideological orientation 127
  intimidation by online mobs 460
  legislation, review of constitutionality of 73
  partisanship 73
  political appointments 73, 447–8, 460
  values 385–6
Watergate scandal 305, 309
whistleblowing 290
Universal Declaration of Human Rights (UDHR) 162, 177–8
  American Declaration of Human Rights 177
  civil rights 162

drafting   177
first generation rights   177
freedom of speech, freedom of religion, freedom from fear, and from want   177
French Declaration of the Rights of Man and the Citizen   177
Magna Carta   177
social rights   162
universalism   177–81
  ad hoc criminal tribunals, establishment of   177–8
  citizenship   171, 173
  Council of Europe   178–81
  genocide   178
  individuality   177–81
  International Bill of Rights   177–8
  International Criminal Court (ICC)   178
utilitarianism   69, 107, 125, 190

values
  corporate lawyers   385–7, 393
  definition of the rule of law   12
  government lawyers   462
  legal profession   474–5
  private sector values   120
  professionalism   347
  public service ethos   119–20, 130
  social values   136, 269, 372
  system values   318–19
  Victorian values   376
Vienna Declaration and Programme of Action 1993   470
violence, control of   24

Wales *see* Bar of England and Wales
war crimes   175, 177–8
Washington Consensus   397–9
Watergate scandal   227–30, 305
  adversary system   228, 235
  loyalty, devotion, or zeal, duty of   309
  morality   227–30, 235
  neutrality   228–30, 235
  prosecutors   228
  senior government lawyers   98–100
  standard conception of the lawyer's role   228–30
Weber, Max   17–19, 106–7, 135, 242, 270, 293, 347–8, 386
Wednesbury unreasonableness   71–2
welfare
  Brexit   448
  Chicago School   371–2
  civil service   120–1
  constitution right to welfare   170–1
  corporatized state   376
  fairness   161
  legal aid work   247
  mythology of rights   182
  neoliberalism   349–50, 395
  pro bono work   389
  public investment   350
  public service ethos   265, 267
  public services and social benefits, deconstruction of   445
  rights and liberties   161, 170–1, 183, 247, 265, 386
  social welfare   14, 130, 448
  substantive rule of law   14
  United States   171, 386
  values   386
Whigs
  adversary system   234
  Bank of England   108
  Catholic emancipation   113
  celebrities, lawyers as   150–1, 152, 155–6
  constitutional monarchy   113
  ethics of representation   219
  franchise, extension of   113
  free trade   113
  individualism   156
  lawyers   249
  pamphlets and tracts, publication of   110
  Parliament   113
  Restoration   46
  slave trade   113, 172
  supremacy of Parliament   113
  treason cases   138
whistleblowing   104, 130, 205, 290, 412
witnesses
  barristers   334–5
  fairness   334–5
  jurors   139
  suspect witness testimony   332
  treatment   334–5
women   24, 159, 168, 171
World Bank   373, 397–8, 401
World Justice Project (WJP) Index   399–400, 404, 421, App I
World Trade Organization (WTO)   373
World War II, restrictions on civil liberties during   163–6

zeal *see* loyalty, devotion, or zeal, duty of
Zimbabwe   401

Milton Keynes UK
Ingram Content Group UK Ltd.
UKHW020843180424
441230UK00005B/104